THE
BEDFORD
READER

FOURTH EDITION

THE
BEDFORD
READER

FOURTH EDITION

X. J. Kennedy • *Dorothy M. Kennedy*

Jane E. Aaron

Bedford Books *of* St. Martin's Press

Boston

For Bedford Books

Publisher: Charles H. Christensen
Associate Publisher: Joan E. Feinberg
Managing Editor: Elizabeth M. Schaaf
Developmental Editor: Karen S. Henry
Production Editor: Tara L. Masih
Copyeditor: Barbara Price
Text Design: Anna Post-George
Cover Design: Richard Emery Design, Inc.
Cover Art: Photograph by Jenny Okun

For information, write: St. Martin's Press, Inc.
175 Fifth Avenue, New York, NY 10010

Editorial Offices: Bedford Books *of* St. Martin's Press
29 Winchester Street, Boston, MA 02116

ISBN: 0–312–03585–3

ACKNOWLEDGMENTS

Maya Angelou. "Champion of the World." From *I Know Why the Caged Bird Sings* by Maya Angelou. Copyright © 1969 by Maya Angelou. Reprinted by permission of Random House, Inc. In "Maya Angelou on Writing," excerpts from Sheila Weller. "Work in Progress/Maya Angelou," *Intellectual Digest*, June 1973. Reprinted by permission.

Acknowledgments and copyrights are continued at the back of the book on pages 756–764, which constitute an extension of the copyright page.

PREFACE
FOR INSTRUCTORS

"A writer," declares Saul Bellow, "is a reader moved to emulation." Indeed, the best path for students of writing may well be to read good and lively prose, get stirred up, and want to say something on their own.

As in the past, this fourth edition of *The Bedford Reader* offers more than just model essays to be emulated. It tries to show how effective writing is written — not just theoretically, but in the working practice of many good writers.

In arranging the book's essays according to familiar methods of writing (narrating, describing, explaining, persuading), we are aware that such classifications are merely ways to get started. As the introduction suggests to the student, these rhetorical modes may be regarded not as boxes to stuff full of verbiage but as natural forms that assist in practical tasks of invention and fruition. Instructors familiar with both rhetorical tradition and the findings of recent composition research know that the methods can prompt student writers to discover that they have much to say. We believe that good writers don't arbitrarily choose a method, then set out mechanically to follow it. Instead, such writers continue thinking, feeling, and discovering while they write.

In selecting essays, we let in none that we did not enjoy reading and wouldn't want to teach. Some time-proven essays — those, for instance, by James Thurber, Jessica Mitford, and Bruce Catton — remain, like the Washington Monument, solidly fixed in place. Other, less familiar essays seem likely candidates to rouse a class and inspire writing, though they may have first seen print only a few months ago.

With this edition, the Kennedys would like to welcome Jane Aaron to the book's editorial team. A long-time colleague in text writing and publishing, Jane brings to this book great resources as a writer and editor, as well as first-hand classroom experience. She teaches writing at Parsons School of Design/The New School for Social Research; and she is the principal author of *The Little, Brown Handbook* and the author-editor of *The Compact Reader*, a popular Bedford Book.

WHAT'S THE SAME

In its basic structure and components, this new edition of *The Bedford Reader* should be familiar to instructors who have used previous versions. The book breaks into a general introduction plus eleven chapters, each chapter devoted to a different method of development. In the introduction, we endeavor to get students started by answering some of their likely questions about reading and writing and by demonstrating a method of critical reading on Joan Didion's popular essay "In Bed." Then, at the start of each chapter, we set forth a different writing procedure: what it is (The Method) and how to use it (The Process). To reinforce that these rhetorical methods are flexible, we slip in two paragraphs showing the method in action: one for a general audience on television and one for a more specialized audience in an academic discipline. (Incidentally, if you want to take up the methods in an order different from ours, nothing will hinder you.)

The selections themselves, besides illustrating the appropriate method, also represent the work of many first-rate and well-known writers, such as Jessica Mitford, Alice Walker, Richard Rodriguez, and Tom Wolfe. Works by Shirley Jackson and Emily Dickinson show the methods at work in literature. And three essays by composition students show that professionals are not the only writers to admire and learn from. To help structure students' critical reading of the essays, each one comes with three sets of questions — on meaning, writing strategy, and language. To prompt students' writing, at least three suggestions for writing follow the questions, and even more topics conclude each chapter. (In the questions, writing topics, and elsewhere, SMALL CAPITAL LETTERS refer students to the glossary.)

A hit from the last edition, the Writers on Writing return this time in even greater numbers. In these comments, ranging from a couple of paragraphs to a couple of pages, the essays' authors discuss getting ideas, planning, revising, and other aspects of writing. Besides offering rock-solid advice, the comments also prove that for the pros, too, writing is usually a challenge.

Several useful aids conclude or accompany the book. A glossary (Useful Terms) contains definitions of all the important terms in the book plus others, such as *introductions* and *conclusions*. An alternate table of contents (Essays Arranged by Subject) makes it easy to ignore the rhetorical methods and organize a course by subjects, themes, or genres. (Some of this edition's new features also serve a thematic arrangement — see "What's New.") And a discussion of every method, selection, and Writer on Writing appears in an instructor's manual bound in with the book's Instructor's Edition.

WHAT'S NEW

In revising, we had the advice of nearly a hundred instructors. Some clamored for big changes, as many for none, but through all the comments we discerned some shifts in the way *The Bedford Reader* is being taught and in the students who are using it. Addressing these shifts while also replacing selections for

variety and currency, we ended up altering as much as we preserved. An itemization:

- The most notable change is the availability of two versions of
  The Bedford Reader: a longer edition, with 69 selections, and a
  shorter edition, with 44 selections. The two versions offer the
  same editorial aids. Now, though, you have your choice: a
  bigger book that gives more options and greater variety, or a
  smaller book that can be covered more readily in one term.

- More than half of the selections are new: 40 in the longer edi-
  tion, 23 in the shorter. New authors include Ralph Ellison,
  Virginia Woolf, Anna Quindlen, Mark Crispin Miller, Nikki
  Giovanni, John Berger, and James Fallows. Four of the au-
  thors — Joan Didion, George Orwell, Annie Dillard, and
  Lewis Thomas — are represented by two selections apiece.

- To stimulate class discussion and students' writing, we've
  forged many thematic links among selections. In each chapter, two selections are now related both rhetorically *and* the-
  matically. These pairs, highlighted in the table of contents,
  concern subjects as diverse as homelessness, sports, the media, and the legalization of drugs. In addition, every selection
  has a writing topic labeled Connections that leads students to
  see thematic and rhetorical relations between two or more selections. These topics may be assigned for writing or used for
  class discussion.

- Also for each selection, a question labeled Other Methods
  highlights the ways writers often combine rhetorical methods
  even if one method predominates.

- Many more selections — at least one per chapter — concern
  some aspect of American or global cultural diversity, the intersections of ethnic groups, races, classes, and genders.

- Within each chapter, further, at least one selection is a classroom favorite, one is cross-curricular, one appeals to younger
  college students, and one appeals to nontraditional students.

- We've strengthened the coverage of critical reading and writing. Besides improving the material on reading in the general
  introduction and on argument in Chapter 11, we have split
  the former chapter on division and classification to give divi-

sion/analysis room to breathe in its own chapter (Chap. 6). Now we can pay due attention to the analytical foundation of critical thinking and provide examples of truly critical writing.

- In response to many requests, we have added a literary analysis (by Margot Harrison) to Chapter 6 and an MLA-documented research paper (by Curtis Chang) to Chapter 11. Both authors are students.
- A new index concludes the text, giving you and your students a way to find not only authors and titles but also discussions of concepts or problems such as *analysis* and *revision*. The index provides a handy guide to the Writers on Writing, too.

ACKNOWLEDGMENTS

We have now accumulated debts to hundreds and hundreds of students and teachers for their suggestions over three previous editions. The total was upped considerably by the almost one hundred teachers who gave us ideas (as well as praise and, sometimes, what for) on a detailed questionnaire. To this diverse group we express our most heartfelt thanks: Donna Alden, Susan Avery, Merilee Bartlett, Martha A. Bartter, Ferne Baumgardner, J. Steven Beauchamp, Maureen Bennett, Richard Bernard, Sally J. Bright, Pamela Brown, Mark J. Bruhn, Sally Buckner, Johnnie Butler, Rachel M. Caldwell, Mary Jane Capozzoli, James D. Collins, Charles Cowdrick, Mahlin F. Cummins, Bonnie Cunningham, Richard A. Davis, Larry J. Degler, Emily Dial-Driver, Kelly Dobyns, Thelma Epstein, Scott Foll, Hood Frazier, Lynn C. Furler, Jonathan A. Gates, Reginald L. Gerlica, Lillis Gilmartin, Anthony R. Grassia, Yohma Gray, Karen Healy, Elizabeth M. A. Hodgson, Sharon J. Holstein, Jason Gary Horn, Page Howald, Richard Hull, Deena Hutchinson, Thomas M. Johnson, Sarah Jordan, Reba Kochersperger, Dianne Koehnecke, Douglas Kreinke, Philip K. Lach, Anne A. LaManna, Gail Lathrop, John Lavagnino, Elaine B. Lavender, Bernadette Low, Agnes Lynch, Barbara McGovern, Larry G. Mapp, John P. Mastroni, Ann

Matheson, Joseph Minton, Janice T. Moore, Leonarda Obarski, Dennis J. O'Brien, Lorie V. Odegaard, James O'Neill, Lynne Paris, Dana Peake, Kirsten Pierce, Andreas K. Punzel, Sylvia Rackow, Dorothy Raffel, Ann Rayson, Janis Richardi, Judy Ryan, Sharon Scruta, Janet Seim, Rosemary H. Shellander, Diane L. Silver, Barbara Sloan, Beth Slusser, Ruth Stratton, Susan Swan, Karen Swenson, David Tomlinson, Anthony C. Turrisi, Peter Ulisse, Sharon Warycka, Laurel V. Williamson, John W. Willoughby, Jo Ellen Winters, Ellen Wolff, Sherida Yoder, and Maria Yuen.

Besides these professional critics, many students have generously spelled out for us their likes and dislikes, using the questionnaire at the back of the book. We wish there were room to thank each one individually. Their wishes were carefully weighed and digested, and often acted upon.

Bedford Books again exceeded the call in help, hand-holding, and good humor. It was through Bedford that we obtained the services of the capable and quick Douglas K. Currier, who drafted questions and answers for the new selections. At Bedford, as usual, Charles H. Christensen unlocked his text-publishing secrets to help shape the contents. Karen S. Henry sagely and cheerfully guided every step of the book's development. Ellen Kuhl proved a research whiz and as a result (we like to think) was justly promoted. Tara L. Masih serenely shepherded not one but two books (longer and shorter) through simultaneous production. To all, our deep and abiding thanks.

X. J. Kennedy
Dorothy M. Kennedy
Jane E. Aaron

CONTENTS

◄► Indicates thematic pair in each chapter.

5. PROCESS ANALYSIS: Explaining Step by Step   281

In this feminist view of marriage, the work of a wife is divided into its roles and functions. What a wonderful boon a wife is! Shouldn't every woman have one of her own?

A typical life, between the ages of eighteen and fifty, may be divided into six stages of growth. Among these, very likely, is the one you are writhing through right now.

Virginia Woolf and Annie Dillard both wrote about the death of a moth, in essays collected in Chapter 2. How are the works alike? How different? A prize-winning student writer offers a literary analysis.

◄► Stardom isn't easy. A close reader of the media analyzes celebrity, mass hostility, and the role played in both by television personality Barbara Walters.

◄► What do a photograph of a woman posing nude and a photograph of a chocolate éclair have in common? Both, says this writer on culture and the media, may be pornographic.

What do we do with a third of our lives? We wait. A patient and humorous writer classifies the reasons why.

"Good music is music that I want to hear. Bad music is music that I don't want to hear." As far as this caustic writer is concerned, the only difference between most music and Muzak is the spelling.

A solution is not always a solution. According to this writer and farmer, the solutions proposed for the current agricultural dilemma reveal flaws in our thinking about a host of problems.

10. DEFINITION: Tracing a Boundary   541

11. ARGUMENT AND PERSUASION: Stating Opinions and Proposals   605

OPINIONS

THE
BEDFORD
READER

FOURTH EDITION

INTRODUCTION

WHY READ? WHY WRITE?
WHY NOT PHONE?

In recent years, many prophets have forecast the doom of the written word. Soon, they have argued, books and magazines will become museum pieces. Newspapers will be found only in attics. The mails will be replaced by a computer terminal in every home.

Although the prophets have been making such forecasts for decades, their vision is far from realized. Books remain more easily portable than computer terminals and television sets — cheaper, too, and in need of less upkeep and energy. The newspaper reader continues to obtain far more information in much less time than the viewer of the six o'clock news. Most business is still conducted with the aid of paper. A letter or memorandum leaves no doubt about what its writer is after. It is a permanent record of thought, and it lies on its recipient's desk, expecting something to be done about it.

The day may come when we will all throw away our pens and typewriters, to compose on the glowing screens of word processors and transmit paragraphs over cables; still, it is doubtful that the basic methods of writing will completely change. Whether on paper or on screens, we will need to arrange our thoughts in a clear order. We will still have to explain them to others plainly and forcefully.

That is why, in almost any career or profession you may enter, you will be expected to read continually, and also to write. This book assumes that reading and writing are a unity. Deepen your mastery of one and you deepen your mastery of the other. The experience of carefully reading an excellent writer, noticing not only what the writer has to say but also the quality of its saying, rubs off (if you are patient and perceptive) on your own writing. "We go to college," said poet Robert Frost, "to be given one more chance to learn to read in case we haven't learned in high school. Once we have learned to read, the rest can be trusted to add itself *unto us*."

For any writer, reading is indispensable. It turns up fresh ideas; it stocks the mind with information, understanding, examples, and illustrations; it instills critical awareness of one's surroundings. When you have a well-stocked and girded mental storehouse, you tell truths, even small and ordinary truths, and so write what most readers will find worth reading, instead of building shimmering spires of words in an attempt to make a reader think, "Wow, what a grade A writer." Thornton Wilder, playwright and novelist, put this advice memorably: "If you write to *impress* it will always be bad, but if you write to *express* it will be good."

USING *THE BEDFORD READER*

The Essays

In this book, we trust, you'll find at least a few essays you will enjoy and care to remember. *The Bedford Reader* features work by many of the finest nonfiction writers, past and present.

The essays deal with more than just writing and literature

and such usual concerns of English courses; they cut broadly across a college curriculum. You'll find writings on science, history, business, medicine, law, religion, women's studies, sociology, education, child development, the environment, music, sports, farming, politics, the media, and minority experience. Some writers recall their childhoods, their families, their own college days, their problems and challenges. Some explore matters likely to spark controversy: drug use, the threat of nuclear war, funerals, sex roles, race relations, class distinctions, bilingual schooling, conservation, the death penalty, the perennial complaint that rock music is going to the dogs. Some writers are intently serious; others, funny. In all, these sixty-nine selections — including one story and one poem — reveal kinds of reading you will meet in other college courses. Such reading is the usual diet of well-informed people with lively minds — who, to be sure, aren't found only on campuses.

The essays have been chosen with one main purpose in mind: to show you how good writers write. Don't feel glum if at first you find an immense gap in quality between E. B. White's writing and yours. Of course there's a gap: White is an immortal with a unique style that he perfected over half a century. You don't have to judge your efforts by comparison. The idea is to gain whatever writing techniques you can. If you're going to learn from other writers, why not go to the best of them? You want to know how to define an idea so that the definition is vivid and clear? Read Tom Wolfe on "pornoviolence." You want to know how to tell a story about your childhood and make it stick in someone's memory? Read Maya Angelou. Incidentally, not all the selections in this book are the work of professional writers: As Linnea Saukko, Margot Harrison, and Curtis Chang prove, students too write essays worth studying.

This book has another aim: to provoke your own thinking and so nourish your own writing. Just mulling over the views these writers advance, working out their suggestions, agreeing and disagreeing with them, sets your mind in motion. You may be led to search your own knowledge and experience (or to do some looking up in a library) to discover ideas, points to make, examples you didn't expect to find.

The Methods

As a glance over the table of contents will show, the essays in *The Bedford Reader* illustrate eleven familiar methods of writing, such as DESCRIPTION or CLASSIFICATION or DEFINITION. These methods aren't classroom games; as our explanations of them show, they're practical ways to generate ideas, to say what you have to say, and to give shape to it. To begin with, of course, you'll need something worth saying. The method isn't supposed to be an empty jug to pour full of any old, dull words. Neither is it meant to be a straitjacket woven by fiendish English teachers to pin your writing arm to your side and keep you from expressing yourself naturally. Amazingly, these methods can be ways to discover what you know, what you need to know, and what you'll want to write about. Give them a try. See if they don't help you find more to say, more that you feel is worth saying. Good writers believe their own words. That is why readers, too, believe them.

Suppose, for example, you set out to write about two popular singers — their sounds, their styles, their looks, what they are like offstage — by the method of COMPARISON and CONTRAST. With any luck, you may find the method prompting you to notice similarities and differences between the two singers that you hadn't dreamed of noticing. At least, hundreds of teachers and tens of thousands of students have found that, in fact, these rhetorical methods can help you to invent and discover. Such little miracles of creating and finding take place with heartening regularity.

Reading the essays in *The Bedford Reader*, you'll find that writers rarely stick to one rhetorical method all the way through. NARRATION is the dominant method in Maya Angelou's "Champion of the World," since the writer tells a story from first word to last, but still she uses description, too. In the flow of most expository prose, methods tend to rise, take shape, and disperse like waves in a tide. Often you'll find a writer using one method for a paragraph or two, then switching to another. In "The Black and White Truth about Basketball," Jeff Greenfield mainly compares and contrasts the styles of black and white players, but he begins with a paragraph that follows another method: giving EXAMPLES. Later, he gives still more examples; he briefly describes famous players in action; he defines the terms *rhythm*, *"black" basketball*, and *"white" basketball*. Clearly, Greenfield employs whatever methods suit his purpose: to explain the differences between two playing styles.

In truth, these rhetorical methods are like oxygen, iron, and other elements that make up substances in nature: all around us, but seldom found alone and isolated, in laboratory-pure states. ANALOGY, the method of explaining the unfamiliar in terms of the familiar, is obviously central to Lewis Thomas's "The Attic of the Brain," even though Thomas traces his analogy only in the first part of his essay and departs from it in the last five paragraphs. In this book, don't expect an essay in a chapter called *Description* or *Process Analysis* to describe or analyze a process in every single line. We promise you only that the method will be central to the writer's purpose in the essay — and that you'll find the method amply (and readably) illustrated.

The Questions, Writing Topics, and Glossary

Following every essay, you'll find questions on meaning, writing strategy, and language that can help you analyze the selection and learn from it. (You can see a sample of how these questions work when we analyze Joan Didion's "In Bed" starting on page 16). These questions are followed by at least three suggestions for writing; one of them, labeled "Connections," links the essay with one or two others in the book. Many more writing topics conclude each chapter.

In some of the questions and writing suggestions, certain terms appear in CAPITAL LETTERS. These are words helpful in discussing both the essays in this book and the essays you write. If you'd like to see such a term defined and illustrated, you can find it in the glossary at the back of the book: Useful Terms. This section offers more than just brief definitions. It is there to provide you further information and support.

Writers on Writing

We have tried to give this book another dimension. We wanted to show that Maya Angelou, Jeff Greenfield, and the other writers represented here do not produce their readable and informative prose on the first try, as if by magic, leaving the rest of us to cope with writer's block, awkward sentences, and all the other difficulties of writing. Take comfort and cheer: These writers, too, struggled to make themselves interesting and clear. In proof, we visit their workshops littered with crumpled paper and forgotten coffee cups. Accompanying most essays are statements by the writers, revealing how they write (or wrote), offering their tricks, setting forth things they admire about good writing. Some of these statements were written especially for this book; others are taken from published sources. You'll find the comments after the questions and writing suggestions at the end of the writer's essay.

No doubt you'll soon notice some contradiction in these statements: The writers disagree about when and how to think about their readers, about whether outlines have any value, about whether style follows subject or vice versa. The reason for the difference of opinion is, simply, that no two writers follow the same path to finished work. Even the same writer may take the left instead of the customary right fork if the writing situation demands a change. A key aim of providing writers' statements on writing, then, is to suggest the sheer variety of routes open to you, the many approaches to writing and strategies for succeeding at it. At the very end of the book, an index points you toward the writers' comments on such practical matters as writing introductions, finding your point, and revising sentences.

READING AN ESSAY

Whatever career you enter, most of the reading you will do — for business, not for pleasure — will probably be hasty. You'll skim: glance at words here and there, find essential facts, catch the drift of an argument. To cross oceans of print, you won't have time to paddle: You'll need to hop a jet. By skimming, you'll be able to tear through a pile of junk mail, or quickly locate the useful parts of a long report. You'll keep up with the latest issue of a specialized journal aimed at members of your trade or profession: *Computer Times*, perhaps, or the *Journal of the American Medical Association*, or *Boarding Kennel Proprietor*.

But reading essays, in order to understand them and learn from them how to write better, calls for reading word by word. Your aim is to jimmy open good writers' writings and see what makes them go. You're looking for pointers to sharpen your skills and help you put your own clear, forceful paragraphs together. Unless with one sweeping, analytic look (like that of Sherlock Holmes sizing up a new client) you can take in everything in a rich and complicated essay, expect to spend an hour or two in its company. Does the essay assigned for today remain unread, and does class start in five minutes? "I'll just breeze through this little item," you might tell yourself. But no, give up. You're a goner.

Good writing, as every writer knows, demands toil; and so does analytic reading. Never try to gulp down a rich and potent essay without chewing; all it will give you is indigestion. When you're going to read an essay in depth, seek out some quiet place — a library, a study cubicle, your room (provided it doesn't also hold two roommates playing poker). Flick off the radio, stereo, or television. What writer can outsing Bono or Luciano Pavarotti, or outshout a kung fu movie? The fewer the distractions, the easier your task will be.

How do you read an essay? Exactly how, that is, do you read it analytically, to master its complexities, to learn how a good writer writes, and so write better yourself? To find out, we'll be taking a close look at an actual essay, Joan Didion's "In Bed." It won't be the easiest in this book, but you'll find it rewards the time you spend getting beyond the difficulties.

The Preliminaries

Analytic reading starts before you read the first word of the essay. Like a pilot circling an airfield, you take stock of what's before you, locating clues to the essay's content and the writer's biases.

The Title

Often the title will tell you the writer's subject, as in George Orwell's "A Hanging" or Gail Sheehy's "Predictable Crises of Adulthood." Sometimes it immediately states the THESIS, the main point the writer will make: "I Want a Wife" or "Oppressed Hair Puts a Ceiling on the Brain." It may set forth its thesis as a question: "Why Don't We Complain?" Some titles spell out the method a writer proposes to follow: "Grant and Lee: A Study in Contrasts." The TONE of a title may also reveal the writer's attitude toward the material. If a work is named "A Serious Call to the Devout and Holy Life," the title gives you an idea of the writer's approach, all right; and so does that of an informal, light-hearted essay like "The Sound of Music: Enough Already." The reader, in turn, approaches each work in a different way — with serious intent, or set to chuckle. Some titles reveal more than others. In calling her essay "In Bed," Joan Didion arouses, and then defies, our expectations. The essay isn't about sex, or sleep, or lolling around in the sack all day eating chocolates. Didion's opening sentence arrests us with a touch of IRONY as we sense a discrepancy between what we expected and what we find. Whatever it does, a title sits atop its essay like a neon sign. Usually, it tells you what's inside — or makes you want to venture in. To pick an alluring title for an essay of your own is a skill worth cultivating.

The Author

Whatever you know about a writer — background, special training, previous works, outlook, or ideology — often will help you guess, before you read a word of the essay, the assumptions on which it is built. Is the writer a political conservative? Expect an argument against more taxes. Is the writer a liberal? Expect an argument in favor of more social spending. Is the writer a black activist? A feminist? An athlete? An internationally renowned philosopher? A popular television comedian? By knowing something about a writer's background or beliefs, you may know beforehand a little of what they will say. To help provide such knowledge, this book supplies biographical notes. The one on

Joan Didion immediately before "In Bed" (p. 11) suggests that Didion is a sophisticated Californian able to write both popular entertainments and serious "think" pieces about politics. If after reading the note you guess that "In Bed" will be thought-provoking yet enjoyable and readily understandable, you will be right.

Where the Essay Was First Published

Clearly, it matters to a writer's credibility whether an article called "Living Mermaids: An Amazing Discovery" first saw print in *Scientific American*, a magazine for scientists and for nonscientists who follow what's happening in science, or in a popular tabloid weekly, sold at supermarket checkout counters, that is full of eye-popping sensations. But no less important, finding out where an essay first appeared can tell you for whom the writer was writing. In this book we'll strongly urge you as a writer to think of your readers and to try looking at what you write as if through their eyes. To help you develop this ability, we tell you something about the sources and thus the original readers of each essay you study, in a note just before the essay. (Such a note precedes Didion's "In Bed" on page 11). After you have read the sample essay, we'll further consider how having a sense of your reader helps you write.

When the Essay Was First Published

Knowing in what year an essay was first printed may give you another key to understanding it. A 1988 essay on mermaids will contain statements of fact more recent and more reliable than an essay printed in 1700 — although the older essay might contain valuable information, too, and perhaps some delectable language, folklore, and poetry. In *The Bedford Reader*, the brief introductory note on every essay tells you not only where but also when the essay was originally printed. If you're reading an essay elsewhere — say, in one of the writer's books — you can find this information on the dust jacket or the copyright page.

The First Reading

On first reading an essay, you don't want to bog down over every troublesome particular. Joan Didion's "In Bed" is written for an educated audience, and that means she'll use a few large words when they seem necessary. If you meet any words that look intimidating, take them in your stride. When, in reading a rich and complicated essay, you run into an unfamiliar word or name, see if you can figure it out from its surroundings. If a word stops you cold and you feel lost, circle it in pencil; you can always look it up later. (In a little while we'll come back to the helpful habit of reading with a pencil. Indeed, some readers feel more confident with pencil in hand from the start.)

The first time you read an essay, size up the forest; later, you can squint at the acorns all you like. Glimpse the essay in its entirety. When you start to read "In Bed," don't even think about dissecting it. Just see what the writer has to say. Even nonsufferers of the paralyzing illness Didion describes will find her account vivid and arresting.

JOAN DIDION

A writer whose fame is fourfold — as novelist, essayist, journalist, and screenwriter — JOAN DIDION was born in 1934 in California, where her family has lived for five generations. After graduation from the University of California, Berkeley, she spent a few years in New York, working as a feature editor for *Vogue*, a fashion magazine. In 1964 she returned to California, where she worked as a freelance journalist and wrote four much-discussed novels: *River Run* (1963), *Play It As It Lays* (1971), *A Book of Common Prayer* (1977), and *Democracy* (1984). *Salvador* (1983), her book-length essay based on a visit to war-torn El Salvador, and *Miami* (1987), a study of Cuban exiles in Florida, also received wide attention. With her husband, John Gregory Dunne, Didion has coauthored screenplays, notably for *True Confessions* (1981) and the Barbra Streisand film *A Star Is Born* (1976). She is now living in New York City and working on a new collection of essays.

In Bed

"In Bed" was written in 1968 for the *Saturday Evening Post* and was collected in a book of Didion's essays, *The White Album* (1979). Although Didion's subject is a medical one, she isn't writing as a scientist for an audience of specialists but as an ordinary citizen describing her personal experience to any willing and capable reader.

Three, four, sometimes five times a month, I spend the day in 1 bed with a migraine headache, insensible to the world around me. Almost every day of every month, between these attacks, I feel the sudden irrational irritation and flush of blood into the cerebral arteries which tell me that migraine is on its way, and I take certain drugs to avert its arrival. If I did not take the drugs, I would be able to function perhaps one day in four. The physiological error called migraine is, in brief, central to the given of my life. When I was 15, 16, even 25, I used to think that I could rid myself of this error by simply denying it, character over chemistry. "Do you have headaches *sometimes? frequently? never?*" the application forms would demand. "Check one." Wary of the trap, wanting whatever it was that the successful circumnavigation of that particular form could bring (a job, a scholarship, the respect of mankind and the grace of God), I would check one. "*Sometimes,*" I would lie. That in fact I spent one or two days a week almost unconscious with pain seemed a shameful secret, evidence not merely of some chemical inferiority but of all my bad attitudes, unpleasant tempers, wrongthink.

For I had no brain tumor, no eyestrain, no high blood pressure, nothing wrong with me at all: I simply had migraine headaches, and migraine headaches were, as everyone who did not have them knew, imaginary. I fought migraine then, ignored the warnings it sent, went to school and later to work in spite of it, sat through lectures in Middle English and presentations to advertisers with involuntary tears running down the right side of my face, threw up in washrooms, stumbled home by instinct, emptied ice trays onto my bed and tried to freeze the pain in my right temple, wished only for a neurosurgeon who would do a lobotomy on house call, and cursed my imagination.

It was a long time before I began thinking mechanistically enough to accept migraine for what it was: something with which I would be living, the way some people live with diabetes. Migraine is something more than the fancy of a neurotic imagination. It is an essentially hereditary complex of symptoms, the most frequently noted but by no means the most unpleasant of which is a vascular headache of blinding severity, suffered by a surprising number of women, a fair number of men (Thomas Jefferson had migraine, and so did Ulysses S. Grant, the day he accepted Lee's surrender), and by some unfortunate children as young as two years old. (I had my first when I was eight. It came on during a fire drill at the Columbia School in Colorado Springs, Colorado. I was taken first home and then to the infirmary at Peterson Field, where my father was stationed. The Air Corps doctor prescribed an enema.) Almost anything can trigger a specific attack of migraine: stress, allergy, fatigue, an abrupt change in barometric pressure, a contretemps over a parking ticket. A flashing light. A fire drill. One inherits, of course, only the predisposition. In other words I spent yesterday in bed with a headache not merely because of my bad attitudes, unpleasant tempers and wrongthink, but because both my grandmothers had migraine, my father has migraine and my mother has migraine.

No one knows precisely what it is that is inherited. The 4 chemistry of migraine, however, seems to have some connection with the nerve hormone named serotonin, which is naturally present in the brain. The amount of serotonin in the blood falls sharply at the onset of migraine, and one migraine drug, methysergide, or Sansert, seems to have some effect on serotonin. Methysergide is a derivative of lysergic acid (in fact Sandoz Pharmaceuticals first synthesized LSD-25 while looking for a migraine cure), and its use is hemmed about with so many contraindications and side effects that most doctors prescribe it only in the most incapacitating cases. Methysergide, when it is prescribed, is taken daily, as a preventive; another preventive which works for some people is old-fashioned ergotamine tartrate, which helps to constrict the swelling blood vessels during the "aura," the period which in most cases precedes the actual headache.

Once an attack is under way, however, no drug touches it. 5 Migraine gives some people mild hallucinations, temporarily blinds others, shows up not only as a headache but as a gastrointestinal disturbance, a painful sensitivity to all sensory stimuli, an abrupt overpowering fatigue, a strokelike aphasia, and a crippling inability to make even the most routine connections. When I am in a migraine aura (for some people the aura lasts fifteen minutes, for others several hours), I will drive through red lights, lose the house keys, spill whatever I am holding, lose the ability to focus my eyes or frame coherent sentences, and generally give the appearance of being on drugs, or drunk. The actual headache, when it comes, brings with it chills, sweating, nausea, a debility that seems to stretch the very limits of endurance. That no one dies of migraine seems, to someone deep into an attack, an ambiguous blessing.

My husband also has migraine, which is unfortunate for him 6 but fortunate for me: perhaps nothing so tends to prolong an attack as the accusing eye of someone who has never had a headache. "Why not take a couple of aspirin," the unafflicted will say from the doorway, or "I'd have a headache, too, spending a beautiful day like this inside with all the shades drawn." All of us who have migraine suffer not only from the attacks themselves but from this common conviction that we are perversely refusing to cure ourselves by taking a couple of aspirin, that we are making ourselves sick, that we "bring it on ourselves." And in the most immediate sense, the sense of why we have a headache this Tuesday and not last Thursday, of course we often do. There certainly is what doctors call a "migraine personality," and that personality tends to be ambitious, inward, intolerant of error, rather rigidly organized, perfectionist. "You don't look like a migraine personality," a doctor once said to me. "Your hair's messy. But I suppose you're a compulsive housekeeper." Actually my house is kept even more negligently than my hair, but the doctor was right nonetheless: perfectionism can also take the form of spending most of a week writing and rewriting and not writing a single paragraph.

But not all perfectionists have migraine, and not all migrainous people have migraine personalities. We do not escape heredity. I have tried in most of the available ways to escape my own migrainous heredity (at one point I learned to give myself two daily injections of histamine with a hypodermic needle, even though the needle so frightened me that I had to close my eyes when I did it), but I still have migraine. And I have learned now to live with it, learned when to expect it, how to outwit it, even how to regard it, when it does come, as more friend than lodger. We have reached a certain understanding, my migraine and I. It never comes when I am in real trouble. Tell me that my house is burned down, my husband has left me, that there is gunfighting in the streets and panic in the banks, and I will not respond by getting a headache. It comes instead when I am fighting not an open but a guerrilla war with my own life, during weeks of small household confusions, lost laundry, unhappy help, canceled appointments, on days when the telephone rings too much and I get no work done and the wind is coming up. On days like that my friend comes uninvited.

And once it comes, now that I am wise in its ways, I no longer fight it. I lie down and let it happen. At first every small apprehension is magnified, every anxiety a pounding terror. Then the pain comes, and I concentrate only on that. Right there is the usefulness of migraine, there in that imposed yoga, the concentration on the pain. For when the pain recedes, ten or twelve hours later, everything goes with it, all the hidden resentments, all the vain anxieties. The migraine has acted as a circuit breaker, and the fuses have emerged intact. There is a pleasant convalescent euphoria. I open the windows and feel the air, eat gratefully, sleep well. I notice the particular nature of a flower in a glass on the stair landing. I count my blessings.

Rereadings

When first looking into an essay as rich and complex as "In Bed," you are like a person who arrives at the doorway of a large and lively room, surveying a party going on inside. Taking a look around the room, you catch the overall picture: the locations of the food and the drinks, of people you know, of people you don't know but would certainly like to. You have just taken such an overview of Didion's essay. Now, stepping through the doorway of the essay and going on in, you can head for whatever beckons most strongly.

Well, what will it be? If it is writing skills you want, then go for those elements that took skill or flair or thoughtful decision on the writer's part. Most likely, you'll need to reread the essay more than once, go over the difficult parts several times, with all the care of someone combing a snag from the mane of an admirable horse.

In giving an essay this going-over, many students — some of the best — find a pencil in hand as good as a currycomb. It concentrates the attention wonderfully. If the book is theirs, these students underline any idea that strikes them as essential. They score things with vertical lines; they bracket passages. They vent their feelings ("Bull!" "Says who?"). They jot notes in the margins. Such pencilwork, you'll find, helps you behold the very spine of an essay, as if in an X-ray view. You'll feel you have put your own two cents into it. (If the book is borrowed, you can accomplish the same thing with just a bit more effort by making notes on a separate sheet of paper.) While reading this way, you're being a writer. Your pencil tracks will jog your memory, too, when you review for a test, when you take part in class discussion, or when you want to write about what you've read. Some sophisticates scorn pencils in favor of markers that roll pink or yellow ink over a word or a line, leaving it legible. (But you can't make notes with such markers.)

Whether you read with close attention and a pencil, or with a marker, or with close attention alone, look for elements of meaning, writing strategy, and language. These categories match the groups of questions after each essay, and they will help shape and direct your responses. Using a method of thinking called DIVISION or ANALYSIS (Chap. 6), you'll want to ask what the author's purpose and main idea are, how clear they are and how well supported. You'll want to isolate which writing techniques the author has used to special advantage, what hits you as particularly fresh, clever, or wise — and what *doesn't* work, too. You'll want to know exactly what the writer is saying, how he or she says it, and whether, in the end, it was worth saying. In short, you'll want to use your critical faculties, your fund of knowledge, and your growing experience as a reader to understand, appreciate, and evaluate what you read.

The following comments on Didion's "In Bed" show how such an analysis can work.

Meaning

"No man but a blockhead," declared Samuel Johnson, "ever wrote except for money." Perhaps the industrious critic, journalist, and dictionary maker was remembering his own days as a literary drudge in London's Grub Street; but surely most people who write often do so for other reasons.

When you read an essay, you'll find it rewarding to ask, "What is this writer's PURPOSE?" By purpose, we mean the writer's apparent reason for writing: what he or she was trying to achieve. A purpose is as essential to a good, pointed essay as a destination is to a trip. It affects every choice or decision the writer makes. (On vacation, of course, carefree people sometimes climb into a car without a thought and go happily rambling around; but if a writer rambles like that in an essay, the reader may plead, "Let me out!") In making a simple statement of a writer's purpose, we might say that the writer writes *to entertain*, or *to explain*, or *to persuade*. To state a purpose more fully, we might say that a writer writes not just to persuade but "to tell a story to illustrate the point that when you are being cheated it's a good idea to complain," or not just to entertain but "to tell a horror story to make chills shoot down our spines." If the essay is an argument meant to convince, a fuller statement of its writer's purpose might be "to win us over to the writer's opinion that San Antonio is the most livable city in the United States," or "to persuade us to take action: write our representative and urge more federal spending for the rehabilitation of criminals."

"But," the skeptic might object, "how can I know a writer's purpose? I'm no mind reader, and even if I were, how could I tell what Jonathan Swift was trying to do? He's dead and buried." And yet writers living and dead reveal their purposes in what they write, just as visibly as a hiker leaves footprints.

What is Joan Didion's purpose in writing? If you want to be exact, you can speak of her *main purpose* or *central purpose*, for "In Bed" fulfills more than one. To be sure, Didion keeps us interested. Her recollections of her case history are lively enough: She tells how she "threw up in washrooms, stumbled home by instinct, emptied ice trays onto my bed. . . ." But is her uppermost purpose simply to entertain? This might be a perfectly good purpose for some essays, but certainly Didion's isn't pure fun to read. Parts of it, such as the passage about throwing up in washrooms, might leave us wincing. By the time we finish reading "In Bed," Didion has fulfilled at least three purposes:

1. *To define migraine.* She does so by explaining how the illness affects its victims. She sets forth its possible causes (family history, a personality type) and what doctors can do for it.
2. *To tell the story of her own case.* She starts with her first migraine attack in grade school during a fire drill. She relates how she bore up (or was crushed down) under migraine while in college

and on the job. And in the end she explains how her attitude toward her malady has changed.

3. *To show that she accepts her illness as beneficial.* We think her major purpose is this last, even though it becomes clear only in her conclusion, in the last two paragraphs. But it is the main idea she leaves us with.

How can you tell a writer's purpose? Ask: What is the thesis of this essay — the point made for a purpose, the overwhelming idea that the writer communicates? Some writers will come right out, early on, and sum up this central idea in a sentence or two. George Orwell, in his essay "Politics and the English Language," states the gist of his argument in his second paragraph:

> Modern English, especially written English, is full of bad habits which spread by imitation and which can be avoided if one is willing to take the necessary trouble. If one gets rid of these habits one can think more clearly, and to think clearly is a necessary first step towards political regeneration.

Orwell's thesis is obvious early on. Sometimes, however, a writer will state the main point only in a summing up at the end. Other writers won't come out and state their theses in any neat Orwellian capsule at all. Even so, the main point of a well-unified essay will make itself clear to you — so clear that you can sum it up in a sentence of your own.

Didion's essay holds its main point for the end. A sentence in the middle of paragraph 7 stands out. It seems her important final idea. Speaking of her illness, she affirms, "And I have learned now to live with it, learned when to expect it, how to outwit it, even how to regard it, when it does come, as more friend than lodger." That is the first indication we get that this essay will take an unexpected final twist. And in that sentence, Didion sums up her thesis for us. You can state this main idea in many ways; one might be as follows: Migraine, for all the suffering it causes, has a positive value; the terrible monster is in truth a friend.

It's part of your job as an active reader to discover the writer's purpose and also to judge whether that purpose is actually achieved — whether the thesis or main point comes through, whether it's supported well enough to convince you of its sincerity and its truth, at least in the terms set by the author. (Such conviction is a basic transaction between writer and reader, even when the writer isn't seeking the reader's outright agreement or action.) Sometimes you'll be confused by a writer's point — "What *is* this about?" — and sometimes your confusion won't yield to repeated careful readings. That's when you'll want to toss the book or magazine aside in exasperation, but you won't always have the choice: A school or work assignment or just an urge to figure out the writer's problem may keep you at it. Then it'll be up to you to figure out why the writer fails — in essence, to clarify what's unclear — by discovering, say, where the writer's assumptions are invalid or where facts or examples fall short.

Analyzing writers' purposes and their successes and failures makes you an alert and critical reader. Applied to your own writing, this analysis also gives you a decided advantage, for when you write with a clear-cut purpose in mind, you head toward a goal. The reader may not know it yet, but you do. You thus control the progress of your essay from beginning to end. The more exactly you define this purpose, the easier you'll find it to fulfill. Of course, sometimes you just can't know what you are going to say until you say it, to echo the English novelist E. M. Forster. In such a situation, your purpose emerges as you write.

Writing Strategy

Here's another element to look for in an essay, and to learn from. STRATEGY is an inclusive name for whatever practices make for good writing. Because Joan Didion holds our interest and engages our sympathies, it will pay us to ask: How does she succeed? (When a writer bores or confuses us, we ask why he or she fails.) You'll notice that Didion keeps involving her readers by referring to common, or uncommon but intriguing, experiences. The details she gives involve us. Didion's account of her symptoms (when the period of "aura" begins) is convincingly, unforgettably specific and particular. "I will drive through red lights," she says, "lose the house keys, spill whatever I am holding. . . ." And at the end, Didion leaves us aware of the definite, specific joys of having survived a migraine attack: "I notice the particular nature of a flower in a glass on the stair landing." In her wonderful, and wonderfully specific, last paragraph, Didion sets forth her main point once more: that life is worth cherishing despite migraine attacks, perhaps even because of them. We believe her — she succeeds in her purpose — because of how vivid and precise she has been all along.

Part of a writer's strategy — Didion's, too — is the method or methods used to develop (construct and support) the main idea. Didion draws on a variety of methods that guide her choice of details: She narrates her experiences with migraine; she describes the headache; she defines migraine and explains how it happens (its process); she explores its causes. Some essays in this book illustrate how a single method may dominate, though always other methods crop up within paragraphs or shorter passages. As for Didion, the method or methods help the writer explore the subject and make it live for the reader.

Aside from the details, probably no writing strategy is as crucial to success as finding an appropriate structure. Writing that we find interesting and clear and convincing almost always has UNITY (everything relates to the main idea) and COHERENCE (the relations between parts are clear). When we find an essay wanting, it may be because the writer got lost in digressions or couldn't make the parts fit together. Sometimes structure almost takes care of itself — the method of narration, for instance, usually dictates a chronological sequence — but when it doesn't, the writer must impose an organization. Didion does just this: She molds her information, memories, and impressions into a shape that piques and holds our interest. The structure of her essay, with its surprise ending, is worth admiring. Reading "In Bed," we learn right away that migraine headaches are a living nightmare. But the final idea the writer leaves us with is more interesting. There's a reason for this gradual unfolding. By first showing us the terrors and sufferings of migraine, Didion achieves a much greater and more surprising effect when she finally declares that the headache is her friend. Few readers expect, when they begin the essay, that it will end in a strong, vivid account of how a migraine attack is useful, how it leaves the writer refreshed, joyful, thankful, and serene.

Language

To examine the element of language is often to go even more deeply into an essay and how it was made. Didion, you'll notice, is a writer whose language is rich and varied. It isn't entirely book-ish. Many arrays of common one-syllable words, many expressions from common speech, lend her prose style vigor and naturalness: "Three, four, sometimes five times a month," "Why not take a couple of aspirin." But consult a dictionary if you need help in defining *lobotomy* (para. 2), *vascular, contretemps, predisposition* (3), *contraindications* (4), *gastrointestinal, aphasia* (5), *compulsive* (6), *euphoria* (8). We assure you that, while questions in this book point to troublesome or unfamiliar words, only you can decide if they are worth looking up. We don't expect you to become a slave to your dictionary, only a frequent client of it. As a writer, you can have no trait more valuable to you than a fondness for words, an enjoyment of strange ones, and a yen to enlarge your working word supply.

Besides commanding a vigorous, well-stocked vocabulary, Didion is a master of FIGURES OF SPEECH: bits of colorful language not meant to be taken literally. One such vivid example is her memorable SIMILE (or likening of one thing to another): "The migraine has acted as a circuit breaker . . ." (para. 8). Speaking in paragraph 1 of the "circumnavigation" of a job application form, Didion uses a METAPHOR. In paragraph 7 she introduces another: Daily life is sometimes "not an open but a guerrilla war." Sometimes she resorts to deliberate exaggeration, the figure of speech called HYPERBOLE: She "wished only for a neurosurgeon who would do a lobotomy on house call" (2). Exaggeration lets her make a point with force: "Tell me that my house is burned down, my husband has left me, that there is gunfighting in the streets and panic in the banks, and I will not respond by getting a headache" (7). Sometimes, on the other hand, she resorts to UNDERSTATEMENT, drily remarking, "That no one dies of migraine seems, to someone deep into an attack, an ambiguous blessing" (5). (What would that idea be if stated directly? Perhaps "When I'm in the middle of an attack I wish I might die.") These playful and illustrative uses of language — the colorful comparisons, the under- and overstatements — give Didion's writing flavor and life. (More examples of figures of speech can be found under Useful Terms, page 729).

A writer's language not only sharpens and animates meaning but also conveys and elicits attitudes. *Tone* — the equivalent of tone of voice in speaking — is achieved by choice of words and sentence patterns. Whether it's angry, sarcastic, or sad, joking or serious, it carries almost as much information about the writer's purpose as the words themselves do. Didion's tone is matter-of-fact, almost deadpan, the better to expose the horribleness of the handicap she describes. (A histrionic approach would overwhelm the sensations.) With everything you read, as with "In Bed," it's instructive to study the writer's tone so that you are aware of whether and how it affects you. Pay particular attention to the CONNOTATIONS of words — their implied meanings, their associations. We sympathize when Didion must confront the "accusing eye" of the "unafflicted" (6): We share her mild hostility toward these accusers for their lack of understanding and tact. When one writer calls the homeless "society's downtrodden" and another calls them "human refuse," we know something of their attitudes and can use that knowledge to analyze and evaluate what they say about homelessness.

In reading essays, why not ask yourself: What am I looking for? Information? Ideas to start my own ideas for writing? Unfamiliar words to extend my vocabulary? A demonstration of how an excellent writer writes?

It never hurts to wonder: What's in this essay for me? Joan Didion, among the other writers in this book, has much to offer. Besides explaining how wonderful ordinary life can be (when the petty concerns and stresses have been swept away), she suggests that we might more keenly relish life. In her rich, beautifully exampled essay, Didion seeks not merely to explain migraines (which, after all, no one completely understands). Her audience isn't only other migraine-sufferers; it's everybody. She wakes us up to our blessings, as if to make us more poignantly alive.

Throughout this book, every selection will be followed by "Suggestions for Writing." You may not wish to take these suggestions exactly as worded; they may merely urge your own thoughts toward what you want to say. Here are three possibilities suggested by "In Bed."

SUGGESTIONS FOR WRITING

1. Write a paragraph in which, referring to your own experience, you familiarize your reader with an illness you know intimately. (If you have never had such an illness, pick an unwelcome mood you know: the blues, for instance, or an irresistible desire to giggle during a solemn ceremony.)

2. Demonstrate, as Joan Didion does, that an apparent misfortune can prove to be a friend.

3. CONNECTIONS. "In Bed" is one of three essays in this book that deal with the experience of illness; the others are Richard Selzer's "The Discus Thrower" (p. 152) and Oliver Sacks's "The President's Speech" (p. 306). In an essay, compare one or both of these essays with Didion's, considering these questions: What is the psychological effect of illness on the person who is ill? What does the person lose and gain? To what extent can doctors help the person? What is the writer's view (implied or stated) of the medical profession?

1
NARRATION
Telling a Story

THE METHOD

"What happened?" you ask a friend who sports a luminous black eye. Unless he merely grunts, "A golf ball," he may answer you with a narrative — a story, true or fictional.

"OK," he sighs, "you know The Tenth Round? That night-club down by the docks that smells of formaldehyde? Last night I heard they were giving away $500 to anybody who could stand up for three minutes against this karate expert, the Masked Samurai. And so . . ."

You lean forward. At least, you lean forward *if* you love a story. Most of us do, particularly if the story tells us of people in action or in conflict, and if it is told briskly, vividly, and with insight into the human heart. Narration, or storytelling, is therefore a powerful method by which to engage and hold the attention of listeners — readers as well. A little of its tremendous power flows to the public speaker who starts off with a joke, even a stale joke ("A funny thing happened to me on my way over here . . ."), and to the preacher who at the beginning of a sermon tells of some funny or touching incident. In its opening paragraph, an article in a popular magazine ("Vampires Live Today!") will give us a brief, arresting narrative: perhaps the case history of a car dealer who noticed, one moonlit night, his incisors strangely lengthening.

At least a hundred times a year, you probably resort to narration, not always for the purpose of telling an entertaining story, but usually to explain, to illustrate a point, to report information, to argue, or to persuade. That is, although a narrative can run from the beginning of an essay to the end, more often in your writing (as in your speaking) a narrative is only a part of what you have to say. It is there because it serves a larger purpose. In truth, because narration is such an effective way to put across your ideas, the ability to tell a compelling story — on paper, as well as in conversation — may be one of the most useful skills you can acquire.

The term *narrative* takes in abundant territory. A narrative may be short or long, factual or imagined, as artless as a tale told in a locker room or as artful as a novel by Henry James. A narrative may instruct and inform, or simply divert and regale. It may set forth some point or message, or it may be as devoid of significance as a comic yarn or a horror tale whose sole aim is to curdle your blood.

A novel is a narrative, but a narrative doesn't have to be long. Sometimes an essay will include several brief stories. See, for instance, William F. Buckley, Jr.'s argument "Why Don't We Complain?" (p. 674). A type of story often used to illustrate a point is the ANECDOTE, a short, entertaining account of a single incident. Sometimes told of famous persons, anecdotes add color and life to history, biography, autobiography, and every issue of *People* magazine. Besides being fun to read, an anecdote can be deeply revealing. W. Jackson Bate, in his biography of Samuel Johnson, traces the growth of the great eighteenth-century critic and scholar's ideas and, with the aid of anecdotes, he shows that his subject was human and lovable. As Bate tells us, Dr. Johnson, a portly and imposing gentleman of fifty-five, had walked with some friends to the crest of a hill, where the great man,

> delighted by its steepness, said he wanted to "take a roll down." They tried to stop him. But he said he "had not had a roll for a long time," and taking out of his pockets his keys, a pencil, a purse, and other objects, lay down parallel at the edge of the hill, and rolled down its full length, "turning himself over and over till he came to the bottom."

However small the event it relates, this anecdote is memorable — partly because of its attention to detail, such as the exact list of the contents of Johnson's pockets. In such a brief story, a super- human figure comes down to human size. In one stroke, Bate re- veals an essential part of Johnson: his boisterous, hearty, and boy- ish sense of fun.

An anecdote may be used to explain a point. Asked why he had appointed to a cabinet post Josephus Daniels, the harshest critic of his policies, President Woodrow Wilson replied with an anecdote of an old woman he knew. On spying a strange man uri- nating through her picket fence into her flower garden, she in- vited the offender into her yard because, as she explained to him, "I'd a whole lot rather have you inside pissing out than have you outside pissing in." By telling this story, a rude ANALOGY (see Chapter 8 for more examples), Wilson made clear his situation in regard to his political enemy more succinctly and pointedly than if he had given a more abstract explanation. As a statesman, Woodrow Wilson may have had his flaws; but as a storyteller, he is surely among the less forgettable.

THE PROCESS

So far, we have considered a few uses of narration. Now let us see how you tell an effective story.

Every good story has a purpose. Perhaps the storyteller seeks to explain what it was like to be a black American in a certain time and place (as Maya Angelou does in "Champion of the World" in this chapter); perhaps the teller seeks merely to enter- tain us. Whatever the reason for its telling, an effective story holds the attention of readers or listeners; and to do so, the story-teller shapes that story to appeal to its audience. If, for instance, you plan to tell a few friends of an embarrassing moment you had on your way to campus — you tripped and spilled a load of books into the arms of a passing dean — you know how to proceed. Simply to provide a laugh is your purpose, and your listeners, who need no introduction to you or the dean, need be told only the bare events of the story. Perhaps you'll use some vivid words to convey the surprise on the dean's face when sixty pounds of lit-erary lumber hit her. Perhaps you'll throw in a little surprise of your own. At first, you didn't take in the identity of this passerby on whom you'd dumped a load of literary lumber. Then you real-ized: It was the dean!

Such simple, direct storytelling is so common and habitual that we do it without planning in advance. The *narrator* (or teller) of such a personal experience is the speaker, the one who was there. (Five selections in this chapter — by Maya Angelou, Ralph Ellison, George Orwell, James Thurber, and John Simpson — tell of such experiences. All except Ellison use the first PERSON *I*.) The telling is usually SUBJECTIVE, with details and language chosen to express the writer's feelings. Of course, a personal experience told in the first person can use some artful telling and some structur-ing. (In the course of this discussion, we'll offer advice on telling stories of different kinds.)

When a story isn't your own experience but a recital of some-one else's, or of events that are public knowledge, then you pro-ceed differently. Without expressing opinions, you step back and report, content to stay invisible. Instead of saying, "I did this; I did that," you use the third PERSON, *he, she, it,* or *they*: "The run-ner did this; he did that." You may have been on the scene; if so, you will probably write as a spectator, from your own POINT OF VIEW (or angle of seeing). If you put together what happened from the testimony of others, you tell the story from the point of view of a *nonparticipant* (a witness who didn't take part). Generally, you are OBJECTIVE in setting forth events: unbiased, as accurate and dispassionate as possible.

When you narrate a story in the third person, you aren't a character central in the eyes of your audience. Unlike the first-person writer of a personal experience, you aren't the main actor; you are the camera operator, whose job is to focus on what transpires. Most history books and news stories are third-person narratives, and so is much fiction. (In this chapter, the selections by Calvin Trillin and Shirley Jackson illustrate third-person narration.) An *omniscient narrator*, one who is all-knowing, can see into the minds of the characters. Sometimes, as in a novel or any imagined story, a writer finds it effective to give us people's inmost thoughts. Whether omniscient narration works or not depends on the subject and the storyteller's purpose. In narrating actual events, as Trillin does, writers stick to the facts and do not invent the thoughts of participants (historical novels, though, do mingle fact and fancy in this way). And even writers of fiction and anecdote imagine the thoughts of their characters only if they want to explore psychology. Note how much Woodrow Wilson's anecdote would lose if the teller had gone into the thoughts of his characters: "The old woman was angry and embarrassed at seeing the stranger. . . ."

Whether you tell of your own experience or of someone else's, you need a whole story to tell. Before starting to write, do some searching and discovering. One trusty method to test your memory (or to make sure you have all the necessary elements of a story) is that of a news reporter. Ask yourself:

1. *What* happened?
2. *Who* took part?
3. *When?*
4. *Where?*
5. *Why* did this event (or these events) take place?
6. *How* did it happen?

That last *how* isn't merely another way of asking what happened. It means: In exactly what way or under what circumstances? If the event was a murder, how was it done — with an ax or with a bulldozer? Journalists call this handy list of questions "the five *W*s and the *H*."

Well-prepared storytellers, those who first search their memories (or do some research and legwork), have far more information on hand than they can use. The writing of a good story calls for careful choice. In choosing, remember your purpose and your audience. If you're writing that story of the dean and the books to give pleasure to readers who are your friends, delighted to hear about the discomfort of a pompous administrator, you will probably dwell lovingly on each detail of her consternation. You would tell the story differently if your audience were strangers who didn't know the dean from Adam. They would need more information on her background, reputation for stiffness, and appearance. If, suspected of having deliberately contrived the dean's humiliation, you were writing a report of the incident for the campus police, you'd want to give the plainest possible account of the story — without drama, without adornment, without background, and certainly without any humor whatsoever.

Your purpose and your audience, then, clearly determine which of the two main strategies of narration you're going to choose: to tell a story by *scene* or to tell it by *summary*. When you tell a story in a scene, or in scenes, you visualize each event as vividly and precisely as if you were there — as though it were a scene in a film, and your reader sat before the screen. This is the strategy of most fine novels and short stories — and of much excellent nonfiction as well. Instead of just mentioning people, you portray them. You recall dialogue as best you can, or you invent some that could have been spoken. You include DESCRIPTION (a mode of writing to be dealt with fully in our next chapter).

For a lively example of a well-drawn scene, see Maya Angelou's account of a tense crowd's behavior as, jammed into a small-town store, they listen to a fight broadcast (in "Champion of the World," beginning on page 37). Angelou prolongs one scene for almost her entire essay. Sometimes, though, a writer will draw a scene in only two or three sentences. This is the brevity we find in W. Jackson Bate's glimpse of the hill-rolling Johnson. Unlike Angelou, Bate evidently seeks not to weave a tapestry of detail, but to show, in telling of one brief event, a trait of his hero's character.

When, on the other hand, you tell a story by the method of summary, you relate events concisely. Instead of depicting people and their surroundings in great detail, you set down what happened in relatively spare narrative form. Most of us employ this method in most stories we tell, for it takes less time and fewer words. A summary is to a scene, then, as a simple stick figure is to a portrait in oils. This is not to dismiss simple stick figures as inferior. A story told in summary may be as effective as a story told in scenes, in lavish detail.

Again, your choice of a method depends on your answer to the questions you ask yourself: What is my purpose? Who is my audience? How fully to flesh out a scene, how much detail to include — these choices depend on what you seek to do, and on how much your audience needs to know to follow you. Read the life of some famous person in an encyclopedia, and you will find the article telling its story in summary form. Its writer's purpose, evidently, is to recount the main events of a whole life in a short space. But glance through a book-length biography of the same celebrity, and you will probably find scenes in it. A biographer writes with a different purpose: to present a detailed portrait roundly and thoroughly, bringing the subject vividly to life.

To be sure, you can use both methods in telling a single story. Often, summary will serve a writer who passes briskly from one scene to the next, or hurries over events of lesser importance. Were you to write, let's say, the story of a man's fiendish passion for horse racing, you might decide to give short shrift to most other facts of his life. To emphasize what you consider essential, you might begin a scene with a terse summary: "Seven years went by, and after three marriages and two divorces, Lars found himself again back at Hialeah." (A detailed scene might follow.)

Good storytellers know what to emphasize. They do not fall into a boring drone: "And then I went down to the club and I had a few beers and I noticed this sign, Go 3 Minutes with the Masked Samurai and Win $500, so I went and got knocked out and then I had pizza and went home." In this lazily strung-out summary, the narrator reduces all events to equal unimportance. A more adept storyteller might leave out the pizza and dwell in detail on the big fight.

Some storytellers assume that to tell a story in the present tense (instead of the past tense, traditionally favored) gives events a sense of immediacy. Presented as though everything were happening right now, the story of the Masked Samurai might begin:

"I duck between the ropes and step into the ring. My heart is thudding fast." You can try the present tense, if you like, and see how immediate it seems to you. Be warned, however, that nowadays so many fiction writers write in this fashion that to use the past tense may make your work seem almost fresh and original.

In *The Bedford Reader*, we are concerned with the kind of writing you do every day in college: writing in which you generally explain ideas, or organize information you have learned. Unless you take a creative writing course, you probably won't write fiction — imaginary stories — and yet in fiction we find an enormously popular and appealing use of narration, and certain devices of storytelling from which all storytellers can learn. For these reasons, this chapter includes one celebrated short story by a master storyteller, Shirley Jackson. As Maya Angelou does in her true memoir "Champion of the World," Jackson strives to make the people in her story come alive for us. She does, however, do something that nonfiction narrators ordinarily do not do: She uses a lot of dialogue, letting conversation advance the story. In fiction, an author may pay as much attention to a change of feelings, or a sudden realization, as a historian pays to a decisive battle; and dialogue can reveal feelings.

In historical or fictional narration, the simplest method is to set down events in CHRONOLOGICAL ORDER, the way they happened. To do so is to have your story already organized for you. A chronological order is therefore an excellent sequence to follow unless you can see some special advantage in violating it. Ask: What am I trying to do? If you are trying to capture your reader's attention right away, you might begin *in medias res* (Latin, "in the middle of things"); and open with a colorful, dramatic event, even though it took place late in the chronology. If trying for dramatic effect, you might save the most exciting or impressive event for last, even though it actually happened early. By this means, you can keep your readers in suspense for as long as possible. (You can return to earlier events by a FLASHBACK, an earlier scene recalled.) Let your purpose be your guide.

Calvin Trillin has recalled why, in a narrative titled "The Tunica Treasure," he deliberately chose not to follow a chronology:

I wrote a story on the discovery of the Tunica treasure which I couldn't begin by saying, "Here is a man who works as a prison guard in Angola State Prison, and on his weekends he sometimes looks for buried treasure that is rumored to be around the Indian village." Because the real point of the story centered around the problems caused when an amateur wanders on to professional territory, I thought it would be much better to open with how momentous the discovery was, that it was the most important archeological discovery about Indian contact with the European settlers to date, and *then* to say that it was discovered by a prison guard. So I made a conscious choice *not* to start with Leonard Charrier working as a prison guard, not to go back to his boyhood in Bunkie, Louisiana, not to talk about how he'd always been interested in treasure hunting — hoping that the reader would assume I was about to say that the treasure was found by an archeologist from the Peabody Museum at Harvard.

Trillin, by saving the fact that a prison guard made the earth-shaking discovery, effectively took his reader by surprise.

No matter what order you choose, either following chronology or departing from it, make sure your audience can follow it. The sequence of events has to be clear. This calls for transitions of time, whether they are brief phrases that point out exactly when each event happened ("Seven years later," "A moment earlier"), or whole sentences that announce an event and clearly locate it in time ("If you had known Leonard Charrier ten years earlier, you would have found him voraciously poring over every archeology text he could lay his hands on in the public library").

In writing a news story, a reporter often begins with the conclusion, placing the main event in the *lead*, or opening paragraph. Dramatically, this may be the weakest method to tell the story; yet it is effective in this case because the reporter's purpose is not to entertain but rather to tell quickly what happened, for an audience impatient to learn the essentials. In most other kinds of narration, however, whether fiction or nonfiction, whether to entertain or to make an idea clear, the storyteller builds toward a memorable conclusion. In a story Mark Twain liked to tell aloud, a woman's ghost returns to claim her artificial arm made of gold, which she wore in life and which her greedy husband had unscrewed from her corpse. Carefully, Twain would build up suspense as the ghost pursued the husband upstairs to his bedroom, stood by his bed, breathed her cold breath on him, and intoned, "*Who's got my golden arm?*" Twain used to end his story by suddenly yelling at a member of the audience, "*You've* got it!" — and enjoying the victim's shriek of surprise. That final punctuating shriek may be a technique that will work only in oral storytelling; yet, like Twain, most storytellers like to end with a bang if they can. The final impact, however, need not be so obvious. As Maya Angelou demonstrates in her story in this chapter, you can achieve impact just by leading to a point. In an effective written narrative, a writer usually hits the main events of a story especially hard, often saving the best punch (or the best karate chop) for the very end.

NARRATION IN A PARAGRAPH: TWO ILLUSTRATIONS

Using Narration to Write about Television

Oozing menace from beyond the stars or from the deeps, televised horror powerfully stimulates a child's already frisky imagination. As parents know, a "Creature Double Feature" has an impact that lasts long after the click of the *off* button. Recently a neighbor reported the strange case of her eight-year-old. Discovered late at night in the game room watching *The Exorcist*, the girl was promptly sent to bed. An hour later, her parents could hear her chanting something in the darkness of her bedroom. On tiptoe, they stole to her door to listen. The creak of springs told them that their daughter was swaying rhythmically to and fro and the smell of acrid smoke warned them that something was burning. At once, they shoved open the door to find the room flickering with shadows cast by a lighted candle. Their daughter was sitting up in bed, rocking back and forth as she intoned over and over, "Fiend in human form . . . Fiend in human form . . ." This case may be unique; still, it seems likely that similar events take place each night all over the screen-watching world.

COMMENT. This paragraph, addressed to a general audience — that is, most readers, those who read nonspecialized books or magazines — puts a story to work to support a thesis statement. A brief anecdote, the story of the mesmerized child backs up the claim (in the second sentence) that for children the impact of TV horror goes on and on. The story relates a small, ordinary, but disquieting experience taken from the writer's conversation with friends. A bit of suspense is introduced, and the reader's curiosity is whetted, when the parents steal to the bedroom door to learn why the child isn't asleep. The *crisis* — the dramatic high moment in the story when our curiosity is about to be gratified — is a sensory detail: the smell of smoke. At the end of the paragraph, the writer stresses the importance of these events by suggesting that they are probably universal. In a way, he harks back to his central idea, reminding us of his reason for telling the story. Narration, as you can see, is a method for dramatizing your ideas.

Using Narration in an Academic Discipline

The news media periodically relate the terrifying and often grim details of landslides. On May 31, 1970, one such event occurred when a gigantic rock avalanche buried more than 20,000 people in Yungay and Ranrahirca, Peru. There was little warning of the impending disaster; it began and ended in just a matter of a few minutes. The avalanche started 14 kilometers from Yungay, near the summit of 6,700-meter-high Nevados Huascaran, the loftiest peak in the Peruvian Andes. Triggered by the ground motion from a strong offshore earthquake, a huge mass of rock and ice broke free from the precipitous north face of the mountain. After plunging nearly one kilometer, the material pulverized on impact and immediately began rushing down the mountainside, made fluid by trapped air and melted ice. The initial mass ripped loose additional millions of tons of debris as it roared downhill. The shock waves produced by the event created thunderlike noise and stripped nearby hillsides of vegetation. Although the material followed a previously eroded gorge, a portion of the debris jumped a 200–300-meter-high bedrock ridge that had protected Yungay from past rock avalanches and buried the entire city. After inundating another town in its path, Ranrahirca, the mass of debris finally reached the bottom of the valley where its momentum carried it across the Rio Santa and tens of meters up the opposite bank.

COMMENT. This paragraph of vivid narration enlivens a college textbook, *The Earth: An Introduction to Physical Geology*, by Edward J. Tarbuck and Frederick K. Lutgens (1984). To illustrate the awesome power of a landslide, the writers give this one-paragraph example, choosing one of the most horrendous such catastrophes in history. Not all landslides are so spectacular, of course, and yet this brief narrative serves to set forth traits typical of landslides in general: sudden beginning, fast movement, irresistible force. This paragraph shows another way in which narration can serve: as a memorable example, making the point that landslides concern people and can cost lives, and as a means to enlist the reader's immediate attention to a discussion that otherwise might seem dry and abstract.

MAYA ANGELOU

MAYA ANGELOU was born Marguerite Johnson in St. Louis in 1928. After an unpleasantly eventful youth by her account ("from a broken family, raped at eight, unwed mother at sixteen"), she went on to join a dance company, star in an off-Broadway play (*The Blacks*), write six books of poetry, produce a series on Africa for PBS-TV, act in the television-special series *Roots*, serve as a coordinator for the Southern Christian Leadership Conference at the request of Martin Luther King, Jr., and accept several honorary doctorates. She is best known, however, for the five books of her searching, frank, and joyful autobiography — beginning with *I Know Why the Caged Bird Sings* (1970), which she adapted for television, through *All God's Children Need Traveling Shoes* (1986). She is Reynolds Professor of American Studies at Wake Forest University.

Champion of the World

"Champion of the World" is the nineteenth chapter in *I Know Why the Caged Bird Sings*; the title is a phrase taken from the chapter. Remembering her childhood, the writer tells how she and her older brother, Bailey, grew up in a town in Arkansas. The center of their lives was Grandmother and Uncle Willie's store, a gathering place for the black community. On the night when this story takes place, Joe Louis, the "Brown Bomber" and the hero of his people, defends his heavyweight boxing title against a white contender.

The last inch of space was filled, yet people continued to wedge themselves along the walls of the Store. Uncle Willie had turned the radio up to its last notch so that youngsters on the porch wouldn't miss a word. Women sat on kitchen chairs, dining-room chairs, stools, and upturned wooden boxes. Small children and babies perched on every lap available and men leaned on the shelves or on each other.

37

The apprehensive mood was shot through with shafts of gai- ²
ety, as a black sky is streaked with lightning.

"I ain't worried 'bout this fight. Joe's gonna whip that cracker ³
like it's open season."

"He gone whip him till that white boy call him Momma." ⁴

At last the talking finished and the string-along songs ⁵
about razor blades were over and the fight began.

"A quick jab to the head." In the Store the crowd grunted. ⁶
"A left to the head and a right and another left." One of the listeners cackled like a hen and was quieted.

"They're in a clinch, Louis is trying to fight his way out." ⁷

Some bitter comedian on the porch said, "That white man ⁸
don't mind hugging that niggah now, I betcha."

"The referee is moving in to break them up, but Louis finally ⁹
pushed the contender away and it's an uppercut to the chin. The
contender is hanging on, now he's backing away. Louis catches
him with a short left to the jaw."

A tide of murmuring assent poured out the door and into the ¹⁰
yard.

"Another left and another left. Louis is saving that mighty ¹¹
right . . ." The mutter in the Store had grown into a baby roar
and it was pierced by the clang of a bell and the announcer's
"That's the bell for round three, ladies and gentlemen."

As I pushed my way into the Store I wondered if the an- ¹²
nouncer gave any thought to the fact that he was addressing as
"ladies and gentlemen" all the Negroes around the world who sat
sweating and praying, glued to their "master's voice."[1]

There were only a few calls for RC Colas, Dr Peppers, and ¹³
Hires root beer. The real festivities would begin after the fight.
Then even the old Christian ladies who taught their children and
tried themselves to practice turning the other cheek would buy
soft drinks, and if the Brown Bomber's victory was a particularly
bloody one they would order peanut patties and Baby Ruths also.

---

[1]"His master's voice," accompanied by a picture of a little dog listening to
a phonograph, was a familiar advertising slogan. (The picture still appears on
RCA Victor records.) — Eds.

Bailey and I laid the coins on top of the cash register. Uncle   14
Willie didn't allow us to ring up sales during a fight. It was too
noisy and might shake up the atmosphere. When the gong rang
for the next round we pushed through the near-sacred quiet to
the herd of children outside.

"He's got Louis against the ropes and now it's a left to the   15
body and a right to the ribs. Another right to the body, it looks
like it was low . . . Yes, ladies and gentlemen, the referee is signal-
ing but the contender keeps raining the blows on Louis. It's another to the body, and it looks like Louis is going down."

My race groaned. It was our people falling. It was another   16
lynching, yet another Black man hanging on a tree. One more
woman ambushed and raped. A Black boy whipped and maimed.
It was hounds on the trail of a man running through slimy
swamps. It was a white woman slapping her maid for being forget-
ful.

The men in the Store stood away from the walls and at atten-   17
tion. Women greedily clutched the babes on their laps while on
the porch the shufflings and smiles, flirtings and pinching of a few
minutes before were gone. This might be the end of the world. If
Joe lost we were back in slavery and beyond help. It would all be
true, the accusations that we were lower types of human beings.
Only a little higher than apes. True that we were stupid and ugly
and lazy and dirty and, unlucky and worst of all, that God Himself hated us and ordained us to be hewers of wood and drawers
of water, forever and ever, world without end.

We didn't breathe. We didn't hope. We waited.   18

"He's off the ropes, ladies and gentlemen. He's moving   19
towards the center of the ring." There was no time to be relieved.
The worst might still happen.

"And now it looks like Joe is mad. He's caught Carnera with   20
a left hook to the head and a right to the head. It's a left jab to the
body and another left to the head. There's a left cross and a right
to the head. The contender's right eye is bleeding and he can't
seem to keep his block up. Louis is penetrating every block. The
referee is moving in, but Louis sends a left to the body and it's an
uppercut to the chin and the contender is dropping. He's on the
canvas, ladies and gentlemen."

Babies slid to the floor as women stood up and men leaned 21
toward the radio.

"Here's the referee. He's young. One, two, three, four, five, 22
six, seven . . . Is the contender trying to get up again?"

All the men in the store shouted, "NO." 23

" — eight, nine, ten." There were a few sounds from the au- 24
dience, but they seemed to be holding themselves in against tremendous pressure.

"The fight is all over, ladies and gentlemen. Let's get the mi- 25
crophone over to the referee . . . Here he is. He's got the Brown
Bomber's hand, he's holding it up . . . Here he is . . ."

Then the voice, husky and familiar, came to wash over us — 26
"The winnah, and still heavyweight champeen of the world . . .
Joe Louis."

Champion of the world. A Black boy. Some Black mother's 27
son. He was the strongest man in the world. People drank Coca-
Colas like ambrosia and ate candy bars like Christmas. Some of
the men went behind the Store and poured white lightning in
their soft-drink bottles, and a few of the bigger boys followed
them. Those who were not chased away came back blowing their
breath in front of themselves like proud smokers.

It would take an hour or more before the people would leave 28
the Store and head for home. Those who lived too far had made
arrangements to stay in town. It wouldn't do for a Black man and
his family to be caught on a lonely country road on a night when
Joe Louis had proved that we were the strongest people in the
world.

QUESTIONS ON MEANING

1. What do you take to be the author's PURPOSE in telling this story?
2. What connection does Angelou make between the outcome of the
   fight and the pride of the black race? To what degree do you think
   the author's view is shared by the others in the store listening to the
   broadcast?

3. To what extent are the statements in paragraphs 16 and 17 to be taken literally? What function do they serve in Angelou's narrative?
4. Primo Carnera was probably *not* the Brown Bomber's opponent on the night Maya Angelou recalls. Louis fought Carnera only once, on June 25, 1935, and it was not a title match; Angelou would have been no more than seven years old at the time. Does the author's apparent error detract from her story?

QUESTIONS ON WRITING STRATEGY

1. What details in the opening paragraphs indicate that an event of crucial importance is about to take place?
2. How does Angelou build up SUSPENSE in her account of the fight? At what point were you able to predict the winner?
3. Comment on the IRONY in Angelou's final paragraph.
4. What EFFECT does the author's use of direct quotation have on her narrative?
5. OTHER METHODS. Besides narration, Angelou also relies heavily on the method of description (Chap. 2). Analyze how narration depends on description just in paragraph 27.

QUESTIONS ON LANGUAGE

1. Explain what the author means by "string-along songs about razor blades" (para. 5).
2. How does Angelou's use of NONSTANDARD ENGLISH contribute to her narrative?
3. Be sure you know the meanings of these words: apprehensive (para. 2); assent (10); ambushed, maimed (16); ordained (17); ambrosia, white lightning (27).

SUGGESTIONS FOR WRITING

1. In a brief essay, write about the progress and outcome of a recent sporting event and your reaction to the outcome. Include enough illustrative detail to bring the contest to life.
2. Write an essay based on some childhood experience of your own, still vivid in your memory.
3. CONNECTIONS. Compare Angelou's narrative with Ralph Ellison's "On Being the Target of Discrimination" (p. 43). Using details and quotations from both works as evidence, write an essay on the ways

group identity — even or perhaps especially identity with an oppressed group such as black Americans — strengthens and binds the
group's members.

MAYA ANGELOU ON WRITING

Maya Angelou's writings have shown great variety: She has
done notable work as an autobiographer, poet, short story writer,
screenwriter, journalist, and song lyricist. Asked by interviewer
Sheila Weller, "Do you start each project with a specific idea?"
Angelou replied:

"It starts with a definite subject, but it might end with something entirely different. When I start a project, the first thing I do
is write down, in longhand, everything I know about the subject,
every thought I've ever had on it. This may be twelve or fourteen
pages. Then I read it back through, for quite a few days, and find
— given that subject — what its rhythm is. 'Cause everything in
the universe has a rhythm. So if it's free form, it still has a
rhythm. And once I hear the rhythm of the piece, then I try to
find out what are the salient points that I must make. And then it
begins to take shape.

"I try to set myself up in each chapter by saying: 'This is what
I want to go from — from B to, say, G-sharp. Or from D to L.'
And then I find the hook. It's like the knitting, where, after you
knit a certain amount, there's one thread that begins to pull. You
know, you can see it right along the cloth. Well, in writing, I
think: 'Now where is that one hook, that one little
thread?' It may be a sentence. If I can catch that, then I'm home-
free. It's the one that tells me where I'm going. It may not even
turn out to be in the final chapter. I may throw it out later or
change it. But if I follow it through, it leads me right out."

FOR DISCUSSION

1. How would you define the word *rhythm* as Maya Angelou uses it?
2. What response would you give a student who said, "Doesn't Angelou's approach to writing waste more time and thought than it's
   worth?"

RALPH ELLISON

RALPH WALDO ELLISON is best known for his award-winning novel *Invisible Man* (1952), about a black man who seeks his identity somewhere beyond white and black stereotypes. Born in 1919, Ellison studied music and read literature at Tuskegee Institute in Alabama but left before graduating for lack of money. He began publishing stories in the late 1930s and has written essays of autobiography, criticism, and cultural history that have been collected in *Shadow and Act* (1964) and *Going to the Territory* (1986). At New York University, Ellison was Albert Schweitzer Professor in Humanities for almost a decade, and he has lectured at Rutgers, Yale, and many other universities. His second novel, long awaited by his readers, has appeared in tantalizing excerpts over the years. Ellison lives in New York City and western Massachusetts.

On Being the Target of Discrimination

Ellison grew up in Oklahoma, where he felt that "relationships between the races were more fluid and thus more human than in the old slave states." Still, as a boy he knew discrimination in "brief impersonal encounters, stares, vocal inflections, hostile laughter, or public reversals of private expectations." Some of these slights are recounted in this essay, which first appeared in 1989 in *A World of Difference*, a special *New York Times* supplement devoted to reducing racial and ethnic prejudice.

It got to you first at the age of six, and through your own curiosity. With kindergarten completed and the first grade ahead, you were eagerly anticipating your first day of public school. For months you had been imagining your new experience and the children, known and unknown, with whom you would study and play. But the physical framework of your imagining, an elementary school in the process of construction, lay close at hand on the block-square site across the street from your home. For over a year you had watched it rise and spread in the air to become a

handsome structure of brick and stone, then seen its broad encir-
cling grounds arrayed with seesaws, swings, and baseball diamonds. You had imagined this picture-book setting as the scene
of your new experience, and when enrollment day arrived, with
its grounds astir with bright colors and voices of kids like yourself,
it did, indeed, become the site of your very first lesson in public
schooling — though not within its classrooms, as you had imagined, but well outside its walls. For while located within a fairly
mixed neighborhood this new public school was exclusively for
whites.

It was then you learned that you would attend a school lo-   2
cated far to the south of your neighborhood, and that reaching it
involved a journey which took you over, either directly or by way
of a viaduct which arched head-spinning high above, a broad expanse of railroad tracks along which a constant traffic of freight-
cars, switch engines, and passenger trains made it dangerous for a
child to cross. And that once the tracks were safely negotiated
you continued past warehouses, factories, and loading docks, and
then through a notorious red-light district where black prostitutes
in brightly colored housecoats and Mary Jane shoes supplied the
fantasies and needs of a white clientele. Considering the fact that
you couldn't attend school with white kids this made for a confusion that was further confounded by the giggling jokes which
older boys whispered about the district's peculiar form of integration. For you it was a grown-up's mystery, but streets being no
less schools than routes to schools, the district would soon add a
few forbidden words to your vocabulary.

It took a bit of time to forget the sense of incongruity aroused   3
by your having to walk *past* a school to get *to* a school, but soon
you came to like your school, your teachers, and most of your
schoolmates. Indeed, you soon enjoyed the long walks and anticipated the sights you might see, the adventures you might encounter, and the many things not taught in school that could be
learned along the way. Your school was not nearly so fine as that
which faced your home but it had its attractions. Among them its
nearness to a park, now abandoned by whites, in which you pic-
nicked and played. And there were the two tall cylindrical fire-
escapes on either wing of its main building down which it was a

joy to lie full-length and slide, spiraling down and around three stories to the ground — providing no outraged teacher was waiting to strap your legs once you sailed out of its chute like a shot off a fireman's shovel. Besides, in your childish way you were learning that it was better to take self-selected risks and pay the price than be denied the joy or pain of risk-taking by those who begrudged your existence.

Beginning when you were four or five you had known the joy of trips to the city's zoo, but one day you would ask your mother to take you there and have her sigh and explain that it was now against the law for Negro kids to view the animals. Had someone done something bad to the animals? No. Had someone tried to steal them or feed them poison? No. Could white kids still go? Yes! So why? Quit asking questions, it's the law and only because some white folks are out to turn this state into a part of the South.   4

This sudden and puzzling denial of a Saturday's pleasure was disappointing and so angered your mother that later, after the zoo was moved north of the city, she decided to do something about it. Thus one warm Saturday afternoon with you and your baby brother dressed in your best she took you on a long streetcar ride which ended at a strange lakeside park, in which you found a crowd of noisy white people. Having assumed that you were on your way to the integrated cemetery where at the age of three you had been horrified beyond all tears or forgetting when you saw your father's coffin placed in the ground, you were bewildered. But now as your mother herded you and your brother in to the park you discovered that you'd come to the zoo and were so delighted that soon you were laughing and babbling as excitedly as the kids around you.   5

Your mother was pleased and as you moved through the crowd of white parents and children she held your brother's hand and allowed as much time for staring at the cages of rare animals as either of you desired. But once your brother began to tire she herded you out of the park and toward the streetcar line. And then it happened.   6

Just as you reached the gate through which crowds of whites were coming and going you had a memorable lesson in the   7 strange ways of segregated-democracy as instructed by a guard in civilian clothes. He was a white man dressed in a black suit and a white straw hat, and when he looked at the fashion in which your mother was dressed, then down to you and your brother, he stiffened, turned red in the face, and stared as though at something dangerous.

"Girl," he shouted, "where are your *white* folks!" 8

"*White* folks," your mother said, "What white folks? I don't 9 *have* any white folks, I'm a Negro!"

"Now don't you get smart with me, colored gal," the white 10 man said, "I mean where are the white folks you come *out* here with!"

"But I just told you that I didn't come here with any white 11 people," your mother said, "I came here with my boys . . ."

"Then what are you doing in this park," the white man said. 12

And now when your mother answered you could hear the fa- 13 miliar sound of anger in her voice.

"I'm here," she said, "because I'm a *taxpayer*, and I thought it 14 was about time that my boys have a look at those animals. And for that I didn't *need* any *white* folks to show me the way!"

"Well," the white man said, "*I'm* here to tell you that you're 15 breaking the law! So now you'll have to leave. Both you and your chillun too. The rule says no niggers is allowed in the zoo. That's the law and I'm enforcing it!"

"Very well," your mother said, "we've seen the animals 16 anyway and were on our way to the streetcar line when you stopped us."

"That's fine," the white man said, "and when that car comes 17 you be sure that you get on it, you hear? You and your chillun too!"

So it was quite a day. You had enjoyed the animals with 18 your baby brother and had another lesson in the sudden ways good times could be turned into bad when white people looked at your color instead of *you*. But better still, you had learned something of your mother's courage and were proud that she had broken an unfair law and stood up for her right to do so. For while the white man kept staring until the streetcar arrived she ignored him and answered your brother's questions about the various animals. Then the car came with its crowd of white parents and children, and when you were entrained and rumbling home past the fine lawns and houses your mother gave way to a gale of laughter; in which, hesitantly at first, and then with assurance and pride, you joined. And from that day the incident became the source of a family joke that was sparked by accidents, faux pas, or obvious lies. Then one of you was sure to frown and say, "Well, I think you'll have to go now, both you and your chillun too!" And the family would laugh hilariously. Discrimination teaches one to discriminate between discriminators while countering absurdity with black (Negro? Afro-American? African-American?) comedy.

When you were eight you would move to one of the white   19 sections through which you often passed on the way to your father's grave and your truly last trip to the zoo. For now your mother was the custodian of several apartments located in a building which housed on its street floor a drug store, a tailor shop, a Piggly Wiggly market, and a branch post office. Built on a downward slope, the building had at its rear a long driveway which led from the side street past an empty lot to a group of garages in which the apartments' tenants stored their cars. Built at an angle with wings facing north and east, the structure supported a servant's quarters which sat above its angle like a mock watchtower atop a battlement, and it was there that you now lived.

Reached by a flight of outside stairs, it consisted of four small   20 rooms, a bath, and a kitchen. Windows on three of its sides provided a view across the empty frontage to the street, of the back yards behind it, and of the back wall and windows of the building in which your mother worked. It was quite comfortable but you secretly disliked the idea of your mother living in service and missed your friends who now lived far away. Nevertheless, the neighborhood was pleasant, served by a sub-station of the street-car line, and marked by a variety of activities which challenged your curiosity. Even its affluent alleys were more exciting to explore than those of your old neighborhood, and the one white friend you were to acquire in the area lived nearby.

This friend was a brilliant but sickly boy who was tutored at   21

home, and with him you shared your new interest in building radios, a hobby at which he was quite skilled. Your friendship eased
your loneliness and helped dispel some of the mystery and resentment imposed by segregation. Through access to his family,
headed by an important Episcopalian minister, you learned more
about whites and thus about yourself. With him you could make
comparisons that were not so distorted by the racial myths which
obstructed your thrust toward self-perception; compare their differences in taste, discipline, and manners with those of Negro
families of comparable status and income; observe variations
between your friend's boyish lore and your own, and measure
his intelligence, knowledge, and ambitions against your own.
For you this was a most important experience and a rare privilege, because up to now the prevailing separation of the races
had made it impossible to learn how you and your Negro
friends compared with boys who lived on the white side of
the color line. It was said by word of mouth, proclaimed in
newsprint, and dramatized by acts of discriminatory law that
you were inferior. You were barred from vying with them
in sports and games, competing in the classroom or the world
of art. Yet what you saw, heard, and smelled of them left irrepres-
sible doubts. So you ached for objective proof, for a fair field of
testing.

    Even your school's proud marching band was denied partici-   22
pation in the statewide music contests so popular at the time, as
though so airy and earth-transcending an art as music would be
contaminated if performed by musicians of different races.

    Which was especially disturbing because after the father of a   23
friend who lived next door in your old neighborhood had taught
you the beginner's techniques required to play valved instruments you had decided to become a musician. Then shortly before moving among whites your mother had given you a brass
cornet, which in the isolation of the servant's quarters you practiced hours on end. But you yearned to play with other musicians
and found none available. Now you lived less than a block from a
white school with a famous band, but there was no one in the
neighborhood with whom to explore the mysteries of the horn.
You could hear the school band's music and watch their march-

ing, but joining in making the thrilling sounds was impossible. Nor did it help that you owned the scores to a few of their marches and could play with a certain facility and fairly good tone. So there, surrounded by sounds but unable to share a sound, you went it alone. You turned yourself into a one-man band.

You played along as best you could with the phonograph, 24 read the score to *The Carnival of Venice* while listening to Del Steigers executing triple-tongue variations on its themes; played the trumpet parts of your bandbook's marches while humming in your head the supporting voices of horns and reeds. And since your city was a seedbed of Southwestern jazz you played Kansas City riffs, bugle calls, and wha-wha-muted imitations of blues singers' pleas. But none of this made up for your lack of fellow musicians. And then, late one Saturday afternoon when your mother and brother were away, and when you had dozed off while reading, you awoke to the nearby sound of live music. At first you thought you were dreaming, and then that you were listening to the high school band, but that couldn't be the source because, instead of floating over building tops and bouncing off wall and windowpane, the sounds you heard rose up, somewhat muffled, from below.

With that you ran to a window which faced the driveway, 25 and looking down through the high windowpane of the lighted post office you could see the metal glint of instruments. Then you were on your feet and down the stairs, keeping to the shadows as you drew close and peeped below. And there you looked down upon a room full of men and women postal workers who were playing away at a familiar march. It was like the answer to a silent prayer because you could tell by the sound that they were beginners like yourself and the covers of the thicket of bandbooks revealed that they were of the same set as yours. For a while you listened and hummed along, unseen but shaking with excitement in the dimming twilight. And then, hardly before the idea formed in your head, you were skipping up the stairs to grab your cornet, lyre, and bandbook and hurtling down again to the drive.

For a while you listened, hearing the music come to a pause 26 and the sound of the conductor's voice. Then came a rap on a music stand and once again the music. And now turning to the march by the light from the window, you snapped score to lyre, raised horn to lip, and began to play; at first silently tonguing the notes through the mouthpiece and then, carried away with the thrill of stealing a part of the music, you tensed your diaphragm and blew. And as you played, keeping time with your foot on the concrete drive, you realized that you were a better cornetist than some in the band and grew bold in the pride of your sound. Now in your mind you were marching along a downtown street to the flying of flags, the tramping of feet, and the cheering of excited crowds. For at last by an isolated act of brassy cunning you had become a member of the band.

Yes, but unfortunately you then let yourself become so car- 27 ried away that you forgot to listen for the conductor's instructions which you were too high and hidden to see. Suddenly the music faded and you opened your ears to the fact that you were now rendering a lonely solo in the startled quietness. And before you could fully return to reality there came the sound of table legs across a floor and a rustle of movement ending in the appearance of a white startled face in the opened window. Then you heard a man's voice exclaim, "I'll be damn, it's a little nigger!" whereupon you took off like quail at the sound of sudden shotgun fire.

Next thing you knew, you were up the stairs and on your 28 bed, crying away in the dark your guilt and embarrassment. You cried and cried, asking yourself how could you have been so lacking in pride as to shame yourself and your entire race by butting in where you weren't wanted. And this just to make some amateur music. To this you had no answers but then and there you made a vow that it would never happen again. And then, slowly, slowly, as you lay in the dark, your earlier lessons in the absurd nature of racial relations came to your aid. And suddenly you found yourself laughing, both at the way you'd run away and the shock you'd caused by joining unasked in the music.

Then you could hear yourself intoning in your eight-year- 29 old's imitation of a white Southern accent. "Well boy, you broke the law, so you have to go, and that means you and your chillun too!"

QUESTIONS ON MEANING

1. What do you see as Ellison's PURPOSE in writing this essay?
2. What does the phrase "You and your chillun too" mean in paragraph 17? What does it come to mean in the writer's family? What does it mean at the end of the essay?
3. How does the writer's self-image change from the beginning of the narrative to the end?

QUESTIONS ON WRITING STRATEGY

1. What is the narrator's POINT OF VIEW? What PERSON does the narrator use? What EFFECT does this choice of person have on you as reader?
2. Why do you think this essay was published in a newspaper supplement designed to reduce discrimination (see the note on the essay, page 43)? How did the essay affect your understanding of or attitude toward discrimination?
3. Why does Ellison narrate several events instead of just one? What is the point of each incident?
4. How do we learn that the narrator's father is dead? Is this fact important to the narrative? Is the narrator's handling of it effective?
5. OTHER METHODS. Comment on Ellison's use of examples (Chap. 3) in paragraphs 3 and 24. What do they add?

QUESTIONS ON LANGUAGE

1. What do the description and dialogue in paragraphs 7–17 tell you about Ellison's attitude toward the white zoo guard?
2. What is generally meant by "black comedy" or "black humor"? What joke is Ellison making at the end of paragraph 18?
3. Define: astir (para. 1); viaduct, clientele (2); incongruity, begrudged (3); faux pas (18); battlement (19); lore, vying (21); intoning (29).

SUGGESTIONS FOR WRITING

1. Write a narrative about a childhood event in which you discovered something about your place in the world. Give careful consideration to POINT OF VIEW and the use of dialogue.

2. Relate an incident from your childhood that illustrates how you felt about a particular environment — a house, rooftop, school, neighborhood, clearing in the woods. Use description (Chap. 2) to create a clear picture of the place.

3. CONNECTIONS. If you haven't already, read Maya Angelou's "Champion of the World" (p. 37). Compare and contrast the ways the black people in Ellison's and Angelou's essays find their value as human beings.

RALPH ELLISON ON WRITING

In his introduction to his collection of essays, *Shadow and Act* (1964), Ralph Ellison talks about how he came to be a writer. "When the first of these essays [reprinted in *Shadow and Act*] was published I regarded myself — in my most secret heart at least — a musician. . . . Writing was far from a serious matter. . . . Nor had I invested in writing any long hours of practice and study. Rather it was a reflex of reading, an extension of a source of pleasure, escape, and instruction. . . . It was not, then, the *process* of writing which initially claimed my attention, but the finished creations, the artifacts — poems, plays, novels. . . . The pleasure I derived from reading had long been a necessity, and in the *act* of reading, that marvelous collaboration between the writer's artful vision and the reader's sense of life, I had become acquainted with other possible selves — freer, more courageous and ingenuous and, during the course of the narrative at least, even wise."

The process of writing did not attract Ellison as strongly until he actually started writing. "Once involved," he says, "I soon became consciously concerned with craft, with technique. . . . I was gradually led, often reluctantly, to become consciously concerned with the nature of the culture and the society out of which American fiction is fabricated."

For Ellison, "the act of writing requires a constant plunging back into the shadow of the past where time hovers ghostlike. . . . [It is] the agency of my efforts to answer the question: Who am I, what am I, how did I come to be? What shall I make of the life around me, what celebrate, what reject, how confront the snare of good and evil which is inevitable? What does American society *mean* when regarded out of my *own* eyes, when informed by my *own* sense of the past and viewed by my *own* complex sense of the present? How, in other words, should I think of myself and my pluralistic sense of the world, how express my vision of the human predicament?"

FOR DISCUSSION

1. How did reading prepare Ellison for writing?
2. What connection does Ellison see between writing and personal identity?

GEORGE ORWELL

GEORGE ORWELL was the pen name of Eric Blair (1903–1950), born in Bengal, India, the son of an English civil servant. After attending Eton on a scholarship, he joined the British police in Burma, where he acquired a distrust for the methods of the empire. Then followed years of tramping, odd jobs, and near-starvation — recalled in *Down and Out in Paris and London* (1933). From living on the fringe of society and from his reportorial writing about English miners and factory workers, Orwell deepened his sympathy with underdogs.

Severely wounded while fighting in the Spanish Civil War, he wrote a memoir, *Homage to Catalonia* (1938), voicing disillusionment with Loyalists who, he claimed, sought not to free Spain but to exterminate their political enemies. A socialist by conviction, Orwell kept pointing to the dangers of a collective state run by totalitarians. In *Animal Farm* (1945), he satirized Soviet bureaucracy; and in his famous novel *1984* (1949) he foresaw a regimented England whose government perverts truth and spies on citizens by two-way television. (The motto of the state and its leader: Big Brother Is Watching You.)

A Hanging

Orwell's personal experience of serving in the Indian Imperial Police in Burma in the 1920s provided the memorable story he unfolds in "A Hanging." As in virtually all of his political writing, Orwell displays a profound sympathy for the victim, the downtrodden. Be sure to notice the specific details that lend color and conviction to this narrative. It first appeared in *Adelphi* magazine in 1931 and was later gathered into the collection *Shooting an Elephant and Other Essays* (1950).

It was in Burma, a sodden morning of the rains. A sickly light, like yellow tinfoil, was slanting over the high walls into the jail yard. We were waiting outside the condemned cells, a row of sheds fronted with double bars, like small animal cages. Each cell measured about ten feet by ten and was quite bare within except for a plank bed and a pot for drinking water. In some of them brown, silent men were squatting at the inner bars, with their blankets draped round them. These were the condemned men, due to be hanged within the next week or two.

One prisoner had been brought out of his cell. He was a [2] Hindu, a puny wisp of a man, with a shaven head and vague liquid eyes. He had a thick, sprouting mustache, absurdly too big for his body, rather like the mustache of a comic man on the films. Six tall Indian warders were guarding him and getting him ready for the gallows. Two of them stood by with rifles and fixed bayonets, while the others handcuffed him, passed a chain through his handcuffs and fixed it to their belts, and lashed his arms tight to his sides. They crowded very close about him, with their hands always on him in a careful, caressing grip, as though all the while feeling him to make sure he was there. It was like men handling a fish which is still alive and may jump back into the water. But he stood quite unresisting, yielding his arms limply to the ropes, as though he hardly noticed what was happening.

Eight o'clock struck and a bugle call, desolately thin in the [3] wet air, floated from the distant barracks. The superintendent of the jail, who was standing apart from the rest of us, moodily prodding the gravel with his stick, raised his head at the sound. He was an army doctor, with a gray toothbrush mustache and a gruff voice. "For God's sake, hurry up, Francis," he said irritably. "The man ought to have been dead by this time. Aren't you ready yet?"

Francis, the head jailer, a fat Dravidian[1] in a white drill suit [4] and gold spectacles, waved his black hand. "Yes sir, yes sir," he bubbled. "All iss satisfactorily prepared. The hangman iss waiting. We shall proceed."

"Well, quick march, then. The prisoners can't get their break- [5] fast until this job's over."

We set out for the gallows. Two warders marched on either [6] side of the prisoner, with their rifles at the slope; two others marched close against him, gripping him by the arm and shoulder, as though at once pushing and supporting him. The rest of

---

[1]A native speaker of one of the southern Indian languages. — Eds.

us, magistrates and the like, followed behind. Suddenly, when we had gone ten yards, the procession stopped short without any order or warning. A dreadful thing had happened — a dog, come goodness knows whence, had appeared in the yard. It came bounding among us with a loud volley of barks and leapt round us wagging its whole body, wild with glee at finding so many human beings together. It was a large woolly dog, half Airedale, half pariah. For a moment it pranced around us, and then, before anyone could stop it, it had made a dash for the prisoner, and jumping up tried to lick his face. Everybody stood aghast, too taken aback even to grab the dog.

"Who let that bloody brute in here?" said the superintendent   7 angrily. "Catch it, someone!"

A warder detached from the escort, charged clumsily after   8 the dog, but it danced and gamboled just out of his reach, taking everything as part of the game. A young Eurasian jailer picked up a handful of gravel and tried to stone the dog away, but it dodged the stones and came after us again. Its yaps echoed from the jail walls. The prisoner, in the grasp of the two warders, looked on incuriously, as though this was another formality of the hanging. It was several minutes before someone managed to catch the dog. Then we put my handkerchief through its collar and moved off once more, with the dog still straining and whimpering.

It was about forty yards to the gallows. I watched the bare   9 brown back of the prisoner marching in front of me. He walked clumsily with his bound arms, but quite steadily, with that bobbing gait of the Indian who never straightens his knees. At each step his muscles slid neatly into place, the lock of hair on his scalp danced up and down, his feet printed themselves on the wet gravel. And once, in spite of the men who gripped him by each shoulder, he stepped lightly aside to avoid a puddle on the path.

It is curious; but till that moment I had never realized what it   10 means to destroy a healthy, conscious man. When I saw the prisoner step aside to avoid the puddle, I saw the mystery, the unspeakable wrongness, of cutting a life short when it is in full tide. This man was not dying, he was alive just as we are alive. All the organs of his body were working — bowels digesting food, skin renewing itself, nails growing, tissues forming — all toiling away in solemn foolery. His nails would still be growing when he stood on the drop, when he was falling through the air with a tenth-of-a-second to live. His eyes saw the yellow gravel and the gray walls, and his brain still remembered, foresaw, reasoned — even about puddles. He and we were a party of men walking together, seeing, hearing, feeling, understanding the same world; and in two minutes, with a sudden snap, one of us would be gone — one mind less, one world less.

The gallows stood in a small yard, separate from the main grounds of the prison, and overgrown with tall prickly weeds. It was a brick erection like three sides of a shed, with planking on top, and above that two beams and a crossbar with the rope dangling. The hangman, a gray-haired convict in the white uniform of the prison, was waiting beside his machine. He greeted us with a servile crouch as we entered. At a word from Francis the two warders, gripping the prisoner more closely than ever, half led, half pushed him to the gallows and helped him clumsily up the ladder. Then the hangman climbed up and fixed the rope round the prisoner's neck.

We stood waiting, five yards away. The warders had formed in a rough circle round the gallows. And then, when the noose was fixed, the prisoner began crying out to his god. It was a high, reiterated cry of "Ram! Ram! Ram! Ram!"[2] not urgent and fearful like a prayer or cry for help, but steady, rhythmical, almost like the tolling of a bell. The dog answered the sound with a whine. The hangman, still standing on the gallows, produced a small cotton bag like a flour bag and drew it down over the prisoner's face. But the sound, muffled by the cloth, still persisted, over and over again: "Ram! Ram! Ram! Ram! Ram!"

The hangman climbed down and stood ready, holding the lever. Minutes seemed to pass. The steady, muffled crying from the prisoner went on and on, "Ram! Ram! Ram!" never faltering for an instant. The superintendent, his head on his chest, was slowly poking the ground with his stick; perhaps he was counting the cries, allowing the prisoner a fixed number — fifty, perhaps,

11

12

13

[2]The prisoner calls upon Rama, incarnation of Vishnu, Hindu god who sustains and preserves. — EDS.

or a hundred. Everyone had changed color. The Indians had gone gray like bad coffee, and one or two of the bayonets were wavering. We looked at the lashed, hooded man on the drop, and listened to his cries — each cry another second of life; the same thought was in all our minds; oh, kill him quickly, get it over, stop that abominable noise!

Suddenly the superintendent made up his mind. Throwing   14
up his head he made a swift motion with his stick. "Chalo!"[3] he shouted almost fiercely.

There was a clanking noise, and then dead silence. The pris-   15
oner had vanished, and the rope was twisting on itself. I let go of the dog, and it galloped immediately to the back of the gallows; but when it got there it stopped short, barked, and then retreated into a corner of the yard, where it stood among the weeds, look-ing timorously out at us. We went round the gallows to inspect the prisoner's body. He was dangling with his toes pointed straight downwards, very slowly revolving, as dead as a stone.

The superintendent reached out with his stick and poked the   16
bare brown body; it oscillated slightly. "*He's* all right," said the superintendent. He backed out from under the gallows, and blew out a deep breath. The moody look had gone out of his face quite suddenly. He glanced at his wristwatch. "Eight minutes past eight. Well, that's all for this morning, thank God."

The warders unfixed bayonets and marched away. The dog,   17
sobered and conscious of having misbehaved itself, slipped after them. We walked out of the gallows yard, past the condemned cells with their waiting prisoners, into the big central yard of the prison. The convicts, under the command of warders armed with lathis,[4] were already receiving their breakfast. They squatted in long rows, each man holding a tin pannikin,[5] while two warders with buckets marched around ladling out rice; it seemed quite a homely, jolly scene, after the hanging. An enormous relief had come upon us now that the job was done. One felt an impulse to

[3](Hindi) "Hurry up!" — EDS.
[4]Policemen's wooden clubs. — EDS.
[5]Small pan or dish. — EDS.

sing, to break into a run, to snigger. All at once everyone began chattering gaily.

The Eurasian boy walking beside me nodded toward the way   18
we had come, with a knowing smile: "Do you know, sir, our friend" (he meant the dead man) "when he heard his appeal had been dismissed, he pissed on the floor of his cell. From fright. Kindly take one of my cigarettes, sir. Do you not admire my new silver case, sir? From the boxwallah,[6] two rupees eight annas. Classy European style."

Several people laughed — at what, nobody seemed certain.   19

Francis was walking by the superintendent, talking garru-   20
lously: "Well, sir, all has passed off with the utmost satisfactori- ness. It was all finished — flick! Like that. It iss not always so — oah, no! I have known cases where the doctor wass obliged to go beneath the gallows and pull the prissoner's legs to ensure de- cease. Most disagreeable!"

"Wriggling about, eh? That's bad," said the superintendent.   21

"Ach, sir, it iss worse when they become refractory! One   22
man, I recall, clung to the bars of his cage when we went to take him out. You will scarcely credit, sir, that it took six warders to dislodge him, three pulling at each leg. We reasoned with him, 'My dear fellow,' we said, 'think of the all the pain and trouble you are causing to us!' But no, he would not listen! Ach, he wass very troublesome!"

I found that I was laughing quite loudly. Everyone was laugh-   23
ing. Even the superintendent grinned in a tolerant way. "You'd better all come out and have a drink," he said quite genially. "I've got a bottle of whiskey in the car. We could do with it."

We went through the big double gates of the prison into the   24
road. "Pulling at his legs!" exclaimed a Burmese magistrate sud- denly, and burst into a loud chuckling. We all began laughing again. At that moment Francis' anecdote seemed extraordinarily funny. We all had a drink together, native and European alike, quite amicably. The dead man was a hundred yards away.

---

[6]Merchant of jewelry boxes. — EDS.

QUESTIONS ON MEANING

1. What reason does the superintendent give for wanting Francis and the other jailers to hurry? What is the real, unspoken reason?
2. In what ways is the appearance of the dog (para. 6) "a dreadful thing"? What, exactly, makes its presence disturbing to the men who accompany the prisoner?
3. How does the condemned man's stepping aside to avoid a puddle trigger a powerful new insight for the author?
4. Explain why the men react as they do to the prisoner's rhythmic "crying out to his god."
5. How do you account for the animated talking and laughing that follow the hanging?
6. What PURPOSE other than to tell an absorbing story do you find in Orwell's essay?

QUESTIONS ON WRITING STRATEGY

1. What order does Orwell follow in his narrative? Where in his account does he depart from this order?
2. Orwell makes no mention of the crime for which the prisoner has been sentenced to death. Had he done so, would his essay have been more effective?
3. Devoting your attention to just one of the characters in "A Hanging," list the concrete details and IMAGES that lend vividness to Orwell's characterization. Share the list with your classmates.
4. OTHER METHODS. Orwell's narrative is also an argument (Chap. 11) against capital punishment. Why do you think he confines his general statements on the issue to a single paragraph (10)?

QUESTIONS ON LANGUAGE

1. Use a dictionary if you need help defining the following words: warders (para. 2); pariah (6); gamboled (8); servile (11); reiterated (12); abominable (13); timorously (15); oscillated (16); garrulously (20); refractory (22); amicably (24).
2. Notice the SIMILES in the first paragraph: the light "like yellow tinfoil," the cells "like small animal cages." Are these FIGURES OF SPEECH merely decorative, or do they add something vital to your perception of the scene Orwell draws? If so, what?

3. Point to other similes in Orwell's essay that seem to you especially apt. Where does the author use METAPHORS to achieve an effect?
4. Point to a few sentences in which the author uses UNDERSTATEMENT. What, in each case, does this figure of speech contribute to the sentence's EFFECT?
5. What does the author mean when, at the end of paragraph 10, he speaks of "one world less"?
6. Explain the force of the phrase *dead silence* in paragraph 15.

SUGGESTIONS FOR WRITING

1. In an essay, recall an unforgettable public event you have witnessed or taken part in, one that gave you some insight you didn't have before. Such an event could be a wedding, a funeral, a graduation, an accident, the dedication of a monument, or another that you can think of. Make clear what caused the event to stick in your memory.
2. Write several paragraphs in which you agree or disagree with Orwell's attitude toward capital punishment. Be sure to include your reasons for believing as you do.
3. CONNECTIONS. Another essay in this book also takes on the subject of capital punishment: H. L. Mencken's "The Penalty of Death" (p. 623). Despite their wholly different opinions and tones, the two essays do touch on the same issues, such as the problem of delay in execution, the unpleasantness of the execution itself, and the emotional effect on those who bring the condemned to death. In a brief, focused essay, pit the two essays against each other on *one* of these issues. Who makes the better case, and why?

GEORGE ORWELL ON WRITING

Don't miss George Orwell's "Politics and the English Language," a famous argument for more accurate, less pretentious writing, reprinted in full in this book (starting on page 690). Speaking more personally, Orwell explains the motives for his own writing in another essay, "Why I Write" (1946):

"What I have most wanted to do throughout the past ten years is to make political writing into an art. My starting point is always a feeling of partisanship, a sense of injustice. When I sit down to write a book, I do not say to myself, 'I am going to pro-

duce a work of art.' I write it because there is some lie that I want
to expose, some fact to which I want to draw attention, and my
initial concern is to get a hearing. But I could not do the work of
writing a book, or even a long magazine article, if it were not also
an esthetic experience. Anyone who cares to examine my work
will see that even when it is downright propaganda it contains
much that a full-time politician would consider irrelevant. I am
not able, and I do not want, completely to abandon the world-
view that I acquired in childhood. So long as I remain alive and
well I shall continue to feel strongly about prose style, to love the
surface of the earth, and to take a pleasure in solid objects and
scraps of useless information. It is no use trying to suppress that
side of myself. The job is to reconcile my ingrained likes and dislikes with the essentially public, nonindividual activities that this
age forces on all of us.

"It is not easy. It raises problems of construction and of language, and it raises in a new way the problem of truthfulness.
Let me give just one example of the cruder kind of difficulty that
arises. My book about the Spanish civil war, *Homage to Catalonia*, is, of course, a frankly political book, but in the main it is
written with a certain detachment and regard for form. I did try
very hard in it to tell the whole truth without violating my literary instincts. But among other things it contains a long chapter,
full of newspaper quotations and the like, defending the Trotsky-
ists who were accused of plotting with Franco. Clearly such a
chapter, which after a year or two would lose its interest for any
ordinary reader, must ruin the book. A critic whom I respect read
me a lecture about it. 'Why did you put in all that stuff?' he said.
'You've turned what might have been a good book into journalism.' What he said was true, but I could not have done otherwise.
I happened to know, what very few people in England had been
allowed to know, that innocent men were being falsely accused. If
I had not been angry about that I should never have written the
book.

"In one form or another this problem comes up again. The
problem of language is subtler and would take too long to discuss.
I will only say that of late years I have tried to write less pictur-
esquely and more exactly. In any case I find that by the time you

have perfected any style of writing, you have always outgrown it. *Animal Farm* was the first book in which I tried, with full consciousness of what I was doing, to fuse political purpose and artistic purpose into one whole. . . .

"Looking back through the last page or two, I see that I have made it appear as though my motives in writing were wholly public-spirited. I don't want to leave that as the final impression. All writers are vain, selfish, and lazy, and at the very bottom of their motives there lies a mystery. Writing a book is a horrible, exhausting struggle, like a long bout of some painful illness. One would never undertake such a thing if one were not driven on by some demon whom one can neither resist nor understand. For all one knows that demon is simply the same instinct that makes a baby squall for attention. And yet it is also true that one can write nothing readable unless one constantly struggles to efface one's own personality. Good prose is like a windowpane. I cannot say with certainty which of my motives are the strongest, but I know which of them deserve to be followed. And looking back through my work, I see that it is invariably where I lacked a *political* purpose that I wrote lifeless books and was betrayed into purple passages, sentences without meaning, decorative adjectives, and humbug generally."

FOR DISCUSSION

1. What does Orwell mean by his "political purpose" in writing? By his "artistic purpose"? How did he sometimes find it hard to fulfill both purposes?
2. Think about Orwell's remark that "one can write nothing readable unless one constantly struggles to efface one's own personality." From your own experience, have you found any truth in this observation, or any reason to think otherwise?

JAMES THURBER

JAMES THURBER (1894–1961), a native of Columbus, Ohio, made himself immortal with his humorous stories of shy, bumbling men (such as "The Secret Life of Walter Mitty") and his cartoons of men, women, and dogs that look as though he had drawn them with his foot. (In fact, Thurber suffered from weak eyesight and had to draw his cartoons in crayon on sheets of paper two or three feet wide.) As Thurber aged and approached blindness, he drew less and less, and wrote more and more. His first book, written with his friend E. B. White, is a takeoff on self-help manuals, *Is Sex Necessary?* (1929). His later prose includes *My Life and Hard Times* (1933), from which "University Days" is taken; *The Thirteen Clocks*, a fable for children (1950); and *The Years with Ross* (1959), a memoir of his years on the staff of *The New Yorker*.

University Days

Ohio State University during World War I may seem remote from your own present situation, but see if you don't agree that this story of campus frustration is as fresh as the day it was first composed. Notice how, with beautiful brevity, Thurber draws a scene, introduces bits of revealing dialogue, and shifts briskly from one scene to another.

I passed all the other courses that I took at my university, but I could never pass botany. This was because all botany students had to spend several hours a week in a laboratory looking through a microscope at plant cells, and I could never see through a microscope. I never once saw a cell through a microscope. This used to enrage my instructor. He would wander around the laboratory pleased with the progress all the students were making in drawing the involved and, so I am told, interesting structure of flower cells, until he came to me. I would just be standing there. "I can't see anything," I would say. He would begin patiently enough, explaining how anybody can see through a microscope, but he would always end up in a fury, claiming that I could *too* see

64

through the microscope but just pretended that I couldn't. "It takes away from the beauty of flowers anyway," I used to tell him. "We are not concerned with beauty in this course," he would say. "We are concerned solely with what I may call the *mechanics* of flars." "Well," I'd say, " I can't see anything." "Try it just once again," he'd say, and I would put my eye to the microscope and see nothing at all, except now and again a nebulous milky sub-stance — a phenomenon of maladjustment. You were supposed to see a vivid, restless clockwork of sharply defined plant cells. "I see what looks like a lot of milk," I would tell him. This, he claimed, was the result of my not having adjusted the microscope properly, so he would readjust it for me, or rather, for himself. And I would look again and see milk.

I finally took a deferred pass, as they called it, and waited a   2 year and tried again. (You had to pass one of the biological sci-ences or you couldn't graduate.) The professor had come back from vacation brown as a berry, bright-eyed, and eager to explain cell-structure again to his classes. "Well," he said to me, cheerily, when we met in the first laboratory hour of the semester, "we're going to see cells this time, aren't we?" "Yes, sir," I said. Students to right of me and to left of me and in front of me were seeing cells; what's more, they were quietly drawing pictures of them in their notebooks. Of course, I didn't see anything.

"We'll try it," the professor said to me, grimly, "with every ad-   3 justment of the microscope known to man. As God as my wit-ness, I'll arrange this glass so that you see cells through it or I'll give up teaching. In twenty-two years of botany, I — " He cut off abruptly for he was beginning to quiver all over, like Lionel Bar-rymore,[1] and he genuinely wished to hold onto his temper; his scenes with me had taken a great deal out of him.

So we tried it with every adjustment of the microscope   4 known to man. With only one of them did I see anything but blackness or the familiar lacteal opacity, and that time I saw, to my pleasure and amazement, a variegated constellation of flecks, specks, and dots. These I hastily drew. The instructor, noting my activity, came back from an adjoining desk, a smile on his lips

[1]A noted American stage, radio, and screen actor (1878–1954). — EDS.

and his eyebrows high in hope. He looked at my cell drawing. "What's that?" he demanded, with a hint of a squeal in his voice. "That's what I saw," I said. "You didn't, you didn't, you *didn't!*" he screamed, losing control of his temper instantly, and he bent over and squinted into the microscope. His head snapped up. "That's your eye!" he shouted. "You've fixed the lens so that it reflects! You've drawn your eye!"

Another course that I didn't like, but somehow managed to pass, was economics. I went to that class straight from the botany class, which didn't help me any in understanding either subject. I used to get them mixed up. But not as mixed up as another student in my economics class who came there direct from a physics laboratory. He was a tackle on the football team, named Bolenciecwcz. At that time Ohio State University had one of the best football teams in the country, and Bolenciecwcz was one of its outstanding stars. In order to be eligible to play it was necessary for him to keep up in his studies, a very difficult matter, for while he was not dumber than an ox he was not any smarter. Most of his professors were lenient and helped him along. None gave him more hints in answering questions or asked him simpler ones than the economics professor, a thin, timid man named Bassum. One day when we were on the subject of transportation and distribution, it came Bolenciecwcz's turn to answer a question. "Name one means of transportation," the professor said to him. No light came into the big tackle's eyes. "Just any means of transportation," said the professor. Bolenciecwcz sat staring at him. "That is," pursued the professor, "any medium, agency, or method of going from one place to another." Bolenciecwcz had the look of a man who is being led into a trap. "You may choose among steam, horse-drawn, or electrically propelled vehicles," said the instructor. "I might suggest the one which we commonly take in making long journeys across land." There was a profound silence in which everybody stirred uneasily, including Bolenciecwcz and Mr. Bassum. Mr. Bassum abruptly broke this silence in an amazing manner. "Choo-choo-choo," he said, in a low voice, and turned instantly scarlet. He glanced appealingly around the room. All of us, of course, shared Mr. Bassum's desire that Bolenciecwcz should stay abreast of the class in economics,

5

for the Illinois game, one of the hardest and most important of the season, was only a week off. "Toot, toot, too-toooooot!" some student with a deep voice moaned, and we all looked encouragingly at Bolenciecwcz. Somebody else gave a fine imitation of a locomotive letting off steam. Mr. Bassum himself rounded off the little show. "Ding, dong, ding, dong," he said, hopefully. Bolenciecwcz was staring at the floor now, trying to think, his great brow furrowed, his huge hands rubbing together, his face red.

"How did you come to college this year, Mr. Bolenciecwcz?" asked the professor. "*Chuffa* chuffa, *chuffa* chuffa." 6

"M'father sent me," said the football player. 7

"What on?" asked Bassum. 8

"I git an 'lowance," said the tackle, in a low, husky voice, obviously embarrassed. 9

"No, no," said Bassum. "Name a means of transportation. What did you *ride* here on?" 10

"Train," said Bolenciecwcz. 11

"Quite right," said the professor. "Now, Mr. Nugent, will you tell us — " 12

If I went through anguish in botany and economics — for different reasons — gymnasium work was even worse. I don't even like to think about it. They wouldn't let you play games or join the exercises with your glasses on and I couldn't see with mine off. I bumped into professors, horizontal bars, agricultural students, and swinging iron rings. Not being able to see, I could take it but I couldn't dish it out. Also, in order to pass gymnasium (and you had to pass it to graduate) you had to learn to swim if you didn't know how. I didn't like the swimming pool, I didn't like swimming, and I didn't like the swimming instructor, and after all these years I still don't. I never swam but I passed my gym work anyway, by having another student give my gymnasium number (978) and swim across the pool in my place. He was a quiet, amiable blond youth, number 473, and he would have seen through a microscope for me if we could have got away with it, but we couldn't get away with it. Another thing I didn't like about gymnasium work was that they made you strip the day you registered. It is impossible for me to be happy when I am stripped and being asked a lot of questions. Still, I did better than a lanky agricul- 13

tural student who was cross-examined just before I was. They
asked each student what college he was in — that is, whether
Arts, Engineering, Commerce, or Agriculture. "What college are
you in?" the instructor snapped at the youth in front of me.
"Ohio State University," he said promptly.

It wasn't that agricultural student but it was another a   14
whole lot like him who decided to take up journalism, possibly
on the ground that when farming went to hell he could fall back
on newspaper work. He didn't realize, of course, that that would
be very much like falling back full-length on a kit of carpenter's
tools. Haskins didn't seem cut out for journalism, being too embarrassed to talk to anybody and unable to use a typewriter, but
the editor of the college paper assigned him to the cow barns,
the sheep house, the horse pavilion, and the animal husbandry
department generally. This was a genuinely big "beat," for it
took up five times as much ground and got ten times as great a
legislative appropriation as the College of Liberal Arts. The agricultural student knew animals, but nevertheless his stories were
dull and colorlessly written. He took all afternoon on each of
them, on account of having to hunt for each letter on the typewriter. Once in a while he had to ask somebody to help him
hunt. C and L, in particular, were hard letters for him to find.
His editor finally got pretty much annoyed at the farmer-jour-
nalist because his pieces were so uninteresting. "See here,
Haskins," he snapped at him one day, "why is it we never have
anything hot from you on the horse pavilion? Here we have two
hundred head of horses on this campus — more than any other
university in the Western Conference except Purdue — and yet
you never get any real lowdown on them. Now shoot over to
the horse barns and dig up something lively." Haskins shambled
out and came back in about an hour; he said he had something.
"Well, start it off snappily," said the editor. "Something people
will read." Haskins set to work and in a couple of hours brought
a sheet of typewritten paper to the desk; it was a two-hundred-
word story about some disease that had broken out among the
horses. Its opening sentence was simple but arresting. It read:
"Who has noticed the sores on the tops of the horses in the animal husbandry building?"

Ohio State was a land grant university and therefore two   15
years of military drill was compulsory. We drilled with old
Springfield rifles and studied the tactics of the Civil War even
though the World War was going on at the time. At 11 o'clock
each morning thousands of freshmen and sophomores used to deploy over the campus, moodily creeping up on the old chemistry
building. It was good training for the kind of warfare that was
waged at Shiloh but it had no connection with what was going on
in Europe. Some people used to think there was German money
behind it, but they didn't say so or they would have been thrown
in jail as German spies. It was a period of muddy thought and
marked, I believe, the decline of higher education in the Middle
West.

As a soldier I was never any good at all. Most of the cadets   16
were glumly indifferent soldiers, but I was no good at all. Once
General Littlefield, who was commandant of the cadet corps,
popped up in front of me during regimental drill and snapped,
"You are the main trouble with this university!" I think he meant
that my type was the main trouble with the university but he may
have meant me individually. I was mediocre at drill, certainly —
that is, until my senior year. By that time I had drilled longer
than anybody else in the Western Conference, having failed at
military at the end of each preceding year so that I had to do it all
over again. I was the only senior still in uniform. The uniform
which, when new, had made me look like an interurban railway
conductor, now that it had become faded and too tight made me
look like Bert Williams in his bellboy act.[2] This had a definitely
bad effect on my morale. Even so, I had become by sheer practice
little short of wonderful at squad maneuvers.

One day General Littlefield picked our company out of the   17
whole regiment and tried to get it mixed up by putting it through
one movement after another as fast as we could execute them:
squads right, squads left, squads on right into line, squads right
about, squads left front into line, etc. In about three minutes one
hundred and nine men were marching in one direction and I was

---

[2]A popular vaudeville and silent-screen comedian of the time, Williams in
one routine played a hotel porter in a shrunken suit. — EDS.

marching away from them at an angle of forty degrees all alone. "Company, halt!" shouted General Littlefield. "That man is the only man who has it right!" I was made a corporal for my achievement.

The next day General Littlefield summoned me to his office. 18 He was swatting flies when I went in. I was silent and he was silent too, for a long time. I don't think he remembered me or why he had sent for me, but he didn't want to admit it. He swatted some more flies, keeping his eyes on them narrowly before he let go with the swatter. "Button up your coat!" he snapped. Looking back on it now I can see that he meant me although he was looking at a fly, but I just stood there. Another fly came to rest on a paper in front of the general and began rubbing its hind legs together. The general lifted the swatter cautiously. I moved restlessly and the fly flew away. "You startled him!" barked General Littlefield, looking at me severely. I said I was sorry. "That won't help the situation!" snapped the General, with cold military logic. I didn't see what I could do except offer to chase some more flies toward his desk, but I didn't say anything. He stared out the window at the faraway figures of co-eds crossing the campus toward the library. Finally, he told me I could go. So I went. He either didn't know which cadet I was or else he forgot what he wanted to see me about. It may have been that he wished to apologize for having called me the main trouble with the university; or maybe he had decided to compliment me on my brilliant drilling of the day before and then at the last minute decided not to. I don't know. I don't think about it much any more.

QUESTIONS ON MEANING

1. In what light does Thurber portray himself in "University Days?" Is his self-portrait sympathetic?
2. Are Bolenciecwcz and Haskins stereotypes? Discuss.
3. To what extent does Thurber sacrifice believability for humorous ·EFFECT? What is his main PURPOSE?

QUESTIONS ON WRITING STRATEGY

1. How do Thurber's INTRODUCTION, his TRANSITIONS, and his CONCLUSION heighten the humor of his essay?
2. Criticize the opening sentence of the story Haskins writes about horse disease (quoted in para. 14).
3. Thurber does not explain in "University Days" how he ever did fulfill his biological science requirement for graduation. Is this an important omission? Explain.
4. OTHER METHODS. Each of Thurber's anecdotes is also an example (Chap. 3), but the GENERALIZATION illustrated by these examples is not stated. How would you phrase this generalization? What idea do the examples add up to? (Avoid a vague assertion like "College can be frustrating.") Does the absence of a stated generalization weaken or strengthen the essay?

QUESTIONS ON LANGUAGE

1. Be sure to know what the following words mean: nebulous (para. 1); lacteal opacity, variegated (4).
2. Explain how Thurber's word choices heighten the IRONY in the following phrases: "like falling back full-length on a kit of carpenter's tools" (para. 14); "a genuinely big 'beat' " (14); "the decline of higher education in the Middle West" (15).
3. What is a land grant university (para. 15)?
4. Where in his essay does Thurber use colloquial DICTION? What is its effect?

SUGGESTIONS FOR WRITING

1. How does Thurber's picture of campus life during the days of World War I compare with campus life today? What has changed? What has stayed the same? Develop your own ideas in a brief essay.
2. Write an essay called "High-School Days" in which, with a light touch, you recount two or three related anecdotes from your own experience, educational or otherwise.
3. CONNECTIONS. James Thurber and E. B. White were friends and colleagues at *The New Yorker*, and both are here represented by reminiscences. But Thurber's "University Days" and White's "Once More to the Lake" (p. 159) are very different in substance and TONE.

After reading White's essay, write an essay of your own comparing these two works. What attitudes does each author convey, and how does he do it? (Use quotations and PARAPHRASES from both essays to support your points.)

JAMES THURBER ON WRITING

In an interview with writers George Plimpton and Max Steele, James Thurber fielded some revealing questions. "Is the act of writing easy for you?" the interviewers wanted to know.

"For me," Thurber replied, "it's mostly a question of rewriting. It's part of a constant attempt on my part to make the finished version smooth, to make it seem effortless. A story I've been working on — 'The Train on Track Six,' it's called — was rewritten fifteen complete times. There must have been close to 240,000 words in all the manuscripts put together, and I must have spent two thousand hours working at it. Yet the finished version can't be more than twenty thousand words."

"Then it's rare that your work comes out right the first time?"

"Well," said Thurber, "my wife took a look at the first version of something I was doing not long ago and said, 'Goddamn it, Thurber, that's high-school stuff.' I have to tell her to wait until the seventh draft, it'll work out all right. I don't know why that should be so, that the first or second draft of everything I write reads as if it was turned out by a charwoman. I've only written one piece quickly. I wrote a thing called 'File and Forget' in one afternoon — but only because it was a series of letters just as one would ordinarily dictate. And I'll have to admit that the last letter of the series, after doing all the others that one afternoon, took me a week. It was the end of the piece and I had to fuss over it."

"Does the fact that you're dealing with humor slow down the production?"

"It's possible. With humor you have to look out for traps. You're likely to be very gleeful with what you've first put down, and you think it's fine, very funny. One reason you go over and over it is to make the piece sound less as if you were having a lot of fun with it yourself."

In his own book *Thurber Country*, Thurber set forth, with tongue in cheek, some general principles for comic writing. "I have established a few standing rules of my own about humor," he wrote, "after receiving dozens of humorous essays and stories from strangers over a period of twenty years. (1) The reader should be able to find out what the story is about. (2) Some inkling of the general idea should be apparent in the first five hundred words. (3) If the writer has decided to change the name of his protagonist from Ketcham to McTavish, Ketcham should not keep bobbing up in the last five pages. A good way to eliminate this confusion is to read the piece over before sending it out, and remove Ketcham completely. He is a nuisance. (4) The word "I'll" should not be divided so that the "I" is on one line and " 'll" on the next. The reader's attention, after the breaking up of "I'll," can never be successfully recaptured. (5) It also never recovers from such names as Ann S. Thetic, Maud Lynn, Sally Forth, Bertha Twins, and the like. (6) Avoid comic stories about plumbers who are mistaken for surgeons, sheriffs who are terrified by gunfire, psychiatrists who are driven crazy by women patients, doctors who faint at the sight of blood, adolescent girls who know more about sex than their fathers do, and midgets who turn out to be the parents of a two-hundred-pound wrestler."

FOR DISCUSSION

1. By what means does Thurber make his writing look "effortless"?
2. Is there any serious advice to be extracted from Thurber's "standing rules about humor"? If so, what is it?

CALVIN TRILLIN

CALVIN TRILLIN, distinguished commentator on American life, was born in 1935 in Kansas City, Missouri, where he grew up. After earning his B.A. from Yale in 1957, he worked as a reporter and writer for *Time*. In 1963 he joined *The New Yorker* as a staff writer and ever since has been a contributor to that lively weekly magazine. Since 1978 Trillin has written a column on political affairs for *The Nation*, a liberal review, and in 1986 he became a syndicated newspaper columnist. Some of his political commentary has been gathered in *Uncivil Liberties* (1982) and in *With All Disrespect* (1985). *If You Can't Say Something Nice* (1987) and *Travels with Alice* (1989) collect some of his essays. Trillin has also written (with appetite) about food and drink in *American Fried* (1974) and *Alice, Let's Eat* (1978).

It's Just Too Late

This essay first appeared in Trillin's *New Yorker* column, "U.S. Journal." The author has since included the narrative in *Killings* (1984), a collection of factual chronicles of violent death in America. The book, says Trillin, "is meant to be more about how Americans live than about how some of them die. . . . A killing often seemed to present the best opportunity to write about people one at a time."

Knoxville, Tennessee
March 1979

Until she was sixteen, FaNee Cooper was what her parents 1
sometimes called an ideal child. "You'd never have to correct her," FaNee's mother has said. In sixth grade, FaNee won a spelling contest. She played the piano and the flute. She seemed to believe what she heard every Sunday at the Beaver Dam Baptist Church about good and evil and the hereafter. FaNee was not an outgoing child. Even as a baby, she was uncomfortable when she was held and cuddled. She found it easy to tell her parents that she loved them but difficult to confide in them. Particularly com-

pared to her sister, Kristy, a cheerful, open little girl two and a
half years younger, she was reserved and introspective. The
thoughts she kept to herself, though, were apparently happy
thoughts. Her eighth-grade essay on Christmas — written in a remarkably neat hand — talked of the joys of helping put together
toys for her little brother, Leo, Jr., and the importance of her parents' reminder that Christmas is the birthday of Jesus. Her parents were the sort of people who might have been expected to
have an ideal child. As a boy, Leo Cooper had been called "one
of the greatest high-school basketball players ever developed in
Knox County." He went on to play basketball at East Tennessee
State, and he married the homecoming queen, JoAnn Henson.
After college, Cooper became a high-school basketball coach and
teacher and, eventually, an administrator. By the time FaNee
turned thirteen, in 1973, he was in his third year as the principal
of Gresham Junior High School, in Fountain City — a small
Knox County town that had been swallowed up by Knoxville
when the suburbs began to move north. A tall man, with curly
black hair going on gray, Leo Cooper has an elaborate way of
talking ("Unless I'm very badly mistaken, he has never related to
me totally the content of his conversation") and a manner that
may come from years of trying to leave errant junior-high-school
students with the impression that a responsible adult is magnanimous, even humble, about invariably being in the right. His wife,
a high-school art teacher, paints and does batik, and created the
name FaNee because she liked the way it looked and sounded —
it sounds like "Fawn-*ee*" when the Coopers say it — but the impression she gives is not of artiness but of soft-spoken small-town
gentility. When she found, in the course of cleaning up FaNee's
room, that her ideal thirteen-year-old had been smoking cigarettes, she was, in her words, crushed. "FaNee was such a perfect
child before that," JoAnn Cooper said some time later. "She was
angry that we found out. She knew we knew that she had done
something we didn't approve of, and then the rebellion started. I
was hurt. I was very hurt. I guess it came through as disappointment."

Several months later, FaNee's grandmother died. FaNee had
been devoted to her grandmother. She wrote a poem in her mem-

ory — an almost joyous poem, filled with Christian faith in the afterlife ("Please don't grieve over my happiness / Rejoice with me in the presence of the Angels of Heaven"). She also took some keepsakes from her grandmother's house, and was apparently mortified when her parents found them and explained that they would have to be returned. By then, the Coopers were aware that FaNee was going to have a difficult time as a teenager. They thought she might be self-conscious about the double affliction of glasses and braces. They thought she might be uncomfortable in the role of the principal's daughter at Gresham. In ninth grade, she entered Halls High School, where JoAnn Cooper was teaching art. FaNee was a loner at first. Then she fell in with what could only be considered a bad crowd.

Halls, a few miles to the north of Fountain City, used to be ³ known as Halls Crossroads. It is what Knoxville people call "over the ridge" — on the side of Black Oak Ridge that has always been thought of as rural. When FaNee entered Halls High, the Coopers were already in the process of building a house on several acres of land they had bought in Halls, in a sparsely settled area along Brown Gap Road. Like two or three other houses along the road, it was to be constructed basically of huge logs taken from old buildings — a house that Leo Cooper describes as being, like the name FaNee, "just a little bit different." Ten years ago, Halls Crossroads was literally a crossroads. Then some of the Knoxville expansion that had swollen Fountain City spilled over the ridge, planting subdivisions here and there on roads that still went for long stretches with nothing but an occasional house with a cow or two next to it. The increase in population did not create a town. Halls has no center. Its commercial area is a series of two or three shopping centers strung together on the Maynardville Highway, the four-lane that leads north into Union County — a place almost synonymous in east Tennessee with mountain poverty. Its restaurant is the Halls Freezo Drive-In. The gathering place for the group FaNee Cooper eventually found herself in was the Maynardville Highway Exxon station.

At Halls High School, the social poles were represented by ⁴ the Jocks and the Freaks. FaNee found her friends among the Freaks. "I am truly enlighted upon irregular trains of thought aimed at strange depots of mental wards," she wrote when she was fifteen. "Yes! Crazed farms for the mental off — Oh! I walked through the halls screams & loud laughter fill my ears — Orderlys try to reason with me — but I am unreasonable! The joys of being a *Freak* in a circus of imagination." The little crowd of eight or ten young people that FaNee joined has been referred to by her mother as "the Union County group." A couple of the girls were from backgrounds similar to FaNee's, but all the boys had the characteristics, if not the precise addresses, that Knoxville people associate with the poor whites of Union County. They were the sort of boys who didn't bother to finish high school, or finished it in a special program for slow learners, or got ejected from it for taking a swing at the principal.

"I guess you can say they more or less dragged us down to   5
their level with the drugs," a girl who was in the group — a girl who can be called Marcia — said recently. "And somehow we settled for it. It seems like we had to get ourselves in the pit before we could look out." People in the group used marijuana and Valium and LSD. They sneered at the Jocks and the "prim and proper little ladies" who went with the Jocks. "We set ourselves aside," Marcia now says. "We put ourselves above everyone. How we did that I don't know." In a Knox County high school, teenagers who want to get themselves in the pit need not mainline heroin. The Jocks they mean to be compared to do not merely show up regularly for classes and practice football and wear clean clothes; they watch their language and preach temperance and go to prayer meetings on Wednesday nights and talk about having a real good Christian witness. Around Knoxville, people who speak of well-behaved high-school kids often seem to use words like "perfect," or even "angels." For FaNee's group, the opposite was not difficult to figure out. "We were into wicked things, strange things," Marcia says. "It was like we were on some kind of devil trip." FaNee wrote about demons and vultures and rats. "Slithering serpents eat my sanity and bite my ass," she wrote in an essay called "The Lovely Road of Life," just after she turned sixteen, "while tornadoes derail and ever so swiftly destroy every car in my train of thought." She wrote a lot about death.

FaNee's girl friends spoke of her as "super-intelligent." Her   6
English teacher found some of her writing profound — and disturbing. She was thought to be not just super-intelligent but
super-mysterious, and even, at times, super-weird — an introverted girl who stared straight ahead with deep-brown, nearly
black eyes and seemed to have thoughts she couldn't share. Nobody really knew why she had chosen to run with the Freaks —
whether it was loneliness or rebellion or simple boredom. Marcia
thought it might have had something to do with a feeling that her
parents had settled on Kristy as their perfect child. "I guess she figured she couldn't be the best," Marcia said recently. "So she decided she might as well be the worst."

Toward the spring of FaNee's junior year at Halls, her prob-   7
lems seemed to deepen. Despite her intelligence, her grades were
sliding. She was what her mother called "a mental dropout." Leo
Cooper had to visit Halls twice because of minor suspensions.
Once, FaNee had been caught smoking. Once, having ducked
out of a required assembly, she was spotted by a favorite teacher,
who turned her in. At home, she exchanged little more than
short, strained formalities with Kristy, who shared their parents'
opinion of FaNee's choice of friends. The Coopers had finished
their house — a large house, its size accentuated by the huge old
logs and a great stone fireplace and outsize "Paul Bunyan"-style
furniture — but FaNee spent most of her time there in her own
room, sleeping or listening to rock music through earphones. One
night, there was a terrible scene when FaNee returned from a
concert in a condition that Leo Cooper knew had to be the result
of marijuana. JoAnn Cooper, who ordinarily strikes people as too
gentle to raise her voice, found herself losing her temper regularly.
Finally, Leo Cooper asked a counsellor he knew, Jim Griffin, to
stop in at Halls High School and have a talk with FaNee — unof-
ficially.

Griffin — a young man with a warm, informal manner —   8
worked for the Juvenile Court of Knox County. He had a reputation for being able to reach teenagers who wouldn't talk to their
parents or to school administrators. One Friday in March of
1977, he spent an hour and a half talking to FaNee Cooper. As

Griffin recalls the interview, FaNee didn't seem alarmed by his presence. She seemed to him calm and controlled — Griffin thought it was something like talking to another adult — and, unlike most of the teenagers he dealt with, she looked him in the eye the entire time. Griffin, like some of FaNee's friends, found her eyes unsettling — "the coldest, most distant, but, at the same time, the most knowing eyes I'd ever seen." She expressed affection for her parents, but she didn't seem interested in exploring ways of getting along better with them. The impression she gave Griffin was that they were who they were, and she was who she was, and there didn't happen to be any connection. Several times, she made the same response to Griffin's suggestions: "It's too late."

That weekend, neither FaNee nor her parents brought up the 9 subject of Griffin's visit. Leo Cooper has spoken of the weekend as being particularly happy; a friend of FaNee's who stayed over remembers it as particularly strained. FaNee stayed home from school on Monday because of a bad headache — she often had bad headaches — but felt well enough on Monday evening to drive to the library. She was to be home at nine. When she wasn't, Mrs. Cooper began to phone her friends. Finally, around ten, Leo Cooper got into his other car and took a swing around Halls — past the teenage hangouts like the Exxon station and the Pizza Hut and the Smoky Mountain Market. Then he took a second swing. At eleven, FaNee was still not home.

She hadn't gone to the library. She had picked up two girl 10 friends and driven to the home of a third, where everyone took five Valium tablets. Then the four girls drove over to the Exxon station, where they met four boys from their crowd. After a while, the group bought some beer and some marijuana and reassembled at Charlie Stevens's trailer. Charlie Stevens was five or six years older than everyone else in the group — a skinny, slow-thinking young man with long black hair and a sparse beard. He was married and had a child, but he and his wife had separated; she was back in Union County with the baby. Stevens had remained in their trailer — parked in the yard near his mother's house, in a back-road area of Knox County dominated by de-

crepit, unpainted sheds and run-down trailers and rusted-out automobiles. Stevens had picked up FaNee at home once or twice
— apparently, more as a driver for the group than as a date —
and the Coopers, having learned that his unsuitability extended
to being married, had asked her not to see him.

In Charlie's trailer, which had no heat or electricity, the 11
group drank beer and passed around joints, keeping warm with
blankets. By eleven or so, FaNee was what one of her friends has
called "super-messed-up." Her speech was slurred. She was having
trouble keeping her balance. She had decided not to go home.
She had apparently persuaded herself that her parents intended
to send her away to some sort of home for incorrigibles. "It's too
late," she said to one of her friends. "It's just too late." It was decided that one of the boys, David Munsey, who was more or less
the leader of the group, would drive the Coopers' car to FaNee's
house, where FaNee and Charlie Stevens would pick him up in
Stevens's car — a worn Pinto with four bald tires, one light, and a
dragging muffler. FaNee wrote a note to her parents, and then,
perhaps because her handwriting was suffering the effects of beer
and marijuana and Valium, asked Stevens to rewrite it on a large
piece of paper, which would be left on the seat of the Coopers'
car. The Stevens version was just about the same as FaNee's, except that Stevens left out a couple of sentences about trying to
work things out ("I'm willing to try") and, not having won any
spelling championships himself, he misspelled a few words, like
"tomorrow." The note said, "Dear Mom and Dad. Sorry I'm late.
Very late. I left your car because I thought you might need it tomorrow. I love you all, but this is something I just had to do. The
man talked to me privately for one and a half hours and I was really scared, so this is something I just had to do, but don't worry,
I'm with a very good friend. Love you all. FaNee. P.S. Please try
to understand I love you all very much, really I do. Love me if you
have a chance."

At eleven-thirty or so, Leo Cooper was sitting in his living 12
room, looking out the window at his driveway — a long gravel
road that runs almost four hundred feet from the house to Brown
Gap Road. He saw the car that FaNee had been driving pull into
the driveway. "She's home," he called to his wife, who had just

left the room. Cooper walked out on the deck over the garage. The car had stopped at the end of the driveway, and the lights had gone out. He got into his other car and drove to the end of the driveway. David Munsey had already joined Charlie Stevens and FaNee, and the Pinto was just leaving, traveling at a normal rate of speed. Leo Cooper pulled out on the road behind them.

Stevens turned left on Crippen Road, a road that has a field [13] on one side and two or three small houses on the other, and there Cooper pulled his car in front of the Pinto and stopped, blocking the way. He got out and walked toward the Pinto. Suddenly, Stevens put the car in reverse, backed into a driveway a hundred yards behind him, and sped off. Cooper jumped in his car and gave chase. Stevens raced back to Brown Gap Road, ran a stop sign there, ran another stop sign at Maynardville Highway, turned north, veered off onto the old Andersonville Pike, a nearly abandoned road that runs parallel to the highway, and then crossed back over the highway to the narrow, dark country roads on the other side. Stevens sometimes drove with his lights out. He took some of the corners by suddenly applying his hand brake to make the car swerve around in a ninety-degree turn. He was in familiar territory — he actually passed his trailer — and Cooper had difficulty keeping up. Past the trailer, Stevens swept down a hill into a sharp left turn that took him onto Foust Hollow Road, a winding, hilly road not much wider than one car.

At a fork, Cooper thought he had lost the Pinto. He started [14] to go right, and then saw what seemed to be a spark from Stevens's dragging muffler off to the left, in the darkness. Cooper took the left fork, down Salem Church Road. He went down a hill, and then up a long, curving hill to a crest, where he saw the Stevens car ahead. "I saw the car airborne. Up in the air," he later testified. "It was up in the air. And then it completely rolled over one more time. It started to make another flip forward, and just as it started to flip to the other side it flipped back this way, and my daughter's body came out."

Cooper slammed on his brakes and skidded to a stop up [15] against the Pinto. "Book!" Stevens shouted — the group's equivalent of "Scram!" Stevens and Munsey disappeared into the darkness. "It was dark, no one around, and so I started yelling for Fa-

Nee," Cooper has testified. "I thought it was an eternity before I
could find her body, wedged under the back end of that car. . . . I
tried everything I could, and saw that I couldn't get her loose. So
I ran to a trailer back up to the top of the hill back up there to try
to get that lady to call to get me some help, and then apparently
she didn't think that I was serious. . . . I took the jack out of my
car and got under, and it was dark, still couldn't see too much
what was going on . . . and started prying and got her loose, and I
don't know how. And then I dragged her over to the side, and, of
course, at the time I felt reasonably assured that she was gone, because her head was completely — on one side just as if you had
taken a sledgehammer and just hit it and bashed it in. And I did
have the pleasure of one thing. I had the pleasure of listening to
her breathe about the last three times she ever breathed in her
life."

David Munsey did not return to the wreck that night, but   16
Charlie Stevens did. Leo Cooper was kneeling next to his daughter's body. Cooper insisted that Stevens come close enough to see
FaNee. "He was kneeling down next to her," Stevens later testified. "And he said, 'Do you know what you've done? Do you really know what you've done?' Like that. And I just looked at her,
and I said, 'Yes,' and just stood there. Because I couldn't say nothing." There was, of course, a legal decision to be made about who
was responsible for FaNee Cooper's death. In a deposition,
Stevens said he had been fleeing for his life. He testified that
when Leo Cooper blocked Crippen Road, FaNee had said that
her father had a gun and intended to hurt them. Stevens was
bound over and eventually indicted for involuntary manslaugh-
ter. Leo Cooper testified that when he approached the Pinto on
Crippen Road, FaNee had a strange expression that he had never
seen before. "It wasn't like FaNee, and I knew something was
wrong," he said. "My concern was to get FaNee out of the car."
The district attorney's office asked that Cooper be bound over for
reckless driving, but the judge declined to do so. "Any father
would have done what he did," the judge said. "I can see no criminal act on the part of Mr. Cooper."

Almost two years passed before Charlie Stevens was brought   17
to trial. Part of the problem was assuring the presence of David
Munsey, who had joined the Navy but seemed inclined to assign
his own leaves. In the meantime, the Coopers went to court with
a civil suit — they had "uninsured-motorist coverage," which requires their insurance company to cover any defendant who has
no insurance of his own — and they won a judgment. There were
ways of assigning responsibility, of course, which had nothing to
do with the law, civil or criminal. A lot of people in Knoxville
thought that Leo Cooper had, in the words of his lawyer, "done
what any daddy worth his salt would have done." There were
others who believed that FaNee Cooper had lost her life because
Leo Cooper had lost his temper. Leo Cooper was not among
those who expressed any doubts about his actions. Unlike his
wife, whose eyes filled with tears at almost any mention of FaNee,
Cooper seemed able, even eager to go over the details of the accident again and again. With the help of a school-board security
man, he conducted his own investigation. He drove over the
route dozens of times. "I've thought about it every day, and I
guess I will the rest of my life," he said as he and his lawyer and
the prosecuting attorney went over the route again the day before
Charlie Stevens's trial finally began. "But I can't tell any alternative for a father. I simply wanted her out of that car. I'd have done
the same thing again, even at the risk of losing her."

Tennessee law permits the family of a victim to hire a special   18
prosecutor to assist the district attorney. The lawyer who acted
for the Coopers in the civil case helped prosecute Charlie
Stevens. Both he and the district attorney assured the jurors that
the presence of a special prosecutor was not to be construed to
mean that the Coopers were vindictive. Outside the courtroom,
Leo Cooper said that the verdict was of no importance to him —
that he felt sorry, in a way, for Charlie Stevens. But there were
people in Knoxville who thought Cooper had a lot riding on the
prosecution of Charlie Stevens. If Stevens was not guilty of FaNee
Cooper's death — found so by twelve of his peers — who was?

At the trial, Cooper testified emotionally and remarkably   19

graphically about pulling FaNee out from under the car and
watching her die in his arms. Charlie Stevens had shaved his
beard and cut his hair, but the effort did not transform him into
an impressive witness. His lawyer — trying to argue that it would
have been impossible for Stevens to concoct the story about Fa-
Nee's having mentioned a gun, as the prosecution strongly implied — said, "His mind is such that if you ask him a question you
can hear his mind go around, like an old mill creaking." Stevens
did not deny the recklessness of his driving or the sorry condition
of his car. It happened to be the only car he had available to flee
in, he said, and he had fled in fear for his life.

    The prosecution said that Stevens could have let FaNee out   20
of the car when her father stopped them, or could have gone to
the commercial strip on the Maynardville Highway for protection. The prosecution said that Leo Cooper had done what he
might have been expected to do under the circumstances —
alone, late at night, his daughter in danger. The defense said precisely the same about Stevens: He had done what he might have
been expected to do when being pursued by a man he had reason
to be afraid of. "I don't fault Mr. Cooper for what he did, but I'm
sorry he did it," the defense attorney said. "I'm sorry the girl said
what she said." The jury deliberated for eighteen minutes. Charlie Stevens was found guilty. The jury recommended a sentence of
from two to five years in the state penitentiary. At the announcement, Leo Cooper broke down and cried. JoAnn Cooper's eyes
filled with tears; she blinked them back and continued to stare
straight ahead.

    In a way, the Coopers might still strike a casual visitor as an   21
ideal family — handsome parents, a bright and bubbly teenage
daughter, a little boy learning the hook shot from his father, a
warm house with some land around it. FaNee's presence is there,
of course. A picture of her, with a small bouquet of flowers over
it, hangs in the living room. One of her poems is displayed in a
frame on a table. Even if Leo Cooper continues to think about
that night for the rest of his life, there are questions he can never
answer. Was there a way that Leo and JoAnn Cooper could have
prevented FaNee from choosing the path she chose? Would she

still be alive if Leo Cooper had not jumped into his car and driven to the end of the driveway to investigate? Did she in fact tell Charlie Stevens that her father would hurt them — or even that her father had a gun? Did she want to get away from her family even at the risk of tearing around dark country roads in Charlie Stevens's dismal Pinto? Or did she welcome the risk? The poem of FaNee's that the Coopers have displayed is one she wrote a week before her death:

> I think I'm going to die
> And I really don't know why.
> But look in my eye
> When I tell you good-bye.
> I think I'm going to die.

QUESTIONS ON MEANING

1. Which appears to be the dominant PURPOSE of Trillin's essay: to report a death, to tell why it happened, or to tell a revealing story?
2. How would you characterize Leo and JoAnn Cooper?
3. Of all the people who talk about FaNee and her problems, who seems to understand her best?
4. In paragraph 18, Trillin hints that Leo Cooper might have felt threatened had Charlie Stevens won acquittal. What, exactly, is the threat?
5. What do the samples of FaNee's writing that appear in Trillin's essay (paras. 2, 4, 5, 11, 21) contribute to your understanding of her behavior?

QUESTIONS ON WRITING STRATEGY

1. What do the direct quotations — from Leo and JoAnn Cooper; the friend called Marcia; the counselor, Jim Griffin; FaNee herself; Charlie Stevens; Cooper's lawyer — contribute to Trillin's narrative, other than local color?
2. Does Trillin seem to be biased against or in favor of anyone in his narrative? Or does he conceal all bias? Muster EVIDENCE for your answer.

3. In his introduction to *Killings*, Trillin recalls that local newspaper reporters he met while working on the story of FaNee Cooper did not understand his interest in the case. "They couldn't imagine why I had come all the way from New York to write about a death that probably hadn't even made their front page. Only one person had died, and she had not been an important person." How might the AUDIENCE of *The New Yorker*, a nationally circulated magazine of nonfiction, fiction, poetry, and humor, read about a killing with expectations different from those of readers of a local newspaper?

4. OTHER METHODS. In his last paragraph, Trillin asks a number of questions about causes and effects (Chap. 9). Do you have answers for any of these questions? Do they provide a satisfactory CONCLUSION to Trillin's narrative? Discuss.

QUESTIONS ON LANGUAGE

1. Consult your dictionary if you need help defining the following: introspective, errant, magnanimous, gentility (para. 1); affliction (2); decrepit (10); incorrigibles (11); deposition, indicted (16); construed, vindictive (18).

2. What do the Jocks mean when they "talk about having a real good Christian witness" (para. 5)?

3. What do you infer about the author's feelings toward Leo Cooper when he describes Cooper as having "a manner that may come from years of trying to leave errant junior-high-school students with the impression that a responsible adult is magnanimous, even humble, about invariably being in the right" (para. 1)?

SUGGESTIONS FOR WRITING

1. Suppose that Mr. Cooper had been able to stop Charlie Stevens's car before FaNee was killed — and that you, as the reporter, beginning after paragraph 13 in "It's Just Too Late," have to tell what happened next. Imagine and write a new, briefer ending for Trillin's narrative.

2. As objectively and concretely as you can, narrate the experience of a high-school acquaintance who committed a rebellious act that had dire (but not necessarily fatal) consequences.

3. CONNECTIONS. Both Trillin's "It's Just Too Late" and Shirley Jackson's short story "The Lottery" (p. 100) are at least partly about how people may be both helped and hurt by those they live among. Write an essay exploring the idea of *community* in these two works.

(A suggestion: Consulting a dictionary for the meanings and history of the word *community* may help focus your thinking.)

CALVIN TRILLIN ON WRITING

In a published conversation with his wife, Alice Trillin, Calvin Trillin was asked, "To what extent is the research — the details — important in the finished story?"

He replied: "If the story is a murder story, that has within it its own narrative line — its own beginning, middle, and end, and its own details — then what I try to do when I write is to get out of the way and just let the story tell itself. I try to get as many of the details as cleanly as possible into the story and try to get all the marks of writing off. Sometimes I think of it as trying to change clothes inside a tiny closet.

"But if it's a story about the search for barbecued mutton in western Kentucky, for instance, which is really just based on my notions of eating thrown together with some experiences — there's no beginning, no middle or end — something different than gathering as many facts as possible is called for.

"And then . . . sometimes a story changes along the way, causing the balance between straight reporting and my personal reactions to the reporting to change with it. But usually, except in extreme cases, like western Kentucky's barbecued mutton, it's not easy to tell how a story will turn out when I begin to write. So I still have to do all the reporting and gather as many facts as I can."

Alice Trillin persisted. "What do you usually end up with, then, after you finish reporting and are ready to start writing and what do you do with it?"

"What I have when I get home," said Trillin, "is a notebook full of handwritten notes, and sometimes, if I've been conscientious, some notes which I've typed up either late at night or early in the morning as a way of sharpening my notes a bit. As I type out notes, I remember things that were said or fill out sentences that aren't really carefully done. Also, I find out what I don't know — that there are questions that I will have to ask the next day. In addition to that, I usually have a lot of xeroxes of newspaper clippings, and sometimes I even have copies of court transcripts, brochures, etc. Whatever I have, it is often a fairly sizeable pile. Then, the day after I get home, I do a kind of predraft — what I call a 'vomit-out.' I don't even look at my notes to write it. It . . . starts out, at least, in the form of a story. But it degenerates fairly quickly, and by page four or five sometimes the sentences aren't complete. I write almost the length of the story in this way. The whole operation takes no more than an hour at the typewriter, but it sometimes takes me all day to do it because I'm tired and I've put it off a bit. Sometimes I don't even look at the vomit-out for the rest of the week and I have an absolute terror of anybody seeing it. It's a very embarrassing document. I tear it up at the end of the week.

"I don't write a predraft for fiction or for humor, but I can't seem to do without one for nonfiction. I've tried to figure out why I need it, what purpose it serves. I think it gives me an inventory of what I want to say and an opportunity to see which way the tone of the story is going to go, which is very important. Also, this is about the time that I begin to see technical problems that will come up — for example, that one part of the story doesn't lead into the next, or that I should write the story in the first person, or start it in a different way."

FOR DISCUSSION

1. What, according to Trillin, are the advantages of writing a "vomit-out"?
2. In what ways does "It's Just Too Late" reflect Trillin's method of telling a murder story: trying "to get out of the way and just let the story tell itself"? To what extent does the writer himself remain invisible? Does he succeed in making you forget that the story required notetaking, legwork, extensive conversations with people?

JOHN SIMPSON

An English news correspondent and editor, JOHN SIMPSON is foreign affairs editor for the British Broadcasting Corporation in London. He was born John Cody Fidler-Simpson in 1944 and educated at St. Paul's School and at Magdalene College of Cambridge University, where he earned a master's degree. Since joining the BBC as a radio correspondent, Simpson has worked all over the globe, reporting from and on Ireland, Belgium, South Africa, Iran, Argentina, and China. Besides numerous articles, Simpson has written two nonfiction books: *The Disappeared: Military Repression in Argentina* (1985) and *Inside Iran: Life Under Khomeini's Regime* (1986). He is also author of two novels, *Moscow Requiem* (1981) and *A Fine and Private Place* (1983).

Tiananmen Square

This harrowing essay first appeared in Autumn 1989 in *Granta*, a magazine of contemporary fiction and nonfiction. Just a few months before, Simpson had been in China, where in early June he witnessed the demonstrations and battles in and around Beijing's Tiananmen Square. Students protesting against corruption and repression had been occupying the huge city square on and off for nearly two months. There and in demonstrations elsewhere in China, students had been joined by workers and other citizens to form protesting crowds numbering as high as one million. Subject to its own internal struggles, the government vacillated between toleration and threats. When it finally sent the army to quell the unrest in Beijing and expel the protestors from Tiananmen Square, the soldiers were at first held back by the angry crowds. But on June 4, troops and tanks broke through. To this day, the facts of who and how many were killed, and where, remain in dispute. Simpson recounts the small part of the events that he saw and heard.

It was humid and airless, and the streets around our hotel 1 were empty. We had set out for Tiananmen Square: a big, con-

spicuous European television team — reporter, producer, cameraman, sound-recordist, translator, lighting man, complete with
gear. A cyclist rode past, shouting and pointing. What it meant
we couldn't tell. Then we came upon a line of soldiers. Some of
them had bleeding faces; one cradled a broken arm. They were
walking slowly, limping. There had been a battle somewhere, but
we couldn't tell where.

When we reached Changan Avenue, the main east-west 2
thoroughfare, it was as full of people as in the days of the great
demonstrations — a human river. We followed the flow of it to
the Gate of Heavenly Peace, under the bland, moonlike portrait
of Chairman Mao. There were hundreds of small groups, each
concentrated around someone who was haranguing or lecturing
the others, using the familiar, heavy public gestures of the Chinese. Other groups had formed around radios tuned to foreign
stations. People were moving from group to group, pushing in,
crushing round a speaker, arguing, moving on, passing along any
new information.

For the most part these were not students. They were from 3
the factories, and the red cloths tied around their heads made
them look aggressive, even piratical. Trucks started arriving from
the outskirts of the city, full of more young workers, waving the
banners of their factories, singing, chanting, looking forward to
trouble.

People were shouting: There was a battle going on between 4
tanks and the crowd, somewhere to the east of the city center.
Details differed, and I had trouble finding out what was being
said: I watched the animated faces, everyone pushing closer to
each new source of information, pulling at each other's sleeves or
shoulders. Tanks and armored personnel carriers, they were saying, were heading toward the square. They were coming from two
directions, east and west. The crowds that gathered couldn't stop
them.

"It's a different army. It's not the Thirty-eighth!" The man 5
who said this was screaming it, clutching at our translator, holding on to him, trying to make him understand the significance of
it. "It is *not* the Thirty-eighth!" It had been the Thirty-eighth
Army that had tried to recapture the city twice before. The sol-

diers had been unarmed: The commander, the father of a student
in the square, had ordered that operations be carried out peace-
fully.

We pushed our way toward the square where, despite the ru-   6
mors and the panic, we saw something very different: several
thousand people standing in silence, motionless, listening to a
large loudspeaker, bolted to a street lamp:

> Go home and save your life. You will fail. You are not behav-
> ing in the correct Chinese manner. This is not the West, it is
> China. You should behave like a good Chinese. Go home and
> save your life. Go home and save your life.

The voice was expressionless, epicene, metallic, like that of a hypnotist. I looked at these silent, serious faces, illuminated by the orange light of the street lamps, studying the loudspeaker. Even the
small children, brought there with the rest of the family, stared
intently. The order was repeated again and again. It was a voice
the people of China had been listening to for forty years, and
continued listening to even now. But now no one did what the
hypnotist said. No one moved.

And then, suddenly, everything changed: The loudspeaker's   7
spell was broken by shouts that the army was coming. There was
the sound of a violent scraping, and across the avenue I saw people pulling at the railings that ran along the roadway and dragging them across the pavement to build a barricade. Everyone
moved quickly, a crowd suddenly animated, its actions fast and
decisive, sometimes brutal. They blocked off Changan Avenue
and the square itself, and we began filming — flooding the sweating enthusiasts with our camera-light. People danced around us,
flaunting their weaponry: coshes,[1] knives, crude spears, bricks. A
boy rushed up to our camera and opened his shabby green windcheater like a black marketeer to reveal a row of Coca-Cola bottles strapped to his waist, filled with petrol and plugged with rags.
He laughed, and mimed the action of pulling out each bottle and

---

[1]*Cosh* is a British word for a blackjack or bludgeon. A *windcheater* (later in
the sentence) is a windbreaker. — EDS.

throwing it. I asked him his age. He was sixteen. Why was he against the government? He couldn't answer. He gripped another of his Molotov cocktails, laughing all the time.

That the army was coming was no longer rumor but fact and   8
our translator heard that it would move in at one o'clock. It was half-past midnight. In the distance, above the noise of the crowd, I thought I could hear the sound of guns. I wanted to find a vantage point from which we could film, without being spotted by the army. But the tension that was bonding members of the crowd together did not have the same effect on the members of our small team. It was hot and noisy. We argued. We started shouting, and I headed off on my own.

I pushed through the crowds, immediately feeling better for   9
being on my own. There were very few foreign journalists left in the square by now, and I felt especially conspicuous. But I also felt good. People grabbed my hand, thanking me for being with them. I gave them a V for Victory sign and was applauded by everyone around me. It was hard to define the mood. There was still a spirit of celebration, that they were out on the streets, defying the government, but the spirit was also giving way to a terrible foreboding. There was also something else. Something I hadn't seen before: a reckless ferocity of purpose.

I crossed back into the main part of Tiananmen Square, the   10
village of student tents. There were sticks and cardboard and broken glass underfoot. The smells were familiar and strong — woodsmoke, urine, and heavy disinfectant. A couple clung to each other, her head on his shoulder. I passed in front of them, but they didn't raise their eyes. A student asked me to sign his T-shirt, a craze from earlier days. He had thick glasses and a bad complexion, and he spoke English. "It will be dangerous tonight," he said. "We are all very afraid here."

I finished signing his shirt, at the back below the collar. He   11
grabbed my hand and shook it excitedly. His grip was bony and clammy. I asked him what he thought would happen.

"We will all die."   12

He straightened up and shook my hand again, and slipped   13
away between the tents.

The camp was dark. There were a few students left; most of 14
them had gathered in the center of the square, around the Monument to the People's Heroes. I could hear their speeches and the occasional burst of singing — the Internationale, as always. Here, though, it was quiet. This was where the students had chosen to build their statue of the Goddess of Democracy, with her sightless eyes, her torch held in both hands. The symbol of all our aspirations, one of the student leaders called her: the fruit of our struggle. To me, she looked very fragile.

The speeches and the songs continued in the distance. Then 15
suddenly they stopped. There was a violent grinding and a squealing sound — the familiar sound of an armored personnel carrier. I heard screaming, and behind me, in the avenue, everyone started running. When I finally spotted the vehicle, I could see that it was making its way with speed down the side of the square. It seemed uncertain of its direction — one moment driving straight for the square, and then stopping, turning, stopping again, as if looking for a way to escape. There was a sudden angry roar, and I know it was because the vehicle had crushed someone under its tracks. It then turned in my direction — it was pointed at me — and I felt a different kind of panic. The action was starting and I was separated from my colleagues: It is an article of faith to stay with your camera crew in times of danger.

The vehicle carried on, careering back and forth. It must 16
have knocked down six or seven people. By now it was on fire, having been hit repeatedly by Molotov cocktails. Somehow, though, it escaped and headed off to the west.

Then a second armored personnel carrier came along 17
Changan Avenue, alone and unsupported like the first. This time everyone turned and ran hard toward the vehicle, knowing that they, with their numbers and their petrol bombs, had the power to knock it out. They screamed with anger and hate as the vehicle swung randomly in different directions, threatening to knock people down as it made its way through the square. The Molotov cocktails arched above our heads, spinning over and over, exploding on the thin shell of armor that protected the men inside. Still the vehicle carried on, zigzagging, crossing the avenue, trying to find a way through the barricade. A pause, and it charged,

head-on, straight into a block of concrete — and then stuck, its engine whirring wildly. A terrible shout of triumph came from the crowd: primitive and dark, its prey finally caught. The smell of petrol and burning metal and sweat was in the air, intoxicating and violent. Everyone around me was pushing and fighting to get to the vehicle. At first I resisted; then, close beside it, I saw the light of a camera, just where the crowd was starting to swarm. There were only three cameramen still filming in the entire square, and I knew that my colleague was the only one crazy enough to be that close. Now I was the one fighting, struggling to get through the crowd, pulling people back, pushing them out of my path, swearing, a big brutal Englishman stronger than any of them. I tore one man's shirt and punched another in the back. All around me the men seemed to be yelling at the sky, their faces lit up; the vehicle had caught fire. A man — his torso bare — climbed up the side of the vehicle and stood on top of it, his arms raised in victory, the noise of the mob welling up around him. They knew they had the vehicle's crew trapped inside. Someone started beating at the armored glass with an iron bar.

I reached the cameraman and pulled hard at his arm to get   18
his attention. He scarcely noticed me, amid the buffeting and the noise and the violence, and carried on filming. He and his sound recordist and the Chinese lighting man were a few feet from the vehicle: close enough to be killed if it exploded or if the soldiers came out shooting. But I couldn't make them step back, and so we stayed there, the four of us, the heat beating against our faces as people continued to pour petrol on the bonnet and roof and smashed at the doors and the armored glass. What was it like in-side? I imagined the soldiers half-crazed with the noise and the heat and the fear of being burned alive.

The screaming around me rose even louder: the handle of the   19
door at the rear of the vehicle had turned a little, and the door began to open. A soldier pushed the barrel of a gun out, but it was snatched from his hands, and then everyone started grabbing his arms, pulling and wrenching until finally he came free, and then he was gone: I saw the arms of the mob, flailing, raised above their heads as they fought to get their blows in. He was dead within seconds, and his body was dragged away in triumph. A

second soldier showed his head through the door and was then immediately pulled out by his hair and ears and the skin on his face. This soldier I could see: His eyes were rolling, and his mouth was open, and he was covered with blood where the skin had been ripped off. Only his eyes remained — white and clear — but then someone was trying to get them as well, and someone else began beating his skull until the skull came apart, and there was blood all over the ground, and his brains, and still they kept beating and beating what was left.

Then the horrible sight passed away, and the ground was wet 20 where he had been.

There was a third soldier inside. I could see his face in the 21 light of the flames, and some of the crowd could too. They pulled him out, screaming, wild at having missed killing the other soldiers. It was his blood they wanted, I was certain, it was to feel the blood running over their hands. Their mouths were open and panting, like dogs, and their eyes were expressionless. They were shouting, the Chinese lighting man told me afterwards, that the soldier they were about to kill wasn't human, that he was just a thing, an object, which had to be destroyed. And all the time the noise and the heat and the stench of oil burning on hot metal beat at us, overwhelming our senses, deadening them.

Just as the third soldier was lifted out of the vehicle, almost 22 fainting, an articulated bus rushed toward us, stopping with great skill, so that its rear door opened just beside the group with the soldier. The students had heard what was happening, and a group had raced the bus over to save whomever they could. The mob did not want to give up its prize. The students tried to drag the soldier on board, and the crowd held on to him, pulling him back. By some mischance the bus door started closing and it seemed that he must be killed.

I had seen people die in front of me before. But I had never seen 23 three people die, one after the other, in this way. Once again the members of the crowd closed around the soldier, their arms raised over their heads to beat him to death. The bus and the safety it promised were so close. It seemed to me then that I couldn't look on any longer, a passive observer, watching another man's skin torn away or his head broken open, and do nothing. I saw the soldier's face, expressing only horror and pain as he sank under the blows of the people around him, and I started to move forward. The ferocity of the crowd had entered me, but I felt it was the crowd that was the animal, that it wasn't properly human. The soldier had sunk down to the ground, and a man was trying to break his skull with a half-brick, bringing it down with full force. I screamed obscenities at the man — stupid obscenities, as no one except my colleagues could have understood them — and threw myself at him, catching him with his arm up, poised for another blow. He looked at me blankly, and his thin arm went limp in my grasp. I stopped shouting. He relaxed his grip on the brick, and I threw it under the bus. It felt wet. A little room had been created around the soldier, and the student who had tried to rescue him before could now get to him. The rest of the mob hadn't given up, but the students were able to pull the soldier away and get him on to the bus by the other door. He was safe.

The vehicle burned for a long time, its driver and the man beside him burning with it. The flames lit up the square and reflected on the face of the monument where the students had taken their stand. The crowd in Changan Avenue had been sated. The loudspeakers had stopped telling people to save their lives. There was silence. 24

The students sang the Internationale. It would be for the last time, and it sounded weak and faint in the vastness of the square. Many were crying. No doubt some students joined in the attacks on the army, but those in the square kept to their principle of nonviolence. Although the army suffered the first casualties, it was the students who would be the martyrs that night. 25

My colleagues and I wanted to save our pictures in case we were arrested, and I told the others that we should go back to the Beijing Hotel and come out again later. I now feel guilty about the decision; it was wrong: We ought to have stayed in the square, even though the other camera crews had already left and it might have cost us our lives. Someone should have been there when the massacre took place, filming what happened, showing the courage of the students as they were surrounded by tanks and the army advancing, firing as it went. 26

Instead, we took up our position on the fourteenth floor of 27
the Beijing Hotel. From there, everything seemed gray and distant. We saw most of what happened, but we were separated from
the fear and the noise and the stench of it. We saw the troops
pouring out of the Gate of Heavenly Peace, bayonets fixed, shooting first into the air and then straight ahead of them. They
looked like automata, with their rounded dark helmets. We
filmed them charging across and clearing the northern end of the
square, where I had signed the student's T-shirt. We filmed the
tanks as they drove over the tents where some of the students had
taken refuge, among them, perhaps, the young couple I had seen
sitting silently, their arms around each other. Dozens of people
seem to have died in that way, and those who saw it said they
could hear the screams of the people inside the tents over the
noise of the tanks. We filmed as the lights in the square were
switched off at four A.M. They were switched on again forty minutes later, when the troops and the tanks moved toward the monument itself, shooting first in the air and then, again, directly at
the students themselves, so that the steps of the monument and
the heroic reliefs which decorated it were smashed by bullets.

Once or twice, we were ourselves shot at, and during the night 28
the security police sent men to our room to arrest us: But I
shouted at them in English, and they went away, uncertain of the
extent of their powers. Below us, people still gathered in the avenue, shouting their defiance at the troops who were massed at the
farther end. Every now and then the crack of a rifle would bring
down another demonstrator, and the body would be rescued by a
trishaw[2] driver or the crew of an ambulance. Below us, the best
and noblest political protest since Czechoslovakia in 1968 was being crushed as we watched. I knelt on the balcony, beside the
cameraman and a Chinese woman, one of the student leaders.

She had taken refuge in our room because we were foreigners. 29
I shouted at her to go back inside, but she refused, turning her
head from me so that I wouldn't see she was crying, her hands
clenched tight enough to hurt, intent on watching the rape of her
country and the movement she and her friends had built up in

[2]A small carriage. — Eds.

the course of twenty-two days. I had seen the river of protest running along Changan Avenue in that time; I had seen a million
people in the streets, demanding a way of life that was better than
rule by corruption and secret police. I recalled the lines of the
T'ang dynasty poet Li Po, that if you cut water with a sword you
merely made it run faster. But the river of change had been
dammed, and below me, in the avenue where it had run, people
were dying. Beside me, the cameraman spotted something and
started filming. Down in the square, in the early light, the soldiers
were busy unrolling something and lifting it up. Soon a great curtain of black cloth covered the entrance to Tiananmen Square.
What was happening there was hidden from us.

QUESTIONS ON MEANING

1. What was Simpson's PURPOSE in writing "Tiananmen Square" — to
   report an event, or something more?
2. In what ways was Simpson handicapped as a witness?
3. The loudspeaker message quoted in paragraph 6 orders those in the
   square to behave like "good Chinese." What do you gather this
   means?
4. Why does Simpson feel guilty about leaving the square (para. 26)?
   Do you think he should feel guilty?

QUESTIONS ON WRITING STRATEGY

1. How would you describe Simpson's POINT OF VIEW? Rewrite paragraph 9 in the third PERSON (*he*) instead of the first PERSON (*I*) used by
   Simpson. How does the paragraph change? Does it seem more or
   less like fact or fiction?
2. Simpson clearly is not merely an objective observer of events: In
   paragraph 23, he abandons any role as "a passive observer." Why do
   you think he is so up-front about his subjectivity? Does it weaken or
   strengthen his narrative?
3. Lack of communication and understanding seems to operate as a
   major theme throughout the essay. What examples from the text
   support this statement? How do they relate to the conclusion?

4. What assumptions does Simpson make about his AUDIENCE? Where do his sympathies lie? Does he expect readers to share these sympathies?
5. OTHER METHODS. Analyze Simpson's description of the crowd in paragraphs 17–23. How does Simpson's vocabulary convey his own feelings?

QUESTIONS ON LANGUAGE

1. Define the following: conspicuous (para. 1); piratical (3); epicene (6); flaunting (7); vantage point (8); foreboding (9); careering, Molotov cocktails (16); welling (17); mischance (22); sated (24); martyrs (25); automata, reliefs (27).
2. Simpson writes, "Below us, the best and noblest political protest since Czechoslovakia in 1968 was being crushed as we watched" (para. 28). What does this sentence say about the author? How does he define a "noble" protest? How do you?
3. Examine Simpson's IMAGES in paragraphs 2 and 29. How effective do you find the METAPHOR of the river in opening and closing the essay?

SUGGESTIONS FOR WRITING

1. Use the first PERSON (*I*) to narrate an event that shocked you into doing something you would not normally do.
2. "The reporter's active participation in the events of Tiananmen Square was both unjustified and useless." Agree or disagree with this statement, supporting your opinion with examples from the text and your own reading and experience.
3. Turn the television on to an action show (the kind featuring cops and robbers). Watch long enough to get the idea of the plot, and then turn the volume all the way down for ten or fifteen minutes. Jot down a narrative of what you suppose is happening; then check your impressions by raising the volume again. Write an analysis of the visual cues and miscues that helped or hindered your attempt to understand without sound.
4. CONNECTIONS. Both John Simpson and Calvin Trillin (in the previous essay) serve as reporters of their respective stories, but they produce quite different results. Analyze their essays' differences in TONE, PERSON, POINT OF VIEW, and OBJECTIVE versus SUBJECTIVE emphasis. (Use quotations and PARAPHRASES from the essays as your support.) What are the pluses and minuses of each approach for the reader?

SHIRLEY JACKSON

SHIRLEY JACKSON was a fiction writer best known for horror stories that probe the dark side of human nature and social behavior. But she also wrote humorously about domestic life, a subject she knew well as a wife and the mother of four children. Born in 1919 in California, Jackson moved as a teenager to Syracuse, New York, and graduated from Syracuse University in 1940. She started writing as a young girl and was highly disciplined and productive all her life. She began publishing stories in 1941, and eventually her fiction appeared in *The New Yorker, Harper's, Good Housekeeping*, and many other magazines. Her tales of family life appeared in two books, *Life among the Savages* (1953) and *Raising Demons* (1957). Her more popular (and to her more significant) suspense novels included *The Haunting of Hill House* (1959) and *We Have Always Lived in the Castle* (1962). After her death in 1965, her husband, the literary critic Stanley Edgar Hyman, published two volumes of stories, novels, and lectures, *The Magic of Shirley Jackson* (1966) and *Come Along with Me* (1968).

The Lottery

By far Jackson's best-known work and indeed one of the best-known short stories ever, "The Lottery" first appeared in *The New Yorker* in 1948 to loud applause and louder cries of outrage. Jackson's husband, denying that her work purveyed "neutoric fantasies," argued instead that it was fitting "for our distressing world of concentration camps and The Bomb." See if you agree.

The morning of June 27th was clear and sunny, with the   1
fresh warmth of a full-summer day; the flowers were blossoming profusely and the grass was richly green. The people of the village began to gather in the square, between the post office and the bank, around ten o'clock; in some towns there were so many people that the lottery took two days and had to be started on June 26th, but in this village, where there were only about three hun-

drcd pcuple, the whole lottery took less than two hours, so it could begin at ten o'clock in the morning and still be through in time to allow the villagers to get home for noon dinner.

The children assembled first, of course. School was recently   2
over for the summer, and the feeling of liberty sat uneasily on most of them; they tended to gather together quietly for a while before they broke into boisterous play, and their talk was still of the classroom and the teacher, of books and reprimands. Bobby Martin had already stuffed his pockets full of stones, and the other boys soon followed his example, selecting the smoothest and roundest stones; Bobby and Harry Jones and Dickie Delacroix — the villagers pronounced this name "Dellacroy" — eventually made a great pile of stones in one corner of the square and guarded it against the raids of the other boys. The girls stood aside, talking among themselves, looking over their shoulders at the boys, and the very small children rolled in the dust or clung to the hands of their older brothers or sisters.

Soon the men began to gather, surveying their own children,   3
speaking of planting and rain, tractors and taxes. They stood together, away from the pile of stones in the corner, and their jokes were quiet and they smiled rather than laughed. The women, wearing faded house dresses and sweaters, came shortly after their menfolk. They greeted one another and exchanged bits of gossip as they went to join their husbands. Soon the women, standing by their husbands, began to call to their children, and the children came reluctantly, having to be called four or five times. Bobby Martin ducked under his mother's grasping hand and ran, laughing, back to the pile of stones. His father spoke up sharply, and Bobby came quickly and took his place between his father and his oldest brother.

The lottery was conducted — as were the square dances, the   4
teenage club, the Halloween program — by Mr. Summers, who had time and energy to devote to civic activities. He was a round-faced, jovial man and he ran the coal business, and people were sorry for him, because he had no children and his wife was a scold. When he arrived in the square, carrying the black wooden box, there was a murmur of conversation among the villagers, and he waved and called, "Little late today, folks." The postmas-

ter, Mr. Graves, followed him, carrying a three-legged stool, and
the stool was put in the center of the square and Mr. Summers set
the black box down on it. The villagers kept their distance, leaving a space between themselves and the stool, and when Mr.
Summers said, "Some of you fellows want to give me a hand?"
there was a hesitation before two men, Mr. Martin and his oldest
son, Baxter, came forward to hold the box steady on the stool
while Mr. Summers stirred up the papers inside it.

The original paraphernalia for the lottery had been lost long   5
ago, and the black box now resting on the stool had been put
into use even before Old Man Warner, the oldest man in town,
was born. Mr. Summers spoke frequently to the villagers about
making a new box, but no one liked to upset even as much tradition as was represented by the black box. There was a story that
the present box had been made with some pieces of the box that
had preceded it, the one that had been constructed when the first
people settled down to make a village here. Every year, after the
lottery, Mr. Summers began talking again about a new box, but
every year the subject was allowed to fade off without anything's
being done. The black box grew shabbier each year; by now it
was no longer completely black but splintered badly among one
side to show the original wood color, and in some places faded or
stained.

Mr. Martin and his oldest son, Baxter, held the black box se-   6
curely on the stool until Mr. Summers had stirred the papers
thoroughly with his hand. Because so much of the ritual had
been forgotten or discarded, Mr. Summers had been successful in
having slips of paper substituted for the chips of wood that had
been used for generations. Chips of wood, Mr. Summers had argued, had been all very well when the village was tiny, but now
that the population was more than three hundred and likely to
keep on growing, it was necessary to use something that would fit
more easily into the black box. The night before the lottery, Mr.
Summers and Mr. Graves made up the slips of paper and put
them in the box, and it was then taken to the safe of Mr. Summer's coal company and locked up until Mr. Summers was ready
to take it to the square next morning. The rest of the year, the
box was put away, sometimes one place, sometimes another; it

had spent one year in Mr. Graves's barn and another year underfoot in the post office, and sometimes it was set on a shelf in the Martin grocery and left there.

There was a great deal of fussing to be done before Mr. Summers declared the lottery open. There were the lists to make up — of heads of families, heads of households in each family, members of each household in each family. There was the proper swearing-in of Mr. Summers by the postmaster, as the official of the lottery; at one time, some people remembered, there had been a recital of some sort, performed by the official of the lottery, a perfunctory, tuneless chant that had been rattled off duly each year; some people believed that the official of the lottery used to stand just so when he said or sang it, others believed that he was supposed to walk among the people, but years and years ago this part of the ritual had been allowed to lapse. There had been, also, a ritual salute, which the official of the lottery had had to use in addressing each person who came up to draw from the box, but this also had changed with time, until now it was felt necessary only for the official to speak to each person approaching. Mr. Summers was very good at all this; in his clean white shirt and blue jeans, with one hand resting carelessly on the black box, he seemed very proper and important as he talked interminably to Mr. Graves and the Martins. 7

Just as Mr. Summers finally left off talking and turned to the assembled villagers, Mrs. Hutchinson came hurriedly along the path to the square, her sweater thrown over her shoulders, and slid into place in the back of the crowd. "Clean forgot what day it was," she said to Mrs. Delacroix, who stood next to her, and they both laughed softly. "Thought my old man was out back stacking wood," Mrs. Hutchinson went on, "and then I looked out the window and the kids was gone, and then I remembered it was the twenty-seventh and came a-running." She dried her hands on her apron, and Mrs. Delacroix said, "You're in time, though. They're still talking away up there." 8

Mrs. Hutchinson craned her neck to see through the crowd and found her husband and children standing near the front. She tapped Mrs. Delacroix on the arm as a farewell and began to make her way through the crowd. The people separated good- 9 humoredly to let her through, two or three people said, in voices just loud enough to be heard across the crowd, "Here comes your Missus, Hutchinson," and "Bill, she made it after all." Mrs. Hutchinson reached her husband, and Mr. Summers, who had been waiting, said cheerfully, "Thought we were going to have to get on without you, Tessie." Mrs. Hutchinson said, grinning, "Wouldn't have me leave m'dishes in the sink, now, would you, Joe?" and soft laughter ran through the crowd as the people stirred back into position after Mrs. Hutchinson's arrival.

"Well now," Mr. Summers said soberly, "guess we better get   10
started, get this over with, so's we can go back to work. Anybody ain't here?"

"Dunbar," several people said. "Dunbar, Dunbar."   11

Mr. Summers consulted his list. "Clyde Dunbar," he said.   12
"That's right. He's broke his leg, hasn't he? Who's drawing for him?"

"Me, I guess," a woman said, and Mr. Summers turned to   13
look at her. "Wife draws for her husband," Mr. Summers said. "Don't you have a grown boy to do it for you, Janey?" Although Mr. Summers and everyone else in the village knew the answer perfectly well, it was the business of the official of the lottery to ask such questions formally. Mr. Summers waited with an expression of polite interest while Mrs. Dunbar answered.

"Horace's not but sixteen yet," Mrs. Dunbar said regretfully.   14
"Guess I gotta fill in for the old man this year."

"Right," Mr. Summers said. He made a note on the list he   15
was holding. Then he asked, "Watson boy drawing this year?"

A tall boy in the crowd raised his hand. "Here," he said. "I'm   16
drawing for m'mother and me." He blinked his eyes nervously and ducked his head as several voices in the crowd said things like "Good fellow, Jack," and "Glad to see your mother's got a man to do it."

"Well," Mr. Summers said, "guess that's everyone. Old Man   17
Warner make it?"

"Here," a voice said, and Mr. Summers nodded.   18

A sudden hush fell on the crowd as Mr. Summers cleared his   19
throat and looked at the list. "All ready?" he called. "Now, I'll read the names — heads of families first — and the men come up

and take a paper out of the box. Keep the paper folded in your hand without looking at it until everyone has had a turn. Everything clear?"

The people had done it so many times that they only half lis- 20 tened to the directions, most of them were quiet, wetting their lips, not looking around. Then Mr. Summers raised one hand high and said, "Adams." A man disengaged himself from the crowd and came forward. "Hi, Steve," Mr. Summers said, and Mr. Adams said, "Hi, Joe." They grinned at one another humorlessly and nervously. Then Mr. Adams reached into the black box and took out a folded paper. He held it firmly by one corner as he turned and went hastily back to his place in the crowd, where he stood a little apart from his family, not looking down at his hand.

"Allen," Mr. Summers said, "Anderson. . . . Bentham."   21

"Seems like there's no time at all between lotteries any more," 22 Mrs. Delacroix said to Mrs. Graves in the back row. "Seems like we got through with the last one only last week."

"Time sure goes fast," Mrs. Graves said.   23

"Clark. . . . Delacroix."   24

"There goes my old man," Mrs. Delacroix said. She held her 25 breath while her husband went forward.

"Dunbar," Mr. Summers said, and Mrs. Dunbar went stead- 26 ily to the box while one of the women said, "Go on Janey," and another said, "There she goes."

"We're next," Mrs. Graves said. She watched while Mr. 27 Graves came around from the side of the box, greeted Mr. Summers gravely, and selected a slip of paper from the box. By now, all through the crowd there were men holding the small folded papers in their large hands, turning them over and over nervously. Mrs. Dunbar and her two sons stood together, Mrs. Dunbar holding the slip of paper.

"Harburt. . . . Hutchinson."   28

"Get up there, Bill," Mrs. Hutchinson said, and the people 29 near her laughed.

"Jones."   30

"They do say," Mr. Adams said to Old Man Warner, who 31 stood next to him, "that over in the north village they're talking of giving up the lottery."

Old Man Warner snorted. "Pack of crazy fools," he said. 32
"Listening to the young folks, nothing's good enough for *them*.
Next thing you know, they'll be wanting to go back to living in
caves, nobody work any more, live *that* way for a while. Used to
be a saying about 'Lottery in June, corn be heavy soon.' First
thing you know, we'd all be eating stewed chickweed and
acorns. There's *always* been a lottery," he added petulantly.
"Bad enough to see young Joe Summers up there joking with everybody."

"Some places have already quit lotteries," Mrs. Adams said. 33

"Nothing but trouble in *that*," Old Man Warner said stoutly. 34
"Pack of young fools."

"Martin." And Bobby Martin watched his father go forward. 35
"Overdyke. . . . Percy."

"I wish they'd hurry," Mrs. Dunbar said to her older son. "I 36
wish they'd hurry."

"They're almost through," her son said. 37

"You get ready to run tell Dad," Mrs. Dunbar said. 38

Mr. Summers called his own name and then stepped forward 39
precisely and selected a slip from the box. Then he called,
"Warner."

"Seventy-seventh year I been in the lottery," Old Man 40
Warner said as he went through the crowd. "Seventy-seventh
time."

"Watson," The tall boy came awkwardly through the 41
crowd. Someone said. "Don't be nervous, Jack," and Mr. Summers said, "Take your time, son."

"Zanini." 42

After that, there was a long pause, a breathless pause, until 43
Mr. Summers, holding his slip of paper in the air, said, "All right,
fellows." For a minute, no one moved, and then all the slips of paper were opened. Suddenly, all the women began to speak at
once, saying, "Who is it?" "Who's got it?" "Is it the Dunbars?" "Is
it the Watsons?" Then the voices began to say, "It's Hutchinson.
It's Bill," "Bill Hutchinson's got it."

"Go tell your father," Mrs. Dunbar said to her older son. 44

People began to look around to see the Hutchinsons. Bill 45
Hutchinson was standing quiet, staring down at the paper in his

hand. Suddenly, Tessie Hutchinson shouted to Mr. Summers, "You didn't give him time enough to take any paper he wanted. I saw you. It wasn't fair!"

"Be a good sport, Tessie," Mrs. Delacroix called, and Mrs. 46
Graves said, "All of us took the same chance."

"Shut up, Tessie," Bill Hutchinson said. 47

"Well, everyone," Mr. Summers said, "that was done pretty 48
fast, and now we've got to be hurrying a little more to get done in time." He consulted his next list. "Bill," he said, "you draw for the Hutchinson family. You got any other households in the Hutchinsons?"

"There's Don and Eva," Mrs. Hutchinson yelled. "Make 49
them take their chance!"

"Daughters drew with their husband's families, Tessie," Mr. 50
Summers said gently. "You know that as well as anyone else."

"It wasn't *fair*," Tessie said. 51

"I guess not, Joe," Bill Hutchinson said regretfully. "My 52
daughter draws with her husband's family, that's only fair. And I've got no other family except the kids."

"Then, as far as drawing for families is concerned, it's you," 53
Mr. Summers said in explanation, "and as far as drawing for households is concerned, that's you, too. Right?"

"Right," Bill Hutchinson said. 54

"How many kids, Bill?" Mr. Summers asked formally. 55

"Three," Bill Hutchinson said. "There's Bill, Jr., and Nancy, 56
and little Dave. And Tessie and me."

"All right, then," Mr. Summer said. "Harry, you got their 57
tickets back?"

Mr. Graves nodded and held up the slips of paper. "Put them 58
in the box, then," Mr. Summers directed. "Take Bill's and put it in."

"I think we ought to start over," Mrs. Hutchinson said, as 59
quietly as she could. "I tell you it wasn't *fair*. You didn't give him time enough to choose. *Every*body saw that."

Mr. Graves had selected the five slips and put them in the 60
box, and he dropped all the papers but those onto the ground, where the breeze caught them and lifted them off.

"Listen, everybody," Mrs. Hutchinson was saying to the peo- 61
ple around her.

"Ready, Bill?" Mr. Summers asked, and Bill Hutchinson,   62
with one quick glance around at his wife and children, nodded.

"Remember," Mr. Summers said, "take the slips and keep   63
them folded until each person has taken one. Harry, you help little Dave." Mr. Graves took the hand of the little boy, who came
willingly with him up to the box. "Take a paper out of the box,
Davy," Mr. Summers said. Davy put his hand into the box and
laughed. "Take just *one* paper," Mr. Summers said. "Harry, you
hold it for him." Mr. Graves took the child's hand and removed
the folded paper from the tight fist and held it while little Dave
stood next to him and looked up at him wonderingly.

"Nancy next," Mr. Summers said. Nancy was twelve, and her   64
school friends breathed heavily as she went forward, switching
her skirt, and took a slip daintily from the box. "Bill, Jr.," Mr.
Summers said, and Billy, his face red and his feet overlarge, nearly
knocked the box over as he got a paper out. "Tessie," Mr. Summers said. She hesitated for a minute, looking around defiantly,
and then set her lips and went up to the box. She snatched a paper out and held it behind her.

"Bill," Mr. Summers said, and Bill Hutchinson reached into   65
the box and felt around, bringing his hand out at last with the
slip of paper in it.

The crowd was quiet. A girl whispered, "I hope it's not   66
Nancy," and the sound of the whisper reached the edges of the
crowd.

"It's not the way it used to be," Old Man Warner said clearly.   67
"People ain't the way they used to be."

"All right," Mr. Summers said. "Open the papers. Harry, you   68
open little Dave's."

Mr. Graves opened the slip of paper and there was a general   69
sigh through the crowd as he held it up and everyone could see
that it was blank. Nancy and Bill, Jr., opened theirs at the same
time, and both beamed and laughed, turning around to the
crowd and holding their slips of paper above their heads.

"Tessie," Mr. Summers said. There was a pause, and then   70
Mr. Summers looked at Bill Hutchinson, and Bill unfolded his
paper and showed it. It was blank.

"It's Tessie," Mr. Summers said, and his voice was hushed.   71
"Show us her paper, Bill."

Bill Hutchinson went over to his wife and forced the slip of 72
paper out of her hand. It had a black spot on it, the black spot
Mr. Summers had made the night before with the heavy pencil in
the coal-company office. Bill Hutchinson held it up and there was
a stir in the crowd.

"All right, folks," Mr. Summers said. "Let's finish quickly." 73

Although the villagers had forgotten the ritual and lost the 74
original black box, they still remembered to use stones. The pile
of stones the boys had made earlier was ready; there were stones
on the ground with the blowing scraps of paper that had come
out of the box. Mrs. Delacroix selected a stone so large she had to
pick it up with both hands and turned to Mrs. Dunbar. "Come
on," she said. "Hurry up."

Mrs. Dunbar had small stones in both hands, and she said, 75
gasping for breath, "I can't run at all. You'll have to go ahead and
I'll catch up with you."

The children had stones already, and someone gave little 76
Davy Hutchinson a few pebbles.

Tessie Hutchinson was in the center of a cleared space by 77
now, and she held her hands out desperately as the villagers
moved in on her. "It isn't fair," she said. A stone hit her on the
side of the head.

Old Man Warner was saying, "Come on, come on, every- 78
one." Steve Adams was in front of the crowd of villagers, with
Mrs. Graves beside him.

"It isn't fair, it isn't right," Mrs. Hutchinson screamed and 79
then they were upon her.

QUESTIONS ON MEANING

1. The PURPOSE of all fiction might be taken as entertainment or self-expression. Does Jackson have any other purpose in "The Lottery"?
2. When does the reader know what is actually going to occur?
3. Describe this story's community on the basis of what Jackson says of it.
4. What do the villagers' attitudes toward the black box indicate about their feelings toward the lottery?

QUESTIONS ON WRITING STRATEGY

1. Jackson uses the third PERSON (*he, she, it, they*) to narrate the story, and she does not enter the minds of her characters. Why do you think she keeps this distant POINT OF VIEW?
2. On your first reading of the story, what did you make of the references to rocks in paragraphs 2–3? Do you think they effectively forecast the ending?
3. Jackson has a character introduce a controversial notion in paragraph 31. Why does she do this?
4. OTHER METHODS. Jackson is exploring — or inviting us to explore — causes and effects (Chap. 9). Why do the villagers participate in the lottery every year? What does paragraph 32 hint might have been the original reason for it?

QUESTIONS ON LANGUAGE

1. Dialogue provides much information not stated elsewhere in the story. Give three examples of such information about the community and its interactions.
2. Check a dictionary for definitions of the following words: profusely (para. 1); boisterous, reprimand (2); jovial, scold, paraphernalia (4); perfunctory, duly, interminably (7); petulantly (32).
3. Jackson admits to setting the story in her Vermont village in the present time (that is, 1948). Judging from the names of the villagers, where did these people's ancestors originally come from? What do you make of the names Delacroix and Zanini? What is their significance?
4. Unlike much fiction, "The Lottery" contains few FIGURES OF SPEECH. Why do you think this is?

SUGGESTIONS FOR WRITING

1. Write an imaginary narrative, perhaps set in the future, of a ritual that demonstrates something about the people who participate in it. The ritual can be but need not be as sinister as Jackson's lottery; yours could concern bathing, eating, dating, going to school, driving, growing older.
2. Choose an actual ritual familiar to you concerning a holiday, a meal, a religion, an observance, a vacation — anything repeated and traditional. Write a narrative about the last time you participated in this ritual. Use description and dialogue to convey the sig-

nificance of the ritual and your own and other participants' attitudes toward it.

3. In his 1974 book *Obedience to Authority*, the psychologist Stanley Milgram reported and analyzed the results of a study he had conducted that caused a furor among psychologists and the general public. Under orders from white-coated "experimenters," many subjects administered what they believed to be life-threatening electric shocks to other people whom they could hear but not see. In fact, the "victims" were actors and received no shocks, but the subjects thought otherwise and many continued to administer stronger and stronger "shocks" when ordered to do so. Find *Obedience to Authority* in the library and compare and contrast the circumstances of Milgram's experiment with those of Jackson's lottery. For instance, who or what is the order-giving authority in the lottery? What is the significance of seeing or not seeing one's victim?

4. CONNECTIONS. As its title might suggest, "Why Don't We Complain?" by William F. Buckley, Jr. (p. 674), touches on some of the same issues as "The Lottery." Write an essay applying Buckley's explanations for why we don't complain to the situation in Jackson's story — or arguing that they don't apply.

SHIRLEY JACKSON ON WRITING

Come Along with Me, a posthumous collection of her work, contains a lecture by Shirley Jackson titled "Biography of a Story" — specifically, a biography of "The Lottery." Far from being born in cruelty or cynicism, the story had quite benign origins. Jackson wrote the story, she recalled, "on a bright June morning when summer seemed to have come at last, with blue skies and warm sun and no heavenly signs to warn me that my morning's work was anything but just another story. The idea had come to me while I was pushing my daughter up the hill in her stroller — it was, as I say, a warm morning, and the hill was steep, and beside my daughter the stroller held the day's groceries — and perhaps the effort of that last fifty yards up the hill put an edge on the story; at any rate, I had the idea fairly clearly in my mind when I put my daughter in her playpen and the frozen vegetables in the refrigerator, and, writing the story, I found that it went quickly and easily, moving from beginning to end without pause. As a matter of fact, when I read it over later I decided that except for one or two minor corrections, it needed no changes, and the story I finally typed up and sent off to my agent the next day was almost word for word the original draft. This, as any writer of stories can tell you, is not a usual thing. All I know is that when I came to read the story over I felt strongly that I didn't want to fuss with it. I didn't think it was perfect, but I didn't want to fuss with it. It was, I thought, a serious, straightforward story, and I was pleased and a little surprised at the ease with which it had been written; I was reasonably proud of it, and hoped that my agent would sell it to some magazine and I would have the gratification of seeing it in print."

After the story was published, however, Jackson was surprised to find both it and herself the subject of "bewilderment, speculation, and plain old-fashioned abuse." She wrote that "one of the most terrifying aspects of publishing stories and books is the realization that they are going to be read, and read by strangers. I had never fully realized this before, although I had of course in my imagination dwelt lovingly upon the thought of the millions and millions of people who were going to be uplifted and enriched and delighted by the stories I wrote. It had simply never occurred to me that these millions and millions of people might be so far from being uplifted that they would sit down and write me letters I was downright scared to open; of the three-hundred-odd letters that I received that summer I can count only thirteen that spoke kindly to me, and they were mostly from friends."

Jackson's favorite letter was one concluding, "Our brothers feel that Miss Jackson is a true prophet and disciple of the true gospel of the redeeming light. When will the next revelation be published?" Jackson's answer: "Never. I am out of the lottery business for good."

FOR DISCUSSION

1. What lesson can we draw about creative inspiration from Jackson's anecdote about the origins of "The Lottery"?
2. What seemed to have alarmed Jackson about readers' reactions to her story? Do you think she was naive in expecting otherwise?

ADDITIONAL WRITING TOPICS

Narration

1. Write a narrative with one of the following as your subject. It may be (as your instructor may advise) either a first-person memoir or a story written in the third person, observing the experience of someone else. Decide before you begin whether you are writing (1) an anecdote; (2) an essay consisting mainly of a single narrative; or (3) an essay that includes more than one story.

   A memorable experience from your early life
   A lesson you learned the hard way
   A trip into unfamiliar territory
   An embarrassing moment that taught you something
   A brush with death
   A monumental misunderstanding
   An accident
   An unexpected encounter
   A story about a famous person, or someone close to you
   A conflict or contest
   An assassination attempt
   A historic event of significance

2. Tell a true story of your early or recent school days, either humorous or serious, showing what a struggle school or college has been for you. (For comparable stories, see Ellison's "On Being the Target of Discrimination," Thurber's "University Days," or, in Chapter 11, Richard Rodriguez's "Aria.")

2
DESCRIPTION
Writing with Your Senses

THE METHOD

Like narration, description is a familiar method of expression, already a working part of you. In any talk-fest with friends, you probably do your share of describing. You depict in words someone you've met by describing her clothes, the look on her face, the way she walks. You describe somewhere you've been, something you admire, something you just can't abide. In a diary or in a letter to a friend, you describe your college (cast concrete buildings, crowded walks, pigeons rattling their wings); or perhaps you describe your brand-new secondhand car, from the snakelike glitter of its hubcaps to the odd antiques in its trunk, bequeathed by its previous owner. You hardly can live a day without describing (or hearing described) some person, place, or thing. Small wonder that, in written discourse, description is almost as indispensable as paper.

Description reports the testimony of your senses. It invites your readers to imagine that they too not only see, but perhaps also hear, taste, smell, and touch the subject you describe. Usually, you write a description for either of two purposes: (1) to convey information without bias or emotion; or (2) to convey it with feeling.

In writing with the first purpose in mind, you write an OBJECTIVE (or *impartial, public,* or *functional*) description. You describe your subject so clearly and exactly that your reader will understand it or recognize it, and you leave your emotions out. Technical or scientific descriptive writing is usually objective: a manual detailing the parts of an internal combustion engine, a biologist's report of a previously unknown species of frog. You write this kind of description in sending a friend directions for finding your house: "Look for the green shutters on the windows and a new garbage can at the front door." Although in a personal letter describing your house you might very well become emotionally involved with it (and call it, perhaps, a "fleabag"), in writing an objective description your purpose is not to convey your feelings. You are trying to make the house easily recognized.

The other type of descriptive writing is SUBJECTIVE (or *emotional, personal,* or *impressionistic*) description. This is the kind included in a magazine advertisement for a new car. It's what you write in your letter to a friend setting forth what your college is like — whether you are pleased or displeased with it. In this kind of description, you may use biases and personal feelings — in fact, they are essential. Let us consider a splendid example: a subjective description of a storm at sea. Charles Dickens, in his memoir *American Notes,* conveys his passenger's-eye view of an Atlantic steamship on a morning when the ocean is wild:

> Imagine the ship herself, with every pulse and artery of her huge body swollen and bursting . . . sworn to go on or die. Imagine the wind howling, the sea roaring, the rain beating; all in furious array against her. Picture the sky both dark and wild, and the clouds in fearful sympathy with the waves, making another ocean in the air. Add to all this the clattering on deck

and down below; the tread of hurried feet; the loud hoarse shouts of seamen; the gurgling in and out of water through the scuppers; with every now and then the striking of a heavy sea upon the planks above, with the deep, dead, heavy sound of thunder heard within a vault; and there is the head wind of that January morning.

I say nothing of what may be called the domestic noises of the ship; such as the breaking of glass and crockery, the tumbling down of stewards, the gambols, overhead, of loose casks and truant dozens of bottled porter, and the very remarkable and far from exhilarating sounds raised in their various staterooms by the seventy passengers who were too ill to get up to breakfast.

Notice how many *sounds* are included in this primarily ear-minded description. We can infer how Dickens feels about the storm. It is a terrifying event that reduces the interior of the vessel to chaos; and yet the writer (in hearing the loose barrels and beer bottles merrily gambol, in finding humor in the seasick passengers' plight) apparently delights in it. Writing subjectively, he intrudes his feelings. Think of what a starkly different description of the very same storm the captain might set down — objectively — in the ship's log: "At 0600 hours, watch reported a wind from due north of 70 knots. Whitecaps were noticed, in height two ells above the bow. Below deck, much gear was reported adrift, and ten casks of ale were broken and their staves strewn about. Mr. Liam Jones, chief steward, suffered a compound fracture of the left leg. . . ." But Dickens, not content simply to record information, strives to ensure that the mind's eye is dazzled and the mind's ear regaled.

Description is usually found in the company of other methods of writing. Often, for instance, it will enliven narration and make the people in the story and the setting unmistakably clear. Writing an argument in his essay "Why Don't We Complain?" William F. Buckley, Jr., begins with a description of eighty suffering commuters perspiring in an overheated train; the description makes the argument more powerful. Description will help a writer in examining the effects of a flood, or in comparing and contrasting two towns. Keep the method of description in mind when you come to try expository and argumentative writing.

THE PROCESS

Understand, first of all, your purpose in writing a description. Are you going to write a subjective description, expressing your personal feelings? Or, instead, do you want to write an objective description, trying only to see and report, leaving out your emotions and biases?

Give a little thought to your audience. What do your readers need to be told, if they are to share the feelings you would have them share, if they are clearly to behold what you want them to? If, let's say, you are describing a downtown street on a Saturday night for an audience of fellow students who live in the same city and know it well, then you need not dwell on the street's familiar geography. What must you tell? Only those details that make the place different on a Saturday night. But if you are remembering your home city, and writing for readers who don't know it, you'll need to establish a few central landmarks to sketch (in their minds) an unfamiliar street on a Saturday night.

Before you begin to write a description, go look at your subject. If that is not possible, your next best course is to spend a few minutes imagining the subject until, in your mind's eye, you can see every flyspeck on it.

Then, having fixed your subject in mind, ask yourself which of its features you'll need to report to your particular audience, for your particular purpose. If you plan to write a subjective description of an old house, laying weight on its spooky atmosphere for readers you wish to make shiver, then you might mention its squeaking bats and its shadowy halls, leaving out any reference to its busy swimming pool and the stomping disco music that billows from its interior. If, however, you are describing the house in a classified ad, for an audience of possible buyers, you might focus instead on its eat-in kitchen, working fireplace, and proximity to public transportation. Details have to be carefully selected. Feel no grim duty to include every perceptible detail. To do so would only invite chaos — or perhaps, for the reader, mere tedium. Pick out the features that matter most. One revealing, hard-to-forget detail (such as Dickens's truant porter bottles) is, like a single masterly brush stroke, worth a whole coat of dull paint. In selecting or discarding details, ask, What am I out to accomplish? What main impression of my subject am I trying to give?

Let your description, as a whole, convey this one DOMINANT IMPRESSION. (The swimming pool and the disco music might be details useful in a description meant to convey that the house is full of merriment.) Perhaps many details will be worth noticing; if so, you will want to arrange them so that your reader will see which matter most. In his description of the storm at sea — a subjective description — Charles Dickens sorts out the pandemonium for us. He groups the various sounds into two classes: those of sea and sailors, and the "domestic noises" of the ship's passengers — their smashing dishes, their rolling bottles, the crashing of stewards who wait on them. Like many effective descriptions, this one clearly reveals a principle of organization.

In organizing your description, you may find it helpful to be aware of your POINT OF VIEW — the physical angle from which you're perceiving and describing. In the previous chapter, on narration, we spoke of point of view: how essential it is for a story to have a narrator — one who, from a certain position, reports what takes place. A description, too, needs a consistent point of view: that of an observer who stays put and observes steadily. For instance, when describing a landscape as seen from the air, do not swoop suddenly to earth.

You can organize a description in several ways. Some writers, as they describe something, make a carefully planned inspection tour of its details, moving spatially (from left to right, from near to far, from top to bottom, from center to periphery), or perhaps moving from prominent objects to tiny ones, from dull to bright, from commonplace to extraordinary — or vice versa. The plan you choose is the one that best fulfills your purpose. If you were to describe, for instance, a chapel in the middle of a desert, you might begin with the details of the lonely terrain. Then, as if approaching the chapel with the aid of a zoom lens, you might detail its exterior and then go on inside. That might be a workable method to write a description *if* your purpose were to emphasize the sense that the chapel is an island of beauty and warmth in the midst of desolation. Say, however, that your purpose was quite different: to emphasize the interior design of the chapel. You might then begin your description inside the structure, perhaps with its most prominent feature, the stained glass windows. You might mention the surrounding desert later in your description, but only incidentally. An effective description makes a definite impression. The writer arranges details so that the reader is firmly left with the feeling the writer intends to convey.

Whatever method you follow in arranging details, stick with it all the way through. Don't start out describing a group of cats by going from old cats to kittens, then switch in the middle of your description and line up the cats according to color. If your arrangement would cause any difficulty for the reader, you need to rearrange your details. If a writer, in describing a pet shop, should skip about wildly from clerks to cats to customers to cat food to customers to cat food to clerks, the reader may quickly be lost. Instead, the writer might group clerks together with customers, and cats together with cat food (or in some other clear order). But suppose (the writer might protest) it's a wildly confused pet shop I'm trying to describe? No matter — the writer nevertheless has to write in an orderly manner, if the reader is to understand. Dickens describes a scene of shipboard chaos, yet his prose is orderly.

Luckily, to write a memorable description, you don't need a storm at sea or any other awe-inspiring subject. As E. B. White demonstrates in his essay in this chapter, "Once More to the Lake," you can write about a summer cabin on a lake as effectively as you can write about a tornado. The secret is in the vividness, the evocativeness, of the details. Like most masters of description, White relies heavily on IMAGES (language calling up concrete sensory experiences), including FIGURES OF SPEECH (expressions that do not mean literally what they say, often describing one thing in terms of another). White writes of motorboats that "whined about one's ears like mosquitoes" (a SIMILE) and of "small waves . . . chucking the rowboat under the chin" (a METAPHOR). Another writer, the humorist S. J. Perelman, uses metaphor to convey the garish brightness of a certain low-rent house. Notice how he makes clear the spirit of the place: "After a few days, I could have sworn that our faces began to take on the hue of Kodachromes, and even the dog, an animal used to bizarre surroundings, developed a strange, off-register look, as if he were badly printed in overlapping colors."

When you, too, write an effective description, you'll convey your sensory experience as exactly as possible. Find vigorous, specific words, and you will enable your reader to behold with the mind's eye — and to feel with the mind's fingertips.

DESCRIPTION IN A PARAGRAPH: TWO ILLUSTRATIONS

Using Description to Write about Television

At 2:59 this Monday afternoon, a thick hush settles like cigarette smoke inside the sweat-scented TV room of Harris Hall. First to arrive, freshman Lee Ann squashes down into the catbird seat in front of the screen. Soon she is flanked by roommates Lisa and Kate, silent, their mouths straight lines, their upturned faces lit by the nervous flicker of a detergent ad. To the left and right of the couch, Pete and Anse crouch on the floor, leaning forward like runners awaiting a starting gun. Behind them, stiff standees line up at attention. Farther back still, English majors and jocks compete for an unobstructed view. Fresh from class, shirttail flapping, arm crooking a bundle of books, Dave barges into the room demanding, "Has it started? Has it started yet?" He is shushed. Somebody shushes a popped-open can of Dr Pepper whose fizz is distractingly loud. What do these students so intently look forward to — the announcement of World War III? A chord of music climbs and the screen dissolves to a title: *General Hospital.*

COMMENT. Although in the end the anticipated mind-blower turns out to be merely an installment of a gripping soap opera, the purpose of this description is to build one definite impression: that something vital is about to arrive. Details are selected accordingly: "thick hush," "nervous flicker," people jostling one another for a better view. The watchers are portrayed as tense and expectant, their mouths straight lines, their faces upturned, the men on the floor crouching forward. The chief appeal is to our visual imaginations, but a few details address our auditory imaginations (the fizz of a can of soda, people saying *Shhh-h-h!*) and our olfactory imaginations ("sweat-scented").

In organizing this description, the writer's scrutiny moves outward from the television screen: first to the students immediately in front of it, then to those on either side, next to the second row, then to the third, and finally to the last anxious arrival. By this arrangement, the writer presents the details to the reader in a natural order. The main impression is enforced, since the TV screen is the center for all eyes.

Using Description in an Academic Discipline

While working on *The Battle of Anghiari*, Leonardo painted his most famous portrait, the *Mona Lisa*. The delicate *sfumato* already noted in the *Madonna of the Rocks* is here so perfected that it seemed miraculous to the artist's contemporaries. The forms are built from layers of glazes so gossamer-thin that the entire panel seems to glow with a gentle light from within. But the fame of the *Mona Lisa* comes not from this pictorial subtlety alone; even more intriguing is the psychological fascination of the sitter's personality. Why, among all the smiling faces ever painted, has this particular one been singled out as "mysterious"? Perhaps the reason is that, as a portrait, the picture does not fit our expectations. The features are too individual for Leonardo to have simply depicted an ideal type, yet the element of idealization is so strong that it blurs the sitter's character. Once again the artist has brought two opposites into harmonious balance. The smile, too, may be read in two ways: as the echo of a momentary mood, and as a timeless, symbolic expression (somewhat like the "Archaic smile" of the Greeks . . .). Clearly, the *Mona Lisa* embodies a quality of maternal tenderness which was to Leonardo the essence of womanhood. Even the landscape in the background, composed mainly of rocks and water, suggests elemental generative forces.

COMMENT. Taken from H. W. Janson's *History of Art: A Survey of the Major Visual Arts from the Dawn of History to the Present Day* (2nd ed., 1979), this paragraph describes the world's most famous portrait in oils, the *Mona Lisa*. In a section of the book dealing with the achievement of Leonardo da Vinci, the author makes clear that this painting amply demonstrates the artist's genius. He does so by describing both the picture's subject and some of the painting techniques that bring it alive — the *sfu-mato*, or soft gradations of lights and darks, the layering of glazes, the tension the viewer can discern between Mona Lisa the individual and Mona Lisa the ideal type. Note the words and phrases he uses that appeal to the senses: "delicate," "gossamer-thin," "glow with a gentle light." By directing the readers' attention to the painting's details, Janson has used description as a teaching tool of tremendous usefulness.

VIRGINIA WOOLF

Generally regarded as one of the greatest twentieth-century writers, VIRGINIA WOOLF earned her acclaim by producing uncommon fiction and nonfiction, the first sensitive and complex, the second poetic and immediate. Born Virginia Stephen in London in 1882, Woolf and her sister Vanessa were educated at home, largely by their father, Sir Leslie Stephen, an author and editor. The two sisters were central to the Bloomsbury Group, an informal society of writers and artists that included the economist John Maynard Keynes and the novelist E. M. Forster. Virginia married Leonard Woolf, a member of the group, in 1912, and the two soon founded the Hogarth Press, publisher of Virginia Woolf and many other notable writers of the day. Woolf's most innovative novels include *Mrs. Dalloway* (1925), *To the Lighthouse* (1927), *Orlando* (1928), *The Waves* (1931), and *Between the Acts* (1941). Her exemplary critical and meditative essays appear in *The Common Reader* (1925), *The Second Common Reader* (1933), and many other collections. Subject to severe depression all her adult life, in 1941 Woolf committed suicide.

The Death of the Moth

One of Woolf's most famous works of nonfiction, "The Death of the Moth" was published in *The Death of the Moth and Other Essays* (1942). Though brief as the life of the moth Woolf observes, the essay is typically evocative, intense, and enduring.

Moths that fly by day are not properly to be called moths;   1
they do not excite that pleasant sense of dark autumn nights and
ivy-blossom which the commonest yellow-underwing asleep in
the shadow of the curtain never fails to rouse in us. They are hybrid creatures, neither gay like butterflies nor somber like their
own species. Nevertheless the present specimen, with his narrow
hay-colored wings, fringed with a tassel of the same color, seemed
to be content with life. It was a pleasant morning, mid-September, mild, benignant, yet with a keener breath than that of the

summer months. The plough was already scoring the field opposite the window, and where the share had been, the earth was pressed flat and gleamed with moisture. Such vigor came rolling in from the fields and the down beyond that it was difficult to keep the eyes strictly turned upon the book. The rooks too were keeping one of their annual festivities; soaring round the tree tops until it looked as if a vast net with thousands of black knots in it had been cast up into the air; which, after a few moments sank slowly down upon the trees until every twig seemed to have a knot at the end of it. Then, suddenly, the net would be thrown into the air again in a wider circle this time, with the utmost clamor and vociferation, as though to be thrown into the air and settle slowly down upon the tree tops were a tremendously exciting experience.

The same energy which inspired the rooks, the ploughmen, the horses, and even, it seemed, the lean bare-backed downs, sent the moth fluttering from side to side of his square of the windowpane. One could not help watching him. One, was, indeed, conscious of a queer feeling of pity for him. The possibilities of pleasure seemed that morning so enormous and so various that to have only a moth's part in life, and a day moth's at that, appeared a hard fate, and his zest in enjoying his meager opportunities to the full, pathetic. He flew vigorously to one corner of his compartment, and, after waiting there a second, flew across to the other. What remained for him but to fly to a third corner and then to a fourth? That was all he could do, in spite of the size of the downs, the width of the sky, the far-off smoke of houses, and the romantic voice, now and then, of a steamer out at sea. What he could do he did. Watching him, it seemed as if a fiber, very thin but pure, of the enormous energy of the world had been thrust into his frail and diminutive body. As often as he crossed the pane, I could fancy that a thread of vital light became visible. He was little or nothing but life. 2

Yet, because he was so small, and so simple a form of the energy that was rolling in at the open window and driving its way through so many narrow and intricate corridors in my own brain and in those of other human beings, there was something marvelous as well as pathetic about him. It was as if someone had taken 3 a tiny bead of pure life and decking it as lightly as possible with down and feathers, had set it dancing and zigzagging to show us the true nature of life. Thus displayed one could not get over the strangeness of it. One is apt to forget all about life, seeing it humped and bossed and garnished and cumbered so that it has to move with the greatest circumspection and dignity. Again, the thought of all that life might have been had he been born in any other shape caused one to view his simple activities with a kind of pity.

After a time, tired by his dancing apparently, he settled on 4 the window ledge in the sun, and, the queer spectacle being at an end, I forgot about him. Then, looking up, my eye was caught by him. He was trying to resume his dancing, but seemed either so stiff or so awkward that he could only flutter to the bottom of the windowpane; and when he tried to fly across it he failed. Being intent on other matters I watched these futile attempts for a time without thinking, unconsciously waiting for him to resume his flight, as one waits for a machine, that has stopped momentarily, to start again without considering the reason of its failure. After perhaps a seventh attempt he slipped from the wooden ledge and fell, fluttering his wings, on to his back on the windowsill. The helplessness of his attitude roused me. It flashed upon me that he was in difficulties; he could no longer raise himself; his legs struggled vainly. But, as I stretched out a pencil, meaning to help him to right himself, it came over me that the failure and awkwardness were the approach of death. I laid the pencil down again.

The legs agitated themselves once more. I looked as if for the 5 enemy against which he struggled. I looked out of doors. What had happened there? Presumably it was midday, and work in the fields had stopped. Stillness and quiet had replaced the previous animation. The birds had taken themselves off to feed in the brooks. The horses stood still. Yet the power was there all the same, massed outside, indifferent, impersonal, not attending to anything in particular. Somehow it was opposed to the little hay-colored moth. It was useless to try to do anything. One could only watch the extraordinary efforts made by those tiny legs against an oncoming doom which could, had it chosen, have submerged an entire city, not merely a city, but masses of human beings; nothing, I knew had any chance against death. Nevertheless after a pause of exhaustion the legs fluttered again. It was superb this last protest, and so frantic that he succeeded at last in righting himself. One's sympathies, of course, were all on the side of life. Also, when there was nobody to care or to know, this gigantic effort on the part of an insignificant little moth, against a power of such magnitude, to retain what no one else valued or desired to keep, moved one strangely. Again, somehow, one saw life, a pure bead. I lifted the pencil again, useless though I knew it to be. But even as I did so, the unmistakable tokens of death showed themselves. The body relaxed, and instantly grew stiff. The struggle was over. The insignificant little creature now knew death. As I looked at the dead moth, this minute wayside triumph of so great a force over so mean an antagonist filled me with wonder. Just as life had been strange a few minutes before, so death was now as strange. The moth having righted himself now lay most decently and uncomplainingly composed. O yes, he seemed to say, death is stronger than I am.

QUESTIONS ON MEANING

1. Why does Woolf choose to write about something as insignificant as a moth's death? Does she have a PURPOSE other than relating a simple observation?
2. Why, in paragraph 2, does Woolf say that the moth was "little or nothing but life"? Why is the moth pitiable?
3. What does the moth in his square windowpane represent to the author? How does Woolf's description in the essay make this clear?
4. How does Woolf's outlook change in paragraph 5? Why?

QUESTIONS ON WRITING STRATEGY

1. Is Woolf's essay an OBJECTIVE or a SUBJECTIVE description? Give details from the essay to support your answer.
2. What is the EFFECT of Woolf's scene-setting in paragraph 1? How does this description influence our perception of the moth?

3. Which of the five senses does Woolf's description principally rely on? Why, do you think?
4. OTHER METHODS. This essay is a description in the framework of a narrative (Chap. 1). Sumarize the changes in Woolf's perceptions of the moth that occur in the narrative.

QUESTIONS ON LANGUAGE

1. Analyze the writing in paragraph 5. How do sentence structure and words create a mood different from that in earlier paragraphs?
2. Analyze Woolf's IMAGES in describing the moth and her substitutions for the word *moth*, such as "the present specimen" in paragraph 1. How do these reinforce Woolf's changing perceptions as you outlined them in question 4 above?
3. You may find Woolf's vocabulary more difficult than that of some other writers in this book. Look up any unfamiliar words in the following list: rouse, hybrid, benignant, plough, share, down, rooks, clamor, vociferation (para. 1); meager, pathetic, diminutive (2); decking, cumbered, circumspection (3); spectacle, futile, vainly (4); animation, righting, magnitude, minute, mean, antagonist (5).

SUGGESTIONS FOR WRITING

1. In an essay of your own, respond to the ideas about life and death in Woolf's essay. First explain what you understand these ideas to be. Then use examples from your reading and experience to support or contest Woolf's ideas.
2. Watch something over an extended period of time and describe it — its physical attributes, movements, surroundings. Draw on as many of your five senses as you like, but make your description as OBJECTIVE as possible by keeping your feelings out of it.
3. Use the same subject as in the previous suggestion, or choose a new one. This time, write a SUBJECTIVE description in which your feelings influence your selection of details and what you say about them. Again, draw on as many senses as you like. Use word IMAGES to convey your perception.
4. CONNECTIONS. Read Annie Dillard's "Death of a Moth," which follows this essay. Of the two highly subjective essays, which is more personal? Write a brief essay answering this question, and support your answer with quotations and PARAPHRASES from both essays.

VIRGINIA WOOLF ON WRITING

A diary keeper from her youth, Virginia Woolf used the form not only to record and reflect on events but also to do a kind of "rough & random" writing she otherwise had little chance for. (Today this kind of writing is often called *freewriting*, a term given wide currency by Peter Elbow [see p. 319].) Woolf wrote in her diary on April 20, 1919, that "the habit of writing thus for my own eye only is good practice. It loosens the ligaments. Never mind the misses & the stumbles. Going at such a pace as I do I must make the most direct & instant shots at my object, & thus have to lay hands on words, choose them, & shoot them with no more pause than is needed to put my pen in the ink. I believe that during the past year I can trace some increase of ease in my professional writing which I attribute to my casual half hours after tea."

Thirteen years later, Woolf felt just as strongly about the value of writing freely, without censorship. In "A Letter to a Young Poet," she advises against writing solely for "a severe and intelligent public." Follow the excitement of "actual life," she urges. "Write then, now that you are young, nonsense by the ream. Be silly, be sentimental, imitate Shelley, imitate Samuel Smiles; give the rein to every impulse; commit every fault of style, grammar, taste, and syntax; pour out; tumble over; loose anger, love, satire, in whatever words you can catch, coerce, or create, in whatever meter, prose, poetry, or gibberish that comes to hand. Thus you will learn to write."

FOR DISCUSSION

1. What does Woolf gain from diary writing? What does she mean that such writing "loosens the ligaments"?
2. Do you think Woolf seriously believed that young writers should write "nonsense by the ream"? (A *ream*, incidentally, is about five hundred sheets of paper.) What might the young writer learn from such freedom?
3. These excerpts do not discuss the writer's work between the loose, private writing Woolf recommends and writing for others. In your view, what does that work consist of?

ANNIE DILLARD

Annie Dillard is accomplished as a prose writer, poet, and literary critic. Born in 1945, she earned a B.A. (1967) and an M.A. (1968) from Hollins College in Virginia. She now teaches writing at Wesleyan University in Connecticut. Dillard's first published prose, *Pilgrim at Tinker Creek* (1974), is a work alive with close, intense, and poetic descriptions of the natural world. It won her a Pulitzer Prize and comparison with Thoreau. Since then, Dillard's entranced and entrancing writing has appeared regularly in *Harper's, American Scholar, The Atlantic Monthly*, and other magazines and in her books: *Tickets for a Prayer Wheel* (1975), poems; *Holy the Firm* (1978), a prose poem; *Living by Fiction* (1982), literary criticism; *Teaching a Stone to Talk* (1982), nonfiction; *Encounters with Chinese Writers* (1984), an account of a trip to China; *An American Childhood* (1987), an autobiography; and *The Writing Life* (1989), anecdotes and metaphors about writing. Dillard is now working on her first novel.

Death of a Moth

Early in life, Annie Dillard began training her powers of description. "When I worked as a detective in Pittsburgh," she recalls, "(strictly freelance, because I was only ten years old), I drew suspects' faces from memory." These powers are evident in all Dillard's writing, including this essay, first published in 1976 in *Harper's*.

I live alone with two cats, who sleep on my legs. There is a 1 yellow one, and a black one whose name is Small. In the morning I joke to the black one, Do you remember last night? Do you remember? I throw them both out before breakfast, so I can eat.

There is a spider, too, in the bathroom, of uncertain lineage, 2 bulbous at the abdomen and drab, whose six-inch mess of web works, works somehow, works miraculously, to keep her alive and me amazed. The web is in a corner behind the toilet, connecting tile wall to tile wall. The house is new, the bathroom im-maculate, save for the spider, her web, and the sixteen or so corpses she's tossed to the floor.

The corpses appear to be mostly sow bugs, those little arma-dillo creatures who live to travel flat out in houses, and die round. In addition to sow-bug husks, hollow and sipped empty of color, there are what seem to be two or three wingless moth bodies, one new flake of earwig, and three spider carcasses crinkled and clenched.

I wonder on what fool's errand an earwig, or a moth, or a sow bug, would visit that clean corner of the house behind the toilet; I have not noticed any blind parades of sow bugs blundering into corners. Yet they do hazard there, at a rate of more than one a week, and the spider thrives. Yesterday she was working on the earwig, mouth on gut; today he's on the floor. It must take a cer-tain genius to throw things away from there, to find a straight line through that sticky tangle to the floor.

Today the earwig shines darkly, and gleams, what there is of him: a dorsal curve of thorax and abdomen, and a smooth pair of pincers by which I knew his name. Next week, if the other bodies are any indication, he'll be shrunk and gray, webbed to the floor with dust. The sow bugs beside him are curled and empty, fragile, a breath away from brittle fluff. The spiders lie on their sides, translucent and ragged, their legs drying in knots. The moths stagger against each other, headless, in a confusion of arcing strips of chitin like peeling varnish, like a jumble of buttresses for cathedral vaults, like nothing resembling moths, so that I would hesitate to call them moths, except that I have had some experi-ence with the figure Moth reduced to a nub.

Two summers ago I was camped alone in the Blue Ridge Mountains of Virginia. I had hauled myself and gear up there to read, among other things, *The Day on Fire*, by James Ullman, a novel about Rimbaud[1] that had made me want to be a writer when I was sixteen; I was hoping it would do it again. So I read

[1]Arthur Rimbaud (1854–1891) was a French poet, adventurer, and mer-chant-trader. — Eds.

every day sitting under a tree by my tent, while warblers sang in the leaves overhead and bristle worms trailed their inches over the twiggy dirt at my feet; and I read every night by candlelight, while barred owls called in the forest and pale moths seeking mates massed round my head in the clearing, where my light made a ring.

Moths kept flying into the candle. They would hiss and re-   7
coil, reeling upside down in the shadows among my cooking pans. Or they would singe their wings and fall, and their hot wings, as if melted, would stick to the first thing they touched — a pan, a lid, a spoon — so that the snagged moths could struggle only in tiny arcs, unable to flutter free. These I could release by a quick flip with a stick; in the morning I would find my cooking stuff deco-rated with torn flecks of moth wings, ghostly triangles of shiny dust here and there on the aluminum. So I read, and boiled wa-ter, and replenished candles, and read on.

One night a moth flew into the candle, was caught, burnt   8
dry, and held. I must have been staring at the candle, or maybe I looked up when a shadow crossed my page; at any rate, I saw it all. A golden female moth, a biggish one with a two-inch wing-spread, flapped into the fire, drooped abdomen into the wet wax, stuck, flamed, and frazzled in a second. Her moving wings ignited like tissue paper, like angels' wings, enlarging the circle of light in the clearing and creating out of the darkness the sudden blue sleeves of my sweater, the green leaves of jewelweed by my side, the ragged red trunk of a pine; at once the light contracted again and the moth's wings vanished in a fine, foul smoke. At the same time, her six legs clawed, curled, blackened, and ceased, disap-pearing utterly. And her head jerked in spasms, making a spatter-ing noise; her antennae crisped and burnt away and her heaving mouthparts cracked like pistol fire. When it was all over, her head was, so far as I could determine, gone, gone the long way of her wings and legs. Her head was a hole lost to time. All that was left was the glowing horn shell of her abdomen and thorax — a fray-ing, partially collapsed gold tube jammed upright in the candle's round pool.

And then this moth-essence, this spectacular skeleton, began   9
to act as a wick. She kept burning. The wax rose in the moth's

body from her soaking abdomen to her thorax to the shattered hole where her head should have been, and widened into flame, a saffron-yellow flame that robed her to the ground like an immolating monk. That candle had two wicks, two winding flames of identical light, side by side. The moth's head was fire. She burned for two hours, until I blew her out.

She burned for two hours without changing, without swaying or kneeling — only glowing within, like a building fire glimpsed through silhouetted walls, like a hollow saint, like a flame-faced virgin gone to God, while I read by her light, kindled, while Rimbaud in Paris burnt out his brain in a thousand poems, while night pooled wetly at my feet.

So. That is why I think those hollow shreds on the bathroom floor are moths. I believe I know what moths look like, in any state.

I have three candles here on the table which I disentangle from the plants and light when visitors come. The cats avoid them, although Small's tail caught fire once; I rubbed it out before she noticed. I don't mind living alone. I like eating alone and reading. I don't mind sleeping alone. The only time I mind being alone is when something is funny; then, when I am laughing at something funny, I wish someone were around. Sometimes I think it is pretty funny that I sleep alone.

QUESTIONS ON MEANING

1. Why did Dillard retreat to the mountains? What is the significance of this information to the essay?
2. What or whom does the burning moth represent? How does Dillard reveal her meaning?
3. What would you say is the unstated THESIS of this essay? What point is Dillard making?
4. In the beginning and end of her essay, Dillard emphasizes that she lives alone. Why? How does this fact relate to the idea of the essay?

QUESTIONS ON WRITING STRATEGY

1. Why do you think Dillard devotes so much of this essay to her domestic arrangements?
2. Dillard's IMAGES are mostly visual. Find three images that belong to other senses. What is their EFFECT?
3. Pick out all the SIMILES in paragraphs 8–10, the episode of the moth. How do they change?
4. The preceding essay, by Virginia Woolf, is titled "The Death of the Moth" (p. 124). Dillard's title — undoubtedly written in full knowledge of Woolf's essay — is "Death of a Moth." What is the significance of the difference?
5. **OTHER METHODS.** In "Death of a Moth" Dillard offers a kind of definition (Chap. 10). What does she define?

QUESTIONS ON LANGUAGE

1. Analyze the TONE of paragraphs 1–5 and 8–10. How does vocabulary alone contribute to the difference in these two sections?
2. What are "sudden blue sleeves" (para. 8)? How can this be said more conventionally? Why is the author's phrase more effective?
3. Define the following: lineage, immaculate (para. 2); earwig (3); dorsal, thorax, pincers, translucent, chitin, buttresses (5); singe, replenished (7); spasms, antennae (8); robed, immolating (9); silhouetted (10).

SUGGESTIONS FOR WRITING

1. Write an essay describing a thing (object, animal, plant) that serves as a SYMBOL of an important event or period in your life — a pet, a flannel shirt, a spider plant, a bottle cap, whatever. Describe both the circumstances and the object so that readers grasp and care about their relationship.
2. In a few paragraphs, describe a friend, relative, or acquaintance in terms of an animal or plant. This topic will require liberal use of FIGURES OF SPEECH.
3. **CONNECTIONS.** Both "The Death of the Moth" by Virginia Woolf (p. 124) and "Death of a Moth" by Annie Dillard are ostensibly about a moth's death. Compare and contrast the moths in both essays as symbols.

ANNIE DILLARD ON WRITING

"Description's not too hard," according to Annie Dillard, "if you mind your active verbs, keep ticking off as many sense impressions as you can, and omit feelings." In descriptive writing, apparently, she believes in paying attention first of all to the world outside herself.

Writing for *The Bedford Reader*, Dillard has testified to her work habits. Rarely satisfied with an essay until it has gone through many drafts, she sometimes goes on correcting and improving it even after it has been published. "I always have to condense or toss openings," she affirms; "I suspect most writers do. When you begin something, you're so grateful to have begun you'll write down anything, just to prolong the sensation. Later, when you've learned what the writing is really about, you go back and throw away the beginning and start over."

Often she replaces a phrase or sentence with a shorter one. In one essay, to tell how a drop of pond water began to evaporate on a microscope slide, she first wrote, "Its contours pulled together." But that sentence seemed to suffer from "tortured abstraction." She made the sentence read instead, "Its edges shrank." Dillard observes, "I like short sentences. They're forceful, and they can get you out of big trouble."

More words by Annie Dillard on writing appear in Chapter 5, page 327.

FOR DISCUSSION

1. Why, according to Dillard, is it usually necessary for writers to revise the opening paragraphs of what they write?
2. Dillard says that short sentences "can get you out of big trouble." What kinds of "big trouble" do you suppose she means?

MICHAEL J. ARLEN

MICHAEL J. ARLEN has been called "a literary critic of television" for the breadth and perception of his writing on the medium. His work has appeared in *The New Yorker* since 1966 and in several books, including *Living-Room War* (1969), analyzing TV coverage of the war in Vietnam; *The View from Highway 1* (1976), collected essays; and *Thirty Seconds* (1980), dissecting the production of an AT&T commercial for long-distance calling. Arlen was born in London in 1930, the son of the Armenian-born novelist and playwright Michael Arlen. The family emigrated to the United States, and Arlen was educated here, at St. Paul's School and Harvard. He has written about his parents in *Exiles* (1970) and about Armenia in *Passage to Ararat* (1975), which won the National Book Award. Arlen's writing has appeared as well in *Esquire, The Atlantic Monthly, The Nation*, and many other magazines.

Ode to Thanksgiving

Although not exactly about television, "Ode to Thanksgiving" is surely about *The Camera Age*, the title of the collection in which the essay appeared in 1981. Arlen offers a wry, not entirely hateful account of the holiday some people love to hate.

It is time, at last, to speak the truth about Thanksgiving, and 1 the truth is this. Thanksgiving is really not such a terrific holiday. Consider the traditional symbols of the event: Dried cornhusks hanging on the door! Terrible wine! Cranberry jelly in little bowls of extremely doubtful provenance which everyone is required to handle with the greatest of care! Consider the participants, the merrymakers: men and women (also children) who have survived passably well throughout the years, mainly as a result of living at considerable distances from their dear parents and beloved siblings, who on this feast of feasts must apparently forgather (as if beckoned by an aberrant Fairy Godmother), usually by circuitous

routes, through heavy traffic, at a common meeting place, where
the very moods, distempers, and obtrusive personal habits that
have kept them all happily apart since adulthood are then and
there encouraged to slowly ferment beneath the cornhusks, and
gradually rise with the aid of the terrible wine, and finally burst
forth out of control under the stimulus of the cranberry jelly! No,
it is a mockery of a holiday. For instance: *Thank you, O Lord, for
what we are about to receive.* This is surely not a gala concept.
There are no presents, unless one counts Aunt Bertha's sweet
rolls a present, which no one does. There is precious little in the
way of costumery: miniature plastic turkeys and those witless Pilgrim hats. There is no sex. Indeed, Thanksgiving is the one day of
the year (a fact known to everybody) when all thoughts of sex
completely vanish, evaporating from apartments, houses, condo-
miniums, and mobile homes like steam from a bathroom mirror.

Consider also the nowhereness of the time of year: the last   2
week or so in November. It is obviously not yet winter: winter,
with its death-dealing blizzards and its girls in tiny skirts pirouetting on the ice. On the other hand, it is certainly not much use to
anyone as fall: no golden leaves or Oktoberfests, and so forth. Instead, it is a no-man's-land between the seasons. In the cold and
sobersided northern half of the country, it is a vaguely unsettling
interregnum of long, mournful walks beneath leafless trees: the
long, mournful walks following the midday repast with the dread
inevitability of pie following turkey, and the leafless trees looming
or standing about like eyesores, and the ground either as hard as
iron or slightly mushy, and the light snow always beginning to fall
when one is halfway to the old green gate — flecks of cold, watery
stuff plopping between neck and collar, for the reason that, it being not yet winter, one has forgotten or not chosen to bring along
a muffler. It is a corollary to the long, mournful Thanksgiving
walk that the absence of this muffler is quickly noticed and that
four weeks or so later, at Christmastime, instead of the Sony Be-
tamax one had secretly hoped the children might have chipped in
to purchase, one receives another muffler: by then the thirty-
third. Thirty-three mufflers! Some walk! Of course, things are
more fun in the warm and loony southern part of the country.
No snow there of any kind. No need of mufflers. Also, no long,

mournful walks, because in the warm and loony southern part of the country everybody drives. So everybody drives over to Uncle Jasper's house to watch the Cougars play the Gators, a not entirely unimportant conflict which will determine whether the Gators get a Bowl bid or must take another post-season exhibition tour of North Korea. But no sooner do the Cougars kick off (an astonishing end-over-end squiggly thing that floats lazily above the arena before plummeting down toward K. C. McCoy and catching him on the helmet) than Auntie Em starts hustling turkey. Soon Cousin May is slamming around the bowls and platters, and Cousin Bernice is oohing and ahing about "all the fixin's," and Uncle Bob is making low, insincere sounds of appreciation: "Yummy, yummy, Auntie Em, I'll have me some more of these delicious yams!" Delicious yams? Uncle Bob's eyes roll wildly in his head. Billy Joe Quaglino throws his long bomb in the middle of Grandpa Morris saying grace, Grandpa Morris speaking so low nobody can hear him, which is just as well, since he is reciting what he can remember of his last union contract. And then, just as J. B. (Speedy) Snood begins his ninety-two-yard punt return, Auntie Em starts dealing everyone second helpings of her famous stuffing, as if she were pushing a controlled substance, which it well might be, since there are no easily recognizable ingredients visible to the naked eye.

Consider for a moment the Thanksgiving meal itself. It has become a sort of refuge for endangered species of starch: cauliflower, turnips, pumpkin, mince (whatever "mince" is), those blessed yams. Bowls of luridly colored yams, with no taste at all, lying torpid under a lava flow of marshmallow! And then the sacred turkey. One might as well try to construct a holiday repast around a fish — say, a nice piece of boiled haddock. After all, turkey tastes very similar to haddock: same consistency, same quite remarkable absence of flavor. But then, if the Thanksgiving *pièce de résistance* were a nice piece of boiled haddock instead of turkey, there wouldn't be all that fun for Dad when Mom hands him the sterling-silver, bone-handled carving set (a wedding present from her parents and not sharpened since) and then everyone sits around pretending not to watch while he saws and tears away at the bird as if he were trying to burrow his way into or out of some grotesque, fowl-like prison.

What of the good side to Thanksgiving, you ask. There is always a good side to everything. Not to Thanksgiving. There is only a bad side and then a worse side. For instance, Grandmother's best linen tablecloth is a bad side: the fact that it is produced each year, in the manner of a red flag being produced before a bull, and then is always spilled upon by whichever child is doing poorest at school that term and so is in need of greatest reassurance. Thus: "Oh, my God, *Veronica*, you just spilled grape juice [or plum wine or tar] on Grandmother's best linen tablecloth!" But now comes worse. For at this point Cousin Bill, the one who lost all Cousin Edwina's money on the car dealership three years ago and has apparently been drinking steadily since Halloween, bizarrely chooses to say: "Seems to me those old glasses are always falling over." To which Auntie Meg is heard to add: "Somehow I don't remember receivin' any of those old glasses." To which Uncle Fred replies: "That's because you and George decided to go on vacation to Hawaii the summer Grandpa Sam was dying." Now Grandmother is sobbing, though not so uncontrollably that she can refrain from murmuring: "I think that volcano painting I threw away by mistake got sent me from Hawaii, heaven knows why." But the gods are merciful, even the Pilgrim-hatted god of cornhusks and soggy stuffing, and there is an end to everything, even to Thanksgiving. Indeed, there is a grandeur to the feelings of finality and doom which usually settle on a house after the Thanksgiving celebration is over, for with the completion of Thanksgiving Day the year itself has been properly terminated: shot through the cranium with a high-velocity candied yam. At this calendrical nadir, all energy on the planet has gone, all fun has fled, all the terrible wine has been drunk.

But then, overnight, life once again begins to stir, emerging, even by the next morning, in the form of Japanese window displays and Taiwanese Christmas lighting, from the primeval ooze of the nation's department stores. Thus, a new year dawns, bringing with it immediate and cheering possibilities of extended consumer debt, office-party flirtations, good — or, at least, mediocre

— wine, and visions of Supersaver excursion fares to Montego Bay. It is worth noting, perhaps, that this true new year always starts with the same mute, powerful mythic ceremony: the surreptitious tossing out, in the early morning, of all those horrid aluminum-foil packages of yams and cauliflower and stuffing and red, gummy cranberry substance which have been squeezed into the refrigerator as if a reenactment of the siege of Paris were shortly expected. Soon afterward, the phoenix of Christmas can be observed as it slowly rises, beating its drumsticks, once again goggle-eyed with hope and unrealistic expectations.

QUESTIONS ON MEANING

1. What is Arlen's apparent PURPOSE in writing "Ode to Thanksgiving"?
2. What is the author's THESIS? How does it relate to the purpose?
3. In general, what is Arlen's humor based on? Do you find the essay funny?

QUESTIONS ON WRITING STRATEGY

1. Is this a SUBJECTIVE or an OBJECTIVE description? Which would the writer say it was?
2. How would you describe Arlen's TONE? What contributes to it?
3. What is the author's principal assumption about his AUDIENCE? What other things does he assume?
4. OTHER METHODS. Arlen organizes his description by classification (Chap. 7). What classes of features does he identify?

QUESTIONS ON LANGUAGE

1. Arlen's essay teems with ALLUSIONS. Locate half a dozen or so and explain their implications.
2. In paragraph 2, Arlen sends up the traditional Thanksgiving football games. What does he seem to think of football? What language tips you off?
3. Look up the following words in a dictionary: provenance, forgather, aberrant, circuitous, distempers, ferment, costumery, witless (para.

1); pirouetting, sobersided, interregnum, repast, corollary (2); luridly, torpid, grotesque (3); grandeur, cranium, calendrical, nadir (4); primeval, mediocre, surreptitious (5).

SUGGESTIONS FOR WRITING

1. Following Arlen's model, select a subject that is conventionally valued and write a descriptive essay portraying it negatively. You may, but need not, use humor. Your subject may be a wedding, say, or a child's birthday party, or an object such as an automobile or a national monument.
2. Take the opposite approach: Describe a subject no one likes — exams, subway travel, hot nights, a bad meal, even a funeral — and portray it as enjoyable or funny. Try to use opportunities for humor.
3. Do you agree with Arlen's view of Thanksgiving? If you strongly disagree, write an essay about the holiday, addressing Arlen's notions and establishing your own.
4. CONNECTIONS. Arlen's "Ode" resembles Fran Lebowitz's "The Sound of Music: Enough Already" (p. 394): Both authors stage attacks on subjects generally regarded as inoffensive, even desirable. Based on Arlen's and Lebowitz's "instruction," write an essay on how to write such an attack, considering especially the use of humor and the techniques of TONE. (If you need guidance on writing a how-to essay, consult the introduction to Chapter 5, "Process Analysis," page 281.)

JOAN DIDION

For a biographical note, see page 11.

The Liquid City

This selection (titled by the editors) is Chapter 3 in Joan Didion's book *Miami* (1987). Didion is often drawn to enigmatic
places: Los Angeles and El Salvador are two examples, and Miami is no exception. Interweaving conversations she's over-
heard with news items and her own sensory impressions, she
creates a distinctive vision of a "lurid" and fantastic city.

During the spring when I began visiting Miami all of Florida   1
was reported to be in drought, with dropping water tables and
unfilled aquifers and Save Water signs, but drought, in a part of
the world which would be in its natural state a shelf of porous oolitic limestone covered most of the year by a shallow sheet flow of
fresh water, proved relative. During this drought the city of Coral
Gables continued, as it had every night since 1924, to empty and
refill its Venetian Pool with fresh unchlorinated water, 820,000
gallons a day out of the water supply and into the storm sewer.
There was less water than there might have been in the Biscayne
Aquifer but there was water everywhere above it. There were
rains so hard that windshield wipers stopped working and cars
got swamped and stalled on I-95. There was water roiling and
bubbling over the underwater lights in decorative pools. There
was water sluicing off the six-story canted window at the Omni, a
hotel from which it was possible to see, in the Third World way,
both the slums of Overtown and those island houses with the
Unusual Security and Ready Access to the Ocean, equally wet.
Water splashed off banana palms, water puddled on flat roofs,
water streamed down the Carne U.S. Good & U.S. Standard
signs on Flagler Street. Water rocked the impounded drug boats
which lined the Miami River and water lapped against the causeways on the bay. I got used to the smell of incipient mildew in my

clothes. I stuffed Kleenex in wet shoes and stopped expecting them to dry.

A certain liquidity suffused everything about the place. 2 Causeways and bridges and even Brickell Avenue did not stay put but rose and fell, allowing the masts of ships to glide among the marble and glass facades of the unleased office buildings. The buildings themselves seemed to swim free against the sky: there had grown up in Miami during the recent money years an architecture which appeared to have slipped its moorings, a not inappropriate style for a terrain with only a provisional claim on being land at all. Surfaces were reflective, opalescent. Angles were oblique, intersecting to disorienting effect. The Arquitectonica office, which produced the celebrated glass condominium on Brickell Avenue with the fifty-foot cube cut from its center, the frequently photographed "sky patio" in which there floated a palm tree, a Jacuzzi, and a lipstick-red spiral staircase, accompanied its elevations with crayon sketches, all moons and starry skies and airborne maidens, as in a Chagall. Skidmore, Owings, and Merrill managed, in its Southeast Financial Center, the considerable feat of rendering fifty-five stories of polished gray granite incorporeal, a sky-blue illusion.

Nothing about Miami was exactly fixed, or hard. Hard con-   3 sonants were missing from the local speech patterns, in English as well as in Spanish. Local money tended to move on hydraulic verbs: When it was not being washed it was being diverted, or channeled through Mexico, or turned off in Washington. Local stories tended to turn on underwater plot points, submerged snappers: on unsoundable extradition proceedings in the Bahamas, say, or fluid connections with the Banco Nacional de Colombia. I recall trying to touch the bottom of one such story in the *Herald*, about six hand grenades which had just been dug up in the bay-front backyard of a Biscayne Boulevard pawnbroker who had been killed in his own bed a few years before, shot at close range with a .25-caliber automatic pistol.

There were some other details on the surface of this story, for   4 example the wife who fired the .25-caliber automatic pistol and the nineteen-year-old daughter who was up on federal weapons charges and the flight attendant who rented the garage apartment

and said that the pawnbroker had collected "just basic things like
rockets, just defused things," but the underwater narrative included, at last sounding, the Central Intelligence Agency (with
which the pawnbroker was said to have been associated), the British intelligence agency MI6 (with which the pawnbroker was said
to have been associated), the late Anastasio Somoza Debayle
(whose family the pawnbroker was said to have spirited into Miami shortly before the regime fell in Managua), the late shah of
Iran (whose presence in Panama was said to have queered an arms
deal about which the pawnbroker had been told), Dr. Josef
Mengele (for whom the pawnbroker was said to be searching),
and a Pompano Beach resident last seen cruising Miami in a cin-
namon-colored Cadillac Sedan de Ville and looking to buy, he
said for the Salvadoran insurgents, a million rounds of ammuni-
tion, thirteen thousand assault rifles, and "at least a couple" of
jeep-mounted machine guns.

In this mood Miami seemed not a city at all but a tale, a ro-   5
mance of the tropics, a kind of waking dream in which any possibility could and would be accommodated. The most ordinary
morning, say at the courthouse, could open onto the distinctly lurid. "I don't think he came out with me, that's all," I recall hearing someone say one day in an elevator at the Miami federal
courthouse. His voice had kept rising. "What happened to all
that stuff about how next time, he gets twenty keys, he could run
wherever-it-is-Idaho, now he says he wouldn't know what to do
with five keys, what is this shit?" His companion had shrugged.
We had continued in silence to the main floor. Outside one
courtroom that day a group of Colombians, the women in silk
shirts and Chanel necklaces and Charles Jourdan suede pumps,
the children in appliquéd dresses from Baby Dior, had been waiting for the decision in a pretrial detention hearing, one in which
the government was contending that the two defendants, who
between them lived in houses in which eighty-three kilos of cocaine and a million-three in cash had been found, failed to qualify
as good bail risks.

"That doesn't make him a longtime drug dealer," one of the   6
two defense lawyers, both of whom were Anglo and one of whom

drove a Mercedes 380 SEL with the license plate "Defense," had argued about the million-three in cash. "That could be one transaction." Across the hall that day closing arguments were being heard in a boat case, a "boat case" being one in which a merchant or fishing vessel has been boarded and drugs seized and eight or ten Colombian crew members arrested, the kind of case in which pleas were typically entered so that one of the Colombians would get eighteen months and the others deported. There were never any women in Chanel necklaces around a boat case, and the lawyers (who were usually hired and paid for not by the defendants but by the unnamed owner of the "load," or shipment) tended to be Cuban. "You had the great argument, you got to give me some good ideas," one of the eight Cuban defense lawyers on this case joked with the prosecutor during a recess. "But you haven't heard my argument yet," another of the defense lawyers said. "The stuff about communism. Fabulous closing argument."

Just as any morning could turn lurid, any moment could turn final, again as in a dream. "I heard a loud, short noise and then there was just a plain moment of dullness," the witness to a shooting in a Miami Beach supermarket parking lot told the *Herald.* "There was no one around except me and two bagboys." I happened to be in the coroner's office one morning when autopsies were being performed on the bodies of two Mariels,[1] shot and apparently pushed from a car on I-95 about nine the evening before, another plain moment of dullness. The story had been on television an hour or two after it happened: I had seen the crime site on the eleven o'clock news, and had not expected to see the victims in the morning. "When he came here in Mariel he stayed at our house but he didn't get along with my mom," a young girl was saying in the anteroom to one of the detectives working the case. "These two guys were killed together," the detective had pressed. "They probably knew each other."

"For sure," the young girl had said, agreeably. Inside the autopsy room the hands of the two young men were encased in the brown paper bags which indicated that the police had not yet

---

[1]Mariels are immigrants who were part of the huge emigration in 1980 from the Port of Mariel in Cuba to the United States. — EDS.

taken what they needed for laboratory studies. Their flesh had the marbelized yellow look of the recently dead. There were other bodies in the room, in various stages of autopsy, and a young woman in a white coat taking eyes, for the eye bank. "Who are we going to start on next?" one of the assistant medical examiners was saying. "The fat guy? Let's do the fat guy."

It was even possible to enter the waking dream without leaving the house, just by reading the *Herald*. A Mariel named Jose "Coca-Cola" Yero gets arrested, with nine acquaintances, in a case involving 1,664 pounds of cocaine, a thirty-seven-foot Cigarette boat named *The Connection*, two Lamborghinis, a million-six in cash, a Mercedes 500 SEL with another $350,000 in cash in the trunk, one dozen Rolex watches color-coordinated to match Jose "Colca-Cola" Yero's wardrobe, and various houses in Dade and Palm Beach counties, a search of one of which turns up not just a photograph of Jose "Colca-Cola" Yero face down in a pile of white powder but also a framed poster of Al Pacino as Tony Montana, the Mariel who appears at a dramatic moment in *Scarface* face down in a pile of white powder. "They got swept up in the fast lane," a Metro-Dade narcotics detective advises the *Herald*. "The fast lane is what put this whole group in jail." A young woman in South Palm Beach goes out to the parking lot of her parents' condominium and gets into her 1979 Pontiac Firebird, opens the T-top, starts the ignition and loses four toes when the bomb goes off. "She definitely knows someone is trying to kill her," the sheriff's investigator tells the *Herald*. "She knew they were coming, but she didn't know when."

Surfaces tended to dissolve here. Clear days ended less so. I recall an October Sunday when my husband and I were taken, by Gene Miller, a *Herald* editor who had won two Pulitzer Prizes for investigative reporting and who had access to season tickets exactly on the fifty-yard line at the Orange Bowl, to see the Miami Dophins beat the Pittsburgh Steelers, 21–17. In the row below us the former Dolphin quarterback Earl Morrall signed autographs for the children who wriggled over seats to slip him their programs and steal surreptitious glances at his Super Bowl ring. A few rows back an Anglo teenager in sandals and shorts and a

black T-shirt smoked a marijuana cigarette in full view of the Hispanic police officer behind him. Hot dogs were passed, and Coca-
Cola spilled. Sony Watchmans were compared, for the definition
on the instant replay. The NBC cameras dollied along the side-
lines and the Dolphin cheerleaders kneeled on their white pom-
poms and there was a good deal of talk about red dogging and
weak secondaries and who would be seen and what would be
eaten in New Orleans, come Super Bowl weekend.

The Miami on display in the Orange Bowl that Sunday after-   11
noon would have seemed another Miami altogether, one with less
weather and harder, more American surfaces, but by dinner we
were slipping back into the tropical: in a virtually empty restaurant on top of a virtually empty condominium off Biscayne Boulevard, with six people at the table, one of whom was Gene Miller
and one of whom was Martin Dardis, who as the chief investiga-
tor for the state attorney's office in Miami had led Carl Bernstein[2]
through the local angles on Watergate and who remained a walking data bank on CDs at the Biscayne Bank and on who called
who on what payoff and on how to follow a money chain, we sat
and we talked and we watched a storm break over Biscayne Bay.
Sheets of warm rain washed down the big windows. Lightning began to fork somewhere around Bal Harbour. Gene Miller mentioned the Alberto Duque trial, then entering its fourth week at
the federal courthouse, the biggest bank fraud case ever tried in
the United States. Martin Dardis mentioned the ESM Government Securities collapse, just then breaking into a fraud case
maybe bigger than the Duque.

The lightning was no longer forking now but illuminating the   12
entire sky, flashing a dead strobe white, turning the bay fluorescent and the islands black, as if in negative. I sat and I listened to
Gene Miller and Martin Dardis discuss these old and new turns
in the underwater narrative and I watched the lightning backlight
the islands. During the time I had spent in Miami many people
had mentioned, always as something extraordinary, something I

---

[2]Bernstein is a reporter who, with his colleague Bob Woodward, broke
the Watergate scandal of the early 1970s that ended in President Richard Nixon's resignation. — EDS.

should have seen if I wanted to understand Miami, the *Surrounded Islands* project executed in Biscayne Bay in 1983 by the Bulgarian artist Christo. *Surrounded Islands*, which had involved surrounding eleven islands with two-hundred-foot petals, or skirts, of pink polypropylene fabric, had been mentioned both by people who were knowledgeable about conceptual art and by people who had not before heard and could not then recall the name of the man who had surrounded the islands. All had agreed. It seemed that the pink had shimmered in the water. It seemed that the pink had kept changing color, fading and reemerging with the movement of the water and the clouds and the sun and the night lights. It seemed that this period when the pink was in the water had for many people exactly defined, as the backlit islands and the fluorescent water and the voices at the table were that night defining for me, Miami.

QUESTIONS ON MEANING

1. What is Didion trying to do in this selection from *Miami?* What is her PURPOSE?
2. What two FIGURES OF SPEECH govern Didion's description of Miami? How are these two images similar?
3. How are the INTRODUCTION of this selection and its CONCLUSION related?
4. In Didion's view, what is it about Miami that makes it different from other American cities?

QUESTIONS ON WRITING STRATEGY

1. How does Didion organize the examples of wateriness in paragraphs 1–4? What does she accomplish with this order?
2. What is Didion's TONE? What do you think is her attitude toward Miami?
3. What kinds of EVIDENCE does Didion use to support her impressions? What evidence do you find most convincing? Least convincing?

4. **OTHER METHODS.** Didion relies heavily on examples (Chap. 3). Choose two of the examples in paragraphs 3–9 and analyze how each supports Didion's impression of liquidity.

QUESTIONS ON LANGUAGE

1. Analyze how Didion uses words to keep the IMAGES of water and dream alive throughout the essay, even when she doesn't explicitly discuss the images.
2. Whom does Didion quote? What do her choices imply about Miami?
3. Look up any of these words that are unfamiliar: aquifers, oolitic, roiling, sluicing, canted, plashed, incipient (para. 1); suffused, opalescent, oblique, incorporeal (2); hydraulic, extradition, pawnbroker (3); insurgents (4); surreptitious (10); polypropylene (12).

SUGGESTIONS FOR WRITING

1. Think of a city or town where you have lived. In an essay, describe this place so as to create a DOMINANT IMPRESSION. If you choose, your central image may be, like Didion's, a FIGURE OF SPEECH.
2. Read through an issue of a newspaper that concentrates on local news. Based on the newspaper, write a description of the area it covers — the kinds of people who live there, their attitudes, cultural life, education, politics, economic status, and so on. Be as specific as possible, and use quotations liberally.
3. **CONNECTIONS.** Didion's writing is always remarkable for its TONE. In an essay, compare and contrast the tones of "The Liquid City" and "In Bed" (p. 11), also by Didion. How are they alike and different? How do the different subjects account for any differences in tone? In your essay, use specific examples from both essays to support your analysis.

JOAN DIDION ON WRITING

In "Why I Write," an essay published by the *New York Times Book Review*, adapted from her Regents' Lecture at the University of California at Berkeley, Joan Didion writes, "Of course I stole the title for this talk, from George Orwell [excerpts of which appear on pages 61–62]. One reason I stole it was that I like the sound of the words: Why I Write. There you have three short unambiguous words that share a sound, and the sound they share is this:

I

I

I

In many ways writing is the act of saying *I*, of imposing oneself upon other people, of saying *listen to me, see it my way, change your mind.* . . .

Didion's "way," though, comes not from notions of how the world works or should work but from its observable details. She writes, "I am not in the least an intellectual, which is not to say that when I hear the word 'intellectual' I reach for my gun, but only to say that I do not think in abstracts. During the years when I was an undergraduate at Berkeley I tried, with a kind of hopeless late-adolescent energy, to buy some temporary visa into the world of ideas, to forge for myself a mind that could deal with the abstract. . . . In short, I tried to think. I failed. My attention veered inexorably back to the specific, to the tangible, to what was generally considered, by everyone I knew then and for that matter have known since, the peripheral. I would try to contemplate the Hegelian dialectic and would find myself concentrating instead on the flowering pear tree outside my window and the particular way the petals fell on my floor.

Later in the essay, Didion writes, "During those years I was traveling on what I knew to be a very shaky passport, forged papers: I knew that I was no legitimate resident in any world of ideas. I knew I couldn't think. All I knew then was what I wasn't, and it took me some years to discover what I was.

"Which was a writer.

"By which I mean not a 'good' writer or a 'bad' writer but simply a writer, a person whose most absorbed and passionate hours are spent arranging words on pieces of paper. Had my credentials been in order I would never have become a writer. Had I been blessed with even limited access to own my mind there would have been no reason to write. I write entirely to find out what I'm thinking, what I'm looking at, what I see, and what it means. What I want and what I fear. . . . *What is going on in these pictures in my mind?*"

In the essay, Didion emphasizes that these mental pictures have a grammar. ". . . Grammar is a piano I play by ear, since I seem to have been out of school the year the rules were mentioned. All I know about grammar is its infinite power. To shift the structure of a sentence alters the meaning of that sentence, as definitely and inflexibly as the position of a camera alters the meaning of the object photographed. Many people know about camera angles now, but not so many know about sentences. The arrangement of the words matters, and the arrangement you want can be found in the picture in your mind. The picture dictates the arrangement. The picture dictates whether this will be a sentence with or without clauses, a sentence that ends hard or a dying-fall sentence, long or short, active or passive. The picture tells you how to arrange the words and the arrangement of the words tells you, or tells me, what's going on in the picture."

FOR DISCUSSION

1. What is Didion's definition of thinking? Do you agree with it?
2. To what extent does Didion's writing support her remarks about how and why she writes?
3. What does Didion mean when she says that grammar has "infinite power"? Power to do what?

RICHARD SELZER

RICHARD SELZER trained to be a doctor and practiced surgery from 1960 to 1985, when he gave it up for his other vocation, writing. He was born in Troy, New York, in 1928 and attended Union College and Albany Medical College before entering private practice and before beginning to teach surgery at Yale University in 1961. Selzer began writing when he was forty years old and set about, he says, "to learn the craft of writing much as I had learned the craft of surgery." A book of short stories, *Rituals of Surgery*, was published in 1974 and followed by collections of essays: *Mortal Lessons* (1976), *Confessions of a Knife* (1979), *Letters to a Young Doctor* (also including some fiction, 1981), and *Taking the World in for Repairs* (1986).

The Discus Thrower

Selzer made the difficult decision to quit surgery, he told an interviewer, "because the surgeon must be anesthetized, but the writer must feel *everything*. . . . It is unbearable to gaze at the events of surgery with the dilated pupils of a writer." Selzer's "dilated pupils" have taken in both the grotesqueness and the mystery of the medical world, and he has written of it both frankly and poetically. "The Discus Thrower," a brief and powerful example, first appeared in *Harper's* magazine in 1977 and was republished in *Confessions of a Knife* (1979).

I spy on my patients. Ought not a doctor to observe his patients by any means and from any stance, that he might the more fully assemble evidence? So I stand in the doorways of hospital rooms and gaze. Oh, it is not all that furtive an act. Those in bed need only look up to discover me. But they never do.

From the doorway of Room 542 the man in the bed seems deeply tanned. Blue eyes and close-cropped white hair give him the appearance of vigor and good health. But I know that his skin is not brown from the sun. It is rusted, rather, in the last stage of containing the vile repose within. And the blue eyes are frosted,

152

looking inward like the windows of a snowbound cottage. This man is blind. This man is also legless — the right leg missing from midthigh down, the left from just below the knee. It gives him the look of a bonsai, roots and branches pruned into the dwarfed fac-simile of a great tree.

Propped on pillows, he cups his right thigh in both hands. 3 Now and then he shakes his head as though acknowledging the intensity of his suffering. In all of this he makes no sound. Is he mute as well as blind?

The room in which he dwells is empty of all possessions — no 4 get-well cards, small, private caches of food, day-old flowers, slip-pers, all the usual kickshaws of the sickroom. There is only the bed, a chair, a nightstand, and a tray on wheels that can be swung across his lap for meals.

"What time is it?" he asks.   5

"Three o'clock."   6

"Morning or afternoon?"   7

"Afternoon."   8

He is silent. There is nothing else he wants to know.   9

"How are you?" I say.   10

"Who is it?" he asks.   11

"It's the doctor. How do you feel?"   12

He does not answer right away.   13

"Feel?" he says.   14

"I hope you feel better," I say.   15

I press the button at the side of the bed.   16

"Down you go," I say.   17

"Yes, down," he says.   18

He falls back upon the bed awkwardly. His stumps, un- 19 weighted by legs and feet, rise in the air, presenting themselves. I unwrap the bandages from the stumps, and begin to cut away the black scabs and the dead, glazed fat with scissors and forceps. A shard of white bone comes loose. I pick it away. I wash the wounds with disinfectant and redress the stumps. All this while, he does not speak. What is he thinking behind those lids that do not blink? Is he remembering a time when he was whole? Does he dream of feet? Of when his body was not a rotting log?

He lies solid and inert. In spite of everything, he remains im-   20
pressive, as though he were a sailor standing athwart a slanting
deck.

"Anything more I can do for you?" I ask.   21

For a long moment he is silent.   22

"Yes," he says at last and without the least irony. "You can   23
bring me a pair of shoes."

In the corridor, the head nurse is waiting for me.   24

"We have to do something about him," she says. "Every   25
morning he orders scrambled eggs for breakfast, and, instead of
eating them, he picks up the plate and throws it against the wall."

"Throws his plate?"   26

"Nasty. That's what he is. No wonder his family doesn't   27
come to visit. They probably can't stand him any more than we
can."

She is waiting for me to do something.   28

"Well?"   29

"We'll see," I say.   30

The next morning I am waiting in the corridor when the   31
kitchen delivers his breakfast. I watch the aide place the tray on
the stand and swing it across his lap. She presses the button to
raise the head of the bed. Then she leaves.

In time the man reaches to find the rim of the tray, then on   32
to find the dome of the covered dish. He lifts off the cover and
places it on the stand. He fingers across the plate until he probes
the eggs. He lifts the plate in both hands, sets it on the palm of his
right hand, centers it, balances it. He hefts it up and down
slightly, getting the feel of it. Abruptly, he draws back his right
arm as far as he can.

There is the crack of the plate breaking against the wall at the   33
foot of his bed and the small wet sound of the scrambled eggs
dropping to the floor.

And then he laughs. It is a sound you have never heard. It is   34
something new under the sun. It could cure cancer.

Out in the corridor, the eyes of the head nurse narrow.   35

"Laughed, did he?"   36

She writes something down on her clipboard.   37

A second aide arrives, brings a second breakfast tray, puts it 38
on the nightstand, out of his reach. She looks over at me shaking
her head and making her mouth go. I see that we are to be accom-
plices.

"I've got to feed you," she says to the man. 39

"Oh, no you don't," the man says. 40

"Oh, yes I do," the aide says, "after the way you just did. 41
Nurse says so."

"Get me my shoes," the man says. 42

"Here's oatmeal," the aide says. "Open." And she touches 43
the spoon to his lower lip.

"I ordered scrambled eggs," says the man. 44

"That's right," the aide says. 45

I step forward. 46

"Is there anything I can do?" I say. 47

"Who are you?" the man asks. 48

In the evening I go once more to that ward to make my 49
rounds. The head nurse reports to me that Room 542 is deceased.
She has discovered this quite by accident, she says. No, there had
been no sound. Nothing. It's a blessing, she says.

I go into his room, a spy looking for secrets. He is still there in 50
his bed. His face is relaxed, grave, dignified. After a while, I turn
to leave. My gaze sweeps the wall at the foot of the bed, and I see
the place where it has been repeatedly washed, where the wall
looks very clean and very white.

―――――

QUESTIONS ON MEANING

1. This essay originally bore the subtitle "Do Not Go Gentle," an allusion to these lines by the poet Dylan Thomas: "Do not go gentle
   into that good night. / Rage, rage against the dying of the light."
   What does this information contribute to your understanding of
   Selzer's essay?
2. What do you see as Selzer's PURPOSE?

3. The doctor twice refers to himself as a "spy" (paras. 1, 50). What do you think he is looking for? What does he find?
4. Why might the patient ask twice for a pair of shoes (paras. 23, 42)?
5. When the doctor asks how the patient is or if he can help, why might the patient respond, "Who is it?" (para. 11), or "Who are you?" (48)?

QUESTIONS ON WRITING STRATEGY

1. Why do you think Selzer tells us so little about the patient — not even the name and nature of his disease?
2. What role does the head nurse play in this essay?
3. What is the EFFECT of Selzer's closing sentence? What do you think it means in the context of the essay as a whole?
4. OTHER METHODS. In "The Discus Thrower," the description is organized in a narrative (Chap. 1). How does the narrator's POINT OF VIEW affect the essay?

QUESTIONS ON LANGUAGE

1. Define the following words: furtive (para. 1); vile, bonsai, facsimile (2); caches, kickshaws (4); shard (19); athwart (20).
2. Would you say this doctor *sounds* like a doctor? What is the effect of Selzer's language?
3. Study the IMAGE in paragraph 20: ". . . he remains impressive, as though he were a sailor standing athwart a slanting deck." Why is this a fitting image for this patient?

SUGGESTIONS FOR WRITING

1. Compare and contrast the doctor's and the head nurse's attitudes toward patients. You will have to go beyond what the essay actually says to consider the implications.
2. On a bus or in a cafeteria or wherever you can, observe a stranger for long enough to form a sharp mental picture of him or her. (Be as inconspicuous as possible to avoid offending or frightening your subject.) In a brief essay, describe this person as clearly and concretely as you can.
3. Think of a time when you witnessed what would generally be considered unacceptable behavior — a child throwing a tantrum, a street person ranting at the wind, a shop clerk treating a customer

rudely, whatever. Describe the person's behavior and, in doing so, see if you can figure out why he or she might have acted in that way.

4. CONNECTIONS. Virginia Woolf's "The Death of the Moth" (p. 124) also concerns the struggle of life against death. Write an essay in which you compare and contrast Selzer's and Woolf's essays on any points of your choosing. Some suggestions: What differences result from taking a moth or a human being as subject? What similarities persist despite the different subjects? Why is Woolf so much freer with interpretation than Selzer? What are the similarities and differences in how the two authors see life? Death?

RICHARD SELZER ON WRITING

Richard Selzer freely discusses his dual profession of doctor and writer, partly because he sees the two as more similar than most people do. "In medicine," he writes in an essay titled "The Pen and the Scalpel," "there is a procedure called transillumination. If, in a darkened room, a doctor holds bright light against a hollow part of the body, he will see through the outer tissues to the structures within that cavity — arteries, veins, projecting shelves of bone. . . . Unlike surgery, which opens the body to direct examination, transillumination gives an indirect vision, calling into play the simplest perceptions of the doctor. To write about a patient is like transillumination. You hold the lamp of language against the body and gaze through the covering layers at the truths within."

Selzer began thinking about the illuminating power of language as a child. "Despite that I did not begin to write until the middle of my life, I think I must have always been a writer. Like my father, who was a general practitioner during the Depression in Troy, N.Y., and who wrote a novel. Father's office was on the ground floor of an old brownstone, and we lived upstairs. At night after office hours, my brother Billy and I (we were 10 and 9 years old) would sneak downstairs to Father's darkened consultation room and there, shamefaced, by the light of a candle stub, we would take down from the shelves his medical textbooks. . . . It was there that I first became aware of the rich language of medicine. Some of the best words began with the letter *c*. *Carcinoma*, I read, and thought it was that aria from *Rigoletto* that Mother used to sing while she washed and dried the dishes. *Cerebellum*. I said the word aloud, letting it drip off the end of my tongue like melted chocolate. And I read *choledochojejunostomy*, which later I was to learn as the name of an operation. . . . I do not use these words in my writing, but I do try to use language that evokes the sounds of the body — *lub-dup*, *lub-dup* of the garrulous heart, the gasp and wheeze of hard breathing, all the murmur and splash of anatomy and physiology. And I have tried to make use of the poetic potential in scientific language."

In another article, a commencement address to medical students, Selzer cautions that language — technical or not — takes care. "To acquire a love of language," he says, "one must know precisely what each word means, and knowing the origin or derivation of a word helps even more. I shall give one example — the word *patient*, which comes from the Latin *patior*, to suffer. Implicit in the word *patient* is suffering. Doctors have patients. Above all this is what distinguishes us from lawyers, who have clients. *Client* comes from the Latin *cliens*, which is the term given to the vassals of a feudal lord for whom services, such as protection, were rendered in return for payment. We have patients; they suffer."

FOR DISCUSSION

1. How, in Selzer's view, are medicine and writing related?
2. Why might a person who believes in precision in language be drawn to medicine as a profession?

E. B. WHITE

ELWYN BROOKS WHITE (1899–1985) for half a century was a regular contributor to *The New Yorker*, and his essays, editorials, anonymous features for "The Talk of the Town," and fillers helped build the magazine a reputation for wit and good writing. If as a child you read *Charlotte's Web* (1952), you have met E. B. White before. The book reflects some of his own life on a farm in North Brooklin, Maine. His *Letters* were collected in 1976, his *Essays* in 1977, and his *Poems and Sketches* in 1981. On July 4, 1963, President Kennedy named White in the first group of Americans to receive the Presidential Medal of Freedom, with a citation that called him "an essayist whose concise comment on men and places has revealed to yet another age the vigor of the English sentence."

Once More to the Lake

"The essayist," says White in a foreword to his *Essays*, "is a self-liberated man, sustained by the childish belief that everything he thinks about, everything that happens to him, is of general interest." In White's case this belief is soundly justified. Perhaps if a duller writer had written "Once More to the Lake," or an essay by that title, we wouldn't much care about it, for at first its subject seems as personal, flat, and ordinary as a letter home. White's loving and exact description, however, brings this lakeside camp to life for us. In the end, the writer arrives at an awareness that shocks him — shocks us, too, with a familiar sensory detail.

August 1941

One summer, along about 1904, my father rented a camp on 1 a lake in Maine and took us all there for the month of August. We all got ringworm from some kittens and had to rub Pond's Extract on our arms and legs night and morning, and my father rolled over in a canoe with all his clothes on; but outside of that the vacation was a success and from then on none of us ever thought there was any place in the world like that lake in Maine.

We returned summer after summer — always on August 1 for one month. I have since become a salt-water man, but sometimes in summer there are days when the restlessness of the tides and the fearful cold of the sea water and the incessant wind that blows across the afternoon and into the evening make me wish for the placidity of a lake in the woods. A few weeks ago this feeling got so strong I bought myself a couple of bass hooks and a spinner and returned to the lake where we used to go, for a week's fishing and to revisit old haunts.

I took along my son, who had never had any fresh water up   2 his nose and who had seen lily pads only from train windows. On the journey over to the lake I began to wonder what it would be like. I wondered how time would have marred this unique, this holy spot — the coves and streams, the hills that the sun set behind, the camps and the paths behind the camps. I was sure that the tarred road would have found it out, and I wondered in what other ways it would be desolated. It is strange how much you can remember about places like that once you allow your mind to return into the grooves that lead back. You remember one thing, and that suddenly reminds you of another thing. I guess I remembered clearest of all the early mornings, when the lake was cool and motionless, remembered how the bedroom smelled of the lumber it was made of and of the wet woods whose scent entered through the screen. The partitions in the camp were thin and did not extend clear to the top of the rooms, and as I was always the first up I would dress softly so as not to wake the others, and sneak out into the sweet outdoors and start out in the canoe, keeping close along the shore in the long shadows of the pines. I remembered being very careful never to rub my paddle against the gunwale for fear of disturbing the stillness of the cathedral.

The lake had never been what you would call a wild lake.   3 There were cottages sprinkled around the shores, and it was in farming country although the shores of the lake were quite heavily wooded. Some of the cottages were owned by nearby farmers, and you would live at the shore and eat your meals at the farmhouse. That's what our family did. But although it wasn't wild, it was a fairly large and undisturbed lake and there were places in it that, to a child at least, seemed infinitely remote and primeval.

I was right about the tar: It led to within half a mile of the   4
shore. But when I got back there, with my boy, and we settled
into a camp near a farmhouse and into the kind of summertime I
had known, I could tell that it was going to be pretty much the
same as it had been before — I knew it, lying in bed the first
morning smelling the bedroom and hearing the boy sneak quietly
out and go off along the shore in a boat. I began to sustain the illusion that he was I, and therefore, by simple transposition, that I
was my father. This sensation persisted, kept cropping up all the
time we were there. It was not an entirely new feeling, but in this
setting it grew much stronger. I seemed to be living a dual existence. I would be in the middle of some simple act, I would be
picking up a bait box or laying down a table fork, or I would be
saying something and suddenly it would be not I but my father
who was saying the words or making the gesture. It gave me a
creepy sensation.

We went fishing the first morning. I felt the same damp moss   5
covering the worms in the bait can, and saw the dragonfly alight on
the tip of my rod as it hovered a few inches from the surface of the
water. It was the arrival of this fly that convinced me beyond any
doubt that everything was as it always had been, that the years
were a mirage and that there had been no years. The small waves
were the same, chucking the rowboat under the chin as we fished at
anchor, and the boat was the same boat, the same color green and
the ribs broken in the same places, and under the floorboards the
same fresh water leavings and debris — the dead hellgrammite, the
wisps of moss, the rusty discarded fishhook, the dried blood from
yesterday's catch. We stared silently at the tips of our rods, at the
dragonflies that came and went. I lowered the tip of mine into the
water, tentatively, pensively dislodging the fly, which darted two
feet away, poised, darted two feet back, and came to rest again a
little farther up the rod. There had been no years between the
ducking of this dragonfly and the other one — the one that was
part of memory. I looked at the boy, who was silently watching his
fly, and it was my hands that held his rod, my eyes watching. I felt
dizzy and didn't know which rod I was at the end of.

We caught two bass, hauling them in briskly as though they   6
were mackerel, pulling them over the side of the boat in a busi-

nesslike manner without any landing net, and stunning them
with a blow on the back of the head. When we got back for a
swim before lunch, the lake was exactly where we had left it, the
same number of inches from the dock, and there was only the
merest suggestion of a breeze. This seemed an utterly enchanted
sea, this lake you could leave to its own devices for a few hours
and come back to, and find that it had not stirred, this constant
and trustworthy body of water. In the shallows, the dark, water-
soaked sticks and twigs, smooth and old, were undulating in clusters on the bottom against the clean ribbed sand, and the track of
the mussel was plain. A school of minnows swam by, each min-
now with its small individual shadow, doubling the attendance,
so clear and sharp in the sunlight. Some of the other campers
were in swimming, along the shore, one of them with a cake of
soap, and the water felt thin and clear and unsubstantial. Over
the years there had been this person with the cake of soap, this
cultist, and here he was. There had been no years.

Up to the farmhouse to dinner through the teeming dusty   7
field, the road under our sneakers was only a two-track road. The
middle track was missing, the one with the marks of the hooves
and the splotches of dried, flaky manure. There had always been
three tracks to choose from in choosing which track to walk in;
now the choice was narrowed down to two. For a moment I
missed terribly the middle alternative. But the way led past the
tennis court, and something about the way it lay there in the sun
reassured me; the tape had loosened along the backline, the alleys
were green with plantains and other weeds, and the net (installed
in June and removed in September) sagged in the dry noon, and
the whole place steamed with midday heat and hunger and emp-
tiness. There was a choice of pie for dessert, and one was blue-
berry and one was apple, and the waitresses were the same country girls, there having been no passage of time, only the illusion of
it as in a dropped curtain — the waitresses were still fifteen; their
hair had been washed, that was the only difference — they had
been to the movies and seen the pretty girls with the clean hair.

Summertime, oh, summertime, pattern of life indelible with   8
fade-proof lake, the wood unshatterable, the pasture with the
sweetfern and the juniper forever and ever, summer without end;

this was the background, and the life along the shore was the design, the cottages with their innocent and tranquil design, their tiny docks with the flagpole and the American flag floating against the white clouds in the blue sky, the little paths over the roots of the trees leading from camp to camp and the paths leading back to the outhouses and the can of lime for sprinkling, and at the souvenir counters at the store the miniature birchbark canoes and the postcards that showed things looking a little better than they looked. This was the American family at play, escaping the city heat, wondering whether the newcomers in the camp at the head of the cove were "common" or "nice," wondering whether it was true that the people who drove up for Sunday dinner at the farmhouse were turned away because there wasn't enough chicken.

It seemed to me, as I kept remembering all this, that those times and those summers had been infinitely precious and worth saving. There had been jollity and peace and goodness. The arriving (at the beginning of August) had been so big a business in itself, at the railway station the farm wagon drawn up, the first smell of the pine-laden air, the first glimpse of the smiling farmer, and the great importance of the trunks and your father's enormous authority in such matters, and the feel of the wagon under you for the long ten-mile haul, and at the top of the last long hill catching the first view of the lake after eleven months of not seeing this cherished body of water. The shouts and cries of the other campers when they saw you, and the trunks to be unpacked, to give up their rich burden. (Arriving was less exciting nowadays, when you sneaked up in your car and parked it under a tree near the camp and took out the bags and in five minutes it was all over, no fuss, no loud wonderful fuss about trunks.)

Peace and goodness and jollity. The only thing that was wrong now, really, was the sound of the place, an unfamiliar nervous sound of the outboard motors. This was the note that jarred, the one thing that would sometimes break the illusion and set the years moving. In those other summertimes all motors were inboard; and when they were at a little distance, the noise they made was a sedative, an ingredient of summer sleep. They were one-cylinder and two-cylinder engines, and some were make-and-break and some were jump-spark, but they all made a sleepy sound across the lake. The one-lungers throbbed and fluttered, and the twin-cylinder ones purred and purred, and that was a quiet sound, too. But now the campers all had outboards. In the daytime, in the hot mornings, these motors made a petulant, irritable sound; at night in the still evening when the afterglow lit the water, they whined about one's ears like mosquitoes. My boy loved our rented outboard, and his great desire was to achieve single-handed mastery over it, and authority, and he soon learned the trick of choking it a little (but not too much), and the adjustment of the needle valve. Watching him I would remember the things you could do with the old one-cylinder engine with the heavy flywheel, how you could have it eating out of your hand if you got really close to it spiritually. Motorboats in those days didn't have clutches, and you would make a landing by shutting off the motor at the proper time and coasting in with a dead rudder. But there was a way of reversing them, if you learned the trick, by cutting the switch and putting it on again exactly on the final dying revolution of the flywheel, so that it would kick back against compression and begin reversing. Approaching a dock in a strong following breeze, it was difficult to slow up sufficiently by the ordinary coasting method, and if a boy felt he had complete mastery over his motor, he was tempted to keep it running beyond its time and then reverse it a few feet from the dock. It took a cool nerve, because if you threw the switch a twentieth of a second too soon you would catch the flywheel when it still had speed enough to go up past center, and the boat would leap ahead, charging bull-fashion at the dock.

We had a good week at the camp. The bass were biting well 11 and the sun shone endlessly, day after day. We would be tired at night and lie down in the accumulated heat of the little bedrooms after the long hot day and the breeze would stir almost imperceptibly outside and the smell of the swamp drift in through the rusty screens. Sleep would come easily and in the morning the red squirrel would be on the roof, tapping out his gay routine. I kept remembering everything, lying in bed in the mornings — the small steamboat that had a long rounded stern like the lip of a Ubangi, and how quietly she ran on the moonlight sails, when the older boys played their mandolins and the girls sang and we ate doughnuts dipped in sugar, and how sweet the music was on the water in the shining night, and what it had felt like to think about girls then. After breakfast we would go up to the store and the things were in the same place — the minnows in a bottle, the plugs and spinners disarranged and pawed over by the youngsters from the boys' camp, the Fig Newtons and the Beeman's gum. Outside, the road was tarred and cars stood in front of the store. Inside, all was just as it had always been, except there was more Coca-Cola and not so much Moxie and root beer and birch beer and sarsaparilla. We would walk out with the bottle of pop apiece and sometimes the pop would backfire up our noses and hurt. We explored the streams, quietly, where the turtles slid off the sunny logs and dug their way into the soft bottom; and we lay on the town wharf and fed worms to the tame bass. Everywhere we went I had trouble making out which was I, the one walking at my side, the one walking in my pants.

One afternoon while we were at that lake a thunderstorm 12 came up. It was like the revival of an old melodrama that I had seen long ago with childish awe. The second-act climax of the drama of the electrical disturbance over a lake in America had not changed in any important respect. This was the big scene, still the big scene. The whole thing was so familiar, the first feeling of oppression and heat and a general air around camp of not wanting to go very far away. In midafternoon (it was all the same) a curious darkening of the sky, and a lull in everything that had made life tick; and then the way the boats suddenly swung the other way at their moorings with the coming of a breeze out of the new quarter, and the premonitory rumble. Then the kettle drum, then the snare, then the bass drum and cymbals, then crackling light against the dark, and the gods grinning and licking their chops in the hills. Afterward the calm, the rain steadily rustling in the calm lake, the return of light and hope and spirits, and the campers running out in joy and relief to go swimming in the rain, their bright cries perpetuating the deathless joke about how they were getting simply drenched, and the children screaming with delight at the new sensation of bathing in the rain, and the joke about getting drenched linking the generations in a strong indestructible chain. And the comedian who waded in carrying an umbrella.

When the others went swimming my son said he was going ₁₃ in, too. He pulled his dripping trunks from the line where they had hung all through the shower and wrung them out. Languidly, and with no thought of going in, I watched him, his hard little body, skinny and bare, saw him wince slightly as he pulled up around his vitals the small, soggy, icy garment. As he buckled the swollen belt, suddenly my groin felt the chill of death.

QUESTIONS ON MEANING

1. How do you account for the distortions that creep into the author's sense of time?
2. What does the discussion of inboard and outboard motors (para. 10) have to do with the author's divided sense of time?
3. To what degree does White make us aware of the impression that this trip to the lake makes on his son?
4. What do you take to be White's main PURPOSE in this essay? At what point do you become aware of it?

QUESTIONS ON WRITING STRATEGY

1. In paragraph 4, the author first introduces his confused feeling that he has gone back in time to his own childhood, an idea that he repeats and expands throughout his account. What is the function of these repetitions?
2. Try to describe the impact of the essay's final paragraph. By what means is it achieved?
3. To what extent is this essay written to appeal to any but middle-aged readers? Is it comprehensible to anyone whose vacations were never spent at a Maine summer cottage?
4. What is the TONE of White's essay?
5. OTHER METHODS. White's essay is both a description and a comparison (Chap. 4) of the lake when he was a boy and when he revisits it with his son. What changes does he find at the lake? What things have stayed the same?

QUESTIONS ON LANGUAGE

1. Be sure you know the meanings of the following words: incessant, placidity (para. 1); gunwale (2); primeval (3); transposition (4); hellgrammite (5); undulating, cultist (6); indelible, tranquil (8); petulant (10); imperceptibly (11); premonitory (12); languidly (13).
2. Comment on White's DICTION in his reference to the lake as "this unique, this holy spot" (para. 2).
3. Explain what White is describing in the sentence that begins, "Then the kettle drum . . ." (para. 12). Where else does the author use METAPHORS?
4. Find effective IMAGES that are not FIGURES OF SPEECH.

SUGGESTIONS FOR WRITING

1. In a descriptive paragraph, try to appeal to each of your reader's five senses.
2. Describe in a brief essay a place you loved as a child. Or, if you have ever returned to a favorite old haunt, describe the experience. Was it pleasant or painful — or both? What, exactly, made it so?
3. CONNECTIONS. As he depicts it in "Once More to the Lake," White experienced a very different childhood from that portrayed by Richard Rodriguez in "Aria: A Memoir of a Bilingual Childhood" (p. 657). After reading Rodriguez's essay, write about the differing childhoods these two men had, focusing on each one's feelings about family, sense of security, and sense of place. Use examples from each essay as EVIDENCE for your ideas. If you want to explore this topic further, use the two essays as the basis for a broader examination of whether and why one experience of childhood is preferable to another.

E. B. WHITE ON WRITING

"You asked me about writing — how I did it," E. B. White replied to a seventeen-year-old who had written to him, wanting to become a professional writer but feeling discouraged. "There is no trick to it. If you like to write and want to write, you write, no matter where you are or what else you are doing or whether anyone pays any heed. I must have written half a million words (mostly in my journal) before I had anything published, save for a couple of short items in *St. Nicholas.*[1] If you want to write about feelings, about the end of the summer, about growing, write about it. A great deal of writing is not 'plotted' — most of my essays have no plot structure, they are a ramble in the woods, or a ramble in the basement of my mind. You ask, 'Who cares?' Everybody cares. You say, 'It's been written before.' Everything has been written before. . . . Henry Thoreau, who wrote *Walden*, said, 'I learned this at least by my experiment: that if one advances confidently in the direction of his dreams and endeavors to live the life which he has imagined, he will meet with a success unexpected in common hours.' The sentence, after more than a hundred years, is still alive. So, advance confidently."

In trying to characterize his own writing, White was modest in his claims. To his brother Stanley Hart White, he once remarked, "I discovered a long time ago that writing of the small things of the day, the trivial matters of the heart, the inconsequential but near things of this living, was the only kind of creative work which I could accomplish with any sincerity or grace. As a reporter, I was a flop, because I always came back laden not with facts about the case, but with a mind full of the little difficulties and amusements I had encountered in my travels. Not till *The New Yorker* came along did I ever find any means of expressing those impertinences and irrelevancies. Thus yesterday, setting out to get a story on how police horses are trained, I ended by writing a story entitled "How Police Horses Are Trained" which never even mentions a police horse, but has to do entirely with my own absurd adventures at police headquarters. The rewards

---

[1]A magazine for children, popular early in the century. — Eds.

of such endeavor are not that I have acquired an audience or a following, as you suggest (fame of any kind being a Pyrrhic victory), but that sometimes in writing of myself — which is the only subject anyone knows intimately — I have occasionally had the exquisite thrill of putting my finger on a little capsule of truth, and heard it give the faint squeak of mortality under my pressure, an antic sound."

FOR DISCUSSION

1. Sometimes young writers are counseled to study the market and then try to write something that will sell. How would you expect E. B. White to have reacted to such advice?
2. What, exactly, does White mean when he says, "Everything has been written before"? How might an aspiring writer take this remark as encouragement?
3. What interesting distinction does White make between reporting and essay writing?

EMILY DICKINSON

For most of her life, EMILY DICKINSON (1830–1886) kept to the shadowy privacy of her family mansion in Amherst, Massachusetts, a farming village and the site of Amherst College. Her father, an eminent lawyer, was for a time a United States congressman. One brief trip to Philadelphia and Washington, two semesters at New England Female Seminary (ending with Emily's refusal to declare herself a Christian despite pressure on her), and a few months with nieces in Cambridge, Massachusetts, while having her eyes treated, were all the poet's travels away from home. Her work on her brilliantly original poems intensified in the years 1858–1862. In later years, Emily Dickinson withdrew more and more from the life of the town into her private thoughts, correspondence with friends, and the society of only her closest family. After her death, her poems were discovered in manuscript (stitched into little booklets), and a first selection was published in 1890. Since then, her personal legend and the devotion of readers have grown vastly and steadily.

A narrow Fellow
in the Grass

In her lifetime, Emily Dickinson published only seven of her more than a thousand poems. "A narrow Fellow in the Grass," one of this handful, was first printed anonymously in 1866 in a newspaper, the *Springfield Republican*. There, without the poet's consent, it was titled "The Snake" and rearranged into eight-line stanzas. Such high-handed treatment seems to have confirmed Dickinson in her dread of publication. For the rest of her life, she preferred to store her poems in the attic. In shape, this poem and most of her others owe much to hymn tunes she had heard in church as a girl. Like "A narrow Fellow in the Grass," about half her poems fall into "common meter": stanzas of four lines, alternating eight syllables and six syllables, the shorter lines rhyming either exactly or roughly. Notice the lively verbs in this poem, its images, its sense of the physical world. On first reading it, Samuel Bowles, the poem's first editor, admiringly wondered aloud: "How did that girl ever know that a boggy field wasn't good for corn?"

A narrow Fellow in the Grass   1
Occasionally rides–
You may have met Him–did you not
His notice sudden is–

The Grass divides as with a Comb–   5
A spotted shaft is seen–
And then it closes at your feet
And opens further on–

He likes a Boggy Acre
A Floor too cool for Corn–   10
Yet when a Boy, and Barefoot–
I more than once at Noon

Have passed, I thought, a Whip lash
Unbraiding in the Sun
When stooping to secure it   15
It wrinkled, and was gone–

Several of Nature's People
I know, and they know me–
I feel for them a transport
Of cordiality–   20

But never met this Fellow
Attended, or alone
Without a tighter breathing
And Zero at the Bone–

QUESTIONS ON MEANING

1. How would you sum up the poet's attitude toward this Fellow? Is she
   playful, serious, or both? Point to lines in the poem to support your
   view.
2. Recast in your own words the thought in Dickinson's lines 17–24.

QUESTIONS ON WRITING STRATEGY

1. By what details does the poet make the snake seem elusive and mysterious?
2. What does the poem gain from the speaker's claim to have once been a barefoot boy? By her PERSONIFICATION of the snake as a Fellow, one of Nature's People?
3. OTHER METHODS. Dickinson is narrating as well as describing her encounters with the snake. What EFFECT does she achieve by using present-tense verbs such as *is* and *closes*?

QUESTIONS ON LANGUAGE

1. Besides PERSONIFICATION, what other FIGURES OF SPEECH enrich this poem?
2. Which pairs of rhyming words chime exactly? Which rhymes seem rough or far out? Dickinson's early editors tried to regularize her inexact rhymes. But how might these rhymes be defended?
3. Can you see any justification for the poet's personal, homemade system of punctuation — the half-dashes?

SUGGESTIONS FOR WRITING

1. What do you feel about snakes? Write a brief essay describing a snake. (If you haven't got one already in mind, go to the zoo or look in a book or tip over a rock.) Agree or disagree with Dickinson's IMAGES if you like.
2. Have you written poetry? Try it now, choosing as your subject an object or animal to describe — something you (like Dickinson) have strong feelings about, such as a favorite tree, a beloved cat, a loathed cockroach. Don't worry too much about meter and rhyme; concentrate instead on images.
3. CONNECTIONS. In two or three paragraphs, analyze Emily Dickinson's and E. B. White's expressions of dread — Dickinson's in lines 23–24 and White's in the last two sentences of "Once More to the Lake" (p. 166). What do their images have in common? How are they different? Which do you find more effective, and why?

EMILY DICKINSON ON WRITING

Although Emily Dickinson never spelled out in detail her methods of writing, her practices are clear to us from the work of scholars who have studied her manuscripts. Evidently she liked to rewrite extensively both poetry and prose, with the result that many poems and some letters exist in multiple versions. Usually, a poem proceeded through three stages: a first, worksheet draft; a semifinal draft; and final copy. Occasionally, in later years, she would return to a poem, tinkering, striving for improvements. (In a few cases, she reduced a previously finished poem to a permanent confusion.)

Her admiration for the work of writer and lecturer Thomas Wentworth Higginson began after he published his "Letter to a Young Contributor" in *The Atlantic Monthly* in 1862. In it, he advised novice writers, "Charge your style with life." Echoing Higginson's remark with approval, Dickinson sent him some of her poems and asked, "Are you too deeply occupied to say if my Verse is alive?" Writers might attain liveliness, Higginson had maintained, by choosing plain words, as few of them as possible. We might expect this advice to find favor with Emily Dickinson, who once wrote:

> A word is dead
> When it is said,
> Some say.
> I say it just
> Begins to live
> That day.

FOR DISCUSSION

1. In what sense might a word "begin to live" when it's said?
2. If *you* had been advised to "charge your style with life," how would you go about it?

ADDITIONAL WRITING TOPICS
Description

1. This is an in-class writing experiment. Describe another person in the room so clearly and unmistakably that when you read your description aloud, your subject will be recognized. (Be OBJECTIVE. No insulting descriptions, please!)
2. Write three paragraphs describing one subject from *each* of the following categories. It will be up to you to make the general subject refer to a particular person, place, or thing. Write at least one paragraph as an OBJECTIVE description and at least one as a SUBJECTIVE description. (Identify your method in each case, so that your instructor can see how well you carry it out.)

   Person

   A friend or roommate
   A typical high-school student
   One of your parents
   An elderly person you know
   A prominent politician
   A historic figure

   Place

   A classroom
   A college campus
   A vacation spot
   A hospital emergency room
   A forest
   A waiting room

   Thing

   A dentist's drill
   A painting or photograph
   A foggy day
   A season of the year
   A musical instrument
   A train

3. In a brief essay, describe your ideal place: an apartment, a bookstore, a dorm room, a vacation spot, a classroom, a restaurant, a

gym, a supermarket or convenience store, a garden, a golf course. With concrete details, try to make the ideal seem actual.

Narration and Description

4. Use a combination of narration and description to develop any one of the following topics:

My first day on the job
My first day at college
Returning to an old neighborhood
Getting lost
A brush with a celebrity
Delivering bad (or good) news

3
EXAMPLE
Pointing to Instances

THE METHOD

"There have been many women runners of distinction," a writer begins, and quickly goes on, "among them Joan Benoit, Mary Decker, Grete Waitz. . . ."

You have just seen examples at work. An *example* (from the Latin *exemplum*: "one thing selected from among many") is an instance that reveals a whole type. By selecting an example, a writer shows the nature or character of the group from which it is taken. In a written essay, an example will often serve to illustrate a general statement, or GENERALIZATION. Here, for instance, the writer Linda Wolfe makes a point about the food fetishes of Roman emperors (Domitian and Claudius ruled in the first century A.D.).

> The emperors used their gastronomical concerns to indicate their contempt of the country and the whole task of governing it. Domitian humiliated his cabinet by forcing them to

attend him at his villa to help solve a serious problem. When they arrived he kept them waiting for hours. The problem, it finally appeared, was that the emperor had just purchased a giant fish, too large for any dish he owned, and he needed the learned brains of his ministers to decide whether the fish should be minced or whether a larger pot should be sought. The emperor Claudius one day rode hurriedly to the Senate and demanded they deliberate the importance of a life without pork. Another time he sat in his tribunal ostensibly administering justice but actually allowing the litigants to argue and orate while he grew dreamy, interrupting the discussions only to announce, "Meat pies are wonderful. We shall have them for dinner."

Wolfe might have allowed the opening sentence of her paragraph — the TOPIC SENTENCE — to remain a vague generalization. Instead, she supports it with three examples, each an anecdote briefly narrating an instance of an emperor's contemptuous behavior. With these examples, Wolfe not only explains and supports her generalization, she animates it.

The method of giving examples — of illustrating what you're saying with a "for instance" — is not merely helpful to practically all kinds of writing, it is indispensable. Bad writers — those who bore us, or lose us completely — often have an ample supply of ideas; their trouble is that they never pull their ideas down out of the clouds. A dull writer, for instance, might declare, "The emperors used food to humiliate their governments," and then, instead of giving examples, go on, "They also manipulated their families," or something — adding still another large, unillustrated idea. Specific examples are *needed* elements in good prose. Not only do they make ideas understandable, but they also keep readers awake. (The previous paragraphs have tried — by giving examples from Linda Wolfe and from "a dull writer" — to illustrate this point.)

THE PROCESS

Where do you find examples? In anything you know — or care to learn. Start close to home. Seek examples in your own immediate knowledge and experience. When assigned an

Example   **179**

elephant-sized subject that you think you know nothing about — ethical dilemmas, for instance — rummage your memory and you may discover that you know more than you thought. In what ethical dilemmas have you ever found yourself? Deciding whether or not to date your best friend's fiancé (or fiancée) when your best friend is out of town? Being tempted to pilfer from the jelly jar of a small boy's Kool-Aid stand when you need a quarter for a bus? No doubt you can supply your own examples. It is the method — exemplifying — that matters. To bring some huge and ethereal concept down to earth may just set your expository faculties galloping over the plains of your own life to the sound of "hi-ho, Silver!" For different examples, you can explore your conversations with others, your studies, and the storehouse of information you have gathered from books, newspapers, magazines, radio, and TV, and from popular hearsay: proverbs and sayings, bits of wisdom you've heard voiced in your family, folklore, popular song.

Now and again, you may feel an irresistible temptation to make up an example out of thin air. This procedure is risky, but can work wonderfully — if, that is, you have a wonder-working imagination. When Henry David Thoreau, in *Walden*, attacks Americans' smug pride in the achievements of nineteenth-century science and industry, he wants to illustrate that kind of invention or discovery "which distracts our attention from serious things." And so he makes up the examples — farfetched, but pointed — of a transatlantic speaking tube and what it might convey: "We are eager to tunnel under the Atlantic and bring the Old World some weeks nearer to the New; but perchance the first news that will leak through into the broad, flapping American ear will be that the Princess Adelaide has the whooping cough."

These examples (and the sarcastic phrase about the American ear) bespeak genius; but, of course, not every writer can be a Thoreau — or needs to be. A hypothetical example may well be better than no example at all; yet, as a rule, an example from fact or experience is likely to carry more weight. Suppose you have to write about the benefits — any benefits — that recent science has conferred upon the nation. You might imagine one such benefit: the prospect of one day being able to vacation in outer space and drift about in free-fall like a soap bubble. That imagined benefit would be all right, but it is obviously a conjecture that you dreamed up without going to the library. Do a little digging in recent books and magazines (for the latter, with the aid of the *Readers' Guide to Periodical Literature*). Your reader will feel better informed to be told that science — specifically, the NASA space program — has produced useful inventions. You add:

> Among these are the smoke detector, originally developed as Skylab equipment; the inflatable air bag to protect drivers and pilots, designed to cushion astronauts in splashdowns; a walk-ing chair that enables paraplegics to mount stairs and travel over uneven ground, derived from the moonwalkers' surface buggy; the technique of cryosurgery, the removal of cancerous tissue by fast freezing.

By using specific examples like these, you render the idea of "ben-efits to society" more concrete and more definite. Such examples are not prettifications of your essay; they are necessary if you are to hold your readers' attention and convince them that you are worth listening to.

When giving examples, you'll find the methods of NARRATION (Chap. 1) and DESCRIPTION (Chap. 2) particularly useful. Some-times, as in the paragraph by Linda Wolfe, an example takes the form of a narrative: a brief story, an ANECDOTE, or a case history. Sometimes it embodies a vivid description of a person, place, or thing. Still another method, ANALOGY, dealt with in Chapter 8, is sometimes invaluable. It uses a familiar, simple example to make an unfamiliar or complicated thing clear.

Lazy writers think, "Oh well, I can't come up with any exam-ple here — I'll just leave it to the reader to find one." The flaw in this assumption is that the reader may be as lazy as the writer. As a result, a perfectly good idea may be left suspended in the strato-sphere. The linguist and writer S. I. Hayakawa tells the story of a professor who, in teaching a philosophy course, spent a whole se-mester on the theory of beauty. When students asked him for a few examples of beautiful paintings, symphonies, or works of na-ture, he refused, saying, "We are interested in principles, not in particulars." The professor himself may well have been interested in principles, but it is a safe bet that his classroom resounded with

Example   **181**

snores. In written exposition, it is undoubtedly the particulars — the pertinent examples — that keep a reader awake and having a good time, and taking in the principles besides.

EXAMPLE IN A PARAGRAPH:
TWO ILLUSTRATIONS
Using Example to Write about Television

To simulate reality must be among television's main concerns, for the airwaves glow with programs that create a smooth and enjoyable imitation of life. Take, for example, wrestling. Stripped to their essentials (and to their gaudy tights), the heroes and villains of TV wrestling matches parade before us like walking abstractions: the Sly Braggart, the Well-Barbered Athlete, the Evil Russian. Larger than life, wrestlers are also louder. They seldom speak; they bellow instead. Part of our enjoyment comes from recognizing the phoniness of it all: When blows fail to land, the intended recipients groan anyway. On Saturday mornings we can even enjoy a simulation of a simulation: a cartoon version of the living sport, *Hulk Hogan's Rock 'n' Wrestling!* Some simulations are less obvious: for instance, the long-running *People's Court.* "What you're about to see is real," a voice-over tells us. In fact, the litigants are not professional actors but people who have filed to appear in a small claims court. Enticed to drop their complaints and instead appear on *People's Court* before the admirably fair Judge Wapner, they play themselves and are rewarded with instant fame and a paycheck. We enjoy the illusion that a genuine legal dispute can be as dramatic as a soap opera. And happily, it can always be settled in exactly ten minutes, between commercials.

COMMENT. To explain the general notion that television often gives us a glossy imitation of life, this paragraph uses three chief examples: wrestling, a cartoon show, and "People's Court." (The examples come from Michael Sorkin's "Faking It," in *Watching Television*, ed. Todd Gitlin [1986].) Inside a brief discussion of wrestling, the writer exemplifies still further, mentioning and inventing names for familiar types of wrestling champions (the Sly Braggart and others). The result is that, in only a few

lines, the intangible idea of simulating life becomes clear and unmistakable. So does the still more abstract idea of simulating a
simulation — thanks to the example of the Hulk Hogan animated
cartoon. Fun to read, these examples also pack weight: They convince us that the writer knows the subject.

Using Example in an Academic Discipline

The primary function of the market is to bring together
suppliers and demanders so that they can trade with one another. Buyers and sellers do not necessarily have to be in face-
to-face contact; they can signal their desires and intentions
through various intermediaries. For example, the demand for
green beans in California is not expressed directly by the green
bean consumers to the green bean growers. People who want
green beans buy them at the grocery store; the store orders
them from a vegetable wholesaler; the wholesaler buys them
from a bean cooperative, whose manager tells local farmers of
the size of the current demand for green beans. The demanders
of green beans are able to signal their demand schedule to the
original suppliers, the farmers who raise the beans, without any
personal communication between the two parties.

COMMENT. Taken from Lewis C. Solmon's *Microeconomics*
(3rd ed., 1980), this paragraph uses a simple example to demonstrate how the market works. By showing step-by-step how green
bean growers are brought together with green bean buyers, the
author can make clear in a single paragraph a concept that
would take much longer to explain in abstract terms — thus doing his audience a favor. Most readers can more easily grasp a
concept when they are shown rather than merely told how it
works. In this case, by personalizing the three intermediaries between the buyers and sellers of green beans, the author lends life
and vigor as well as clarity to his explanation.

BARBARA LAZEAR ASCHER

BARBARA LAZEAR ASCHER was born in 1946 and educated at Bennington College and Cardozo School of Law. She practiced law for two years in a private firm, where she found herself part of a power structure in which those on top resembled "the two-year-old with the biggest plastic pail and shovel on the beach. It's a life of nervous guardianship." Ascher quit the law to devote herself to writing, to explore, as she says, "what really matters." Her essays have appeared in the *New York Times*, the *Yale Review*, *Vogue*, and other periodicals and have been collected in *Playing after Dark* (1987) and *The Habit of Loving* (1989). She lives with her family in New York City.

On Compassion

Ascher often writes about life in New York City, where human problems sometimes seem larger and more stubborn than in other places. But this essay concerns an experience most of us have had, wherever we live: responding to those who need help. First published in *Elle* magazine in 1988, the essay was later reprinted in *The Habit of Loving*. (The essay following this one, Anna Quindlen's "Homeless," addresses the same issue.)

The man's grin is less the result of circumstance than dreams   1
or madness. His buttonless shirt, with one sleeve missing, hangs outside the waist of his baggy trousers. Carefully plaited dreadlocks bespeak a better time, long ago. As he crosses Manhattan's Seventy-ninth Street, his gait is the shuffle of the forgotten ones held in place by gravity rather than plans. On the corner of Madison Avenue, he stops before a blond baby in an Aprica stroller. The baby's mother waits for the light to change and her hands close tighter on the stroller's handle as she sees the man approach.

The others on the corner, five men and women waiting for   2
the crosstown bus, look away. They daydream a bit and gaze into the weak rays of November light. A man with a briefcase lifts and

lowers the shiny toe of his right shoe, watching the light reflect, trying to catch and balance it, as if he could hold and make it his, to ease the heavy gray of coming January, February, and March. The winter months that will send snow around the feet, calves, and knees of the grinning man as he heads for the shelter of Grand Central or Pennsylvania Station.

But for now, in this last gasp of autumn warmth, he is still. 3
His eyes fix on the baby. The mother removes her purse from her shoulder and rummages through its contents: lipstick, a lace handkerchief, an address book. She finds what she's looking for and passes a folded dollar over her child's head to the man who stands and stares even though the light has changed and traffic navigates about his hips.

His hands continue to dangle at his sides. He does not know 4
his part. He does not know that acceptance of the gift and gratitude are what make this transaction complete. The baby, weary of the unwavering stare, pulls its blanket over its head. The man does not look away. Like a bridegroom waiting at the altar, his eyes pierce the white veil.

The mother grows impatient and pushes the stroller before 5
her, bearing the dollar like a cross. Finally, a black hand rises and closes around green.

Was it fear or compassion that motivated the gift? 6

Up the avenue, at Ninety-first Street, there is a small French 7
bread shop where you can sit and eat a buttery, overpriced croissant and wash it down with rich cappuccino. Twice when I have stopped here to stave hunger or stay the cold, twice as I have sat and read and felt the warm rush of hot coffee and milk, an old man has wandered in and stood inside the entrance. He wears a stained blanket pulled up to his chin, and a woolen hood pulled down to his gray, bushy eyebrows. As he stands, the scent of stale cigarettes and urine fills the small, overheated room.

The owner of the shop, a moody French woman, emerges 8
from the kitchen with steaming coffee in a Styrofoam cup, and a small paper bag of . . . of what? Yesterday's bread? Today's croissant? He accepts the offering as silently as he came, and is gone.

Twice I have witnessed this, and twice I have wondered, what 9
compels this woman to feed this man? Pity? Care? Compassion?

Or does she simply want to rid her shop of his troublesome presence? If expulsion were her motivation she would not reward his
arrival with gifts of food. Most proprietors do not. They chase the
homeless from their midst with expletives and threats.

As winter approaches, the mayor of New York City is mov-   10
ing the homeless off the streets and into Bellevue Hospital. The
New York Civil Liberties Union is watchful. They question
whether the rights of these people who live in our parks and doorways are being violated by involuntary hospitalization.

I think the mayor's notion is humane, but I fear it is some-   11
thing else as well. Raw humanity offends our sensibilities. We
want to protect ourselves from an awareness of rags with voices
that make no sense and scream forth in inarticulate rage. We do
not wish to be reminded of the tentative state of our own well-
being and sanity. And so, the troublesome presence is removed
from the awareness of the electorate.

Like other cities, there is much about Manhattan now that   12
resembles Dickensian London. Ladies in high-heeled shoes pick
their way through poverty and madness. You hear more cocktail
party complaints than usual, "I just can't take New York anymore." Our citizens dream of the open spaces of Wyoming, the
manicured exclusivity of Hobe Sound.

And yet, it may be that these are the conditions that finally   13
give birth to empathy, the mother of compassion. We cannot
deny the existence of the helpless as their presence grows. It is impossible to insulate ourselves against what is at our very doorstep.
I don't believe that one is born compassionate. Compassion is
not a character trait like a sunny disposition. It must be learned,
and it is learned by having adversity at our windows, coming
through the gates of our yards, the walls of our towns, adversity
that becomes so familiar that we begin to identify and empathize
with it.

For the ancient Greeks, drama taught and reinforced com-   14
passion within a society. The object of Greek tragedy was to inspire empathy in the audience so that the common response to
the hero's fall was: "There, but for the grace of God, go I." Could
it be that this was the response of the mother who offered the dollar, the French woman who gave the food? Could it be that the

homeless, like those ancients, are reminding us of our common humanity? Of course, there is a difference. This play doesn't end — and the players can't go home.

QUESTIONS ON MEANING

1. What do the two men in Ascher's essay exemplify?
2. What is Ascher's THESIS? What is her PURPOSE?
3. What solution to homelessness is introduced in paragraph 10? What does Ascher think of this possibility?
4. How do you interpret Ascher's last sentence? Is she optimistic or pessimistic about whether people will learn compassion?

QUESTIONS ON WRITING STRATEGY

1. Which comes first, the GENERALIZATIONS or the supporting examples? Why has Ascher chosen this order?
2. What assumptions does the author make about her AUDIENCE?
3. Why do the other people at the bus stop look away (para. 2)? What does Ascher's description of their activities say about them?
4. OTHER METHODS. Ascher explores causes and effects (Chap. 9). Do you agree with her that exposure to others' helplessness increases our compassion? Why, or why not?

QUESTIONS ON LANGUAGE

1. What is the difference between empathy and compassion? Why does Ascher say that "empathy [is] the mother of compassion" (para. 13)?
2. Find definitions for the following words: plaited, dreadlocks, bespeaks (para. 1); stave, stay (7); expletives (9); inarticulate, electorate (11).
3. What are the implications of Ascher's ALLUSION to "Dickensian London"?
4. Examine the language Ascher uses to describe the two homeless men. Is it OBJECTIVE? Sympathetic? Negative?

SUGGESTIONS FOR WRITING

1. Write an essay on the problem of homelessness in your town or city. Use examples to support your view of the problem and a possible solution.
2. Have you had a personal experience with misfortune? Have you needed to beg on the street, been evicted from an apartment, had to scrounge for food? Have you worked in a soup kitchen, been asked for money by beggars, helped in a city hospital? Write an essay on your experience, using examples to convey the effect the experience had on you.
3. Ascher refers to the efforts of New York City to move the homeless off the streets (para. 10). In October 1987, one of New York's homeless, Joyce Brown, was taken off the sidewalk where she lived to Bellevue Hospital. The American Civil Liberties Union sued on her behalf, claiming that she was not a danger to herself or to others — the grounds for involuntary hospitalization. Although Brown was eventually released in January 1988, the issue of the city's right to hospitalize her was never resolved. Consult the *New York Times Index* and the *Times* itself for news articles and editorials on this situation. Write an essay arguing for or against Joyce Brown's freedom to live on the street, supporting your argument with evidence from the newspaper and from your own experience.
4. CONNECTIONS. The next essay, Anna Quindlen's "Homeless," also uses examples to make a point about homelessness. What are some of the differences in the examples each writer uses? In a brief essay, explore whether and how these differences create different TONES in the two works.

ANNA QUINDLEN

Anna Quindlen was born in 1952 and graduated from Barnard College in 1974. She worked as a reporter for the *New York Post* and the *New York Times* before taking over the *Times*'s "About New York" column, serving as the paper's deputy metropolitan editor, and in 1986 creating her own weekly column, "Life in the Thirties." Many of the essays from this popular column were collected in *Living Out Loud* (1988). After taking some time off to care for her third child, in 1989 Quindlen began a weekly op-ed column for the *Times*, on social and political issues. She is also working on her first novel.

Homeless

In this essay from *Living Out Loud*, Quindlen explores the same topic as Barbara Lazear Ascher (p. 183), but with a different slant. Typically for Quindlen, she mingles a reporter's respect for details with a passionate regard for life.

Her name was Ann, and we met in the Port Authority Bus 1 Terminal several Januarys ago. I was doing a story on homeless people. She said I was wasting my time talking to her; she was just passing through, although she'd been passing through for more than two weeks. To prove to me that this was true, she rummaged through a tote bag and a manila envelope and finally unfolded a sheet of typing paper and brought out her photographs.

They were not pictures of family, or friends, or even a dog or 2 cat, its eyes brown-red in the flashbulb's light. They were pictures of a house. It was like a thousand houses in a hundred towns, not suburb, not city, but somewhere in between, with aluminum siding and a chain-link fence, a narrow driveway running up to a one-car garage and a patch of backyard. The house was yellow. I looked on the back for a date or a name, but neither was there. There was no need for discussion. I knew what she was trying to tell me, for it was something I had often felt. She was not adrift, alone, anonymous, although her bags and her raincoat with the

188

grime shadowing its creases had made me believe she was. She had a house, or at least once upon a time had had one. Inside were curtains, a couch, a stove, potholders. You are where you live. She was somebody.

I've never been very good at looking at the big picture, taking   3
the global view, and I've always been a person with an overactive sense of place, the legacy of an Irish grandfather. So it is natural that the thing that seems most wrong with the world to me right now is that there are so many people with no homes. I'm not simply talking about shelter from the elements, or three square meals a day or a mailing address to which the welfare people can send the check — although I know that all these are important for survival. I'm talking about a home, about precisely those kinds of feelings that have wound up in cross-stitch and French knots on samplers over the years.

Home is where the heart is. There's no place like it. I love my   4
home with a ferocity totally out of proportion to its appearance or location. I love dumb things about: the hot-water heater, the plastic rack you drain dishes in, the roof over my head, which occasionally leaks. And yet it is precisely those dumb things that make it what it is — a place of certainty, stability, predictability, privacy, for me and for my family. It is where I live. What more can you say about a place than that? That is everything.

Yet it is something that we have been edging away from grad-   5
ually during my lifetime and the lifetimes of my parents and grandparents. There was a time when where you lived often was where you worked and where you grew the food you ate and even where you were buried. When that era passed, where you lived at least was where your parents had lived and where you would live with your children when you became enfeebled. Then, suddenly where you lived was where you lived for three years, until you could move on to something else and something else again.

And so we have come to something else again, to children   6
who do not understand what it means to go to their rooms because they have never had a room, to men and women whose fantasy is a wall they can paint a color of their own choosing, to old people reduced to sitting on molded plastic chairs, their skin blue-white in the lights of a bus station, who pull pictures of

houses out of their bags. Homes have stopped being homes. Now they are real estate.

People find it curious that those without homes would rather   7
sleep sitting up on benches or huddled in doorways than go to shelters. Certainly some prefer to do so because they are emotionally ill, because they have been locked in before and they are damned if they will be locked in again. Others are afraid of the violence and trouble they may find there. But some seem to want something that is not available in shelters, and they will not compromise, not for a cot, or oatmeal, or a shower with special soap that kills the bugs. "One room," a woman with a baby who was sleeping on her sister's floor, once told me, "painted blue." That was the crux of it; not size or location, but pride of ownership. Painted blue.

This is a difficult problem, and some wise and compassionate   8
people are working hard at it. But in the main I think we work around it, just as we walk around it when it is lying on the sidewalk or sitting in the bus terminal — the problem, that is. It has been customary to take people's pain and lessen our own participation in it by turning it into an issue, not a collection of human beings. We turn an adjective into a noun: the poor, not poor people; the homeless, not Ann or the man who lives in the box or the woman who sleeps on the subway grate.

Sometimes I think we would be better off if we forgot about   9
the broad strokes and concentrated on the details. Here is a woman without a bureau. There is a man with no mirror, no wall to hang it on. They are not the homeless. They are people who have no homes. No drawer that holds the spoons. No window to look out upon the world. My God. That is everything.

QUESTIONS ON MEANING

1. What is Quindlen's THESIS?
2. What distinction is Quindlen making in her CONCLUSION with the sentences "They are not the homeless. They are people without homes"?

3. Why does Quindlen feel a home is so important? Do you agree with her that a home is "everything"?

QUESTIONS ON WRITING STRATEGY

1. Why do you think Quindlen begins with the story of Ann? How else might Quindlen have begun her essay?
2. What is the EFFECT of Quindlen's examples of her own home?
3. What key assumptions does the author make about her AUDIENCE? Are the assumptions reasonable? Where does she specifically address an assumption that might undermine her view?
4. **OTHER METHODS**. Quindlen uses examples to support an argument (Chap. 11). What position does she want readers to recognize and accept?

QUESTIONS ON LANGUAGE

1. What is the EFFECT of "My God" in the last paragraph?
2. How might Quindlen be said to give new meaning to the old CLICHÉ "Home is where the heart is" (para. 4)?
3. What is meant by "crux" (para. 7)? Where does the word come from?

SUGGESTIONS FOR WRITING

1. Describe your living space — house, apartment, or room — in a way that conveys its importance or lack of importance to you.
2. Have you ever moved from one place to another? What sort of experience was it? Write an essay about leaving an old home and moving to a new one. Was there an activity or a piece of furniture that helped ease the transition?
3. Address Quindlen's contention that turning homelessness into an issue avoids the problem, that we might "be better off if we forgot about the broad strokes and concentrated on the details."
4. **CONNECTIONS**. Compare and contrast the views of homelessness and its solution in Quindlen's "Homeless" and Barbara Lazear Ascher's "On Compassion" (p. 183). Use specific passages from each essay to support your comparison.

ANNA QUINDLEN ON WRITING

Anna Quindlen started her writing career as a newspaper reporter. "I had wanted to be a writer for most of my life," she recalls in the introduction to her book, *Living Out Loud*, "and in the service of the writing I became a reporter. For many years I was able to observe, even to feel, life vividly, but at secondhand. I was able to stand over the chalk outline of a body on a sidewalk dappled with black blood; to stand behind the glass and look down into an operating theater where one man was placing a heart in the yawning chest of another; to sit in the park on the first day of summer and find myself professionally obligated to record all the glories of it. Every day I found answers: who, what, when, where, and why."

Quindlen was a good reporter, but the business of finding answers did not satisfy her personally. "In my own life," she continues, "I had only questions." Then she switched from reporter to columnist at the *New York Times*. It was "exhilarating," she says, that "my work became a reflection of my life. After years of being a professional observer of other people's lives, I was given the opportunity to be a professional observer of my own. I was permitted — and permitted myself — to write a column, not about my answers, but about my questions. Never did I make so much sense of my life as I did then, for it was inevitable that as a writer I would find out most clearly what I thought, and what I only thought I thought, when I saw it written down. . . . After years of feeling secondhand, of feeling the pain of the widow, the joy of the winner, I was able to allow myself to feel those emotions for myself."

FOR DISCUSSION

1. What were the advantages and disadvantages of news reporting, according to Quindlen?
2. What does Quindlen feel she can accomplish in a column that she could not accomplish in a news report? What evidence of this difference do you see in her essay "Homeless"?

LANCE MORROW

Lance Morrow has worked at *Time* magazine since 1965, for
many years as a senior writer responsible for dozens of cover
stories and essays. He was born in 1935 in Lewisburg, Pennsylvania, and graduated from Harvard. After a stint as a reporter
for the *Washington Star*, Morrow joined *Time*. His essays for
the magazine earned him a National Magazine Award in 1981
and have been collected in *Fishing in the Tiber* (1988). Morrow
has published two other books: *America: A Rediscovery* (1987)
and *The Chief* (1985), the latter a memoir of his father, Hugh
Morrow, a journalist himself and political consultant. Lance
Morrow lives in New York City.

Advertisements for Oneself

One of Morrow's *Time* essays, "Advertisements for Oneself"
was reprinted in *Fishing in the Tiber*. With typical insight and
liveliness, Morrow studies personal ads — those classifieds for
courtship in the back of magazines.

It is an odd and compact art form, and somewhat unnatural.   1
A person feels quite uncomfortable composing a little song of
himself for the classifieds. The personal ad is like haiku of self-celebration, a brief solo played on one's own horn. Someone else
should be saying these things. It is for others to pile up the extravagant adjectives ("sensitive, warm, witty, vibrant, successful,
handsome, accomplished, incredibly beautiful, cerebral, and sultry") while we stand demurely by. But someone has to do it. One
competes for attention. One must advertise. One must chum the
waters and bait the hook, and go trolling for love and laughter,
for caring and sharing, for long walks and quiet talks, for Bach
and brie. Nonsmokers only. Photo a must.

There are poetic conventions and clichés and codes in com-   2
posing a personal ad. One specifies DWF (divorced white female),

SBM (single black male), GWM (gay white male) and so on, to describe marital status, race, sex. Readers should understand the euphemisms. "Zaftig" or "Rubenesque," for example, usually means fat. "Unpretentious" is liable to mean boring. "Sensuous" means the party likes sex.

Sometimes the ads are quirkily self-conscious. "Ahem," be-   3
gan one suitor in the *New York Review of Books*. "Decent, soft-spoken sort, sanely silly, philosophish, seeks similar." Then he started to hit his stride: "Central Jersey DM WASP professional, 38, 6'2", slow hands, student of movies and Marx, gnosis and news, craves womanish companionship. . . ."

The sociology of personals has changed in recent years. One   4
reason that people still feel uncomfortable with the form is that during the sixties and early seventies personal ads had a slightly sleazy connotation. They showed up in the back of underground newspapers and sex magazines, the little billboards through which wife swappers and odd sexual specialists communicated. In the past several years, however, personal ads have become a pop-ular and reputable way of shopping for new relationships. The *Chicago Tribune* publishes them. So does the conservative *National Review*, although a note from the publisher advises, "*NR* extends maximum freedom in this column, but *NR's* maximum freedom may be another man's straitjacket. *NR* reserves the right to reject any copy deemed unsuitable." *National Review* would likely have turned down a West Coast entreaty: "Kinky Boy Scout seeks Kinky Girl Scout to practice knots. Your rope or mine?" *National Review's* personals are notably chaste, but so are those in most other magazines. The emphasis is on "traditional values," on "long-term relationships" and "nest building." The sexual revolution has cooled down to a domestic room tempera-ture. The raciest item might call for a woman with "Dolly Parton-like figure." One ad in Los Angeles stated: "Branflake patent holder tired of money and what it can buy seeks intellectual stim-ulation from big-bosomed brunette. Photo please." The *Village Voice* rejected the language of a man who wanted a woman with a "big ass." A few days later the man returned with an ad saying he sought a "callipygian" woman.

Every week *New York* magazine publishes five or six pages of   5
personals. The *New York Review of Books* publishes column after

column of some of the most entertaining personals. Many of them are suffused with a soft-focus romanticism. Firelight plays over the fantasy. Everyone seems amazingly successful. The columns are populated by Ph.D.s. Sometimes one encounters a millionaire. Occasionally a satirical wit breaks the monotony: "I am DWM, wino, no teeth, smell bad, age 40 — look 75. Live in good cardboard box in low-traffic alley. You are under 25, tall, sophisticated, beautiful, talented, financially secure, and want more out of life. Come fly with me."

Humor helps, especially in a form that usually gives off a flat   6 glare of one-dimensional optimism. It is hard not to like the "well read, well shaped, well disposed widow, early sixties, not half bad in the dusk with the light behind me." She sought a "companionable, educated, professional man of wit and taste," and she probably deserved him. Her self-effacement is fairly rare in personals. The ads tend sometimes to be a little nervous and needing, and anxiously hyperbolic. Their rhetoric tends to get overheated and may produce unintended effects. A man's hair stands on end a bit when he encounters "Alarmingly articulate, incorrigibly witty, overeducated, but extremely attractive NYC woman." A female reader of *New York* magazine might enjoy a chuckling little shudder at this: "I am here! A caring, knowing, daffy, real, tough, vulnerable, and handsome brown-eyed psychoanalyst." One conjures up the patient on the couch and a Freudian in the shape of Daffy Duck shouting: "You're desPICable!"

The struggle is composing one's ad is to be distinctive and re-   7 lentlessly self-confident. What woman could resist the "rugged rascal with masculine determined sensual viewpoint"? An ad should not overreach, however, like the woman who began: "WANTED: One Greek god of refined caliber."

Not all the ads are jaunty or dewy-eyed. One begins: "Have   8 herpes?" Some are improbably specialized: "Fishing Jewish woman over 50 seeks single man to share delights of angling." Or: "Literate snorkeler . . . have room in my life for one warm, secure, funny man."

Anyone composing a personal ad faces an inherent credibility   9 problem. While we are accustomed to the self-promotions of politicians, say, we sense something bizarre when ordinary people erupt in small rhapsodies of self-celebration that are occasioned by loneliness and longing. One is haunted by almost piteous cries that come with post-office-box number attached: "Is there anyone out there? Anyone out there for me?"

Composing an ad with oneself as the product is an interesting 10 psychological exercise, and probably good training in self-asser-tion. Truth will endure a little decorative writing, perhaps. The personals are a form of courtship that is more efficient, and easier on the liver, than sitting in bars night after night, hoping for a lucky encounter. Yet one feels sometimes a slightly disturbed and forlorn vibration in those columns of chirpy pleading. It is inor-ganic courtship. There is something severed, a lost connection. One may harbor a buried resentment that there are not parents and aunts and churches and cotillions to arrange the meetings in more seemly style.

That, of course, may be mere sentimentalism. Whatever 11 works. Loneliness is the Great Satan. Jane Austen,[1] who knew ev-erything about courtship, would have understood the personals columns perfectly. Her novel *Emma*, in fact, begins, "Emma Woodhouse, handsome, happy, clever, and rich, with a comfort-able home and happy disposition." The line might go right into the *New York Review of Books*.

QUESTIONS ON MEANING

1. What overall GENERALIZATION do Morrow's examples illustrate? What would you say is the essay's THESIS?
2. What do you see as Morrow's PURPOSE in this essay?
3. What reservations does Morrow have about personal ads?

QUESTIONS ON WRITING STRATEGY

1. What is the EFFECT of Morrow's using brief quotations from many ads?
2. Why do you think Morrow often gives the sources of the personal ads he quotes?

[1]Austen (1775–1817) was a great English novelist. — EDS.

3. Do you think Morrow uses or writes personal ads? Do you think he assumes his AUDIENCE does? How does his TONE help you answer these questions?
4. **OTHER METHODS.** Morrow roughly classifies personal ads (Chap. 7). What classes does he identify?

QUESTIONS ON LANGUAGE

1. Define any of the following words you don't know: haiku, cerebral, sultry, demurely (para. 1); euphemisms (2); gnosis (3); entreaty, chaste (4); suffused, satirical (5); effacement, hyperbolic, rhetoric, incorrigibly (6); caliber (7); herpes (8); cotillions (10).
2. What is the meaning of "callipygian" (para. 4)? Where does the word come from?
3. What is the effect of Morrow's many short sentences (for example, in para. 5)?

SUGGESTIONS FOR WRITING

1. According to Morrow, "Composing an ad with oneself as the product is an interesting psychological exercise." It could be a good writing exercise, too. Try your hand at a short paragraph describing yourself as if for a personal ad. Or, if you can't bear to describe yourself, describe a good friend.
2. Study the personal ads in a newspaper or magazine. Create a classification scheme that the ads can be sorted into, and explain and illustrate it in an essay. (See Chapter 7 if you need help with classification.)
3. Have you ever written a personal ad? Do you know people who have? If so, write about such ads (pro or con) from a personal point of view.
4. **CONNECTIONS.** Based on Morrow's essay and your own reading of personal ads, write ads for a sloppy person and a neat person as described in Suzanne Britt's "Neat People vs. Sloppy People" (p. 229) and for the "I" who wants a wife in Judy Brady's essay (p. 342). When writing the ads, convey specific information both about the advertiser and about what he or she wants.

LANCE MORROW ON WRITING

In his introduction to *Fishing in the Tiber*, Lance Morrow discusses the particular demands of the essay, the form he has contributed for well over a decade to *Time* magazine. "The essay is supposed to be a meditative form. Sometimes working for a weekly newsmagazine, one is forced to meditate very fast — in a few hours on deadline on a Friday afternoon, before the magazine's weekly closing. . . . I sometimes even prefer to write that way, a little scared, under the agitation of a deadline. It seems to give some energy to the writing."

The clock is not Morrow's only master; the ruler also governs. "All of us who write for *Time* are forced to discipline ourselves to be concise, to write within the confines of the magazine's available space. . . . Normally one must fit the essay into a page, or two pages, of the magazine. Over the years, I have learned the pace of the form, like a runner who instinctively knows how to run a 220-yard race, as opposed to a 440 or a mile."

FOR DISCUSSION

1. What does Morrow gain by writing "a little scared"? What is "energy" in writing?
2. What might Morrow mean by "the pace of the form"? What information does his comparison with a runner contribute?

BRENT STAPLES

BRENT STAPLES is a member of the editorial board of the *New York Times*. Born in 1951 in Chester, Pennsylvania, Staples has a B.A. in behavioral science from Widener University in Chester and a Ph.D. in psychology from the University of Chicago. Before joining the *New York Times* in 1985, he worked for the *Chicago Sun-Times*, the *Chicago Reader*, *Chicago* magazine, and *Down Beat* magazine. At the *Times*, Staples writes on culture and politics. He also contributes often to the *New York Times Magazine*, *New York Woman*, *Ms.*, and *Harper's*. In 1991 he published *Parallel Time: A Memoir*.

Black Men and Public Space

"Black Men and Public Space" appeared in the December 1987 issue of *Harper's* magazine. It was originally published, in a slightly different version, in *Ms.* magazine (September 1986) under the title "Just Walk on By." The essay relates incidents Staples has experienced "as a night walker in the urban landscape."

My first victim was a woman — white, well dressed, probably in her late twenties. I came upon her late one evening on a deserted street in Hyde Park, a relatively affluent neighborhood in an otherwise mean, impoverished section of Chicago. As I swung onto the avenue behind her, there seemed to be a discreet, uninflammatory distance between us. Not so. She cast back a worried glance. To her, the youngish black man — a broad six feet two inches with a beard and billowing hair, both hands shoved into the pockets of a bulky military jacket — seemed menacingly close. After a few more quick glimpses, she picked up her pace and was soon running in earnest. Within seconds she disappeared into a cross street.

That was more than a decade ago. I was twenty-two years old, a graduate student newly arrived at the University of Chicago. It was in the echo of that terrified woman's footfalls that I first began to know the unwieldy inheritance I'd come into — the ability to alter public space in ugly ways. It was clear that she thought herself the quarry of a mugger, a rapist, or worse. Suffering a bout of insomnia, however, I was stalking sleep, not defenseless wayfarers. As a softy who is scarcely able to take a knife to a raw chicken — let alone hold one to a person's throat — I was surprised, embarrassed, and dismayed all at once. Her flight made me feel like an accomplice in tyranny. It also made it clear that I was indistinguishable from the muggers who occasionally seeped into the area from the surrounding ghetto. That first encounter, and those that followed, signified that a vast, unnerving gulf lay between nighttime pedestrians — particularly women — and me. And I soon gathered that being perceived as dangerous is a hazard in itself. I only needed to turn a corner into a dicey situation, or crowd some frightened, armed person in a foyer somewhere, or make an errant move after being pulled over by a policeman. Where fear and weapons meet — and they often do in urban America — there is always the possibility of death.

In that first year, my first away from my hometown, I was to 3 become thoroughly familiar with the language of fear. At dark, shadowy intersections, I could cross in front of a car stopped at a traffic light and elicit the *thunk, thunk, thunk, thunk* of the driver — black, white, male, or female — hammering down the door locks. On less traveled streets after dark, I grew accustomed to but never comfortable with people crossing to the other side of the street rather than pass me. Then there were the standard unpleasantries with policemen, doormen, bouncers, cabdrivers, and others whose business it is to screen out troublesome individuals *before* there is any nastiness.

I moved to New York nearly two years ago and I have re- 4 mained an avid night walker. In central Manhattan, the near-constant crowd cover minimizes tense one-on-one street encounters. Elsewhere — in SoHo, for example, where sidewalks are narrow and tightly spaced buildings shut out the sky — things can get very taut indeed.

After dark, on the warrenlike streets of Brooklyn where I live, 5 I often see women who fear the worst from me. They seem to have set their faces on neutral, and with their purse straps strung across their chests bandolier-style, they forge ahead as though bracing themselves against being tackled. I understand, of course, that the danger they perceive is not a hallucination. Women are particularly vulnerable to street violence, and young black males are drastically overrepresented among the perpetrators of that violence. Yet these truths are no solace against the kind of alienation that comes of being ever the suspect, a fearsome entity with whom pedestrians avoid making eye contact.

It is not altogether clear to me how I reached the ripe old age   6
of twenty-two without being conscious of the lethality nighttime pedestrians attributed to me. Perhaps it was because in Chester, Pennsylvania, the small, angry industrial town where I came of age in the 1960s, I was scarcely noticeable against a backdrop of gang warfare, street knifings, and murders. I grew up one of the good boys, had perhaps a half-dozen fistfights. In retrospect, my shyness of combat has clear sources.

As a boy, I saw countless tough guys locked away; I have   7
since buried several, too. They were babies, really — a teenage cousin, a brother of twenty-two, a childhood friend in his mid-twenties — all gone down in episodes of bravado played out in the streets. I came to doubt the virtues of intimidation early on. I chose, perhaps unconsciously, to remain a shadow — timid, but a survivor.

The fearsomeness mistakenly attributed to me in public   8
places often has a perilous flavor. The most frightening of these confusions occurred in the late 1970s and early 1980s, when I worked as a journalist in Chicago. One day, rushing into the office of a magazine I was writing for with a deadline story in hand, I was mistaken for a burglar. The office manager called security and, with an ad hoc posse, pursued me through the labyrinthine halls, nearly to my editor's door. I had no way of proving who I was. I could only move briskly toward the company of someone who knew me.

Another time I was on assignment for a local paper and kill-   9
ing time before an interview. I entered a jewelry store on the city's affluent Near North Side. The proprietor excused herself and returned with an enormous red Doberman pinscher straining at the end of a leash. She stood, the dog extended toward me, silent to

my questions, her eyes bulging nearly out of her head. I took a cursory look around, nodded, and bade her good night.

Relatively speaking, however, I never fared as badly as another black male journalist. He went to nearby Waukegan, Illinois, a couple of summers ago to work on a story about a murderer who was born there. Mistaking the reporter for the killer, police officers hauled him from his car at gunpoint and but for his press credentials would probably have tried to book him. Such episodes are not uncommon. Black men trade tales like this all the time.   10

Over the years, I learned to smother the rage I felt at so often being taken for a criminal. Not to do so would surely have led to madness. I now take precautions to make myself less threatening. I move about with care, particularly late in the evening. I give a wide berth to nervous people on subway platforms during the wee hours, particularly when I have exchanged business clothes for jeans. If I happen to be entering a building behind some people who appear skittish, I may walk by, letting them clear the lobby before I return, so as not to seem to be following them. I have been calm and extremely congenial on those rare occasions when I've been pulled over by the police.   11

And on late-evening constitutionals I employ what has proved to be an excellent tension-reducing measure: I whistle melodies from Beethoven and Vivaldi and the more popular classical composers. Even steely New Yorkers hunching toward nighttime destinations seem to relax, and occasionally they even join in the tune. Virtually everybody seems to sense that a mugger wouldn't be warbling bright, sunny selections from Vivaldi's *Four Seasons*. It is my equivalent of the cowbell that hikers wear when they know they are in bear country.   12

QUESTIONS ON MEANING

1. What is the PURPOSE of this essay? Do you think Staples believes that he (or other black men) will cease "to alter public space in ugly ways" in the near future? Does he suggest any long-term solu-

tion for "the kind of alienation that comes of being ever the suspect" (para. 5)?

2. In paragraph 5, Staples says he understands that the danger women fear when they see him "is not a hallucination." Do you take this to mean that Staples perceives himself to be dangerous? Explain.

3. Staples says, "I chose, perhaps unconsciously, to remain a shadow — timid, but a survivor" (para. 7). What are the usual CONNOTATIONS of the word *survivor*? Is "timid" one of them? How can you explain this apparent discrepancy?

QUESTIONS ON WRITING STRATEGY

1. The concept of altering public space is relatively abstract. How does Staples convince you that this phenomenon really takes place?

2. The author employs a large number of examples in a fairly small space. He cites three specific instances that involved him, several general situations, and one incident involving another black male journalist. How does Staples avoid having the piece sound like a list? How does he establish COHERENCE among all these examples? (Look, for example, at TRANSITIONS.)

3. OTHER METHODS. Many of Staples's examples are actually ANECDOTES — brief narratives (Chap. 1). The opening paragraph is especially notable. Why is it so effective?

QUESTIONS ON LANGUAGE

1. What does the author accomplish by using the word *victim* in the essay's first paragraph? Is the word used literally? What TONE does it set for the essay?

2. Be sure you know how to define the following words, as used in this essay: affluent, uninflammatory (para. 1); unwieldy, tyranny, pedestrians (2); intimidation (7); congenial (11); constitutionals (12).

3. The word *dicey* (para. 2) comes from British slang. Without looking it up in your dictionary, can you figure out its meaning from the context in which it appears?

SUGGESTIONS FOR WRITING

1. Write an essay explaining what it means to alter public space, considering these questions along with Staples's essay: Isn't there a certain amount of power implicit in this ability? It seems clear that

Staples would rather not have this power, but would such power always be undesirable? Can you imagine an instance in which the ability to alter public space might be a *good* thing? Whatever your response, be sure to illustrate your answer with specific examples.

2. Are you aware of any incident in which *you* altered public space? That is, where your entry into a situation, or simply your presence, brought about changes in peoples' attitudes or behavior? Write a narrative essay describing this experience. Or write an essay about witnessing someone else altering public space, whether in a negative or positive way. What changes did you observe in the behavior of the people around you? Was your behavior similarly affected? In retrospect, do you feel your reactions were justified?

3. CONNECTIONS. Like Staples, Barbara Lazear Ascher, in "On Compassion" (p. 183), also considers how people regard and respond to "the Other," the one who is regarded as different. In an essay, compare and contrast the POINTS OF VIEW of these two authors. How does point of view affect each author's selection of details and TONE?

BRENT STAPLES ON WRITING

In comments written especially for *The Bedford Reader*, Brent Staples talks about the writing of "Black Men and Public Space." "I was only partly aware of how I felt when I began this essay. I knew only that I had this collection of experiences (facts) and that I felt uneasy with them. I sketched out the experiences one by one and strung them together. The bridge to the essay — what I wanted to say, but did not know when I started — sprang into life quite unexpectedly as I sat looking over these experiences. The crucial sentence comes right after the opening anecdote, in which my first 'victim' runs away from me: 'It was in the echo of that woman's footfalls that I first began to know the unwieldy inheritance I'd come into — the ability to alter public space in ugly ways.' 'Aha!' I said, 'This is why I feel bothered and hurt and frustrated when this happens. I don't want people to think I'm stalking them. I want some fresh air. I want to stretch my legs. I want to be as anonymous as any other person out for a walk in the night.'"

A news reporter and editor by training and trade, Staples sees much similarity between the writing of a personal essay like

"Black Men and Public Space" and the writing of, say, a murder story for a daily newspaper. "The newspaper murder," he says, "begins with standard newspaper information: the fact that the man was found dead in an alley in such-and-such a section of the city; his name, occupation, and where he lived; that he died of gunshot wounds to such-and-such a part of his body; that arrests were or were not made; that such-and-such a weapon was found at the scene; that the police have established no motive; etc.

"Personal essays take a different tack, but they, too, begin as assemblies of facts. In 'Black Men and Public Space,' I start out with an anecdote that crystalizes the issue I want to discuss — what it is like to be viewed as a criminal all the time. I devise a sentence that serves this purpose and also catches the reader's attention: 'My first victim was a woman — white, well dressed, probably in her late twenties.' The piece gives examples that are meant to illustrate the same point and discusses what those examples mean.

"The newspaper story stacks its details in a specified way, with each piece taking a prescribed place in a prescribed order. The personal essay begins often with a flourish, an anecdote, or the recounting of a crucial experience, then goes off to consider related experiences and their meanings. But both pieces rely on reporting. Both are built of facts. Reporting is the act of finding and analyzing facts.

"A fact can be a state of the world — a date, the color of someone's eyes, the arc of a body that flies through the air after having been struck by a car. A fact can also be a feeling — sorrow, grief, confusion, the sense of being pleased, offended, or frustrated. 'Black Men and Public Space' explores the relationship between two sets of facts: (1) the way people cast worried glances at me and sometimes run away from me on the streets after dark, and (2) the frustration and anger I feel at being made an object of fear as I try to go about my business in the city."

Personal essays and news stories share one other quality as well, Staples thinks: They affect the writer even when the writing is finished. "The discoveries I made in 'Black Men and Public Space' continued long after the essay was published. Writing about the experiences gave me access to a whole range of internal concerns and ideas, much the way a well-reported news story opens the door onto a given neighborhood, a situation, or set of issues."

FOR DISCUSSION

1. In recounting how his essay developed, what does Staples reveal about his writing process?
2. How, according to Staples, are essay writing and news writing similar? How are they different?
3. What does Staples mean when he says that "writing about the experiences gave me access to a whole range of internal concerns and ideas"?

EDWARD T. HALL

EDWARD T. HALL is an anthropologist whose research and writing have done much to illuminate the differences and similarities among cultures. Born in 1914 in Webster Groves, Missouri, Hall attended Pomona College and the University of Denver (B.A., 1936), the University of Arizona (M.A., 1938), and Columbia University (Ph.D., 1942). He has conducted anthropological research among Native Americans in the Southwest and among Micronesians in the Pacific. He has worked in and advised both business and government on intercultural relations. And he has taught at the University of Denver, Bennington College, Harvard Business School, the Illinois Institute of Technology, and Northwestern University, where he is now emeritus professor. Besides scholarly publications, Hall has written several books for the general public, notably *The Silent Language* (1959), on nonverbal communication; *The Hidden Dimension* (1966), on human perceptions of space; and *The Dance of Life* (1983), on concepts of time.

Proxemics in the Arab World

In *The Hidden Dimension*, Hall introduced *proxemics*, the study of spatial relations among people and between them and their environment. "Proxemics in the Arab World," a self-contained section of the book, illustrates how concepts of space can cause cultural misunderstandings.

In spite of over two thousand years of contact, Westerners and Arabs still do not understand each other. Proxemic research reveals some insights into this difficulty. Americans in the Middle East are immediately struck by two conflicting sensations. In public they are compressed and overwhelmed by smells, crowding, and high noise levels; in Arab homes Americans are apt to rattle around, feeling exposed and often somewhat inadequate because of too much space! (The Arab houses and apartments of the middle and upper classes which Americans stationed abroad commonly occupy are much larger than the dwellings such Americans usually inhabit.) Both the high sensory stimulation which is experienced in public places and the basic insecurity which comes from being in a dwelling that is too large provide Americans with an introduction to the sensory world of the Arab.

Pushing and shoving in public places is characteristic of Middle Eastern culture. Yet it is not entirely what Americans think it is (being pushy and rude) but stems from a different set of assumptions concerning not only the relations between people but how one experiences the body as well. Paradoxically, Arabs consider northern Europeans and Americans pushy, too. This was very puzzling to me when I started investigating these two views. How could Americans who stand aside and avoid touching be considered pushy? I used to ask Arabs to explain this paradox. None of my subjects was able to tell me specifically what particulars of American behavior were responsible, yet they all agreed that the impression was widespread among Arabs. After repeated unsuccessful attempts to gain insight into the cognitive world of the Arab on this particular point, I filed it away as a question that only time would answer. When the answer came, it was because of a seemingly inconsequential annoyance.

While waiting for a friend in a Washington, D.C., hotel lobby and wanting to be both visible and alone, I had seated myself in a solitary chair outside the normal stream of traffic. In such a setting most Americans follow a rule, which is all the more binding because we seldom think about it, that can be stated as follows: As soon as a person stops or is seated in a public place, there balloons around him a small sphere of privacy which is considered inviolate. The size of the sphere varies with the degree of crowding, the age, sex, and the importance of the person, as well as the general surroundings. Anyone who enters this zone and stays there is intruding. In fact, a stranger who intrudes, even for a specific purpose, acknowledges the fact that he has intruded by beginning his request with "Pardon me, but can you tell me . . . ?"

To continue, as I waited in the deserted lobby, a stranger walked up to where I was sitting and stood close enough so that not only could I easily touch him but I could even hear him breathing. In addition, the dark mass of his body filled the pe-

2

3

4

ripheral field of vision on my left side. If the lobby had been crowded with people, I would have understood his behavior, but in an empty lobby his presence made me exceedingly uncomfortable. Feeling annoyed by this intrusion, I moved my body in such a way as to communicate annoyance. Strangely enough, instead of moving away, my actions seemed only to encourage him, because he moved even closer. In spite of the temptation to escape the annoyance, I put aside thoughts of abandoning my post, thinking, "To hell with it. Why should I move? I was here first and I'm not going to let this fellow drive me out even if he is a boor." Fortunately, a group of people soon arrived whom my tormentor immediately joined. Their mannerisms explained his behavior, for I knew from both speech and gestures that they were Arabs. I had not been able to make this crucial identification by looking at my subject when he was alone because he wasn't talking and he was wearing American clothes.

In describing the scene later to an Arab colleague, two con-   5
trasting patterns emerged. My concept and my feelings about my own circle of privacy in a "public" place immediately struck my Arab friend as strange and puzzling. He said, "After all, it's a public place, isn't it?" Pursuing this line of inquiry, I found that in Arab thought I had no rights whatsoever by virtue of occupying a given spot; neither my place nor my body was inviolate! For the Arab, there is no such thing as an intrusion in public. Public means public. With this insight, a great range of Arab behavior that had been puzzling, annoying, and sometimes even frightening began to make sense. I learned, for example, that if A is standing on a street corner and B wants his spot, B is within his rights if he does what he can to make A uncomfortable enough to move. In Beirut only the hardy sit in the last row in a movie theater, because there are usually standees who want seats and who push and shove and make such a nuisance that most people give up and leave. Seen in this light, the Arab who "intruded" on my space in the hotel lobby had apparently selected it for the very reason I had: It was a good place to watch two doors and the elevator. My show of annoyance, instead of driving him away, had only encouraged him. He thought he was about to get me to move.

Another silent source of friction between Americans and Ar-   6
abs is in an area that Americans treat very informally — the manners and rights of the road. In general, in the United States we
tend to defer to the vehicle that is bigger, more powerful, faster,
and heavily laden. While a pedestrian walking along a road may
feel annoyed he will not think it unusual to step aside for a fast-
moving automobile. He knows that because he is moving he does
not have the right to the space around him that he has when he is
standing still (as I was in the hotel lobby). It appears that the reverse is true with the Arabs who apparently *take on rights to space
as they move.* For someone else to move into a space an Arab is
also moving into is a violation of his rights. It is infuriating to an
Arab to have someone else cut in front of him on the highway. It
is the American's cavalier treatment of moving space that makes
the Arab call him aggressive and pushy.

The experience described above and many others suggested   7
to me that Arabs might actually have a wholly contrasting set of
assumptions concerning the body and the rights associated with
it. Certainly the Arab tendency to shove and push each other in
public and to feel and pinch women in public conveyances would
not be tolerated by Westerners. It appeared to me that they must
not have any concept of a private zone outside the body. This
proved to be precisely the case.

In the Western world, the person is synonymous with an in-   8
dividual inside a skin. And in northern Europe generally, the
skin and even the clothes may be inviolate. You need permission
to touch either if you are a stranger. This rule applies in some
parts of France where the mere touching of another person during an argument used to be legally defined as assault. For the
Arab the location of the person in relation to the body is quite
different. The person exists somewhere down inside the body.
The ego is not completely hidden, however, because it can be
reached very easily with an insult. It is protected from touch but
not from words. The dissociation of the body and the ego may explain why the public amputation of a thief's hand is tolerated as
standard punishment in Saudi Arabia. It also sheds light on why
an Arab employer living in a modern apartment can provide his

servant with a room that is a boxlike cubicle approximately 5 by 10 by 4 feet in size that is not only hung from the ceiling to conserve floor space but has an opening so that the servant can be spied on.

As one might suspect, deep orientations toward the self such 9 as the one just described are also reflected in the language. This was brought to my attention one afternoon when an Arab colleague who is the author of an Arab-English dictionary arrived in my office and threw himself into a chair in a state of obvious exhaustion. When I asked him what had been going on, he said: "I have spent the entire afternoon trying to find the Arab equivalent of the English word 'rape.' There is no such word in Arabic. All my sources, both written and spoken, can come up with no more than an approximation, such as 'He took her against her will.' There is nothing in Arabic approaching your meaning as it is expressed in that one word."

Differing concepts of the placement of the ego in relation to 10 the body are not easily grasped. Once an idea like this is accepted, however, it is possible to understand many other facets of Arab life that would otherwise be difficult to explain. One of these is the high population density of Arab cities like Cairo, Beirut, and Damascus. . . . While it is probable that Arabs are suffering from population pressures, it is also just as possible that continued pressure from the desert has resulted in a cultural adaptation to high density which takes the form described above. Tucking the ego down inside the body shell not only would permit higher population densities but would explain why it is that Arab communications are stepped up as much as they are when compared to northern European communication patterns. Not only is the sheer noise level much higher, but the piercing look of the eyes, the touch of the hands, and the mutual bathing in the warm moist breath during conversation represent stepped-up sensory inputs to a level which many Europeans find unbearably intense.

The Arab dream is for lots of space in the home, which un- 11 fortunately many Arabs cannot afford. Yet when he has space, it is very different from what one finds in most American homes. Arab spaces inside their upper-middle-class homes are tremendous by our standards. They avoid partitions because Arabs *do not like to be alone.* The form of the home is such as to hold the family together inside a single protective shell, because Arabs are deeply involved with each other. Their personalities are intermingled and take nourishment from each other like the roots and soil. If one is not with people and actively involved in some way, one is deprived of life. An old Arab saying reflects this value: "Paradise without people should not be entered because it is Hell." Therefore, Arabs in the United States often feel socially and sensorially deprived and long to be back where there is human warmth and contact.

Since there is no physical privacy as we know it in the Arab   12
family, not even a word for privacy, one could expect that the Arabs might use some other means to be alone. Their way to be alone is to stop talking. Like the English, an Arab who shuts himself off in this way is not indicating that anything is wrong or that he is withdrawing, only that he wants to be alone with his own thoughts or does not want to be intruded upon. One subject said that her father would come and go for days at a time without saying a word, and no one in the family thought anything of it. Yet for this very reason, an Arab exchange student visiting a Kansas farm failed to pick up the cue that his American hosts were mad at him when they gave him the "silent treatment." He only discovered something was wrong when they took him to town and tried forcibly to put him on a bus to Washington, D.C., the headquarters of the exchange program responsible for his presence in the United States.

Like everyone else in the world, Arabs are unable to formu-   13
late specific rules for their informal behavior patterns. In fact, they often deny that there are any rules, and they are made anxious by suggestions that such is the case. Therefore, in order to determine how the Arab sets distances, I investigated the use of each sense separately. Gradually, definite and distinctive behavioral patterns began to emerge.

Olfaction occupies a prominent place in the Arab life. Not   14
only is it one of the distance-setting mechanisms, but it is a vital part of a complex system of behavior. Arabs consistently breathe on people when they talk. However, this habit is more than a

matter of different manners. To the Arab good smells are pleasing and a way of being involved with each other. To smell one's friend is not only nice but desirable, for to deny him your breath is to act ashamed. Americans, on the other hand, trained as they are not to breathe in people's faces, automatically communicate shame in trying to be polite. Who would expect that when our highest diplomats are putting on their best manners they are also communicating shame? Yet this is what occurs constantly, because diplomacy is not only "eyeball to eyeball' but breath to breath.

By stressing olfaction, Arabs do not try to eliminate all the body's odors, only to enhance them and use them in building human relationships. Nor are they self-conscious about telling others when they don't like the way they smell. A man leaving his house in the morning may be told by his uncle, "Habib, your stomach is sour and your breath doesn't smell too good. Better not talk too close to people today." Smell is even considered in the choice of a mate. When couples are being matched for marriage, the man's go-between will sometimes ask to smell the girl, who may be turned down if she doesn't "smell nice." Arabs recognize that smell and disposition may be linked.

In a word, the olfactory boundary performs two roles in Arab life. It enfolds those who want to relate and separates those who don't. The Arab finds it essential to stay inside the olfactory zone as a means of keeping tabs on changes in emotion. What is more, he may feel crowded as soon as he smells something unpleasant. While not much is known about "olfactory crowding," this may prove to be as significant as any other variable in the crowding complex because it is tied directly to the body chemistry and hence to the state of health and emotions. . . . It is not surprising, therefore, that the olfactory boundary constitutes for the Arabs an informal distance-setting mechanism in contrast to the visual mechanisms of the Westerner.

One of my earliest discoveries in the field of intercultural communication was that the position of the bodies of people in conversation varies with the culture. Even so, it used to puzzle me that a special Arab friend seemed unable to walk and talk at the same time. After years in the United States, he could not bring himself to stroll along, facing forward while talking. Our progress would be arrested while he edged ahead, cutting slightly in front of me and turning sideways so we could see each other. Once in this position, he would stop. His behavior was explained when I learned that for the Arabs, to view the other person peripherally is regarded as impolite, and to sit or stand back-to-back is considered very rude. You must be involved when interacting with Arabs who are friends.

One mistaken American notion is that Arabs conduct all 18 conversations at close distances. This is not the case at all. On social occasions, they may sit on opposite sides of the room and talk across the room to each other. They are, however, apt to take offense when Americans use what are to them ambiguous distances, such as the four- to seven-foot social-consultative distance. They frequently complain that Americans are cold or aloof or "don't care." This was what an elderly Arab diplomat in an American hospital thought when the American nurses used "professional" distance. He had the feeling that he was being ignored, that they might not take good care of him. Another Arab subject remarked, referring to American behavior, "What's the matter? Do I smell bad? Or are they afraid of me?"

Arabs who interact with Americans report experiencing a 19 certain flatness traceable in part to a very different use of the eyes in private and in public as well as between friends and strangers. Even though it is rude for a guest to walk around the Arab home eyeing things, Arabs look at each other in ways which seem hostile or challenging to the American. One Arab informant said that he was in constant hot water with Americans because of the way he looked at them without the slightest intention of offending. In fact, he had on several occasions barely avoided fights with American men who apparently thought their masculinity was being challenged because of the way he was looking at them. . . . Arabs look each other in the eye when talking with an intensity that makes most Americans highly uncomfortable.

As the reader must gather by now, Arabs are involved with 20 each other on many different levels simultaneously. Privacy in a public place is foreign to them. Business transactions in the bazaar, for example, are not just between buyer and seller, but are participated in by everyone. Anyone who is standing around may join in. If a grownup sees a boy breaking a window, he must stop him even if he doesn't know him. Involvement and participation are expressed in other ways as well. If two men are fighting, the crowd must intervene. On the political level, *to fail to intervene* when trouble is brewing is to take sides, which is what our State Department always seems to be doing. Given the fact that few people in the world today are even remotely aware of the cultural mold that forms their thoughts it is normal for Arabs to view our behavior as though it stemmed from *their* own hidden set of assumptions.

In the course of my interviews with Arabs the term *tomb* kept   21 cropping up in conjunction with enclosed space. In a word, Arabs don't mind being crowded by people but hate to be hemmed in by walls. They show a much greater overt sensitivity to architectural crowding than we do. Enclosed space must meet at least three requirements that I know of if it is to satisfy the Arabs: There must be plenty of unobstructed space in which to move around (possibly as much as a thousand square feet); very high ceilings — so high in fact that they do not normally impinge on the visual field; and, in addition, there must be an unobstructed view. It was spaces such as these in which the Americans referred to earlier felt so uncomfortable. One sees the Arab's need for a view expressed in many ways, even negatively, for to cut off a neighbor's view is one of the most effective ways of spiting him. In Beirut one can see what is known locally as the "spite house." It is nothing more than a thick, four-story wall, built at the end of a long fight between neighbors, on a narrow strip of land for the express purpose of denying a view of the Mediterranean to any house built on the land behind. According to one of my informants, there is also a house on a small plot of land between Beirut and Damascus which is completely surrounded by a neighbor's wall built high enough to cut off the view from all windows!

Proxemic patterns tell us other things about Arab culture.   22 For example, the whole concept of the boundary as an abstraction is almost impossible to pin down. In one sense, there are no boundaries. "Edges" of towns, yes, but permanent boundaries out in the country (hidden lines), no. In the course of my work with Arab subjects I had a difficult time translating our concept of a boundary into terms which could be equated with theirs. In order to clarify the distinctions between the two very different definitions, I thought it might be helpful to pinpoint acts which constituted trespass. To date, I have been unable to discover anything even remotely resembling our own legal concept of trespass.

Arab behavior in regard to their own real estate is apparently   23
an extension of, and therefore consistent with, their approach to the body. My subjects simply failed to respond whenever trespass was mentioned. They didn't seem to understand what I meant by this term. This may be explained by the fact that they organize relationships with each other according to closed social systems rather than spatially. For thousands of years Moslems, Marinites, Druses, and Jews have lived in their own villages, each with strong kin affiliations. Their hierarchy of loyalties is: first to one's self, then to kinsman, townsman, or tribesman, coreligionist and/ or countryman. Anyone not in these categories is a stranger. Strangers and enemies are very closely linked, if not synonymous, in Arab thought. Trespass in this context is a matter of who you are, rather than a piece of land or a space with a boundary that can be denied to anyone and everyone, friend and foe alike.

In summary, proxemic patterns differ. By examining them it   24
is possible to reveal hidden cultural frames that determine the structure of a given people's perceptual world. Perceiving the world differently leads to differential definitions of what constitutes crowded living, different interpersonal relations, and a different approach to both local and international politics.

QUESTIONS ON MEANING

1. What is Hall's THESIS? What is his PURPOSE?
2. Summarize the key differences Hall sees between Arabs and Westerners.

3. Hall devotes more attention to Arab than to Western perceptions of space. In paragraph 21, what can you infer about Western perceptions and attitudes?

QUESTIONS ON WRITING STRATEGY

1. What kind of examples does Hall use in paragraphs 3–4 and 17? What is their EFFECT?
2. What other kinds of EVIDENCE might Hall have used besides examples? Why do you think he did not?
3. Would this essay be especially helpful to an Arab about to visit the United States? Why, or why not?
4. OTHER METHODS. Hall's essay compares and contrasts (Chap. 4). However, as we noted before, Hall does not give equal time to both cultures. Why is that? Is it a weakness of the essay?

QUESTIONS ON LANGUAGE

1. Would you characterize Hall's writing STYLE as formal or informal? Cite passages from the text to support your opinion.
2. Hall does not try to avoid all technical terms. What do you make of words and phrases such as olfaction (para. 14) and social-consultative distance (18)? Does the occasional technical language help or hurt the essay?
3. Consult your dictionary, if necessary, for the meanings of the following words: sensory (para. 1); paradoxically, cognitive (2); inviolate (3); peripheral, boor (4); cavalier (6); conveyances (7); dissociation (8); sensorially (11); impinge, spiting (21); affiliations, hierarchy, coreligionist (23).

SUGGESTIONS FOR WRITING

1. Write your own essay on proxemics. Compare and contrast the concepts or attitudes toward space of two groups or even two people. Use examples to support your GENERALIZATIONS.
2. Write a narrative about an incident in which you misread the customs in unfamiliar surroundings: a friend's or stranger's home, a new restaurant, a business meeting, a city street, whatever. What was your mistake? How did others react? What did you learn from your mistake?
3. CONNECTIONS. In "America: The Multinational Society" (p. 649), Ishmael Reed claims that the number and variety of ethnic groups

in the United States makes it "unique in the world: The world is here." In your view, is there such a thing as an American culture? Do you think Hall's generalizations about Westerners and particularly Americans are valid today? Taking Reed's essay into account, write an essay of your own in which you answer these questions, supporting your ideas with examples from your reading and experience.

EDWARD T. HALL ON WRITING

Authors commonly thank their spouses in their prefaces, but not often as revealingly as Edward T. Hall does in *The Hidden Dimension*. On the way to acknowledging the assistance of his wife, Mildred Reed Hall, he admits the value of an objective, patient reader between drafts.

"The nature of communication," Hall says, "is such that in its early, ill-defined stages any utterance lies partly revealed on paper while the rest, and often the most essential part, is hidden in the author's mind. He does not know this, however, because in reading his own manuscript he automatically inserts the missing parts. The first need for an author, therefore, is for someone to stick with him and to put up with his exasperated and often hostile response when it is pointed out that he has failed to distinguish clearly between what he knows and what he has written."

FOR DISCUSSION

1. What can this "someone" Hall mentions do for a writer?
2. If you have participated in "collaborative learning" (group work in evaluating and solving problems in writing), what have you gained from it?

ADDITIONAL WRITING TOPICS

Example

1. Select one of the following general statements, or set forth a general statement of your own that one of these inspires. Making it your central idea (or THESIS), maintain it in an essay full of examples. Draw your examples from your reading, your studies, your conversation, or your own experience.

   People one comes to admire don't always at first seem likable.
   Fashions this year are loonier than ever before.
   Bad habits are necessary to the nation's economy.
   Each family has its distinctive life-style.
   Certain song lyrics, closely inspected, will prove obscene.
   Comic books are going to the dogs.
   At some point in life, most people triumph over crushing difficulties.
   Churchgoers aren't perfect.
   TV commercials suggest: Buy this product and your love life will improve like crazy.
   Home cooking can't win over fast food.
   Ordinary lives sometimes give rise to legends.
   Some people I know are born winners (or losers).
   Books can change our lives.
   Certain machines *do* have personalities.
   Some road signs lead drivers astray.

2. In a brief essay, make some GENERALIZATION about either the terrors or the joys that ethnic minorities seem to share. To illustrate your generalization, draw examples from personal experience, from outside reading, or from two or three of the following *Bedford Reader* essays: Maya Angelou's "Champion of the World" and Ralph Ellison's "On Being the Target of Discrimination" in Chapter 1; Brent Staples's "Black Men and Public Space" and Edward T. Hall's "Proxemics in the Arab World" in Chapter 3; Alice Walker's "Oppressed Hair Puts a Ceiling on the Brain" in Chapter 8; Nikki Giovanni's "Pioneers" in Chapter 10; Richard Rodriguez's "Aria," Curtis Chang's "Streets of Gold," and Martin Luther King, Jr.'s "I Have a Dream" in Chapter 11.

4
COMPARISON
AND CONTRAST
Setting Things Side by Side

THE METHOD

Should we pass laws to regulate pornography, or just let pornography run wild? Which team do you place your money on, the Dolphins or the Colts? To go to school full-time or part-time: What are the rewards and drawbacks of each way of life? How do the Republican and the Democratic platforms stack up against each other? How is the work of Picasso like or unlike that of Matisse? These are questions that may be addressed by the dual method of comparison and contrast. In comparing, you point to similar features of the subjects; in contrasting, to different features. (The features themselves you identify by the method of DIVISION or ANALYSIS; see Chapter 6.)

With the aid of comparison and contrast, you can show why you prefer one thing to another, one course of action to another, one idea to another. In an argument in which you support one of two possible choices, a careful and detailed comparison and contrast of the choices may be extremely convincing. In an expository essay, it can demonstrate that you understand your subjects thoroughly. That is why, on exams that call for essay answers, often you will be asked to compare and contrast. Sometimes the examiner will come right out and say, "Compare and contrast nineteenth-century methods of treating drug addiction with those of the present day." Sometimes, however, comparison and contrast won't even be mentioned by name; instead, the examiner will ask, "What resemblances and differences do you find between John Updike's short story 'A & P' and the Grimm fairy tale 'Godfather Death'?" Or, "Evaluate the relative desirability of holding a franchise as against going into business as an independent proprietor." But those — as you realize when you begin to plan your reply — are just other ways of asking you to compare and contrast.

In practice, the two methods are usually inseparable. A little reflection will show you why you need both. Say you intend to write a portrait-in-words of two people. No two people are in every respect exactly the same, or entirely dissimilar. Simply to compare them, or to contrast them, would not be true to life. To set them side by side and portray them accurately, you must consider both similarities and differences.

A good essay in comparing and contrasting serves a purpose. Most of the time, the writer of such an essay has one of two purposes in mind:

1. *The purpose of showing each of two subjects distinctly by considering both, side by side.* Writing with such a purpose, the writer doesn't necessarily find one of the subjects better than the other. In "The Black and White Truth about Basketball" in this chapter, Jeff Greenfield details two styles of playing the game; and his conclusion is not that either "black" or "white" basketball is the more beautiful, but that the two styles can complement each other on the same court.

2. *The purpose of evaluating, or judging between two things.* In daily life, we often compare and contrast two possibilities to choose between them: which college course to elect, which movie to see, which luncheon special to take — chipped beef over green noodles or fried smelt on a bun? Our thinking on a matter such as

the last is quick and informal: "Hmmmm, the smelt *looks* better. Red beef, green noodles — ugh, what a sight! Smelt has bones, but the beef is rubbery. Still, I don't like the smell of that smelt. I'll go for the beef (or maybe just grab a hamburger after class)." In essays, too, a writer, by comparing points, decides which of two things is more admirable: "Organic Gardening, Yes; Gardening with Chemical Fertilizers, No!" — or "Skydiving versus the Safe, Sane Life." In writing, as in thinking, you need to consider the main features of both subjects, the positive features and the negative, and to choose the subject whose positive features more clearly predominate.

THE PROCESS

The first step in comparing and contrasting is to select subjects that will display a clear basis for comparison. In other words, you have to pick two subjects that have enough in common to be worth placing side by side. You'll have the best luck if you choose two of a kind: two California wines, two mystery writers, two schools of political thought. It can sometimes be effective to find similarities between evidently unlike subjects — a city and a country town, say, or liberal and conservative solutions for homelessness — but you must have a valid reason for bringing the two together. From the title of his essay "Grant and Lee," Bruce Catton leads us to expect insights into the characters of the two Civil War generals. But in an essay called "General Grant and Mick Jagger," you would be hard-pressed to find any real basis for comparison. Although you might wax ingenious and claim, "Like Grant, Jagger has posed a definite threat to Nashville," the ingenuity would wear thin and soon the yoking together of general and rock star would fall apart.

The basis for comparison has to be carefully limited. You would be overly ambitious to try to compare and contrast the Soviet way of life with the American way of life in 500 words; you probably couldn't include all the important similarities and differences. In a brief paper, you would be wise to select a single point: to show, for instance, how day care centers in Russia and the United States are both alike and dissimilar.

Students occasionally groan when asked to compare and contrast things; but, in fact, this method isn't difficult. You have only
to plan your paper carefully, make an outline (in your head or on
paper), and then follow it. Here are two common ways to compare and contrast:

1. *Subject by subject.* Set forth all your facts about subject A,
then do the same for subject B. Next, sum up their similarities
and differences. In your conclusion, state what you think you
have shown. This procedure works for a paper of a few paragraphs, but for a longer one, it has a built-in disadvantage. Readers need to remember all the facts about subject A while they read
about subject B. If the essay is long and lists many facts, this procedure may burden the reader.

2. *Point by point.* Usually more workable in writing a long paper than the first method, a different method is to compare and
contrast as you go. You consider one point at a time, taking up
your two subjects alternately. In this way, you continually bring
the subjects together, perhaps in every paragraph. Your outline
might look like this:

TITLE: "Jed and Jake: Two Bluegrass Banjo-pickers"

PURPOSE: To show the distinct identities of the two musicians

INTRODUCTION: Who are Jed and Jake?

1. *Training*

   Jed: studied under Scruggs
   Jake: studied under Segovia

2. *Choice of material*

   Jed: traditional
   Jake: innovative

3. *Technical dexterity*

   Jed: highly skilled
   Jake: highly skilled

4. *Playing style*

   Jed: likes to show off
   Jake: keeps work simple

5. *On-stage manner*

Jed: theatrical
Jake: cool and reserved

CONCLUSION

And your conclusion might be: Although similar in degree of skill, the two differ greatly in aims and in personalities. Jed is better suited to the Grand Ol' Opry; Jake, to a concert hall. Now, this is a more extensive outline than you would need for a brief (say, 250-word) essay; but it might be fine for an essay of seven substantial paragraphs. (If you were writing only 250 words, you might use a subject-by-subject organization, just saying your say about Jed, doing the same for Jake, then concluding.) Another way to organize a longer paper would be to group together all the similarities, then group together all the differences.

No matter how you group your points, they have to balance; you can't discuss Jed's on-stage manner without discussing Jake's too. If you have nothing to say about Jake's on-stage manner, then you might as well omit the point. A sure-fire loser is the paper that proposes to compare and contrast two subjects but then proceeds to discuss quite different elements in each: Jed's playing style and Jake's choice of material, Jed's fondness for smelt on a bun and Jake's hobby of antique car collecting. The writer of such a paper doesn't compare and contrast the two musicians at all, but provides two quite separate discussions.

By the way, a subject-by-subject organization works most efficiently for a *pair* of subjects. If you want to write about *three* banjo-pickers, you might first consider Jed and Jake, then Jake and Josh, then Josh and Jed — but it would probably be easiest to compare and contrast all three point by point.

As you write, an outline will help you see the shape of your paper and keep your procedure in mind. But don't be the simple tool of your outline. Few essays are more boring to read than the long comparison-and-contrast written mechanically. The reader comes to feel like a weary tennis spectator, whose head has to swivel from side to side: now Jed, now back to Jake; now Jed again, now back to Jake again. No law decrees that an outline has to be followed in lock step order, nor that a list of similarities and a list of differences must be of the same length, nor that if you spend fifty words discussing Jed's banjo-picking skill, you are obliged to give Jake his fifty, too. Your essay, remember, doesn't need to be as symmetrical as a pair of salt and pepper shakers. What is your outline but a simple means to organize your account of a complicated reality? As you write, keep casting your thoughts upon a living, particular world — not twisting and squeezing that world into a rigid scheme, but moving through it with open senses, being patient and faithful and exact in your telling of it.

COMPARISON AND CONTRAST
IN A PARAGRAPH: TWO ILLUSTRATIONS
Using Comparison and Contrast
to Write about Television

Seen on aged 16-millimeter film, the original production of Paddy Chayevsky's *Marty* makes clear the differences between television drama of 1953 and that of today. Today there's no weekly Goodyear Playhouse to showcase original one-hour plays; most scriptwriters write serials about familiar characters. *Marty* features no car chases, no bodice ripping, no *Dallas* mansion. Instead, it simply shows the awakening of love between a heavyset butcher and a mousy high-school teacher: both single, lonely, and shy, never twice dating the same person. Unlike the writer of today, Chayevsky couldn't set scenes outdoors or on location. In one small studio, in slow lingering takes (some five minutes long — not eight to twelve seconds, as we now expect), the camera probes the faces of two seated characters as Marty and his pal Angie plan Saturday night ("What do you want to do?" — "I dunno, what do *you?*"). Oddly, the effect is spellbinding. To bring such scenes to life, the actors must project with vigor; and like the finer actors of today, Rod Steiger as Marty exploits each moment. In 1953, plays were telecast live. Today, well-edited videotape may eliminate blown lines, but a chill slickness prevails. Technically, *Marty* is primitive, yet it probes souls. Most televised drama today displays a physically larger world — only to nail a box around it.

COMMENT. The writer of this closely knit paragraph compares and contrasts televised drama of today with drama of television's so-called Golden Age — in particular, *Marty*, an out-standing example. Most of the paragraph is taken up with differences. That both eras of television have actors who make the most of their time on screen is the one similarity noted. In building the paragraph, the writer followed this outline:

1. *Today*: mostly serials
   Then: Goodyear Playhouse, weekly series of new plays
2. *Today*: violence, sex, luxury
   Then: simplicity
3. *Today*: scenes outdoors, on location
   Then: one small studio
4. *Today*: brief takes
   Then: long, slow takes
5. *Today*: good acting
   Then: good acting
6. *Today*: plays videotaped
   Then: plays telecast live
7. *Conclusion*: TV drama today shows a more limited world.

In fulfilling this outline, the writer didn't proceed in a rigid, me-chanical alternation of *Today* and *Then*, but took each point in whatever order came naturally. This is a long outline, as a para-graph so full and meaty required, and it might have sufficed for a whole essay had the writer wanted to compare at greater length with the aid of other examples.

Using Comparison and Contrast in an Academic Discipline

In Russia, too, modernists fell into two camps. They squared off against each other in public debate and in Vkhute-mas, a school of architecture organized in 1920 along lines parallel to the Bauhaus. "The measure of architecture is archi-tecture," went the motto of one camp. They believed in an un-fettered experimentalism of form. The rival camp had a prob-lem-solving orientation. The architect's main mission, in their view, was to share in the common task of achieving the trans-formation of society promised by the October Revolution [of 1917]. They were keen on standardization, user interviews, and ideological prompting. They worked on new building programs that would consolidate the social order of communism. These they referred to as "social condensers."

COMMENT. Taken from *A History of Architecture* by Spiro Kostof (1985), this paragraph explains the key difference in the philosophies of two groups of architects working in Russia just after the Russian Revolution in 1917. Notice how the paragraph is organized: The author first introduces the topic; then, following a subject-by-subject structure, he specifies the views of one group at a time. The discussion of the "problem-solving" group comes last and is more detailed because, as Kostof goes on to discuss, it eventually prevailed.

SUZANNE BRITT

Suzanne Britt was born in Winston-Salem, North Carolina, and studied at Salem College and Washington University, where she earned an M.A. in English. She writes a regular column for *North Carolina Gardens & Homes* and for the *Dickens Dispatch*, a national newsletter for Charles Dickens disciples, and she occasionally contributes to *Books and Religion*, a newspaper of social and theological comment, published by Duke University. Britt has written for the *New York Times*, *Newsweek*, the *Boston Globe*, and many other publications. She teaches English part-time at Meredith College in North Carolina and has published two English textbooks. Her other books are collections of her essays: *Show and Tell* (1983) and *Skinny People Are Dull and Crunchy like Carrots* (1982).

Neat People
vs.
Sloppy People

"Neat People vs. Sloppy People" appears in Britt's collection *Show and Tell*. Mingling humor with seriousness (as she often does), Britt has called the book a report on her journey into "the awful cave of self: You shout your name and voices come back in exultant response, telling you their names." In this essay about certain inescapable personality traits, you may recognize some aspects of your *own* self, awful or otherwise.

I've finally figured out the difference between neat people and sloppy people. The distinction is, as always, moral. Neat people are lazier and meaner than sloppy people.

Sloppy people, you see, are not really sloppy. Their sloppiness is merely the unfortunate consequence of their extreme moral rectitude. Sloppy people carry in their mind's eye a heavenly vision, a precise plan, that is so stupendous, so perfect, it can't be achieved in this world or the next.

Sloppy people live in Never-Never Land. Someday is their   3
métier. Someday they are planning to alphabetize all their books
and set up home catalogs. Someday they will go through their
wardrobes and mark certain items for tentative mending and certain items for passing on to relatives of similar shape and size.
Someday sloppy people will make family scrapbooks into which
they will put newspaper clippings, postcards, locks of hair, and
the dried corsage from their senior prom. Someday they will file
everything on the surface of their desks, including the cash receipts from coffee purchases at the snack shop. Someday they will
sit down and read all the back issues of *The New Yorker.*

For all these noble reasons and more, sloppy people never get   4
neat. They aim too high and wide. They save everything, planning someday to file, order, and straighten out the world. But
while these ambitious plans take clearer and clearer shape in their
heads, the books spill from the shelves onto the floor, the clothes
pile up in the hamper and closet, the family mementos accumulate in every drawer, the surface of the desk is buried under
mounds of paper and the unread magazines threaten to reach the
ceiling.

Sloppy people can't bear to part with anything. They give   5
loving attention to every detail. When sloppy people say they're
going to tackle the surface of the desk, they really mean it. Not a
paper will go unturned; not a rubber band will go unboxed. Four
hours or two weeks into the excavation, the desk looks exactly
the same, primarily because the sloppy person is meticulously creating new piles of papers with new headings and scrupulously
stopping to read all the old book catalogs before he throws them
away. A neat person would just bulldoze the desk.

Neat people are bums and clods at heart. They have cavalier   6
attitudes toward possessions, including family heirlooms. Everything is just another dust-catcher to them. If anything collects
dust, it's got to go and that's that. Neat people will toy with the
idea of throwing the children out of the house just to cut down
on the clutter.

Neat people don't care about process. They like results. What   7
they want to do is get the whole thing over with so they can sit
down and watch the rasslin' on TV. Neat people operate on two

unvarying principles: Never handle any item twice, and throw everything away.

The only thing messy in a neat person's house is the trash   8
can. The minute something comes to a neat person's hand, he will look at it, try to decide if it has immediate use and, finding none, throw it in the trash.

Neat people are especially vicious with mail. They never go   9
through their mail unless they are standing directly over a trash can. If the trash can is beside the mailbox, even better. All ads, catalogs, pleas for charitable contributions, church bulletins and money-saving coupons go straight into the trash can without being opened. All letters from home, postcards from Europe, bills and paychecks are opened, immediately responded to, then dropped in the trash can. Neat people keep their receipts only for tax purposes. That's it. No sentimental salvaging of birthday cards or the last letter a dying relative ever wrote. Into the trash it goes.

Neat people place neatness above everything, even eco-   10
nomics. They are incredibly wasteful. Neat people throw away several toys every time they walk through the den. I knew a neat person once who threw away a perfectly good dish drainer because it had mold on it. The drainer was too much trouble to wash. And neat people sell their furniture when they move. They will sell a La-Z-Boy recliner while you are reclining in it.

Neat people are no good to borrow from. Neat people buy ev-   11
erything in expensive little single portions. They get their flour and sugar in two-pound bags. They wouldn't consider clipping a coupon, saving a leftover, reusing plastic nondairy whipped cream containers or rinsing off tin foil and draping it over the un-moldy dish drainer. You can never borrow a neat person's newspaper to see what's playing at the movies. Neat people have the paper all wadded up and in the trash by 7:05 A.M.

Neat people cut a clean swath through the organic as well as   12
the inorganic world. People, animals, and things are all one to them. They are so insensitive. After they've finished with the pantry, the medicine cabinet, and the attic, they will throw out the red geranium (too many leaves), sell the dog (too many fleas), and send the children off to boarding school (too many scuff-marks on the hardwood floors).

QUESTIONS ON MEANING

1. "Suzanne Britt believes that neat people are lazy, mean, petty, callous, wasteful, and insensitive." How would you respond to this statement?
2. Is the author's main PURPOSE to make fun of neat people, to assess the habits of neat and sloppy people, to help neat and sloppy people get along better, to defend sloppy people, to amuse and entertain, or to prove that neat people are morally inferior to sloppy people? Discuss.
3. What is meant by "as always" in the sentence "The distinction is, as always, moral" (para. 1)? Does the author seem to be suggesting that any and all distinctions between people are moral?

QUESTIONS ON WRITING STRATEGY

1. What is the general TONE of this essay? What words and phrases help you determine that tone?
2. Britt mentions no similarities between neat and sloppy people. Does that mean this is not a good comparison and contrast essay? Why might a writer deliberately focus on differences and give very little or no time to similarities?
3. Consider the following GENERALIZATIONS: "For all these noble reasons and more, sloppy people never get neat" (para. 4) and "The only thing messy in a neat person's house is the trash can" (para. 8). How can you tell that these statements are generalizations? Look for other generalizations in the essay. What is the EFFECT of using so many?
4. OTHER METHODS. Although filled with generalizations, Britt's essay does not lack for examples (Chap. 3). Study the examples in paragraph 11 and explain how they do and don't work the way examples are supposed to, to bring the generalizations about people down to earth.

QUESTIONS ON LANGUAGE

1. Consult your dictionary for definitions of these words: rectitude (para. 2); métier, tentative (3); accumulate (4); excavation, meticulously, scrupulously (5); salvaging (9).

2. How do you understand the use of the word *noble* in the first sentence of paragraph 4? Is it meant literally? Are there other words in the essay that appear to be written in a similar tone?

SUGGESTIONS FOR WRITING

1. Write an essay in which you compare and contrast two apparently dissimilar groups of people: for example, blue-collar workers and white-collar workers, people who write letters and people who don't write letters, runners and football players, readers and TV watchers, or any other variation you choose. Your approach may be either lighthearted or serious, but make sure you come to some conclusion about your subjects. Which group do you favor? Why?
2. Analyze the similarities and differences between two characters in your favorite novel, story, film, or television show. Which aspects of their personalities make them work well together, within the context in which they appear? Which characteristics work against each other, and therefore provide the necessary conflict to hold the readers' or viewers' attention?
3. CONNECTIONS. Write an essay about the humor gained from exaggeration, relying on Britt's essay and James Thurber's "University Days" (p. 64) for examples. Consider why exaggeration is often funny and what qualities humorous exaggeration often has. Use quotations and PARAPHRASES from Britt's and Thurber's essays as your support.

SUZANNE BRITT ON WRITING

Asked to tell how she writes, Suzanne Britt contributed the following comment to *The Bedford Reader.*

"The question 'How do you write?' gets a snappy, snappish response from me. The first commandment is 'Live!' And the second is like unto it: 'Pay attention!' I don't mean that you have to live high or fast or deep or wise or broad. And I certainly don't mean you have to live true and upright. I just mean that you have to suck out all the marrow of whatever you do, whether it's picking the lint off the navy-blue suit you'll be wearing to Cousin Ione's funeral or popping an Aunt Jemimah frozen waffle into the toaster oven or lying between sand dunes, watching the way the sea oats slice the azure sky. The ominous question put to me by students on all occasions of possible accountability is 'Will this count?' My answer is rock bottom and hard: 'Everything counts,' I say, and silence falls like prayers across the room.

"The same is true of writing. Everything counts. Despair is good. Numbness can be excellent. Misery is fine. Ecstasy will work — or pain or sorrow or passion. The only thing that won't work is indifference. A writer refuses to be shocked and appalled by anything going or coming, rising or falling, singing or soundless. The only thing that shocks me, truth to tell, is indifference. How dare you not fight for the right to the crispy end piece on the standing-rib roast? How dare you let the fragrance of Joy go by without taking a whiff of it? How dare you not see the old woman in the snap-front housedress and the rolled-down socks, carrying her Polident and Charmin in a canvas tote that says, simply, elegantly, Le Bag?

"After you have lived, paid attention, seen connections, felt the harmony, writhed under the dissonance, fixed a Diet Coke, popped a big stick of Juicy Fruit in your mouth, gathered your life around you as a mother hen gathers her brood, as a queen settles the folds in her purple robes, you are ready to write. And what you will write about, even if you have one of those teachers who makes you write about, say, Guatemala, will be something very exclusive and intimate — something just between you and Guatemala. All you have to find out is what that small intimacy might be. It is there. And having found it, you have to make it count.

"There is no rest for a writer. But there is no boredom either. A Sunday morning with a bottle of extra-strength aspirin within easy reach and an ice bag on your head can serve you very well in writing. So can a fly buzzing at your ear or a heart-stopping siren in the night or an interminable afternoon in a biology lab in front of a frog's innards.

"All you need, really, is the audacity to believe, with your whole being, that if you tell it right, tell it truly, tell it so we can all see it, the 'it' will play in Peoria, Poughkeepsie, Pompeii, or Podunk. In the South we call that conviction, that audacity, an act of faith. But you can call it writing."

FOR DISCUSSION

1. What advice does Britt offer a student assigned to write a paper about, say, Guatemala? If you were that student, how would you go about taking her advice?
2. Where in her comment does the author use colorful and effective FIGURES OF SPEECH?
3. What is the TONE of Britt's remarks? Sum up her attitude toward her subject, writing.

BRUCE CATTON

Bruce Catton (1899–1978) became America's best-known historian of the Civil War. As a boy in Benzonia, Michigan, Catton acted out historical battles on local playing fields. In his memoir *Waiting for the Morning Train* (1972), he recalls how he would listen by the hour to the memories of Union Army veterans. His studies at Oberlin College interrupted by service in World War I, Catton never finished his bachelor's degree. Instead, he worked as a reporter, columnist, and editorial writer for the *Cleveland Plain Dealer* and other newspapers, then became a speechwriter and information director for government agencies. Of Catton's eighteen books, seventeen were written after his fiftieth year. *A Stillness at Appomattox* (1953) won him both a Pulitzer Prize for history and a National Book Award; other notable works include *This Hallowed Ground* (1956) and *Gettysburg: The Final Fury* (1974). From 1954 until his death, Catton edited *American Heritage*, a magazine of history. President Gerald Ford awarded him a Medal of Freedom for his life's accomplishment.

Grant and Lee:
A Study in Contrasts

"Grant and Lee: A Study in Contrasts" first appeared in *The American Story*, a book of essays written by eminent historians. In his discussion of the two great Civil War generals, Catton contrasts not only two very different men, but the conflicting traditions they represented. Catton's essay builds toward the conclusion that, in one outstanding way, the two leaders were more than a little alike.

When Ulysses S. Grant and Robert E. Lee met in the parlor   1
of a modest house at Appomattox Court House, Virginia, on
April 9, 1865, to work out the terms for the surrender of Lee's
Army of Northern Virginia, a great chapter in American life
came to a close, and a great new chapter began.

These men were bringing the Civil War to its virtual finish. 2
To be sure, other armies had yet to surrender, and for a few days
the fugitive Confederate government would struggle desperately
and vainly, trying to find some way to go on living now that its
chief support was gone. But in effect it was all over when Grant
and Lee signed the papers. And the little room where they wrote
out the terms was the scene of one of the poignant, dramatic contrasts in American history.

They were two strong men, these oddly different generals, 3
and they represented the strengths of two conflicting currents
that, through them, had come into final collision.

Back of Robert E. Lee was the notion that the old aristocratic 4
concept might somehow survive and be dominant in American
life.

Lee was tidewater Virginia, and in his background were fam- 5
ily, culture, and tradition . . . the age of chivalry transplanted to a
New World which was making its own legends and its own
myths. He embodied a way of life that had come down through
the age of knighthood and the English country squire. America
was a land that was beginning all over again, dedicated to nothing much more complicated than the rather hazy belief that all
men had equal rights, and should have an equal chance in the
world. In such a land Lee stood for the feeling that it was somehow of advantage to human society to have a pronounced
inequality in the social structure. There should be a leisure
class, backed by ownership of land; in turn, society itself should
be keyed to the land as the chief source of wealth and influence. It would bring forth (according to this ideal) a class of men
with a strong sense of obligation to the community; men who
lived not to gain advantage for themselves, but to meet the solemn obligations which had been laid on them by the very fact
that they were privileged. From them the country would get its
leadership; to them it could look for the higher values — of
thought, of conduct, of personal deportment — to give it
strength and virtue.

Lee embodied the noblest elements of this aristocratic ideal. 6
Through him, the landed nobility justified itself. For four years,
the Southern states had fought a desperate war to uphold the

ideals for which Lee stood. In the end, it almost seemed as if the Confederacy fought for Lee; as if he himself was the Confederacy . . . the best thing that the way of life for which the Confederacy stood could ever have to offer. He had passed into legend before Appomattox. Thousands of tired, underfed, poorly clothed Confederate soldiers, long-since past the simple enthusiasm of the early days of the struggle, somehow considered Lee the symbol of everything for which they had been willing to die. But they could not quite put this feeling into words. If the Lost Cause, sanctified by so much heroism and so many deaths, had a living justification, its justification was General Lee.

Grant, the son of a tanner on the Western frontier, was everything Lee was not. He had come up the hard way, and embodied nothing in particular except the eternal toughness and sinewy fiber of the men who grew up beyond the mountains. He was one of a body of men who owed reverence and obeisance to no one, who were self-reliant to a fault, who cared hardly anything for the past but who had a sharp eye for the future.   7

These frontier men were the precise opposites of the tidewater aristocrats. Back of them, in the great surge that had taken people over the Alleghenies and into the opening Western country, there was a deep, implicit dissatisfaction with a past that had settled into grooves. They stood for democracy, not from any reasoned conclusion about the proper ordering of human society, but simply because they had grown up in the middle of democracy and knew how it worked. Their society might have privileges, but they would be privileges each man had won for himself. Forms and patterns meant nothing. No man was born to anything, except perhaps to a chance to show how far he could rise. Life was competition.   8

Yet along with this feeling had come a deep sense of belonging to a national community. The Westerner who developed a farm, opened a shop, or set up in business as a trader could hope to prosper only as his own community prospered — and his community ran from the Atlantic to the Pacific and from Canada down to Mexico. If the land was settled, with towns and highways and accessible markets, he could better himself. He saw his fate in terms of the nation's own destiny. As its horizons   9 expanded, so did his. He had, in other words, an acute dollars-and-cents stake in the continued growth and development of his country.

And that, perhaps, is where the contrast between Grant and Lee becomes most striking. The Virginia aristocrat, inevitably, saw himself in relation to his own region. He lived in a static society which could endure almost anything except change. Instinctively, his first loyalty would go to the locality in which that society existed. He would fight to the limit of endurance to defend it, because in defending it he was defending everything that gave his own life its deepest meaning.   10

The Westerner, on the other hand, would fight with an equal tenacity for the broader concept of society. He fought so because everything he lived by was tied to growth, expansion, and a constantly widening horizon. What he lived by would survive or fall with the nation itself. He could not possibly stand by unmoved in the face of an attempt to destroy the Union. He would combat it with everything he had, because he could only see it as an effort to cut the ground out from under his feet.   11

So Grant and Lee were in complete contrast, representing two diametrically opposed elements in American life. Grant was the modern man emerging; beyond him, ready to come on the stage, was the great age of steel and machinery, of crowded cities and a restless, burgeoning vitality. Lee might have ridden down from the old age of chivalry, lance in hand, silken banner fluttering over his head. Each man was the perfect champion of his cause, drawing both his strengths and his weaknesses from the people he led.   12

Yet it was not all contrast, after all. Different as they were — in background, in personality, in underlying aspiration — these two great soldiers had much in common. Under everything else, they were marvelous fighters. Furthermore, their fighting qualities were really very much alike.   13

Each man had, to begin with, the great virtue of utter tenacity and fidelity. Grant fought his way down the Mississippi Valley in spite of acute personal discouragement and profound military handicaps. Lee hung on in the trenches at Petersburg after hope itself had died. In each man there was an indomitable quality . . .   14 the born fighter's refusal to give up as long as he can still remain on his feet and lift his two fists.

Daring and resourcefulness they had, too; the ability to think   15
faster and move faster than the enemy. These were the qualities
which gave Lee the dazzling campaigns of Second Manassas and
Chancellorsville and won Vicksburg for Grant.

Lastly, and perhaps greatest of all, there was the ability, at the   16
end, to turn quickly from war to peace once the fighting was over.
Out of the way these two men behaved at Appomattox came the
possibility of a peace of reconciliation. It was a possibility not
wholly realized, in the years to come, but which did, in the end,
help the two sections to become one nation again . . . after a war
whose bitterness might have seemed to make such a reunion
wholly impossible. No part of either man's life became him more
than the part he played in their brief meeting in the McLean
house at Appomattox. Their behavior there put all succeeding
generations of Americans in their debt. Two great Americans,
Grant and Lee — very different, yet under everything very much
alike. Their encounter at Appomattox was one of the great moments of American history.

QUESTIONS ON MEANING

1. What is Bruce Catton's PURPOSE in writing: to describe the meeting
   of two generals at a famous moment in history; to explain how the
   two men stood for opposing social forces in America; or to show
   how the two differed in personality?
2. Summarize the background and the way of life that produced Robert E. Lee; then do the same for Ulysses S. Grant. According to Catton, what ideals did each man represent?
3. In the historian's view, what essential traits did the two men have in
   common? Which trait does Catton think most important of all? For
   what reason?
4. How does this essay help you understand why Grant and Lee were
   such determined fighters?
5. Although slavery, along with other issues, helped precipitate the
   Civil War, Catton in this particular essay does not deal with it. If he

had recalled the facts of slavery, would he have destroyed his thesis that Lee had a "strong sense of obligation to the community"? (*What* community?)

QUESTIONS ON WRITING STRATEGY

1. From the content of this essay, and from knowing where it first appeared, what can you infer about Catton's original AUDIENCE? At what places in his essay does the writer expect of his readers a great familiarity with United States history?
2. What effect does the writer achieve by setting both his INTRODUCTION and his CONCLUSION in Appomattox?
3. For what reasons does Catton contrast the two generals *before* he compares them? Suppose he had reversed his outline, and had dealt first with Grant and Lee's mutual resemblances. Why would his essay have been less effective?
4. Pencil in hand, draw a single line down the margin of every paragraph in which you find the method of contrast. Then draw a *double* line next to every paragraph in which you find the method of comparison. How much space does Catton devote to each method? Why didn't he give comparison and contrast equal time?
5. Closely read the first sentence of every paragraph and underline each word or phrase in it that serves as a TRANSITION. Then review your underlinings. How much COHERENCE has Catton given his essay?
6. What is the TONE of this essay — that is, what is the writer's attitude toward his two subjects? Is Catton poking fun at Lee by imagining the Confederate general as a knight of the Middle Ages, "lance in hand, silken banner fluttering over his head" (para. 12)?
7. OTHER METHODS. In identifying "two conflicting currents," Catton uses classification (Chap. 7) to sort Civil War–era Americans into two groups represented by Lee and Grant. Catton then uses analysis (Chap. 6) to tease out the characteristics of each current, each type. How do classification and analysis serve Catton's comparison and contrast?

QUESTIONS ON LANGUAGE

1. In his opening paragraph, Catton uses a METAPHOR: American life is a book containing chapters. Find other FIGURES OF SPEECH in his essay. What do they contribute?

2. Look up *poignant* in the dictionary. Why is it such a fitting word in paragraph 2? Why wouldn't *touching*, *sad*, or *teary* have been as good?
3. What information do you glean from the sentence, "Lee was tidewater Virginia" (para. 5)?
4. Define *aristocratic* as Catton uses it in paragraphs 4 and 6.
5. Define *obeisance* (para. 7); *indomitable* (14).

SUGGESTIONS FOR WRITING

1. Compare and contrast two other figures of American history with whom you are familiar: Franklin D. Roosevelt and John F. Kennedy, Lincoln and Douglas, or Susan B. Anthony and Elizabeth Cady Stanton — to suggest only a few.
2. In a brief essay full of specific examples, discuss: Do the "two diametrically opposed elements in American life" (as Catton calls them) still exist in the country today? Are there still any "landed nobility"?
3. In your thinking and your attitudes, whom do you more closely resemble — Grant or Lee? Compare and contrast your outlook with that of one famous American or the other. (A serious tone for this topic isn't required.)
4. CONNECTIONS. Read James Fallows's "Freedom, Control, and Success: Asia and America" (p. 529). Catton and Fallows both address American values and ideals of individualism and community, but their views differ, in part because of their different subjects and time periods (internal conflict versus international competition, the Civil War versus the present). Write an essay discussing which of the qualities that Catton identifies in Grant and in Lee seem, today (according to Fallows), to be working for or against U.S. success in the global economy.

BRUCE CATTON ON WRITING

Most of Bruce Catton's comments on writing, those that have been preserved, refer to the work of others. As editor of *American Heritage*, he was known for his blunt, succinct comments on unsuccessful manuscripts: "This article can't be repaired and wouldn't be much good if it were." Or: "The high-water mark of this piece comes at the bottom of page one, where the naked Indian nymph offers the hero strawberries. Unfortunately, this level is not maintained."

In a memoir published in *Bruce Catton's America* (1979), Catton's associate Oliver Jensen has marveled that, besides editing *American Heritage* for twenty-four years (and contributing to nearly every issue), Catton managed to produce so many substantial books. "Concentration was no doubt the secret, that and getting an early start. For many years Catton was always the first person in the office, so early that most of the staff never knew when he did arrive. On his desk the little piles of yellow sheets grew slowly, with much larger piles in the wastebasket. A neat and orderly man, he preferred to type a new page than correct very much in pencil."

His whole purpose as a writer, Catton once said, was "to reexamine [our] debt to the past."

FOR DISCUSSION

1. To which of Catton's traits does Oliver Jensen attribute the historian's impressive output?
2. Which characteristics of Catton the editor would you expect to have served him well as a writer?

ELLEN GOODMAN

ELLEN GOODMAN was born in Brookline, Massachusetts, in 1941. After her graduation from Radcliffe in 1963, she worked as a reporter-researcher for *Newsweek*; and from 1965 to 1971 she was a reporter for the *Detroit Free Press*. She joined the *Boston Globe* as a full-time columnist in 1971, and her twice-weekly column is now syndicated in more than 400 newspapers across the country. Goodman has earned many honors, among them the 1980 Pulitzer Prize for distinguished commentary. She is the author of *Turning Points* (1979), a study of life changes culled from interviews with over a hundred and fifty people. She has collected her essays in *Close to Home* (1979), *At Large* (1981), *Keeping in Touch* (1985), and *Making Sense* (1989).

Sin, Salvation, and a Good Shrink

When Goodman wrote this essay in March 1988, the television evangelist Jimmy Swaggart was about to be forced to resign his ministry after admitting to an unspecified sin and "moral failure." He followed other televangelists (as they are called for short) who had also resigned because of immoral conduct. The two whom Goodman mentions — Jim Bakker (his wife is Tammy Bakker) and Marvin Gorman — had, ironically, been exposed and denounced by Swaggart less than a year before his own fall. Goodman's essay was reprinted in *Making Sense*.

When Jimmy Swaggart fell from grace, the event resounded as loudly as a golden idol hitting a marble temple floor. The fall, like the rise of this evangelical, made for high televised drama. At its peak, he cried out, "I know that so many of you will ask, 'Why? Why?' I have asked myself that 10,000 times through 10,000 tears." 1

Swaggart had preached mightily against sin, unforgivingly against weaknesses in his brother preachers and bitterly against pornography. "Pornography titillates and captivates the sickest of the sick and makes them slaves to their own consuming lusts . . . 2

ensnares its victims in a living hell," he once wrote. It appears now he knew a good deal about that living hell.

But it wasn't just Swaggart's flock that asked "Why? Why?" as they found out the details — the motel strip he cruised regularly, the $13-an-hour motel room where he is said to have paid a prostitute to perform pornographic acts, all in the shadow of a billboard that reads, "Your Eternity Is at Stake." The most cynical and secular people I know seemed somewhat bewildered. Listing the sex-scandal ministers alphabetically from Jimmy Bakker to Marvin Gorman to Jimmy Swaggart, many of them asked, "What's with these guys?" 3

In the weeks that followed, I watched two distinct sets of answers to that question and to Swaggart's "Why?" emerge. They reveal a split in American society that runs deeper even than the split in Swaggart's life. A split between those who analyze human failings in the terms of psychology and those who analyze them in the terms of scripture. 4

To the millions who worship in Swaggart's church and through his televised ministry, the minister lost a round in the battle between God and the Devil. To the secular millions who've absorbed psychoanalytic terms into their everyday vocabulary, he lost in a battle between the superego and the id. 5

To the first group, he was a sinner. To the second group, he was screwed up. The first group described a struggle between the forces of light and darkness. The second described the subconscious urges that led to the motel strip where he was caught by his arch-rival. 6

These two American cultures spoke in their own distinct languages. Even words like *healing* and *counseling* have different meanings in their dictionaries. If, for example, Jimmy Swaggart's wife had written to Ann Landers that her minister-husband had an obsession with pornography, she would have been directed to "seek help." But it would have been a very different sort than the "counseling" prescribed by the Assemblies of God. As distant as prayer is from psychotherapy. 7

The fundamentalist and therapeutic cultures in this country are not always crisply divided. Confession has much in common with what Freud called "the talking cure." One group's soul is the other's psyche. Most of us are at least somewhat bilingual. The 8 therapeutic language has infiltrated fundamentalist speech, the words of a moral code are rampant in a secular world.

Fundamentalist Tammy Bakker described her use of contributions for personal shopping as "therapy." More than one secular supporter judged Gary Hart's behavior as both a character and a moral flaw, two parts stupid, one part wrong.[1] At their edges, feel-good fundamentalism and feel-good therapy offer the same promises.

But between the hard-core groups, there are more than differences of vocabulary. There are conflicts as great as one's focus on the afterlife and the other's focus on the here and now. Swaggart himself railed against psychology as a modern devil. There are therapists, in turn, who accept everyone and everything except religious self-righteousness.

The gap is particularly great in regard to sex, the centerpiece for the Bakker-Gorman-Swaggart trilogy. Swaggart said more than once, "Victory over flesh does not come easily." But no child of the Freudian era would speak of victory over flesh as if Eros were the enemy of Psyche.[2] Indeed Freud believed that trouble came when sexuality was in conflict with the spirit.

The Swaggart story is the essence of a larger melodrama, played before two American cultures. One that thinks the preacher has been led astray and another that thinks he's a neurotic mess. One thinks he can be saved and the other thinks he could use a good shrink. And it isn't just one congregation in Louisiana that speaks in tongues that sound strange to outsiders.

QUESTIONS ON MEANING

1. Is Goodman's PURPOSE more to explain two perspectives, to evaluate them, or to judge one as preferable to the other?

---

[1]Gary Hart was a front-runner for the Democratic presidential nomination in 1987 when a sex scandal forced him to withdraw from the race. — EDS.

[2]Eros was the Greek god of love. As Cupid in Roman mythology, he was the lover of Psyche. The names symbolize sexual love and spirit, respectively. — EDS.

2. In your own words, what are the "two American cultures" Goodman identifies?
3. What is the role of Jimmy Swaggart in this comparison?

QUESTIONS ON WRITING STRATEGY

1. Is Goodman's comparison organized subject by subject or point by point? What is the advantage of this structure?
2. Which does Goodman do more: compare or contrast? Why, do you think?
3. What assumption about her AUDIENCE does Goodman reveal when she says, "Most of us are at least somewhat bilingual" (para. 8)?
4. Why does Goodman save sex for last?
5. OTHER METHODS. Goodman's comparison rests on examples (Chap. 3). Which examples do you find most effective? Are there places where you would have liked more examples?

QUESTIONS ON LANGUAGE

1. Define any of these words that are unfamiliar: idol, evangelical (para. 1); titillates (2); secular (3); superego, id (5); therapeutic, fundamentalist, rampant (8); trilogy (11); melodrama, neurotic (12).
2. Analyze the words Goodman uses to characterize the views of both groups. What do they contribute to the TONE of the essay?
3. What is the EFFECT of Goodman's quoting and paraphrasing Swaggart to define the fundamentalist position (paras. 2, 10, 11)?

SUGGESTIONS FOR WRITING

1. Goodman maintains that the responses to the Swaggart scandal "reveal a split in American society that runs deeper than the split in Swaggart's life." Do you agree with her observation? Is this split an important division in American society? Write a brief essay responding to Goodman's.
2. Select a difference in outlook or a controversy that you think divides American society into two or more groups. Compare and contrast the groups using examples as support. Try to be OBJECTIVE in your comparison.
3. CONNECTIONS. Read Lewis Thomas's "The Attic of the Brain" (p. 445), which urges that we leave some "untidy" areas of our minds free from the penetration and control of psychological analysis. In an essay, use or dispute the ideas of Goodman and Thomas in your

own argument for or against psychological therapy. Bolster your case with examples from your own experience and reading.

ELLEN GOODMAN ON WRITING

As a newspaper columnist, Ellen Goodman finds she needs "the pacing of a long-distance runner to write day after day, week after week, year after year." In the introduction to *Close to Home*, Goodman notes that her twice-weekly column demands "two opinions a week, although I assure you that some weeks I overflow with ideas, percolate opinions, while other weeks I can't decide what I think about the weather. Moreover, I have to fit these thoughts into a carefully reserved piece of newspaper property. I am allotted approximately the same number of words whether I am writing about life, love, or the world-shattering problem of a zucchini that is sterile."

Goodman does not, however, allow the restrictions to discourage her. "I tend to go through life like a vacuum cleaner," she writes, "inhaling all the interesting tidbits in my path, using almost everything I observe, read, or report." Later, in *Making Sense*, Goodman returns to this point. "The starter dough for many of [my] columns is the daily news. A Washington woman has a forced cesarean. A safe-sex club opens in Michigan. An unwed father asks the Supreme Court for visitation rights. The texts of the times contain at least one necessary ingredient for this work. They tweak my curiosity.

"Most of these columns began with a question: Why? What's going on here? I write to figure that out for myself and others. Why has character become the dominant political theme of the past four years? Why are we less concerned about public morality and more about private ethics? Why do we head into the 1990s still wrestling with the sixties?"

Her columns, Goodman continues, "are my attempts to chronicle and understand changes like these. To put them in context, my own and my country's. . . . In an era of great divides, many of [my] columns seek common ground. They are infused less with a set political perspective than with a set of values. I leave the manufacture of great 'isms' to others. I prefer to use my tools in these modest attempts at making sense."

FOR DISCUSSION

1. What does Goodman mean when she talks about "going through life like a vacuum" and "percolating ideas"? How do her FIGURES OF SPEECH relate to her goals in writing?
2. Goodman gets much inspiration from the news. How does she convert the news into a column?
3. By avoiding dogmatic conclusions in her columns, is Goodman also avoiding commitment to her ideas, is she trying to remain OBJECTIVE, or is her goal something else?

WILLIAM OUCHI

Born in 1943 in Honolulu, WILLIAM OUCHI earned a B.A. from Williams College, an M.B.A. from Stanford University, and a doctorate in business administration from the University of Chicago. He has taught in the graduate business schools at Chicago and Stanford, and he is now a professor in the Graduate School of Management at UCLA. Ouchi is a prominent business consultant, and he has served on the editorial boards of several scholarly journals. His two books for business and general audiences have been published in fourteen languages: *Theory Z: How American Business Can Meet the Japanese Challenge* (1981) and *The M-Form Society: How American Teamwork Can Recapture the Competitive Edge* (1984).

Japanese and American Workers: Two Casts of Mind

"Japanese and American Workers: Two Casts of Mind" (editors' title) is excerpted from *Theory Z*. In the book Ouchi compares Japanese collectivism with American individualism and traces the influence of both traditions on industrial productivity. His thesis is that, with sensitive regard for cultural differences, the best of both worlds can be combined in one excellent system.

Collective Values

Perhaps the most difficult aspect of the Japanese for Western-   1
ers to comprehend is the strong orientation to collective values, particularly a collective sense of responsibility. Let me illustrate with an anecdote about a visit to a new factory in Japan owned and operated by an American electronics company. The American company, a particularly creative firm, frequently attracts attention within the business community for its novel approaches to planning, organizational design, and management systems. As a consequence of this corporate style, the parent company deter-

mined to make a thorough study of Japanese workers and to design a plant that would combine the best of East and West. In
their study they discovered that Japanese firms almost never
make use of individual work incentives, such as piecework or
even individual performance appraisal tied to salary increases.
They concluded that rewarding individual achievement and individual ability is always a good thing.

In the final assembly area of their new plant long lines of   2
young Japanese women wired together electronic products on a
piece-rate system: The more you wired, the more you got paid.
About two months after opening, the head foreladies approached
the plant manager. "Honorable plant manager," they said humbly as they bowed, "we are embarrassed to be so forward, but we
must speak to you because all of the girls have threatened to quit
work this Friday." (To have this happen, of course, would be a
great disaster for all concerned.) "Why," they wanted to know,
"can't our plant have the same compensation system as other Japanese companies? When you hire a new girl, her starting wage
should be fixed by her age. An eighteen-year-old should be paid
more than a sixteen-year-old. Every year on her birthday, she
should receive an automatic increase in pay. The idea that any
one of us can be more productive than another must be wrong,
because none of us in final assembly could make a thing unless all
of the other people in the plant had done their jobs right first. To
single one person out as being more productive is wrong and is
also personally humiliating to us." The company changed its
compensation system to the Japanese model.

Another American company in Japan had installed a sugges-   3
tion system much as we have in the United States. Individual
workers were encouraged to place suggestions to improve productivity into special boxes. For an accepted idea the individual received a bonus amounting to some fraction of the productivity
savings realized from his or her suggestion. After a period of six
months, not a single suggestion had been submitted. The American managers were puzzled. They had heard many stories of the
inventiveness, the commitment, and the loyalty of Japanese
workers, yet not one suggestion to improve productivity had appeared.

The managers approached some of the workers and asked   4
why the suggestion system had not been used. The answer: "No
one can come up with a work improvement idea alone. We work
together, and any ideas that one of us may have are actually developed by watching others and talking to others. If one of us was
singled out for being responsible for such an idea, it would embar-
rass all of us." The company changed to a group suggestion system, in which workers collectively submitted suggestions. Bo-
nuses were paid to groups which would save bonus money until
the end of the year for a party at a restaurant or, if there was
enough money, for family vacations together. The suggestions
and productivity improvements rained down on the plant.

One can interpret these examples in two quite different ways.   5
Perhaps the Japanese commitment to collective values is an
anachronism that does not fit with modern industrialism but
brings economic success despite that collectivism. Collectivism
seems to be inimical to the kind of maverick creativity exemplified
in Benjamin Franklin, Thomas Edison, and John D. Rockefeller.
Collectivism does not seem to provide the individual incentive to
excel which has made a great success of American enterprise. Entirely apart from its economic effects, collectivism implies a loss of
individuality, a loss of the freedom to be different, to hold fundamentally different values from others.

The second interpretation of the examples is that the Japa-   6
nese collectivism is economically efficient. It causes people to
work well together and to encourage one another to better efforts. Industrial life requires interdependence of one person on
another. But a less obvious but far-reaching implication of the
Japanese collectivism for economic performance has to do with
accountability.

In the Japanese mind, collectivism is neither a corporate or   7
individual goal to strive for nor a slogan to pursue. Rather, the
nature of things operates so that nothing of consequence occurs
as a result of individual effort. Everything important in life happens as a result of teamwork or collective effort. Therefore, to attempt to assign individual credit or blame to results is unfounded.
A Japanese professor of accounting, a brilliant scholar trained at
Carnegie-Mellon University who teaches now in Tokyo, re-

marked that the status of accounting systems in Japanese industry is primitive compared to those in the United States. Profit centers, transfer prices, and computerized information systems are barely known even in the largest Japanese companies, whereas they are a commonplace in even small United States organizations. Though not at all surprised at the difference in accounting systems, I was not at all sure that the Japanese were primitive. In fact, I thought their system a good deal more efficient than ours.

Most American companies have basically two accounting systems. One system summarizes the overall financial state to inform stockholders, bankers, and other outsiders. That system is not of interest here. The other system, called the managerial or cost accounting system, exists for an entirely different reason. It measures in detail all of the particulars of transactions between departments, divisions, and key individuals in the organization, for the purpose of untangling the interdependencies between people. When, for example, two departments share one truck for deliveries, the cost accounting system charges each department for part of the cost of maintaining the truck and driver, so that at the end of the year, the performance of each department can be individually assessed, and the better department's manager can receive a larger raise. Of course, all of this information processing costs money, and furthermore may lead to arguments between the departments over whether the costs charged to each are fair.

In a Japanese company a short-run assessment of individual performance is not wanted, so the company can save the considerable expense of collecting and processing all of that information. Companies still keep track of which department uses a truck how often and for what purposes, but like-minded people can interpret some simple numbers for themselves and adjust their behavior accordingly. Those insisting upon clear and precise measurement for the purpose of advancing individual interests must have an elaborate information system. Industrial life, however, is essentially integrated and interdependent. No one builds an automobile alone, no one carries through a banking transaction alone. In a sense the Japanese value of collectivism fits naturally into an industrial setting, whereas the Western individualism provides constant conflicts. The image that comes to mind is of

Chaplin's silent film *Modern Times* in which the apparently insignificant hero played by Chaplin successfully fights against the unfeeling machinery of industry. Modern industrial life can be aggravating, even hostile, or natural: All depends on the fit between our culture and our technology.

A Difference of Tradition

The *shinkansen* or "bullet train" speeds across the rural areas 10 of Japan giving a quick view of cluster after cluster of farmhouses surrounded by rice paddies. This particular pattern did not develop purely by chance, but as a consequence of the technology peculiar to the growing of rice, the staple of the Japanese diet. The growing of rice requires the construction and maintenance of an irrigation system, something that takes many hands to build. More importantly, the planting and the harvesting of rice can only be done efficiently with the cooperation of twenty or more people. The "bottom line" is that a single family working alone cannot produce enough rice to survive, but a dozen families working together can produce a surplus. Thus the Japanese have had to develop the capacity to work together in harmony, no matter what the forces of disagreement or social disintegration, in order to survive.

Japan is a nation built entirely on the tips of giant, suboceanic 11 volcanoes. Little of the land is flat and suitable for agriculture. Terraced hillsides make use of every available square foot of arable land. Small homes built very close together further conserve the land. Japan also suffers from natural disasters such as earthquakes and hurricanes. Traditionally homes are made of light construction materials, so a house falling down during a disaster will not crush its occupants and also can be quickly and inexpensively rebuilt. During the feudal period until the Meiji restoration of 1868, each feudal lord sought to restrain his subjects from moving from one village to the next for fear that a neighboring lord might amass enough peasants with which to produce a large agricultural surplus, hire an army and pose a threat. Apparently bridges were not commonly built across rivers and streams until the late nineteenth century, since bridges increased mobility between villages.

Taken all together, this characteristic style of living paints the 12
picture of a nation of people who are homogeneous with respect
to race, history, language, religion, and culture. For centuries and
generations these people have lived in the same village next door
to the same neighbors. Living in close proximity and in dwellings
which gave very little privacy, the Japanese survived through
their capacity to work together in harmony. In this situation, it
was inevitable that the one most central social value which
emerged, the one value without which the society could not continue, was that an individual does not matter.

To the Western soul this is a chilling picture of society. Sub- 13
ordinating individual tastes to the harmony of the group and
knowing that individual needs can never take precedence over
the interests of all is repellent to the Western citizen. But a frequent theme of Western philosophers and sociologists is that individual freedom exists only when people willingly subordinate
their self-interests to the social interest. A society composed entirely of self-interested individuals is a society in which each person is at war with the other, a society which has no freedom. This
issue, constantly at the heart of understanding society, comes up
in every century, and in every society, whether the writer be
Plato, Hobbes, or B. F. Skinner. The question of understanding
which contemporary institutions lie at the heart of the conflict
between automatism and totalitarianism remains. In some ages,
the kinship group, the central social institution, mediated between these opposing forces to preserve the balance in which freedom was realized; in other times the church or the government
was most critical. Perhaps our present age puts the work organization as the central institution.

In order to complete the comparison of Japanese and Ameri- 14
can living situations, consider flight over the United States. Looking out of the window high over the state of Kansas, we see a pattern of a single farmhouse surrounded by fields, followed by
another single homestead surrounded by fields. In the early 1800s
in the state of Kansas there were no automobiles. Your nearest
neighbor was perhaps two miles distant; the winters were long,
and the snow was deep. Inevitably, the central social values were
self-reliance and independence. Those were the realities of that
place and age that children had to learn to value.

The key to the industrial revolution was discovering that 15
nonhuman forms of energy substituted for human forms could increase the wealth of a nation beyond anyone's wildest dreams.
But there was a catch. To realize this great wealth, nonhuman energy needed huge complexes called factories with hundreds, even
thousands of workers collected into one factory. Moreover, several factories in one central place made the generation of energy
more efficient. Almost overnight, the Western world was transformed from a rural and agricultural country to an urban and industrial state. Our technological advance seems to no longer fit
our social structure: In a sense, the Japanese can better cope with
modern industrialism. While Americans still busily protect our
rather extreme form of individualism, the Japanese hold their individualism in check and emphasize cooperation.

QUESTIONS ON MEANING

1. What reasons does Ouchi give for the Japanese workers' discomfort
   with the piece-rate system?
2. According to Ouchi, what changes did the American plant managers have to make in their suggestion system before the Japanese
   workers would accept it?
3. Explain the differences the author has observed between Japanese
   and American systems of accounting.
4. Sum up Ouchi's view of Japanese collectivism and American individualism as natural outgrowths of each country's history and traditions.
5. Do you think the Japanese approach to work would succeed in the
   American factory system? Why, or why not?

QUESTIONS ON WRITING STRATEGY

1. What is the TONE of Ouchi's essay? How appropriate is the author's
   tone to his subject?
2. To what extent does the EVIDENCE Ouchi introduces into his essay
   justify his CONCLUSION?

3. Who is the writer's probable AUDIENCE? What can you infer about the probable interests, general knowledge, and level of education of his readers?

4. In his comparison, Ouchi devotes more attention to Japanese attitudes and methods than to American. How do you explain this? Is it a flaw in the essay?

5. OTHER METHODS. How does Ouchi use narration in his comparison of Japanese and American business methods? To what extent does the author make use of description and example?

QUESTIONS ON LANGUAGE

1. Examine Ouchi's use of "accountability" in paragraph 6, and "accounting" in paragraphs 7 and 8. Explain the subtle difference in meaning between the two words.

2. Define the following words, referring to your dictionary if necessary: orientation, collective, incentives (para. 1); anachronism, inimical, maverick (5); implication (6); arable (11); homogeneous, proximity, inevitable (12); precedence, repellent (13).

3. What does Ouchi mean by these *isms*: collectivism, industrialism (para. 5); automatism, totalitarianism (13)?

SUGGESTIONS FOR WRITING

1. Marshaling evidence of your own, write a paragraph in which you maintain that American individualism is better preparation for industrialized living than is Japanese collectivism. (Remember, offer EVIDENCE — no Fourth of July oratory, please.)

2. Choose any task: harvesting apples, assembling a wardrobe, organizing a term paper, finding a job, obtaining a neighbor's cooperation. In a brief essay, compare and contrast two approaches to the task and decide which one is better. Give evidence to support your conclusion.

3. CONNECTIONS. James Fallows's "Freedom, Control, and Success" (p. 529) also explores underlying differences between Japan and the United States. Fallows continues where Ouchi leaves off, by examining how the differences affect national economic performance. In a comparison essay drawing on Ouchi's and Fallows's ideas and examples, lay out the differences clearly, point by point. A suggestion: Organize your essay from small to large scale, from the differences in land use discussed by Ouchi (paras. 10–11, 14) to the differences in economic systems discussed by Fallows.

JEFF GREENFIELD

Jeff Greenfield, born in 1943, graduated from the University of Wisconsin and Yale University School of Law. He became a sportswriter, humorist, and media commentator for CBS-TV, and now he is a political and media analyst for ABC News, a regular guest anchor on the news show *Nightline*, and a syndicated columnist. Earlier in his career, he served as a staff aide and writer of speeches for both John V. Lindsay, former mayor of New York City, and the late attorney general Robert F. Kennedy. His books include *A Populist Manifesto* (1972), *Where Have You Gone, Joe DiMaggio?* (1973), *The World's Greatest Team* (history of the Boston Celtics, 1976), *Television: The First 50 Years* (1977), *Playing to Win: An Insider's Guide to Politics* (1980), and *The Real Campaign* (1982).

The Black and White Truth about Basketball

When Jeff Greenfield's survey of "black" and "white" basketball, subtitled "A Skin-Deep Theory of Style," was first published in *Esquire* in 1975, it provoked immediate interest and controversy. Greenfield updated the essay in 1989 for Bedford Books. (His thesis is unchanged.) For a complimentary view of two other American sports—football and baseball—see the essay following this one, by Murray Ross.

The dominance of black athletes over professional basketball 1 is beyond dispute. Two-thirds of the players are black, and the number would be greater were it not for the continuing practice of picking white bench warmers for the sake of balance. Over the last two decades, no more than three white players have been among the ten starting players on the National Basketball Association's All-Star team, and in the last quarter century, only two white players — Dave Cowens and Larry Bird of the Boston Celtics — have ever been chosen as the NBA's Most Valuable Player.

And at a time when a baseball executive can lose his job for 2

258

asserting that blacks lack "the necessities" to become pro sports executives and when the National Football League only in 1989 had its first black head coach, the NBA stands as a pro sports league that hired its first black head coach in 1968 (Bill Russell) and its first black general manager in the early 1970s (Wayne Embry of the Milwaukee Bucks). What discrimination remains—lack of equal opportunity for speaking engagements and product endorsements—has more to do with society than with basketball.

This dominance reflects a natural inheritance: Basketball is a   3 pastime of the urban poor. The current generation of black athletes are heirs to a tradition more than half a century old. In a neighborhood without the money for bats, gloves, hockey sticks and ice skates, or shoulder pads, basketball is an eminently accessible sport. "Once it was the game of the Irish and Italian Catholics in Rockaway and the Jews on Fordham Road in the Bronx," writes David Wolf in his brilliant book, *Foul!* "It was recreation, status, and a way out." But now the ethnic names have been changed: Instead of the Red Holzmans, Red Auerbachs, and the McGuire brothers, there are Julius Ervings and Michael Jordans, Ralph Sampsons and Kareem Abdul-Jabbars. And professional basketball is a sport with national television exposure and million-dollar salaries.

But the mark on basketball of today's players can be measured by more than money or visibility. It is a question of style. For there is a clear difference between "black" and "white" styles of play that is as clear as the difference between 155th Street at Eighth Avenue and Crystal City, Missouri. Most simply (remembering we are talking about culture, not chromosomes), "black" basketball is the use of superb athletic skill to adapt to the limits of space imposed by the game. "White" ball is the pulverization of that space by sheer intensity.[1]

[1]This distinction has nothing to do with the question of whether whites can play as "well" as blacks. In 1987, the Detroit Pistons' Isiah Thomas quipped that the Celtics' Larry Bird was "a pretty good player," but would be much less celebrated and wealthy if he were black. As Thomas later said, Bird is one of the greatest pro players in history. Nor is this distinction about "smart," although the Los Angeles Lakers' Magic Johnson is right in saying that too many journalists ascribe brilliant strategy by black players to be solely due to "innate" ability.

It takes a conscious effort to realize how constricted the space   5
is on a basketball court. Place a regulation court (ninety-four by
fifty feet— on a football field, and it will reach from the back of
the end zone to the twenty-one-yard line; its width will cover less
than a third of the field. On a baseball diamond, a basketball
court will reach from home plate to first base. Compared to its
principal indoor rival, ice hockey, basketball covers about one-
fourth the playing area. Moreover, during the normal flow of the
game, most of the action takes place on the third of the court
nearest the basket. It is in this dollhouse space that ten men, each
of them half a foot taller than the average man, come together to
battle each other.

There is, thus, no room; basketball is a struggle for the edge: 6
the half step with which to cut around the defender for a lay-up,
the half second of freedom with which to release a jump shot, the
instant a head turns allowing a pass to a teammate breaking for
the basket. It is an arena for the subtlest of skills: the head fake,
the shoulder fake, the shift of body weight to the right and the
sudden cut to the left. Deception is crucial to success; and to
young men who have learned early and painfully that life is a battle for survival, basketball is one of the few pursuits in which the
weapon of deception is a legitimate tactic rather than the source
of trouble.

If there is, then, the need to compete in a crowd, to battle for   7
the edge, then the surest strategy is to develop the *unexpected*: to
develop a shot that is simply and fundamentally different from
the usual methods of putting the ball in the basket. Drive to the
hoop, but go under it and come up the other side; hold the ball at
waist level and shoot from there instead of bringing the ball up to
eye level; leap into the air, but fall away from the basket instead of
toward it. All these tactics, which a fan can see embodied in the
astonishing play of the Chicago Bulls' Michael Jordan, take maximum advantage of the crowding on the court. They also stamp
uniqueness on young men who may feel it nowhere else.

"For many young men in the slums," David Wolf writes, "the   8
school yard is the only place they can feel true pride in what they
do, where they can move free of inhibitions and where they can,
by being spectacular, rise for the moment against the drabness

and anonymity of their lives. Thus, when a player develops extraordinary 'school yard' moves and shots . . . [they] become his measure as a man."

So the moves that begin as tactics for scoring soon become 9 calling cards. You don't just lay the ball in for an uncontested basket; you take the ball in both hands, leap as high as you can, and slam the ball through the hoop. When you jump in the air, fake a shot, bring the ball back to your body, and throw up a shot, all without coming back down, you have proven your worth in uncontestable fashion.

This liquid grace is an integral part of "black" ball, almost ex- 10 clusively the province of the playground player. Some white stars like Bob Cousy, Billy Cunningham, and Doug Collins had it, and the Celtics' Kevin McHale has it now: the body control, the moves to the basket, the free-ranging mobility. Most of them also possessed the surface ease that is integral to the "black" style; an incorporation of the ethic of mean streets—to "make it" is not just to have wealth but to have it without strain. Whatever the muscles and organs are doing, the face of the "black" star almost never shows it. Magic Johnson of the Lakers can bring the ball downcourt with two men on him, whip a pass through an invisible opening, cut to the basket, take a return pass, and hit the shot all with no more emotion than a quick smile. So stoic was San Antonio Spurs' great George Gervin that he earned the nickname "Ice Man." (Interestingly, a black coach like former Celtics' coach K. C. Jones exhibited far less emotion on the bench than a white counterpart like Dick Motta or Jack Ramsey.)

If there is a single trait that characterizes "black" ball it is leap- 11 ing ability. Bob Cousy, ex-Celtic great and former pro coach, says that "when coaches get together, one is sure to say, 'I've got the one black kid in the country who can't jump.' When coaches see a white boy who can jump or who moves with extraordinary quickness, they say, 'He should have been born black, he's that good.'"

Don Nelson, now a top executive with the Golden State 12 Warriors, recalls that back in 1970, Dave Cowens, then a relatively unknown graduate of Florida State, prepared for his rookie pro season by playing in the Rucker League, an outdoor competition in Harlem playgrounds that pits pros against college kids and playground stars. So ferocious was Cowens's leaping ability, Nelson says, that "when the summer was over, everyone wanted to know who the white son of a bitch was who could jump so high." That's another way to overcome a crowd around the basket—just go over it.

Speed, mobility, quickness, acceleration, "the moves"—all of 13 these are catch-phrases that surround the "black" playground athlete, the style of play. So does the most racially tinged of attributes, "rhythm." Yet rhythm is what the black stars themselves talk about: feeling the flow of the game, finding the tempo of the dribble, the step, the shot. It is an instinctive quality (although it stems from hundreds of hours of practice), and it is one that has led to difficulty between system-oriented coaches and free-form players. "Cats from the street have their own rhythm when they play," said college dropout Bill Spivey, onetime New York high school star. "It's not a matter of somebody setting you up and you shooting. You *feel* the shot. When a coach holds you back, you lose the feel and it isn't fun anymore."

When legendary Brooklyn playground star Connie Hawkins 14 was winding up his NBA career under Laker coach Bill Sharman, he chafed under the methodical style of play. "He's systematic to the point where it begins to be a little too much. It's such an action-reaction type of game that when you have to do everything the same way, I think you lose something."

There is another kind of basketball that has grown up in 15 America. It is not played on asphalt playgrounds with a crowd of kids competing for the court; it is played on macadam driveways by one boy with a ball and a backboard nailed over the garage; it is played in gyms in the frigid winter of the rural Midwest and on Southern dirt courts. It is a mechanical, precise development of skills (when Don Nelson was an Iowa farm boy, his incentive to make his shots was that an errant rebound would land in the middle of chicken droppings). It is a game without frills, without flow, but with effectiveness. It is "white" basketball: jagged, sweaty, stumbling, intense. Where a "black" player overcomes an obstacle with finesse and body control, a "white" player reacts by outrunning or overpowering the obstacle.

By this definition, the Boston Celtics are a classically "white" 16
team. They rarely suit up a player with dazzling moves; indeed
such a player would probably make Red Auerbach swallow his cigar. Instead, the Celtics wear you down with execution, with constant running, with the same play run again and again and again.
The rebound by Robert Parrish triggers the fast break, as everyone races downcourt; the ball goes to Larry Bird, who pulls up
and takes the shot or who drives and then finds Reggie Lewis or
Kevin McHale free for an easy basket.

Perhaps the most definitively "white" position is that of the 17
quick forward, one without great moves to the basket, without
highly developed shots, without the height and mobility for re-
bounding effectiveness. So what does he do?

He runs. He runs from the opening jump to the final buzzer. 18
He runs up and down the court, from base line to base line, back
and forth under the basket, looking for the opening, the pass, the
chance to take a quick step, the high-percentage shot. To watch
San Antonio's Mark Olberding or Detroit's Bill Lambeer, players
without speed or obvious moves, is to wonder what they are doing in the NBA—until you see them swing free and throw up a
shot that, without demanding any apparent skill, somehow goes
in the basket more frequently than the shots of many of their
more skilled teammates. And to have watched the New York
Knicks' (now U.S. Senator) Bill Bradley, or the Celtics' John
Havlicek, is to have watched "white" ball at its best.

Havlicek or Lambeer, or the Phoenix Suns' Kurt Rambis, 19
stands in dramatic contrast to Michael Jordan or to the Philadelphia 76ers' legend, Julius Erving. Erving had the capacity to make
legends come true, leaping from the foul line and slam-dunking
the ball on his way down; going up for a lay-up, pulling the ball to
his body, and driving under and up the other side of the rim, defying gravity and probability with impossible moves and jumps.
Michael Jordan of the Chicago Bulls has been seen by thousands
spinning a full 360 degrees in midair before slamming the ball
through the hoop.

When John Havlicek played, by contrast, he was the living 20
embodiment of his small-town Ohio background. He would bring
the ball downcourt, weaving left, then right, looking for a path.

He would swing the ball to a teammate, cut behind the pick, take the pass, and release the shot in a flicker of time. It looked plain, unvarnished. But it was a blend of skills that not more than half a dozen other players in the league possessed.

To former pro Jim McMillian, a black who played quick for- 21 ward with "white" attributes, "it's a matter of environment. Julius Erving grew up in a different environment from Havlicek. John came from a very small town in Ohio. There everything was done the easy way, the shortest distance between two points. It's nothing fancy; very few times will he go one-on-one. He hits the layup, hits the jump shot, makes the free throw, and after the game you look up and say, 'How did he hurt us that much?'"

"White" ball, then, is the basketball of patience, method, and 22 sometimes brute strength. "Black" ball is the basketball of electric self-expression. One player has all the time in the world to perfect his skills, the other a need to prove himself. These are slippery categories, because a poor boy who is black can play "white" and a white boy of middle-class parents can play "black." Bill Cartwright of the Chicago Bulls and Steve Alford of the Golden State Warriors are athletes who seem to defy these categories.

And what makes basketball the most intriguing of sports is 23 how these styles do not necessarily clash; how the punishing intensity of "white" players and the dazzling moves of the "blacks" can fit together, a fusion of cultures that seems more and more difficult in the world beyond the out-of-bounds line.

QUESTIONS ON MEANING

1. According to Greenfield, how did black athletes come to dominate professional basketball?
2. What differences does the author discern between "black" and "white" styles of play? How do exponents of the two styles differ in showing emotion?
3. Does Greenfield stereotype black and white players? Where in his essay does he admit there are players who don't fit neatly into his two categories?

4. Do you agree with the author's observations about playing style? Can you think of any EVIDENCE to the contrary?

QUESTIONS ON WRITING STRATEGY

1. How much do we have to know about professional basketball to appreciate Greenfield's essay? Is it written only for basketball fans, or for a general AUDIENCE?
2. In what passage in his essay does Greenfield begin comparing and contrasting? What is the function of the paragraphs that come before this passage?
3. In paragraph 5 the author compares a basketball court to a football field, a baseball diamond, and an ice hockey arena. What is the basis for his comparison?
4. OTHER METHODS. In addition to comparison and contrast and a good deal of description (Chap. 2), Greenfield uses cause and effect (Chap. 9) when he accounts for the differences in playing style. Sum up in your own words the author's point about school yards (para. 8) and his point about macadam driveways, gyms, and dirt courts (para. 15). Explain "the ethic of mean streets" (para. 10).

QUESTIONS ON LANGUAGE

1. Consult the dictionary if you need help in defining the following words: ethnic (para. 3); constricted (5); inhibitions, anonymity (8); uncontestable (9); finesse (15); execution (16); embodiment (20).
2. Talk to someone who knows basketball if you need help in understanding the head fake, the shoulder fake (para. 6); fast break (16); high-percentage shot (18); jump shot (21). What kind of DICTION do you find in these instances?
3. When Greenfield says, "We are talking about culture, not chromosomes" (para. 4), how would you expect him to define these terms?
4. Explain the author's reference to the word *rhythm* as "the most racially tinged of attributes" (para. 13).

SUGGESTIONS FOR WRITING

1. In a paragraph or two, discuss how well you think Greenfield has surmounted the difficulties facing any writer who makes GENERALIZATIONS about people.

2. Compare and contrast a college basketball and professional basketball team, or the styles of two athletes in any sport.

3. Compare and contrast the styles of two people in the same line of work, showing how their work is affected by their different personalities. You might take, for instance, two singers, two taxi drivers, two bank tellers, two evangelists, two teachers, or two symphony orchestra conductors.

4. CONNECTIONS. The following essay, Murray Ross's "Football Red and Baseball Green," proposes that "each sport contains a fundamental myth which it elaborates for its fans." First, read Ross's essay so that you understand just what he means by the myths in sports. Then write your own interpretation of the myths represented by the "black" and "white" styles of basketball play; or, if you prefer, write about the myth represented by the entire sport of basketball.

JEFF GREENFIELD ON WRITING

For *The Bedford Reader*, Jeff Greenfield told how he gathered his information for "The Black and White Truth about Basketball" from basketball professionals, and how he tried to contrast the two styles of play with humor and goodwill. "In the early 1970s," he commented, "I was spending a good deal of time playing hookey from my work as a political consultant writing books and magazine articles; and no writing was more enjoyable than sports reporting. . . . Coming from the world of politics where everything was debatable — who would win, whose position was right, who was engaging in 'desperation smear tactics' — I relished the world of sports, where winners and losers were clearly identifiable. . . .

"It was while writing about various star basketball players of the time — men like the New York Knicks' Willis Reed, the Boston Celtics' Dave Cowens — that I first began noticing how often offhand, utterly unmalicious racial references were being thrown about. A white player in practice would miss a rebound, and a black teammate would joke, 'Come on, man, jump like a brother.' A black player would lose a footrace for a ball, and someone would quip, 'Looks black, plays white.' It slowly became

clear to me that many of those in the basketball world freely acknowledged that there were different styles of play that broke
down, roughly speaking, into black and white characteristics.

"At first, it did not even occur to me that this would make a
publishable magazine piece. For one thing, I came from a typical
postwar liberal family, repulsed by the racial stereotypes which
still dominated 'respectable' conversation. In a time when black
Americans were heavily portrayed as happy-go-lucky, shiftless,
childlike adults, consigned to success as athletes and tap-dancers,
the idea that there was anything like a 'black' or 'white' way to
play basketball would have seemed something out of a segrega-
tionist manifesto.

"For another, I have always been an enthusiastic follower of
the sports pages and had never seen any such analysis in the
many newspapers I read. Apparently, most sportswriters felt
equally uncomfortable with a foray into race; it had, after all,
taken baseball more than a half a century to admit blacks into its
ranks. Indeed, one of the more common assertions of bigots in
the 1930s and 1940s was that blacks could not be great athletes
because 'they couldn't take the pressure.' It is easy to understand
why race was not a comfortable basis on which to analyze athletic
grace.

"In the end, I decided to write about 'black' and 'white' basketball because it made the game more enjoyable to me. Clearly,
there *were* different ways to play the game; clearly the kind of self-
assertion represented by the spectacular moves of black school-
yard ball was a reflection of how important the game was to an
inner-city kid, for whom the asphalt court was the cheapest —
maybe the only — release from a nasty, sometimes brutish, existence. And books such as Pete Axthelm's *The City Game*
and David Wolf's *Foul!* had brilliantly explored the significance
of basketball in the urban black world of modern America.

"I talked with players and sportswriters alike when I wrote the
article; without exception, they approached the subject as I did:
with humor, un-self-consciously. Perhaps it is a measure of the
progress we have made in racial matters that no one — black or
white — thought it insulting or offensive to remark on the different styles of play, to note that the gravity-defying slam-dunks of a

Julius Erving and the carefully calibrated shots of a Kevin McHale are two facets of the same game."

FOR DISCUSSION

1. What gave Greenfield the idea for his essay?
2. What aspects of his topic made Greenfield hesitant to write about it? What persuaded him to go ahead?

MURRAY ROSS

Born in 1942 in Pasadena, California, MURRAY ROSS was educated at Williams College and the University of California at Berkeley. In 1975 he was hired by the University of Colorado at Colorado Springs to found and direct a theater program, and he has been there ever since teaching English, humanities, and theater. He has published articles on film and Elizabethan drama, but most of his creative attention, he says, goes to directing plays. As artistic director of Theatreworks, the resident theater company at Colorado Springs, he has directed fourteen of Shakespeare's plays and aspires to complete the entire canon.

Football Red and Baseball Green

By his own testimony, Murray Ross's only involvement in football and baseball "is confined to the couch." But as this essay shows, spectating can afford a powerful position from which to see and understand. Like Jeff Greenfield in "The Black and White Truth about Basketball" (p. 258), Ross perceives that sports represent more in American life than "just games." "Football Red and Baseball Green" first appeared in *Chicago Review* in 1971. Murray Ross revised and updated it for this edition of *The Bedford Reader*.

Every Superbowl played in the 1980s rates among the top television draws of the decade — pro football's championship game is right up there on the charts with blockbusters like *Star Wars*, *Batman*, and the *Rockys*. This revelation is one way of indicating just how popular spectator sports are in this country. Americans, or American men anyway, seem to care about the games they watch as much as the Elizabethans cared about their plays, and I suspect for some of the same reasons. There is, in sport, some of the rudimentary drama found in popular theater: familiar plots, type characters, heroic and comic action spiced with new and unpredictable variations. And common to watching both activities is the sense of participation in a shared tradition and in shared fantasies. If sport exploits these fantasies without significantly transcending them, it seems no less satisfying for all that.

It is my guess that sport spectating involves something more   2
than the vicarious pleasures of identifying with athletic prowess. I suspect that each sport contains a fundamental myth which it elaborates for its fans, and that our pleasure in watching such games derives in part from belonging briefly to the mythical world which the game and its players bring to life. I am especially interested in baseball and football because they are so popular and so uniquely *American*; they began here and unlike basketball they have not been widely exported. Thus whatever can be said, mythically, about these games would seem to apply to our culture.

Baseball's myth may be the easier to identify since we have a   3
greater historical perspective on the game. It was an instant success during the Industrialization, and most probably it was a reaction to the squalor, the faster pace, and the dreariness of the new conditions. Baseball was old-fashioned right from the start; it seems conceived in nostalgia, in the resuscitation of the Jeffersonian dream. It established an artificial rural environment, one removed from the toil of an urban life, which spectators could be admitted to and temporarily breathe in. Baseball is a *pastoral* sport, and I think the game can be best understood as this kind of art. For baseball does what all good pastoral does — it creates an atmosphere in which everything exists in harmony.

Consider, for instance, the spatial organization of the game.   4
A kind of controlled openness is created by having everything fan out from home plate, and the crowd sees the game through an arranged perspective that is rarely violated. Visually this means that the game is always seen as a constant, rather calm whole, and that the players and the playing field are viewed in relationship to each other. Each player has a certain position, a special area to tend, and the game often seems to be as much a dialogue between the fielders and the field as it is a contest between the players themselves: Will that ball get through the hole? Can that outfielder run under that fly? As a moral genre, pastoral asserts the

virtue of communion with nature. As a competitive game, baseball asserts that the team which best relates to the playing field (by hitting the ball in the right places) will win.

Having established its landscape, pastoral art operates to   5
eliminate any reference to that bigger, more disturbing, more real world it has left behind. All games are to some extent insulated from the outside by having their own rules, but baseball has a circular structure as well which furthers its comfortable feeling of self-sufficiency. By this I mean that every motion of extention is also one of return — a ball hit outside is a *home* run, a full circle. Home — familiar, peaceful, secure — it is the beginning and end. You must go out but you must come back; only the completed movement is registered.

Time is a serious threat to any form of pastoral. The genre   6
poses a timeless world of perpetual spring, and it does its best to silence the ticking of clocks which remind us that in time the green world fades into winter. One's sense of time is directly related to what happens in it, and baseball is so structured as to stretch out and ritualize whatever action it contains. Dramatic moments are few, and they are almost always isolated by the routine texture of normal play. It is certainly a game of climax and drama, but it is perhaps more a game of repeated and predictable action: the foul balls, the walks, the pitcher fussing around on the mound, the lazy fly ball to center field. This is, I think, as it should be, for baseball exists as an alternative to a world of too much action, struggle, and change. It is a merciful release from a more grinding and insistent tempo, and its time, as William Carlos Williams suggests, makes a virtue out of idleness simply by providing it:

> The crowd at the ball game
> is moved uniformly
> by a spirit of uselessness
> Which delights them. . . .

Within this expanded and idle time the baseball fan is at lib-   7
erty to become a ceremonial participant and a lover of style. Because the action is normalized, how something is done becomes as important as the action itself. Thus baseball's most delicate and

detailed aspects are often, to the spectator, the most interesting. The pitcher's windup, the anticipatory crouch of the infielders, the quick waggle of the bat as it poises for the pitch — these subtle miniature movements are as meaningful as the home runs and the strikeouts. It somehow matters in baseball that all the tiny rituals are observed: The shortstop must kick the dirt and the umpire must brush the plate with his pocket broom. In a sense baseball is largely a continuous series of small gestures, and I think it characteristic that the game's most treasured moment came when Babe Ruth pointed to where he subsequently hit a home run.

Baseball is a game where the little things mean a lot, and this, together with its clean serenity, its open space, and its ritualized action is enough to place it in a world of yesterday. Baseball evokes for us a past which may never have been ours, but which we believe was, and certainly that is enough. In the Second World War, supposedly, we fought for "Baseball, Mom, and Apple Pie," and considering what baseball means, that phrase is a good one. We fought then for the right to believe in a green world of tranquility and uninterrupted contentment, where the little things would count. But now the possibilities of such a world are more remote, and it seems that while the entertainment of such a dream has an enduring appeal, it is no longer sufficient for our fantasies. I think this may be why baseball is no longer our preeminent national pastime, and why its myth is being replaced by another more appropriate to the new realities (and fantasies) of our time. 8

Football, especially professional football, is the embodiment of a newer myth, one which in many respects is opposed to baseball's. The fundamental difference is that football is not a pastoral game; it is a heroic one. Football wants to convert men into gods; it suggests that magnificence and glory are as desirable as happiness. Football is designed, therefore, to impress its audience rather differently than baseball. 9

As a pastoral game, baseball attempts to close the gap between the players and the crowd. It creates the illusion, for instance, that with a lot of hard work, a little luck, and possibly some extra talent, the average spectator might well be playing, not watching. For most of us can do a few of the things the ball 10 players do: catch a pop-up, field a ground ball, and maybe get a hit once in a while. As a heroic game, football is not concerned with a shared community of near-equals. It seeks almost the opposite relationship between its spectators and players, one which stresses the distance between them. We are not allowed to identify directly with the likes of Jim Brown, the legendary running back for the Cleveland Browns, any more than we are with Zeus, because to do so would undercut his stature as something more than human. Pittsburgh's Mean Joe Green, in a classic commercial from the seventies, walks off the battlefield like Achilles, clouded by combat. A little boy offers him a Coke, reluctantly accepted but enthusiastically drunk, and Green tosses the boy his jersey afterwards — the token of a generous god. Football encourages us to see its players much as the little boy sees Mean Joe: We look up to them with something approaching awe. For most of us could not begin to imagine ourselves playing their game without risking imminent humiliation. The players are all much bigger and much faster and much stronger than we are, and even as fans we have trouble enough just figuring out what's going on. In baseball what happens is what meets the eye, but in football each play means eleven men acting against eleven other men: It's too much for a single set of eyes to follow. We now are provided with several television commentators to explain the action to us, with the help of the ubiquitous slow-motion instant replay. Even the coaches need their spotters in the stands and their long postgame film analyses to arrive at something like full comprehension of the game they direct and manage.

If football is distanced from its fans by its intricacy and its "superhuman" play, it nonetheless remains an intense spectacle. Baseball, as I have implied, dissolves time and urgency in a green expanse, thereby creating a luxurious and peaceful sense of leisure. As is appropriate to a heroic enterprise, football reverses this procedure and converts space into time. The game is ideally played in an oval stadium, not in a "park," and the difference is the elimination of perspective. This makes football a perfect television game, because even at first hand it offers a flat, perpetually moving foreground (wherever the ball is). The eye in baseball viewing opens up; in football it zeroes in. There is no democratic vista in football, and spectators are not asked to relax, but to concentrate. You are encouraged to watch the drama, not a medley of ubiquitous gestures, and you are constantly reminded that this event is taking place in time. The third element in baseball is the field; in football this element is the clock. Traditionally heroes do reckon with time, and football players are no exceptions. Time in football is wound up inexorably until it reaches the breaking point in the last minutes of a close game. More often than not it is the clock which emerges as the real enemy, and it is the sense of time running out that regularly produces a pitch of tension uncommon in baseball.

A further reason for football's intensity is that the game is 12 played like a war. The idea is to win by going through, around, or over the opposing team and the battle lines, quite literally, are drawn on every play. Violence is somewhere at the heart of the game, and the combat quality is reflected in football's army language ("blitz," "trap," "zone," "bomb," "trenches," etc.). Coaches often sound like generals when they discuss their strategy. Woody Hayes, the former coach of Ohio State, explained his quarterback option play as if it had been conceived in the Pentagon: "You know," he said, "the most effective kind of warfare is siege. You have to attack on broad fronts. And that's all the option is — attacking on a broad front. You know General Sherman ran an option through the South."

Football like war is an arena for action, and like war football 13 leaves little room for personal style. It seems to be a game which projects "character" more than personality, and for the most part football heroes, publicly, are a rather similar lot. They tend to become personifications rather than individuals, and, with certain exceptions, they are easily read emblematically as embodiments of heroic qualities such as "strength," "confidence," "grace," etc. — clichés really, but forceful enough when represented by the play of a Lawrence Taylor, a Joe Montana, or a Jim Rice. Perhaps this simplification of personality results in part from the heroes' total identification with their mission, to the extent that they become more characterized by what they do than by what they intrinsically "are." At any rate football does not make as many allowances for the idiosyncrasies that baseball actually seems to encourage, and as a result there have been few football players as uniquely crazy or human as, say, Casey Stengel or Dizzy Dean.

A further reason for the underdeveloped qualities of football 14 personalities, and one which gets us to the heart of the game's modernity, is that football is very much a game of modern technology. Football's action is largely interaction, and the game's complexity requires that its players mold themselves into a perfectly coordinated unit. The smoothness and precision of play execution are insatiable preoccupations, and most coaches believe that the team which makes the fewest mistakes will be the team that wins. Individual identity thus comes to be associated with the team or unit that one plays for to a much greater extent than in baseball. Darryl Strawberry is mostly Darryl Strawberry, but Dan Hampton is mostly a Chicago Bear. The latter metaphor is a precise one, since football heroes stand out not only because of purely individual acts, but also because they epitomize the action and style of the groups they are connected to. Ideally a football team should be what Camelot was supposed to have been, a group of men who function as equal parts of a larger whole, dependent on each other for total meaning.

The humanized machine as hero is something very new in 15 sport, for in baseball anything approaching a machine has always been suspect. The famous Yankee teams of the fifties were almost flawlessly perfect, yet they never were especially popular. Their admirers took pains to romanticize their precision into something more natural than plain mechanics — Joe DiMaggio, for instance, became the "Yankee Clipper." Even so, most people seemed to want the Brooklyn Dodgers (the "bums") to thrash them in the World Series. One of the most memorable triumphs in recent decades — the victory of the Amazin' Mets in 1969 — was memorable precisely because it was the triumph of a random collection of inspired rejects over the superbly skilled, fully integrated, and almost homogenized Baltimore Orioles. In baseball, machinery seems tantamount to villainy, whereas in football this smooth perfection is part of the unexpected integration a championship team must attain.

It is not surprising, really, that we should have a game 16

which asserts the heroic function of a mechanized group, since we have become a country where collective identity is a reality. Yet football's collective pattern is only one aspect of the way in which it seems to echo our contemporary environment. The game, like our society, can be thought of as cluster of people living under great tension in a state of perpetual flux. The potential for sudden disaster or triumph is as great in football as it is in our own age, and although there is something ludicrous in equating interceptions with assassinations and long passes with moonshots, there is also something valid and appealing in the analogies. It seems to me that football does successfully reflect those salient and common conditions which affect us all, and it does so with the end of making us feel better about them and our lot. For one thing, it makes us feel that something can be released and connected in all this chaos; out of the accumulated pile of bodies something can emerge — a runner breaks into the clear or a pass finds its way to a receiver. To the spectator, plays such as these are human and dazzling. They suggest to the audience what it has hoped for (and been told) all along, that technology is still a tool and not a master. Fans get living proof of this every time a long pass is completed; they appreciate that it is the result of careful planning, perfect integration, and an effective "pattern," but they see too that it is human and that what counts as well is man, his desire, his natural skill, and his "grace under pressure." Football metaphysically yokes heroic action and technology by violence to suggest that they are mutually supportive. It's a doubtful proposition, but given how we live, it has its attractions.

Football, like the space program, is a game in the grand manner. Homer would have chronicled it; Beowulf would have played fullback. Baseball's roots are at least as deep; it's a variation of the Satyr play, it's a feast of fools. But today their mythic resonance has been eroded by commercial success. Like so much else in America, their character has been modified by money.   17

More and more, both baseball and football are being played indoors on rugs in multipurpose spaces. It doesn't make good business sense to play outside where it might rain and snow and do terrible things; it isn't really prudent to play on a natural field   18 that can be destroyed in a single afternoon; and why build a whole stadium or park that's good for only one game? The fans in these stadiums are constantly diverted by huge whiz-bang scoreboards that dominate and describe the action, while the fans at home are constantly being reminded by at least three lively sportscasters of the other games, the other sports, and the other shows that are coming up later on the same stations. Both pro football and pro baseball now play vastly extended seasons, so that the World Series now takes place on chilly October nights and football is well under way before the summer ends. From my point of view all this is regrettable, because these changes tend to remove the games from their intangible but palpable mythic contexts. No longer clearly set in nature, no longer given the chance to breathe and steep in their own special atmospheres, both baseball and football risk becoming demythologized. As fans we seem to participate a little less in mythic ritual these days, while being subjected even more to the statistics, the hype, and the salary disputes that proceed from a jazzed-up, inflated, yet somehow flattened sporting world — a world that looks too much like the one we live in all the time.

Still, there is much to be thankful for, and every season seems   19 to bring its own contribution to mythic lore. Some people will think this nonsense, and I must admit there are good reasons for finding both games simply varieties of decadence.

In its preoccupation with mechanization, and in its open dis-   20 play of violence, football is the more obvious target for social moralists, but I wonder if this is finally more "corrupt" than the seductive picture of sanctuary and tranquility that baseball has so artfully drawn for us. Almost all sport is vulnerable to such criticism because it is not strictly ethical in intent, and for this reason there will always be room for puritans like the Elizabethan John Stubbes who howled at the "wanton fruits which these cursed pastimes bring forth." As a long-time dedicated fan of almost anything athletic, I confess myself out of sympathy with most of this; which is to say, I guess, that I am vulnerable to those fantasies which these games support, and that I find happiness in the company of people who feel as I do.

A final note. It is interesting that the heroic and pastoral con-   21 ventions which underlie our most popular sports are almost classically opposed. The contrasts are familiar: city versus country, aspirations versus contentment, activity versus peace, and so on. Judging from the rise of professional football, we seem to be slowly relinquishing that unfettered rural vision of ourselves that baseball so beautifully mirrors, and we have come to cast ourselves in a genre more reflective of a nation confronted by constant and unavoidable challenges. Right now, like the Elizabethans, we seem to share both heroic and pastoral yearnings, and we reach out to both. Perhaps these divided needs account in part for the enormous attention we as a nation now give to spectator sports. For sport provides one place where we can have our football and our baseball too.

QUESTIONS ON MEANING

1. Summarize the features Ross mentions for both baseball and football. Do the two sports have any similarities?
2. What do you see as Ross's principal PURPOSE?
3. What is Ross's THESIS? Where does he state it?
4. What problem does Ross introduce in paragraph 17? To what does he attribute the coexistence of football and baseball in his CONCLUSION?

QUESTIONS ON WRITING STRATEGY

1. Does Ross give equal treatment to baseball and football? To similarities and differences? What explains his strategy?
2. What types of EVIDENCE does Ross use to support his opinions?
3. What does Ross assume about his AUDIENCE? Does he seem to address only sports fans or nonfans as well?
4. What is the author's TONE? How does he achieve it? Is it effective, do you think?
5. OTHER METHODS. Ross uses many analogies (Chap. 8) to help the reader understand various points. Select two or three of the analogies and discuss their EFFECT.

QUESTIONS ON LANGUAGE

1. How does Ross use language to extend his SIMILE that "the game is played like a war" (para. 12)?
2. Study Ross's ALLUSIONS — for instance, to Elizabethan theater (para. 1), the "Jeffersonian dream" (5), Babe Ruth pointing his bat (7), Zeus (10), Homer and Beowulf (17). What does each one refer to? What do they add to the essay?
3. How much baseball and football does the reader need to know to follow Ross's essay? Did you have problems with any terms or names?
4. Consult your dictionary if any of these words are unfamiliar: revelation, rudimentary (para. 1); vicarious, prowess (2); squalor, resuscitation, pastoral (3); preeminent (8); embodiment (9); imminent, ubiquitous (10); inexorably (11); emblematically, idiosyncrasies (13); epitomize (14); tantamount (15); flux, ludicrous, salient (16); intangible, palpable (18); decadence (19); sanctuary (20); aspirations, relinquishing, unfettered (21).

SUGGESTIONS FOR WRITING

1. Select two sports or other activities you enjoy watching or participating in: football and hockey, dance and swimming, music and dance, whatever. Write an essay comparing and contrasting the two activities on some point, such as what they represent, what they demand, or what they give the spectator or participant.
2. Respond to Ross's essay by taking issue with it: Does baseball have its military side? Does football have its pastoral side? Does either embody other myths besides those Ross considers? Does such mythologizing harm sport in some way?
3. CONNECTIONS. Write an essay comparing and contrasting two essays on sport: Ross's "Football Red and Baseball Green" and Jeff Greenfield's "The Black and White Truth about Basketball" (p. 258). How are the two authors' attitudes toward sports the same or different? Which is the more ambitious essay, do you think? Which is the more successful?

ADDITIONAL WRITING TOPICS
Comparison and Contrast

1. In an essay replete with examples, compare and contrast the two subjects in any one of the following pairs:

   The main characters of two films, stories, or novels
   Women and men as consumers
   The styles of two runners
   Alexander Hamilton and Thomas Jefferson: their opposing views of central government
   How city dwellers and country dwellers spend their leisure time
   The presentation styles of two television news commentators

2. Approach a comparison and contrast essay on one of the following general subjects by explaining why you prefer one thing to the other:

   Two buildings on campus or in town
   Two football teams
   German-made cars and Detroit-made cars
   Two horror movies
   Television when you were a child and television today
   City life and small-town or rural life
   Malls and main streets
   Two neighborhoods
   Two sports

3. Write an essay in which you compare a reality with an ideal. For instance:

   The house you live in and the house of your dreams
   A real vacation and an ideal one
   The job you have and the job you dream of
   The car you own and the car you'd love to own
   Some present ability and some ideal ability
   Your study habits and those you wish you had

5
PROCESS ANALYSIS
Explaining Step by Step

THE METHOD

A chemist working for a soft-drink firm is asked to improve on a competitor's product, Orange Quench. First, she chemically tests a sample to figure out what's in the drink. This is the method of DIVISION or ANALYSIS, the separation of something into its parts in order to understand it (see the following chapter). Then the chemist writes a report telling her boss how to make a drink like Orange Quench, but better. This recipe is a special kind of analysis, called *process analysis*: explaining step by step how to do something or how something is done.

Like any type of analysis, process analysis divides a subject into its components. It divides a continuous action into stages. Processes much larger and more involved than the making of an orange drink also may be analyzed. When geologists explain how the Grand Canyon was formed — a process that occurred over several hundred million years — they describe the successive layers of sediment deposited by oceans, floods, and wind; then the great uplift of the entire region by underground forces; and then the erosion, visible to us today, by the Colorado River and its tributaries, by little streams and flash floods, by crumbling and falling rock, and by wind. Exactly what are the geologists doing in this explanation? They are taking a complicated event (or process) and dividing it into parts. They are telling us what happened first, second, and third, and what is still happening today.

Because it is useful in explaining what is complicated, process analysis is a favorite method of scientists such as geologists. The method, however, may be useful to anybody. Two kinds of process analysis are very familiar to you. The first (or *directive*) kind tells a reader how to do something or make something. You meet it when you read a set of instructions for assembling newly purchased stereo components, or follow the directions to a stereo store ("Turn right at the blinker and follow Patriot Boulevard for 2.4 miles . . ."). The second (or *informative*) kind of process analysis tells us how something is done, or how it takes place. This is the kind we often read out of curiosity. Such an essay may tell of events beyond our control: how atoms behave when split, how lions hunt, how a fertilized egg develops into a child. In this chapter, you will find examples of both kinds of process analysis — both the "how to" and the "how." In a practical directive, Peter Elbow tells you how to write when a deadline looms and you absolutely have to produce. Jessica Mitford, in a spellbinding informative essay, explains how corpses are embalmed; but, clearly, she doesn't expect you to rush down to your basement and give her instructions a try.

Sometimes the method is used very imaginatively. Foreseeing that the sun eventually will cool, the earth shrink, the oceans freeze, and all life perish, an astronomer who cannot possibly behold the end of the world nevertheless can write a process analysis of it. An exercise in learned guesswork, such an essay divides a vast and almost inconceivable event into stages that, taken one at a time, become clearer and more readily imaginable.

Whether it is useful or useless (but fun to imagine), an effective essay in process analysis holds a certain fascination. Leaf through a current issue of a newsstand magazine, and you will find that process analysis abounds in it. You may meet, for instance, articles telling you how to tenderize cuts of meat, sew homemade designer jeans, lose fat, cut hair, play the money markets, arouse a bored mate, and program a computer. Less practical, but not necessarily less interesting, are the informative articles: how brain surgeons work, how diamonds are formed, how cities fight crime. Readers, it seems, have an unslakable thirst for process analysis. In every issue of the *New York Times Book Review*, we find an entire best-seller list devoted to "Advice, How-to and Miscellaneous," including books on how to make money in real estate, how to lose weight, how to find a good mate, and how to lose a bad one. Evidently, if anything will still make an American crack open a book, it is a step-by-step explanation of how he or she, too, can be a success at living.

THE PROCESS

Here are suggestions for writing an effective process analysis of your own. (In fact, what you are about to read is itself a process analysis.)

1. Understand clearly the process you are about to analyze. Think it through. This preliminary survey will make the task of writing far easier for you.

2. If you are giving a set of detailed instructions, ask yourself: Are there any preparatory steps a reader ought to take? If there are, list them. (These might include, "Remove the packing from the components," or, "First, lay out three eggs, one pound of Sheboygan bratwurst. . . .")

3. List the steps or stages in the process. Try setting them down in chronological order, one at a time — if this is possible. Some processes, however, do not happen in an orderly sequence, but occur all at once. If, for instance, you are writing an account of a typical earthquake, what do you mention first? The shifting of underground rock strata? Cracks in the earth? Falling houses? Bursting water mains? Toppling trees? Mangled cars? Casualties? (Here is a subject for which the method of CLASSIFICATION, to be discussed in Chapter 7, may come to your aid. You might sort out

apparently simultaneous events into categories: injury to people; damage to homes, to land, to public property.)

4. Now glance back over your list, making sure you haven't omitted anything or instructed your reader to take the steps in the wrong order. Sometimes a stage of a process may contain a number of smaller stages. Make sure none has been left out. If any seems particularly tricky or complicated, underline it on your list to remind yourself when you write your essay to slow down and detail it with extra care.

5. Ask yourself: Will I use any specialized or technical terms? If you will, be sure to define them. You'll sympathize with your reader if you have ever tried to work a Hong Kong–made short-wave radio that comes with an instruction booklet written in translatorese, full of unexplained technical jargon; or if you have ever tried to assemble a plastic tricycle according to a directive that reads, "Position sleeve casing on wheel center in fork with shaft in tong groove, and gently but forcibly tap in medium pal nut head. . . ."

6. Use time-markers or TRANSITIONS. These words or phrases indicate *when* one stage of a process stops and the next begins, and they greatly aid your reader in following you. Here, for example, is a paragraph of plain medical prose that makes good use of the helpful time-markers printed in *italics*. (The paragraph is adapted from Alan F. Guttmacher's *Pregnancy and Birth*, 1970).

> In the human, *thirty-six hours after* the egg is fertilized, a two-cell egg appears. A twelve-cell development takes place *in seventy-two hours*. The egg is *still* round and has increased little in diameter. In this respect it is like a real estate development. *At first* a road bisects the whole area; *then* a cross road divides it into quarters, and *later* other roads divide it into eighths and twelfths. This happens without the taking of any more land, simply by subdivision of the original tract. *On the third or fourth day*, the egg passes from the Fallopian tube into the uterus. *By the fifth day* the original single large cell has subdivided into sixty small cells and floats about the slitlike uterine cavity *a day or two longer*, *then* adheres to the cavity's inner lining. *By the twelfth day* the human egg is already firmly implanted. Impregnation is *now* completed, *as yet* unbeknown to the woman. *At present*, she has not even had time to miss her first menstrual

period, and other symptoms of pregnancy are *still several days distant.*

Brief as these time-markers are, they define each stage of the human egg's journey. Note how the writer, after declaring in the second sentence that the egg forms twelve cells, backtracks for a moment and retraces the process by which the egg has subdivided, comparing it (by a brief analogy) to a piece of real estate. (For more examples of ANALOGY, see Chapter 8.) When using time-markers, vary them so that they won't seem mechanical. If you can, avoid the monotonous repetition of a fixed phrase (*In the fourteenth stage . . . , In the fifteenth stage . . .*). Even boring time-markers, though, are better than none at all. As in any chronological narrative, words and phrases such as *in the beginning, first, second, next, after that, three seconds later, at the same time,* and *finally* can help a process to move smoothly in the telling and lodge firmly in the reader's mind.

7. When you begin writing a first draft, state your analysis in generous detail, even at the risk of being wordy. When you revise, it will be easier to delete than to amplify.

8. Finally, when your essay is finished, reread it carefully. If it is a simple *directive* ("How to Eat an Ice Cream Cone without Dribbling"), ask a friend to try it out. See if somebody else can follow your instructions without difficulty. If you have written an *informative* process analysis ("How a New Word Enters the Dictionary"), however, ask others to read your essay and tell you whether the process unfolds as clearly in their minds as it does in yours.

PROCESS ANALYSIS IN A PARAGRAPH: TWO ILLUSTRATIONS

Using Process Analysis to Write about Television

The timer on your videocassette recorder permits you to record up to eight programs over a two-week period even when you are not at home. For each program you wish to record in your absence, locate an empty program number by pushing the P button until a flashing number appears on the TV screen.

The next four steps set the information for the program. First, push the *Day* button until the day and date show on the screen. The screen will flash *On* until you set the starting time. (Be sure the time is set correctly for A.M. or P.M.) Then push the *Off* button and set the ending time (again, watching A.M. or P.M.). When the times have been set, push the *Chan* button and set the channel using the unit's channel selector. You may review the program information by pushing the *Check* button. When you are satisfied that the settings are correct, push *Timer* to set the timer to operate. (The unit cannot be operated manually while the timer is on.)

COMMENT. In this directive process analysis adapted from a VCR user's manual, the writer neatly lays out the steps necessary to program a machine for timed recording. (Of course, drawings would accompany any such instructions in an actual manual to make the steps even clearer.) The writer introduces the purpose of the process in the first sentence, pauses once to preview "the next four steps," and provides a way of checking that the process has been performed correctly — all to help users understand the instructions and avoid mistakes. The separate steps are indicated with time-markers ("first," "until you set," "then," "When the times have been set," "When you are satisfied"). Notice that the writer avoids any temptation to digress to other functions of the machine (as, indeed, one real and almost useless VCR manual did by stopping midstream to explain three different speeds for taping). By the way, the writer's use of the second person ("you") along with sentences of command ("Push the *Day* button . . .") is quite usual in directive process analyses.

Using Process Analysis in an Academic Discipline

The generation of rain by the coalescence process depends on the occurrence of oversize water droplets that are larger than twenty micrometers in radius. An oversize droplet falls just a bit faster than the typical droplet, and it grows by colliding with and sweeping up smaller droplets in its path. Rising currents of air carry the swelling droplets upward faster than they can fall out of the cloud, allowing them more time to grow. A droplet requires about half an hour to grow to raindrop size by coalescence, and the rain cloud must be at least 2.5 km (1.6 miles) thick to contain the growing drops long enough for them to become raindrops. Thinner clouds limit the growth of drops by coalescence, resulting in *drizzle*, a form of precipitation that consists of very tiny drops that "float" rather than fall to the surface. Pavements made wet by drizzle can be very hazardous for motorists, but drizzle never produces significant quantities of precipitation.

COMMENT. This paragraph, from Robert A. Muller and Theodore M. Oberlander's *Physical Geography Today: A Portrait of a Planet* (3rd ed., 1984), clearly illustrates the method of informative process analysis. In it, the authors detail one of the ways in which minuscule water droplets coalesce to form raindrops large enough to fall to earth. The most interesting detail, perhaps, is that the droplets have to travel upward and collide and combine with other droplets before they have enough weight to fall down. In organizing their analysis, the authors proceed step by step, making the point as they move through the process that conditions have to be right: The clouds have to be thick enough. If they aren't the end result will be drizzle rather than rain.

JESSICA MITFORD

Born in Batsford Mansion, England, in 1917, the daughter of
Lord and Lady Redesdale, JESSICA MITFORD devoted much of
her early life to defying her aristocratic upbringing. In her autobiography *Daughters and Rebels* (1960), she tells how she received a genteel schooling at home, then as a young woman
moved to Loyalist Spain during the violent Spanish Civil War.
Later, she emigrated to America, where for a time she worked
in Miami as a bartender. She has since become one of her
adopted country's most noted reporters: *Time* called her
"Queen of the Muckrakers." Exposing with her typewriter
what she regards as corruption, abuse, and absurdity, Mitford
has written *The American Way of Death* (1963), *Kind and Unusual Punishment: The Prison Business* (1973), and *Poison Penmanship* (1979), a collection of articles from *The Atlantic, Harper's*, and other magazines. *A Fine Old Conflict* (1976) is the
second volume of Mitford's autobiography. A recent novel,
Grace Had an English Heart (1989), examines how the media
transform ordinary people into celebrities.

Behind the
Formaldehyde Curtain

The most famous (or notorious) thing Jessica Mitford has written is *The American Way of Death*. The following essay is a self-
contained selection from it. In the book, Mitford criticizes the
mortuary profession; and when her work landed on bestseller
lists, the author was the subject of bitter attacks from funeral
directors all over North America. To finish reading the essay,
you will need a stable stomach as well as an awareness of Mitford's outrageous sense of humor. "Behind the Formaldehyde
Curtain" is a clear, painstaking process analysis, written with
masterly style.

The drama begins to unfold with the arrival of the corpse at   1
the mortuary.

Alas, poor Yorick! How surprised he would be to see how his   2 counterpart of today is whisked off to a funeral parlor and is in short order sprayed, sliced, pierced, pickled, trussed, trimmed, creamed, waxed, painted, rouged, and neatly dressed — transformed from a common corpse into a Beautiful Memory Picture. This process is known in the trade as embalming and restorative art, and is so universally employed in the United States and Canada that the funeral director does it routinely, without consulting corpse or kin. He regards as eccentric those few who are hardy enough to suggest that it might be dispensed with. Yet no law requires embalming, no religious doctrine commends it, nor is it dictated by considerations of health, sanitation, or even of personal daintiness. In no part of the world but in Northern America is it widely used. The purpose of embalming is to make the corpse presentable for viewing in a suitably costly container; and here too the funeral director routinely, without first consulting the family, prepares the body for public display.

Is all this legal? The processes to which a dead body may be subjected are after all to some extent circumscribed by law. In most states, for instance, the signature of next of kin must be obtained before an autopsy may be performed, before the deceased may be cremated, before the body may be turned over to a medical school for research purposes; or such provision must be made in the decedent's will. In the case of embalming, no such permission is required nor is it ever sought.[1] A textbook, *The Principles and Practices of Embalming*, comments on this: "There is some question regarding the legality of much that is done within the preparation room." The author points out that it would be most unusual for a responsible member of a bereaved family to instruct the mortician, in so many words, to "embalm" the body of a deceased relative. The very term *embalming* is so seldom used that the mortician must rely upon custom in the matter. The author concludes that unless the family specifies otherwise, the act of en-

3

---

[1]Partly because of Mitford's attack, the Federal Trade Commission now requires the funeral industry to provide families with itemized price lists, including the price of embalming, to state that embalming is not required, and to obtain the family's consent to embalming before charging for it. — Eds.

trusting the body to the care of a funeral establishment carries with it an implied permission to go ahead and embalm.

Embalming is indeed a most extraordinary procedure, and one must wonder at the docility of Americans who each year pay hundreds of millions of dollars for its perpetuation, blissfully ignorant of what it is all about, what is done, how it is done. Not one in ten thousand has any idea of what actually takes place. Books on the subject are extremely hard to come by. They are not to be found in most libraries or bookshops.

In an era when huge television audiences watch surgical operations in the comfort of their living rooms, when, thanks to the animated cartoon, the geography of the digestive system has become familiar territory even to the nursery school set, in a land where the satisfaction of curiosity about almost all matters is a national pastime, the secrecy surrounding embalming can, surely, hardly be attributed to the inherent gruesomeness of the subject. Custom in this regard has within this century suffered a complete reversal. In the early days of American embalming, when it was performed in the home of the deceased, it was almost mandatory for some relative to stay by the embalmer's side and witness the procedure. Today, family members who might wish to be in attendance would certainly be dissuaded by the funeral director. All others, except apprentices, are excluded by law from the preparation room.

A close look at what does actually take place may explain in large measure the undertaker's intractable reticence concerning a procedure that has become his major *raison d'être*. Is it possible he fears that public information about embalming might lead patrons to wonder if they really want this service? If the funeral men are loath to discuss the subject outside the trade, the reader may, understandably, be equally loath to go on reading at this point. For those who have the stomach for it, let us part the formaldehyde curtain. . . .

The body is first laid out in the undertaker's morgue — or rather, Mr. Jones is reposing in the preparation room — to be readied to bid the world farewell.

The preparation room in any of the better funeral establishments has the tiled and sterile look of a surgery, and indeed the embalmer–restorative artist who does his chores there is beginning to adopt the term *dermasurgeon* (appropriately corrupted by some mortician-writers as "demi-surgeon") to describe his calling. His equipment, consisting of scalpels, scissors, augers, forceps, clamps, needles, pumps, tubes, bowls, and basins, is crudely imitative of the surgeon's, as is his technique, acquired in a nine- or twelve-month post-high-school course in an embalming school. He is supplied by an advanced chemical industry with a bewildering array of fluids, sprays, pastes, oils, powders, creams, to fix or soften tissue, shrink or distend it as needed, dry it here, restore the moisture there. There are cosmetics, waxes, and paints to fill and cover features, even plaster of Paris to replace entire limbs. There are ingenious aids to prop and stabilize the cadaver: a Vari-Pose Head Rest, the Edwards Arm and Hand Positioner, the Repose Block (to support the shoulders during the embalming), and the Throop Foot Positioner, which resembles an old-fashioned stocks.

Mr. John H. Eckels, president of the Eckels College of Mortuary Science, thus describes the first part of the embalming procedure: "In the hands of a skilled practitioner, this work may be done in a comparatively short time and without mutilating the body other than by slight incision — so slight that it scarcely would cause serious inconvenience if made upon a living person. It is necessary to remove the blood, and doing this not only helps in the disinfecting, but removes the principal cause of disfigurements due to discoloration."   9

Another textbook discusses the all-important time element: "The earlier this is done, the better, for every hour that elapses between death and embalming will add to the problems and complications encountered. . . ." Just how soon should one get going on the embalming? The author tells us, "On the basis of such scanty information made available to this profession through its rudimentary and haphazard system of technical research, we must conclude that the best results are to be obtained if the subject is embalmed before life is completely extinct — that is, before cellular death has occurred. In the average case, this would mean within an hour after somatic death." For those who feel that there is something a little rudimentary, not to say haphazard,   10 about this advice, a comforting thought is offered by another writer. Speaking of fears entertained in early days of premature burial, he points out, "One of the effects of embalming by chemical injection, however, has been to dispel fears of live burial." How true; once the blood is removed, chances of live burial are indeed remote.

To return to Mr. Jones, the blood is drained out through the 11 veins and replaced by embalming fluid pumped in through the arteries. As noted in *The Principles and Practices of Embalming*, "every operator has a favorite injection and drainage point — a fact which becomes a handicap only if he fails or refuses to forsake his favorites when conditions demand it." Typical favorites are the carotid artery, femoral artery, jugular vein, subclavian vein. There are various choices of embalming fluid. If Flextone is used, it will produce a "mild, flexible rigidity. The skin retains a velvety softness, the tissues are rubbery and pliable. Ideal for women and children." It may be blended with B. and G. Products Company's Lyf-Lyk tint, which is guaranteed to reproduce "nature's own skin texture . . . the velvety appearance of living tissue." Suntone comes in three separate tints: Suntan; Special Cosmetic Tint, a pink shade "especially indicated for female subjects"; and Regular Cosmetic Tint, moderately pink.

About three to six gallons of a dyed and perfumed solution of 12 formaldehyde, glycerin, borax, phenol, alcohol, and water is soon circulating through Mr. Jones, whose mouth has been sewn together with a "needle directed upward between the upper lip and gum and brought out through the left nostril," with the corners raised slightly "for a more pleasant expression." If he should be bucktoothed, his teeth are cleaned with Bon Ami and coated with colorless nail polish. His eyes, meanwhile, are closed with flesh-tinted eye caps and eye cement.

The next step is to have at Mr. Jones with a thing called a tro- 13 car. This is a long, hollow needle attached to a tube. It is jabbed into the abdomen, poked around the entrails and chest cavity, the contents of which are pumped out and replaced with "cavity fluid." This done, and the hole in the abdomen sewn up, Mr. Jones's face is heavily creamed (to protect the skin from burns which may be caused by leakage of the chemicals), and he is covered with a sheet and left unmolested for a while. But not for long — there is more, much more, in store for him. He has been embalmed, but not yet restored, and the best time to start the restorative work is eight to ten hours after embalming, when the tissues have become firm and dry.

The object of all this attention to the corpse, it must be remembered, is to make it presentable for viewing in an attitude of healthy repose. "Our customs require the presentation of our dead in the semblance of normality . . . unmarred by the ravages of illness, disease, or mutilation," says Mr. J. Sheridan Mayer in his *Restorative Art*. This is rather a large order since few people die in the full bloom of health, unravaged by illness and unmarked by some disfigurement. The funeral industry is equal to the challenge: "In some cases the gruesome appearance of a mutilated or disease-ridden subject may be quite discouraging. The task of restoration may seem impossible and shake the confidence of the embalmer. This is the time for intestinal fortitude and determination. Once the formative work is begun and affected tissues are cleaned or removed, all doubts of success vanish. It is surprising and gratifying to discover the results which may be obtained." 14

The embalmer, having allowed an appropriate interval to elapse, returns to the attack, but now he brings into play the skill and equipment of sculptor and cosmetician. Is a hand missing? Casting one in plaster of Paris is a simple matter. "For replacement purposes, only a cast of the back of the hand is necessary; this is within the ability of the average operator and is quite adequate." If a lip or two, a nose, or an ear should be missing, the embalmer has at hand a variety of restorative waxes with which to model replacements. Pores and skin texture are simulated by stippling with a little brush, and over this cosmetics are laid on. Head off? Decapitation cases are rather routinely handled. Ragged edges are trimmed, and head joined to torso with a series of splints, wires, and sutures. It is a good idea to have a little something at the neck — a scarf or a high collar — when time for viewing comes. Swollen mouth? Cut out tissue as needed from inside the lips. If too much is removed, the surface contour can easily be restored by padding with cotton. Swollen necks and cheeks are reduced by removing tissue through vertical incisions made 15 down each side of the neck. "When the deceased is casketed, the pillow will hide the suture incisions . . . as an extra precaution against leakage, the suture may be painted with liquid sealer."

The opposite condition is more likely to present itself — that   16
of emaciation. His hypodermic syringe now loaded with massage cream, the embalmer seeks out and fills the hollowed and sunken areas by injection. In this procedure the backs of the hands and fingers and the under-chin area should not be neglected.

Positioning the lips is a problem that recurrently challenges   17
the ingenuity of the embalmer. Closed too tightly, they tend to give a stern, even disapproving expression. Ideally, embalmers feel, the lips should give the impression of being ever so slightly parted, the upper lip protruding slightly for a more youthful appearance. This takes some engineering, however, as the lips tend to drift apart. Lip drift can sometimes be remedied by pushing one or two straight pins through the inner margin of the lower lip and then inserting them between the two front upper teeth. If Mr. Jones happens to have no teeth, the pins can just as easily be anchored in his Armstrong Face Former and Denture Replacer. Another method to maintain lip closure is to dislocate the lower jaw, which is then held in its new position by a wire run through holes which have been drilled through the upper and lower jaws at the midline. As the French are fond of saying, *il faut souffrir pour être belle.*[2]

If Mr. Jones has died of jaundice, the embalming fluid will   18
very likely turn him green. Does this deter the embalmer? Not if he has intestinal fortitude. Masking pastes and cosmetics are heavily laid on, burial garments and casket interiors are color-cor-related with particular care, and Jones is displayed beneath rose-colored lights. Friends will say "How *well* he looks." Death by carbon monoxide, on the other hand, can be rather a good thing from the embalmer's viewpoint: "One advantage is the fact that this type of discoloration is an exaggerated form of a natural pink coloration." This is nice because the healthy glow is already present and needs but little attention.

---

[2]You have to suffer to be beautiful. — Eds.

The patching and filling completed, Mr. Jones is now 19
shaved, washed, and dressed. Cream-based cosmetic, available in
pink, flesh, suntan, brunette, and blond, is applied to his hands
and face, his hair is shampooed and combed (and, in the case of
Mrs. Jones, set), his hands manicured. For the horny-handed son
of toil special care must be taken; cream should be applied to remove ingrained grime, and the nails cleaned. "If he were not in
the habit of having them manicured in life, trimming and shaping
is advised for better appearance — never questioned by kin."

Jones is now ready for casketing (this is the present participle 20
of the verb "to casket"). In this operation his right shoulder
should be depressed slightly "to turn the body a bit to the right
and soften the appearance of lying flat on the back." Positioning
the hands is a matter of importance, and special rubber positioning blocks may be used. The hands should be cupped slightly for
a more lifelike, relaxed appearance. Proper placement of the body
requires a delicate sense of balance. It should lie as high as possible in the casket, yet not so high that the lid, when lowered, will
hit the nose. On the other hand, we are cautioned, placing the
body too low "creates the impression that the body is in a box."

Jones is next wheeled into the appointed slumber room where a 21
few last touches may be added — his favorite pipe placed in his
hand or, if he was a great reader, a book propped into position. (In
the case of little Master Jones a Teddy bear may be clutched.) Here
he will hold open house for a few days, visiting hours 10 A.M. to 9 P.M.

All now being in readiness, the funeral director calls a staff 22
conference to make sure that each assistant knows his precise duties.
Mr. Wilber Kriege writes: "This makes your staff feel that they are a
part of the team, with a definite assignment that must be properly
carried out if the whole plan is to succeed. You never heard of a
football coach who failed to talk to his entire team before they go on
the field. They have drilled on the plays they are to execute for hours
and days, and yet the successful coach knows the importance of
making even the benchwarming third-string substitute feel that he
is important if the game is to be won." The winning of *this* game is
predicated upon glass-smooth handling of the logistics. The funeral
director has notified the pallbearers whose names were furnished by
the family, has arranged for the presence of clergyman, organist,

and soloist, has provided transportation for everybody, has organized and listed the flowers sent by friends. In *Psychology of Funeral
Service* Mr. Edward A. Martin points out, "He may not always do as
much as the family thinks he is doing, but it is his helpful guidance
that they appreciate in knowing they are proceeding as they should.
. . . The important thing is how well his services can be used to make
the family believe they are giving unlimited expression to their own
sentiment."

The religious service may be held in a church or in the chapel   23
of the funeral home; the funeral director vastly prefers the latter
arrangement, for not only is it more convenient for him but it af-
fords him the opportunity to show off his beautiful facilities to the
gathered mourners. After the clergyman has had his say, the
mourners queue up to file past the casket for a last look at the deceased. The family is *never* asked whether they want an open-
casket ceremony; in the absence of their instruction to the contrary, this is taken for granted. Consequently well over 90 per
cent of all American funerals feature the open casket — a custom
unknown in other parts of the world. Foreigners are astonished
by it. An English woman living in San Francisco described her reaction in a letter to the writer:

> I myself have attended only one funeral here — that of an
> elderly fellow worker of mine. After the service I could not un-
> derstand why everyone was walking towards the coffin (sorry, I
> mean casket), but thought I had better follow the crowd. It
> shook me rigid to get there and find the casket open and poor
> old Oscar lying there in his brown tweed suit, wearing a suntan
> makeup and just the wrong shade of lipstick. If I had not been
> extremely fond of the old boy, I have a horrible feeling that I
> might have giggled. Then and there I decided that I could never
> face another American funeral — even dead.

The casket (which has been resting throughout the service on a   24
Classic Beauty Ultra Metal Casket Bier) is now transferred by a hydraulically operated device called Porto-Lift to a balloon-tired,
Glide Easy casket carriage which will wheel it to yet another convey-
ance, the Cadillac Funeral Coach. This may be lavender, cream,
light green — anything but black. Interiors, of course, are color-
correlated, "for the man who cannot stop short of perfection."

At graveside, the casket is lowered into the earth. This office, 25 once the prerogative of friends of the deceased, is now performed by a patented mechanical lowering device. A "Lifetime Green" artificial grass mat is at the ready to conceal the sere earth, and overhead, to conceal the sky, is a portable Steril Chapel Tent ("resists the intense heat and humidity of summer and the terrific storms of winter . . . available in Silver Gray, Rose, or Evergreen"). Now is the time for the ritual scattering of earth over the coffin, as the solemn words "earth to earth, ashes to ashes, dust to dust" are pronounced by the officiating cleric. This can today be accomplished "with a mere flick of the wrist with the Gordon Leak-Proof Earth Dispenser. No grasping of a handful of dirt, no soiled fingers. Simple, dignified, beautiful, reverent! The modern way!" The Gordon Earth Dispenser (at $5) is of nickel-plated brass construction. It is not only "attractive to the eye and long wearing"; it is also "one of the 'tools' for building better public relations" if presented as "an appropriate non-commercial gift" to the clergyman. It is shaped something like a saltshaker.

Untouched by human hand, the coffin and the earth are now 26 united.

It is in the function of directing the participants through this 27 maze of gadgetry that the funeral director has assigned to himself his relatively new role of "grief therapist." He has relieved the family of every detail, he has revamped the corpse to look like a living doll, he has arranged for it to nap for a few days in a slumber room, he has put on a well-oiled performance in which the concept of *death* has played no part whatsoever — unless it was inconsiderately mentioned by the clergyman who conducted the religious service. He has done everything in his power to make the funeral a real pleasure for everybody concerned. He and his team have given their all to score an upset victory over death.

QUESTIONS ON MEANING

1. What was your emotional response to this essay? Can you analyze your feelings?

2. To what does the author attribute the secrecy that surrounds the process of embalming?
3. What, according to Mitford, is the mortician's intent? What common obstacles to fulfilling it must be surmounted?
4. What do you understand from Mitford's remark in paragraph 10, on dispelling fears of live burial: "How true; once the blood is removed, chances of live burial are indeed remote"?
5. Do you find any implied PURPOSE in this essay? Does Mitford seem primarily out to rake muck, or does she offer any positive suggestions to Americans?

QUESTIONS ON WRITING STRATEGY

1. What is Mitford's TONE? In her opening two paragraphs, exactly what shows her attitude toward her subject?
2. Why do you think Mitford goes into so much grisly detail? How does it serve her purpose?
3. What is the EFFECT of calling the body Mr. Jones (or Master Jones)?
4. Paragraph by paragraph, what time-markers does the author employ? (If you need a refresher on this point, see the discussion of time-markers on pages 284–285.)
5. Into what stages has the author divided the embalming process?
6. To whom does Mitford address her process analysis? How do you know she isn't writing for an AUDIENCE of professional morticians?
7. Consider one of the quotations from the journals and textbooks of professionals and explain how it serves the author's general purpose.
8. OTHER METHODS. In paragraph 8, Mitford uses classification (Chap. 7) in listing the embalmer's equipment and supplies. What groups does she identify, and why does she bother sorting the items at all?

QUESTIONS ON LANGUAGE

1. Explain the ALLUSION to Yorick in paragraph 2.
2. What IRONY do you find in Mitford's statement in paragraph 7, "The body is first laid out in the undertaker's morgue — or rather, Mr. Jones is reposing in the preparation room"? Pick out any other words or phrases in the essay that seem ironic. Comment especially on those you find in the essay's last two sentences.
3. Why is it useful to Mitford's purpose that she cites the brand names of morticians' equipment and supplies (the Edwards Arm and Hand

Positioner, Lyf-Lyk tint)? List all the brand names in the essay that are memorable.

4. Define the following words or terms: counterpart (para. 2); circumscribed, autopsy, cremated, decedent, bereaved (3); docility, perpetuation (4); inherent, mandatory (5); intractable, reticence, *raison d'être*, formaldehyde (6); "dermasurgeon," augers, forceps, distend, stocks (8); somatic (10); carotid artery, femoral artery, jugular vein, subclavian vein, pliable (11); glycerin, borax, phenol, bucktoothed (12); trocar, entrails (13); stippling, sutures (15); emaciation (16); jaundice (18); predicated (22); queue (23); hydraulically (24); cleric (25); therapist (27).

SUGGESTIONS FOR WRITING

1. Defend the ritual of the American funeral, or of the mortician's profession, against Mitford's sarcastic attack.

2. With the aid of the *Readers' Guide to Periodical Literature*, find information about the recent phenomenon of quick-freezing the dead. Set forth this process, including its hoped-for result of reviving the corpses in the far future.

3. Analyze some other process whose operations may not be familiar to everyone. (Have you ever held a job, or helped out in a family business, that has taken you behind the scenes? How is fast food prepared? How are cars serviced? How is a baby sat? How is a house constructed?) Detail it step by step in an essay that includes time-markers.

4. CONNECTIONS. Mitford is not the only writer of IRONY in this book: James Thurber (p. 64), Judy Brady (p. 342), Fran Lebowitz (p. 394), H. L. Mencken (p. 623), and Jonathan Swift (p. 713) also employ it. Based on Mitford's essay and essays by at least two of these others, define *irony*. If you need a boost, supplement the definition in this book's glossary with one in a dictionary of literary or rhetorical terms. But go beyond others' definitions to construct one of your own, using quotations from the essays as your support.

JESSICA MITFORD ON WRITING

"Choice of subject is of cardinal importance," declares Jessica Mitford in *Poison Penmanship*. "One does by far one's best work when besotted by and absorbed in the matter at hand." After *The American Way of Death* was published, Mitford received hundreds of letters suggesting alleged rackets that ought to be exposed, and to her surprise, an overwhelming majority of these letters complained about defective and overpriced hearing aids. But Mitford never wrote a book blasting the hearing aid industry. "Somehow, although there may well be need for such an exposé, I could not warm up to hearing aids as a subject for the kind of thorough, intensive, long-range research that would be needed to do an effective job." She once taught a course at Yale in muckraking, with each student choosing a subject to investigate. "Those who tackled hot issues on campus, such as violations of academic freedom or failure to implement affirmative-action hiring policies, turned in some excellent work; but the lad who decided to investigate 'waste in the Yale dining halls' was predictably unable to make much of this trivial topic." (The editors interject: We aren't sure that the topic is necessarily trivial, but obviously not everyone would burn to write about it!)

The hardest problem Mitford faced in writing *The American Way of Death*, she recalls, was doing her factual, step-by-step account of the embalming process. She felt "determined to describe it in all its revolting details, but how to make this subject palatable to the reader?" Her solution was to cast the whole process analysis in the official jargon of the mortuary industry, drawing on lists of taboo words and their euphemisms (or acceptable synonyms), as published in the trade journal *Casket & Sunnyside*: "Mr., Mrs., Miss Blank, not corpse or body; preparation room, not morgue; reposing room, not laying-out room. . . ." The story of Mr. Jones thus took shape; and Mitford's use of jargon, she found, added macabre humor to the proceedings.

FOR DISCUSSION

1. What seem to be Mitford's criteria for an effective essay or book?
2. What is muckraking? Why do you suppose anyone would want to do it?

MARVIN HARRIS

Marvin Harris is an influential and often controversial cultural anthropologist with a particular interest in how the "practical problems of earthly existence" — getting food, for instance — determine human cultures. Harris was born in Brooklyn, New York, in 1927 and received a B.A. (1949) and Ph. D. (1953) from Columbia University. He taught at Columbia for almost three decades and is now graduate research professor of anthropology at the University of Florida. Harris has traveled extensively, conducting research in South America, Africa, Asia, and East Harlem, New York City. His seventeen books comprise scholarly works such as *The Rise of Anthropological Theory* (1968) and textbooks such as *Culture, People, Nature* (now in its fifth edition). But Harris is best known for books intended for general audiences: *Cows, Pigs, Wars, and Witches: The Riddles of Culture* (1974); *Cannibals and Kings: The Origins of Cultures* (1977); and *Good to Eat* (1986) and *The Sacred Cow and the Abominable Pig* (1987), both subtitled *Riddles of Food and Culture*.

How Our Skins Got Their Color

This essay comes from Harris's latest book, *Our Kind: Who We Are, Where We Came from, Where We Are Going* (1988). Typically for Harris's writing, the book tackles big questions about human evolution with insight and information. In this selection, Harris sets the record straight on race.

Most human beings are neither very fair nor very dark, but 1 brown. The extremely fair skin of northern Europeans and their descendants, and the very black skins of central Africans and their descendants, are probably special adaptations. Brown-skinned ancestors may have been shared by modern-day blacks and whites as recently as ten thousand years ago.

Human skin owes its color to the presence of particles known 2 as melanin. The primary function of melanin is to protect the upper levels of the skin from being damaged by the sun's ultraviolet rays. This radiation poses a critical problem for our kind because we lack the dense coat of hair that acts as a sunscreen for most mammals. Hairlessness exposes us to two kinds of radiation hazards: ordinary sunburn, with its blisters, rashes, and risk of infection; and skin cancers, including malignant melanoma, one of the deadliest diseases known. Melanin is the body's first line of defense against these afflictions. The more melanin particles, the darker the skin, and the lower the risk of sunburn and all forms of skin cancer. This explains why the highest rates for skin cancer are found in sun-drenched lands such as Australia, where light-skinned people of European descent spend a good part of their lives outdoors wearing scanty attire. Very dark-skinned people such as heavily pigmented Africans of Zaire seldom get skin cancer, but when they do, they get it on depigmented parts of their bodies — palms and lips.

If exposure to solar radiation had nothing but harmful effects, 3 natural selection would have favored inky black as the color for all human populations. But the sun's rays do not present an unmitigated threat. As it falls on the skin, sunshine converts a fatty substance in the epidermis into vitamin D. The blood carries vitamin D from the skin to the intestines (technically making it a hormone rather than a vitamin), where it plays a vital role in the absorption of calcium. In turn, calcium is vital for strong bones. Without it, people fall victim to the crippling diseases rickets and osteomalacia. In women, calcium deficiencies can result in a deformed birth canal, which makes childbirth lethal for both mother and fetus.

Vitamin D can be obtained from a few foods, primarily the 4 oils and livers of marine fish. But inland populations must rely on the sun's rays and their own skins for the supply of this crucial substance. The particular color of a human population's skin, therefore, represents in large degree a trade-off between the hazards of too much versus too little solar radiation: acute sunburn and skin cancer on the one hand, and rickets and osteomalacia on the other. It is this trade-off that largely accounts for the preponderance of brown people in the world and for the general tendency for skin color to be darkest among equatorial populations and lightest among populations dwelling at higher latitudes.

At middle latitudes, the skin follows a strategy of changing colors with the seasons. Around the Mediterranean basin, for example, exposure to the summer sun brings high risk of cancer but low risk for rickets; the body produces more melanin and people grow darker (i.e., they get suntans). Winter reduces the risk of sunburn and cancer; the body produces less melanin, and the tan wears off.

The correlation between skin color and latitude is not perfect because other factors — such as the availability of foods containing vitamin D and calcium, regional cloud cover during the winter, amount of clothing worn, and cultural preferences — may work for or against the predicted relationship. Arctic-dwelling Eskimo, for example, are not as light-skinned as expected, but their habitat and economy afford them a diet that is exceptionally rich in both vitamin D and calcium.

Northern Europeans, obliged to wear heavy garments for protection against the long, cold, cloudy winters, were always at risk for rickets and osteomalacia from too little vitamin D and calcium. This risk increases sometime after 6000 B.C., when pioneer cattle herders who did not exploit marine resources began to appear in northern Europe. The risk would have been especially great for the brown-skinned Mediterranean peoples who migrated northward along with the crops and farm animals. Samples of Caucasian skin (infant penile foreskin obtained at the time of circumcision) exposed to sunlight on cloudless days in Boston (42°N) from November through February produced no vitamin D. In Edmonton (52°N) this period extended from October to March. But further south (34°N) sunlight was effective in producing vitamin D in the middle of the winter. Almost all of Europe lies north of 42°N. Fair-skinned, nontanning individuals who could utilize the weakest and briefest doses of sunlight to synthesize vitamin D were strongly favored by natural selection. During the frigid winters, only a small circle of a child's face could be left to peek out at the sun through the heavy clothing, thereby favoring the survival of individuals with translucent patches of pink on their cheeks characteristic of many northern Europeans. . . .

If light-skinned individuals on the average had only 2 percent   8
more children survive per generation, the changeover in their
skin color could have begun five thousand years ago and reached
present levels well before the beginning of the Christian era. But
natural selection need not have acted alone. Cultural selection
may also have played a role. It seems likely that whenever people
consciously or unconsciously had to decide which infants to
nourish and which to neglect, the advantage would go to those
with lighter skin, experience having shown that such individuals
tended to grow up to be taller, stronger, and healthier than their
darker siblings. White was beautiful because white was healthy.

To account for the evolution of black skin in equatorial lati-   9
tudes, one has merely to reverse the combined effects of natural
and cultural selection. With the sun directly overhead most of the
year, and clothing a hindrance to work and survival, vitamin D
was never in short supply (and calcium was easily obtained from
vegetables). Rickets and osteomalacia were rare. Skin cancer was
the main problem, and what nature started, culture amplified.
Darker infants were favored by parents because experience
showed that they grew up to be freer of disfiguring and lethal ma-
lignancies. Black was beautiful because black was healthy.

QUESTIONS ON MEANING

1. What is Harris's THESIS? How does process analysis develop this idea?
2. How does the author explain the development of very light-skinned
   and very dark-skinned people?
3. With what is skin color most closely associated? Why is this correlation not perfect?
4. What point does Harris make about cultural selection? What do you
   think he means by this term?

QUESTIONS ON WRITING STRATEGY

1. What historical movement of people does Harris refer to? Why does
   he mention this movement?

2. What kind of EVIDENCE does Harris use? Do you find the evidence convincing?
3. How does the example of Australia (para. 2) fit into Harris's process analysis?
4. What is the ALLUSION in Harris's last sentence? What does that sentence suggest about Harris's PURPOSE?
5. **OTHER METHODS.** Harris compares and contrasts people with different skin colors. Does he have a bias — either personal or biologically based — toward any particular color?

QUESTIONS ON LANGUAGE

1. What is the TONE of this essay? Is it appropriate, do you think?
2. Examine how Harris introduces technical vocabulary. What can you tell about the meanings of the following terms from what Harris says: melanin, malignant, melanoma (para. 2); radiation, epidermis, hormone, calcium, rickets, osteomalacia (3); latitudes (4); correlation, habitat (6); siblings (8).
3. Be sure you know the meanings of these words as well: afflictions (para. 2); unmitigated (3); preponderance (4); translucent (7).
4. When, if at all, does Harris use the words "whites" and "blacks"? What words does he use to describe skin color? Why?

SUGGESTIONS FOR WRITING

1. Write a process analysis of how something came to be the way it is — for instance, a city street pattern, the furless bodies of humans, automated bank tellers, or the basic design of the automobile. Conduct whatever research is necessary, and explain the process clearly and with ample detail.
2. Respond to Harris's essay in one of several possible ways: (a) Explain the EFFECT the essay had on you. (b) Explain how you think skin color is viewed in this country, with examples. (c) List individuals or groups of people you think should read this essay, and explain why in each case.
3. **CONNECTIONS.** Several essays in this book address perceptions of skin color in American society — for instance, Ralph Ellison's "On Being the Target of Discrimination" (p. 43), Brent Staples's "Black Men and Public Space" (p. 199), and Curtis Chang's "Streets of Gold" (p. 635). In an essay of your own based on two or more of these works, analyze what skin color seems to signify in the United States. In your opinion, to what extent, if at all, is skin color regarded as biological?

OLIVER SACKS

OLIVER SACKS is a doctor, medical researcher, and writer whom the critic Anatole Broyard has called "the poet laureate of contemporary medicine." He was born in 1933 in London to parents who were both doctors. He attended Oxford University, where he earned several bachelor's and master's degrees, and he trained as a physician at Middlesex Hospital. In 1960 Sacks came to the United States to study neurology at UCLA, and in 1965 he took up teaching at Albert Einstein Medical College in New York, where he is still a professor of neurology. While treating patients, Sacks grew increasingly aware of the complex interrelations of mind and body — two spheres usually kept distinct by modern medicine and psychology. This belief in the wholeness of the individual pervades all of Sacks's work and his writing. His books include *Migraine: The Evolution of a Common Disorder* (1970); *Awakenings* (1973, republished 1987), about Sacks's work with patients who had sleeping sickness; *A Leg to Stand On* (1984), an autobiographical account of dealing with a crippling leg injury; *The Man Who Mistook His Wife for a Hat* (1985), essays on people with disorders of the nervous system; and *Seeing Voices: A Journey into the World of the Deaf* (1989).

The President's Speech

In this essay from *The Man Who Mistook His Wife for a Hat*, Sacks pursues his interest in disorders that affect the patient's sense of self. He writes what he calls "romantic science," science that welcomes what most scientists claim to reject: "the judgmental, the particular, the personal." The result in this case is a process analysis both clear and sensitive.

What was going on? A roar of laughter from the aphasia ward, just as the President's speech was coming on, and they had all been so eager to hear the President speaking. . . .

There he was, the old Charmer, the Actor, with his practiced rhetoric, his histrionisms, his emotional appeal — and all the patients were convulsed with laughter. Well, not all: Some looked bewildered, some looked outraged, one or two looked apprehensive, but most looked amused. The President was, as always, moving — but he was moving them, apparently, mainly to laughter. What could they be thinking? Were they failing to understand him? Or did they, perhaps, understand him all too well?

It was often said of these patients, who though intelligent had the severest receptive or global aphasia, rendering them incapable of understanding words as such, that they nonetheless understood most of what was said to them. Their friends, their relatives, the nurses who knew them well, could hardly believe, sometimes, that they *were* aphasic.

This was because, when addressed naturally, they grasped some or most of the meaning. And one does speak "naturally," naturally.

Thus to demonstrate their aphasia, one had to go to extraordinary lengths, as a neurologist, to speak and behave unnaturally, to remove all the extraverbal cues — tone of voice, intonation, suggestive emphasis or inflection, as well as all visual cues (one's expressions, one's gestures, one's entire, largely unconscious, personal repertoire and posture): One had to remove all of this (which might involve total concealment of one's person, and total depersonalization of one's voice, even to using a computerized voice synthesizer) in order to reduce speech to pure words, speech totally devoid of what Frege called "tone-color" (*Klangenfarben*) or "evocation." With the most sensitive patients, it was only with such a grossly artificial, mechanical speech — somewhat like that of the computers in *Star Trek* — that one could be wholly sure of their aphasia.

Why all this? Because speech — natural speech — does *not* consist of words alone, nor (as Hughlings Jackson thought) "propositions" alone. It consists of *utterance* — an uttering-forth of one's whole meaning with one's whole being — the understanding of which involves infinitely more than mere word-recognition. And this was the clue to aphasiacs' understanding, even when they might be wholly uncomprehending of words as such. For though the words, the verbal constructions, *per se*, might convey nothing, spoken language is normally suffused with "tone," embedded in an expressiveness which transcends the verbal — and it is precisely this expressiveness, so deep, so various, so complex, so subtle, which is perfectly preserved in aphasia, though understanding of words be destroyed. Preserved — and often more: preternaturally enhanced. . . .

This too becomes clear — often in the most striking, or   7
comic, or dramatic way — to all those who work or live closely with aphasiacs: their families or friends or nurses or doctors. At first, perhaps, we see nothing much the matter; and then we see that there has been a great change, almost an inversion, in their understanding of speech. Something has gone, has been devastated, it is true — but something has come, in its stead, has been immensely enhanced, so that — at least with emotionally laden utterance — the meaning may be fully grasped even when every word is missed. This, in our species *Homo loquens*,[1] seems almost an inversion of the usual order of things: an inversion, and perhaps a reversion too, to something more primitive and elemental. And this perhaps is why Hughlings Jackson compared aphasiacs to dogs (a comparison that might outrage both!) though when he did this he was chiefly thinking of their linguistic incompetencies, rather than their remarkable, and almost infallible, sensitivity to "tone" and feeling. Henry Head, more sensitive in this regard, speaks of "feeling-tone" in his (1926) treatise on aphasia, and stresses how it is preserved, and often enhanced, in aphasiacs.

Thus the feeling I sometimes have — which all of us who   8
work closely with aphasiacs have — that one cannot lie to an aphasiac. He cannot grasp your words, and so cannot be deceived by them; but what he grasps he grasps with infallible precision, namely the *expression* that goes with the words, that total, spontaneous, involuntary expressiveness which can never be simulated or faked, as words alone can, all too easily. . . .

We recognize this with dogs, and often use them for this pur-   9
pose — to pick up falsehood, or malice, or equivocal intentions, to tell us who can be trusted, who is integral, who makes sense, when we — so susceptible to words — cannot trust our own instincts.

And what dogs can do here, aphasiacs do too, and at a human   10
and immeasurably superior level. "One can lie with the mouth,"

---

[1]Latin: "speaking man." — EDS.

Nietzsche writes, "but with the accompanying grimace one never-theless tells the truth." To such a grimace, to any falsity or impropriety in bodily appearance or posture, aphasiacs are preternaturally sensitive. And if they cannot see one — this is especially true of our blind aphasiacs — they have an infallible ear for every vocal nuance, the tone, the rhythm, the cadences, the music, the subtlest modulations, inflections, intonations, which can give — or remove — verisimilitude to or from a man's voice.

In this, then, lies their power of understanding — under-   11 standing, without words, what is authentic or inauthentic. Thus it was the grimaces, the histrionisms, the false gestures and, above all, the false tones and cadences of the voice, which rang false for these wordless but immensely sensitive patients. It was to these (for them) most glaring, even grotesque, incongruities and improprieties that my aphasic patients responded, undeceived and undeceivable by words.

This is why they laughed at the President's speech.   12

If one cannot lie to an aphasiac, in view of his special sensitiv-   13 ity to expression and "tone," how is it, we might ask, with patients — if there are such — who *lack* any sense of expression and "tone," while preserving, unchanged, their comprehension for words: patients of an exactly opposite kind? We have a number of such patients, also on the aphasia ward, although, technically, they do not have aphasia, but, instead, a form of *agnosia*, in particular a so-called "tonal" agnosia. For such patients, typically, the expressive qualities of voices disappear — their tone, their timbre, their feeling, their entire character — while words (and grammatical constructions) are perfectly understood. Such tonal agnosias (or "atonias") are associated with disorders of the *right* temporal lobe of the brain, whereas the aphasias go with disorders of the *left* temporal lobe.

Among the patients with tonal agnosia on our aphasia ward   14 who also listened to the President's speech was Emily D., with a glioma in her right temporal lobe. A former English teacher, and poetess of some repute, with an exceptional feeling for language, and strong powers of analysis and expression, Emily D. was able to articulate the opposite situation — how the President's speech sounded to someone with tonal agnosia. Emily D. could no longer tell if a voice was angry, cheerful, sad — whatever. Since voices now lacked expression, she had to look at people's faces, their postures and movements when they talked, and found herself doing so with a care, an intensity, she had never shown before. But this, it so happened, was also limited, because she had a malignant glaucoma, and was rapidly losing her sight too.

What she then found she had to do was to pay extreme attention to exactness of words and word use, and to insist that those around her did just the same. She could less and less follow loose speech or slang — speech of an allusive or emotional kind — and more and more required of her interlocutors that they speak *prose* — "proper words in proper places." Prose, she found, might compensate, in some degree, for lack of perceived tone or feeling.   15

In this way she was able to preserve, even enhance, the use of "expressive" speech — in which the meaning was wholly given by the apt choice and reference of words — despite being more and more lost with "evocative" speech (where meaning is wholly given in the use and sense of tone).   16

Emily D. also listened, stony-faced, to the President's speech, bringing to it a strange mixture of enhanced and defective perceptions — precisely the opposite mixture to those of our aphasiacs. It did not move her — no speech now moved her — and all that was evocative, genuine or false, completely passed her by. Deprived of emotional reaction, was she then (like the rest of us) transported or taken in? By no means. "He is not cogent," she said. "He does not speak good prose. His word-use is improper. Either he is brain-damaged, or he has something to conceal." Thus the President's speech did not work for Emily D. either, due to her enhanced sense of formal language use, propriety as prose, any more than it worked for our aphasiacs, with their word-deafness but enhanced sense of tone.   17

Here then was the paradox of the President's speech. We normals — aided, doubtless, by our wish to be fooled, were indeed well and truly fooled (*"Populus vult decipi, ergo decipiatur"*[2]). And so cunningly was deceptive word-use combined with deceptive tone, that only the brain-damaged remained intact, undeceived.   18

[2]Latin: "The population wants to be deceived, therefore let it be deceived." — Eds.

QUESTIONS ON MEANING

1. What is the THESIS of the essay? The PURPOSE?
2. What is the PARADOX of the President's speech? Where do we first get wind of it?
3. Summarize the difference between a person with aphasia and one with tonal agnosia. How was Emily D. an exceptional agnosia patient?
4. In paragraph 7, Sacks says that Hughlings Jackson's comparison of aphasiacs and dogs "might outrage them both." Why, then, does Sacks go on to further the comparison (9–10)? How is his comparison different?

QUESTIONS ON WRITING STRATEGY

1. What process(es) does Sacks analyze? What related process(es) does he leave uncovered? How is this omission consistent with Sacks's purpose?
2. Does it matter that Sacks does not identify the President by name?
3. What assumptions does Sacks make about his AUDIENCE? Are they valid?
4. What kind of EVIDENCE does Sacks provide? What is its EFFECT?
5. OTHER METHODS. This process analysis depends heavily on definition (Chap. 10). What does Sacks define? Why?

QUESTIONS ON LANGUAGE

1. How would you characterize the TONE of this essay?
2. A few of Sacks's sentences are very short ("Why all this?" para. 6). Many others are quite long and involved ("Something has gone, has been devastated, it is true — but something has come, in its stead, has been immensely enhanced, so that — at least with emotionally laden utterance — the meaning may be fully grasped even when every word is missed," 7). What is the EFFECT of these long sentences?
3. Some of the following words may be new to you: histrionisms (para. 2); extraverbal, devoid, repertoire, synthesizer (5); utterance, suffused, embedded, preternaturally (6); stead, reversion, infallible, treatise (7); integral, susceptible (9); impropriety, nuance, cadences, verisimilitude (10); timbre (13); glioma, glaucoma, malignant (14); allusive, interlocutors (15); cogent (17).

SUGGESTIONS FOR WRITING

1. Watch a politician or any public figure on television (*MacNeil/ Lehrer Newshour, Nightline,* or another news show with interviews would be a good source). Turn down the volume and see what you can understand simply from what Sacks calls "visual cues." Then raise the volume and turn your back to the set, listening for "extraverbal cues" such as tone, emphasis, and inflection. Write a brief essay in which you explain what these cues add to spoken words, using specific examples from your experiment.

2. Write a process analysis of a particular form of communication — how a cat gets what it wants, say, or how some parents you know control their child, or how a store clerk deals with rude customers. The subject should be something you're familiar with from observation or experience so that you can generalize from instances to principles. You may wish to explain how the communication works in different situations (a cat wanting to be fed, let out, let in) or in a sequence of steps (parents causing and then quieting a child's tantrum).

3. CONNECTIONS. Read Richard Selzer's "The Discus Thrower" (p. 152). Write an essay in which you analyze and compare Selzer's and Sacks's attitudes toward their patients as evidenced both by *what* they say and *how* they say it.

OLIVER SACKS ON WRITING

In interviews, Oliver Sacks describes himself as working from example to generalization. "I don't have a systematic sort of mind," he says. "I need a plight, a predicament, a human situation to kindle me and direct me on to more general things." The writer and the doctor use the same material: "I think of myself as a reporter, a describer of things, a journalist of biological predicaments and the adaptations — often remarkable and sometimes creative — that go with them. I have always written journals and have always had a pen in hand. I write at odd times, in restaurants, on planes, and my books are my form of foreign travel. Being a doctor bestows an enormous privilege — one hears lives, predicaments, struggles, and wonderful stories."

Starting from the instance, the particular patient, means that

Sacks usually does not know what he will write next. "I love the feeling of organic growth, of something happening outside my will," he said in another interview. His method also means he can get sidetracked, but he doesn't mind in the least. In *Seeing Voices* he confesses, "I have never found it possible to tell a story, or pursue a line of thought, without taking innumerable side trips or excursions along the way, and finding my journey the richer for this."

FOR DISCUSSION

1. What would you say is the advantage of Sacks's approach to writing? The disadvantage?
2. What parallels do you see between Sacks's approach to writing and the scientific method?

LINNEA SAUKKO

LINNEA SAUKKO was born in Warren, Ohio, in 1956. After receiving a degree in environmental quality control from Muskingum Area Technical College, she spent three years as an environmental technician, developing hazardous waste programs and acting as adviser on chemical safety at a large corporation. Concerned about the lack of safe methods for disposing of hazardous waste, Saukko went back to school to earn a B.A. in geology (Ohio State University, 1985) so that she could help address this issue. She currently lives in Hilliard, Ohio, and works as supervisor of the Groundwater Division of the Ohio Environmental Protection Division, evaluating various sites for possible contamination of the groundwater.

How to Poison the Earth

"How to Poison the Earth" was written in response to an assignment given in a freshman composition class and was awarded a 1983 Bedford Prize in Student Writing. It was one of thirty-one winners chosen from over 1,100 essays submitted to this nationwide contest and was subsequently published in *Student Writers at Work: The Bedford Prizes*, edited by Nancy Sommers and Donald McQuade (1984). In this satirical essay, Saukko shares with readers some of what she has learned on the job, and suggests one way we can guarantee the fate of the earth.

Poisoning the earth can be difficult because the earth is always trying to cleanse and renew itself. Keeping this in mind, we should generate as much waste as possible from substances such as uranium-238, which has a half-life (the time it takes for half of the substance to decay) of one million years, or plutonium, which has a half-life of only 0.5 million years but is so toxic that if distributed evenly, ten pounds of it could kill every person on the earth. Because the United States generates about eighteen tons of plutonium per year, it is about the best substance for long-term 1 poisoning of the earth. It would help if we would build more nuclear power plants because each one generates only 500 pounds of plutonium each year. Of course, we must include persistent toxic chemicals such as polychlorinated biphenyl (PCB) and dichloro-diphenyl trichloroethane (DDT) to make sure we have enough toxins to poison the earth from the core to the outer atmosphere. First, we must develop many different ways of putting the waste from these nuclear and chemical substances in, on, and around the earth.

Putting these substances in the earth is a most important step   2
in the poisoning process. With deep-well injection we can ensure that the earth is poisoned all the way to the core. Deep-well injection involves drilling a hole that is a few thousand feet deep and injecting toxic substances at extremely high pressures so they will penetrate deep into the earth. According to the Environmental Protection Agency (EPA), there are about 360 such deep injection wells in the United States. We cannot forget the groundwater aquifers that are closer to the surface. These must also be contaminated. This is easily done by shallow-well injection, which operates on the same principle as deep-well injection, only closer to the surface. The groundwater that has been injected with toxins will spread the contamination beneath the earth. The EPA estimates that there are approximately 500,000 shallow injection wells in the United States.

Burying the toxins in the earth is the next best method. The   3
toxins from landfills, dumps, and lagoons slowly seep into the earth, guaranteeing that contamination will last a long time. Because the EPA estimates there are only about 50,000 of these dumps in the United States, they should be located in areas where they will leak to the surrounding ground and surface water.

Applying pesticides and other poisons on the earth is another   4
part of the poisoning process. This is good for coating the earth's surface so that the poisons will be absorbed by plants, will seep into the ground, and will run off into surface water.

Surface water is very important to contaminate because it will   5
transport the poisons to places that cannot be contaminated directly. Lakes are good for long-term storage of pollutants while they release some of their contamination to rivers. The only trou-

ble with rivers is that they act as a natural cleansing system for the earth. No matter how much poison is dumped into them, they will try to transport it away to reach the ocean eventually.

The ocean is very hard to contaminate because it has such a 6 large volume and a natural buffering capacity that tends to neutralize some of the contamination. So in addition to the pollution from rivers, we must use the ocean as a dumping place for as many toxins as possible. The ocean currents will help transport the pollution to places that cannot otherwise be reached.

Now make sure that the air around the earth is very polluted. 7 Combustion and evaporation are major mechanisms for doing this. We must continuously pollute because the wind will disperse the toxins while rain washes them from the air. But this is good because a few lakes are stripped of all living animals each year from acid rain. Because the lower atmosphere can cleanse itself fairly easily, we must explode nuclear test bombs that shoot radioactive particles high into the upper atmosphere where they will circle the earth for years. Gravity must pull some of the particles to earth, so we must continue exploding these bombs.

So it is that easy. Just be sure to generate as many poisonous 8 substances as possible and be sure they are distributed in, on, and around the entire earth at a greater rate than it can cleanse itself. By following these easy steps we can guarantee the poisoning of the earth.

QUESTIONS ON MEANING

1. Is the author's main PURPOSE to amuse and entertain, to inform readers of ways they can make better use of natural resources, to warn readers about threats to the future of our planet, or to make fun of scientists? Support your answer with EVIDENCE from the essay.

2. Describe at least three of the earth's mechanisms for cleansing its land, water, and atmosphere, as presented in this essay.

3. According to Saukko, many of our actions are detrimental, if not outright destructive, to our environment. Identify these practices

and discuss them. If these activities are harmful to the earth, why are they permitted? Do they serve some other important goal or purpose? If so, what? Are there other ways that these goals might be reached?

QUESTIONS ON WRITING STRATEGY

1. How is Saukko's essay organized? Follow the process carefully to determine whether it happens chronologically, with each step depending on the one before it, or whether it follows another order. How effective is this method of organization and presentation?
2. For what AUDIENCE is this essay intended? How can you tell?
3. What is the TONE of this essay? Consider especially the title and the last paragraph as well as examples from the body of the essay. How does the tone contribute to Saukko's SATIRE?
4. How detailed and specific are Saukko's instructions for poisoning the earth? Which steps in this process would you be able to carry out, once you finished reading the essay? In what instances might an author choose *not* to provide concrete, comprehensive instructions for a procedure? Relate your answer to the tone and purpose of this essay.
5. OTHER METHODS. Saukko doesn't mention every possible pollutant but instead focuses on certain examples (Chap. 3). Why do you think she chooses these particular examples? What serious pollutants can you think of that Saukko doesn't mention specifically?

QUESTIONS ON LANGUAGE

1. How do the phrases "next best method" (para. 3), "another part of the poisoning process" (4), and "lakes are good for long-term storage of pollutants" (5) signal the tone of this essay? Should they be read literally, ironically, metaphorically, or some other way?
2. Be sure you know how to define the following words: generate, nuclear, toxins (para. 1); lagoons, contamination (3); buffering, neutralize (6); combustion (7).

SUGGESTIONS FOR WRITING

1. Write a satirical essay in which you propose the solution to a problem or the means to an end. Make sure your tone signals your satiric intent. Describe your solution in detail, using time-markers to indicate the order of steps or events.

2. Write an essay defending and justifying the use of nuclear power plants, pesticides, or another pollutant Saukko mentions. This essay will require some research because you will need to argue that the benefits of these methods outweigh their hazardous and destructive effects. Be sure to support your claims with factual information and statistics. Or, approach the issue from the same point of view that Saukko did, and argue against the use of nuclear power plants or pesticides. Substantiate your argument with data and facts, and make sure to propose alternative sources of power or alternative methods of insect control.

3. CONNECTIONS. Compare Linnea Saukko's essay and Jonathan Swift's "A Modest Proposal" (p. 713) as SATIRES. In your essay, explain what satire is (consult a literary or rhetorical dictionary if you need more information than our glossary provides), and explain how each author uses satire. What are the differences and similarities between the two essays?

LINNEA SAUKKO ON WRITING

"After I have chosen a topic," says Linnea Saukko, "the easiest thing for me to do is to write about how I really feel about it. The goal of 'How To Poison the Earth' was to inform people, or more specifically, to open their eyes.

"As soon as I decided on my topic, I made a list of all the types of pollution and I sat down and basically wrote the paper in less than two hours. The information seemed to pour from me onto the page. Of course I did a lot of editing afterward, but I never changed the idea and the tone that I started with."

FOR DISCUSSION

1. When have you had the experience of writing on a subject that compelled your words to pour forth with little effort? What was the subject? What did you learn from this experience?

PETER ELBOW

PETER ELBOW is well known as a director of writing programs for community groups and for college students. Born in 1935, he received his education at Williams College and at Brandeis, Harvard, and Oxford. He has taught at Wesleyan University, MIT, Franconia College, and the Harvard Graduate School of Education, as well as at Evergreen State College in Olympia, Washington. Recently he started the highly acclaimed "Workshop in Language and Thinking" at Bard College, and served as director of the Writing Program at the State University of New York, Stony Brook. He is the author of many articles and of the influential *Writing without Teachers* (1973), *Writing with Power* (1981), and *Embracing Contraries: Explorations in Learning and Teaching* (1986). Currently, he teaches at the University of Massachusetts, Amherst.

Desperation Writing

What do you do when you have a paper due but can't think of a word to say about the assigned subject? This is a problem faced by most college students at one time or another. But take heart. Peter Elbow has come up with a solution. What's more, if you try to follow his advice, you will find it much less painful than you expected. "Desperation Writing" has offered solace and help to thousands since it first appeared in *Writing without Teachers*. (The next essay, Annie Dillard's "Writing and Vision," also offers writing help, though of a different sort.)

I know I am not alone in my recurring twinges of panic that I 1 won't be able to write something when I need to, I won't be able to produce coherent speech or thought. And that lingering doubt is a great hindrance to writing. It's a constant fog or static that clouds the mind. I never got out of its clutches till I discovered that it was possible to write something — not something great or pleasing but at least something usable, workable — when my mind is out of commission. The trick is that you have to do all

your cooking out on the table: Your mind is incapable
of doing any inside. It means using symbols and pieces of paper
not as a crutch but as a wheelchair.

The first thing is to admit your condition: Because of some   2
mood or event or whatever, your mind is incapable of anything
that could be called thought. It can put out a babbling kind of
speech utterance, it can put a simple feeling, perception, or sort-
of-thought into understandable (though terrible) words. But it is
incapable of considering anything in relation to anything else.
The moment you try to hold that thought or feeling up against
some other to see the relationship, you simply lose the picture —
you get nothing but buzzing lines or waving colors.

So admit this. Avoid anything more than one feeling, percep-   3
tion, or thought. Simply write as much as possible. Try simply to
steer your mind in the direction or general vicinity of the thing
you are trying to write about and start writing and keep writing.

Just write and keep writing. (Probably best to write on only   4
one side of the paper in case you should want to cut parts out
with scissors — but you probably won't.) Just write and keep writing. It will probably come in waves. After a flurry, stop and take a
brief rest. But don't stop too long. Don't think about what you
are writing or what you have written or else you will overload the
circuit again. Keep writing as though you are drugged or drunk.
Keep doing this till you feel you have a lot of material that might
be useful; or, if necessary, till you can't stand it any more — even
if you doubt that there's anything useful there.

Then take a pad of little pieces of paper — or perhaps 3×5 5
cards — and simply start at the beginning of what you were writing, and as you read over what you wrote, every time you come to
any thought, feeling, perception, or image that could be gathered
up into one sentence or one assertion, do so and write it by itself
on a little sheet of paper. In short, you are trying to turn, say, ten
or twenty pages of wandering mush into twenty or thirty hard little crab apples. Sometimes there won't be many on a page. But if
it seems to you that there are none on a page, you are making a
serious error — the same serious error that put you in this comatose state to start with. You are mistaking lousy, stupid, second-
rate, wrong, childish, foolish, worthless ideas for no ideas at all.

Your job is not to pick out *good* ideas but to pick out ideas. As long as you were conscious, your words will be full of things that could be called feelings, utterances, ideas — things that can be squeezed into one simple sentence. This is your job. Don't ask for too much.

After you have done this, take those little slips or cards, read   6
through them a number of times — not struggling with them, simply wandering and mulling through them; perhaps shifting them around and looking through them in various sequences. In a sense these are cards you are playing solitaire with, and the rules of this particular game permit shuffling the unused pile.

The goal of this procedure with the cards is to get them to dis-   7
tribute themselves in two or three or ten or fifteen different piles on your desk. You can get them to do this almost by themselves if you simply keep reading through them in different orders; certain cards will begin to feel like they go with other cards. I emphasize this passive, thoughtless mode because I want to talk about desperation writing in its pure state. In practice, almost invariably at some point in the procedure, your sanity begins to return. It is often at this point. You actually are moved to have thoughts or — and the difference between active and passive is crucial here — to *exert* thought; to hold two cards together and *build* or *assert* a relationship. It is a matter of bringing energy to bear.

So you may start to be able to do something active with these   8
cards, and begin actually to think. But if not, just allow the cards to find their own piles with each other by feel, by drift, by intuition, by mindlessness.

You have now engaged in the two main activities that will   9
permit you to get something cooked out on the table rather than in your brain: writing out into messy words, summing up into single assertions, and even sensing relationships between assertions. You can simply continue to deploy these two activities.

If, for example, after that first round of writing, assertion-   10
making, and pile-making, your piles feel as though they are useful and satisfactory for what you are writing — paragraphs or sections or trains of thought — then you can carry on from there. See if you can gather each pile up into a single assertion. When you can, then put the subsidiary assertions of that pile into their

best order to fit with that single unifying one. If you *can't* get the
pile into one assertion, then take the pile as the basis for doing
some more writing out into words. In the course of this writing,
you may produce for yourself the single unifying assertion
you were looking for; or you may have to go through the cycle
of turning the writing into assertions and piles and so forth. Perhaps more than once. The pile may turn out to want to be two or
more piles itself; or it may want to become part of a pile you
already have. This is natural. This kind of meshing into one
configuration, then coming apart, then coming together and
meshing into a different configuration — this is growing and
cooking. It makes a terrible mess, but if you can't do it in
your head, you have to put up with a cluttered desk and a lot of
confusion.

If, on the other hand, all that writing *didn't* have useful mate-   11
rial in it, it means that your writing wasn't loose, drifting, quirky,
jerky, associative enough. This time try especially to let things
simply remind you of things that are seemingly crazy or unrelated. Follow these odd associations. Make as many metaphors as
you can — be as nutty as possible — and explore the metaphors
themselves — open them out. You may have all your energy tied
up in some area of your experience that you are leaving out.
Don't refrain from writing about whatever else is on your mind:
how you feel at the moment, what you are losing your mind over,
randomness that intrudes itself on your consciousness, the pattern on the wallpaper, what those people you see out the window
have on their minds — though keep coming back to the what-
everitis you are supposed to be writing about. Treat it, in short,
like ten-minute writing exercises. Your best perceptions and
thoughts are always going to be tied up in whatever is really occupying you, and that is also where your energy is. You may end up
writing a love poem — or a hate poem — in one of those little
piles while the other piles will finally turn into a lab report
on data processing or whatever you have to write about. But
you couldn't, in your present state of having your head shot off,
have written that report without also writing the poem. And
the report will have some of the juice of the poem in it and vice
versa.

QUESTIONS ON MEANING

1. On what assumptions does Elbow base his advice?
2. Where in his essay does the author reveal his PURPOSE?
3. What value does Elbow discern in "lousy, stupid, second-rate, wrong, childish, foolish, worthless ideas" (para. 5)?
4. In your own words, describe the role of the unconscious in the process Elbow analyzes. Where in the process does the conscious mind have to do its part?
5. How does the author justify writing a poem when the assignment is to write a lab report?

QUESTIONS ON WRITING STRATEGY

1. What EFFECT does the author achieve by opening his essay in the first PERSON?
2. At what AUDIENCE does Elbow direct his advice?
3. Into how many steps does the author break down the process he analyzes? What are they?
4. Point to effective samples of time-markers in this essay. (Time-markers are discussed on pages 284–285.)
5. Point to phrases or sentences in the essay that seem to you designed to offer encouragement and comfort.
6. OTHER METHODS. When Elbow says that he wants "to talk about desperation writing in its pure state," he calls attention to a developing definition (Chap. 10). In your own words, what is "pure" desperation writing?

QUESTIONS ON LANGUAGE

1. Where in his essay does the author make good use of FIGURES OF SPEECH?
2. Using a dictionary if necessary, define the following words: coherent, hindrance (para. 1); assertion, comatose (5); configuration (10).

SUGGESTIONS FOR WRITING

1. Approach a writing assignment for any one of your classes by following Peter Elbow's advice. Write steadily in the manner prescribed

for at least ten minutes; then sort out any ideas you may have brought forth. If you have no class assignment that involves writing, work instead on a journal entry about some recent event, book, idea, or experience that impressed you. When your exercise has been completed, write a paragraph in which you evaluate how well Elbow's method succeeded for you. Did it lead to any good results? Any surprises?

2. In a brief essay, explain how to tackle any job you're not in the mood for: researching a paper, preparing a speech, performing a lab experiment, studying for a test, cleaning your house, washing your car, getting up in the morning. The process should involve at least three steps.

3. CONNECTIONS. Elbow's "Desperation Writing" and the next essay, Annie Dillard's "Writing and Vision," present different but not contradictory views of the writing process. What attitudes and beliefs do the two writers share? Where do they diverge? What GENERALIZA-TIONS about the writing process can you make based on these two essays? In writing your responses to these questions, use specific examples from both essays. (Use examples from your own experience, too, if they extend Elbow's and Dillard's.)

PETER ELBOW ON WRITING

Peter Elbow's best-known work is devoted, like "Desperation Writing," to encouraging people to write. Much of his advice comes from his writing experience. His own life is the source for a recent article, "Closing My Eyes as I Speak: An Argument for Ignoring Audience."

That it often helps writers to be aware of their readers is an article of faith for many college writing instructors; it is an assumption we make in *The Bedford Reader*. Without denying that a sense of audience is sometimes valuable, Elbow makes a persuasive case for sometimes trying to forget that an audience is there. "When I am talking to a person or a group," he begins, "and struggling to find words or thoughts, I often find myself involuntarily closing my eyes as I speak. I realize now that this behavior is an instinctive attempt to blot out awareness of audience when I need all my concentration for just trying to figure out or express what I want to say. Because the audience is so imperiously *present* in a speaking situation, my instinct reacts with this active attempt to avoid audience awareness. This behavior — in a sense impolite or antisocial — is not so uncommon. Even when we write, alone in a room to an absent audience, there are occasions when we are struggling to figure something out and need to push aside awareness of those absent readers."

Some audiences — like a readership of close friends — are helpful to keep in mind. "When we think about them from the start, we think of more and better things to say." But other audiences are powerfully inhibiting, and keeping them in mind as we write may put up writer's blocks. "For example, when we have to write to someone we find intimidating (and of course students often perceive teachers as intimidating), we often start thinking wholly defensively. As we write down each thought or sentence, our mind fills with thoughts of how the intended reader will criticize or object to it. So we try to qualify or soften what we've just written — or write out some answer to a possible objection. Our writing becomes tangled. Sometimes we get so tied in knots that we cannot even figure out what we think."

The solution? "We can ignore that audience altogether during the *early* stages of writing and direct our words only to ourselves or to no one in particular — or even to the 'wrong' audience, that is, to an *inviting* audience of trusted friends or allies. . . . Putting audience out of mind is of course a traditional practice: Serious writers have long used private journals for early explorations of feeling, thinking, or language." In contrast, inferior newspaper or business writing often reminds us of "the ineffective actor whose consciousness of self distracts us: He makes us too aware of his own awareness of us. When we read such prose, we wish the writer would stop thinking about us — would stop trying to adjust or fit what he is saying to our frame of reference. 'Damn it, put all your attention on what you are saying,' we want to say, 'and forget about us and how we are reacting.'

"When we examine really good student or professional writing, we can often see that its goodness comes from the writer's having gotten sufficiently wrapped up in her meaning and her language as to forget all about audience needs: The writer manages to 'break through.'"

To overcome the problem of being painfully conscious of readers, if it is a problem you've met, Elbow advises writing more than one draft of everything. "*After* we have figured out our thinking in copious exploratory or draft writing — perhaps finding the right voice or stance as well — *then* we can follow the traditional rhetorical advice: Think about readers and revise carefully to adjust our words and thoughts to our intended audience."

FOR DISCUSSION

1. How closely do Peter Elbow's observations reflect your own writing experience? Do you ever worry so hard about what your reader will think that you become pen-tied? Or do you usually close your eyes to your audience, and just write?
2. What is wrong with the following attempt to state Elbow's thesis: "A writer should simply forget about audience"?
3. If you feel uncomfortable when you write, too keenly aware of the reader "looking over your shoulder," what advice of Elbow's might you follow? Can you suggest any other advice to relieve a writer's self-consciousness?

ANNIE DILLARD

For a biographical note, see page 130.

Writing and Vision

This selection comprises three related sections of Dillard's *The Writing Life* (1989); the title is the editors'. Like Peter Elbow in the preceding essay, Dillard writes out of her own experience of writing. In applying her unusual descriptive powers to her writing process, she actually tells of two processes: the wrong and right way to chop wood; and what happens to a writer's idea, to "vision," during drafting. The two processes *may* seem unrelated, but read on.

Once, in order to finish a book I was writing and yet not live   1
in the same room with it, I begged a cabin to use as a study. I finished the book there, wrote some other things, and learned to split wood. All this was on a remote and sparsely populated island on Haro Strait, where I moved when I left Virginia. The island was in northern Puget Sound, Washington State, across the water from Canadian islands.

The cabin was a single small room near the water. Its walls   2
were shrunken planks, not insulated; in January, February, and March, it was cold. There were two small metal beds in the room, two cupboards, some shelves over a little counter, a wood stove, and a table under a window, where I wrote. The window looked out on a bit of sandflat overgrown with thick, varicolored mosses; there were a few small firs where the sandflat met the cobble beach; and there was the water: Puget Sound, and all the sky over it and all the other wild islands in the distance under the sky. It was very grand. But you get used to it. I don't much care where I work. I don't notice things. The door used to blow open and startle me witless. I did, however, notice the cold.

I tried to heat the cabin with the wood stove and a kerosene   3
heater, but I never was warm. I used to work wearing a wool cap,

long wool tights, sweaters, a down jacket, and a scarf. I was too
lazy to stick a damper in the wood stove chimney; I kept putting
off the task for a warm day. Thoreau said that his firewood
warmed him twice — because he labored to cut his own. Mine
froze me twice, for the same reason. After I learned to split wood,
in a manner I am shortly to relate — after I learned to split wood,
I stepped out into the brute northeaster and split just enough alder to last me through working hours, which was not enough
splitting to warm me. Then I came in and kindled a fire in the
stove, all the heat of which vanished up the chimney.

At first, in the good old days, I did not know how to split   4
wood. I set a chunk of alder on the chopping block and harassed
it, at enormous exertion, into tiny wedges that flew all over the
sandflat and lost themselves. What I did was less like splitting
wood than chipping flints. After a few whacks my alder chunk
still stood serene and unmoved, its base untouched, its tip a
thorn. And then I actually tried to turn the sorry thing over and
balance it on its wee head while I tried to chop its feet off before it
fell over. God save us.

All this was a very warm process. I removed my down jacket,   5
my wool hat and scarf. Alas, those early wood-splitting days,
when I truly warmed myself, didn't last long. I lost the knack.

I did not know it at the time, but during those first weeks   6
when I attacked my wood every morning, I was collecting a
crowd — or what passed on the island for a crowd. At the sound
of my ax, Doe and Bob — real islanders, proper, wood-splitting islanders — paused in their activities and mustered, unseen, across
the sandflat, under the firs. They were watching me (oh, the idleness) try to split wood. It must have been a largely silent comedy.
Later, when they confessed, and I railed at them, Bob said inno-
cently that the single remark he had ever permitted himself had
been, "I love to watch Annie split wood."

One night, while all this had been going on, I had a dream in   7
which I was given to understand, by the powers that be, how to split
wood. You aim, said the dream — of course! — at the chopping
block. It is true. You aim at the chopping block, not at the wood;
then you split the wood, instead of chipping it. You cannot do the
job cleanly unless you treat the wood as the transparent means to

an end, by aiming past it. But then, alas, you easily split your day's wood in a few minutes, in the freezing cold, without working up any heat; then you utterly forfeit your only chance of getting warm.

The knack of splitting wood was the only useful thing I had   8
ever learned from any dream, and my attitude toward the powers that be was not entirely grateful. The island comedy was over; everybody had to go back to work; and I never did get warm. . . .

Here is a fairly sober version of what happens in the small   9
room between the writer and the work itself. It is similar to what happens between a painter and the canvas.

First you shape the vision of what the projected work of art   10
will be. The vision, I stress, is no marvelous thing: It is the work's intellectual structure and aesthetic surface. It is a chip of mind, a pleasing intellectual object. It is a vision of the work, not of the world. It is a glowing thing, a blurred thing of beauty. Its structure is at once luminous and translucent; you can see the world through it. After you receive the initial charge of this imaginary object, you add to it at once several aspects, and incubate it most gingerly as it grows into itself.

Many aspects of the work are still uncertain, of course; you   11
know that. You know that if you proceed you will change things and learn things, that the form will grow under your hands and develop new and richer lights. But that change will not alter the vision or its deep structures; it will only enrich it. You know that, and you are right.

But you are wrong if you think that in the actual writing, or   12
in the actual painting, you are filling in the vision. You cannot fill in the vision. You cannot even bring the vision to light. You are wrong if you think that you can in any way take the vision and tame it to the page. The page is jealous and tyrannical; the page is made of time and matter; the page always wins. The vision is not so much destroyed, exactly, as it is, by the time you have finished, forgotten. It has been replaced by this changeling, this bastard, this opaque lightless chunky ruinous work.

Here is how it happens. The vision is, *sub specie aeternitatis*,[1] a   13

---

[1]Latin: "under the aspect of eternity." — EDS.

set of mental relationships, a coherent series of formal possibilities. In the actual rooms of time, however, it is a page or two of
legal paper filled with words and questions; it is a terrible diagram, a few books' names in a margin, an ambiguous doodle, a
corner folded down in a library book. These are memos from the
thinking brain to witless hope.

Nevertheless, ignoring the provisional and pathetic nature of   14
these scraps, and bearing the vision itself in mind — having it before your sights like the very Grail — you begin to scratch out the
first faint marks on the canvas, on the page. You begin the work
proper. Now you have gone and done it. Now the thing is no
longer a vision: It is paper.

Words lead to other words and down the garden path. You   15
adjust the paints' values and hues not to the world, not to the vision, but to the rest of the paint. The materials are stubborn and
rigid; push is always coming to shove. You can fly — you can fly
higher than you thought possible — but you can never get off the
page. After every passage another passage follows, more sentences,
more everything on drearily down. Time and materials hound the
work; the vision recedes ever farther into the dim realms.

And so you continue the work, and finish it. Probably by   16
now you have been forced to toss the most essential part of the
vision. But this is a concern for mere nostalgia now: For before
your eyes, and stealing your heart, is this fighting and frail finished product, entirely opaque. You can see nothing through it. It
is only itself, a series of well-known passages, some colored paint.
Its relationship to the vision that impelled it is the relationship between any energy and any work, anything unchanging to anything temporal.

The work is not the vision itself, certainly. It is not the vision   17
filled in, as if it had been a coloring book. It is not the vision re-
produced in time; that were impossible. It is rather a simulacrum
and a replacement. It is a golem. You try — you try every time
to reproduce the vision, to let your light so shine before men. But
you can only come along with your bushel and hide it.

Who will teach me to write? a reader wanted to know.   18
The page, the page, that eternal blankness, the blankness of   19

eternity which you cover slowly, affirming time's scrawl as a right and your daring as necessity; the page, which you cover wood-enly, ruining it, but asserting your freedom and power to act, ac-knowledging that you ruin everything you touch but touching it nevertheless, because acting is better than being here in mere opacity; the page, which you cover slowly with the crabbed thread of your gut; the page in the purity of its possibilities; the page of your death, against which you pit such flawed excellences as you can muster with all your life's strength: That page will teach you to write.

There is another way of saying this. Aim for the chopping   20 block. If you aim for the wood, you will have nothing. Aim past the wood, aim through the wood; aim for the chopping block.

QUESTIONS ON MEANING

1. How is splitting wood like writing?
2. What happens in paragraphs 14–16?
3. Why, after all her talk of vision, does Dillard stress the page as the teacher of writing?
4. What is Dillard's PURPOSE, do you think?

QUESTIONS ON WRITING STRATEGY

1. Outline the steps in the writing process as Dillard presents them.
2. "An understanding of the writing process is a mixed blessing." What EVIDENCE from the essay supports this statement?
3. What is the EFFECT of the concluding paragraph?
4. How and why does Dillard's TONE change from the beginning of the selection to the end?
5. OTHER METHODS. Dillard uses two analogies (Chap. 8). What are they? What purpose does each serve?

QUESTIONS ON LANGUAGE

1. What is the meaning of two of Dillard's ALLUSIONS, "Grail" (para. 14) and "golem" (17)?

2. How does Dillard use language in paragraphs 10–11 to stress the relation between a painter's and a writer's "vision"?
3. What is the effect of the omitted commas in "opaque lightless chunky ruinous work" (para. 12)?
4. Look in the dictionary for any of these words you do not know: forfeit (para. 7); aesthetic, translucent, incubate, gingerly (10); changeling (12); coherent (13); provisional (14); temporal (16); simulacrum (17).

SUGGESTIONS FOR WRITING

1. Write a process analysis of your own writing process. Consider your TONE and use FIGURES OF SPEECH to make your attitudes concrete.
2. Choose some other largely mental process — making a difficult decision, solving a mathematical problem, meditating, reading. Think of an analogy between it and a physical activity (if you need help with this part, see Chap. 8). Write an essay that explains the mental process in terms of the physical process.
3. CONNECTIONS. Read Peter Elbow's "Desperation Writing" (p. 319) if you have not already. Drawing on it and Dillard's essay as well as on your own experience, write briefly about what can be accomplished, and what may be lost, if, as Elbow puts it, you "just write and keep writing."
4. CONNECTIONS. What, if anything, of the struggle Dillard defines in this selection do you see in her essay "Death of a Moth" (p. 130)? Or, if you prefer, how is the Dillard in "Writing and Vision" the same as or different from the Dillard in "Death of a Moth"? Answer either or both questions in an essay that uses quotations as EVIDENCE.

ADDITIONAL WRITING TOPICS
Process Analysis

1. Write a *directive* process analysis (a "how-to" essay) in which, drawing on your own knowledge, you instruct someone in doing or making something. Divide the process into steps and be sure to detail each step thoroughly. Some possible subjects (any of which may be modified or narrowed with the approval of your instructor):

   How to enlist people's confidence
   How to bake bread
   How to meditate
   How to teach a child to swim
   How to select a science fiction novel
   How to select a rental video tape
   How to drive a car
   How to prepare yourself to take an intelligence test
   How to compose a photograph
   How to judge cattle
   How to buy a used motorcycle
   How to enjoy an opera
   How to organize your own rock group
   How to eat an artichoke
   How to groom a horse
   How to bellydance
   How to make a movie or videotape
   How to build (or fly) a kite
   How to start weight training
   How to aid a person who is choking
   How to behave on a first date
   How to get your own way
   How to kick a habit
   How to lose weight
   How to win at poker
   How to make an effective protest or complaint

   Or, if you don't like any of those topics, what else do you know that others might care to learn from you?

2. Step by step, working in chronological order, write a careful *informative* analysis of any one of the following processes. (This is not to be

a "how-to" essay, but an essay that explains how something happens.) Make use of description wherever necessary, and be sure to include frequent time-markers. If one of these topics gives you a better idea for a paper, discuss your choice of subject with your instructor.

How a student is processed during orientation or registration
How the student newspaper gets published
How a professional umpire (or an insurance underwriter, or some other professional) does his or her job
How an amplifier (or other stereo component) works
How an air conditioner (or other household appliance) works
How a political candidate runs for office
How birds teach their young (or some other process in the natural world: how sharks feed, how a snake swallows an egg, how the human liver works)
How police control crowds
How people usually make up their minds when shopping for new cars (or new clothes)

3. Write a directive process analysis in which you use a light TONE. Although you need not take your subject in deadly earnest, your humor will probably be effective only if you take the method of process analysis seriously. Make clear each stage of the process and explain it in sufficient detail.

How to get through the month of November (or March)
How to flunk out of college swiftly and efficiently
How to outwit a pinball machine
How to choose a mate
How to go broke
How to sell something that nobody wants

6
DIVISION OR ANALYSIS
Slicing into Parts

THE METHOD

A chemist working for a soft-drink company is asked to improve on a competitor's product, Orange Quench. (In the last chapter, the same chemist was working on a different part of the same problem.) To do the job, the chemist first has to figure out what's in the drink. She smells the stuff and tastes it. Then she tests a sample chemically to discover the actual ingredients: water, corn syrup, citric acid, sodium benzoate, coloring. Methodically, the chemist has performed division or analysis: She has separated the beverage into its components. Orange Quench stands revealed, understood, ready to be bettered.

Analysis is a key skill in learning and in life. It is an instrument allowing you to slice a large and complicated subject into smaller parts that you can grasp and relate to one another. With analysis you comprehend — and communicate — the structure of

things. And when it works, you find in the parts an idea or conclusion about the subject that makes it clearer, truer, more comprehensive, or more vivid than before you started.

If you have worked with the previous two chapters, you have
already used division or analysis in explaining a process (Chap. 5)
and in comparing and contrasting (Chap. 4). To make a better
Orange Quench (a process), the chemist might prepare a recipe
that divides the process into separate steps or actions ("First, boil
a gallon of water . . ."). When the batch was done, she might
taste-test the two drinks, analyzing and then comparing their orange flavor, sweetness, and acidity. As you'll see in following
chapters, too, division or analysis figures in all the other methods
of developing ideas, for it is basic to any concerted thought, explanation, or evaluation.

Although division or analysis always works the same way —
separating a whole, singular subject into its elements, slicing it
into parts — the method can be more or less difficult depending
on how unfamiliar, complex, and abstract the subject is. Obviously, it's going to be much easier to analyze a chicken (wings,
legs, thighs . . .) than a poem by T. S. Eliot (this image, that allusion . . .), easier to analyze why you won a swimming race than
why the French and then the Americans got involved in Vietnam. Just about any subject *can* be analyzed and will be the
clearer for it. In "I Want a Wife," an essay in this chapter, Judy
Brady divides the role of a wife into its various functions or services. In an essay called "Teacher" from his book *Pot Shots at
Poetry* (1980), Robert Francis divides the knowledge of poetry he
imparted to his class into six pie sections. The first slice is what
he told his students that they knew already.

> The second slice is what I told them that they could have
> found out just as well or better from books. What, for instance,
> is a sestina?
>
> The third slice is what I told them that they refused to ac-
> cept. I could see it on their faces, and later I saw the evidence in
> their writing.
>
> The fourth slice is what I told them that they were willing
> to accept and may have thought they accepted but couldn't ac-
> cept since they couldn't fully understand. This also I saw in

their faces and in their work. Here, no doubt, I was mostly to blame.

The fifth slice is what I told them that they discounted as whimsy or something simply to fill up time. After all, I was being paid to talk.

The sixth slice is what I didn't tell them, for I didn't try to tell them all I knew. Deliberately I kept back something — a few professional secrets, a magic formula or two.

There are always multiple ways to divide or analyze a subject, just as there are many ways to slice a pie. Francis could have divided his knowledge of poetry into knowledge of rhyme, knowledge of meter, knowledge of imagery, and so forth — basically following the components of a poem. In other words, the outcome of an analysis depends on the rule or principle used to do the slicing. This fact accounts for some of the differences among academic disciplines: A psychologist, say, may look at the individual primarily as a bundle of drives and needs, whereas a sociologist may emphasize the individual's roles in society. Even within disciplines, different factions analyze differently, using different principles of division. Some psychologists are interested mainly in thought, others mainly in behavior; some psychologists focus mainly on emotional development, others mainly on moral development.

We said earlier that analysis is a "key skill," but we have yet to mention its fundamental role in CRITICAL THINKING. *Critical* here does not mean "negative" but (according to *Webster's New World Dictionary*) "characterized by careful analysis and judgment." In fact, *analysis* and *criticism* are deeply related: The first comes from a Greek word meaning "to undo," the second from a Greek word meaning "to separate."

Critical thinking goes beneath the surface of the object, word, image, or whatever the subject is. It not only seeks the literal or obvious parts or meanings but also teases out their relations and tests their quality. Say a campaign brochure quotes a candidate as favoring "reasonable government expenditures on reasonable highway projects." The candidate will support new roads, right? Wrong. A critical reader of the brochure quickly senses something fishy in the use (twice) of "reasonable." An in-

formed reader knows (or finds out) that the candidate has consistently opposed new roads, so the chances of her finding a highway
project "reasonable" are slim. At the same time, her stand has
been unpopular, so of course she wants to seem "reasonable" on
the issue. Through critical thinking like this, you unearth the
buried meanings, interpretations, assumptions, or biases that define the essence of something — whether a campaign promise or a
short story, a sociological case study or an environmental impact
report.

If you've read this far in this book, you've already done quite
a bit of critical thinking as you've read and analyzed the essays. In
this chapter, several of the essays themselves — by Margot Harrison, a student, and Mark Crispin Miller and Rosalind Coward,
both writers on the media — show a fair range of concerted critical thinking.

THE PROCESS

Keep an eye out for writing assignments requiring division or
analysis — in college and work, they won't be few or hard to find.
They will probably include the word *analyze* or a word implying
analysis such as *evaluate, interpret, discuss,* or *criticize.* Any time
you spot such a term, you know your job is to separate the subject
into its elements, to explore the relations among them, and to
draw a conclusion about the subject.

Almost any coherent entity — object, person, place, concept
— is a fit subject for division or analysis *if* the analysis will add to
the subject's meaning or significance. Little is deadlier than the
rote analytical exercise that leaves the parts neatly dissected and
the subject comatose on the page. As a writer, you have to ani-
mate the subject, and that means finding your interest. What
about your subject seems curious? What's appealing? Or mysterious? Or awful?

Such questions can help you find your analytical framework,
the rule or principle you will use to divide the subject into parts.
(As we mentioned before, there's more than one way to slice most
subjects.) Say you're contemplating a hunk of bronze in the park.
What elements of its creation and physical form make this sculp-

ture art? Or what is the point of such public art? Or what does this sculpture do for this park? Or vice versa? Any of these questions would give you an angle of vision, a slant on your subject, and get your analysis moving.

In developing an essay by division or analysis, having an outline at your elbow can be a help. You don't want to overlook any parts or elements that should be included in your framework. (You needn't mention every feature in your final essay or give them all equal treatment, but any omissions or variations should be conscious.) And you want to use your framework consistently, not switching carelessly (and confusingly) from, say, the form of the sculpture to the function of public art. In writing her brief essay "I Want a Wife," Judy Brady must have needed an outline to work out carefully the different activities of a wife, so that she covered them all and clearly distinguished them.

Making a valid analysis is chiefly a matter of giving your subject thought, but for the result to seem useful and convincing to your readers, it will have to refer to the concrete world. The method requires not only cogitation, but open eyes and a willingness to provide EVIDENCE. The nature of the evidence will depend entirely on what you are analyzing — physical details for a sculpture, quotations for a poem, financial data for a business case study, statistics for a psychology case study, and so forth. The idea is to supply enough evidence to justify and support your particular slant on the subject.

Be sure your readers know what that slant is, too. Why did you go to the trouble of analyzing the sculpture, anyway, and what conclusion can you draw from the work? Usually, you'll state that conclusion as your THESIS close to the beginning of your essay — for instance, "Like much public art today, this bronze sculpture seems chiefly intended to make people feel good." It doesn't hurt to reassemble your divided subject at the end of the essay, too: That gives you a chance to place your subject in a larger context or speculate on its influence or affirm its significance.

A final caution: It's possible to get carried away with one's own analysis, to become so enamored of the details that the subject itself becomes dim or distorted. You can avoid this danger by keeping the subject literally in front of you as you work (or at least imagining it vividly) and by maintaining an outline. In the end, your subject must be truly represented by your analysis, not twisted, diminished, inflated, or obliterated. The reader should be intrigued by your subject, yes, but also able to recognize it on the street.

DIVISION OR ANALYSIS IN A PARAGRAPH: TWO ILLUSTRATIONS

Using Division or Analysis to Write about Television

Most television comedies, even some that boast live audiences, rely on the laugh machine to fill too-quiet moments on the soundtrack. The effect of a canned laugh comes from its four overlapping elements. The first is style, from titter to belly laugh. The second is intensity, the volume, ranging from mild to medium to ear splitting. The third ingredient is duration, the length of the laugh, whether quick, medium, or extended. And finally, there's the number of laughers, from a lone giggler to a roaring throng. According to rumor (for its exact workings are a secret), the machine contains a bank of thirty-two tapes. Furiously working keys and tromping pedals, the operator plays the tapes singly or in combination to blend the four ingredients, as a maestro weaves a symphony out of brass, woodwinds, percussion, and strings.

COMMENT. This paragraph illustrates a fairly simple form of division or analysis: The four simultaneous parts of a canned laugh are separated out and explained. The writer's principle of analysis — the rule for dividing the subject — is clear and consistently applied: Any canned laugh has four overlapping elements. (The writer might have begun with an altogether different principle, such as the sequence of an individual laugh — beginning, crescendo, end — and that would have produced an altogether different paragraph.) Notice that each element of the laugh is adequately detailed for us to understand it clearly. Because of the analysis, we may not hear television laugh tracks — or even our own laughter — the same way again.

Using Division or Analysis
in an Academic Discipline

The model of social relationship which fits these conditions [of realistic equality between patient and doctor] is that of
the contract or convenant. The notion of contract should not
be loaded with legalistic implications, but taken in its more
symbolic form as in the traditional religious or marriage "contract" or "covenant." Here two individuals or groups are interacting in a way where there are obligations and expected benefits for both parties. The obligations and benefits are limited in
scope, though, even if they are expressed in somewhat vague
terms. The basic norms of freedom, dignity, truth-telling,
promise-keeping, and justice are essential to a contractual relationship. The premise is trust and confidence even though it is
recognized that there is not a full mutuality of interests. Social
sanctions institutionalize and stand behind the relationship, in
case there is a violation of the contract, but for the most part
the assumption is that there will be a faithful fulfillment of the
obligations.

COMMENT. This paragraph by Robert M. Veatch comes
from "Models for Medicine in a Revolutionary Age" (1972), an
article that first appeared in a scholarly journal, *Hastings Center
Report*, and then was reprinted in a textbook on medical ethics.
The author divides or analyzes the idea of the contract as it
might pertain to the relation between doctor and patient. That,
indeed, is the principle of analysis: What elements of a typical
contractual relation might apply to the basic medical relation?
The question is a complicated one, and Veatch clearly itemizes
the elements: interacting individuals or groups with mutual but
limited obligations and expectations; freedom, dignity, and other
"norms"; trust and confidence; the support of social sanctions
(meaning that society upholds the relation); and good faith. The
analysis accomplishes two interlocking goals. It explains contractual arrangements such as the marriage covenant Veatch mentions. And it reconfigures the doctor-patient relation so that, as
Veatch goes on to propose, patients and doctors can share decision making.

JUDY BRADY

JUDY BRADY, born in 1937 in San Francisco, where she now lives, earned a B.F.A. in painting from the University of Iowa in 1962. Drawn into political action by her work in the feminist movement, she went to Cuba in 1973, where she studied class relationships as a way of understanding change in a society. "I am not a 'writer,'" Brady declares, "but really am a disenfranchised (and fired) housewife, now secretary." Despite her disclaimer, Brady does publish articles occasionally — on union organizing, abortion, education in Cuba, and other topics. In 1990 she also published *Women and Cancer*, an anthology of writings by women.

I Want a Wife

"I Want a Wife" first appeared in the Spring 1972 issue of *Ms.* magazine and has been reprinted there, most recently in 1990. The essay is one of the best-known manifestos in popular feminist writing. In it, Brady trenchantly divides the work of a wife into its multiple duties and functions, leading to an inescapable conclusion.

I belong to that classification of people known as wives. I am   1
A Wife. And, not altogether incidentally, I am a mother.

Not too long ago a male friend of mine appeared on the scene   2
fresh from a recent divorce. He had one child, who is, of course, with his ex-wife. He is looking for another wife. As I thought about him while I was ironing one evening, it suddenly occurred to me that I, too, would like to have a wife. Why do I want a wife?

I would like to go back to school so that I can become eco-   3
nomically independent, support myself, and, if need be, support those dependent upon me. I want a wife who will work and send me to school. And while I am going to school I want a wife to take care of my children. I want a wife to keep track of the children's doctor and dentist appointments. And to keep track of mine, too. I want a wife to make sure my children eat properly and are kept

clean. I want a wife who will wash the children's clothes and keep them mended. I want a wife who is a good nurturant attendant to my children, who arranges for their schooling, makes sure that they have an adequate social life with their peers, takes them to the park, the zoo, etc. I want a wife who takes care of the children when they are sick, a wife who arranges to be around when the children need special care, because, of course, I cannot miss classes at school. My wife must arrange to lose time at work and not lose the job. It may mean a small cut in my wife's income from time to time, but I guess I can tolerate that. Needless to say, my wife will arrange and pay for the care of the children while my wife is working.

I want a wife who will take care of *my* physical needs. I want a   4
wife who will keep my house clean. A wife who will pick up after my children, a wife who will pick up after me. I want a wife who will keep my clothes clean, ironed, mended, replaced when need be, and who will see to it that my personal things are kept in their proper place so that I can find what I need the minute I need it. I want a wife who cooks the meals, a wife who is a *good* cook. I want a wife who will plan the menus, do the necessary grocery shopping, prepare the meals, serve them pleasantly, and then do the cleaning up while I do my studying. I want a wife who will care for me when I am sick and sympathize with my pain and loss of time from school. I want a wife to go along when our family takes a vacation so that someone can continue to care for me and my children when I need a rest and change of scene.

I want a wife who will not bother me with rambling com-   5
plaints about a wife's duties. But I want a wife who will listen to me when I feel the need to explain a rather difficult point I have come across in my course of studies. And I want a wife who will type my papers for me when I have written them.

I want a wife who will take care of the details of my social life.   6
When my wife and I are invited out by my friends, I want a wife who will take care of the babysitting arrangements. When I meet people at school that I like and want to entertain, I want a wife who will have the house clean, will prepare a special meal, serve it to me and my friends, and not interrupt when I talk about things that interest me and my friends. I want a wife who will have ar-

ranged that the children are fed and ready for bed before my guests arrive so that the children do not bother us. I want a wife who takes care of the needs of my guests so that they feel comfortable, who makes sure that they have an ashtray, that they are passed the hors d'oeuvres, that they are offered a second helping of the food, that their wine glasses are replenished when necessary, that their coffee is served to them as they like it. And I want a wife who knows that sometimes I need a night out by myself.

I want a wife who is sensitive to my sexual needs, a wife who   7
makes love passionately and eagerly when I feel like it, a wife who makes sure that I am satisfied. And, of course, I want a wife who will not demand sexual attention when I am not in the mood for it. I want a wife who assumes the complete responsibility for birth control, because I do not want more children. I want a wife who will remain sexually faithful to me so that I do not have to clutter up my intellectual life with jealousies. And I want a wife who understands that *my* sexual needs may entail more than strict adherence to monogamy. I must, after all, be able to relate to people as fully as possible.

If, by chance, I find another person more suitable as a wife   8
than the wife I already have, I want the liberty to replace my present wife with another one. Naturally, I will expect a fresh, new life; my wife will take the children and be solely responsible for them so that I am left free.

When I am through with school and have a job, I want my   9
wife to quit working and remain at home so that my wife can more fully and completely take care of a wife's duties.

My God, who *wouldn't* want a wife?   10

QUESTIONS ON MEANING

1. Sum up the duties of a wife as Brady sees them.
2. To what inequities in the roles traditionally assigned to men and to women does "I Want a Wife" call attention?
3. What is the THESIS of this essay? Is it stated or implied?
4. Is Brady unfair to men?

QUESTIONS ON WRITING STRATEGY

1. What EFFECT does Brady obtain with the title "I Want a Wife"?
2. What do the first two paragraphs accomplish?
3. What is the TONE of this essay?
4. How do you explain the fact that Brady never uses the pronoun *she* to refer to a wife? Does this make her prose unnecessarily awkward?
5. What principle does Brady use to analyze the role of wife? Can you think of some other principle for analyzing the job?
6. Knowing that this essay was first published in *Ms.* magazine in 1972, what can you guess about its intended readers? Does "I Want a Wife" strike a college AUDIENCE today as revolutionary?
7. OTHER METHODS. Although she mainly divides or analyzes the role of wife, Brady also uses classification (Chap. 7) to sort the many duties and responsibilities into manageable groups. What are the groups?

QUESTIONS ON LANGUAGE

1. What is achieved by the author's frequent repetition of the phrase "I want a wife"?
2. Be sure you know how to define the following words as Brady uses them: nurturant (para. 3); replenished (6); adherence, monogamy (7).
3. In general, how would you describe the DICTION of this essay? How well does it suit the essay's intended audience?

SUGGESTIONS FOR WRITING

1. Write a brief essay entitled "I Want a Husband" in which, using examples as Brady does, you enumerate the stereotyped roles traditionally assigned to men in our society.
2. Imagining that you want to employ someone to do a specific job, divide the task into its duties and functions. Then, guided by your analysis, write an accurate job description in essay form.
3. CONNECTIONS. Rosalind Coward's "Naughty but Nice," later in this chapter (p. 374), also deals with gender roles and stereotypes. Write an essay agreeing or disagreeing with the assumption of both Brady and Coward that women do not rank with men in what Coward calls our "sexually divided and hierarchical society." Anchor your essay in specifics (such as quotations from Brady, Coward, and other writers), statistics, and examples from your own experience.

GAIL SHEEHY

GAIL SHEEHY was born in 1937. She earned her B.S. degree from the University of Vermont in 1958 and was a fellow in Columbia University's Journalism School in 1970. A contributor to the *New York Times Magazine, Esquire, McCall's, Ms., Cosmopolitan, Rolling Stone,* and other magazines, she has also written a novel, *Lovesounds* (1970), and several popular studies of contemporary life: *Speed Is of the Essence* (1971), *Panthermania* (1971), *Hustling* (1973), *Passages* (1976), *Pathfinders* (1981), and *Character: America's Search for Leadership* (1988). In *The Spirit of Survival* (1986), Sheehy has written a history of strife and deprivation in Cambodia. The book includes a narrative told from the point of view of Mohm, a twelve-year-old Cambodian child adopted by Sheehy and her husband, Clay Felker, a New York editor.

Predictable Crises of Adulthood

"Predictable Crises of Adulthood" is adapted from the second chapter of *Passages.* In the essay, Sheehy identifies six stages that most people experience between the ages of eighteen and fifty. The author, as she herself makes clear, is not a theorist or a scholar; she is an artful reporter, in this case of findings in a new social science, adult development. Not everyone goes through the stages Sheehy traces at exactly the same time, but see whether any of the following crises sound familiar to you.

We are not unlike a particularly hardy crustacean. The lobster grows by developing and shedding a series of hard, protective shells. Each time it expands from within, the confining shell must be sloughed off. It is left exposed and vulnerable until, in time, a new covering grows to replace the old.

With each passage from one stage of human growth to the next we, too, must shed a protective structure. We are left exposed and vulnerable — but also yeasty and embryonic again, capable of stretching in ways we hadn't known before. These sheddings may take several years or more. Coming out of each passage, though, we enter a longer and more stable period in which we can expect relative tranquility and a sense of equilibrium regained. . . .

As we shall see, each person engages the steps of development 3 in his or her own characteristic *step-style*. Some people never complete the whole sequence. And none of us "solves" with one step — by jumping out of the parental home into a job or marriage, for example — the problems in separating from the caregivers of childhood. Nor do we "achieve" autonomy once and for all by converting our dreams into concrete goals, even when we attain those goals. The central issues or tasks of one period are never fully completed, tied up, and cast aside. But when they lose their primacy and the current life structure has served its purpose, we are ready to move on to the next period.

Can one catch up? What might look to others like listlessness, 4 contrariness, a maddening refusal to face up to an obvious task may be a person's own unique detour that will bring him out later on the other side. Developmental gains won can later be lost — and rewon. It's plausible, though it can't be proven, that the mastery of one set of tasks fortifies us for the next period and the next set of challenges. But it's important not to think too mechanistically. Machines work by units. The bureaucracy (supposedly) works step by step. Human beings, thank God, have an individual inner dynamic that can never be precisely coded.

Although I have indicated the ages when Americans are 5 likely to go through each stage, and the differences between men and women where they are striking, do not take the ages too seriously. The stages are the thing, and most particularly the sequence.

Here is the briefest outline of the developmental ladder. 6

Pulling Up Roots

Before 18, the motto is loud and clear: "I have to get away 7 from my parents." But the words are seldom connected to action. Generally still safely part of our families, even if away at school, we feel our autonomy to be subject to erosion from moment to moment.

After 18, we begin Pulling Up Roots in earnest. College, military service, and short-term travels are all customary vehicles our society provides for the first round trips between family and a base of one's own. In the attempt to separate our view of the world from our family's view, despite vigorous protestations to the contrary — "I know exactly what I want!" — we cast about for any beliefs we can call our own. And in the process of testing those beliefs we are often drawn to fads, preferably those most mysterious and inaccessible to our parents. 8

Whatever tentative memberships we try out in the world, the fear haunts us that we are really kids who cannot take care of ourselves. We cover that fear with acts of defiance and mimicked confidence. For allies to replace our parents, we turn to our contemporaries. They become conspirators. So long as their perspective meshes with our own, they are able to substitute for the sanctuary of the family. But that doesn't last very long. And the instant they diverge from the shaky ideals of "our group," they are seen as betrayers. Rebounds to the family are common between the ages of 18 and 22. 9

The tasks of this passage are to locate ourselves in a peer group role, a sex role, an anticipated occupation, an ideology or world view. As a result, we gather the impetus to leave home physically and the identity to *begin* leaving home emotionally. 10

Even as one part of us seeks to be an individual, another part longs to restore the safety and comfort of merging with another. Thus one of the most popular myths of this passage is: We can piggyback our development by attaching to a Stronger One. But people who marry during this time often prolong financial and emotional ties to the family and relatives that impede them from becoming self-sufficient. 11

A stormy passage through the Pulling Up Roots years will probably facilitate the normal progression of the adult life cycle. If one doesn't have an identity crisis at this point, it will erupt during a later transition, when the penalties may be harder to bear. 12

The Trying Twenties

The Trying Twenties confront us with the question of how to 13
take hold in the adult world. Our focus shifts from the interior
turmoils of late adolescence — "Who am I?" "What is truth?" —
and we become almost totally preoccupied with working out the
externals. "How do I put my aspirations into effect?" "What is the
best way to start?" "Where do I go?" "Who can help me?" "How
did *you* do it?"

In this period, which is longer and more stable compared 14
with the passage that leads to it, the tasks are as enormous as they
are exhilarating: To shape a Dream, that vision of ourselves
which will generate energy, aliveness, and hope. To prepare for a
lifework. To find a mentor if possible. And to form the capacity
for intimacy, without losing in the process whatever consistency
of self we have thus far mustered. The first test structure must be
erected around the life we choose to try.

Doing what we "should" is the most pervasive theme of the 15
twenties. The "shoulds" are largely defined by family models, the
press of the culture, or the prejudices of our peers. If the prevailing cultural instructions are that one should get married and settle down behind one's own door, a nuclear family is born. If instead the peers insist that one should do one's own thing, the
25-year-old is likely to harness himself onto a Harley-Davidson
and burn up Route 66 in the commitment to have no commitments.

One of the terrifying aspects of the twenties is the inner con- 16
viction that the choices we make are irrevocable. It is largely a
false fear. Change is quite possible, and some alteration of our
original choices is probably inevitable.

Two impulses, as always, are at work. One is to build a firm, 17
safe structure for the future by making strong commitments, to
"be set." Yet people who slip into a ready-made form without
much self-examination are likely to find themselves *locked in.*

The other urge is to explore and experiment, keeping any 18
structure tentative and therefore easily reversible. Taken to the
extreme, these are people who skip from one trial job and one

limited personal encounter to another, spending their twenties in the *transient* state.

Although the choices of our twenties are not irrevocable, they do set in motion a Life Pattern. Some of us follow the lock-in pattern, others the transient pattern, the wunderkind pattern, the caregiver pattern, and there are a number of others. Such patterns strongly influence the particular questions raised for each person during each passage. . . . 19

Buoyed by powerful illusions and belief in the power of the will, we commonly insist in our twenties that what we have chosen to do is the one true course in life. Our backs go up at the merest hint that we are like our parents, that two decades of parental training might be reflected in our current actions and attitudes. 20

"Not me," is the motto, "I'm different." 21

Catch-30

Impatient with devoting ourselves to the "shoulds," a new vitality springs from within as we approach 30. Men and women alike speak of feeling too narrow and restricted. They blame all sorts of things, but what the restrictions boil down to are the outgrowth of career and personal choices of the twenties. They may have been choices perfectly suited to that stage. But now the fit feels different. Some inner aspect that was left out is striving to be taken into account. Important new choices must be made, and commitments altered or deepened. The work involves great change, turmoil, and often crisis — a simultaneous feeling of rock bottom and the urge to bust out. 22

One common response is the tearing up of the life we spent most of our twenties putting together. It may mean striking out on a secondary road toward a new vision or converting a dream of "running for president" into a more realistic goal. The single person feels a push to find a partner. The woman who was previously content at home with children chafes to venture into the world. The childless couple reconsiders children. And almost everyone who is married, especially those married for seven years, feels a discontent. 23

If the discontent doesn't lead to a divorce, it will, or should, 24
call for a serious review of the marriage and of each partner's aspirations in their Catch-30 condition. The gist of that condition
was expressed by a 29-year-old associate with a Wall Street law
firm:

"I'm considering leaving the firm. I've been there four years 25
now; I'm getting good feedback, but I have no clients of my own. I
feel weak. If I wait much longer, it will be too late, too close to
that fateful time of decision on whether or not to become a partner. I'm success-oriented. But the concept of being 55 years old
and stuck in a monotonous job drives me wild. It drives me crazy
now, just a little bit. I'd say that 85 percent of the time I thoroughly enjoy my work. But when I get a screwball case, I come
away from court saying, 'What am I doing here?' It's a *visceral* reaction that I'm wasting my time. I'm trying to find some way to
make a social contribution or a slot in city government. I keep
saying, 'There's something more.' "

Besides the push to broaden himself professionally, there is 26
a wish to expand his personal life. He wants two or three more
children. "The concept of a home has become very meaningful
to me, a place to get away from troubles and relax. I love my
son in a way I could not have anticipated. I never could live
alone."

Consumed with the work of making his own critical life-steer- 27
ing decisions, he demonstrates the essential shift at this age: an
absolute requirement to be more self-concerned. The self has new
value now that his competency has been proved.

His wife is struggling with her own age-30 priorities. She 28
wants to go to law school, but he wants more children. If she is
going to stay home, she wants him to make more time for the
family instead of taking on even wider professional commitments.
His view of the bind, of what he would most like from his wife, is
this:

"I'd like not to be bothered. It sounds cruel, but I'd like not to 29
have to worry about what she's going to do next week. Which is
why I've told her several times that I think she should do something. Go back to school and get a degree in social work or geography or whatever. Hopefully that would fulfill her, and then I

wouldn't have to worry about her line of problems. I want her to be decisive about herself."

The trouble with his advice to his wife is that it comes out of 30 concern with *his* convenience, rather than with *her* development. She quickly picks up on this lack of goodwill: He is trying to dispose of her. At the same time, he refuses her the same latitude to be "selfish" in making an independent decision to broaden her horizons. Both perceive a lack of mutuality. And that is what Catch-30 is all about for the couple.

Rooting and Extending

Life becomes less provisional, more rational and orderly 31 in the early thirties. We begin to settle down in the full sense. Most of us begin putting down roots and sending out new shoots. People buy houses and become very earnest about climbing career ladders. Men in particular concern themselves with "making it." Satisfaction with marriage generally goes downhill in the thirties (for those who have remained together) compared with the highly valued, vision-supporting marriage of the twenties. This coincides with the couple's reduced social life outside the family and the in-turned focus on raising their children.

The Deadline Decade

In the middle of the thirties we come upon a crossroads. We 32 have reached the halfway mark. Yet even as we are reaching our prime, we begin to see there is a place where it finishes. Time starts to squeeze.

The loss of youth, the faltering of physical powers we have al- 33 ways taken for granted, the fading purpose of stereotyped roles by which we have thus far identified ourselves, the spiritual dilemma of having no absolute answers — any or all of these shocks can give this passage the character of crisis. Such thoughts usher in a decade between 35 and 45 that can be called the Deadline Decade. It is a time of both danger and opportunity. All of us have the chance to rework the narrow identity by which we defined ourselves in the first half of life. And those of us who make the most of the opportunity will have a full-out authenticity crisis.

To come through this authenticity crisis, we must reexamine 34
our purposes and reevaluate how to spend our resources from now on. "Why am I doing all this? What do I really believe in?" No matter what we have been doing, there will be parts of ourselves that have been suppressed and now need to find expression. "Bad" feelings will demand acknowledgment along with the good.

It is frightening to step off onto the treacherous footbridge 35
leading to the second half of life. We can't take everything with us on this journey through uncertainty. Along the way, we discover that we are alone. We no longer have to ask permission because we are the providers of our own safety. We must learn to give ourselves permission. We stumble upon feminine or masculine aspects of our natures that up to this time have usually been masked. There is grieving to be done because an old self is dying. By taking in our suppressed and even our unwanted parts, we prepare at the gut level for the reintegration of an identity that is ours and ours alone — not some artificial form put together to please the culture or our mates. It is a dark passage at the beginning. But by disassembling ourselves, we can glimpse the light and gather our parts into a renewal.

Women sense this inner crossroads earlier than men do. The 36
time pinch often prompts a woman to stop and take an all-points survey at age 35. Whatever options she has already played out, she feels a "my last chance" urgency to review those options she has set aside and those that aging and biology will close off in the *now foreseeable* future. For all her qualms and confusion about where to start looking for a new future, she usually enjoys an exhilaration of release. Assertiveness begins rising. There are so many firsts ahead.

Men, too, feel the time push in the mid-thirties. Most men re- 37
spond by pressing down harder on the career accelerator. It's "my last chance" to pull away from the pack. It is no longer enough to be the loyal junior executive, the promising young novelist, the lawyer who does a little *pro bono* work on the side. He wants now

to become part of top management, to be recognized as an established writer, or an active politician with his own legislative program. With some chagrin, he discovers that he has been too anxious to please and too vulnerable to criticism. He wants to put
together his own ship.

During this period of intense concentration on external ad-   38
vancement, it is common for men to be unaware of the more difficult, gut issues that are propelling them forward. The survey that
was neglected at 35 becomes a crucible at 40. Whatever rung of
achievement he has reached, the man of 40 usually feels stale,
restless, burdened, and unappreciated. He worries about his
health. He wonders, "Is this all there is?" He may make a series of
departures from well-established lifelong base lines, including
marriage. More and more men are seeking second careers in
midlife. Some become self-destructive. And many men in their
forties experience a major shift of emphasis away from pouring all
their energies into their own advancement. A more tender, feeling side comes into play. They become interested in developing
an ethical self.

Renewal or Resignation

Somewhere in the mid-forties, equilibrium is regained. A new   39
stability is achieved, which may be more or less satisfying.

If one has refused to budge through the midlife transition, the   40
sense of staleness will calcify into resignation. One by one, the
safety and supports will be withdrawn from the person who is
standing still. Parents will become children; children will become
strangers; a mate will grow away or go away; the career will become just a job — and each of these events will be felt as an aban-
donment. The crisis will probably emerge again around 50. And
although its wallop will be greater, the jolt may be just what is
needed to prod the resigned middle-ager toward seeking revital-
ization.

On the other hand . . .   41

If we have confronted ourselves in the middle passage and   42
found a renewal of purpose around which we are eager to build a
more authentic life structure, these may well be the best years.

Personal happiness takes a sharp turn upward for partners who can now accept the fact: "I cannot expect *anyone* to fully understand me." Parents can be forgiven for the burdens of our childhood. Children can be let go without leaving us in collapsed silence. At 50, there is a new warmth and mellowing. Friends become more important than ever, but so does privacy. Since it is so often proclaimed by people past midlife, the motto of this stage might be "No more bullshit."

QUESTIONS ON MEANING

1. In your own words, summarize each of Sheehy's six predictable stages of adult life.
2. According to the author, what happens to people who fail to experience a given stage of growth at the usual time?
3. How would you characterize Sheehy's attitude toward growth and change in adult life?

QUESTIONS ON WRITING STRATEGY

1. Why does Sheehy employ the method of division? How does it serve her readers, too?
2. What, if anything, does the author gain by writing her essay in the first PERSON plural (*we, us*)?
3. What difficulties go along with making GENERALIZATIONS about human beings? To what extent does Sheehy surmount these difficulties?
4. How much knowledge of psychology does Sheehy expect of her AUDIENCE?
5. OTHER METHODS. Sheehy's first two paragraphs constitute an analogy (Chap. 8). How effective is this analogy, do you think?

QUESTIONS ON LANGUAGE

1. Consult your dictionary if you need help in defining the following words: crustacean (para. 1); embryonic, tranquility, equilibrium (2); autonomy, primacy (3); plausible (4); inaccessible (8); sanctuary (9);

impetus (10); exhilarating, mentor (14); pervasive (15); irrevocable (16); tentative (18); wunderkind (19); visceral (25); mutuality (30); dilemma (33); *pro bono*, chagrin, vulnerable (37); crucible (38); calcify (40).

2. What is a "nuclear family" (para. 15)?

3. The author coins a few phrases of her own. Refer to the context in which they appear to help you define the following: step-style (para. 3); Stronger One (11); Catch-30 (24); authenticity crisis (33).

SUGGESTIONS FOR WRITING

1. From your experience, observation, or reading, test the accuracy of one of Sheehy's accounts of a typical period of crisis.

2. Inspired by Sheehy's division of life after 18 into phases, look back on your own earlier life or that of a younger person you know, and detail a series of phases in it. Invent names for the phases.

3. CONNECTIONS. You may have noticed the similarity between Sheehy's characterization of the Catch-30 couple (paras. 22–30) and Judy Brady's analysis in "I Want a Wife" (p. 342). Use the information provided by Sheehy (about other stages as well, if you like) to analyze the particular crisis of the "I" who wants a wife in Brady's essay. Support your ideas with EVIDENCE from both essays.

MARGOT HARRISON

A 1990 graduate of Harvard University, MARGOT HARRISON majored in comparative literature. She was born in New York City and has lived in New York State, Indiana, and other places. A constant reader since childhood, Harrison reports feeling sometimes that "the world within the pages was more real than the one outside." She began writing as a child, too, and in high school and college won several awards for stories and critical essays. She intends to earn a Ph.D. in comparative literature so that she can teach at the college level, while continuing to write criticism and fiction "on the side."

The Death of a Moth: Two Visions

This essay (titled by the editors) is a perceptive critical analysis of two essays printed earlier in this book: Virginia Woolf's "The Death of the Moth" (p. 124) and Annie Dillard's "Death of a Moth" (p. 130). Harrison's essay was first written for a course in freshman compositon and then won a 1987 Bedford Prize in Student Writing. It was subsequently printed in the third edition of *Student Writers at Work*, edited by Nancy Sommers and Donald McQuade (1989). Originally, Harrison's parenthetical page references were to the anthology in which she read the essays and that she cites at the end of her analysis: *Elements of Literature*, edited by Carl H. Klaus. For convenience, the page references have been changed to match *The Bedford Reader*.

At first glance, Virginia Woolf's essay "The Death of the   1
Moth" and Annie Dillard's "Death of a Moth" seem to demand comparison. But for one small article, after all, the titles are identical, and a reading reveals general similarities in the essays themselves. Each uses the death of a moth as its focus, and in each this small, normally unnoticed incident — about which, as Woolf, says, there is "nobody to care or to know" (127) — becomes a concentrated moment of pure insight for the author, something

comparable to what Wordsworth calls a "spot of time." It arouses philosophical reflection and religious awe; to Woolf, it is a dramatization of the struggle between life and death, to Dillard, a "transfiguration."

Yet although both essays are centered around a "spot of time," they vary substantially in the way this moment is framed and depicted. A difference is suggested already in the small distinction between the titles: Woolf's "*the* moth" is emphasized and definite, indicating the moth's importance as a symbol (just as "The Rape of *the* Lock" sets Pope's mock-heroic mood better than "The Rape of *a* Lock" would have done), while Dillard's "*a* moth" is vaguer, more equivocal about this particular moth's significance. Woolf, as her title implies, makes the moth's death very clearly her focus and states its symbolic meaning to us: The moth is "dancing and zigzagging to show us the true nature of life" (126), then illustrates the fact that "nothing, I knew, had any chance against death" (127). The incident inspires "wonder" because it is a display in microcosm of "an oncoming doom which could, had it chosen, have submerged an entire city . . . masses of human beings" (126–127). The author exists purely to observe, to feel and record this wonder. There is an "I," a first-person narrator, but her reasons for sitting at the window with a book are unimportant and she is often eclipsed by impersonal forms: "the eyes strictly turned upon the book" (125) rather than "my eyes" and "my book," the frequent use of "one." This impersonality seems to serve to point out the moth's universal significance, the implication being that, although Woolf is the only one on hand to witness this particular death, any one of us would have seen it as she does. When she writes, "Nothing, I knew, had any chance against death" (127), or "One's sympathies, of course, were all on the side of life" (127), she uses the assumption that each of us accepts these facts to invite us to step into her place before the window and become ourselves the observer.

In dealing with "universal" concepts and telling us directly 3
that she is doing so, Woolf runs the risk of making a simplified, self-evident statement — "nothing has a chance against death" — and nothing more. But, almost as if in disdain of subtlety and concealment, she says what she means and then digs deeper into

the "self-evident," using images to give concrete, perceptible form to the abstract concepts which otherwise might have become meaningless catchwords. She states flatly that the entire landscape is "inspired" by "energy," that the moth is "a tiny bead of pure life" (126), but she shows us at the same time what she means by "energy" and "life" in descriptions such as that of the rising and settling of a flock of rooks. Here there are evocations of motion ("soaring . . . sank . . . thrown into the air"), sound ("utmost clamor and vociferation"), and emotion ("tremendously exciting") (125). Perhaps most graphic is the description of life in its diluted and less energetic form: "humped and bossed and garnished and cumbered so that it has to move with the greatest circumspection and dignity" (126). In this image an abstract, general quality becomes concrete — "life" appears before the mind's eye as a ponderous, ornate piece of machinery, the spontaneity of its movement crushed by the weight of human custom. When this machine image is opposed to that of the tiny, flitting moth, the contrast between everyday life and "pure life" is as sharply visible to us as it is to Woolf's narrator, visible in terms of shape, size, and motion. Death becomes equally concrete and visible when it is depicted in terms of a loss of motion, the sudden relaxation and stiffening of a corpse. Woolf's aim thus seems less to make new philosophical observations about mortality than to give us a vivid, sensual experience of the abstract.

While Woolf makes abstractions concrete, Dillard begins with concrete objects — a moth, a candle — and draws from them the abstract concept of transfiguration. Since Woolf also takes the concrete body of the moth and gives it symbolic significance, one could say that this is generally true for both essays. The difference lies primarily in structure: Woolf states the significance of the moth almost immediately, while Dillard brings it in as a revelation, literally a sudden burst of light as the moth sizzles and the candle flares. Unlike Woolf's speaker, Dillard's has a definite identity, and this revelatory moment is framed by descriptions of her daily life which bear no obvious relation to it. The essay begins with the statement that she lives alone ("I live alone with two cats, who sleep on my legs" [130]) and ends with a return to that fact ("Sometimes I think it is pretty funny that I sleep alone" [133]). Nowhere in this prologue or epilogue to the description of the moth's death does there seem to be any of its emotion. The speaker claims that she is only telling the story of the moth in order to explain her ability to identify moth corpses left by a spider, but this is clearly an excuse for a striking image which becomes the essay's centerpiece. The descriptions up to this point, such as the catalogue of the spider's victims, have been detached and emotionless, carrying the implication that chance rather than any master plan determines acts of nature: "I wonder on what fool's errand an earwig, or a moth, or a sow bug, would visit that clean corner of the house" (131). As the moth burns, however, Dillard's imagery and tone become passionate and religious; the moth is "like an immolating monk," "like a hollow saint, like a flame-faced virgin gone to God" (133). While Woolf calmly reflects on the moth's vitality and its struggle against death, Dillard is carried away by the force of the moment she describes, her imagery becoming more and more lyrical until, like a poet rather than an essayist, she is no longer responsible for telling us why the corpse should resemble a "flame-faced virgin"; we sense that the image is appropriate and understand intuitively. We have the sense that it is actually the author who is being transfigured in this passage, baring to us the deep significance which the burning moth holds for her as an individual.

After a series of fiery religious images, it is jarring to be returned abruptly at the end of the essay to a discussion of the pros and cons of living alone. Is this an unintentional anticlimax? Or is there an implicit connection between the moth's transfiguration and the author's life? Dillard's narrator clearly establishes such a connection when, in a deadpan tone which suggests a kind of compulsive coyness, a reluctance to point, as Woolf does, directly to symbolic meaning, she calls the reader's attention to the "three candles here on the table" which echo the image of immolation (133). Why should it matter to us that Dillard's house contains candles? Perhaps living alone itself is seen here as a sort of death and transfiguration. Celibacy ("sleeping alone") represents death in that it involves a removal of oneself from the normal flow of social life and the continuance of that life which sexual reproduction ensures. The "flame-faced virgin" and the "immolating monk" are, like Dillard's narrator, celibate, and their death is at the same time a transfiguration, a rebirth as light which is made possible by their purity, their sacrifice of earthly concerns. Death, literal or symbolic, becomes a way of achieving sainthood.

Dillard herself undergoes no literal transfiguration in flames,   6
but the mentions of Rimbaud in the essay strongly suggest that a transfiguration of analogous nature is available to her. The camping trip on which the moment of the moth's immolation occurs is a quest for artistic inspiration: Dillard takes with her "a novel about Rimbaud that had made me want to be a writer when I was sixteen; I was hoping it would do it again" (131). The connection between art and transfiguration is later made more explicit: "Rimbaud in Paris burnt out his brain in a thousand poems," just as the moth burns out its husk in the candle-flame (133). Neither art nor light is born without a sacrifice of the more earthly elements. Thus the transfiguration which Dillard shows us is also that of her own life as a writer, and it is made all the more startling and dramatic by the impassive descriptions of everyday life which surround it. Dillard seems almost to carry off a quiet deception on us, beginning her essay with what appears to be earthy realism — close description of cats, a house, a spider — and showing within the essay that writing itself provides an abstract way to transcend the earth and life altogether.

The tone of Dillard's essay is generally deadpan, with one   7
sudden burst of emotion in sharp contrast, while Woolf's is constant throughout, tranquil and yet quietly awed. There is a corresponding difference in their visual styles. Woolf's moth is a day moth, and her setting is suffused with light and energy. She focuses in on the moth as a harmonious part of this setting which contains its essence in miniature, including the inevitable tendency — not directly shown but perhaps implied in the landscape — of life to end in death. Dillard's moth is a night moth and lights up the darkness with its burning; rather than emphasizing detail of a harmonious picture, she describes one of the most potent images of creation: light out of darkness. From the death of a moth comes rebirth, the creation of a new being and transfiguration of the old.

A basic difference between Woolf and Dillard seems to be be-   8

tween close observation and creation, reflection and transfiguration. A revelation, a transcendence of the ordinary, occurs in
both essays, but while Woolf's revelation seems to come naturally
and calmly from her observations of what is around her, Dillard's
is born of a violent combination of elements — her own mind,
the flaming moth, Rimbaud. And yet on another, deeper level
the two essays are alike, for Woolf's redefining of familiar concepts in terms of sensual imagery also has a subjective, creative
component. She makes us, as Shelley wrote about the role of a
poet, "imagine what we know," while Dillard implicitly takes the
abstract, imagined idea of transfiguration and assimilates it into
the reality of her own life, suggesting that, even in the twentieth
century, the eternal and transcendent are not beyond our reach.

Works Cited

Dillard, Annie. "Death of a Moth." *Elements of Literature*. Ed. Carl H.
    Klaus. New York: Oxford UP, 1986. 107–09.
Woolf, Virginia. "The Death of the Moth." *Elements of Literature*. Ed.
    Carl H. Klaus. New York: Oxford UP, 1986. 57–59.

QUESTIONS ON MEANING

1. What is Harrison's PURPOSE in this essay? Why does the author
   say that the two essays analyzed "seem to demand comparison"
   (para. 1)?
2. What is the author's THESIS? Where is it stated in the essay?
3. Summarize the similarities and differences Harrison sees in Woolf's
   and Dillard's essays. (*Suggestion*: It may help to use a side-by-side
   listing.)

QUESTIONS ON WRITING STRATEGY

1. What key elements of each essay does Harrison's analysis focus on?
2. What is Harrison's principal EVIDENCE for her analysis of the essays?
3. Is Harrison's analysis of the two essays evaluative? Does she seem to
   prefer one over another? If so, does she supply the evidence to back
   up her preference?

4. Harrison has said that she set out to examine the "narrative methods" in the two essays, "which seemed to me in one case to run the risk of leaving too much unsaid and, in the other, of saying too much." Which essay is which in this comment? Does Harrison make it clear why the methods don't fail after all?

5. OTHER METHODS. Harrison's essay is also clearly a comparison and contrast (Chap. 4). Why is it perhaps more appropriate to classify it as an analysis?

QUESTIONS ON LANGUAGE

1. Harrison's original title for this essay was "Creative Transfiguration in the Death of a Moth." What is a "creative transfiguration" in the context of this essay?

2. Harrison uses many quotations from Woolf's and Dillard's essays. Examine the ways she works these quotations into her own sentences. Is it consistently clear which are her thoughts and which the other authors'? Is the integration of text and quotation consistently smooth? Cite examples in your answers.

3. Define the following: equivocal, microcosm, (para. 2); subtlety, catchwords, evocations (3); lyrical (4); anticlimax, implicit, deadpan, coyness, immolation, celibacy, earthly (5); explicit, earthy (6); suffused (7).

SUGGESTIONS FOR WRITING

1. Following Harrison's example, choose one of the following essays in this book and analyze it, using evidence from it to support your interpretation of its meaning: George Orwell's "A Hanging" (p. 54); Joan Didion's "The Liquid City" (p. 142); Richard Selzer's "The Discus Thrower" (p. 152); Anna Quindlen's "Homeless" (p. 188); Alice Walker's "Oppressed Hair Puts a Ceiling on the Brain" (p. 437); Richard Rodriguez's "Aria" (p. 657).

2. Do you agree with Harrison's analysis of Woolf's and Dillard's essays? Does Harrison leave out elements of either essay? Does she read too much into either one? Write an analysis of Harrison's analysis.

3. CONNECTIONS. Add your voice to the Woolf–Dillard–Harrison discussion. After reading the essays by all three, take issue with Harrison, extend her ideas, or, if you prefer, take a wholly different approach. Whatever course you choose, support your ideas with summaries of and quotations from the essays you cite.

MARGOT HARRISON ON WRITING

For *Student Writers at Work*, Margot Harrison was asked what advice she would give other college students about writing. "One thing I think is essential to good writing," she responded, "is to write about something you *like* — 'like' in the sense that it generally interests you, that you want to examine it in detail. Nor should you feel like a slave to your topic; you should believe — whether true or not — that you have something original to contribute not only to the class but to the world at large. It's depressing to be modest and feel as if you're only saying what professors of English have said or can say better, and I don't think that this kind of modesty contributes to good writing, however 'realistic' it may be. It pays to think hard about what you are going to write about and to make it something that you can individualize, although the topic shouldn't quite become a slave to your personal expression, either. A balance has to be achieved."

Harrison had one more bit of advice, this concerning revision. "It helps incredibly to get rid of stock phrases and clichés, to express things in energetic and original language. The more you can make the essay yours — even if it means breaking some of the rules you learned in high school — the better."

FOR DISCUSSION

1. What is the "balance" that Harrison feels is so important in writing?
2. What might Harrison mean by "breaking some of the rules you learned in high school"? Can you think of an example of such a rule that can profitably be broken?

MARK CRISPIN MILLER

Applying his academic training as a Renaissance scholar to contemporary culture, MARK CRISPIN MILLER produces fresh and provocative cultural criticism. He was born in 1949 in Chicago and grew up there and in Boston. He received a B.A. in 1971 from Northwestern University, and an M.A. in 1973 and Ph.D. in 1977 from the Johns Hopkins University. After several years at the University of Pennsylvania, Miller now teaches in the writing seminars at Johns Hopkins. Miller's critical essays on rock music, film, television, and advertising appear frequently in *The New Republic*, *The Nation*, *Mother Jones*, *The New York Review of Books*, and other magazines. Some of the essays are collected in the volume *Boxed In: The Culture of TV* (1987). Miller edited an anthology, *Seeing through Movies* (1990), and is writing a book on modern advertising.

Barbara Walters's Theater of Revenge

Published first in *Savvy Woman* in October 1989 and then adapted for *Harper's* the next month, this essay exemplifies Miller's close readings of contemporary popular culture. Television especially grabs his attention because after the 1970s, he says, "it was no longer a mere stain or imposition on some pre-existent cultural environment, but had itself become the environment"; it "was not only 'on the air,' but had become the very air we breathe."

In Hollywood today, being beautiful is not enough; the stars 1 also must exhibit "a self-mocking sense of humor." So say Hollywood's casting directors, as surveyed recently by *TV Guide*. Self-mockery, they have noticed, is "a key ingredient in star quality. 'Tom Selleck has it,' says HBO's [head of casting], 'and so do Burt Reynolds and Paul Newman.' And they *have* to have it, she says, because it allows the audience to forgive them for their looks."

That explanation points up a sobering fact about Celebrity 2 today: The stars are obligated not just to tantalize their fans but also to appease them. The stars must seem to pay us back for the envy they've been paid to make us feel. While basking in success, they must also seem to shrug it off, or to atone for it, so as to blunt the deep resentment that is the obverse of our "love."

Such mass ambivalence is at least as old as the star system it- 3 self. In the thirties, Nathanael West sensed the hatred simmering among the movies' most passionate fans: "The police force would have to be doubled when the stars started to arrive," he writes of the hellish "world premiere" in *The Day of the Locust*. "At the sight of their heroes and heroines, the crowd would turn demoniac. Some little gesture, either too pleasing or too offensive, would start it moving and then nothing but machine guns would stop it."

Throughout Hollywood's heyday, the press functioned to 4 contain that great mass animus, channeling the audience's wrath according to the needs of the studio executives. Read by millions, "reporters" like Louella Parsons, Hedda Hopper, and Sheilah Graham, among others, did not just hype the stars but also helped supervise them, by standing as the righteous tribunes of the movie-going populace. In 1950, one of Hedda Hopper's legmen gleefully called her attacks "a healthy disciplinary medium among the stars and big shots who sometimes delude themselves they're entitled to special privileges, like, for instance, adultery, taking dope, and indulging in strange sex aberrations." Through the columnists, the audience could act out its revenge against the privileged movie colony. And so the stars had to abase themselves before those hard columnists, regarding them, as Leo Rosten wrote in 1941, with "a combination of cunning, fear, hate, and propitiation."

If anything, that mass hostility seems to have increased, now 5 that TV tantalizes everyone nonstop. Through TV, the dazzling image of Celebrity has become inescapable, a glow pervading every home and haunting every mind, with a thoroughness that was not possible when the stars were beckoning only from the screens of crowded movie theaters. The same medium that appears to bring the stars within our reach also (of course) withholds them — a kind of teasing that makes people angry. This may, in part, explain why stardom has, with the spread of TV, become more dangerous, a status that today requires not just the occasional instruments of crowd control but a staff of live-in body-guards.

Only a few fans, of course, have vented their anger in the 6 kind of kamikaze operation that has felled John Lennon, Ronald Reagan, Theresa Saldana, Rebecca Schaeffer. The psychotic assault on Celebrity is only the most extreme symptom of the widespread resentment, which usually finds less violent release in the same media spectacle that also rouses that resentment. While a few carry guns and keep mad diaries, millions simply feed on lurid fantasies of retribution, available at any supermarket checkout line, as well as on television.

Of all the features in today's theater of revenge, however, 7 there is none as popular, or as subtle, as the quarterly ritual staged by Barbara Walters — an edgy televisual ceremony in which Walters acts out, and exploits, the viewers' ambivalence toward the superstars. A throwback to the likes of Hedda Hopper, Walters, on our behalf, seems to penalize the stars for their success — right after, or even in the midst of, hyping it.

Thus the Walters interview usually begins with what she calls 8 "the tour," i.e., a bald exhibition of fantastic wealth, the camera panning reverently across stupendous lawns, vast marble foyers, bedrooms like the tombs of emperors, etc., while Walters, in voice-over, extols the property as if trying to sell it.

After this display, however, Walters must stage a punishment 9 for the affluence she has just eyed so worshipfully. Most often, Walters will, after a little fawning, suddenly confront the subject with a very rude personal question, just as a child or imbecile would. At these moments, the interviewer actively personifies the viewing audience at its nosiest. It is, in fact, her genius to intuit the wonderings of the tactless oaf within each one of us and then to become that oaf, speaking its "mind" right in the star's home, right in the star's face.

Here, for instance, is an exchange that Walters conducted, in 10 1977, with Elizabeth Taylor and Senator John Warner, then newlyweds, "in the spacious kitchen of their elegant farmhouse":

> B.W.: [*to Liz, out of nowhere*]: Are you worried about putting on weight?

LIZ: No. [*tense giggling*]

B.W.: Does it matter to you?

LIZ: No, it doesn't. Because I'm so happy, and I enjoy eating. I like to cook — um — and I enjoy eating, and I love it —

B.W.: You wouldn't care if you got *fat?*

LIZ: I *am* fat!

B.W.: I didn't want to say it.

LIZ: I can hardly get into any of my clothes!

B.W.: But you don't *care?*

LIZ: Not really.

B.W.: [*changing tactics*]: Do you worry about getting older?

LIZ: No, not at all. I'm forty-four years old, and I'll be forty-five next Sunday —

[*Cut to an extreme close-up, letting us enjoy the sight of Liz Taylor's laugh lines and double chin while she sits there trying to sound liberated.*]

"Why didn't you get your nose fixed?" Walters once asked 11 Barbra Streisand. On a show featuring Bo Derek, Cheryl Ladd, Farrah Fawcett, and Bette Midler, Walters — referring to Derek's hit movie — asked Midler to rate, one to ten, her own looks. "Fifty-five!" Midler sang out genially, whereupon Walters, seeing as the oaf sees, was ostentatiously nonplussed: "Er — *really?*" she gasped, and Midler was clearly — and understandably — offended.

Obviously, Walters's purpose is not to regale the public with 12 good conversation but to abuse the stars as that same public would, and often does, abuse them: "People can be very cruel," Barbra Streisand once told Walters. "They treat performers sometimes as if they're not alive." Tellingly, Walters used that sound bite to kick off her gala Fiftieth Special, as if to advertise the cruelty of her own approach. Her callousness shows itself not just in childish personal remarks but in even grosser moments of impertinence: "Can you have sex?" Walters asked the paraplegic singer Teddy Pendergrass.

When trying to justify such invasiveness (which she does not 13 do often), Walters will lay the blame on us: "I *hate* to do this," she insisted to Fawn Hall (having asked her if she was dating anyone), "but *you* know people want to know." In thus voicing the abrasive curiosity of the oaf multitude, Walters recalls the Hollywood newsbags, who were also merciless inquirers. The difference is, of course, that the columnists would leave, in print, no trace of their own prying, whereas Barbara Walters asks those nervy questions right on camera — indeed, the asking often *makes* the story. Walters wants visceral responses: a gulp, a sob or two, or preferably a fit of keening. For this payoff, she will move in — often indirectly — on the most painful memories, which she will bring up with a fixed look of clammy pseudo-sympathy and in the Standard Condolatory Murmur used by people who enjoy funerals. "Betty, did you know from the first there was no hope?" Thus Walters delicately opened up the subject of Betty White's eventual widowhood.

Why do those stars go through with it? In part, of course, 14 they want the exposure, and Walters offers a unique promotional bonanza. Moreover, it would be a sentimental error to imply that the stars are mere victims here, because Walters often stages the star's punishment with the star's own complicity — just as the Hollywood "reporters" used to do. The ambush mode is not Walters's only means of bringing down Celebrity. Just as often, she will help some star evade the mass resentment by getting her to tell us how she's Been Through Hell — a confession of past misery that permits the star to go on having all that fame and fortune ("She deserves it, with what she's been through!"), and that also reassures us oafs that we're all better off just as we are: working (if we're lucky) nine to five, waiting on line in supermarkets, watching television.

But while she generally has the women sell themselves as erst- 15 while victims, she tends to bring the males down in a different way. As spokesperson for the masses, Walters often moralizes, promoting the same tidy Code of Family Values that Hopper/Parsons used to push so hypocritically. Usually, however, Walters defends the code not by railing at the stars' loose behavior but by having them — the men, that is — give dewy-eyed avowals of their deep longing for domestic life. This is exactly how the stars of yore, however randy, mollified their leery public through the gossip columns. And so Sylvester Stallone told Walters what would make him happy: "I would like to be able to have a home life that is really beautiful, that is — the whole storybook, white-picket-fence bit. I really would. I would like to go for that," said the man who had married Brigitte Nielsen.

The whole pseudo-populist spectacle, all the prying and the 16 piety, has a fundamentally elitist purpose. Although posing as a journalist, Walters is, like Hopper and the others, in the business not of public information but of popular delusion. Through her, we only seem to be allowed inside a world of peace and luxury, a world whose real inhabitants, through her, we only seem to punish for our actual exclusion. And yet there is no peace within that world, because of us. Even for the stars, in other words, the specials offer no real benefit. They sit down with Walters not only for the vast exposure but as a form of public penance, hoping thereby to pacify the eerie rage of their adoring audience. The stars are in hiding from us, and so they meet uneasily with Barbara Walters.

QUESTIONS ON MEANING

1. What is Miller actually analyzing in this essay? What is his THESIS?
2. How has television contributed to the public's ambivalence toward celebrities?
3. What is Barbara Walters's relationship with the stars she interviews? Is she a friend? Enemy? Something else?
4. How does Walters help female stars "evade the mass resentment"? How does she help male stars? Why the difference?

QUESTIONS ON WRITING STRATEGY

1. What is the function of paragraphs 3 and 4? Are they necessary, do you think?
2. What is the TONE of the essay? Support your answer with quotations from the essay.
3. What does Miller use for EVIDENCE? How effective is it? Comment especially on the excerpt in paragraph 10. How does Miller "doctor" this interview?
4. "It is, in fact, her genius to intuit the wonderings of the tactless oaf within each one of us and then to become that oaf" (para. 9). Ana-

lyze Miller's use of "us" in this sentence. How do you think Miller conceives of himself and his AUDIENCE?

5. OTHER METHODS. Like most analyses, Miller's makes good use of examples (Chap. 3). What is the EFFECT of including the names of the celebrities Walters is questioning? Would the examples be as effective without the names?

QUESTIONS ON LANGUAGE

1. Why does Miller capitalize "Celebrity" (para. 2), "Standard Condolatory Murmur" (13), "Been Through Hell" (14), and "Code of Family Values" (15)?
2. How does the language in the description of "the tour" in paragraph 8 typify Miller's tone?
3. Miller uses the prefix "pseudo-" twice in the essay: "pseudo-sympathy" (13) and "pseudo-populist" (16). What does this prefix mean? Why is Miller's use of it appropriate?
4. Define the following: appease, atone, obverse (para. 2); ambivalence (3); heyday, animus, aberrations, abase, propitiation (4); kamikaze (6); extols (8); fawning (9); ostentatiously, nonplussed (11); callousness (12); visceral, keening, condolatory (13); erstwhile, avowals, mollified (15).

SUGGESTIONS FOR WRITING

1. Analyze the interviewing style of another television journalist or talk-show host, such as Oprah Winfrey, Bryant Gumbel, David Letterman, or Arsenio Hall. Following Miller's example, state what you think the interviewer and the style represent and back up your opinions with detailed examples.
2. Watch Barbara Walters on her other show, 20/20. Is her performance different from that described by Miller? In an essay, compare and contrast Walters's performance on the two shows. Or, if you prefer, take issue with Miller's analysis of Walters's celebrity interviews, using examples and quotations to support your argument.
3. Write an imaginary dialogue with Mark Crispin Miller as interviewer and Barbara Walters as subject. Make it as funny or serious as you choose.
4. CONNECTIONS. Like Miller's essay, Rosalind Coward's "Naughty but Nice" (p. 374) also deals with the communications media. After reading both essays, write an essay of your own that examines whether the media *shape* or *reflect* the attitudes of their audiences.

Use EVIDENCE from Miller and Coward as well as from your own observations and experiences.

MARK CRISPIN MILLER ON WRITING

Mark Miller learned the art of analysis while studying literature in graduate school. "I learned to know the poem," he recalls in the introduction to *Boxed In*, "to (try to) divine its every implication, to trace its terms and images back through their respective secret histories, and then finally to compose a reading, so that the old text might dance clear of the impediments of age. Such, at any rate, was the ideal." The procedure sometimes resembled an autopsy, Miller admits; but it "could also illuminate what had been dark, for there was, in the erotic sense, a certain madness in that method, which demanded the near-maniacal attentiveness of a yearning lover."

While thus engaged in Renaissance poetry, Miller was also attracted by "the different sort of text piling up all over the place, covering the world like snow, or uncollected trash . . . — the interminable text of television, usually somewhere in view, never out of earshot." This text, too, demanded close reading, for "TV has all but boxed us in, . . . overwhelming the mind . . . , making it only half-aware."

In his writing, Miller has attempted to set out a "critical approach that would take TV seriously (without extolling it), a method of deciphering TV's component images, requiring both a meticulous attention to concrete detail, and a sense of TV's historical situation. . . . The reading of TV contains and necessitates a reading of our moment and its past."

For Miller, "critical analysis can just as easily reclaim a marvel . . . as it can devastate a lie. . . . The critical impulse can help also to replenish the minds within its sphere. . . . Those who have grown up watching television are not, because of all that gaping, now automatically adept at visual interpretation. That spectatorial 'experience' is passive, mesmeric, undiscriminating, and therefore not conducive to the refinement of the critical faculties: logic and imagination, linguistic precision, historical awareness, and a capacity for long, intense absorption. These — and not the abilities to compute, apply, or memorize — are the true desiderata of any higher education, and it is critical thinking that can best realize them."

FOR DISCUSSION

1. How is Renaissance poetry like television?
2. In your own words, what does Miller mean by "critical analysis"?
3. What are the "desiderata of higher education"? How does critical thinking help one realize them?

ROSALIND COWARD

An English writer focusing mainly on sexuality, health, and contemporary culture, ROSALIND COWARD was born in London in 1952 and studied at Cambridge University (B.A., 1974) and Birmingham University (Ph.D., 1977). She taught communications and media studies in several British universities between 1980 and 1988 before turning to writing full-time. Besides articles in *Feminist Review*, the *New Statesman*, the *Guardian*, and other periodicals, Coward has written both scholarly and general-interest books: *Language and Materialism: Developments in Semiology and the Theory of the Subject* (with John Ellis; 1977); *Patriarchial Precedents: Sexuality and Social Relations* (1983); *Female Desires: How They Are Sought, Bought, and Packaged* (1985); and *The Whole Truth: The Myths of Alternative Health* (1991).

Naughty but Nice: Food Pornography

Food pornography? In this essay from *Female Desires*, Coward explores the "illicit" images of food in magazines pitched to women, especially magazines on "slimming," or dieting. "Pleasure is this society's permanent Special Offer," says Coward. "To be a woman is to be constantly addressed, to be constantly scrutinized, to have our desire constantly courted." Here she analyzes the "courting" that occurs in advertising, photographing, and writing about food.

There's a full-page spread in a woman's magazine. It's captioned Breakfast Special, and shows a picture of every delicious breakfast imaginable. The hungry eye can delight in croissants with butter, exquisitely prepared bacon and eggs, toasted waffles with maple syrup. But over the top of the pictures there's a sinister message: 430 calories for the croissants; 300 for the waffles. The English breakfast takes the biscuit with a top score of 665 calories. It must be a galling sight for the readers of this particular magazine. Because it's *Slimmer* magazine. And one presumes the reader looks on these pleasures in the full knowledge that they had better not be indulged.

This pleasure in looking at the supposedly forbidden is reminiscent of another form of guilty-but-indulgent looking, that of sexual pornography. Sexual pornography as a separate realm of imagery exists because our society defines some explicit pictures of sexual activity or sexual parts as "naughty," "illicit." These images are then made widely available through a massive and massively profitable industry.

The glossy pictures in slimming magazines show in glorious Technicolor all the illicit desires which make us fat. Many of the articles show almost life-size pictures of the real baddies of the dieting world — bags of crisps, peanuts, bars of chocolate, cream puddings. Diet foods are advertised as sensuously as possible. The food is made as appetizing as possible, often with explicit sexual references: "Tip Top. For Girls Who Used to Say No"; "Grapefruits. The Least Forbidden Fruit."

Pictures in slimming magazines and those circulated around the slimming culture are only the hard core of food pictures which are in general circulation in women's magazines. Most women's magazines carry articles about food, recipes, or advertising. All are accompanied by larger-than-life, elaborate pictures of food, cross-sections through a cream and strawberry sponge, or close-ups of succulent Orange and Walnut Roast Beef. Recipe books often dwell on the visual impact of food. Robert Carrier has glossy cards showing the dish in question and carrying the recipe on the back — just the right size for the pocket. In the street, billboards confront us with gargantuan cream cakes.

But it is only the unfortunate readers of the slimming magazines who are supposed to use the pictures as a substitute for the real thing. While other forms of food photography are meant to stimulate the desire to prepare and eat the food, for the slimmers it is a matter of feasting the eyes only.

Like sexual pornography, pictures of food provide a photographic genre geared toward one sex. And like sexual pornography, it is a regime of "pleasure" which is incomprehensible to the opposite sex. This is because these pornographies are creating and indulging "pleasures" which confirm or trap men and women in their respective positions of power and subordination.

Sexual pornography is an industry dealing in images geared toward men. Sexual pornography is dominated by pictures of women. It shows bits of women's bodies, women engaged in sex acts, women masturbating, women supposedly having orgasms. When the women look at the camera, it is with an expression of sexual arousal, interest, and availability. The way in which women are posed for these images presupposes a male viewer, behind the camera, as it were, about to move in on the act.   7

Pornography is only the extreme end of how images of women are circulated in general in this society. Pornography is defined as being illicit, naughty, unacceptable for public display (though definitions of what is acceptable vary from one epoch to the next). It shows things which generally available images don't — penetration, masturbation, women's genitals. The porn industry then thrives on marketing and circulating these "illicit" images. But if pornography is meant to be illicit, and hidden, the kinds of images it shows differ little from the more routinely available images of women. Page three nudes in daily papers, advertisements showing women, the representation of sex in nonpornographic films, all draw on the conventions by which women are represented in pornography. Women are made to look into the camera in the same way, their bodies are arranged in the same way, the same glossy photographic techniques are used, there is the same fragmentation of women's bodies, and a concomitant fetishistic concentration on bits of the body.   8

Many women now think that the way male arousal is catered for in these images is a problem. These images feed a belief that men have depersonalized sexual needs, like sleeping or going to the lavatory. Pornography as it is currently practiced suggests that women's bodies are available to meet those needs. Men often say that porn is just fantasy, a harmless way of having pleasure as a substitute for the real thing. But women have begun to question this use of the term *pleasure*. After all, the pleasure seems conditional on feeling power to use women's bodies. And maybe there's only a thin line between the fantasy and the lived experi-   9 ence of sexuality where men do sometimes force their sexual attentions on women.

If sexual pornography is a display of images which confirm 10 men's sense of themselves as having power over women, food pornography is a regime of pleasurable images which has the opposite effect on its viewers — women. It indulges a pleasure which is linked to servitude and therefore confirms the subordinate position of women. Unlike sexual pornography, however, food porn cannot even be used without guilt. Because of pressures to diet, women have been made to feel guilty about enjoying food.

The use of food pornography is surprisingly widespread. All 11 the women I have talked to about food have confessed to enjoying it. Few activities it seems rival relaxing in bed with a good recipe book. Some indulged in full color pictures of gleaming bodies of Cold Mackerel Basquaise lying invitingly on a bed of peppers, or perfectly formed chocolate mousse topped with mounds of cream. The intellectuals expressed a preference for erotica, Elizabeth David's historical and literary titillation. All of us used the recipe books as aids to oral gratification, stimulants to imagine new combinations of food, ideas for producing a lovely meal.

Cooking food and presenting it beautifully is an act of servi- 12 tude. It is a way of expressing affection through a gift. In fact, the preparation of a meal involves intensive domestic labor, the most devalued labor in this society. That we should aspire to produce perfectly finished and presented food is a symbol of a willing and enjoyable participation in servicing other people.

Food pornography exactly sustains these meanings relating to 13 the preparation of food. The kinds of pictures used always repress the process of production of a meal. They are always beautifully lit, often touched up. The settings are invariably exquisite — a conservatory in the background, fresh flowers on the table. The dishes are expensive and look barely used.

There's a whole professional ideology connected with food 14 photography. The *Focal Encyclopaedia of Photography* tells us that in a "good food picture," "the food must be both perfectly cooked and perfectly displayed" if it is to appeal to the magazine reader. The photographer "must decide in advance on the correct style and arrangement of table linen, silver, china, flowers. Close attention to such details is vital because the final pictures must survive the critical inspection of housewives and cooks." Food photographers are supposed to be at the service of the expert chef, but sometimes "the photographer learns by experience that certain foodstuffs do not photograph well." And in such circumstances, "he must be able to suggest reasonable substitutes." Glycerine-covered green paper is a well-known substitute for lettuce, which wilts under the bright lights of a studio. And fast-melting foods like ice cream pose interesting technical problems for the food photographer. Occasionally, they do get caught out — I recently saw a picture of a sausage dinner where a nail was clearly visible, holding the sausage to its surroundings! Virtually all meals shown in these photos are actually inedible. If not actually made of plaster, most are sprayed or treated for photographing. How ironic to think of the perfect meal destined for the dustbin.

Food photographs are the culinary equivalent of the removal   15
of unsightly hairs. Not only do hours of work go into the preparation of the settings and the dishes, but the finished photos are touched up and imperfections removed to make the food look succulent and glistening. The aim of these photos is the display of the perfect meal in isolation from the kitchen context and the process of its production. There are no traces of the hours of shopping, cleaning, cutting up, preparing, tidying up, arranging the table and the room which in fact go into the production of a meal. Just as we know that glamorous models in the adverts don't really look as they appear, so we know perfectly well about the hours of untidy chaos involved in the preparation of a meal. We know that photos of glamour models are touched up, skin blemishes removed, excess fat literally cut out of the picture. And — subconsciously at least — we probably realize the same process has been at work on the Black Forest Gâteau. But the ideal images still linger in our minds as a lure. A meal should really look like the pictures. And that's how the images produce complicity in our subordination. We aim at giving others pleasure by obliterating the traces of our labor.

But it is not as if, even if we could produce this perfect meal,   16
we could wholeheartedly enjoy it. Because at the same time as food is presented as the one legitimate sensual pleasure for women

we are simultaneously told that women shouldn't eat too much. Food is Naughty but Nice, as the current Real Dairy Cream advertisement announces.

This guilt connected with eating has become severe over the 17 last few decades. It's a result of the growing pressure over these years toward the ideal shape of women. This shape is more like an adolescent than a woman, a silhouette rather than a soft body. There's a current dictum in slimming circles: "If you can pinch an inch, you may need to lose weight." This seems a particularly vicious control of female contours in a society obsessed with eating and uninterested in physical exertion. Dieting is the forcible imposition of an ideal shape on a woman's body.

The presentation of food sets up a particular trap for women. 18 The glossy, sensual photography legitimates oral desires and pleasures for women in a way that sexual interest for women is never legitimated. At the same time, however, much of the food photography constructs a direct equation between food and fat, an equation which can only generate guilt about oral pleasures. Look at the way advertising presents food, drawing a direct equation between what women eat and what shape they will be. Tab is the low-calorie drink from Coca-Cola. Its advertising campaign shows a glass of the stuff which is in the shape of a woman's body! Beside the glass are the statistics 35″ 22″ 35″. A Sweetex advertisement shows two slender women and exhorts "Take the lumps out of your life. Take Sweetex"! Heinz promotes its "Slimway Mayonnaise" with a picture of a very lurid lobster and the caption "Mayonnaise without guilt." Tea even "adds a little weight to the slimming argument." Another soft-drink company exhorts: "Spoil yourself, not your figure," which is a common promise for slimming foods. Nor is this phenomenon confined to slimming foods. Women's magazines have articles about whether "your taste buds are ruining your figure," and creamy foods are offered as wicked but worth it.

An equation is set up in this kind of writing and these pic- 19 tures between what goes into the mouth and the shape your body will be. It is as if we swallow a mouthful and it goes immediately, without digestion, to join the "cellulite." If we give this a moment's thought, we realize it is nonsense. There's no direct correlation between food into the mouth and fat; that's about the *only* thing on which all the diet experts agree. People have different metabolisms, use food differently. Different things in different people's lives affect what they eat and what effect that eating has on overall health. But the simplistic ideologies behind food and dieting cultures reinforce the guilt associated with food for women. Oral pleasures are only really permissible when tied to the servicing of others in the production of a meal. Women are controlled and punished if they indulge themselves.

The way images of food are made and circulated is not just an innocent catering for pleasures. They also meddle in people's sense of themselves and their self-worth. In a sexually divided and hierarchical society, these pleasures are tied to positions of power and subordination.   20

QUESTIONS ON MEANING

1. What is Coward's THESIS? Where is it stated?
2. PARAPHRASE paragraph 10. Which pornography does Coward consider the more subversive? Why?
3. How does Coward's discussion of photography support her comparison of food pornography and sexual pornography?
4. Why does Coward feel that pornography — food and sexual — subordinates women? What does pornography represent for Coward?

QUESTIONS ON WRITING STRATEGY

1. Why does Coward use sexual pornography to analyze food pornography? How does the comparison serve her PURPOSE in this essay?
2. Why does Coward provide more EVIDENCE of food pornography than of sexual pornography? What kind of evidence does she use?
3. What is the TONE of this essay? Is it appropriate, do you think?
4. "'Naughty but Nice' was written for an AUDIENCE of women." Do you agree or disagree with this statement? If you agree, does that mean that men can't gain anything from the essay?
5. OTHER METHODS. Coward compares and contrasts (Chap. 4). What key difference does she find between the two kinds of pornography?

QUESTIONS ON LANGUAGE

1. Coward writes, "The food is made as appetizing as possible, often with explicit sexual references" (para. 3). How does she use sexual ALLUSIONS to describe food pornography?
2. Coward sometimes uses a feminist vocabulary in this essay. Find some examples and analyze their EFFECT on the essay.
3. Use a dictionary to define any of the following words that are unfamiliar: galling (para. 1); illicit (2); gargantuan (4); genre (6); epoch, concomitant, fetishistic (8); erotica (11); conservatory (13); culinary (15); dictum (17); exhorts (18); correlation (19).

SUGGESTIONS FOR WRITING

1. Can you think of another type of pornography — clothes pornography, hair pornography, employment pornography, family pornography? After consulting a dictionary, write a definition of *pornography* that accounts for Coward's and your own use of the word. Then analyze the form of pornography you've identified.
2. Pick up a women's magazine such as *Cosmopolitan, Vogue, Redbook,* or *Mademoiselle* and analyze the image of women presented in the magazine's advertisements, text, and illustrations. Or analyze the image of men in a men's magazine such as *GQ, Playboy,* or *Esquire.*
3. Do you agree with Coward's analysis of sexual pornography? Write a short essay agreeing or disagreeing with the author's observations.
4. CONNECTIONS. In "Barbara Walters's Theater of Revenge" (p. 365), Mark Crispin Miller observes that female celebrities "sell themselves" as urchins, while male celebrities broadcast their respect for traditional values (paras. 14–15). Write an essay in which you relate these observations of Miller's to the issues of male and female relations and self-esteem discussed by Rosalind Coward. What is the possible connection, for instance, between men's "sense of themselves as having power over women" (Coward, 10) and Sylvester Stallone's wish for "a home life that is really beautiful" (Miller, 15), or between women's being "controlled and punished if they indulge themselves" (Coward, 19) and their confessing to "past misery" so that they may "go on having all that fame and fortune" (Miller, 14)?

ADDITIONAL WRITING TOPICS
Division or Analysis

Write an essay by the method of division or analysis using one of the following subjects (or choose your own subject). In your essay, make sure your purpose and your principle of division or analysis is clear to your readers. Explain the parts of your subject so that readers know how each relates to the others and contributes to the whole.

1. A typical TV commercial for a product such as laundry soap, deodorant, beer, or an economy car
2. An appliance or machine, such as a stereo speaker, a motorcycle, a microwave oven, or a camera
3. An organization or association, such as a social club, a sports league, or a support group
4. The characteristic appearance of a rock singer or a classical violinist
5. A year in the life of a student
6. Your favorite poem
7. A short story, a play, or a dramatic film that made you think
8. The government of your community
9. The most popular bookstore (or other place of business) in town
10. The Bible
11. A band or orchestra
12. A famous painting or statue

7
CLASSIFICATION
Sorting into Kinds

THE METHOD

To *classify* is to make sense of the world by arranging many units — trucks, chemical elements, wasps, students — into more manageable groups. Zoologists classify animals, botanists classify plants — and their classifications help us to understand a vast and complex subject: life on earth. To help us find books in a library, librarians classify books into categories: fiction, biography, history, psychology, and so forth. For the convenience of readers, newspapers run classified advertising, grouping many small ads into categories such as Help Wanted and Cars for Sale.

The subject of a classification is always a number of things, such as peaches or political systems. (In contrast, DIVISION or ANALYSIS, the topic of the last chapter, usually deals with a solitary subject, a coherent whole, such as *a* peach or *a* political system.) The job of classification is to sort the things into groups or classes based on their similarities and differences. Say, for instance, you're going to write an essay about how people write. After interviewing a lot of writers, you determine that writers' processes differ widely, mainly in the amount of planning and rewriting they entail. (Notice that this determination involves analyzing the process of writing, separating it into steps. See Chapter 5.) On the basis of your findings, you create groups for planners, one-drafters, and rewriters. Once your groups are defined (and assuming they are valid), your subjects (the writers) almost sort themselves out.

Classification is done for a purpose. In a New York City guidebook, Joan Hamburg and Norma Ketay discuss low-priced hotels. (Notice that already they are examining the members of a group: low-priced as opposed to medium- and high-priced hotels.) They cast the low-priced hotels into categories: Rooms for Singles and Students, Rooms for Families, Rooms for Servicemen, and Rooms for General Occupancy. Always their purpose is evident: to match up the visitor with a suitable kind of room. When a classification has no purpose, it seems a silly and hollow exercise.

Just as you can analyze a subject (divide a pie) in many ways, you can classify a subject according to many principles. A different New York guidebook might classify all hotels according to price: grand luxury, luxury, commercial, low-priced (Hamburg and Ketay's category), fleabag, and flophouse. The purpose of this classification would be to match visitors to hotels fitting their pocketbooks. The principle you use in classifying things depends on your purpose. A linguist might write an essay classifying the languages of the world according to their origins (Romance languages, Germanic languages, Coptic languages . . .), but a student battling with a college language requirement might write a humorous essay classifying them into three groups: hard to learn, harder to learn, and unlearnable.

The simplest method of classification is *binary* (or *two-part*) *classification*, in which you sort things out into (1) those with a certain distinguishing feature and (2) those without it. You might classify a number of persons, let's say, into smokers and non-smokers, blind people and sighted people, runners and non-runners, believers and nonbelievers. Binary classification is most useful when your subject is easily divisible into positive and negative categories.

Classification can be complex as well. As Jonathan Swift reminds us,

> So, naturalists observe, a flea
> Hath smaller fleas that on him prey,
> And these have smaller yet to bite 'em.
> And so proceed *ad infinitum.*

In being faithful to reality, you will sometimes find that you have to sort out the members of categories into subcategories. Hamburg and Ketay did something of the kind when they subclassified the class of low-priced New York hotels. Writing about the varieties of one Germanic language, such as English, a writer could identify the subclasses of British English, North American English, Australian English, and so on.

As readers, we all enjoy watching a clever writer sort things into categories, or break things into elements. We like to meet classifications that strike us as true and familiar. This pleasure may account for the appeal of magazine articles that classify things ("The Seven Common Garden Varieties of Moocher," "Five Embarrassing Types of Social Blunder"). Usefulness as well as pleasure may explain the popularity of classifications that evaluate things. In a survey of current movies, a newspaper critic might classify the films into categories: "Don't Miss," "Worth Seeing," "So-So," and "Never Mind." The magazine *Consumer Reports* uses this method of classifying in its comments on different brands of stereo speakers or canned tuna. Products are sorted into groups (excellent, good, fair, poor, and not acceptable), and the merits of each are discussed by the method of description. (Of a frozen pot pie: "Bottom crust gummy, meat spongy when chewed, with nondescript old-poultry and stale-flour flavor.")

THE PROCESS

Classification will usually come into play when you want to impose order on a numerous and unwieldy subject. (In separate essays in this chapter, Robert Reich and Ralph Whitehead, Jr.,

classify a huge subject, the people of the United States.) Sometimes you may use classification humorously, as Tom Bodett and
Fran Lebowitz do in other essays in this chapter, to give a charge
to familiar experiences. Whichever use you make of classification,
though, do it for a reason. The files of composition instructors are
littered with student essays in which nothing was ventured and
nothing gained by classification.

Things may be classified into categories that reveal truth, or
into categories that don't tell us a thing. To sort out ten U.S. cities according to their relative freedom from air pollution, or their
cost of living, or the degree of progress they have made in civil
rights might prove highly informative and useful. Such a classification might even tell us where we'd want to live. But to sort out
the cities according to a superficial feature such as the relative size
of their cat and dog populations wouldn't interest anyone, probably, except a veterinarian looking for a job.

Your purpose, your thesis, and your principle of classification
will all overlap at the point where you find your interest in your
subject. Say you're curious about how other students write. Is
your interest primarily in the materials they use (word processor,
typewriter, pencil), in where and when they write, or in how
much planning and rewriting they do? Any of these could lead to
a principle for sorting the students into groups. In the essay itself,
let readers in on your principle of classification and explain why
you have chosen it.

For a workable classification, make sure that the categories
you choose don't overlap. If you were writing a survey of popular
magazines for adults and you were sorting your subject into categories that included women's magazines and sports magazines,
you might soon run into trouble. Into which category would you
place *Women's Sports*? The trouble is that both categories take in
the same item. To avoid this problem, you'll need to reorganize
your classification on a different principle. You might sort out the
magazines by their audiences: magazines mainly for women, magazines mainly for men, magazines for both women and men. Or
you might group them according to subject matter: sports magazines, literary magazines, astrology magazines, fashion magazines,
TV fan magazines, trade journals, and so on. *Women's Sports*

would fit into either of those classification schemes, but into only one category in each scheme.

When you draw up a scheme of classification, be sure also that you include all essential categories. Omitting an important category can weaken the effect of your essay, no matter how well-written it is. It would be a major oversight, for example, if you were to classify the residents of a dormitory according to their religious affiliations and not include a category for the numerous nonaffiliated. Your reader might wonder if your sloppiness in forgetting a category extended to your thinking about the topic as well.

Some form of outline can be helpful to keep the classes and their members straight as you develop ideas and write. You might experiment with a diagram in which you jot down headings for the groups, with plenty of space around them, and then let each heading accumulate members as you think of them, the way a magnet attracts paperclips. This kind of diagram offers more flexibility than a vertical list or outline, and it may be a better aid for keeping categories from overlapping or disappearing.

CLASSIFICATION IN A PARAGRAPH:
TWO ILLUSTRATIONS

Using Classification
to Write about Television

Most canned laughs produced by laugh machines fall into one of five reliable types. There are *titters*, light vocal laughs with which an imaginary audience responds to a comedian's least wriggle or grimace. Some producers rely heavily on *chuckles*, deeper, more chesty responses. Most profound of all, *belly laughs* are summoned to acclaim broader jokes and sexual innuendos. When provided at full level of sound and in longest duration, the belly laugh becomes the Big Boffola. There are also *wild howls* or *screamers*, extreme responses used not more than three times per show, lest they seem fake. These are crowd laughs, and yet the machine also offers *freaky laughs*, the piercing, eccentric screeches of solitary kooks. With them, a producer affirms that even a canned audience may include one thorny individualist.

COMMENT. This paragraph relates to one in the previous chapter (p. 340) about the laugh machine used by producers of television comedies to make jokes seem funny. In the earlier, analytical paragraph, style was identified as one of the components of the canned laugh. Now in this paragraph the writer classifies the *styles* of canned laughs. (Choosing a different principle of classification, the writer might also have examined different volumes or durations of canned laughs.) The labels for the five categories clearly distinguish them, as do the descriptions and examples. Simple but memorable, the categories register in our minds.

Using Classification
in an Academic Discipline

Sheldon described three types of physical physique: the *endomorph*, who is overweight, with poorly developed bones and muscles; the *mesomorph*, muscular, strong, and athletic; and the thin, fragile *ectomorph*. He then came up with three clusters of personality traits: *viscerotonia* (comfort-loving, food-oriented, sociable, relaxed); *somatotonia* (aggressive, adventure-loving, risk-taking); and *cerebrotonia* (restrained, self-conscious, introverted). When Sheldon rated men according to where they stood with regard to both body types and personality traits, he found high correlations. Extremely endomorphic men were likely to be viscerotonic, mesomorphs tended to be somatotonic, and ectomorphs were cerebrotonic.

COMMENT. In this paragraph from their textbook *Psychology* (1985), the authors Diane E. Papalia and Sally Wendkos Olds, are explaining the research of a medical doctor and scholar named William H. Sheldon. Sheldon used two different principles of classification to sort men into groups: physique and personality. The point of the paragraph is that he found correspondences between classes in each scheme. Papalia and Olds go on in a subsequent paragraph to say that later researchers found fewer correlations between body type and personality than Sheldon did; but his classification contains enough of the truth, apparently, to be still worth mentioning.

TOM BODETT

A self-proclaimed "generic American," TOM BODETT was born in 1955 in Champagne, Illinois, and grew up in Sturgis, Michigan. He attended Michigan State University before heading to Oregon and then Alaska, working as a logger, deckhand, and contractor. Known for his good-natured, folksy humor, Bodett is a regular contributor to National Public Radio and hosts a weekly show from his local radio station in Homer, Alaska. He has published three collections of humorous essays: *As Far as You Can Go without a Passport* (1985), *Small Comforts* (1987), and *The End of the Road* (1989). His down-home voice on radio spots for Motel 6 ("We'll leave the light on for you") has gained him something of a cult following.

Wait Divisions

Classification is often put to humorous ends, as this essay by Bodett illustrates. "Wait Divisions" first appeared in *Small Comforts*. In it, Bodett shows what the commentator Andrei Codrescu calls "the crisp freshness of someone at home in the world."

I read somewhere that we spend a full third of our lives waiting. I've also read where we spend a third of our lives sleeping, a third working, and a third at our leisure. Now either somebody's lying, or we're spending all our leisure time waiting to go to work or sleep. That can't be true or league softball and Winnebagos never would have caught on.

So where are we doing all of this waiting and what does it mean to an impatient society like ours? Could this unseen waiting be the source of all our problems? A shrinking economy? The staggering deficit? Declining mental health and moral apathy? Probably not, but let's take a look at some of the more classic "waits" anyway.

The very purest form of waiting is what we'll call the *Watched-Pot Wait*. This type of wait is without a doubt the most annoying of all. Take filling up the kitchen sink. There is absolutely nothing you can do while this is going on but keep both eyes glued to the sink until it's full. If you try to cram in some extracurricular activity, you're asking for it. So you stand there, your hands on the faucets, and wait. A temporary suspension of duties. During these waits it's common for your eyes to lapse out of focus. The brain disengages from the body and wanders around the imagination in search of distraction. It finds none and springs back into action only when the water runs over the edge of the counter and onto your socks.

The phrase "A watched pot never boils" comes of this experi-   4
ence. Pots don't care whether they are watched or not; the problem is that nobody has ever seen a pot actually come to a boil. While they are waiting, their brains turn off.

Other forms of the Watched-Pot Wait would include waiting   5
for your drier to quit at the laundromat, waiting for your toast to pop out of the toaster, or waiting for a decent idea to come to mind at a typewriter. What they all have in common is that they render the waiter helpless and mindless.

A cousin to the Watched-Pot Wait is the *Forced Wait*. Not for   6
the weak of will, this one requires a bit of discipline. The classic Forced Wait is starting your car in the winter and letting it slowly idle up to temperature before engaging the clutch. This is every bit as uninteresting as watching a pot, but with one big difference. You have a choice. There is nothing keeping you from racing to work behind a stone-cold engine save the thought of the early demise of several thousand dollars' worth of equipment you haven't paid for yet. Thoughts like that will help you get through a Forced Wait.

Properly preparing packaged soup mixes also requires a   7
Forced Wait. Directions are very specific on these mixes. "Bring three cups water to boil, add mix, simmer three minutes, remove from heat, let stand five minutes." I have my doubts that anyone has ever actually done this. I'm fairly spineless when it comes to instant soups and usually just boil the bejeezus out of them until the noodles sink. Some things just aren't worth a Forced Wait.

All in all Forced Waiting requires a lot of a thing called *pa-*   8
tience, which is a virtue. Once we get into virtues I'm out of my

element, and can't expound on the virtues of virtue, or even lie about them. So let's move on to some of the more far-reaching varieties of waiting.

The *Payday Wait* is certainly a leader in the long-term antici- 9 pation field. The problem with waits that last more than a few minutes is that you have to actually do other things in the meantime. Like go to work. By far the most aggravating feature of the Payday Wait is that even though you must keep functioning in the interludes, there is less and less you are able to do as the big day draws near. For some of us the last few days are best spent alone in a dark room for fear we'll accidentally do something that costs money. With the Payday Wait comes a certain amount of hope that we'll make it, and faith that everything will be all right once we do.

With the introduction of faith and hope, I've ushered in the 10 most potent wait class of all, the *Lucky-Break Wait,* or the *Wait for One's Ship to Come In.* This type of wait is unusual in that it is for the most part voluntary. Unlike the Forced Wait, which is also voluntary, waiting for your lucky break does not necessarily mean that it will happen.

Turning one's life into a waiting game of these proportions re- 11 quires gobs of the aforementioned faith and hope, and is strictly for the optimists among us. For these people life is the thing that happens to them while they're waiting for something to happen to them. On the surface it seems as ridiculous as following the directions on soup mixes, but the Lucky-Break Wait performs an outstanding service to those who take it upon themselves to do it. As long as one doesn't come to rely on it, wishing for a few good things to happen never hurt anybody.

In the end it is obvious that we certainly do spend a good deal 12 of our time waiting. The person who said we do it a third of the time may have been going easy on us. It makes a guy wonder how anything at all gets done around here. But things do get done, people grow old, and time boils on whether you watch it or not.

The next time you're standing at the sink waiting for it to fill 13 while cooking soup mix that you'll have to eat until payday or until a large bag of cash falls out of the sky, don't despair. You're probably just as busy as the next guy.

QUESTIONS ON MEANING

1. Is Bodett's PURPOSE to inform or to entertain?
2. What is the difference between the Watched-Pot Wait and the Forced Wait? The Forced Wait and the Lucky-Break Wait?
3. What is Bodett's CONCLUSION? How does he relate it to the INTRODUCTION?

QUESTIONS ON WRITING STRATEGY

1. How does Bodett's introduction justify his essay?
2. Are Bodett's categories complete? Do they encompass all forms of waiting?
3. What is the point of paragraph 8?
4. **OTHER METHODS.** Bodett clarifies his categories with examples (Chap. 3). What can you infer about his assumed AUDIENCE from his choice of examples? Where does he use the method of DIVISION?

QUESTIONS ON LANGUAGE

1. How, in paragraph 2, does Bodett typify "all of our problems"? Where might he have gotten these phrases? What is their EFFECT?
2. What is Bodett's TONE? What words in the essay support your answer?
3. A few of these words may be unfamiliar: apathy (para. 2); render (5); demise (6); aggravating (9); potent (10); aforementioned (11).

SUGGESTIONS FOR WRITING

1. Choose a different aspect of everyday life (classrooms, study habits, meals, dates) and break that aspect into different categories. Follow Bodett's example and think up appropriate descriptive names for your categories.
2. Write an essay about what Bodett calls the Lucky-Break Wait (paras. 10–11). Is it a good thing, do you think, to wait for a lucky break, or (as Bodett hints) do people wait away their lives waiting for a break? Support your opinion with examples from your own experience and observations.
3. **CONNECTIONS.** Read the next essay, Fran Lebowitz's "The Sound of Music: Enough Already." Both Bodett and Lebowitz classify for

humorous purposes, but they go about it quite differently. Contrast the two essays in terms of TONE: What are the differences? Are there any similarities? How does each author achieve his or her tone?

TOM BODETT ON WRITING

In his introduction to *Small Comforts*, Tom Bodett claims that "reading a list of national averages is like leafing through my résumé." For the reference book *Contemporary Authors*, he wrote, "I consider myself a normal person with a normal life, and I write, normally, about typical things. I assume my audience is made up of normal people."

Why then does Bodett write? He answers in *Small Comforts*: "We've all had our moments when reading, at the theater, or listening to a gifted storyteller when we've stopped to say to ourselves, 'Yeah, it's just like that.' Such moments serve, for a time, to take bit of the loneliness out of being human. This sharing of experience seems to me the only real purpose to produce or consume art of any kind.

"Not having been trained as either an artist or a writer, I am all too aware of the audacity invoked in presenting this collection of my thoughts on the world at large. I am not well educated or even particularly experienced in the wider scope of things. I've yet to commit an idea to paper that I didn't read later and think, 'Who really cares?' I'm always pleasantly surprised when anyone does. It helps keep me going despite my lack of credentials."

But Bodett does have credentials. He's a "card-carrying member of life as we know it." All he really wants from his readers is that "at least once you stop to think, 'Yeah, it's just like that.'"

FOR DISCUSSION

1. What can a "normal" person like Tom Bodett bring to writing?
2. Do you get that spark of recognition from Bodett's essay? What writers, artists, or musicians have provided that spark for you?

FRAN LEBOWITZ

Fran Lebowitz is a satirist best known for her witty attacks on contemporary urban life. Born in 1950 in Morristown, New Jersey, Lebowitz finished high school there and skipped college. Instead, she worked in New York City at a series of jobs, including taxi driver and apartment cleaner. A writer since grade school, Lebowitz began publishing in *Changes* magazine — book and movie reviews, mostly — and then in 1972 started a regular column for Andy Warhol's *Interview* magazine. From 1977 to 1979 Lebowitz contributed to *Interview* and also to *Mademoiselle*, but by 1981 she had left both posts to concentrate on fiction writing. Her essays are collected in *Metropolitan Life* (1978) and *Social Studies* (1981). Lebowitz lectures and reads at colleges and universities across the country and is often a guest on *Late Night with David Letterman*. She is at work on her first novel, which she once predicted "should be done when I'm about ninety-seven."

The Sound of Music: Enough Already

Lebowitz's reviewers often disagree over her work. "Sour grapes," says one. "Brittle humor, drained of compassion," says another. But still another says, "Lebowitz is . . . a funny, urbane, intelligent one-woman bulwark against ticky-tack, creeping mellowness, and the excesses of what Mencken dubbed 'boobus Americanus.'" See what you think of this essay from *Metropolitan Life*.

First off, I want to say that as far as I am concerned, in instances where I have not personally and deliberately sought it out, the only difference between music and Muzak is the spelling. Pablo Casals practicing across the hall with the door open — being trapped in an elevator, the ceiling of which is broadcasting "Parsley, Sage, Rosemary, and Thyme" — it's all the same to me. Harsh words? Perhaps. But then again these are not gentle times we live in. And they are being made no more gentle by this incessant melody that was once real life.

There was a time when music knew its place. No longer. Possibly this is not music's fault. It may be that music fell in with a bad crowd and lost its sense of common decency. I am willing to consider this. I am willing even to try and help. I would like to do my bit to set music straight in order that it might shape up and leave the mainstream of society. The first thing that music must understand is that there are two kinds of music — good music and bad music. Good music is music that I want to hear. Bad music is music that I don't want to hear.

So that music might more clearly see the error of its ways I offer the following. If you are music and you recognize yourself on this list, you are bad music.

1. Music in Other People's Clock Radios

There are times when I find myself spending the night in the home of another. Frequently the other is in a more reasonable line of work than I and must arise at a specific hour. Ofttimes the other, unbeknownst to me, manipulates an appliance in such a way that I am awakened by Stevie Wonder. On such occasions I announce that if I wished to be awakened by Stevie Wonder I would sleep with Stevie Wonder. I do not, however, wish to be awakened by Stevie Wonder and that is why God invented alarm clocks. Sometimes the other realizes that I am right. Sometimes the other does not. And that is why God invented *many* others.

2. Music Residing in the Hold Buttons of Other People's Business Telephones

I do not under any circumstances enjoy hold buttons. But I am a woman of reason. I can accept reality. I can face the facts. What I cannot face is the music. Just as there are two kinds of music — good and bad — so there are two kinds of hold buttons — good and bad. Good hold buttons are hold buttons that hold one silently. Bad hold buttons are hold buttons that hold one musically. When I hold I want to hold silently. That is the way it was meant to be, for that is what God was talking about when he said, "Forever hold your peace." He would have added, "and quiet," but he thought you were smarter.

3. Music in the Streets

The past few years have seen a steady increase in the number   6
of people playing music in the streets. The past few years have also seen a steady increase in the number of malignant diseases. Are these two facts related? One wonders. But even if they are not — and, as I have pointed out, one cannot be sure — music in the streets has definitely taken its toll. For it is at the very least disorienting. When one is walking down Fifth Avenue, one does not expect to hear a string quartet playing a Strauss waltz. What one expects to hear while walking down Fifth Avenue is traffic. When one does indeed hear a string quartet playing a Strauss waltz while one is walking down Fifth Avenue, one is apt to become confused and imagine that one is not walking down Fifth Avenue at all but rather that one has somehow wound up in Old Vienna. Should one imagine that one is in Old Vienna one is likely to become quite upset when one realizes that in Old Vienna there is no sale at Charles Jourdan. And that is why when I walk down Fifth Avenue I want to hear traffic.

4. Music in the Movies

I'm not talking about musicals. Musicals are movies that   7
warn you by saying, "Lots of music here. Take it or leave it." I'm talking about regular movies that extend no such courtesy but allow unsuspecting people to come to see them and then assault them with a barrage of unasked-for tunes. There are two major offenders in this category: black movies and movies set in the fifties. Both types of movies are afflicted with the same misconception. They don't know that movies are supposed to be movies. They think that movies are supposed to be records with pictures. They have failed to understand that if God had wanted records to have pictures, he would not have invented television.

5. Music in Public Places Such as Restaurants, Supermarkets, Hotel Lobbies, Airports, Etc.

When I am in any of the above-mentioned places I am not there to hear music. I am there for whatever reason is appropriate to the respective place. I am no more interested in hearing "Mack the Knife" while waiting for the shuttle to Boston than someone sitting ringside at the Sands Hotel is interested in being forced to choose between sixteen varieties of cottage cheese. If God had meant for everything to happen at once, he would not have invented desk calendars. 8

Epilogue

Some people talk to themselves. Some people sing to themselves. Is one group better than the other? Did not God create all people equal? Yes, God created all people equal. Only to some he gave the ability to make up their own words. 9

QUESTIONS ON MEANING

1. What is Lebowitz's PURPOSE? To change the places where we hear music? To express herself? To entertain the reader, or what?
2. What is Lebowitz's THESIS?
3. What does the author admit in the first paragraph? What does this say about her judgments in the essay?

QUESTIONS ON WRITING STRATEGY

1. Lebowitz gives each category a heading. What is the EFFECT of these headings?
2. Lebowitz's categories are actually subcategories of a larger class she identifies early on. What is it?
3. Why does Lebowitz constantly evoke God? Might some readers consider this offensive?

4. How could you characterize the TONE of this essay? Does the author admit to being humorous?
5. OTHER METHODS. To what extent is "The Sound of Music" an argument (Chap. 11)?

QUESTIONS ON LANGUAGE

1. Look up any of these words that you do not find familiar: incessant (para. 1); malignant, disorienting (6); barrage, afflicted, misconception (7); respective (8).
2. What ALLUSION does Lebowitz make when she says, "What I cannot face is the music" (para. 5)?
3. How does Lebowitz use PERSONIFICATION in paragraph 2? Why?

SUGGESTIONS FOR WRITING

1. What is your taste in music? Following Lebowitz's example (but not her criteria), classify good and bad music, and subclassify bad music. You can be humorous or serious, as you like.
2. Select some aspect of your life that really irks you, perhaps other people's pets, restaurant servers, customers, bus drivers, car drivers, dorm residents, household pests. Write an essay classifying this irksome thing, being careful to supply details and to indicate your feelings in your TONE.
3. Since Lebowitz wrote "The Sound of Music" over a decade ago, musical soundtracks have become almost required for nonmusical films. Write an essay agreeing or disagreeing with Lebowitz's contention that such movies are "records with pictures" rather than movies (para. 7). Use specific examples to support your position.
4. CONNECTIONS. Fran Lebowitz and Suzanne Britt in "Neat People vs. Sloppy People" (p. 229) both establish classifications in which they personally side with one class: Lebowitz with "good music," Britt with "sloppy people." Compare and contrast the ways each writer characterizes the class she does not like, "bad music" or "neat people." What are the qualities of the class? What kinds of words describe it? Which writer is funnier, and why?

FRAN LEBOWITZ ON WRITING

Interviewing Fran Lebowitz in 1983, Jean W. Ross noted that her "very funny writing seems to grow out of a genuine irritation." Lebowitz acknowledged as much: "I've always been enraged. . . . Not only have I always been in a state of rage, but I genuinely don't understand why everyone isn't. I don't think of it as being unusual; I think it's the only logical response to life. I think of my writing as an organized and rarefied form of a tantrum. It's the only thing that keeps me from being a murderer. There is a very thin line that divides the comic writer from the mass murderer, and, you know, I really have that impulse all the time. So I guess writing or making wisecracks and jokes is a way of not ending up in prison.

"People have always told me I'm going to have a heart attack because I get angry and blow up," Lebowitz continued, explaining the source of her attitude. "Every time you get on the subway in New York, it stops between the stations for no reason. You sit there for twenty minutes. No one ever tells you why, and everyone just sits there. But I don't. I walk to the front of the train and start screaming at the conductor. Of course it doesn't get any results. People ask me what I hope to achieve from my writing. I never for a second imagined that I was going to change anyone's mind. And I also never for a second imagined that any complaint I would ever make in writing or talking would have any effect. Which further enrages me. The last writer who managed to move people to action was Thomas Paine, and the time of the pamphleteer is gone. I think of myself as a kind of pamphleteer, though the likelihood of affecting people by writing in a country where people are basically illiterate is not very great."

FOR DISCUSSION

1. How is Lebowitz's behavior in a stalled subway car similar to her attitude about writing?
2. What is a pamphleteer? How is Lebowitz like one?
3. What do you think Lebowitz means by "illiterate"? What do you think of her characterization of the American people as "basically illiterate"?

WENDELL BERRY

WENDELL BERRY is a poet, fiction writer, essayist, and farmer. Born in 1934 in Port Royal, Kentucky, he received a B.A. (1956) and an M.A. (1957) from the University of Kentucky. After several years in California, Italy, and New York City, he returned to Port Royal to teach, write, and farm. His copious writings include the novels *Nathan Coulter* (1960), *A Place on Earth* (1967, revised 1983), *The Memory of Old Jack* (1974), and *The Remembering* (1988); the short stories in *The Wild Birds* (1986); the poems in *The Broken Ground* (1964), *Farming: A Handbook* (1970), *The Wheel* (1982), and other collections; and the essays in *The Long-Legged House* (1969), *Home Economics* (1987), *What Are People For?* (1990), and other collections. All of Berry's work explores the relations of humans to nature and to each other. He is an earnest and persuasive speaker for the changes in values needed to save our environment.

Solving for Pattern

Berry has long championed restoration of traditional farming methods. That is his immediate subject here, but, as you will see, farming is not just farming: It represents a host of environmental and cultural problems and solutions. This selection is actually the self-contained opening of a longer essay with the same title. It was first published in *The New Farm* in 1980 and then was reprinted in Berry's collection *The Gift of Good Land* (1981).

Our dilemma in agriculture now is that the industrial meth- 1
ods that have so spectacularly solved some of the problems of food production have been accompanied by "side effects" so damaging as to threaten the survival of farming. Perhaps the best clue to the nature and the gravity of this dilemma is that it is not limited to agriculture. My immediate concern here is with the irony of agricultural methods that destroy, first, the health of the soil and, finally, the health of human communities. But I could just as easily be talking about sanitation systems that pollute, school sys-

tems that graduate illiterate students, medical cures that cause disease, or nuclear armaments that explode in the midst of the people they are meant to protect. This is a kind of surprise that is characteristic of our time: The cure proves incurable; security results in the evacuation of a neighborhood or a town. It is only when it is understood that our agricultural dilemma is characteristic not of our agriculture but of our time that we can begin to understand why these surprises happen, and to work out standards of judgment that may prevent them.

To the problems of farming, then, as to other problems of our time, there appear to be three kinds of solutions: 2

There is, first, the solution that causes a ramifying series of new problems, the only limiting criterion being, apparently, that the new problems should arise beyond the purview of the expertise that produced the solution — as, in agriculture, industrial solutions to the problem of production have invariably caused problems of maintenance, conservation, economics, community health, etc., etc. 3

If, for example, beef cattle are fed in large feed lots, within the boundaries of the feeding operation itself a certain factorylike order and efficiency can be achieved. But even within those boundaries that mechanical order immediately produces biological disorder, for we know that health problems and dependence on drugs will be greater among cattle so confined than among cattle on pasture. 4

And beyond those boundaries, the problems multiply. Pen feeding of cattle in large numbers involves, first, a manure-removal problem, which becomes at some point a health problem for the animals themselves, for the local watershed, and for the adjoining ecosystems and human communities. If the manure is disposed of without returning it to the soil that produced the feed, a serious problem of soil fertility is involved. But we know too that large concentrations of animals in feed lots in one place tend to be associated with, and to promote, large cash-grain monocultures in other places. These monocultures tend to be accompanied by a whole set of specifically agricultural problems: soil erosion, soil compaction, epidemic infestations of pests, weeds, and disease. But they are also accompanied by a set of 5

agricultural-economic problems (dependence on purchased technology; dependence on purchased fuels, fertilizers, and poisons;
dependence on credit) — and by a set of community problems, beginning with depopulation and the removal of sources,
services, and markets to more and more distant towns. And
these are, so to speak, only the first circle of the bad effects of a
bad solution. With a little care, their branchings can be traced
on into nature, into the life of the cities, and into the cultural
and economic life of the nation.

   The second kind of solution is that which immediately wors-   6
ens the problem it is intended to solve, causing a hellish symbiosis
in which problem and solution reciprocally enlarge one another
in a sequence that, so far as its own logic is concerned, is limitless
— as when the problem of soil compaction is "solved" by a bigger
tractor, which further compacts the soil, which makes a need for
a still bigger tractor, and so on and on. There is an identical symbiosis between coal-fired power plants and air conditioners. It is
characteristic of such solutions that no one prospers by them but
the suppliers of fuel and equipment.

   These two kinds of solutions are obviously bad. They always   7
serve one good at the expense of another or of several others, and
I believe that if all their effects were ever to be accounted for they
would be seen to involve, too frequently if not invariably, a net
loss to nature, agriculture, and the human commonwealth.

   Such solutions always involve a definition of the problem   8
that is either false or so narrow as to be virtually false. To define
an agricultural problem as if it were solely a problem of agriculture — or solely a problem of production or technology or economics — is simply to misunderstand the problem, either inadvertently or deliberately, either for profit or because of a
prevalent fashion of thought. The whole problem must be solved,
not just some handily identifiable and simplifiable aspect of it.

   Both kinds of bad solutions leave their problems unsolved.   9
Bigger tractors do not solve the problem of soil compaction any
more than air conditioners solve the problem of air pollution.
Nor does the large confinement-feeding operation solve the problem of food production; it is, rather, a way calculated to allow
large-scale ambition and greed to profit from food production.

The real problem of food production occurs within a complex, mutually influential relationship of soil, plants, animals, and people. A real solution to that problem will therefore be ecologically, agriculturally, and culturally healthful.

Perhaps it is not until health is set down as the aim that we   10
come in sight of the third kind of solution: that which causes a ramifying series of solutions — as when meat animals are fed on the farm where the feed is raised, and where the feed is raised to be fed to the animals that are on the farm. Even so rudimentary a description implies a concern for pattern, for quality, which necessarily complicates the concern for production. The farmer has put plants and animals into a relationship of mutual dependence, and must perforce be concerned for balance or symmetry, a reciprocating connection in the pattern of the farm that is biological, not industrial, and that involves solutions to problems of fertility, soil husbandry, economics, sanitation — the whole complex of problems whose proper solutions add up to *health*: the health of the soil, of plants and animals, of farm and farmer, of farm family and farm community, all involved in the same internested, interlocking pattern — or pattern of patterns.

A bad solution is bad, then, because it acts destructively   11
upon the larger patterns in which it is contained. It acts destructively upon those patterns, most likely, because it is formed in ignorance or disregard of them. A bad solution solves for a single purpose or goal, such as increased production. And it is typical of such solutions that they achieve stupendous increases in production at exorbitant biological and social costs.

A good solution is good because it is in harmony with those   12
larger patterns — and this harmony will, I think, be found to have the nature of analogy. A bad solution acts within the larger pattern the way a disease or addiction acts within the body. A good solution acts within the larger pattern the way a healthy organ acts within the body. But it must at once be understood that a healthy organ does not — as the mechanistic or industrial mind would like to say — "give" health to the body, is not exploited for the body's health, but is *a part* of its health. The health of organ and organism is the same, just as the health of organism and ecosystem is the same. And these structures of organ, organism, and

ecosystem belong to a series of analogical integrities that begins with the organelle and ends with the biosphere.

QUESTIONS ON MEANING

1. Would you say Berry's PURPOSE is explanatory, persuasive, or both?
2. Is Berry's THESIS concerned with agriculture or with something else in addition? What is the thesis?
3. What is the meaning of Berry's title, "Solving for Pattern"? What is a "pattern"?
4. In your own words, summarize Berry's three categories of solutions.
5. To what does Berry attribute all bad solutions?

QUESTIONS ON WRITING STRATEGY

1. What EVIDENCE does Berry use to support his classification? Is it ample and authoritative enough?
2. Why does Berry introduce the global aspect of good and bad solutions in his INTRODUCTION?
3. What is the advantage of the analogy (Chap. 8) that Berry uses to conclude the selection?
4. Analyze Berry's organization. How effective is it?
5. OTHER METHODS. How does Berry use cause and effect (Chap. 9) in analyzing his first example (paras. 4–5)?

QUESTIONS ON LANGUAGE

1. A key word in Berry's essay is *ramifying*. What does it mean, and why is it important?
2. Consult your dictionary if you need help defining the following words: criterion, purview (para. 3); watershed, ecosystems, monocultures (5); symbiosis, reciprocally (6); invariably, commonwealth (7); inadvertently, prevalent (8); rudimentary, perforce, symmetry, husbandry (10); stupendous, exorbitant (11); mechanistic, integrities, organelle, biosphere (12).
3. In his conclusion, Berry refers to the "mechanistic or industrial mind." How else does Berry characterize this "mind" (and those who have it) throughout the essay?

4. How and where does Berry associate the words *nature* and *agriculture* in the mind of the reader? What does he gain from this association?

SUGGESTIONS FOR WRITING

1. Berry's classification of solutions illustrates the uses of this method for pinning down GENERAL or ABSTRACT concepts. Choose another such generality — perhaps decisions, responsibilities, goals, or moral choices — and write a classification essay. How does classification help clarify your thinking?
2. In his INTRODUCTION, Berry lists several other areas in which solutions cause fresh problems: sanitation, education, medicine, and nuclear armaments. Choose one of these areas or another that interests you. In a brief essay, explore what you understand to be the ramifications of the methods being used. If possible, use examples from your own experience and observation. Or consult library sources.
3. CONNECTIONS. Both Lewis Thomas in "On the Need for Asylums" (p. 684) and Wendell Berry in this essay speak about the "side effects" of solutions. In your own essay, discuss Thomas's argument as an example of Berry's — that is, explain whether and how the handling of people with serious mental illness, as Thomas describes it, illustrates a "bad" solution.

WENDELL BERRY ON WRITING

In "Standing by Words," an essay in his 1983 collection of the same title, Wendell Berry defines something he calls "tyrannese": language that "accompanies, and in one way or another enables, the taking of power." Tyrannese, says Berry, "is used conscientiously to refer to nothing in particular. . . . It is not language that the user will very likely be required to stand by or to act on, for it does not define any personal ground for standing or acting." Here is an example, an excerpt from a paragraph-length sentence Berry quotes: "It has been logical for humans to employ their minds' progressive discoveries of the cosmic principles governing all physical interattractions, interactions, reactions, and intertransformings." Such language, Berry believes, "works directly against the conventionality, the community life, of language, for it holds in contempt, not only all particular grounds of private fidelity and action, but the common ground of human experience, memory, and understanding from which language rises and on which meaning is shaped."

Both the personal and the common grounds of language originate, Berry believes, in the sentence. "When we reflect that 'sentence' means, literally, 'a way of thinking' (Latin: *sententia*) and that it comes from the Latin *sentire*, to feel, we realize that the concepts of sentence and sentence structure are not merely grammatical or merely academic — not negligible in any sense. A sentence is both the opportunity and the limit of thought — what we have to think with, and what we have to think in. It is, moreover, a *feelable* thought, a thought that impresses its sense not just on our understanding, but on our hearing, our sense of rhythm and proportion. It is a pattern of felt sense."

In tyrannese, though, the sentence "is completely shapeless and therefore a loss of thought, an act of self-abandonment to incoherence." Tyrannese lacks the sentence's and thus the language's "precision of definition, this setting of bounds or ends to thought." As a result, Berry says, when we write tyrannese, "we cannot mean, or say what we mean, or mean what we say; we cannot stand by our words because we cannot utter words that can be stood by; we cannot speak of our own actions as persons, or even as communities, but only of the actions of percentages, large organizations, concepts, historical trends, or the impersonal 'forces' of destiny or evolution."

FOR DISCUSSION

1. Who might write or speak tyrannese? Scour a newspaper for examples, and bring one or two to class for discussion.
2. What are the virtues of the sentence, according to Berry?
3. How is Berry's tyrannese like the bad English defined by George Orwell in "Politics and the English Language" (p. 690)?

ROBERT B. REICH

ROBERT B. REICH is a writer and teacher who is regarded as a leader of the "neoliberals" — those seeking ways for the United States to achieve economic strength without sacrificing social programs. Reich was born in 1946 in Scranton, Pennsylvania, and attended Dartmouth College, Oxford University (as a Rhodes Scholar), and Yale Law School. He was active in liberal politics in the late 1960s and after law school worked in the federal government for some years. He is now a professor of business, political economy, and public policy at Harvard University's John F. Kennedy School of Government. He is also a consultant to business, government, and political candidates. Reich appears often on television and radio as a commentator; contributes regularly to the *Atlantic*, the *Harvard Businss Review*, and *The New Republic*; and has written numerous books, among them *The Next American Frontier* (1983), *Tales of a New America* (1987), *The Power of Public Ideas* (1988), and a collection of essays, *The Resurgent Liberal (and Other Unfashionable Prophesies)* (1989).

Why the Rich Are Getting Richer and the Poor Poorer

This essay first appeared in May 1989 in *The New Republic* and was then reprinted in early 1990 in the *Utne Reader*. Reich outlines a shift in American economic and social classes that means more, not less, distance between them. What's needed, Reich has said elsewhere, is a "true patriotism" that is based on "a common concern for, and investment in, the well-being of our future citizens." (For a complementary view of American classes, see Ralph Whitehead, Jr.'s "Class Acts," p. 419.)

Between 1978 and 1987, the poorest fifth of American families became 8 percent poorer, and the richest fifth became 13 percent richer. That means the poorest fifth now have less than 5 percent of the nation's income, while the richest fifth have more than 40 percent.

This widening gap can't be blamed on the growth in single-   2
parent lower-income families, which in fact slowed markedly after
the late 1970s. Nor is it due mainly to the stingy social policies of
the Reagan years. Granted, food stamp benefits have dropped 13
percent since 1981 (in real terms), and many states have failed to
raise benefits for the poor and unemployed to keep up with inflation. But this doesn't come close to accounting for the growing
persistence of economic inequality in the United States. Rather,
this disturbing trend is connected to a profound change in the
American economy as it merges with the global economy. And
because the merging is far from complete, this trend will not stop
all by itself anytime soon. It is significant that the growth of inequality can be seen most strikingly among Americans who have
jobs. Through most of the postwar era, the wages of Americans at
different income levels rose at about the same pace. Although different workers occupied different steps on the escalator, everyone
moved up together. In those days poverty was the condition of
jobless Americans, and the major economic challenge was to create enough jobs for everyone. Once people were safely in the
work force, their problems were assumed to be over. Thus "full
employment" became a liberal rallying cry.

But in recent years Americans with jobs have been traveling   3
on two escalators — one going up, the other going down. In 1987
the average hourly earnings of nonsupervisory workers (adjusted
for inflation) were lower than in any year since 1966. Middle-level
managers fared much better, although their median real earnings
were only slightly above the levels of the 1970s. Executives, however, did spectacularly well. In 1988 alone, CEOs of the 100 largest publicly held industrial corporations received raises averaging
almost 12 percent.

Between 1978 and 1987, as the real earnings of unskilled   4
workers were declining, the real incomes of investment bankers
and other securities industry workers rose 21 percent. It is not unusual for a run-of-the-mill investment banker to bring home comfortably over a million dollars. Meanwhile, the number of impoverished *working* Americans climbed by nearly two million, or 23
percent, during those same years. Nearly 60 percent of the 20 million people who now fall below the Census Bureau's poverty line

are from families with at least one member in full-time or part-time work.

The American economy now exhibits a wider gap between   5
rich and poor than it has at any other time since World War II.
The most basic reason, put simply, is that America itself is ceasing
to exist as an economic system separate from the rest of the world.
One can no more meaningfully speak of an "American economy"
than of a "Delaware economy." We are becoming but a region —
albeit still a relatively wealthy region — of a global economy. This
is a new kind of economy whose technologies, savings, and in-
vestments move effortlessly across borders, making it harder for
individual nations to control their economic destinies.

We have yet to come to terms with the rise of the global cor-   6
poration, whose managers, shareholders, and employees span the
world. Our debates over the future of American jobs still focus on
topics such as the competitiveness of the American automobile
industry or the future of American manufacturing. But these issues are increasingly irrelevant.

New technologies of worldwide communication and trans-   7
portation have redrawn the economic playing field. American industries no longer compete against Japanese or European industries. Rather, a company with headquarters in the United States,
production facilities in Taiwan, and a marketing force spread
across many nations competes with another, similarly wide-rang-
ing company. So when General Motors, say, is doing well, that
probably is good news for a lot of executives in Detroit, and for
GM shareholders across the globe, but it isn't necessarily good
news for a lot of assembly-line workers in Detroit, because there
may, in fact, be very few GM assembly-line workers in Detroit, or
anywhere else in America. The welfare of assembly-line workers in
Detroit may depend, instead, on the health of corporations based
in Japan or Canada.

More to the point, even if those Canadian and Japanese cor-   8
porations are doing well, those Detroit workers may be in trouble. For they are increasingly part of an international labor market, encompassing Asia, Africa, Western Europe, and, perhaps
before long, Eastern Europe. With relative ease corporations can

relocate their production centers to take advantage of low wages. So American workers find themselves settling for low wages in order to hold on to their jobs. More and more, your "competitiveness" as a worker depends not on the fortunes of any American corporation, or of any American industry, but on what function you serve within the global economy.

In order to see in greater detail what is happening to American jobs, it helps to view the work that most Americans do in terms of new categories that reflect how U.S. workers fit into the global economy. Essentially, three broad categories are emerging. I call them: (1) symbolic-analytic services; (2) routine production services; and (3) routine personal services.   9

1. Symbolic-analytic services are based on the manipulation   10
of information: data, words, and oral and visual symbols. Symbolic analysis comprises some (but by no means all) of the work undertaken by people who call themselves lawyers, investment bankers, commercial bankers, management consultants, research scientists, academics, public-relations executives, real estate developers, and even a few creative accountants. Also, many advertising and marketing specialists, art directors, design engineers, architects, writers and editors, musicians, and television and film producers.

Some of the manipulations of information performed by   11
these symbolic analysts offer ways of more efficiently deploying resources or shifting financial assets, or of otherwise saving time and energy. Other manipulations grab money from people who are too slow or naive to protect themselves. Still others serve to entertain the public.

Most symbolic analysts work alone or in small teams. If they   12
work with others, they often have partners rather than bosses or supervisors. Their work environments tend to be quiet and tastefully decorated, often within tall steel-and-glass buildings. When they are not analyzing, designing, or strategizing, they are in meetings or on the telephone — giving advice or making deals. Many of them spend an inordinate amount of time in jet planes and hotels. They are generally articulate and well groomed. The vast majority are white males.

Symbolic analysis now accounts for more than 40 percent of 13 America's gross national product, and almost 20 percent of our jobs.

The services performed by America's symbolic analysts are in 14 high demand around the world. The Japanese are buying up the insights and inventions of America's scientists and engineers (who are only too happy to sell them at a fat profit). The Europeans, meanwhile, are hiring our management consultants, business strategists, and investment bankers. Developing nations are hiring our civil and design engineers; and almost everyone is buying the output of our pop musicians, television stars, and film producers.

The same thing is happening with the global corporation. 15 The central offices of these sprawling entities, headquartered in America, are filled with symbolic analysts who manipulate information and then export their insights around the world via the corporation's far-flung operations. IBM, for instance, doesn't export machines from the United States; it manufactures its machines in factories all over the globe. IBM world headquarters, in Armonk, New York, exports just strategic planning and related management services.

Thus has the standard of living of America's symbolic analysts risen. They increasingly find themselves part of a global labor market, not a national one. And because the United States has a highly developed economy, and an excellent university system, they find that the services they have to offer are in high demand around the whole world. This ensures that their salaries are quite high.

Those salaries are likely to go even higher in the years ahead, 17 as the world market for symbolic analysis continues to grow. Foreigners are trying to learn these skills and techniques, to be sure, but they still have a long way to go. No other country does a better job of preparing its most fortunate citizens for symbolic analysis than does the United States. None has surpassed America in providing experience and training, often with entire regions specializing in one or another kind of symbolic analysis (New York and Chicago for finance, Los Angeles for music and film, the San Francisco Bay area and greater Boston for science and engineer-

ing). In this we can take pride. But for the second major category
of American workers — the providers of routine production services — the future doesn't bode well.

2. Routine production services involve tasks that are re-   18
peated over and over, as one step in a sequence of steps for producing a finished product. Although we tend to associate these
jobs with manufacturing, they are becoming common in banking,
insurance, wholesaling, retailing, health care — all industries employing millions of people who spend their days processing data,
often putting information into computers or taking it out.

Most people involved in routine production services work   19
with many other people who do similar work, within large, centralized facilities. They are overseen by supervisors, who in turn
are monitored by more senior supervisors. They are usually paid
an hourly wage. Their jobs are often monotonous. Most of the
workers do not have a college education. Those who deal with
metal are mostly white males; those who deal with fabrics or information tend to be female and/or minorities.

Decades ago, those kinds of workers were relatively well paid.   20
But in recent years America's providers of routine production services have found themselves in direct competition with millions
of foreign workers, most of whom work for a fraction of the pay
American workers get. Through the miracle of satellite transmission, even routine data processing can now be undertaken in relatively poor nations, thousands of miles away from the skyscrapers
where the data are finally used. This fact has given management
ever greater power in bargaining talks. If routine production
workers living in America don't agree to reduce their wages, then
the work often goes abroad.

And it has. In 1950, routine production services constituted   21
about 30 percent of our gross national product and well over half
of American jobs. Today such services represent about 20 percent
of the GNP and one fourth of jobs. And the scattering of foreign-
owned factories placed here to circumvent American protectionism isn't going to reverse the trend. So the standard of living of
America's routine production workers will likely keep declining.
The dynamics behind the wage concessions, plant closings, and

union-busting that have become commonplace won't be stopped without a major turnaround in labor organizing or political action.

3. Routine personal services also entail simple, repetitive [22] work, but, unlike routine production services, they are provided in person. Included in this employment category are restaurant and hotel workers, barbers and beauticians, retail sales personnel, cab drivers, household cleaners, day-care workers, hospital attendants and orderlies, truck drivers, and — among the fastest-growing of all careers — custodians and security guards.

Like production workers, providers of personal services are [23] usually paid by the hour. They are also carefully supervised and rarely have more than a high school education. But unlike people in the other two categories of work, they are in direct contact with the ultimate beneficiaries of what they do. And the companies they work for are often small. In fact, some routine personal-service workers become entrepreneurs. (Most new businesses and new jobs in America come from this sector — which now constitutes about 20 percent of GNP and 30 percent of jobs.) Women and minorities make up the bulk of routine personal-service workers.

Apart from the small number who strike out on their own, [24] these workers are paid poorly. They are sheltered from the direct effects of global competition, but not the indirect effects. They often compete with undocumented workers willing to work for low wages, or with former or would-be production workers who can't find well-paying production jobs, or with labor-saving machinery (automated tellers, self-service gas pumps) dreamed up by symbolic analysts in America and manufactured in Asia. And because they tend to be unskilled and dispersed among small businesses, personal-service workers rarely have a union or a powerful lobby group to stand up for their interests. When the economy turns sour, they are among the first to feel the effects.

These workers will continue to have jobs in the years ahead [25] and may experience some small increase in real wages. They will have demographics on their side, as the American work force shrinks. But for all the foregoing reasons, the gap between their earnings and those of the symbolic analysts will continue to grow if present economic trends and labor conditions continue.

These three functional categories — symbolic analysis, rou- 26 tine production services, and routine personal services — cover at least three out of four American jobs. The rest of the nation's work force consists mainly of government employees (including public school teachers), employees in regulated industries (like utility workers), and government-financed workers (engineers working on defense weapons systems), many of whom are sheltered from global competition. One further clarification: Some traditional job categories overlap several of these categories. People called "secretaries," for example, include those who actually spend their time doing symbolic analysis work closely allied to what their bosses do; those who do routine data entry or retrieval of a sort that will eventually be automated or done overseas; and those who provide routine personal services.

The important point is that workers in these three functional 27 categories are coming to have different competitive positions in the world economy. Symbolic analysts hold a commanding position in an increasingly global labor market. Routine production workers hold a relatively weak position in an increasingly global labor market. Routine personal service workers still find themselves in a national labor market, but for various reasons they suffer the indirect effects of competition from workers abroad.

How should we respond to these trends? One response is to 28 accept them as inevitable consequences of change, but to try to offset their polarizing effects through a truly progressive income tax, coupled with more generous income assistance — including health insurance — for poor working Americans. (For a start, we might reverse the extraordinarily regressive Social Security amendments of 1983, through which poor working Americans are now financing the federal budget deficit, often paying more in payroll taxes than in income taxes.)

A more ambitious response would be to guard against class ri- 29 gidities by ensuring that any talented American kid can become a symbolic analyst — regardless of family income or race. But America's gifted but poor children can't aspire to such jobs until the government spends substantially more than it does now to ensure excellent public schools in every city and region and ample financial help when they are ready to attend college.

Of course, it isn't clear that even under those circumstances 30 there would be radical growth in the number of Americans who become research scientists, design engineers, musicians, management consultants, or (even if the world needed them) investment bankers and lawyers. So other responses are also needed. Perhaps the most ambitious would be to increase the numbers of Americans who could apply symbolic analysis to production and to personal services.

There is ample evidence, for example, that access to comput- 31 erized information can enrich production jobs by enabling workers to alter the flow of materials and components in ways that increase efficiency. Production workers who have broader responsibilities and more control over how production is organized cease to be "routine" workers — becoming, in effect, symbolic analysts at a level very close to the production process. The same transformation can occur in personal-service jobs. Consider, for example, the checkout clerk whose computer enables her to control inventory and decide when to reorder items from the factory.

The number of such technologically empowered jobs, of 32 course, is limited by the ability of workers to learn on the job. That means a far greater number of Americans will need a good grounding in mathematics, basic science, reading, and communication skills. So once again, comfortably integrating the American work force into the new world economy turns out to rest heavily on education. (Better health care, especially prenatal and pediatric care, would also figure in here.)

Education and health care for poor children are apt to be 33 costly. Since poorer working Americans, already under a heavy tax load, can't afford it, the cost would have to be borne by wealthier Americans — who also would have to bear the cost of any income redistribution plans designed to neutralize the polarizing domestic effects of a globalized economy. Thus a central question is the willingness of the more fortunate American citizens — espe-

cially symbolic analysts, who constitute much of the most fortunate fifth, with 40 percent of the nation's income — to bear the
burden. But here lies a catch-22. For as our economic fates diverge, the top fifth may be losing its sense of connectedness with
the bottom fifth (or even the bottom half) that would elicit such
generosity.

The conservative tide that has swept the land during the past   34
decade surely has many causes, but the fundamental changes in
our economy should not be discounted as a major factor. It is now
possible for the most fortunate fifth to sell their expertise directly
in the global market, and thus maintain and enhance their standard of living, even as that of other Americans declines. There is
less and less basis for a strong sense of interclass interdependence
in America. Meanwhile, the fortunate fifth have also been able to
insulate themselves from the less fortunate, by living in suburban
enclaves far removed from the effects of poverty. Neither patriotism nor altruism may be sufficient to overcome these realities. Yet
without the active support of at least some of the fortunate fifth,
it will be more difficult to muster the political will necessary for
change. . . .

On withdrawing from the presidential race of 1988, Paul Si-   35
mon of Illinois said, "Americans instinctively know that we are
one nation, one family, and when anyone in that family hurts, all
of us hurt." Sadly, that is coming to be less and less the case.

QUESTIONS ON MEANING

1. What is Reich's PURPOSE in this essay? Is it the same as his reason for
   classifying the American labor force into three new categories?
2. In paragraphs 28 and 33, Reich speaks of "polarizing effects." What
   does he mean? How would polarization relate to his categories?
3. What responses does the author suggest to the problems he identifies? How does he rank these responses?
4. In Reich's opinion, what is needed to implement these responses?

QUESTIONS ON WRITING STRATEGY

1. What EVIDENCE does Reich use to define each of his categories? Does each category receive the same attention?
2. How does Reich deal with jobs that don't fit into his categories, or with more traditional categories that don't match his?
3. This essay first appeared in *The New Republic* and then in the *Utne Reader*, both magazines with a primarily educated, liberal AUDIENCE. In what category do his readers and Reich himself most likely belong? How might his audience have influenced Reich's purpose?
4. OTHER METHODS. Reich uses classification in the service of argument and persuasion (Chap. 11). What APPEALS (RATIONAL and EMOTIONAL) does the author use to bring the reader over to his way of thinking?

QUESTIONS ON LANGUAGE

1. Define these key terms in Reich's essay: global economy (para. 2); inflation, median (3); impoverished (4); shareholders (7); symbolic (10); deploying (11); wholesaling (18); gross national product, protectionism (21); entrepreneurs (23); undocumented workers, lobby (24); demographics (25); progressive income tax, regressive (28); altruism (34).
2. What does the author think of investment bankers? Find language from the essay to support your opinion.
3. What does Reich mean by a *catch-22* (para. 33)? Where does the term come from? What has it come to mean?

SUGGESTIONS FOR WRITING

1. Reich's essay reclassifies a subject (jobs) that has been classified in other ways. Find a traditional classification of something, such as college courses, departments, or schools; staff positions; sections in the college bookstore or local supermarket — classification is everywhere. Reclassify the items according to an alternative principle of classification. You will have to state and perhaps defend your classification, and of course define and illustrate your categories.
2. Reclassify the jobs in the help-wanted or employment section of your local newspaper into Reich's categories: symbolic-analytic, routine production, routine personal, and other (as in paragraph 26). Give reasons for your inclusion of each job opening in each of Reich's categories.

3. What do you think of Reich's assessment of the disconnectedness and responsibilities of the symbolic analysts? Write an essay in which you agree or disagree with Reich, supporting your opinions with EVIDENCE from your own experience and reading as well as from Reich's essay.

4. CONNECTIONS. Both Reich's essay and Ralph Whitehead, Jr.'s "Class Acts" (p. 419) classify American society, and both authors warn of increasing polarization in society. Write an essay comparing and contrasting the two classifications. What is each author's THE-SIS? What categories does each identify? To what extent do the two classifications overlap? Which essay is more effective, and why?

ROBERT B. REICH ON WRITING

In the introduction to his book *Tales of a New America*, Robert Reich explains why he finds it necessary to "probe the public consciousness and examine the reigning public philosophy": This is the terrain, he insists, "in which public problems are defined and public ideals are forged."

In seeking to map this terrain, Reich makes certain demands on his audience. "I am relying on you, the reader, to be an active explorer as well. You will need to ask yourself: How do these illustrations resonate with my experience? Are these interpretations plausible and meaningful to me? Do they help me better understand my own values, or lead me to question them?" In short, "examining what the prevailing vision has been, and what it might be" is a job not just for political scientists and government officials but for critical thinkers and readers as well.

FOR DISCUSSION

1. Why does writing on "public philosophy" demand critical reading of the sort Reich describes?

2. What other kinds of reading require the critical approach Reich asks of his readers?

RALPH WHITEHEAD, JR.

Ralph Whitehead, Jr., is a journalist and a professor of journalism at the University of Massachusetts at Amherst. He grew up and attended school in Wisconsin, and in the late 1960s he became a news reporter in Chicago, covering the social tumult of that period for the *Chicago Sun-Times* and *Chicago Today*. He has also reported for the *Newark Star Ledger* and served as both reporter and news anchor on public and commercial television. When Whitehead began teaching at the University of Massachusetts in 1973, he continued writing for various publications, including the *American Scholar*, the *Columbia Journalism Review*, *The New Republic*, and *Psychology Today*. For most of the 1980s, his knack for understanding and articulating social hierarchies and public opinion earned him speaking engagements and consulting work with politicians, political groups, and labor organizations. He now concentrates on teaching and on finishing a book about the changing American class structure.

Class Acts:
America's Changing Middle Class

In an essay that anticipates his forthcoming book, Whitehead here outlines changes in the American "social ladder" — the hierarchy of social and economic groups. Whitehead's classification complements Robert Reich's in the previous essay (p. 407) and first appeared with it in the January/February 1990 *Utne Reader*.

As we enter the 1990s, American society exhibits a vastly different social and economic makeup from the one that we grew accustomed to in the thirty years that followed World War II. The gap between the top and bottom is far greater now, of course, but the economic position of people in the middle is changing, too. This new social ladder is seen most vividly in the lives of our younger generations, the baby boom and the later baby bust. Be-

cause the new ladder is so much steeper than the old one, it's creating an alarming new degree of polarization in American life.

As it held sway for roughly the first three decades after World   2
War II, the old social ladder was shaped largely by the continuing
expansion of the middle class. For the first time, many people
could afford to buy a house, a car (or two), a washer and dryer, an
outdoor grill, adequate health coverage, maybe a motor boat, and
possibly college for the kids. And for the first time, a growing
number of blacks and Hispanics could enter the middle class.

Within this expanding middle class, there were a couple of   3
fairly well-defined ways of life: white-collar life and blue-collar life.
White-collar life was typified by TV characters like Ward and
June Cleaver and later Mike and Carol Brady. Blue-collar life was
typified by characters like Ralph and Alice Kramden and later
Archie and Edith Bunker.

At the top of the old social ladder stood a small number of   4
rich people. A larger but declining number of poor people stood
at the bottom, and the rest of the ladder was taken up by the middle class. The old social ladder looked roughly like this:

THE RICH

THE EXPANDING MIDDLE CLASS:
White collar
Blue collar

THE POOR

The new social ladder is markedly different. Within the baby   5
boom and baby bust generations, the middle class is no longer expanding. Therefore the new social ladder is shaped by — and at
the same time is helping to shape — a new polarization between
the haves and the have-nots. The social ladder of the 1990s looks
roughly like this:

UPSCALE AMERICA:
The Rich
The Overclass

THE NEW MIDDLE CLASS:
Bright collar
New collar
Blue collar

DOWNSCALE AMERICA:
The Poor
The Underclass

The rich are still on top, of course. But the new generation of rich people is typified by Donald Trump, the billionaire developer of luxury buildings for the newly rich, rather than by someone like his father, Fred Trump, a developer who made millions building modestly priced postwar homes and apartments for the expanding middle class — the kinds of homes in which the Kramdens and Bunkers lived.

The poor are still with us, of course, but they're no longer at the bottom. It's not because they've risen to the middle class but rather because some of them have fallen into the underclass. Because definitions of the underclass vary, so do estimates of its size. However, it does include at least two million people who lead lives that aren't even typified in America's popular culture. To belong to the underclass is to be without a face and without a voice. 6

Just as an underclass has emerged, so has an overclass, which occupies the rung just below the rich. Located chiefly in a dozen metropolises and heavily concentrated in lucrative management and professional jobs, the overclass is roughly the same size as the underclass. Its significance lies not in its numbers, however, but in its immense power throughout American society. The overclass holds the highest level positions in the fields of entertainment, media, marketing, advertising, real estate, finance, and politics. It's pursued for its consumption dollars and cajoled for its investment dollars. It is crudely typified by the media stereotype of the yuppie. 7

What clearly stood out on the old social ladder that shaped American society during the fifties and sixties was the dominant presence of an expanding middle class. What is noticeable about 8 the new social ladder is the unmistakable emergence of distinct upper and lower rungs, and the vast social, economic, and psychological distance between them. Together, the rich and the overclass form Upscale America. Together, the underclass and the poor form Downscale America.

The expanding middle class, with its white and blue collars, has given way in the baby boom and baby bust generations to a new middle class. It consists largely of three kinds of workers: 9

•**Bright collars.** Within the ranks of managerial and professional workers a new category of job has emerged. The white-collar worker is receding and the bright-collar worker is advancing. The bright collars are the 20 million knowledge workers born since 1945: lawyers and teachers, architects and social workers, accountants and budget analysts, engineers and consultants, rising executives and midlevel administrators. They earn their livings by taking intellectual initiatives. They face the luxury and the necessity of making their own decisions on the job and in their personal lives.   10

Bright-collar people lack the touchstones that guided white-collar workers like Ward Cleaver in the 1950s and 1960s. The white collars believed in institutions; bright collars are skeptical of them. The corporate chain of command, a strong force in white-collar life then, is far weaker for bright collars today. They place a premium on individuality, on standing out rather than fitting in. Although the older white collars knew the rules and played by them, bright collars can't be sure what the rules are and must think up their own. The white collars were organization men and women (mostly men); bright collars are entrepreneurs interested in building careers for themselves outside big corporations.   11

Three quarters of the managers and professionals of the 1950s were men. Today half are women. Seven percent are black or Hispanic or Asian. Bright collars make up a third of the baby boom work force. They're typified by figures like *L.A. Law*'s Grace Van Owen, Mike Kuzak, and Victor Sifuentes.   12

•**Blue collars.** Within the manufacturing workplace, blue-collar work endures, but on a much smaller scale. Thirty years ago almost 40 percent of the adult work force did blue-collar work. To-   13 day, after the relative decline of American heavy industry, it's done by less than 25 percent of baby boom workers. During the fifties and sixties, blue-collar wages rose steadily, thus helping fuel the expansion of the middle class. In the past 15 years these wages have been relatively flat. Young blue collars often must live near the economic margins.

The blue-collar world is still a man's world. Roughly three   14 quarters of today's younger blue collars are men — the same percentage as in the 1950s. Twelve percent are black, Hispanic, or Asian. Within a growing number of innovative manufacturing workplaces, new models of blue-collar work have begun to emerge, but they haven't yet advanced enough to trigger a new category of American worker. In the popular culture the new generation of blue collars finds a voice in Bruce Springsteen, but it still hasn't found a face.

•**New collars.** These people aren't managers and professionals,   15 and they don't do physical labor. Their jobs fall between those two worlds. They're secretaries, clerks, telephone operators, keypunch operators, inside salespeople, police officers. They often avoid the grime and regimentation of blue-collar work, but without quite gaining the freedom of bright-collar work. Two thirds of the new collars are women. More than 15 percent are black, Hispanic, or Asian. The new collars make up at least 35 percent of the baby boom work force. They're typified by figures like Lucy Bates and Joe Coffey of *Hill Street Blues*.

Federal Express truck drivers are typical new-collar workers.   16 They design pickup and delivery routes, explain the company's services and fees, provide mailing supplies, and handle relatively sophisticated information technology in their trucks. They aren't traditional truck drivers so much as sales clerks in offices on wheels.

The rise of the new social ladder has helped to drive a num-   17 ber of changes in American life, but one of them, already evident, should be underscored: the dramatic shift of power within both the middle class and the society as a whole.

As members of the expanding middle class of the postwar   18

years, blue collars once held considerable leverage. In the electorate, for every vote cast by the white collars in 1960, the blue collars cast two. In the workplace, they acted through powerful unions. In the marketplace, they were valued as consumers. As a
result, blue collars dealt with white collars as equals. In the fifties
and sixties, whatever class lines still divided the two groups
seemed to be dissolving.

Within the new middle class today, the balance of power is   19
much different. In the electorate, for every vote cast by younger
blue collars in 1988, bright collars cast two. In the workplace,
younger blue-collar workers are losing union power, while bright
collars exert the power of their knowledge and the privilege of
their status. In the marketplace, blue-collar consumers are written
off as too downscale, while the bright-collar consumer is courted
as an aspiring member of the overclass. Deep divisions have
sprung up between bright collars and blue collars. They look a lot
like class lines.

The rise of an overclass throws the decline of blue-collar life   20
into sharper relief, and vice versa. Upscale yuppie haunts spring
up: the health club, the gourmet takeout shop, the pricy bou-
tique, the atrium building. Downscale blue-collar haunts wither:
the union hall, the lodge, the beauty parlor, the mill. The guys
with red suspenders began showing up in the beer commercials
right about the time the loggers and guys with air hammers began
to disappear. The overclass's stock portfolios began to get fat just
as blue-collar families were losing their pensions and health insurance. Condo prices were climbing in Atlanta just as bungalow
prices fell in Buffalo. It seems that there's a battle here, a zero-sum
game, whereby the rise of one comes at the expense of the other.

The contrast between the rich and the underclass is sharper   21
than ever. If you look at the new social ladder in New York, you
see Donald Trump in his penthouse and the homeless people in
the subways.

This situation intensifies the shift of power in society as a   22
whole. With the middle class divided, the center cannot hold.
The dominant forces in society become Upscale America and
Downscale America — or, more precisely, Upscale America *versus* Downscale America. Upscale America uses its power to secure

privileges such as proposed cuts in the capital gains tax. Downscale America strikes back blindly through rising rates of crime. Through the old social ladder, the expanding middle class acted as the nation's glue. With the new social ladder, the new middle class is merely caught in the crossfire.

QUESTIONS ON MEANING

1. What is Whitehead's THESIS? What does "polarization" mean?
2. What is happening to the American middle class, according to Whitehead?
3. What does Whitehead say is the main result of the change he describes?
4. What do you think is Whitehead's PURPOSE in this essay? To inform? To persuade? Both?

QUESTIONS ON WRITING STRATEGY

1. Whitehead provides a classification within a classification. Why?
2. Why does Whitehead use figures from television and music to illustrate the various classes he identifies (paras. 3, 11, 12, 14, 15, 20)? What is the EFFECT of these examples?
3. What attitudes does Whitehead seem to assume his AUDIENCE will have toward his ideas? (It may help to recall that this essay was first published in the *Utne Reader*, a magazine whose essays and articles take a mainly liberal approach to national and international issues.)
4. **OTHER METHODS.** How does Whitehead use comparison and contrast (Chap. 4) to clarify changes in American society?

QUESTIONS ON LANGUAGE

1. Define the phrases *baby boom* and *baby bust* (para. 1). Which generation do you belong to?
2. What is the meaning of the word *collar* to designate classes? What does Whitehead mean by "bright collar"?
3. Use your dictionary to find any of these words that are unfamiliar: lucrative, cajoled (para. 7); initiatives (10); touchstones, skeptical, entrepreneurs (11); regimentation (15); leverage (18).

SUGGESTIONS FOR WRITING

1. Write an essay classifying Americans or some part of American society by a principle of classification other than income — for instance,
   political views, moral values, attitudes toward education. If you like,
   your essay may be humorous, taking as its principle something like
   clothing styles, television preferences, or table manners. Draw on
   your own experiences, observations, and reading, and be sure to
   give plenty of examples of each class.
2. Write an essay taking a stand in relation to Whitehead's classification of middle-class workers. You may want to agree with it by supplying additional detailed examples (Springsteen song lyrics, for instance, or characters from movies). Or you may want to disagree
   with it by providing other categories missed by Whitehead or examples of people who don't fit into his categories.
3. CONNECTIONS. Both Whitehead's essay and Robert B. Reich's
   "Why the Rich Are Getting Richer" (p. 407) discuss the classes in
   American society. When you've read both essays, write an essay of
   your own that answers the following questions: What are the advantages of such classifications? What are the disadvantages? Where
   do you see yourself fitting in Reich's and Whitehead's schemes —
   now and in the future? Does positioning yourself in this way open
   or close options, do you think?

RALPH WHITEHEAD, JR., ON WRITING

Ralph Whitehead, Jr., has a reputation for translating data
about social and economic change into useful ideas for a broad
audience. As he told Scott Heller for the *Chronicle of Higher Education*, "I'm a popularizer, a synthesizer, a middlebrow." Unlike
many writers on politics and society, Whitehead watches and lis-
tens to what's going on outside the narrow circle of journalists,
politicians, media consultants, and academics. Such openness
and a willingness to say what his research told him led Whitehead
in the mid-1980s to articulate the changes outlined in "Class
Acts," which had been overlooked by most other observers.
"There's a danger," he warns, "that this country will be driven by
technocrats who can't get their noses off the sidewalk. Within the
world of politics and policy, I'm a guy people like to have in the
room. There's always a hunger for a generalizer."

FOR DISCUSSION

1. What does Whitehead mean by "a popularizer, a synthesizer, a middlebrow," and "a generalizer"?
2. Popularizers are often disparaged as less important than the scholars whose work they report. How does Whitehead challenge that view?

ADDITIONAL WRITING TOPICS
Classification

Write an essay by the method of classification, in which you sort one of the following subjects into categories of your own devising. Make clear your PURPOSE in classifying and the basis of your classification. Explain each class with definitions and examples (you may find it helpful to make up a name for each group). Check your classes to be sure they neither gap nor overlap.

1. The ills or benefits of city life
2. The recordings you own
3. Families
4. Stand-up comedians
5. Present-day styles of marriage
6. Vacations
7. College students today
8. Paperback novels
9. Waiters you'd never tip
10. Comic strips
11. Movie monsters
12. Sports announcers
13. Inconsiderate people
14. Radio stations
15. Mall millers (people who mill around malls)

8
ANALOGY
Drawing a Parallel

THE METHOD

The photography instructor is perspiring. He is trying to explain the workings of a typical camera to people who barely know how to pop a film cartridge into an Instamatic. "Let me give you an analogy," he offers — and from that moment, the faces of his class start coming alive. They understand him. What helps is his *analogy*: a point-by-point comparison that explains something unknown in terms of something familiar.

"Like the pupil in the human eye," the instructor begins, "the aperture of a camera — that's the opening in front — is adjustable. It contracts or it widens, letting in a lesser or a greater amount of light. The film in the camera is like the retina at the back of the eye — it receives an image. . . ." And the instructor continues, taking up one point at a time, working out the similarities between camera and eye.

To make clear his explanation, the instructor uses an analogy often found in basic manuals of photography. The inner workings of a Minolta Maxxum may be mysterious to a beginning student of photography, but the parts of the eye are familiar to anyone who has looked in a mirror, or has had to draw and label the parts of the eye in sixth grade. Not every time you write an essay, but once in a while, analogy will be a wonderfully useful method. With its help you can explain a subject that is complicated, unfamiliar, or intangible. You can put it into terms as concrete and understandable as nuts and nutcrackers.

Analogy is similar to the method of COMPARISON and CONTRAST (Chap. 4). Both use DIVISION or ANALYSIS (Chap. 6) to identify the distinctive features of two things and then set the features side by side. But in comparing and contrasting, you explain two obviously similar things, considering both their differences and their similarities. You might show, in writing a comparison and contrast, how San Francisco is quite unlike Boston in history, climate, and predominant life-styles, but like it in being a seaport and a city proud of its own (and neighboring) colleges. That isn't the way an analogy works. In an analogy you yoke together two apparently unlike things (eye and camera, the air currents in a storm and the opposing armies in a battle), and all you care about is their major similarities.

If the photography instructor had said, "The human eye is a kind of camera," he would have stated a METAPHOR. As you may recall from having read any poetry, a metaphor is a figure of speech that declares one thing to be another — even though it isn't, in a strictly literal sense — for the purpose of making us aware of similarity. "Hope," says the poet Emily Dickinson, "is the thing with feathers / That perches in the soul" — thus pointing to the similarity between a feeling and a bird (also between the human soul and a tree that birds light in). Such a metaphor is in essence a *short analogy*. And most analogies are, by their nature, extended metaphors: *extended*, because usually they go on longer than a line of poetry and they touch on a number of similarities. Here is an example. In August 1981, after *Voyager 2* transmitted to Earth its spectacular pictures of Saturn, NASA scientists held a news briefing. They wanted to explain to the public the difficulty of what they had achieved. They realized, however, that most people have no clear idea of the distance from Earth to Saturn, nor of the complexities of space navigation; and so they used an analogy. To bring *Voyager 2* within close range of Saturn, they explained, was analogous to sinking a putt from 500 miles away. Extending the metaphor, one scientist added, "Of course, you should allow the golfer to run alongside the ball and make trajectory corrections by blowing on it." A listener can immediately grasp the point: Such a feat is colossally hard.

Scientists explaining their work to nonscientists are particularly fond of such analogies because they deal with matters that an audience without technical training may find difficult. But the method is a favorite, too, of preachers and philosophers, because it can serve to make things beyond the experience of our senses vivid and graspable. We see this happening in one of the most famous passages in medieval literature, an analogy given by the eighth-century English historian Bede. (The quotation here is from *A History of the English Church and People*, 1968). Bede tells how in the year 627 King Edwin of Northumbria summoned a council to decide whether to accept the strange new religion of Christianity. Said one counselor,

> Your Majesty, when we compare the present life of man on earth with that time of which we have no knowledge, it seems to me like the swift flight of a single sparrow through the banqueting-hall where you are sitting at dinner on a winter's day with your thanes and counselors. In the midst there is a comforting fire to warm the hall; outside, the storms of winter rain or snow are raging. This sparrow flies swiftly in through one door of the hall, and out through another. While he is inside, he is safe from the winter storms; but after a few moments of comfort, he vanishes from sight into the wintry world from which he came. Even so, man appears on earth for a little while; but of what went before this life or of what follows, we know nothing. Therefore, if this new teaching has brought any more certain knowledge, it seems only right that we should follow it.

Why, after twelve centuries, has this analogy remained unforgotten? Our minds cannot grasp infinite time, and we hardly can comprehend humankind's relation to it. But we can readily visualize a winter's snow and rain and a sparrow's flight through a banquet hall.

Like a poet, who also discovers metaphors, the writer who draws an analogy gives pleasure by making a comparison that offers a reader a little surprise. In setting forth vigorous, concrete, and familiar EXAMPLES, an analogy strikes us with poemlike force. For this reason, it is sometimes used by a writer who wishes to sway and arouse an audience, to engrave a message in memory. In his celebrated speech, "I Have a Dream," Martin Luther King, Jr., draws a remarkable analogy to express the anger and disappointment of American blacks that, one hundred years after Lincoln's Emancipation Proclamation, their full freedom has yet to be achieved. "It is obvious today," declares King, "that America has defaulted on this promissory note"; and he compares the founding fathers' written guarantee — of the rights of life, liberty, and the pursuit of happiness — to a bad check returned for insufficient funds. (For the entire "I Have a Dream" speech, see Chapter 11.) In a similar use of analogy to persuade, the Canadian journalist Pierre Berton once satirized opponents of public health care by writing in the voice of an after-dinner speaker alarmed by the idea of establishing a public school system — which, of course, already exists:

> Under this foreign system each one of us would be forced by government edict, and under penalty of imprisonment, to send our children to school until each reaches the age of sixteen — whether we wish to or not. . . . Ask yourself, gentlemen, if it is economically sane to hand a free education, no strings attached, to everybody in the nation between the ages of six and sixteen!

Berton's speaker doesn't even mention free public health care, but he echoes accusations made familiar by its opponents. He calls the whole idea "foreign" and too costly; he complains that its advocates are "pie-in-the-sky idealists." We realize that we have heard these accusations before. Free clinics, Berton suggests, are just as practicable as free schools — a system we all take for granted.

Neither King nor Berton pretends that his analogy will prove his case and, indeed, analogies cannot serve as proof in a logical ARGUMENT (see Chap. 11). The stated parallels may suggest others, but in the end the subjects are dissimilar. In Berton's argument, for instance, the analogy between public education and public health care can be taken only so far before the differences (in respective aims, alternatives to public funding, and the like) start to become more important than the similarities. The analogy can make readers more receptive to the argument or inspire them, but the case for public health care must be made on its own merits.

Analogy can be misused even when it's not being offered as logical proof. One of the so-called fallacies of argument is the *false analogy*, the claim of fundamental likeness when none exists. For more on this fallacy, see page 616.

THE PROCESS

When you set forth a subject that you believe will be unfamiliar to your readers, then analogy may come to your aid. In explaining some special knowledge, the method is most likely to be valuable. Have you played some unusual sport? Are you expert in a particular skill, or knowledgeable in some hobby? Did you travel to some place your readers may not have visited? Have you learned the workings of some specialized machine (a mechanical potato peeler, say, or an automatic pinsetter)? Have you had any experience that most people haven't? Is your family background, perhaps, unusual? You may then have a subject that will be made clearer by the method of analogy.

With subject in hand, consider: Exactly what will your analogy be? A bright idea has to dawn on you. If none *does* dawn, then it's far better to write your essay by some other method than to contrive a laborious, forced analogy. "Death is a dollar bill," one writer began — but the analogy that followed seemed a counterfeit. Remember: An effective analogy points to real similarities, not manufactured ones. (The author of the dollar bill essay went on: "Death is a cold condition, like cold, hard cash. . . ." — inflating an already weak currency.)

An analogy likens its subject to something more familiar than itself — as space navigation is likened to a game of golf. Your sub-ject may be an abstraction or a feeling, but in analogy you can't use another abstraction or feeling to explain it. Were a scientist, for instance, to liken the steering of *Voyager 2* to the charting of a person's spiritual course through life, the result might be a fasci-nating essay, but it wouldn't explain the steering of the spacecraft. (If the scientist's main subject were the charting of a spiritual course, and if he were writing for an audience of technicians to whom the steering of *Voyager 2* was familiar, then indeed, he could write an analogy.)

There's one more preliminary test of your idea. Like all good metaphors, an analogy sets forth a writer's fresh discovery. The reader ought to think, "Look at that! Those two things are a lot alike! Who would have thought so?" (You, the writer — that's who.) That is why the analogy of a camera to the human eye (if you haven't heard it before) is striking; and why Bede's compari-son of a life to the flight of a sparrow through a warm room is ef-fective. You could write an essay likening toothpaste to bar soap, and remark that both make suds and float dirt away; but the result would probably put the reader to sleep, and anyhow, it wouldn't be an analogy. Both things would be simple and famil-iar, and too similar. You wouldn't be using one to explain the other. Dissimilarity, as well as similarity, has to be present to make an analogy. And so, before you write, make sure that your subject and what you explain it with are noticeably *unlike* each other.

You now have your bright idea. Next you make a brief out-line, listing your subject, what you'll use to explain it, and their similarities. Most analogies begin by likening the two, then go on to work through the similarities one point at a time. Never mind the differences. If your analogy is to form only a part of your es-say, then later, perhaps, you will want to mention the differences — but wait until you have completed your analogy.

At last, with your outline before you, you are ready to write. As you work, visualize your subject (*if* it can be visualized — Bede's subject, the uncertainty of life, can't). Be sure to hold in your mind's eye the thing with which you explain your subject. Try for the most exact, concrete words you can find. An effective

analogy is definite. It makes something swing wide, as a key un-
locks a door.

ANALOGY IN A PARAGRAPH:
TWO ILLUSTRATIONS

Using Analogy to Write about Television

Public television is hugely more popular in Japan than in
America. In fact, Japanese viewers spend more time in watching the programs of NHK than in watching those of the ninety-
nine commercial-carrying stations put together. NHK has a
high and ambitious goal: not merely to entertain, but to educate and inspire. Independently run, under no government authority, the network dedicates itself to preserving national culture and "furthering world peace and the good of humankind."
In this regard, the Japanese public broadcasting system resembles not an American TV network but an American college.
Although its programming, like a college curriculum, includes
sports — wrestling and baseball are covered faithfully — the
network's central concern is the life of the mind. NHK's schedule reads almost like the course listings in a college catalog. Sev-
enty-five percent of its programming is spent on news and
video lessons (brush calligraphy; musical instruction; courses in
natural history, English, and sociology), while NHK's second
channel is wholly devoted to education: programs for public
schools, serious music, classic drama — both Kabuki plays and
Shakespeare's. Like the campus Mardi Gras or barbecue, fun
has its minor place on NHK. Comedy is popular, and there is
even a fifteen-minute commercial-free soap opera (*Oshin*),
about a farmer's daughter turned grocery magnate. Finally, like
an American college, NHK demands tuition: a voluntary fee,
which practically all Japanese viewers pay willingly.

COMMENT. In its four opening sentences, this paragraph is
devoted to the nature of Japanese television — specifically, NHK,
the unfamiliar subject to be explained. Then the writer helps us
understand the public broadcasting system's "high and ambitious goal" by an analogy — likening NHK to a college. There
are four areas in which North American college life resembles
NHK's programming: in sports, coursework, just-for-fun activities, and tuition fees. What the writer makes clear, without com-

ing out and hitting us over the head with the point, is that watching Japanese television is a little like going to school. This may be an unfamiliar notion to us, but as the analogy makes clear, NHK apparently satisfies its highly literate audience.

Using Analogy in an Academic Discipline

The simplest definition of diabetes begins with that familiar concept, "an abnormally high blood sugar," but it is more accurate to say that diabetes occurs when insulin fails to do its job. Insulin is a hormone, a chemical messenger sent to all parts of the body to regulate the way incoming food is handled. You can think of insulin as being a little like a grocery boy. When nourishment arrives in the intestine and is absorbed into the bloodstream, this hormone is sent out to notify all the relevant cells of the body. Similar to the grocery boy, who runs up to push the doorbell at a house receiving this week's supply of produce, insulin arrives at the outer surface of a cell and touches one of its "receptors." In response, the cell opens its doors (so to speak) and begins to take in the food that it requires. At least two things can go wrong with this system: There may be no grocery boy, or the doorbell may not work. In either case, what happens is the same. While food accumulates on the front porch, within the houses the inhabitants are famished. This is essentially what happens in diabetes. Although an ample supply of nourishment in the form of blood sugar (or *glucose*) is present, it cannot gain access to the interior of cells, which thus behave, biochemically, as though they were starving.

COMMENT. As we have seen, analogy is especially useful for explaining a complicated idea or process in a way that readers will grasp easily. In this paragraph, from *The Harvard Medical School Health Letter*, the author sets out to clarify for readers the medical problem of diabetes. The analogy is between the complex hormone insulin and the familiar figure of a grocery deliverer. Their likeness — the basis for the analogy — is that each signals the "inhabitants" of a cell/house that food is available. When either fails to signal, the food remains outside, while inside the "inhabitants" go hungry. With this simple and concrete analogy, a few sentences explain what might have taken many paragraphs in more technical and abstract language.

ALICE WALKER

Alice Walker gained wide recognition when her novel *The Color Purple* (1982) won both a Pulitzer Prize and an American Book Award and was made into a popular movie. Born in a sharecropping family in Eatonton, Georgia, in 1944, Walker graduated from Sarah Lawrence College and became active in the civil rights movement. At the same time, she pursued her writing and won several important fellowships. In addition to *The Color Purple*, Walker's books include the novels *The Third Life of Grange Copeland* (1970), *Meridian* (1976), and *The Temple of My Familiar* (1989); three volumes of poetry; two short story collections; a biography of the writer Langston Hughes; an anthology of the work of Zora Neale Hurston; and two essay collections, *In Search of Our Mothers' Gardens: Womanist Prose* (1983) and *Living by the Word* (1988). Walker has taught at numerous colleges and universities, including Wellesley, Yale, Brandeis, and the University of California at Berkeley. She lives in San Francisco, where she runs her own publishing company, Wild Trees Press.

Oppressed Hair Puts a Ceiling on the Brain

How does a change in hair style represent spiritual liberation? Alice Walker tells how by recounting her own experience and demonstrates that effective analogies often link unlikely subjects. As the opening paragraphs indicate, this piece was originally a speech, delivered in 1987 at Spelman College, where Walker spent her first college years. The speech was later reprinted in *Living by the Word*.

As some of you no doubt know, I myself was a student here 1
once, many moons ago. I used to sit in these very seats (sometimes still in pajamas, underneath my coat) and gaze up at the light streaming through these very windows. I listened to dozens of encouraging speakers and sang, and listened to, wonderful music. I

believe I sensed I would one day return, to be on this side of the podium. I think that, all those years ago, when I was a student here and still in my teens, I was thinking about what I would say to you now.

It may surprise you that I do not intend (until the question-   2
and-answer period perhaps) to speak of war and peace, the econ-
omy, racism, or sexism, or the triumphs and tribulations of black people or of women. Or even about movies. Though the discern-
ing ear may hear my concern for some of these things in what I am about to say, I am going to talk about an issue even closer to home. I am going to talk to you about hair. Don't give a thought to the state of yours at the moment. Don't be at all alarmed. This is not an appraisal. I simply want to share with you some of my own experiences with our friend hair, and at the most hope to entertain and amuse you.

For a long time, from babyhood through young adulthood   3
mainly, we grow, physically and spiritually (including the intellec-
tual with the spiritual), without being deeply aware of it. In fact, some periods of our growth are so confusing that we don't even recognize that growth is what is happening. We may feel hostile or angry or weepy and hysterical, or we may feel depressed. It would never occur to us, unless we stumbled on a book or person who explained it to us, that we were in fact in the process of change, of actually becoming larger, spiritually, than we were before. Whenever we grow, we tend to feel it, as a young seed must feel the weight and inertia of the earth as it seeks to break out of its shell on its way to becoming a plant. Often the feeling is any-
thing but pleasant. But what is most unpleasant is the not know-
ing what is happening. I remember the waves of anxiety that used to engulf me at different periods in my life, always manifesting itself in physical disorders (sleeplessness, for instance) and how frightened I was because I did not understand how this was possible.

With age and experience, you will be happy to know, growth   4
becomes a conscious, recognized process. Still somewhat frighten-
ing, but at least understood for what it is. Those long periods when something inside ourselves seems to be waiting, holding its breath, unsure about what the next step should be, eventually be-

come the periods we wait for, for it is in those periods that we realize we are being prepared for the next phase of our life and that, in all probability, a new level of the personality is about to be revealed.

A few years ago I experienced one such long period of restlessness disguised as stillness. That is to say, I pretty much withdrew from the larger world in favor of the peace of my personal, smaller one. I unplugged myself from television and newspapers (a great relief!), from the more disturbing members of my extended family, and from most of my friends. I seemed to have reached a ceiling in my brain. And under this ceiling my mind was very restless, although all else about me was calm.

As one does in these periods of introspection, I counted the beads of my progress in this world. In my relationship to my family and the ancestors, I felt I had behaved respectfully (not all of them would agree, no doubt); in my work I felt I had done, to the best of my ability, all that was required of me; in my relationship to the persons with whom I daily shared my life I had acted with all the love I could possibly locate within myself. I was also at least beginning to acknowledge my huge responsibility to the Earth and my adoration of the Universe. What else, then, was required? Why was it that, when I meditated and sought the escape hatch at the top of my brain, which, at an earlier stage of growth, I had been fortunate enough to find, I now encountered a ceiling, as if the route to merge with the infinite I had become used to was plastered over?

One day, after I had asked this question earnestly for half a year, it occurred to me that in my physical self there remained one last barrier to my spiritual liberation, at least in the present phase: my hair.

Not my friend hair itself, for I quickly understood that it was innocent. It was the way I related to it that was the problem. I was always thinking about it. So much so that if my spirit had been a balloon eager to soar away and merge with the infinite, my hair would be the rock that anchored it to Earth. I realized that there was no hope of continuing my spiritual development, no hope of future growth of my soul, no hope of really being able to stare at the Universe and forget myself entirely in the staring (one of the purest joys!) if I still remained chained to thoughts about my hair. I suddenly understood why nuns and monks shaved their heads!

I looked at myself in the mirror and I laughed with happiness!   9 I had broken through the seed skin, and was on my way upward through the earth.

Now I began to experiment: For several months I wore long   10 braids (a fashion among black women at the time) made from the hair of Korean women. I loved this. It fulfilled my fantasy of having very long hair and it gave my short, mildly processed (oppressed) hair a chance to grow out. The young woman who braided my hair was someone I grew to love — a struggling young mother, she and her daughter would arrive at my house at seven in the evening and we would talk, listen to music, and eat pizza or burritos while she worked, until one or two o'clock in the morning. I loved the craft involved in the designs she created for my head. (Basket making! a friend once cried on feeling the intricate weaving atop my head.) I loved sitting between her knees the way I used to sit between my mother's and sister's knees while they braided my hair when I was a child. I loved the fact that my own hair grew out and grew healthy under the "extensions," as the lengths of hair were called. I loved paying a young sister for work that was truly original and very much a part of the black hairstyling tradition. I loved the fact that I did not have to deal with my hair except once every two or three months (for the first time in my life I could wash it every day if I wanted to and not have to do anything further). Still, eventually the braids would have to be taken down (a four- to seven-hour job) and redone (another seven to eight hours); nor did I ever quite forget the Korean women, who, according to my young hairdresser, grew their hair expressly to be sold. Naturally this information caused me to wonder (and, yes, worry) about all other areas of their lives.

When my hair was four inches long, I dispensed with the hair   11 of my Korean sisters and braided my own. It was only then that I became reacquainted with its natural character. I found it to be springy, soft, almost sensually responsive to moisture. As the little braids spun off in all directions but the ones I tried to encourage them to go, I discovered my hair's willfulness, so like my own! I saw that my friend hair, given its own life, had a sense of humor. I discovered I liked it.

Again I stood in front of the mirror and looked at myself and   12 laughed. My hair was one of those odd, amazing, unbelievable, stop-you-in-your-tracks creations — not unlike a zebra's stripes, an armadillo's ears, or the feet of the electric-blue-footed boobie — that the Universe makes for no reason other than to express its own limitless imagination. I realized I had never been given the opportunity to appreciate hair for its true self. That it did, in fact, have one. I remembered years of enduring hairdressers — from my mother onward — doing missionary work on my hair. They dominated, suppressed, controlled. Now, more or less free, it stood this way and that. I would call up my friends around the country to report on its antics. It never thought of lying down. Flatness, the missionary position, did not interest it. It grew. Being short, cropped off near the root, another missionary "solution," did not interest it either. It sought more and more space, more light, more of itself. It loved to be washed; but that was it.

Eventually I knew *precisely* what hair wanted: It wanted to   13 grow, to be itself, to attract lint, if that was its destiny, but to be left alone by anyone, including me, who did not love it as it was. What do you think happened? (Other than that I was now able, as an added bonus, to comprehend Bob Marley[1] as the mystic his music always indicated he was.) The ceiling at the top of my brain lifted; once again my mind (and spirit) could get outside myself. I would not be stuck in restless stillness, but would continue to grow. The plant was above the ground!

This was the gift of my growth during my fortieth year. This   14 and the realization that as long as there is joy in creation there will always be new creations to discover, or to rediscover, and that a prime place to look is within and about the self. That even death, being part of life, must offer at least one moment of delight.

---

[1]Marley (1945–1981) was the leader of the Wailers, the preeminent Jamaican reggae band. He wore his hair in the kind of braids Walker describes. — Eds.

QUESTIONS ON MEANING

1. What is Walker's stated PURPOSE? What other purpose does she seem to have?
2. What does Walker mean when she says, "I suddenly understood why nuns and monks shaved their heads" (para. 8)? Why does she reject this course for herself?
3. To what does the author attribute her "liberation"?

QUESTIONS ON WRITING STRATEGY

1. What is the lesson of Walker's analogy?
2. What does the FIGURE OF SPEECH of the seed accomplish in paragraphs 3, 9, and 13?
3. What is the point of the stage setting in paragraphs 5 and 6?
4. In paragraphs 6 and 13, Walker uses several RHETORICAL QUESTIONS. What is their EFFECT?
5. OTHER METHODS. Walker's essay is strongly narrative (Chap. 1). Why do you think she chooses this structure for the point she wants to make? What stages does she go through in the experience she recounts?

QUESTIONS ON LANGUAGE

1. Look at the words Walker uses to describe her hair throughout the essay. How do they change?
2. How does Walker use PERSONIFICATION to describe her hair? What human attributes does she give it?
3. What ALLUSION is Walker making when she refers to the "missionary work" done on her hair in the past (para. 12)?
4. Use a dictionary to check any of these words if you don't know them: tribulations, discerning, appraised (para. 2); inertia, engulf (3); introspection (6); dispersed, sensually (11); mystic (13).

SUGGESTIONS FOR WRITING

1. You have been asked to speak to a group of eighth graders at your old school. Write your speech using analogy to explain an important aspect of high-school life in terms of something the audience already understands.

2. Write an essay about something in your life that represents liberation, however you want to define that word. The subject could be clothes, a bicycle or car, education, sports, playing an instrument, anything. Make sure readers understand exactly what the connection is between the subject and liberation.

3. CONNECTIONS. In the following essay, "The Attic of the Brain" (p. 445), Lewis Thomas also writes about efforts to liberate the mind, but he is not as enthusiastic as Walker is. In an essay, discuss Walker's and Thomas's views: Where do they appear to agree and disagree? Use quotations and PARAPHRASES from each essay to support your analysis.

ALICE WALKER ON WRITING

In an interview with David Bradley, Alice Walker has described her method of writing as waiting for friendly spirits to visit her. Usually, she doesn't outline or devote much time to preliminary organization. She plunges in with a passion, and she sees a definite purpose in most of her work: to correct injustices. "I was brought up to try to see what was wrong, and right it. Since I am a writer, writing is how I right it. I was brought up to look at things that are out of joint, out of balance, and to try to bring them into balance. And as a writer that's what I do."

An articulate feminist, Walker has written in support of greater rights for women, including blacks. If most of her works are short — stories, essays, and poems — there is a reason: She sees thick, long-winded volumes as alien to a female sensibility. "The books women write can be more like us — much thinner, much leaner, much cleaner."

Much of Alice Walker's writing has emerged from painful experience: She has written of her impoverished early days on a Georgia sharecropper's farm, a childhood accident with a BB gun that cost her the sight of one eye, a traumatic abortion, years as a civil rights worker in Mississippi. "I think," she says, "writing really helps you heal yourself. I think if you write long enough, you will be a healthy person. That is, if you write what you need to write, as opposed to what will make money or what will make fame."

FOR DISCUSSION

1. What does the author mean when she speaks of the importance of writing "what you need to write"?
2. What writers can you think of whose work has helped to right the world's wrongs?
3. Can you cite any exceptions to Walker's GENERALIZATION that long books are alien to women's sensibilities?

LEWIS THOMAS

Lewis Thomas has held teaching, research, and administrative positions at numerous medical schools and hospitals, including Johns Hopkins, Cornell, Harvard, and Massachusetts General. In addition, Thomas has served as dean of the School of Medicine at both Yale and New York universities, and as president of the Sloan-Kettering Cancer Center in New York City. Born in 1913 in Flushing, New York, Thomas attended Princeton University and Harvard Medical School, and most of his early writings were technical papers on his specialty, pathology. He did write poetry, too, and published some of it. Still, it wasn't until 1971, when he began to write a monthly column for the *New England Journal of Medicine*, that Thomas came to the attention of the general public. His column, "Notes of a Biology Watcher," allowed him to explore the less technical, more humanitarian and philosophical issues science sometimes raises. Many of these columns appear in his first book, *Lives of a Cell* (1974), which won a National Book Award — in part because Thomas writes with a unique candor, humor, grace, and style. Other books include *The Medusa and the Snail* (1979), *Late Night Thoughts on Listening to Mahler's Ninth Symphony* (1983), and *Etcetera, Etcetera* (1990), all essay collections; and *The Youngest Science* (1983), a memoir about becoming a doctor.

The Attic of the Brain

"The Attic of the Brain" originally appeared in *Discover* magazine, and is included in Thomas's collection of essays *Late Night Thoughts on Listening to Mahler's Ninth Symphony*. Although Thomas is a scientist, no special knowledge is needed to understand this essay, for his approach to his subject is not technical, and the metaphor he extends is as familiar to most of us as the street on which we grew up. With the help of an analogy, Thomas is able to discuss one of the most complex entities in the world: the human brain.

My parents' house had an attic, the darkest and strangest 1
part of the building, reachable only by placing a stepladder be-

neath the trapdoor and filled with unidentifiable articles too important to be thrown out with the trash but no longer suitable to
have at hand. This mysterious space was the memory of the place.
After many years all the things deposited in it became, one by
one, lost to consciousness. But they were still there, we knew,
safely and comfortably stored in the tissues of the house.

These days most of us live in smaller, more modern houses or   2
in apartments, and attics have vanished. Even the deep closets in
which we used to pile things up for temporary forgetting are
rarely designed into new homes.

Everything now is out in the open, openly acknowledged   3
and displayed, and whenever we grow tired of a memory, an old
chair, a trunkful of old letters, they are carted off to the dump for
burning.

This has seemed a healthier way to live, except maybe for the   4
smoke — everything out to be looked at, nothing strange hidden
under the roof, nothing forgotten because of no place left in im-
penetrable darkness to forget. Openness is the new life-style, no
undisclosed belongings, no private secrets. Candor is the rule in
architecture. The house is a machine for living, and what kind of
a machine would hide away its worn-out, obsolescent parts?

But it is in our nature as human beings to clutter, and we   5
hanker for places set aside, reserved for storage. We tend to accumulate and outgrow possessions at the same time, and it is an
endlessly discomforting mental task to keep sorting out the ones
to get rid of. We might, we think, remember them later and find a
use for them, and if they are gone for good, off to the dump, this
is a source of nervousness. I think it may be one of the reasons we
drum our fingers so much these days.

We might take a lesson here from what has been learned   6
about our brains in this century. We thought we discovered, first
off, the attic, although its existence has been mentioned from
time to time by all the people we used to call great writers. What
we really found was the trapdoor and a stepladder, and off we
clambered, shining flashlights into the corners, vacuuming the
dust out of bureau drawers, puzzling over the names of objects,
tossing them down to the floor below, and finally paying around
fifty dollars an hour to have them carted off for burning.

After several generations of this new way of doing things we took up openness and candor with the febrile intensity of a new religion, everything laid out in full view, and as in the design of our new houses it seemed a healthier way to live, except maybe again for smoke.   7

And now, I think, we have a new kind of worry. There is no place for functionless, untidy, inexplicable notions, no dark comfortable parts of the mind to hide away the things we'd like to keep but at the same time forget. The attic is still there, but with the trapdoor always open and the stepladder in place we are always in and out of it, flashing lights around, naming everything, unmystified.   8

I have an earnest proposal for psychiatry, a novel set of therapeutic rules, although I know it means waiting in line.   9

Bring back the old attic. Give new instructions to the patients who are made nervous by our times, including me, to make a conscious effort to hide a reasonable proportion of thought. It would have to be a gradual process, considering how far we have come in the other direction talking, talking all the way. Perhaps only one or two thoughts should be repressed each day, at the outset. The easiest, gentlest way might be to start with dreams, first by forbidding the patient to mention any dream, much less to recount its details, then encouraging the outright forgetting that there was a dream at all, remembering nothing beyond the vague sense that during sleep there had been the familiar sound of something shifting and sliding, up under the roof.   10

We might, in this way, regain the kind of spontaneity and zest for ideas, things popping into the mind, uncontrollable and ungovernable thoughts, the feel that this notion is somehow connected unaccountably with that one. We could come again into possession of real memory, the kind of memory that can come from jumbled forgotten furniture, old photographs, fragments of music.   11

It has been one of the great errors of our time to think that by thinking about thinking, and then talking about it, we could possibly straighten out and tidy up our minds. There is no delusion more damaging than to get the idea in your head that you understand the functioning of your own brain. Once you acquire such   12 a notion, you run the danger of moving in to take charge, guiding your thoughts, shepherding your mind from place to place, *controlling* it, making lists of regulations. The human mind is not meant to be governed, certainly not by any book of rules yet written; it is supposed to run itself, and we are obliged to follow it along, trying to keep up with it as best we can. It is all very well to be aware of your awareness, even proud of it, but never try to operate it. You are not up to the job.

I leave it to the analysts to work out the techniques for doing   13
what now needs doing. They are presumably the professionals most familiar with the route, and all they have to do is turn back and go the other way, session by session, step by step. It takes a certain amount of hard swallowing and a lot of revised jargon, and I have great sympathy for their plight, but it is time to reverse course.

If after all, as seems to be true, we are endowed with uncon-   14
scious minds in our brains, these should be regarded as normal structures, installed wherever they are for a purpose. I am not sure what they are built to contain, but as a biologist, impressed by the usefulness of everything alive, I would take it for granted that they are useful, probably indispensable organs of thought. It cannot be a bad thing to own one, but I would no more think of meddling with it than trying to exorcise my liver, an equally mysterious apparatus. Until we know a lot more, it would be wise, as we have learned from other fields in medicine, to let them be, above all not to interfere. Maybe, even — and this is the notion I wish to suggest to my psychiatric friends — to stock them up, put more things into them, make *use* of them. Forget whatever you feel like forgetting. From time to time, practice *not* being open, discover new things *not* to talk about, learn reserve, hold the tongue. But above all, develop the human talent for forgetting words, phrases, whole unwelcome sentences, all experiences involving wincing. If we should ever lose the loss of memory, we might lose as well that most attractive of signals ever flashed from the human face, the blush. If we should give away the capacity for embarrassment, the touch of fingertips might be the next to go, and then the suddenness of laughter, the unaccountable sure sense of something gone wrong, and, fi-

nally, the marvelous conviction that being human is the best thing to be.

Attempting to operate one's own mind, powered by such a 15 magical instrument as the human brain, strikes me as rather like using the world's biggest computer to add columns of figures, or towing a Rolls-Royce with a nylon rope.

I have tried to think of a name for the new professional activ- 16 ity, but each time I think of a good one I forget it before I can get it written down. Psychorepression is the only one I've hung on to, but I can't guess at the fee schedule.

QUESTIONS ON MEANING

1. State, in your own words, the THESIS of this essay.
2. In paragraph 4, Thomas links the amount of space we live in to certain aspects of our life-styles. What relationship is he suggesting here? Do you think it's valid, or is he reaching too far for the sake of his analogy? Support your answer with examples from your own experience as well as from the essay.
3. The author works from the premise that we need a place "for functionless, untidy, inexplicable notions" (para. 8). Why does he seem to think that such a place is necessary?
4. According to Thomas, why is it "time to reverse course" (para. 13)? What does he find wrong with the course we're on, and what will we gain by learning reserve, by not being open, by forgetting certain things?

QUESTIONS ON WRITING STRATEGY

1. What analogy does Thomas draw? Identify, as succinctly as possible, the two things he compares.
2. What is the TONE of paragraph 10?
3. What is the tone of the last paragraph, particularly the phrase "each time I think of a good one I forget it before I can get it written down"? Would you label this humor silly, ironic, gentle, or sarcastic? How does Thomas's humor contribute to this essay's effectiveness?

4. The author makes the assumption that the unconscious mind is a normal structure, and therefore useful. As a biologist, however, Thomas surely knows that some living things and structures seem to serve no use at all. Does it weaken his essay that he doesn't address this fact?

5. OTHER METHODS. Thomas is using analogy in the service of an argument (Chap. 11). Given the case he wants to make, why does he concede that living without attics "has seemed a healthier way to live" (para. 4)?

QUESTIONS ON LANGUAGE

1. Consult your dictionary if you need help in defining the following words: candor, obsolescent (para. 4); febrile (7); exorcise, apparatus (14).

2. Consider the last sentence in paragraph 6, which ends "and off we clambered . . . puzzling over the names of objects, tossing them down to the floor below, and finally paying around fifty dollars an hour to have them carted off for burning." Explain the reference to having the objects carted off for burning. Is the author suggesting we'd pay fifty dollars an hour to have someone do *that*? Discuss.

3. Be sure you understand the distinction Thomas makes between being "aware of your awareness" and trying "to operate it" (para. 12).

SUGGESTIONS FOR WRITING

1. Consider Thomas's statement, "it is in our nature as human beings to clutter" (para. 5). Do you agree that this is a fundamental part of human nature? Write an essay responding to this statement. Be sure to provide enough examples to make your case convincing; generalizing from one illustration is not an effective strategy.

2. Thomas approaches this essay with a healthy respect for the human mind and its ability to do what it's supposed to, even if we aren't completely conscious of what that is. Write a brief essay in which you argue that the human mind *does* need to be governed, and that repressing or forgetting things is psychologically damaging. Or, if you prefer, argue in support of Thomas's thesis, taking care to provide fresh EVIDENCE so that you are not merely repeating what Thomas has already said. Whichever topic you choose, see whether a new analogy might help you illustrate any point.

3. CONNECTIONS. Compare and contrast Thomas's essay and Alice Walker's "Oppressed Hair" (p. 437) as analogies. What is each au-

thor's basic METAPHOR that is extended to an analogy? What does each author want to accomplish with analogy? What specific comparisons does each draw? Which is the more effective analogy, in your view, and why?

LEWIS THOMAS ON WRITING

Lewis Thomas has found little similarity between his popular essays and the scientific articles he has written for specialized journals. Some of the latter, he recalls with amusement, have been quoted to illustrate "how awful the prose is in scientific papers."

Still, he admits, his essays do in a way resemble scientific writing: They report experiments in thought. "Although I usually think I know what I'm going to be writing about, what I'm going to say," he told the writer David Hellerstein, "most of the time it doesn't happen that way at all. At some point I get misled down a garden path. I get surprised by an idea that I hadn't anticipated getting, which is a little bit like being in a laboratory. Including, in fact, that the outcome in writing essays, like the outcome in a laboratory, often enough turns out to be a dud."

FOR DISCUSSION

1. Lewis Thomas the essayist has a reputation as a stylist. How do you account for the reaction he reports to some of his scientific papers? Who might have made such a judgment?
2. What important similarities does the author see between scientists in the laboratory and essayists? What new light does this comparison cast on the ordinary citizen's usual view of scientists?

HENRY DAVID THOREAU

HENRY DAVID THOREAU (1817–1862) was born in Concord, Massachusetts, where, except for short excursions, he remained for the whole of his life. After his graduation from Harvard College, he taught school briefly, worked irregularly as surveyor and house painter, and for a time worked in his father's pencil factory (and greatly improved the product). The small sales of his first, self-published book, *A Week on the Concord and Merrimac Rivers* (1849), led him to remark, "I have now a library of nearly nine hundred volumes, over seven hundred of which I wrote myself."

The philosopher Ralph Waldo Emerson befriended his neighbor Thoreau; but although the two agreed that a unity exists between man and nature, they did not always see eye to eye on matters of politics. Unlike Emerson, Thoreau was an activist. He helped escaped slaves flee to Canada; he went to jail rather than pay his poll tax to a government that made war against Mexico. He recounts this brush with the law in his essay "Civil Disobedience" (1849), in which later readers (including Mahatma Gandhi of India and Martin Luther King, Jr.) have found encouragement for their own nonviolent resistance. One other book appeared in Thoreau's lifetime: *Walden* (1854), a searching account of his life in (and around, and beyond) the one-room cabin he built for himself at Walden Pond near Concord. When Thoreau lay dying, an aunt asked whether he had made his peace with God. "I did not know we had quarreled," he replied.

The Battle of the Ants

At Walden Pond, Thoreau mercilessly simplified his needs. Making himself almost self-sustaining, he proved to his own satisfaction that he could write, read Plato, grow beans, and observe in minute detail the natural world. In the following famous section of *Walden*, Thoreau reports a war he happened to observe while going to fetch wood. It is artful reporting, for Thoreau wrote with care: like a craftsman lovingly joining wood to make a cabinet. To revise *Walden*, a relatively short book, took him seven years. Thoreau's is a style marked by a

New England Yankee tightness of lip — indeed, there are no useless words — and by an evident delight in setting forth an analogy.

One day when I went out to my wood-pile, or rather my pile   1
of stumps, I observed two large ants, the one red, the other much larger, nearly half an inch long, and black, fiercely contending with one another. Having once got hold they never let go, but struggled and wrestled and rolled on the chips incessantly. Looking farther, I was surprised to find that the chips were covered with such combatants, that it was not a *duellum*, but a *bellum*,[1] a war between two races of ants, the red always pitted against the black, and frequently two red ones to one black. The legions of these Myrmidons[2] covered all the hills and vales in my wood-yard, and the ground was already strewn with the dead and dying, both red and black. It was the only battle which I have ever witnessed, the only battle-field I ever trod while the battle was raging; internecine war; the red republicans on the one hand, and the black imperialists on the other. On every side they were engaged in deadly combat, yet without any noise that I could hear, and human soldiers never fought so resolutely. I watched a couple that were fast locked in each other's embraces, in a little sunny valley amid the chips, now at noonday prepared to fight till the sun went down, or life went out. The smaller red champion had fastened himself like a vice to his adversary's front, and through all the tumblings on that field never for an instant ceased to gnaw at one of his feelers near the root, having already caused the other to go by the board; while the stronger black one dashed him from side to side, and, as I saw on looking nearer, had already divested him of several of his members. They fought with more pertinacity than bulldogs. Neither manifested the least disposition to retreat. It was evident that their battle-cry was "Conquer or die." In the meanwhile there came along a single red ant

---

[1] Not a hand-to-hand combat, but a whole war. — Eds.

[2] Fierce warriors, originally not men but a tribe of ants. In Homer's *Iliad* the god Zeus, transforming them, sends them to help fight the war against Troy. — Eds.

on the hillside of this valley, evidently full of excitement, who either had dispatched his foe, or had not yet taken part in the battle; probably the latter, for he had lost none of his limbs; whose mother had charged him to return with his shield or upon it. Or perchance he was some Achilles, who had nourished his wrath apart, and had now come to avenge or rescue his Patroclus.[3] He saw this unequal combat from afar — for the blacks were nearly twice the size of the red — he drew near with rapid pace till he stood on his guard within half an inch of the combatants; then, watching his opportunity, he sprang upon the black warrior, and commenced his operations near the root of his right foreleg, leaving the foe to select among his own members; and so there were three united for life, as if a new kind of attraction had been invented which put all other locks and cements to shame. I should not have wondered by this time to find that they had their respective musical bands stationed on some eminent chip, and playing their national airs the while, to excite the slow and cheer the dying combatants. I was myself excited somewhat even as if they had been men. The more you think of it, the less the difference. And certainly there is not the fight recorded in Concord history, at least, if in the history of America, that will bear a moment's comparison with this, whether for the numbers engaged in it, or for the patriotism and heroism displayed. For numbers and for carnage it was an Austerlitz or Dresden.[4] Concord Fight! Two killed on the patriots' side, and Luther Blanchard wounded! Why here every ant was a Buttrick — "Fire! for God's sake fire!" — and thousands shared the fate of Davis and Hosmer.[5] There was not one hireling there. I have no doubt that it was a principle they fought for, as much as our ancestors, and not to avoid a three-penny tax on their tea; and the results of this battle will be as important and memorable to those whom it concerns as those of the battle of Bunker Hill, at least.

---

[3]In the *Iliad* again, the Greek hero Achilles and his slain comrade-in-arms. — EDS.

[4]Battles that Napoleon waged with great loss of life. — EDS.

[5]Minutemen who fought the British redcoats in the Battle of Concord Bridge, 1775. — EDS.

I took up the chip on which the three I have particularly de- 2
scribed were struggling, carried it into my house, and placed it under a tumbler on my window-sill, in order to see the issue. Holding a microscope to the first-mentioned red ant, I saw that,
though he was assiduously gnawing at the near foreleg of his enemy, having severed his remaining feeler, his own breast was all
torn away, exposing what vitals he had there to the jaws of the
black warrior, whose breastplate was apparently too thick for him
to pierce; and the dark carbuncles of the sufferer's eyes shone
with ferocity such as war only could excite. They struggled half an
hour longer under the tumbler, and when I looked again the
black soldier had severed the heads of his foes from their bodies,
and the still living heads were hanging on either side of him like
ghastly trophies at his saddle-bow, still apparently as firmly fastened as ever, and he was endeavoring with feeble struggles, being
without feelers, and with only the remnant of a leg, and I know
not how many other wounds, to divest himself of them, which at
length, after half an hour more, he accomplished. I raised the
glass, and he went off over the window-sill in that crippled state.
Whether he finally survived that combat, and spent the remain-
der of his days in some Hôtel des Invalides,[6] I do not know; but I
thought that his industry would not be worth much thereafter. I
never learned which party was victorious, nor the cause of the
war, but I felt for the rest of that day as if I had my feelings excited
and harrowed by witnessing the struggle, the ferocity and carnage, of a human battle before my door.

Kirby and Spence tell us that the battles of ants have long 3
been celebrated and the date of them recorded, though they say
that Huber[7] is the only modern author who appears to have witnessed them. "Aeneas Sylvius," say they, "after giving a very circumstantial account of one contested with great obstinacy by a
great and small species on the trunk of a pear tree," adds that
"'this action was fought in the pontificate of Eugenius the
Fourth, in the presence of Nicholas Pistoriensis, an eminent law-

[6]In Paris, a home for old soldiers. — EDS.
[7]Three leading entomologists (or zoologists specializing in insects) of Thoreau's day: Kirby and Spence in America, Huber in Switzerland. — EDS.

yer, who related the whole history of the battle with the greatest fidelity.' A similar engagement between great and small ants is recorded by Olaus Magnus, in which the small ones, being victorious, are said to have buried the bodies of their own soldiers, but left those of their giant enemies a prey to the birds. This event happened previous to the expulsion of the tyrant Christian the Second from Sweden." The battle which I witnessed took place in the Presidency of Polk, five years before the passage of Webster's Fugitive-Slave Bill.[8]

QUESTIONS ON MEANING

1. In finding the Battle of Concord Bridge a minor skirmish when compared to the battle of the ants, in crediting the ant soldiers with greater heroism (para. 1), is Thoreau putting down patriotism? Does he hint that the American Revolution didn't matter? What is his point?
2. For what PURPOSE (or purposes) does Thoreau seem to write such a detailed account of so trifling a war?

QUESTIONS ON WRITING STRATEGY

1. "Human soldiers," says Thoreau in paragraph 1, "never fought so resolutely." With what specific examples and observations does he support his GENERALIZATION? Point to memorable details that make us see the ant soldiers' inhuman determination.
2. In drawing his analogy, does Thoreau seek to explain the behavior of ants by comparing it to human war, or to explain human war by comparing it to the behavior of ants? (Which of the two kinds of warfare — ant or human — does Thoreau appear to regard as strange and unfamiliar, and therefore in greater need of explaining?)

---

[8]Daniel Webster (1782–1852) was an American statesman who, as a senator from Massachusetts in 1850, backed a law penalizing anyone who helped a slave escape. Northern abolitionists, including Thoreau, were vehemently opposed to the law. — EDS.

3. What is the TONE of this essay? In his attitude toward the ant war (and human war), does Thoreau seem grim, amused, appalled, disgusted, mocking, or what? How can you tell?

4. Do Thoreau's ALLUSIONS to history and to Greek literature seem decorations meant to show off his knowledge? What do they add to the essay? Look closely at one or two of them.

5. In many anthologies, you will find this selection with paragraph 3 shaved off. Why is Thoreau's CONCLUSION so effective? If it is omitted, what is lost?

6. OTHER METHODS. Paragraph 2 is a famous piece of narration (Chap. 1) and description (Chap. 2). What is the DOMINANT IMPRESSION of this paragraph, and how does Thoreau achieve it?

QUESTIONS ON LANGUAGE

1. What is an "internecine war" (para. 1)?

2. Define any of these other words you may have doubts about: perchance, eminent (para. 1); assiduously, carbuncles, saddlebow, carnage (2); circumstantial, obstinacy (3).

3. In noting that the black ant has a "breastplate" (para. 2), Thoreau sees the ant soldier as wearing armor like a man. What other examples of PERSONIFICATION do you find?

4. Is this essay written in the technical vocabulary of a professional entomologist? Glance again at Thoreau's microscopic description of the ants (para. 2): How specialized are its words?

SUGGESTIONS FOR WRITING

1. In a paragraph, draw an analogy between some *typical* person, whose general sort you've observed, and some animal, bird, or insect. You might consider someone bursting with energy; someone who takes until eleven o'clock in the morning to wake up; a belligerent sort; a talkative scold; a ravenous eater; or — what kind of person interests you?

2. Describe some phenomenon or some creature in the natural world that has fascinated you. If, as you write, an analogy occurs to you, put it in; but don't force one if it doesn't come naturally.

3. Like Thoreau, the ancient Greek writer Aesop was fond of likening animals to persons. Some of his *Fables* may be familiar to you: the one about the hare and the tortoise (with the slow, persistent plodder winning the race), the tale of the fox and the grapes (about the fox who, when he couldn't reach the tempting fruit, decided that it

must be sour anyway), and that of the mice who wanted to bell the cat (but who couldn't get one of their number to volunteer). An Aesop fable usually sums up the point of a story in a closing moral ("Slow and steady is sure to win," "There is comfort in pretending that the unattainable is not worth having," "It is easier to plan than to fulfill"). Read or reread a few of Aesop's fables, then try writing one of your own.

4. CONNECTIONS. Like Thoreau, Virginia Woolf and Annie Dillard also describe life and death in the insect world (see "The Death of the Moth," p. 124, and "Death of a Moth," p. 130). In an essay using the authors' language as your EVIDENCE, explore their respective attitudes toward life and death and how each is affected by what he or she witnesses.

HENRY DAVID THOREAU ON WRITING

"Keep a journal," Emerson had urged Thoreau, and in 1837 the younger writer began making entries. For the rest of his life, he continued to be a faithful journal keeper. Into this intimate volume, kept only for his own eyes, Thoreau poured ideas, opinions, impressions, poems, meditations, passages from his reading that he wished to remember. Much of this raw material found its way into *Walden* and other published works. From Thoreau's *Journal*, here is a provocative sampling of his thoughts about writing. (To help identify each, we have given them subject headings.)

Physical Exercise. "How vain it is to sit down to write when you have not stood up to live! Methinks that the moment my legs begin to move, my thoughts begin to flow, as if I had given vent to the stream at the lower end and consequently new fountains flowed into it at the upper. A thousand rills which have their rise in the sources of thought burst forth and fertilize my brain. . . . The writing which consists with habitual sitting is mechanical, wooden, dull to read." (August 19, 1851)

Not Saying Everything. "It is the fault of some excellent writers — De Quincey's first impressions on seeing London suggest it to me — that they express themselves with too great fullness and detail. They give the most faithful, natural, and lifelike account of their sensations, mental and physical, but they lack moderation and sententiousness. They do not affect us by an intellectual earnestness and a reserve of meaning, like a stutterer; they say all they mean. Their sentences are not concentrated and nutty. Sentences which suggest far more than they say, which have an atmosphere about them, which do not merely report an old, but make a new impression; sentences which suggest as many things and are as durable as a Roman aqueduct: to frame these, that is the *art* of writing. Sentences which are expensive, towards which so many volumes, so much life, went; which lie like boulders on the page, up and down or across; which contain the seed of other sentences, not mere repetition, but creation: which a man might sell his grounds and castles to build." (August 22, 1851)

Writing with Body and Senses. "We cannot write well or truly but what we write with gusto. The body, the senses, must conspire with the mind. Expression is the act of the whole man, that our speech may be vascular. The intellect is powerless to express thought without the aid of the heart and liver and of every member. Often I feel that my head stands out too dry, when it should be immersed. A writer, a man writing, is the scribe of all nature; he is the corn and the grass and the atmosphere of writing. It is always essential that we love what we are doing, do it with a heart." (September 2, 1851)

Drawing Analogies. "Be greedy of occasions to express your thought. Improve the opportunity to draw analogies." (September 4, 1851)

Thought and Style. "Shall I not have words as fresh as my thoughts? Shall I use any other man's word? A genuine thought or feeling can find expression for itself, if it have to invent hieroglyphics. It has the universe for type-metal. It is for want of original thought that one man's style is like another's." (September 8, 1851)

Revision. "In correcting my manuscripts, which I do with sufficient phlegm, I find that I invariably turn out much that is good along with the bad, which it is then impossible for me to distinguish — so much for keeping bad company; but after the lapse of time, having purified the main body and thus created a distinct standard for comparison, I can review the rejected sentences and easily detect those which deserve to be readmitted." (March 1, 1854)

The Value of Lapsed Time. "Often I can give the truest and most interesting account of any adventure I have had after years have elapsed, for then I am not confused, only the most significant facts surviving in my memory. Indeed, all that continues to interest me after such a lapse of time is sure to be pertinent, and I may safely record all that I remember." (March 28, 1857)

Self-Inspiration. "The writer must to some extent inspire himself. Most of his sentences may at first lie dead in his essay, but when all are arranged, some life and color will be reflected on them from the mature and successful lines; they will appear to pulsate with fresh life, and he will be enabled to eke out their slumbering sense, and make them worthy of their neighborhood. . . . Most that is first written on any subject is a mere groping after it, mere rubble-stone and foundation." (February 3, 1859)

Thought Breeds Thought. "The Scripture rule, "Unto him that hath shall be given," is true of composition. The more you have thought and written on a given theme, the more you can still write. Thought breeds thought. It grows under your hands." (February 13, 1860)

FOR DISCUSSION

1. What connection does Thoreau find between life and art?
2. What are the author's views about revision?
3. What does Thoreau recommend for writers who "express themselves with too great fullness and detail"?

JAMES C. RETTIE

The quiet, hardworking life of JAMES C. RETTIE (1904–1969), an economist by profession, has rendered him a man of mystery about whom few facts are known. Although he wrote many scholarly articles and reports, Rettie is mainly remembered as the author of a single famous work: the following essay, often reprinted in textbooks and anthologies. Rettie completed it in 1948 while working at an experimental station of the National Forest Service in Upper Darby, Pennsylvania. Later, during the presidencies of John F. Kennedy and Lyndon B. Johnson, he served as an advisor to the U.S. Department of the Interior.

"But a Watch in the Night": *A Scientific Fable*

In writing his essay, Rettie apparently drew some of his ideas from a U.S. government pamphlet, "To Hold This Soil," prepared by the Department of Agriculture. In it, we are given a relatively matter-of-fact account of soil erosion. But Rettie had a flash of genius and converted the pamphlet's statistics into a remarkable analogy, couched in a science-fiction narrative.

Out beyond our solar system there is a planet called Copernicus. It came into existence some four or five billion years before the birth of our Earth. In due course of time it became inhabited by a race of intelligent men.

About 750 million years ago the Copernicans had developed the motion picture machine to a point well in advance of the stage that we have reached. Most of the cameras that we now use in motion picture work are geared to take twenty-four pictures per second on a continuous strip of film. When such film is run through a projector, it throws a series of images on the screen and these change with a rapidity that gives the visual impression of normal movement. If a motion is too swift for the human eye to see it in detail, it can be captured and artificially slowed down by means of the slow-motion camera. This one is geared to take

461

many more shots per second — ninety-six or even more than that. When the slow-motion film is projected at the normal speed of twenty-four pictures per second, we can see just how the jumping horse goes over a hurdle.

What about motion that is too slow to be seen by the human 3 eye? That problem has been solved by the use of the time-lapse camera. In this one, the shutter is geared to take only one shot per second, or one per minute, or even one per hour — depending upon the kind of movement that is being photographed. When the time-lapse film is projected at the normal speed of twenty-four pictures per second, it is possible to see a bean sprout growing up out of the ground. Time-lapse films are useful in the study of many types of motion too slow to be observed by the unaided, human eye.

The Copernicans, it seems, had time-lapse cameras some 757 4 million years ago and they also had superpowered telescopes that gave them a clear view of what was happening upon this Earth. They decided to make a film record of the life history of Earth and to make it on the scale of one picture per year. The photography has been in progress during the last 757 million years.

In the near future, a Copernican interstellar expedition will 5 arrive upon our Earth and bring with it a copy of the time-lapse film. Arrangements will be made for showing the entire film in one continuous run. This will begin at midnight of New Year's Eve and continue day and night without a single stop until midnight of December 31. The rate of projection will be twenty-four pictures per second. Time on the screen will thus seem to move at the rate of twenty-four years per second; 1440 years per minute; 86,400 years per hour; approximately two million years per day; and sixty-two million years per month. The normal lifespan of individual man will occupy about three seconds. The full period of earth history that will be unfolded on the screen (some 757 million years) will extend from what the geologists call Precambrian times up to the present. This will, by no means, cover the full time-span of the earth's geological history but it will embrace the period since the advent of living organisms.

During the months of January, February, and March the pic- 6 ture will be desolate and dreary. The shape of the land masses and the oceans will bear little or no resemblance to those that we know. The violence of geological erosion will be much in evidence. Rains will pour down on the land and promptly go booming down to the seas. There will be no clear streams anywhere except where the rains fall upon hard rock. Everywhere on the steeper ground the stream channels will be filled with boulders hurled down by rushing waters. Raging torrents and dry stream beds will keep alternating in quick succession. High mountains will seem to melt like so much butter in the sun. The shifting of land into the seas, later to be thrust up as new mountains, will be going on at a grand scale.

Early in April there will be some indication of the presence of single-celled living organisms in some of the warmer and sheltered coastal waters. By the end of the month it will be noticed that some of these organisms have become multicellular. A few of them, including the Trilobites, will be encased in hard shells.

Toward the end of May, the first vertebrates will appear, but they will still be aquatic creatures. In June about 60 percent of the land area that we know as North America will be under water. One broad channel will occupy the space where the Rocky Mountains now stand. Great deposits of limestone will be forming under some of the shallower seas. Oil and gas deposits will be in process of formation — also under shallow seas. On land there will still be no sign of vegetation. Erosion will be rampant, tearing loose particles and chunks of rock and grinding them into sand and silt to be spewed out by the streams into bays and estuaries.

About the middle of July the first land plants will appear and take up the tremendous job of soil building. Slowly, very slowly, the mat of vegetation will spread, always battling for its life against the power of erosion. Almost foot by foot, the plant life will advance, lacing down with its root structures whatever pulverized rock material it can find. Leaves and stems will be giving added protection against the loss of the soil foothold. The increasing vegetation will pave the way for the land animals that will live upon it.

Early in August the seas will be teeming with fish. This will be what geologists call the Devonian period. Some of the races of these fish will be breathing by means of lung tissue instead of

through gill tissues. Before the month is over, some of the lung
fish will go ashore and take on a crude lizardlike appearance. Here
are the first amphibians.

In early September the insects will put in their appearance.   11
Some will look like huge dragonflies and will have a wing spread
of 24 inches. Large portions of the land masses will now be covered with heavy vegetation that will include the primitive spore-
propagating trees. Layer upon layer of this plant growth will build
up, later to appear as the coal deposits. About the middle of this
month, there will be evidence of the first seed-bearing plants and
the first reptiles. Heretofore, the land animals will have been amphibians that could reproduce their kind only by depositing a soft
egg mass in quiet waters. The reptiles will be shown to be freed
from the aquatic bond because they can reproduce by means of a
shelled egg in which the embryo and its nurturing liquids are
sealed and thus protected from destructive evaporation. Before
September is over, the first dinosaurs will be seen — creatures
destined to dominate the animal realm for about 140 million
years and then to disappear.

In October there will be series of mountain uplifts along what   12
is now the eastern coast of the United States. A creature with
feathered limbs — half bird and half reptile in appearance — will
take itself into the air. Some small and rather unpretentious animals will be seen to bring forth their young in a form that is a
miniature replica of the parents and to feed these young on milk
secreted by mammary glands in the female parent. The emergence of this mammalian form of animal life will be recognized as
one of the great events in geologic time. October will also witness
the high water mark of the dinosaurs — creatures ranging in size
from that of the modern goat to monsters like Brontosaurus that
weighed some 40 tons. Most of them will be placid vegetar-
ians, but a few will be hideous-looking carnivores, like Allosaurus
and Tyrannosaurus. Some of the herbivorous dinosaurs will be
clad in bony armor for protection against their flesh-eating com-
rades.

November will bring pictures of a sea extending from the   13
Gulf of Mexico to the Arctic in space now occupied by the Rocky
Mountains. A few of the reptiles will take to the air on batlike

wings. One of these, called Pteranodon, will have a wingspread of 15 feet. There will be a rapid development of the modern flowering plants, modern trees, and modern insects. The dinosaurs will disappear. Toward the end of the month there will be a tremendous land disturbance in which the Rocky Mountains will rise out of the sea to assume a dominating place in the North American landscape.

As the picture runs on into December it will show the mammals in command of the animal life. Seed-bearing trees and grasses will have covered most of the land with a heavy mantle of vegetation. Only the areas newly thrust up from the sea will be barren. Most of the streams will be crystal clear. The turmoil of geologic erosion will be confined to localized areas. About December 25 will begin the cutting of the Grand Canyon of the Colorado River. Grinding down through layer after layer of sedimentary strata, this stream will finally expose deposits laid down in Precambrian times. Thus in the walls of that canyon will appear geological formations dating from recent times to the period when the Earth had no living organisms upon it.

The picture will run on through the latter days of December and even up to its final day with still no sign of mankind. The spectators will become alarmed in the fear that man has somehow been left out. But not so; sometime about noon on December 31 (one million years ago) will appear a stooped, massive creature of manlike proportions. This will be Pithecanthropus, the Java ape man. For tools and weapons he will have nothing but crude stone and wooden clubs. His children will live a precarious existence threatened on the one side by hostile animals and on the other by tremendous climatic changes. Ice sheets — in places 4000 feet deep — will form in the northern parts of North America and Eurasia. Four times this glacial ice will push southward to cover half the continents. With each advance the plant and animal life will be swept under or pushed southward. With each recession of the ice, life will struggle to reestablish itself in the wake of the retreating glaciers. The woolly mammoth, the musk ox, and the caribou all will fight to maintain themselves near the ice line. Sometimes they will be caught and put into cold storage — skin, flesh, blood, bones and all.

The picture will run on through supper time with still very lit- 16
tle evidence of man's presence on the earth. It will be about 11
o'clock when Neanderthal man appears. Another half hour will
go by before the appearance of Cro-Magnon man living in caves
and painting crude animal pictures on the walls of his dwelling.
Fifteen minutes more will bring Neolithic man, knowing how to
chip stone and thus produce sharp cutting edges for spears and
tools. In a few minutes more it will appear that man has domesticated the dog, the sheep, and, possibly, other animals. He will
then begin the use of milk. He will also learn the arts of basket
weaving and the making of pottery and dugout canoes.

The dawn of civilization will not come until about five or six 17
minutes before the end of the picture. The story of the Egyptians,
the Babylonians, the Greeks, and the Romans will unroll during
the fourth, the third, and the second minute before the end. At
58 minutes and 43 seconds past 11:00 P.M. (just 1 minute and 17
seconds before the end) will come the beginning of the Christian
era. Columbus will discover the New World 20 seconds before the
end. The Declaration of Independence will be signed just 7 seconds before the final curtain comes down.

In those few moments of geologic time will be the story of all 18
that has happened since we became a nation. And what a story it
will be! A human swarm will sweep across the face of the continent and take it away from the . . . red men. They will change it
far more radically than it has ever been changed before in a comparable time. The great virgin forests will be seen going down before ax and fire. The soil, covered for eons by its protective mantle of trees and grasses, will be laid bare to the ravages of water
and wind erosion. Streams that had been flowing clear will, once
again, take up a load of silt and push it toward the seas. Humus
and mineral salts, both vital elements of productive soil, will be
seen to vanish at a terrifying rate. The railroads and highways
and cities that will spring up may divert attention, but they cannot cover up the blight of man's recent activities. In great sections
of Asia, it will be seen that man must utilize cow dung and every
scrap of available straw or grass for fuel to cook his food. The forests that once provided wood for this purpose will be gone without a trace. The use of these agricultural wastes for fuel, in place

of returning them to the land, will be leading to increasing soil impoverishment. Here and there will be seen a dust storm darkening the landscape over an area a thousand miles across. Man-creatures will be shown counting their wealth in terms of bits of printed paper representing other bits of a scarce but comparatively useless yellow metal that is kept buried in strong vaults. Meanwhile, the soil, the only real wealth that can keep mankind alive on the face of this earth is savagely being cut loose from its ancient moorings and washed into the seven seas.

We have just arrived upon this earth. How long will we stay?   19

QUESTIONS ON MEANING

1. What is the subject of Rettie's analogy? To what does he liken it?
2. For what reason does the writer include this analogy? To give us a sense of the vast extent of time, to show us how humankind would appear to alien beings, to demonstrate how much has gone into the growth and development of the earth and living things, or what?
3. Sum up the PURPOSE of the essay as a whole. What is Rettie's THESIS?
4. Why does the writer end with a RHETORICAL QUESTION? What answer does he expect us to supply?

QUESTIONS ON WRITING STRATEGY

1. Do you have any trouble accepting Rettie's notion of a movie whose screening takes a year? What commonplace, practical objections to such a movie occur to you? Is Rettie's analogy silly, or does it serve him well?
2. What is the writer's POINT OF VIEW? How does the inclusion of the Copernicans help establish it?
3. What other environmental problems might Rettie have mentioned in his CONCLUSION? Why doesn't he discuss such problems? (What would this have done to his plot summary of the movie?)
4. What kinds of TRANSITIONS are most numerous at the start of paragraphs? Why are they essential in this essay?
5. Can Rettie, in his conclusion, be accused of SENTIMENTALITY?

6. OTHER METHODS. In what section of the essay does the method of process analysis appear? Into what main stages does the writer divide the history of the earth?

QUESTIONS ON LANGUAGE

1. The title of Rettie's essay is an ALLUSION to Psalms 90:4 in the King James Version of the Bible: "For a thousand years in Thy sight are but as yesterday when it is past, and as a watch in the night." Can you explain this quotation? What light does it cast on the essay?
2. What is the value of the essay's subtitle, "A Scientific Fable"? What is a fable?
3. What terms from the vocabulary of science (Precambrian, for example) occur in this essay? Is Rettie writing for an AUDIENCE of trained specialists? Do you think he could have done without such terms?
4. Make sure the following words and phrases are part of your vocabulary: hurdle (para. 2); time-lapse camera (3); interstellar, geological, advent (5); desolate, erosion, torrents (6); multicellular (7); vertebrates, aquatic, rampant, spewed, estuaries (8); pulverized (9); spore-propagating, reptiles, amphibians, realm (11); unpretentious, replica, mammary, mammalian, carnivores, herbivorous (12); mantle, sedimentary (14); precarious, Eurasia, recession (15); domesticated (16); eons, silt, humus, impoverishment, moorings (18).

SUGGESTIONS FOR WRITING

1. In a few paragraphs, respond to Rettie's essay and give reasons for your reaction.
2. Write your own analogy to make some very large subject clear and vivid to readers — the changes wrought by the Industrial Revolution, for instance, or the possible effects of global warming, or problems of waste disposal. (If you need to, consult library sources for details.)
3. CONNECTIONS. Both James C. Rettie and Linnea Saukko (in "How to Poison the Earth," p. 314) address humans' destruction of the environment. Neither attacks directly, however: Saukko uses SATIRE and Rettie uses analogy to make a case. Compare and contrast the two essays in terms of this indirection: What does each author accomplish that a bolder attack might not? What does each author lose by not being direct? Which author's strategy is more effective, and why?

NEIL POSTMAN

A writer and teacher of communication arts and sciences, NEIL POSTMAN is also a well-known critic of education and the media. He was born in 1931 in Brooklyn, New York, and attended the State University of New York at Fredonia and Columbia University, earning a doctorate in education in 1958. Postman first gained a reputation as an education reformer with books such as *Teaching as a Subversive Activity* (1969) and *The Soft Revolution* (1971), both written with Charles Weingartner. He has written countless magazine articles and more than a dozen other books, including *The Disappearance of Childhood* (1982) and *Amusing Ourselves to Death: Public Discourse in the Age of Show Business* (1985). A professor at New York University, Postman has received awards for his teaching and writing, including the George Orwell Award for Clarity in Language.

The Parable of the
Ring around the Collar

This essay comes from Postman's latest collection, *Conscientious Objections: Stirring up Trouble about Language, Technology, and Education* (1988). In a note on the essay, Postman confesses that he is "close to obsessed about television, for it does not seem to me that my countrymen have yet taken its measure. We speak about America as if television has merely been added to it and little else has changed. . . . We have not yet reached the point where we watch ourselves watch it."

Television commercials are a form of religious literature. To comment on them in a serious vein is to practice hermeneutics, the branch of theology concerned with interpreting and explaining the Scriptures. This is what I propose to do here. The heathens, heretics, and unbelievers may move on to something else.

I do not claim, for a start, that every television commercial has religious content. Just as in church the pastor will sometimes call the congregation's attention to nonecclesiastical matters, so there are television commercials that are entirely secular. Someone has something to sell; you are told what it is, where it can be obtained, and what it costs. Though these may be shrill and offensive, no doctrine is advanced and no theology invoked.

But the majority of important television commercials take the form of religious parables organized around a coherent theology. Like all religious parables, they put forward a concept of sin, intimations of the way to redemption, and a vision of Heaven. They also suggest what are the roots of evil and what are the obligations of the holy. 3

Consider, for example, the Parable of the Ring around the Collar. This is to television scripture what the Parable of the Prodigal Son is to the Bible, which is to say it is an archetype containing most of the elements of form and content that recur in its genre. To begin with, the Parable of the Ring around the Collar is short, occupying only about thirty seconds of one's time and attention. There are three reasons for this, all obvious. First, it is expensive to preach on television; second, the attention span of the congregation is not long and is highly vulnerable to distraction; and third, a parable does not need to be long — tradition dictating that its narrative structure be tight, its symbols unambiguous, its explication terse. 4

The narrative structure of the Parable of the Ring around the Collar is, indeed, comfortably traditional. The story has a beginning, a middle, and an end. A married couple is depicted in some relaxed setting — a restaurant, say — in which they are enjoying each other's company and generally having a wonderful time. But then a waitress approaches their table, notices that the man has a dirty collar, stares at it boldly, sneers with cold contempt, and announces to all within hearing the nature of his transgression. The man is humiliated and glares at his wife with scorn, for she is the source of his shame. She, in turn, assumes an expression of self-loathing mixed with a touch of self-pity. This is the parable's beginning: the presentation of the problem. 5

The parable continues by showing the wife at home using a detergent that never fails to eliminate dirt around the collars of men's shirts. She proudly shows her husband what she is doing, 6 and he forgives her with an adoring smile. This is the parable's middle: the solution of the problem. Finally, we are shown the couple in a restaurant once again, but this time they are free of the waitress's probing eyes and bitter social chastisement. This is the parable's end: the moral, the explication, the exegesis. From this, we should draw the proper conclusion.

As in all parables, behind the apparent simplicity there are 7
some profound ideas to ponder. Among the most subtle and important is the notion of where and how problems originate. Embedded in every belief system there is an assumption about the root cause of evil from which the varieties of sinning take form. In science, for example, evil is represented in superstition. In psychoanalysis, we find it in early, neurotic transactions with our parents. In Christianity, it is located in the concept of Original Sin.

In television-commercial parables, the root cause of evil is 8
Technological Innocence, a failure to know the particulars of the beneficent accomplishments of industrial progress. This is the primary source of unhappiness, humiliation, and discord in life. And, as forcefully depicted in the Parable of the Ring, the consequences of technological innocence may strike at any time, without warning, and with the full force of their disintegrating action.

The sudden striking power of technological innocence is a 9
particularly important feature of television-commercial theology, for it is a constant reminder of the congregation's vulnerability. One must never be complacent or, worse, self-congratulatory. To attempt to live without technological sophistication is at all times dangerous, since the evidence of one's naïveté will always be painfully visible to the vigilant. The vigilant may be a waitress, a friend, a neighbor, or even a spectral figure — a holy ghost, as it were — who materializes in your kitchen, from nowhere, to give witness to your sluggardly ignorance.

Technological innocence refers not only to ignorance of de- 10
tergents, drugs, sanitary napkins, cars, salves, and foodstuffs, but also to ignorance of technical machinery such as savings banks and transportation systems. One may, for example, come upon one's neighbors while on vacation (in television-commercial parables, this is always a sign of danger) and discover that they have invested their money in a certain bank of whose special interest

rates you have been unaware. This is, of course, a moral disaster, and both you and your vacation are doomed.

As demonstrated in the Ring Parable, there is a path to re- 11 demption, but it can be entered only on two conditions. The first requires that you be open to advice or social criticism from those who are more enlightened. In the Ring Parable, the waitress serves the function of counselor, although she is, to be sure, exacting and very close to unforgiving. In some parables, the adviser is rather more sarcastic than severe. But in most parables, as for example in all sanitary napkin, mouthwash, shampoo, and aspirin commercials, the advisers are amiable and sympathetic, perhaps all too aware of their own vulnerability on other matters.

The Innocent are required to accept instruction in the spirit 12 in which it is offered. This cannot be stressed enough, for it instructs the congregation in two lessons simultaneously: One must be eager to accept advice, and just as eager to give it. Giving advice is, so to speak, the principal obligation of the holy. In fact, the ideal religious community may be depicted in images of dozens of people, each in his or her turn giving and taking advice on technological advances.

The second condition involves one's willingness to act on the 13 advice given. As in traditional Christian theology, it is not sufficient to hear the gospel or even preach it. One's understanding must be expressed in good works. In the Ring Parable, the once-pitiable wife acts almost immediately, and the Parable concludes by showing the congregation the effects of her action. In the Parable of the Person with Rotten Breath, of which there are several versions, we are shown a woman who, ignorant of the technological solution to her problem, is enlightened by a supportive roommate. The woman takes the advice without delay, with results we are shown in the last five seconds: a honeymoon in Hawaii. In the Parable of the Stupid Investor, we are shown a man who knows not how to make his money make money. Upon enlightenment, he acts swiftly and, at the parable's end, he is rewarded with a car, or a trip to Hawaii, or something approximating peace of mind.

Because of the compactness of commercial parables, the end- 14 ing — that is, the last five seconds — must serve a dual purpose. It is, of course, the moral of the story: If one will act in such a way, this will be the reward. But in being shown the result, we are also shown an image of Heaven. Occasionally, as in the Parable of the Lost Traveler's Checks, we are given a glimpse of Hell: Technological Innocents lost and condemned to eternal wandering far from their native land. But mostly we are given images of a Heaven both accessible and delicious: that is, a Heaven that is here, now, on earth, in America, and quite often in Hawaii.

But Hawaii is only a convenient recurring symbol. Heaven 15 can, in fact, materialize and envelop you anywhere. In the Parable of the Man Who Runs through Airports, Heaven is found at a car-rental counter to which the confounded Runner is shepherded by an angelic messenger. The expression of ecstasy on the Runner's face tells clearly that this moment is as close to transcendence as he can ever hope for.

Ecstasy is the key idea here, for commercial parables depict 16 the varieties of ecstasy in as much detail as you will find in any body of religious literature. At the conclusion of the Parable of the Spotted Glassware, a husband and wife assume such ecstatic countenances as can only be described by the word "beatification." Even in the Ring Parable, which at first glance would not seem to pose as serious a moral crisis as spotted glassware, we are shown ecstasy, pure and serene. And where ecstasy is, so is Heaven. Heaven, in brief, is any place where you have joined your soul with the Deity — the Deity, of course, being Technology.

Just when, as a religious people, we replaced our faith in tradi- 17 tional ideas of God with a belief in the ennobling force of Technology is not easy to say. Television commercials played no role in bringing about this transformation, but they reflect the change, document it, and amplify it. They constitute the most abundant literature we possess of our new spiritual commitment. That is why we have a solemn obligation to keep television commercials under the continuous scrutiny of hermeneutics.

QUESTIONS ON MEANING

1. State, in your own words, the THESIS of Postman's essay.
2. What is Postman's PURPOSE in the essay? Why has he chosen to analyze the ring-around-the-collar commercial?

3. What is a parable? Supplement Postman's definition (para. 3) with another from a dictionary.
4. How does the Technological Innocent find redemption?

QUESTIONS ON WRITING STRATEGY

1. What analogy is Postman drawing? Summarize the points of similarity Postman sees between his subjects.
2. What is the TONE of this essay? How does Postman achieve it?
3. Who are the "heathens, heretics, and unbelievers" Postman refuses to address? Whom does he want in his AUDIENCE?
4. OTHER METHODS. Postman's analogy depends on division or analysis (Chap. 6). What is he analyzing, and why?

QUESTIONS ON LANGUAGE

1. Why does Postman use so many long and difficult words? Look up any of these you are unfamiliar with: heathens, heretics (para. 1); nonecclesiastical (2); intimations, redemption (3); prodigal, archetype, genre, explication (4); transgression, self-loathing (5); chastisement, exegesis (6); neurotic (7); complacent, naïveté, spectral (9); amiable (11); transcendence (15); countenances, beatification (16); ennobling, scrutiny (17).
2. What is the EFFECT of the titles Postman gives the television parables?
3. Find examples of biblical-sounding language. What is its effect?

SUGGESTIONS FOR WRITING

1. Choose a television genre — a soap opera, news program, action series, situation comedy, or a type of public service announcement or commercial. Following Postman's example, explain by analogy the EFFECT you think it is intended to have on the viewer.
2. What do you think of Postman's essay? Do you, for instance, agree or disagree with Postman's specific analogy? Do you agree or disagree that commercials "played no role" in the transformation from belief in God to belief in Technology? Answer one of these questions or another of your own in an essay.
3. Find the Parable of the Prodigal Son in the Bible (Luke 15:11–32). Write an analysis of it using the structure and themes of a parable provided by Postman.
4. CONNECTIONS. If you haven't already done so, read Mark Crispin Miller's "Barbara Walters's Theater of Revenge" (p. 365) and his

comments on writing (p. 372). In an essay of your own, compare and contrast Miller's and Postman's essays as works of television criticism. Which do you find the more enlightening, and why? Support your opinions with quotations and PARAPHRASES from the authors' works.

NEIL POSTMAN ON WRITING

In his preface to *Conscientious Objections*, Neil Postman connects writing and geography. "The two best places for a writer to live," he says, "are America and Russia. Both are dynamic imperial powers prone to making mistakes. I should not like to live in Switzerland. Switzerland does not make mistakes, and therefore deprives a writer of grievances. For a writer, that society is best which is most burdensome. The favor is returned: For a society, that writer is best who is most burdensome."

Postman acknowledges the differences between the United States and the Soviet Union. Still, he contends that the differences do "nothing to change the fact that grievance is the source of all interesting prose. Without grievance, a writer tends to become a celebrant, which is an agreeable but repetitious state. After you have sung two choruses of 'God Bless America,' what else is there to say?

"I must hasten to add that though grievance is a necessary condition for good prose, it is far from sufficient. There are, after all, differences between a writer and a wimp. The differences are easier to notice than to describe, but we may at least say this: A good writer is a wimp who has found a unique and prudent form in which to say 'No.' I use the word *unique* to mean that the form is well suited to the nature of the writer, assuming the writer is sane. I use the word *prudent* to mean that the form is well suited to the nature of the grievance, assuming the grievance is sane."

Criticism should have a positive purpose, Postman believes. "Sometimes it is great fun to complain and, in America, it can even be profitable. But unless one's complaints are grounded in a sense of duty to one's country or to a recognizable humane tradition, they are not worthy of serious attention.

"Therefore," Postman concludes, "I write as a devoted patriot who wishes to celebrate the best by noticing the worst. Readers must decide if I've found a unique and prudent form in which to do this."

FOR DISCUSSION

1. What, according to Postman, are the elements of effective writing?
2. Do you agree with Postman that "grievance is the source of all interesting prose"?
3. What is Postman's conception of the relationship between a writer and the society in which he writes?

ADDITIONAL WRITING TOPICS

Analogy

1. Develop one of these topics by the method of analogy. (You might consider several of these topics, until one of them blooms into a bright idea for an analogy.)

   The behavior of a chemical element
   Watching late-night or morning television
   The body's circulatory system
   The way a rumor spreads
   The way a child learns to walk and talk
   What it's like to get behind in your schoolwork
   Becoming sure of yourself in a new situation
   Trying to understand a difficult concept
   Getting the job done through cooperation instead of competition
   Teaching worthwhile values to a child
   How violent crime intrudes on our lives
   Competition between the sexes
   Building character
   A crushing failure
   The brightest spot in your day
   Learning a new skill
   How your body fights germs
   Being a nonconformist
   Trying to get by without sufficient preparation
   Going into debt
   An allergic reaction
   The experience of unexpected happiness

2. In one meaty paragraph, set forth an analogy between practicing some activity you know well (dancing, playing basketball, climbing a mountain, running, sailing) and some other activity familiar to most people. Your purpose is to explain the nature of the activity to a reader unfamiliar with it. You might show, for example, how trying to sink a basket on a crowded court is like trying to buy a gift on Christmas Eve in a busy department store, or how climbing a mountain is like climbing many flights of cluttered stairs. If you like, you might explain some physical task (taking a photograph, diapering a baby, getting up in the morning, driving a motorcycle).

9
CAUSE AND EFFECT
Asking Why

THE METHOD

Press the button of a doorbell and, inside the house or apartment, chimes sound. Why? Because the touch of your finger on the button closed an electrical circuit. But why did you ring the doorbell? Because you were sent by your dispatcher: You are a bill collector calling on a customer whose payments are three months overdue.

The touch of your finger on the button is the *immediate cause* of the chimes: the event that precipitates another. That you were ordered by your dispatcher to go ring the doorbell is a *remote cause*: an underlying, more basic reason for the event, not apparent to an observer. Probably, ringing the doorbell will lead to some results: The door will open, and you may be given a check — or a kick in the teeth.

To figure out reasons and results is to use the method of *cause and effect*. You try to answer the question Why did something

479

happen? or the question What were the consequences? As part of answering either question, you use DIVISION or ANALYSIS (Chap. 6) to separate the flow of events into causes or effects.

Seeking causes, you can ask, for example, Why did guerrilla warfare erupt in El Salvador? For what reason or reasons do birds migrate? What has caused sales of Detroit-made cars to pick up (or decline) lately? Looking for effects, you can ask What have been the effects of the birth-control pill on the typical American family? What impact has the personal computer had on the nursing profession? You can look to a possible future and ask Of what use might a course in psychology be to me if I become an office manager? Suppose a new comet the size of Halley's were to strike Philadelphia — what would be the probable consequences? Essay exams in history and economics courses tend often to ask for either causes or effects: What were the principal causes of America's involvement in the war in Vietnam? What were the immediate effects on the world monetary system of Franklin D. Roosevelt's removing the United States from the gold standard?

Don't, by the way, confuse cause and effect with the method of process analysis (Chap. 5). Some process analysis essays, too, deal with happenings; but they focus more on *how* (not why) something happened. If you were explaining the process by which the doorbell rings, you might break the happening into stages — (1) the finger presses the button; (2) the circuit closes; (3) the current travels the wire; (4) the chimes make music — and you'd set forth the process in detail. But why did the finger press the button? What happened because the doorbell rang? To answer those questions, you need cause and effect.

Sometimes one event will appear to trigger another, and it in turn will trigger yet another, and another still, in an order we call a *causal chain*. A classic example of such a chain is set forth in a Mother Goose rhyme:

> For want of a nail the shoe was lost,
> For want of a shoe the horse was lost,
> For want of a horse the rider was lost,
> For want of a rider the battle was lost,
> For want of a battle the kingdom was lost —
> And all for the want of a nail.

In reality, causes are seldom so easy to find as that missing nail: They tend to be many and complicated. A battle may be lost for more than one reason. Perhaps the losing general had fewer soldiers, and had a blinding hangover the morning he mapped out his battle strategy. Perhaps winter set in, expected reinforcements failed to arrive, and a Joan of Arc inspired the winning army. The downfall of a kingdom is not to be explained as though it were the toppling of the last domino in a file. Still, one event precedes another in time, and in discerning causes you don't ignore chronological order; you pay attention to it.

In trying to account for some public event (a strike, say, or the outcome of an election), in trying to explain a whole trend in today's society (toward nonsmoking, or late marriage), you can expect to find a whole array of causes — interconnected, perhaps, like the strands of a spiderweb. You'll want to do an honest job of unraveling. This may take time. For a jury to acquit or convict an accused slayer, weeks of testimony from witnesses, detectives, and psychiatrists may be required, then days of deliberation. It took a great historian, Jakob Burckhardt, most of his lifetime to set forth a few reasons for the dawn of the Italian Renaissance. To be sure, juries must take great care when a life hangs in the balance; and Burckhardt, after all, was writing an immense book. To produce a college essay, you don't have forty years; but before you start to write, you will need to devote extra time and thought to seeing which facts are the causes, and which matter most.

To answer the questions Why? and What followed as a result? may sometimes be hard, but it can be satisfying — even illuminating. Indeed, to seek causes and effects is one way for the mind to discover order in a reality that otherwise might seem (as life came to seem to Macbeth) "a tale told by an idiot, full of sound and fury, signifying nothing."

THE PROCESS

In writing an essay that seeks causes or one that seeks effects, first make sure that your subject is manageable. Choose a subject you can get to the bottom of, given the time and information you have. For a 500-word essay due Thursday, the causes of teenage rebellion would be a more unwieldy topic than why a certain thirteen-year-old you know ran away from home. Excellent papers may be written on large subjects, and yet they may be written on smaller, more personal subjects as well. You can ask yourself, for instance, why you behaved in a certain way at a certain moment. You can examine the reasons for your current beliefs and attitudes. Such a paper might be rewarding: You might happen upon a truth you hadn't realized before. In fact, both you and your reader may profit from an essay that seeks causes along the lines of these: "Why I Espouse Nudism," or "Why I Quit College and Why I Returned." Such a paper, of course, takes thought. It isn't easy to research your own motivations. A thoughtful, personal paper that discerns *effects* might follow from a topic such as "Where Nudism Led Me" or "What Happened When I Quit College."

When seeking remote causes, look only as far back as necessary. Explaining why a small town has fallen on hard times, you might confine yourself to the immediate cause of the hardship: the closing of a factory. You might explain what caused the shutdown: a dispute between union and management. You might even go back to the cause of the dispute (announced firings) and the cause of the firings (loss of sales to a Japanese competitor). For a short essay, that might be far enough back in time to go; but if you were writing a whole book (*Pottsville in the 1990s: Its Glorious Past and Its Present Agony*), you might look to causes still more remote. You could trace the beginning of the decline of Pottsville back to the discovery, in Kyoto in 1845, of a better carrot grater. A manageable short paper showing effects might work in the other direction, moving from the factory closing to its impact on the town: unemployment, the closing of stores and the only movie house, people packing up and moving away.

When you can see a number of apparent causes, weigh them and assign each a relative importance. Which do you find matter most? Often, you will see that causes are more important or less so: *major* or *minor*. If Judd acquires a heavy drug habit and also takes up residence in a video arcade, and as a result finds himself penniless, it is probably safe to assume that the drug habit is the major cause of his going broke and his addiction to Tetris a minor one. If you were writing about his sad case, you'd probably emphasize the drug habit by giving it most of your space, perhaps touching on video games in a brief sentence.

You can plan out an essay by arranging events in chronological order (or in reverse order: from a recent event back to past events that cause it). If Judd drops out of college, the most immediate cause might be his inability to meet a tuition payment. But his lack of money might have a cause, too: his having earlier acquired a heavy drug habit. The cause of his addiction might be traced back further still: to a period of depression he suffered, and to an even earlier, more remote cause — the death of a friend in a car accident. In writing about him, you might begin with the accident, and then step by step work out its consequences; or you could begin with Judd's withdrawal from school, and trace a causal chain back to the accident.

In so doing beware of the logical fallacy "after this, therefore because of this" (in Latin, *post hoc, ergo propter hoc*) — that is, don't expect Event A to cause Event B just because A happened before B. This is the error of the superstitious man who decides that he lost his job because a black cat walked in front of him. Another error is to *oversimplify* causes by failing to recognize their full number and complexity — claiming, say, that violent crime is simply a result of "all those gangster shows on TV." Avoid such wrong turns in reasoning by patiently looking for evidence before you write, and by giving it careful thought. (For a fuller list of such LOGICAL FALLACIES, or errors in reasoning, see pages 614–616.)

To understand the deep-down causes of a person's act takes thought. Before you write, you can ask yourself a few searching questions. These have been suggested by the work of the literary critic Kenneth Burke. Burke asks (and answers) the questions in a complicated way, but for most practical purposes, before you write about the cause of a human act, ask yourself these five questions:

1. What act am I trying to explain?
2. What is the character, personality, or mental state of whoever acted?

3. In what scene or location did the act take place, and in what circumstances?
4. What instruments or means did the person use?
5. For what purpose did the person act?

Burke calls these elements a *pentad* (or set of five): the *act*, the *actor*, the *scene*, the *agency*, and the *purpose*. If you are trying to explain, for instance, why a person burned down a liquor shop, it will be revealing to ask about his character and mental state. Was the act committed by the shop's worried, debt-ridden owner? A mentally disturbed anti-alcohol crusader? A drunk who had been denied a purchase? The scene of the burning, too, might tell you something. Was the shop near a church, a mental hospital, or a fireworks factory? And what was the agency (or means of the act): a flaming torch or a flipped-away cigarette butt? To learn the purpose might be illuminating, whether it was to collect insurance on the shop, to get revenge, or to work what the actor believed to be the will of the Lord. You can further deepen your inquiry by seeing relationships between the terms of the pentad. Ask, for instance, what does the actor have to do with this scene? (Is he or she the preacher in the church across the street, who has been staring at the liquor shop resentfully for the past twenty years?).[1]

You can use Burke's pentad to help explain the acts of groups as well as those of individuals. Why, for instance, did the sophomore class revel degenerate into a brawl? Here are some possible answers:

1. *Act:* the brawl
2. *Actors:* the sophs were letting off steam after exams, and a mean, tense spirit prevailed

---

[1] If you are interested and care to explore the possibilities of Burke's pentad, you can pair up its five terms in ten different ways: act to actor, actor to scene, actor to agency, actor to purpose, act to scene, act to agency, act to purpose, scene to agency, scene to purpose, agency to purpose. This approach can go profoundly deep. We suggest you try writing ten questions (one for each pair) in the form, What does act have to do with actor? Ask them of some act you'd like to explain.

3. *Scene:* a keg-beer party outdoors in the quad at midnight on a
   sticky and hot May night
4. *Agencies:* fists and sticks
5. *Purpose:* the brawlers were seeking to punish whoever kicked
   over the keg

Don't worry if not all the questions apply, if not all the answers are immediately forthcoming. Bring the pentad to bear on
the sad case of Judd, and probably only the question about his
character and mental state would help you much. Even a single
hint, though, can help you write. Burke's pentad isn't meant to
be a grim rigmarole; it is a means of discovery, to generate a lot of
possible material for you — insights, observations, hunches to
pursue. It won't solve each and every human mystery, but sometimes it will helpfully deepen your thought.

In stating what you believe to be causes and effects, don't be
afraid to voice a well-considered hunch. Your instructor doesn't
expect you to write, in a short time, a definitive account of the
causes of an event or a belief or a phenomenon — only to write a
coherent and reasonable one. To discern all causes — including
remote ones — and all effects is beyond the power of any one human mind. Still, admirable and well-informed writers on matters
such as politics, economics, and world and national affairs are often canny guessers and brave drawers of inferences. At times,
even the most cautious and responsible writer has to leap boldly
over a void to strike firm ground on the far side. Consider your
evidence. Think about it hard. Look well before leaping. Then
take off.

CAUSE AND EFFECT IN A PARAGRAPH:
TWO ILLUSTRATIONS

Using Cause and Effect
to Write about Television

Why is it that, despite a growing interest in soccer among
American athletes, and despite its ranking as the most popular
sport in the world, commercial television ignores it? To see a
televised North American Soccer League game, you have to
tune at odd hours to public TV. Part of the reason stems from

the basic nature of network television, which exists not to inform and entertain but to sell. During most major sporting events on television — football, baseball, basketball, boxing — producers can take advantage of natural interruptions in the action to broadcast sales pitches; or, if the natural breaks occur too infrequently, the producers can contrive time-outs for the sole purpose of airing lucrative commercials. But soccer is played in two solid halves of forty-five minutes each; not even injury to a player is cause for a time-out. How, then, to insert the requisite number of commercial breaks without resorting to false fouls or other questionable tactics? After CBS aired a soccer match, on May 27, 1967, players reported, according to Stanley Frank, that before the game the referee had instructed them "to stay down every nine minutes." The resulting hue and cry rose all the way to the House Communications Subcommittee. From that day to this, no one has been able to figure out how to screen advertising jingles during a televised soccer game. The result is that the commercial networks have to treat the North American Soccer League as if it didn't exist.

COMMENT. In this paragraph, the writer seeks a cause and the opening sentence poses the Why? question to be answered. The middle portion of the paragraph explains one cause — that soccer, unlike other sports, is difficult to adapt to commercial television. The famous case reported by Frank shows what happened when, for a change, a soccer game was telecast, but was artificially orchestrated so as to allow blank moments for commercials. The cause *and* its effect are stated together in the concluding two sentences. Note how the writer illustrates generalizations with examples. The only unillustrated one is the statement that network TV exists for the purpose of selling things; and this seems an apparent truth we all know already.

Using Cause and Effect
in an Academic Discipline

Many factors played a role in Johnson's fateful decision. But the most obvious explanation is that the new president faced many pressures to expand the American involvement and only a very few to limit it. As the untested successor to a revered and martyred president, he felt obliged to prove his

worthiness for the office by continuing the policies of his prede-
cessor. Aid to South Vietnam had been one of the most prominent of those policies. Johnson also felt it necessary to retain in
his administration many of the important figures of the Kennedy years. In doing so, he surrounded himself with a group of
foreign policy advisers — Secretary of State Dean Rusk, Secretary of Defense Robert McNamara, National Security Adviser
McGeorge Bundy — who strongly believed not only that the
United States had an important obligation to resist communism in Vietnam, but that it possessed the ability and resources
to make that resistance successful. As a result, Johnson seldom
had access to information making clear how difficult the new
commitment might become. A compliant Congress raised little
protest to, and indeed at one point openly endorsed, Johnson's
use of executive powers to lead the nation into war. And for
several years at least, public opinion remained firmly behind
him — in part because Barry Goldwater's bellicose remarks
about the war during the 1964 campaign made Johnson seem
by comparison to be a moderate on the issue. Above all, intervention in South Vietnam was fully consistent with nearly
twenty years of American foreign policy. An anticommunist
ally was appealing to the United States for assistance; all the assumptions of the containment doctrine seemed to require the
nation to oblige. Johnson seemed unconcerned that the government of South Vietnam existed only because the United
States had put it there, and that the regime had never succeeded in acquiring the loyalty of its people. Vietnam, he believed, provided a test of American willingness to fight communist aggression, a test he was determined not to fail.

COMMENT. The ability both to probe causes and to discern effects is fundamental to the study of history, and both are apparent in this paragraph from the sixth edition of *American History:
A Survey*, by Richard N. Current and others (1983). The authors
examine a number of reasons for President Lyndon B. Johnson's
having escalated our country's involvement in Vietnam into
"a full-scale American war" during his first two years in the White
House. The TOPIC SENTENCE, coming right after the transitional
sentence that introduces the paragraph, makes clear the authors'
belief that not one but many causes resulted in this decision on
the part of the president. Succinctly, they list and explain them.

GORE VIDAL

GORE VIDAL was born in 1925 at the U.S. Military Academy at West Point, where his father was an instructor. At the age of nineteen, he wrote his first novel, *Williwaw* (1946), while serving as a warrant officer aboard an army supply ship. Among the later of his twenty-one novels are *Duluth* (1983), *Lincoln* (1984), *Empire* (1987), and *Hollywood* (1989). He has also written mysteries under the pen name Edgar Box. As a playwright, he is best known for *Visit to a Small Planet* (1957), which was made into a film. The grandson of Senator T. P. Gore, who represented Oklahoma for thirty years, Vidal himself entered politics in 1960 and 1982 as a candidate for Congress. A provocative and perceptive literary and social critic, Vidal is a frequent contributor of brilliant, opinionated essays to *The New York Review of Books* and other magazines, and he has published several collections of essays, most recently *At Home* (1988). Vidal divides his time between Italy and America.

Drugs

Vidal, whom some critics have called America's finest living essayist, first published "Drugs" in 1970 on the *New York Times*'s op-ed page (the page opposite the editorial page, reserved for diverse opinions). Vidal included the essay in *Homage to Daniel Shays: Collected Essays 1952–1972*. The essay addresses a problem that has worsened since it was first published. Lately, an increasing number of social scientists, medical professionals, and politicians have urged that we consider just such a radical solution as Vidal proposes. (For an opposing view, see A. M. Rosenthal's "The Case for Slavery," page 494.)

It is possible to stop most drug addiction in the United States 1
within a very short time. Simply make all drugs available and sell them at cost. Label each drug with a precise description of what effect — good and bad — the drug will have on the taker. This will require heroic honesty. Don't say that marijuana is addictive

or dangerous when it is neither, as millions of people know — unlike "speed," which kills most unpleasantly, or heroin, which is addictive and difficult to kick.

For the record, I have tried — once — almost every drug and liked none, disproving the popular Fu Manchu theory that a single whiff of opium will enslave the mind. Nevertheless many drugs are bad for certain people to take and they should be told why in a sensible way.

Along with exhortation and warning, it might be good for our citizens to recall (or learn for the first time) that the United States was the creation of men who believed that each man has the right to do what he wants with his own life as long as he does not interfere with his neighbor's pursuit of happiness. (That his neighbor's idea of happiness is persecuting others does confuse matters a bit.)

This is a startling notion to the current generation of Americans. They reflect a system of public education which has made the Bill of Rights, literally, unacceptable to a majority of high school graduates (see the annual Purdue reports) who now form the "silent majority" — a phrase which that underestimated wit Richard Nixon took from Homer who used it to describe the dead.

Now one can hear the warning rumble begin: If everyone is allowed to take drugs everyone will and the GNP will decrease, the Commies will stop us from making everyone free, and we shall end up a race of zombies, passively murmuring "groovy" to one another. Alarming thought. Yet it seems most unlikely that any reasonably sane person will become a drug addict if he knows in advance what addiction is going to be like.

Is everyone reasonably sane? No. Some people will always become drug addicts just as some people will always become alcoholics, and it is just too bad. Every man, however, has the power (and should have the legal right) to kill himself if he chooses. But since most men don't, they won't be mainliners either. Nevertheless, forbidding people things they like or think they might enjoy only makes them want those things all the more. This psychological insight is, for some mysterious reason, perennially denied our governors.

It is a lucky thing for the American moralist that our coun-   7
try has always existed in a kind of time-vacuum: We have no
public memory of anything that happened before last Tuesday.
No one in Washington today recalls what happened during the
years alcohol was forbidden to the people by a Congress that
thought it had a divine mission to stamp out Demon Rum —
launching, in the process, the greatest crime wave in the country's
history, causing thousands of deaths from bad alcohol, and creating a general (and persisting) contempt among the citizenry for
the laws of the United States.

The same thing is happening today. But the government has   8
learned nothing from past attempts at prohibition, not to mention repression.

Last year when the supply of Mexican marijuana was slightly   9
curtailed by the Feds, the pushers got the kids hooked on heroin
and deaths increased dramatically, particularly in New York.
Whose fault? Evil men like the Mafiosi? Permissive Dr. Spock?
Wild-eyed Dr. Leary? No.

The government of the United States was responsible for   10
those deaths. The bureaucratic machine has a vested interest in
playing cops and robbers. Both the Bureau of Narcotics and the
Mafia want strong laws against the sale and use of drugs because if
drugs are sold at cost there would be no money in it for anyone.

If there was no money in it for the Mafia, there would be no   11
friendly playground pushers, and addicts would not commit
crimes to pay for the next fix. Finally, if there was no money in it,
the Bureau of Narcotics would wither away, something they are
not about to do without a struggle.

Will anything sensible be done? Of course not. The Ameri-   12
can people are as devoted to the idea of sin and its punishment as
they are to making money — and fighting drugs is nearly as big a
business as pushing them. Since the combination of sin and
money is irresistible (particularly to the professional politician),
the situation will only grow worse.

QUESTIONS ON MEANING

1. How readily do you accept Vidal's statement that "each man has a right to do what he wants with his own life" — including, presumably, to be a drug addict — "as long as he does not interefere with his neighbor's pursuit of happiness" (para. 3)? Do you accept Vidal's implicit assumption that people with easy access to drugs are not necessarily threats to their neighbors? Back up you answers with EVIDENCE.
2. For what reasons, according to Vidal, is it unlikely that our drug laws will be eased? Can you suggest other possible reasons why the Bureau of Narcotics favors strict drug laws?
3. Vidal's essay was first published more than two decades ago. Do you find the views expressed in it still timely, or out of date?
4. What do you take to be Vidal's main PURPOSE in writing this essay? How well does he accomplish it?

QUESTIONS ON WRITING STRATEGY

1. How would you characterize Vidal's humor? Find some examples of it.
2. In paragraphs 9 and 10, Vidal asserts that the government of the United States caused heroin deaths among the young in New York. Is the author guilty of oversimplification? (See p. 483.)
3. Where in the essay does Vidal appear to anticipate the response of his AUDIENCE? How can you tell?
4. What function do the essay's RHETORICAL QUESTIONS perform?
5. OTHER METHODS. In paragraph 7, Vidal uses a historical analogy (Chap 8.) to strengthen his case. Spend enough time in the library to learn more about the era of Prohibition in the United States. To what extent does the evidence support Vidal's contention that Prohibition was a bad idea? To what extent are the events that took place during and after Prohibition relevant to the drug problem today?

QUESTIONS ON LANGUAGE

1. Know the definitions of the following terms: exhortation (para. 3); GNP (5); mainliners, perennially (6); curtailed (9).
2. How do you interpret Vidal's use of the phrase *underestimated wit* to describe Richard Nixon?

SUGGESTIONS FOR WRITING

1. Write several paragraphs in which you try to predict both the good and the ill effects you think might result from following Vidal's advice to "make all drugs available and sell them at cost."

2. Research the situation reported by Vidal in paragraphs 9 and 10. (Begin with the *New York Times Index* for the years 1969 and 1970.) Write an essay that clearly and objectively analyzes the causes of the situation.

3. CONNECTIONS. In an essay, compare Vidal's essay with A. M. Rosenthal's "The Case for Slavery" (p. 494). Focus especially on the main assertions of each — the advantages and disadvantages of drug legalization — and on the evidence each provides. Conclude with a statement, backed by reasons, about which essay you think is the more effective.

GORE VIDAL ON WRITING

"Do you find writing easy?" Gerald Clark asked Gore Vidal for the *Paris Review*. "Do you enjoy it?"

"Oh, yes, of course I enjoy it," he shot back. "I wouldn't do it if I didn't. Whenever I get up in the morning, I write for about three hours. I write novels in longhand on yellow pads, exactly like the First Criminal Nixon. For some reason I write plays and essays on the typewriter. The first draft usually comes rather fast. One oddity: I never reread a text until I have finished the first draft. Otherwise it's too discouraging. Also, when you have the whole thing in front of you for the first time, you've forgotten most of it and see it fresh. Rewriting, however, is a slow, grinding business.

"When I first started writing, I used to plan everything in advance, not only chapter to chapter but page to page. Terribly constricting — like doing a film from someone else's meticulous treatment. About the time of *The Judgment of Paris* [a novel published in 1952] I started improvising. I began with a mood. A sentence. The first sentence is all-important. [My novel] *Washington, D.C.* began with a dream, a summer storm at night in a garden above the Potomac — that was Merrywood, where I grew up.

"The most interesting thing about writing is the way that it obliterates time. Three hours seem like three minutes. Then there is the business of surprise. I never know what is coming next. The phrase that sounds in the head changes when it appears on the page. Then I start probing it with a pen, finding new meanings. Sometimes I burst out laughing at what is happening as I twist and turn sentences. Strange business, all in all. One never gets to the end of it. That's why I go on, I suppose. To see what the next sentences I write will be."

FOR DISCUSSION

1. What is it that Vidal seems to enjoy most about writing?
2. What advantage does he find in not planning every page in advance?

A. M. ROSENTHAL

ABRAHAM MICHAEL ROSENTHAL, born in 1922 in Ontario, Canada, came to the United States when he was four. His long association with the *New York Times* began in 1944. Since then, he has served the newspaper as correspondent at the United Nations and in India, Poland, Switzerland, and Japan; as managing editor; as executive editor; and currently as a regular columnist. The author of *38 Witnesses* (1964), Rosenthal also has written articles for the *New York Times Magazine*, *Saturday Evening Post*, and *Foreign Affairs*. In 1960 his reporting of international news won him a Pulitzer Prize.

The Case for Slavery

Like Gore Vidal's "Drugs" (p. 488), this essay was first published on the op-ed page of the *New York Times*. But there the similarity ends. Rosenthal's piece appeared in 1989, almost two decades after Vidal's, and it forcefully opposes what Vidal proposes.

Across the country, a scattered but influential collection of   1
intellectuals is intensely engaged in making the case for slavery.

With considerable passion, these Americans are repeatedly   2
expounding the benefits of not only tolerating slavery but legalizing it:

It would make life less dangerous for the free. It would save a   3
great deal of money. And since the economies could be used to improve the lot of the slaves, in the end they would be better off.

The new antiabolitionists, like their predecessors in the nine-   4
teenth century, concede that those now in bondage do not themselves see the benefits of legalizing their status.

But in time they will, we are assured, because the beautiful   5
part of legalization is that slavery would be designed so as to keep slaves pacified with the very thing that enslaves them!

The form of slavery under discussion is drug addiction. It   6
does not have every characteristic of more traditional forms of

bondage. But they have enough in common to make the comparison morally valid — and the campaign for drug legalization morally disgusting.

Like the plantation slavery that was a foundation of American society for so long, drug addiction largely involves specifiable groups of people. Most of the enchained are children and adolescents of all colors and black and Hispanic adults.   7

Like plantation slavery, drug addiction is passed on from generation to generation. And this may be the most important similarity: Like plantation slavery, addiction can destroy among its victims the social resources most valuable to free people for their own betterment — family life, family traditions, family values.   8

In plantation-time America, mothers were taken from their children. In drug-time America, mothers abandon their children. Do the children suffer less, or the mothers?   9

Antiabolitionists argue that legalization would make drugs so cheap and available that the profit for crime would be removed. Well-supplied addicts would be peaceful addicts. We would not waste billions for jails and could spend some of the savings helping the addicted become drug-free.   10

That would happen at the very time that new millions of Americans were being enticed into addiction by legalization — somehow.   11

Are we really foolish enough to believe that tens of thousands of drug gang members would meekly steal away, foiled by the marvels of the free market?   12

Not likely. The pushers would cut prices, making more money than ever from the ever-growing mass market. They would immediately increase the potency and variety beyond anything available at any government-approved narcotics counters.   13

Crime would increase. Crack produces paranoid violence. More permissiveness equals more use equals more violence.   14

And what will legalization do to the brains of Americans drawn into drug slavery by easy availability?   15

Earlier this year, an expert drug pediatrician told me that after only a few months babies born with crack addiction seemed to recover. Now we learn that stultifying behavioral effects last at least through early childhood. Will they last forever?   16

How long will crack affect neurological patterns in the brains 17
of adult crack users? Dr. Gabriel G. Nahas of Columbia University argues in his new book, *Cocaine: The Great White Plague*,
that the damage may be irreversible. Would it not be an act of
simple intelligence to drop the legalization campaign until we find
out?

Then why do a number of writers and academicians, left to 18
right, support it? I have discussed this with antidrug leaders like
Jesse Jackson, Dr. Mitchell Rosenthal of Phoenix House, and William J. Bennett, who search for answers themselves.

Perhaps the answer is that the legalizers are not dealing with 19
reality in America. I think the reason has to do with class.

Crack is beginning to move into the white middle and upper 20
classes. That is a tragedy for those addicted.

However, it has not yet destroyed the communities around 21
which their lives revolve, not taken over every street and doorway. It has not passed generation to generation among them, killing the continuity of family.

But in ghetto communities poverty and drugs come together 22
in a catalytic reaction that is reducing them to social rubble.

The antiabolitionists, virtually all white and well-to-do, do 23
not see or do not care. Either way they show symptoms of the callousness of class. That can be a particularly dangerous social disorder.

QUESTIONS ON MEANING

1. On what grounds does Rosenthal claim that the analogy between
   drug addiction and slavery is valid? (See Chapter 8 if you need a refresher in analogy.) How does he say the two are alike?
2. Rosenthal records two sets of possible results from the legalization of
   drugs: one from those who favor legalization, the other his own.
   Summarize the two sides.
3. Explain what Rosenthal means when he says that support of drug
   legalization "has to do with class" (para. 19).
4. What is Rosenthal's PURPOSE in writing this essay? Does he fulfill it?

QUESTIONS ON WRITING STRATEGY

1. Would you say Rosenthal is more interested in the causes and effects of drug addiction or in the causes and effects of the legalization argument? Why?
2. When does Rosenthal first introduce his topic? Why does he delay it so long?
3. Analyze the TONE of this essay. Why do you think Rosenthal takes this tone?
4. On what EVIDENCE does Rosenthal's argument principally depend? Is his evidence adequate?
5. **OTHER METHODS.** Rosenthal uses cause and effect to further an argument (Chap. 11). Examine the APPEALS he relies on: are they more rational or emotional? Find examples of each.

QUESTIONS ON LANGUAGE

1. What does Rosenthal achieve by repeatedly calling drug legalization advocates "antiabolitionists"?
2. Typically for newspaper writers, Rosenthal uses very short paragraphs, some only a sentence. In a newspaper's narrow columns, this approach keeps paragraphs short. What is its EFFECT in the wider columns of a book? As an exercise, connect related paragraphs of Rosenthal's into larger paragraphs.
3. Consult your dictionary for the meanings of any unfamiliar words: expounding (para. 2); concede, predecessors (4); pacified (5); specifiable, enchained (7); enticed (11); foiled (12); paranoid (14); stultifying (16); irreversible (17); academicians (18); catalytic (22); callousness (23).

SUGGESTIONS FOR WRITING

1. Analyze Rosenthal's analogy between drug addiction and slavery and, by extension, between legalization and antiabolition. (See Chapter 8 if you need help with analogies.) In your analysis, go beyond Rosenthal to spell out all the similarities and the dissimilarities you can see. Be specific.
2. Choose a controversy that you know something about — it could be local (a college issue such as parking regulations, financial aid, or race relations), national (tax increases, bilingual education), or international (global warming, human rights violations). Take issue with

one side in the controversy by analyzing the possible effects of the position.

3. CONNECTIONS. After reading Gore Vidal's "Drugs" (p. 488) and Rosenthal's "The Case for Slavery," write an essay in which you take sides for or against the legalization of drugs. You may argue from your own experience and observations, using Vidal or Rosenthal as a backup, or you could do some library research to test, extend, and support your opinions.

A. M. ROSENTHAL ON WRITING

In "Learning on the Job," a memoir of his forty years as a newspaper reporter and editor, A. M. Rosenthal has recalled a lesson he learned at the start of his career. "The very first day I was on the job as a reporter — a real reporter, with a press card in my pocket and a light in my heart — I learned all about the First Amendment. It was a Saturday and I was sitting in the *Times*'s newsroom when an assistant editor walked over, told me that there had been a murder or a suicide at the Mayflower Hotel in midtown, and why didn't I go over and see what it was all about. Yes, sir! I rushed out, jumped on a bus, got to the hotel, asked an elevator operator where the trouble was. Ninth floor, he told me, and up I went. A push of the buzzer and the door opened. Standing there was a police detective. He was twelve and a half feet tall. I started to walk in and he put his hand into my face. That hand was just a bit larger than a basketball.

" 'Where are you going, kid?' he said.

" 'I'm a reporter,' I said. '*Times*. I want to see the body.'

"He looked at me, up and down, slowly. 'Beat it,' he proposed.

"Beat it? I hadn't realized anybody talked to *Times* reporters that way. I knew there had to be some misunderstanding. So I smiled, pulled out my press card, and showed it to him. He took it, read it carefully front and back, handed it back, and said: 'Shove it in your ear.'

"Shove it in my ear? I could not comprehend what was taking place. 'But I'm from the *Times*,' I explained. 'A reporter from the *New York Times*. Don't you want me to get the story right?'

" 'Listen, Four Eyes,' he said, 'I don't care if you drop dead.' Then he slammed the door in my face and there I stood, staring at that door. I slunk off to a pay phone in the lobby and called the special reporters' number that had been confided to me — LAckawanna 4-1090, I've never forgotten it — and confessed to the clerk on the city desk that I had not only been unable to crack the case but had never even seen the corpse.

" 'Don't worry about it kid,' he said. 'We got it already from the A.P.[1] They called the police headquarters and got the story. Come on in.'

"Right there at the Mayflower I learned my first lesson about the First Amendment. The First Amendment means I have the right to ask anybody any question I wish. And anybody has the right to tell me to shove it in my ear. I have been involved in First Amendment cases for more than twenty years, but when I began as a reporter I was not answering any call to protect and defend the Constitution of the United States. I was not even thinking about the Constitution of the United States. All I was thinking about was the pleasure and joy of newspapering, of the wonderful zest of being able to run around, see things, find out what was going on, write about it. . . . That was what the newspaper business meant to me then and mostly still does — the delight of discovery, the exhilaration of writing a story and the quick gratification of seeing it in the paper; ink, ink, ink, even if it does rub off on your fingers just a tiny bit.

"We newspaper people are given to talking and writing about journalistic philosophy and I certainly have done my share. . . . But newspapering is not a philosophy, it is a way of spending a lifetime, and most of us in it know that if you really don't love it, love the whole mixture of searching, finding, and telling, love the strange daily rhythm where you have to climb higher and higher during the day instead of slackening off as the day goes on as normal people do, if you don't have a sensation of apprehension when you set out to find a story and a swagger when you sit down to write it, you are in the wrong business. You can make

---

[1]Associated Press. — EDS.

more money as a dentist and cops won't tell you to shove it in your ear."

FOR DISCUSSION

1. What is the First Amendment to the Constitution and exactly what did Rosenthal learn about it?
2. What aspects of being a reporter have the greatest appeal for Rosenthal?
3. As Rosenthal recounts the joys of a reporter's life, he also reveals, directly or indirectly, some of the disadvantages. What are they?

JOHN ROCKWELL

JOHN ROCKWELL is a music critic and writer with an unusually wide range of interests, from opera to contemporary rock, from electronic jazz to Latin American salsa. Born in 1940 in Washington, D.C., Rockwell earned a B.A. from Harvard and an M.A. and Ph.D. from the University of California at Berkeley. His studies were in cultural history, placing music in a broader perspective, and throughout graduate school he wrote about music for the broadcast and print media. Since 1974 he has been a music critic at the *New York Times*. His publications include contributions to works on John Lennon, rock music history, the classical composer Virgil Thomson, and the performance artist Laurie Anderson; the books *All American Music: Composition in the Late Twentieth Century* (1983) and *Sinatra: An American Classic* (1984); and articles in *Rolling Stone*, *Esquire*, *Opera News*, and other periodicals.

Why Rock Remains the Enemy

Rock-and-roll music is not quite the target now that it once was, when, for instance, a national television show would broadcast Elvis Presley only from the waist up. But rock music does not go unnoticed either. In this essay from the January 21, 1990, *New York Times*, Rockwell analyzes the causes of rock's continued bad image.

Those who fret that rock is dead — which usually means that 1 the music they grew up with has been supplanted by something younger folk like — might take comfort in its continued ostracism. On the theory that anything continually attacked must have some life left in it, rock seems very much alive.

Rock's commercial triumph, to be sure, is nearly absolute. It 2 swamps the airwaves, to the pain of lovers of most other kinds of music. It dominates record sales, muscling out jazz and folk and classical product in all but the largest record stores. Except for a few musty bastions like the "Tonight Show" band and the occasional cable or Public Broadcasting Service offering, it defines the music heard on television.

But one can still speak of its patronizing dismissal or worse by the adult mainstream, meaning the guardians of our moral and political and cultural life. From the conservative Parents' Music Resource Center and liberal moralists' attempts to "educate" consumers on rock lyrics' sexual or racial wickedness to the Australian conductor and arts advocate Denis Vaughan warning Britons this month that their country's social ills could be cured by more classical music, there is still a chorus cautioning against rock's dangers.

Mind you, 'twas ever so, and so before rock was even born. Just recently I heard a clever chamber opera by Robert Xavier Rodriguez called "Tango" (1985), whose text consisted of news reports and denunciations, most of them clerical, of the civilization-ending evils of that Argentine dance. Of course, when you think about it, the tango craze took place in 1913 and 1914, and starting in 1914 came a world war that almost *did* end Western civilization.

Then again, that was was triggered by the establishment, not the tango dancers. And those moralists seem ever eager to lambaste rock as the supposed cause of social phenomena that far transcend even music's mighty powers. Elvis and the Beatles didn't unleash the youth rebellions of the 1960s, except maybe for a few short-term disturbances. They were more like Hegelian Silver Surfers, riding the wave of historical destiny.[1]

Mr. Vaughan's fulminations appear in the January issue of that impeccably serious, not to say slightly stuffy, English monthly *The Musical Times*. Although he throws in lip service about liking "some" rock music and about the need for a diversity of musical experience, his notion that rock amplifications and rhythm machines lead inexorably to "a state of complete mental stupor — drugged, numbed, and impervious to feeling" — seems

[1]Rockwell alludes to the theories of Georg Friedrich Wilhelm Hegel (1770–1831), a German philosopher who maintained that history is a dynamic process involving the continual resolution of conflicts toward the realization of human reason and liberty. — EDS.

overwrought at best. And his statements that rock's back beat is "unnatural" and hence injurious to human physiognomy and psyche, or that rock singing is based "albeit unwittingly" on the sound of "lustful ejaculation," approach the kinky.

But my concern here is not for silliness or for repression in the name of moralism. It is to consider why rock still inspires such attacks, in this age when it is supposed to have long since lost its revolutionary bite.   7

One reason is sex. Sex scares a lot of people, and rock and indeed most popular music of this liberated era has been about sex, from the waltz and cancan in the nineteenth century to the tango and the Charleston and the twist right down to the pelvis-grinding lambada of today.   8

Another closely related reason is youth, which tends to practice sex with more enthusiasm and less caution than most other segments of society. Censors scared of curtailing art for adults can justify their censorious urges when the issue of child protection is introduced. Being against child protection is like being for wife beating: it's moralistically inconceivable.   9

Then there's the question of volume, and indeed amplification of any sort. Proponents of most kinds of unamplified or lightly amplified music object to rock's volume, and in the case of musicians and fans who stand for hours daily in front of megaloudspeakers, they have a point, insofar as ear damage is concerned. But they cannot logically argue that volume desensitizes the emotions if they also say that rock fires up the libido.   10

Another source of prejudice is rock's nasty habit of making money. A distinction has persisted between artistic music that confirms its nobility by its inability to attract enough of a public to pay for it, and commercial music that proves its corruption by its very popularity. This distinction derives from religious and Marxist moralists alike, the latter led by Theodor W. Adorno and the Frankfurt School of philosophers, who were implacable in their opposition to popular music.   11

Such a prejudice ignores three things: One, that moneymaking music may indeed speak to the true musical desires of the broader public, rather than to what the Frankfurt School considered tastes perverted by exposure to capitalist promotion and im-   12 age manipulation. Two, that popular music is a social form like church music or academic contemporary music, with composers paid for product. And three, that rock itself now has all manner of marginally commercial or noncommercial subcultures. Among art rockers, in the wake of the Velvet Underground, a sense of self-conscious artistry has by now long since evolved, as happened with the rise of Romantic composers after Beethoven in classical music and with the advent of bop in jazz three decades ago.

The real fear inspired by rock is the fear so many moralists 13 have felt for music per se, from Plato (who wanted it strictly regulated in his Republic) to early Roman Catholic church fathers. Some moralists want music curtailed or eliminated; others — above all, Protestants from Martin Luther to today's gospel-singing Baptists and Pentecostals — hope to harness it to the faith. But they resist letting it speak with its own, or worse yet the devil's voice.

A lot of the subtler, less vocal opposition to rock comes from 14 simple generational or class disdain. Carnegie Hall has been the site of all sorts of important rock events, like the Beatles' first concerts in this country. But the current guardians of that hall, in planning for its centennial season starting this summer [1990], have ignored rock in favor of classical music, with token jazz and folk music. A similar pattern prevails at the National Endowment for the Arts.

Is this a cause for outrage, anger, and protest? Only if you 15 think rock's salvation lies in a welcoming recognition by the very forces it has always fought. The pop-music business has always tended toward innocuous romantic platitudes. Rock has been and continues to be different: a deliberately rude, attitude-striking attestation of generational ideals and desires.

While the slow embrace of rock by the academic and grant- 16 giving establishment is inevitable and on many levels welcome, that embrace won't necessarily be all for the good. It will mark the final subversion of rock's revolutionary impulses: Kiss and kill, one might say. But not to worry: The human need for aggressive, liberating music is eternal. If it's not military marches, it's Beethoven symphonies; if it's not rock-and-roll, it will be something else, equally exciting and equally annoying.

QUESTIONS ON MEANING

1. What is Rockwell's THESIS? Is it stated?
2. Summarize in your own words the main causes of the continued attacks on rock music.
3. What do you take to be Rockwell's opinion of censorship?
4. Why is Rockwell unconcerned about the establishment's eventual acceptance of rock music?

QUESTIONS ON WRITING STRATEGY

1. What do you make of Rockwell's TONE in the essay? How is it related to his CONCLUSION?
2. Explain the relationship of cause and effect in the essay. What causes are Rockwell concerned with? What effects?
3. What does the author assume about his AUDIENCE's attitudes toward and knowledge of music? Does he write for a general reader?
4. OTHER METHODS. Rockwell's essay uses many examples (Chap. 3) but none of contemporary rock music that has been attacked. Why do you think the writer omits such examples?

QUESTIONS ON LANGUAGE

1. Is Rockwell making fun of Vaughan's opinions in *The Musical Times* (para. 6)? What words or phrases support your answer?
2. What do you think of the author's definition of rock in paragraph 15? Is Rockwell a rock fan?
3. Look up the meanings of any unfamiliar words in this list: ostracism (para. 1); musty, bastions (2); patronizing (3); denunciation, lambaste (5); fulminations, impeccably, inexorably, impervious, physiognomy, albeit (6); censorious (9); proponents (10).

SUGGESTIONS FOR WRITING

1. What other elements of popular culture are dismissed by "the adult mainstream"? Perhaps a style of clothing, a dance, a hairstyle, a form of SLANG, a type of movie? Choose one of these or another of your own and write an essay analyzing the causes of its dismissal.
2. Rockwell appears not to agree with "the guardians of our moral and political and cultural life" who would ban music or restrict lyrics

(para. 3). Write an essay on this subject: Do you think certain kinds of music or lyrics should be banned? Which kinds? Why, or why not?

3. Write an essay on a form of art or entertainment that means a lot to you. It could be rock music but need not be. Analyze the causes and effects of your feelings. Be specific: Give examples.

4. CONNECTIONS. Like Rockwell, Fran Lebowitz also discusses music, in "The Sound of Music: Enough Already" (p. 394). But the two authors' attitudes are quite different. Write a brief essay in which, imitating Lebowitz, you respond to Rockwell's implication that rock music is alive and exciting because it is "deliberately rude."

JOHN ROCKWELL ON WRITING

For the reference book *Contemporary Authors*, the interviewer Jean W. Ross asked John Rockwell if he found it especially difficult to write clearly for the general reader. It's his preference, he replied. "In my opinion, an intellectual (which I flatter myself to be) who chooses to work in journalism is making, whether he knows it or not — and I know it — a populist statement: We live in a democracy, and to write journalism means to make a deliberate attempt to purge oneself of obscurantism. I think journalism at its best is a very healthy way of doing that: It's a way of purging yourself of writer's block, because there are deadlines, and it's a way of purging yourself of prolixity, because there are space limitations."

Ross also asked Rockwell whether having to write about a musical performance detracted from his enjoyment of it. "Not at all," Rockwell answered; "quite the reverse. I find at this point that if I go to a concert just because I'm interested in going, but I'm not writing about it, the experience seems incomplete. To formulate an opinion in my own mind and then to articulate it in the course of actually writing out the review is to me the fulfillment of the experience of going to the concert. Therefore, just to go on my own — although I do fairly often — is sort of a strange half-experience."

FOR DISCUSSION

1. What does Rockwell mean that "to purge oneself of obscurantism" and "prolixity" is to make "a populist statement"?
2. How do you think writing might complete Rockwell's experience of a concert? Have you ever experienced a similar effect from writing about something?

STEPHEN JAY GOULD

A paleontologist and collector of snails, STEPHEN JAY GOULD was born in New York City in 1941, went to Antioch College, and took a doctorate from Columbia University. Since the age of twenty-five, Gould has taught biology, geology, and the history of science at Harvard, where his courses are among the most popular. Although he has written for specialists (*Ontogeny and Phylogeny*, 1977), Gould is best known for essays that explore science in prose a layperson can enjoy. He writes a monthly column (called "This View of Life") for *Natural History* magazine, and these and other essays have been collected in *Ever Since Darwin* (1977), *The Panda's Thumb* (1980), *Hens' Teeth and Horses' Toes* (1983), *The Flamingo's Smile* (1985), and *An Urchin in the Storm* (1987). In 1981, Gould received $200,000 (popularly called a "genius grant") from the MacArthur Foundation, which subsidizes the work of original artists and thinkers. His latest book is *Wonderful Life: The Burgess Shale and the Nature of History* (1989).

Sex, Drugs, Disasters, and the Extinction of Dinosaurs

In this essay, Stephen Jay Gould tackles one of the greatest mysteries in the evolution of life on this planet: the extinction of dinosaurs. Working backward from this concrete effect (the fact that dinosaurs are extinct), Gould employs both scholarship and wit to analyze several possible causes. The essay originally appeared in *Discover* magazine in March 1984, and it is included in Gould's fourth collection of essays, *The Flamingo's Smile: Reflections in Natural History* (1985).

Science, in its most fundamental definition, is a fruitful mode 1
of inquiry, not a list of enticing conclusions. The conclusions are the consequence, not the essence.

My greatest unhappiness with most popular presentations of 2
science concerns their failure to separate fascinating claims from the methods that scientists use to establish the facts of nature.

Journalists, and the public, thrive on controversial and stunning statements. But science is, basically, a way of knowing — in P. B. Medawar's apt words, "the art of the soluble." If the growing corps of popular science writers would focus on *how* scientists develop and defend those fascinating claims, they would make their greatest possible contribution to public understanding.

Consider three ideas, proposed in perfect seriousness to explain that greatest of all titillating puzzles — the extinction of dinosaurs. Since these three notions invoke the primally fascinating themes of our culture — sex, drugs, and violence — they surely reside in the category of fascinating claims. I want to show why two of them rank as silly speculation, while the other represents science at its grandest and most useful.

Science works with testable proposals. If, after much compilation and scrutiny of data, new information continues to affirm a hypothesis, we may accept it provisionally and gain confidence as further evidence mounts. We can never be completely sure that a hypothesis is right, though we may be able to show with confidence that it is wrong. The best scientific hypotheses are also generous and expansive: They suggest extensions and implications that enlighten related, and even far distant, subjects. Simply consider how the idea of evolution has influenced virtually every intellectual field.

Useless speculation, on the other hand, is restrictive. It generates no testable hypothesis, and offers no way to obtain potentially refuting evidence. Please note that I am not speaking of truth or falsity. The speculation may well be true; still, if it provides, in principle, no material for affirmation or rejection, we can make nothing of it. It must simply stand forever as an intriguing idea. Useless speculation turns in on itself and leads nowhere; good science, containing both seeds for its potential refutation and implications for more and different testable knowledge, reaches out. But, enough preaching. Let's move on to dinosaurs, and the three proposals for their extinction.

1. *Sex.* Testes function only in a narrow range of temperature (those of mammals hang externally in a scrotal sac because internal body temperatures are too high for their proper function). A worldwide rise in temperature at the close of the

Cretaceous period caused the testes of dinosaurs to stop functioning and led to their extinction by sterilization of males.

2. *Drugs.* Angiosperms (flowering plants) first evolved toward the end of the dinosaurs' reign. Many of these plants contain psychoactive agents, avoided by mammals today as a result of their bitter taste. Dinosaurs had neither means to taste the bitterness nor livers effective enough to detoxify the substances. They died of massive overdoses.

3. *Disasters.* A large comet or asteroid struck the earth some 65 million years ago, lofting a cloud of dust into the sky and blocking sunlight, thereby suppressing photosynthesis and so drastically lowering world temperatures that dinosaurs and hosts of other creatures became extinct.

Before analyzing these three tantalizing statements, we must establish a basic ground rule often violated in proposals for the dinosaurs' demise. *There is no separate problem of the extinction of dinosaurs.* Too often we divorce specific events from their wider contexts and systems of cause and effect. The fundamental fact of dinosaur extinction is its synchrony with the demise of so many other groups across a wide range of habitats, from terrestrial to marine.

The history of life has been punctuated by brief episodes of mass extinction. A recent analysis by University of Chicago paleontologists Jack Sepkoski and Dave Raup, based on the best and most exhaustive tabulation of data ever assembled, shows clearly that five episodes of mass dying stand well above the "background" extinctions of normal times (when we consider all mass extinctions, large and small, they seem to fall in a regular 26-million-year cycle). The Cretaceous debacle, occurring 65 million years ago and separating the Mesozoic and Cenozoic eras of our geological time scale, ranks prominently among the five. Nearly all the marine plankton (single-celled floating creatures) died with geological suddenness; among marine invertebrates, nearly 15 percent of all families perished, including many previously dominant groups, especially the ammonites (relatives of squids in coiled shells). On land, the dinosaurs disappeared after more than 100 million years of unchallenged domination.

In this context, speculations limited to dinosaurs alone ignore   7
the larger phenomenon. We need a coordinated explanation for a
system of events that includes the extinction of dinosaurs as one
component. Thus it makes little sense, though it may fuel our desire to view mammals as inevitable inheritors of the earth, to
guess that dinosaurs died because small mammals ate their eggs (a
perennial favorite among untestable speculations). It seems most
unlikely that some disaster peculiar to dinosaurs befell these massive beasts — and that the debacle happened to strike just when
one of history's five great dyings had enveloped the earth for completely different reasons.

The testicular theory, an old favorite from the 1940s, had its   8
root in an interesting and thoroughly respectable study of temperature tolerances in the American alligator, published in the
staid *Bulletin of the American Museum of Natural History* in 1946
by three experts on living and fossil reptiles — E. H. Colbert,
my own first teacher in paleontology; R. B. Cowles; and C. M.
Bogert.

The first sentence of their summary reveals a purpose beyond   9
alligators: "This report describes an attempt to infer the reactions
of extinct reptiles, especially the dinosaurs, to high temperatures
as based upon reactions observed in the modern alligator." They
studied, by rectal thermometry, the body temperatures of alligators under changing conditions of heating and cooling. (Well,
let's face it, you wouldn't want to try sticking a thermometer under a 'gator's tongue.) The predictions under test go way back to
an old theory first stated by Galileo in the 1630s — the unequal
scaling of surfaces and volumes. As an animal, or any object,
grows (provided its shape doesn't change), surface areas must increase more slowly than volumes — since surfaces get larger as
length squared, while volumes increase much more rapidly, as
length cubed. Therefore, small animals have high ratios of surface
to volume, while large animals cover themselves with relatively
little surface.

Among cold-blooded animals lacking any physiological   10
mechanism for keeping their temperatures constant, small creatures have a hell of a time keeping warm — because they lose so
much heat through their relatively large surfaces. On the other
hand, large animals, with their relatively small surfaces, may lose

heat so slowly that, once warm, they may maintain effectively constant temperatures against ordinary fluctuations of climate. (In fact, the resolution of the "hot-blooded dinosaur" controversy that burned so brightly a few years back may simply be that, while large dinosaurs possessed no physiological mechanism for constant temperature, and were not therefore warm-blooded in the technical sense, their large size and relatively small surface area kept them warm.)

Colbert, Cowles, and Bogert compared the warming rates of small and large alligators. As predicted, the small fellows heated up (and cooled down) more quickly. When exposed to a warm sun, a tiny 50-gram (1.76-ounce) alligator heated up one degree Celsius every minute and a half, while a large alligator, 260 times bigger at 13,000 grams (28.7 pounds), took seven and a half minutes to gain a degree. Extrapolating up to an adult 10-ton dinosaur, they concluded that a one-degree rise in body temperature would take eighty-six hours. If large animals absorb heat so slowly (through their relatively small surfaces), they will also be unable to shed any excess heat gained when temperatures rise above a favorable level.

The authors then guessed that large dinosaurs lived at or near their optimum temperatures; Cowles suggested that a rise in global temperatures just before the Cretaceous extinction caused the dinosaurs to heat up beyond their optimal tolerance — and, being so large, they couldn't shed the unwanted heat. (In a most unusual statement within a scientific paper, Colbert and Bogert then explicitly disavowed this speculative extension of their empirical work on alligators.) Cowles conceded that this excess heat probably wasn't enough to kill or even to enervate the great beasts, but since testes often function only within a narrow range of temperature, he proposed that this global rise might have sterilized all the males, causing extinction by natural contraception.

The overdose theory has recently been supported by UCLA psychiatrist Ronald K. Siegel. Siegel has gathered, he claims, more than 2,000 records of animals who, when given access, administer various drugs to themselves — from a mere swig of alcohol to massive doses of the big H. Elephants will swill the equivalent of twenty beers at a time, but do not like alcohol in concentrations greater than 7 percent. In a silly bit of anthropo-centric speculation, Siegel states that "elephants drink, perhaps, to forget . . . the anxiety produced by shrinking rangeland and the competition for food."

Since fertile imaginations can apply almost any hot idea to 14 the extinction of dinosaurs, Siegel found a way. Flowering plants did not evolve until late in the dinosaurs' reign. These plants also produced an array of aromatic, amino-acid-based alkaloids — the major group of psychoactive agents. Most mammals are "smart" enough to avoid these potential poisons. The alkaloids simply don't taste good (they are bitter); in any case, we mammals have livers happily supplied with the capacity to detoxify them. But, Siegel speculates, perhaps dinosaurs could neither taste the bitter-ness nor detoxify the substances once ingested. He recently told members of the American Psychological Association: "I'm not suggesting that all dinosaurs OD'd on plant drugs, but it certainly was a factor." He also argued that death by overdose may help ex-plain why so many dinosaur fossils are found in contorted posi-tions. (Do not go gentle into that good night.)

Extraterrestrial catastrophes have long pedigrees in the popu- 15 lar literature of extinction, but the subject exploded again in 1979, after a long lull, when the father-son, physicist-geologist team of Luis and Walter Alvarez proposed that an asteroid, some 10 km in diameter, struck the earth 65 million years ago (comets, rather than asteroids, have since gained favor. Good science is self-corrective).

The force of such a collision would be immense, greater by far 16 than the megatonnage of all the world's nuclear weapons. In try-ing to reconstruct a scenario that would explain the simultaneous dying of dinosaurs on land and so many creatures in the sea, the Alvarezes proposed that a gigantic dust cloud, generated by parti-cles blown aloft in the impact, would so darken the earth that photosynthesis would cease and temperatures drop precipitously. (Rage, rage against the dying of the light.) The single-celled pho-tosynthetic oceanic plankton, with life cycles measured in weeks, would perish outright, but land plants might survive through the dormancy of their seeds (land plants were not much affected by the Cretaceous extinction, and any adequate theory must account for the curious pattern of differential survival). Dinosaurs would die by starvation and freezing; small, warm-blooded mammals, with more modest requirements for food and better regulation of body temperature, would squeak through. "Let the bastards freeze in the dark," as bumper stickers of our chauvinistic neighbors in sunbelt states proclaimed several years ago during the Northeast's winter oil crisis.

All three theories, testicular malfunction, psychoactive overdosing, and asteroidal zapping, grab our attention mightily. As pure phenomenology, they rank about equally high on any hit parade of primal fascination. Yet one represents expansive science, the others restrictive and untestable speculation. The proper criterion lies in evidence and methodology; we must probe behind the superficial fascination of particular claims.   17

How could we possibly decide whether the hypothesis of testicular frying is right or wrong? We would have to know things that the fossil record cannot provide. What temperatures were optimal for dinosaurs? Could they avoid the absorption of excess heat by staying in the shade, or in caves? At what temperatures did their testicles cease to function? Were late Cretaceous climates ever warm enough to drive the internal temperatures of dinosaurs close to this ceiling? Testicles simply don't fossilize, and how could we infer their temperature tolerances even if they did? In short, Cowles's hypothesis is only an intriguing speculation leading nowhere. The most damning statement against it appeared right in the conclusion of Colbert, Cowles, and Bogert's paper, when they admitted: "It is difficult to advance any definite arguments against this hypothesis." My statement may seem paradoxical — isn't a hypothesis really good if you can't devise any arguments against it? Quite the contrary. It is simply untestable and unusable.   18

Siegel's overdosing has even less going for it. At least Cowles extrapolated his conclusion from some good data on alligators. And he didn't completely violate the primary guideline of siting dinosaur extinction in the context of a general mass dying — for rise in temperature could be the root cause of a general catastrophe, zapping dinosaurs by testicular malfunction and different groups for other reasons. But Siegel's speculation cannot touch the extinction of ammonites or oceanic plankton (diatoms make   19 their own food with good sweet sunlight; they don't OD on the chemicals of terrestrial plants). It is simply a gratuitous, attention-grabbing guess. It cannot be tested, for how can we know what dinosaurs tasted and what their livers could do? Livers don't fossilize any better than testicles.

The hypothesis doesn't even make any sense in its own context. Angiosperms were in full flower ten million years before dinosaurs went the way of all flesh. Why did it take so long? As for the pains of a chemical death recorded in contortions of fossils, I regret to say (or rather I'm pleased to note for the dinosaurs' sake) that Siegel's knowledge of geology must be a bit deficient: Muscles contract after death and geological strata rise and fall with motions of the earth's crust after burial — more than enough reason to distort a fossil's pristine appearance. 20

The impact story, on the other hand, has a sound basis in evidence. It can be tested, extended, refined, and, if wrong, disproved. The Alvarezes did not just construct an arresting guess for public consumption. They proposed their hypothesis after laborious geochemical studies with Frank Asaro and Helen Michael had revealed a massive increase of iridium in rocks deposited right at the time of extinction. Iridium, a rare metal of the platinum group, is virtually absent from indigenous rocks of the earth's crust; most of our iridium arrives on extraterrestrial objects that strike the earth. 21

The Alvarez hypothesis bore immediate fruit. Based originally on evidence from two European localities, it led geochemists throughout the world to examine other sediments of the same age. They found abnormally high amounts of iridium everywhere — from continental rocks of the western United States to deep sea cores from the South Atlantic. 22

Cowles proposed his testicular hypothesis in the mid-1940s. Where has it gone since then? Absolutely nowhere, because scientists can do nothing with it. The hypothesis must stand as a curious appendage to a solid study of alligators. Siegel's overdose scenario will also win a few press notices and fade into oblivion. The Alvarezes' asteroid falls into a different category altogether, and much of the popular commentary has missed this essential distinction by focusing on the impact and its attendant results, and 23 forgetting what really matters to a scientist — the iridium. If you talk just about asteroids, dust, and darkness, you tell stories no better and no more entertaining than fried testicles or terminal trips. It is the iridium — the source of testable evidence — that counts and forges the crucial distinction between speculation and science.

The proof, to twist a phrase, lies in the doing. Cowles's hypothesis has generated nothing in thirty-five years. Since its proposal in 1979, the Alvarez hypothesis has spawned hundreds of studies, a major conference, and attendant publications. Geologists are fired up. They are looking for iridium at all other extinction boundaries. Every week exposes a new wrinkle in the scientific press. Further evidence that the Cretaceous iridium represents extraterrestrial impact and not indigenous volcanism continues to accumulate. As I revise this essay in November 1984 (this paragraph will be out of date when [it] is published), new data include chemical "signatures" of other isotopes indicating unearthly provenance, glass spherules of a size and sort produced by impact and not by volcanic eruptions, and high-pressure varieties of silica formed (so far as we know) only under the tremendous shock of impact.

My point is simply this: Whatever the eventual outcome (I suspect it will be positive), the Alvarez hypothesis is exciting, fruitful science because it generates tests, provides us with things to do, and expands outward. We are having fun, battling back and forth, moving toward a resolution, and extending the hypothesis beyond its original scope.

As just one example of the unexpected, distant cross-fertilization that good science engenders, the Alvarez hypothesis made a major contribution to a theme that has riveted public attention in the past few months — so-called nuclear winter. In a speech delivered in April 1982, Luis Alvarez calculated the energy that a ten-kilometer asteroid would release on impact. He compared such an explosion with a full nuclear exchange and implied that all-out atomic war might unleash similar consequences.

This theme of impact leading to massive dust clouds and falling temperatures formed an important input to the decision of Carl Sagan and a group of colleagues to model the climatic consequences of nuclear holocaust. Full nuclear exchange would probably generate the same kind of dust cloud and darkening that may have wiped out the dinosaurs. Temperatures would drop precipitously and agriculture might become impossible. Avoidance of nuclear war is fundamentally an ethical and political imperative, but we must know the factual consequences to make firm judgments. I am heartened by a final link across disciplines and deep concerns — another criterion, by the way, of science at its best: A recognition of the very phenomenon that made our evolution possible by exterminating the previously dominant dinosaurs and clearing a way for the evolution of large mammals, including us, might actually help to save us from joining those magnificent beasts in contorted poses among the strata of the earth.

QUESTIONS ON MEANING

1. According to Gould, what constitutes a scientific hypothesis? What constitutes useless speculation? Where in the essay do you find his definitions of these terms?
2. State, in your own words, the THESIS of this essay.
3. What does Gould perceive to be the major flaws in the testicular malfunction and drug overdose theories about the extinction of dinosaurs? Cite his specific reasons for discrediting each theory.
4. What is the connection between nuclear holocaust and the extinction of dinosaurs? (See the essay's last paragraph.)

QUESTIONS ON WRITING STRATEGY

1. How do you understand the phrases "hit parade of primal fascination" (para. 17) and "the hypothesis of testicular frying" (18)? Is the TONE here somber, silly, whimsical, ironic, or what?
2. Paragraphs 14 and 16 both contain references to Dylan Thomas's poem, "Do Not Go Gentle into That Good Night." (The poem's title is used in paragraph 14; "Rage, rage against the dying of the light," one of the poem's refrains, appears in paragraph 16.) If you are not familiar with the poem, look it up. Is it necessary to know the

poem to understand Gould's use of these lines? What is the EFFECT of this ALLUSION?

3. In explaining the Alverezes' hypothesis about the dinosaurs, Gould outlines a causal chain. Draw a diagram to illustrate this chain.
4. OTHER METHODS. The methods of example, comparison and contrast, process analysis, and division or analysis are all at work in this essay. Identify instances of each, and discuss the function each performs in the essay.

QUESTIONS ON LANGUAGE

1. What do you take the sentence "There is no separate problem of the extinction of dinosaurs" (para. 5) to mean? Separate from what? According to Gould, then, what *is* the problem being discussed?
2. Be sure you can define the following words: enticing (para. 1); hypothesis (4); psychoactive, photosynthesis, synchrony (5); paleontology (8); extrapolating (11); empirical (12); gratuitous (19).

SUGGESTIONS FOR WRITING

1. Write a paragraph addressing either the causes or the effects of a situation or circumstance in which you are directly involved. Possible situations might include working in the school cafeteria, taking a psychology class offered only on Wednesday evenings, or anything else that interests you. Make sure that you consider the remote causes or effects as well as the immediate.
2. As Gould himself predicts (para. 24), his summary of the research into the Alvarez hypothesis is now dated: more data have accumulated; the hypothesis has been challenged, tested, revised. Consult the *Readers' Guide to Periodical Literature* for the past five or six years to find articles on the extinction of the dinosaurs. Write an essay updating Gould's in which you summarize the significant EVIDENCE for and against the Alvarez hypothesis.
3. CONNECTIONS. A number of essays in this book are written by science specialists for an AUDIENCE of nonspecialists: for instance, Oliver Sacks's "The President's Speech" (p. 306); Richard Selzer's "The Discus Thrower" (p. 152); Marvin Harris's "How Our Skins Got Their Color" (p. 301); Lewis Thomas's "The Attic of the Brain" (p. 445); and James C. Rettie's " 'But a Watch in the Night' " (p. 461). In an essay, compare Gould's essay with at least one other of these essays in terms of complexity of material, use and explanation of

technical vocabulary, and clarity of explanation. Overall, which essay do you find more (or most) effective in explaining a technical subject?

STEPHEN JAY GOULD ON WRITING

In his prologue to *The Flamingo's Smile*, Stephen Jay Gould positions himself in a long and respectable tradition of writers who communicate scientific ideas to a general audience. To popularize, he says, does not mean to trivialize, cheapen, or adulterate. "I follow one cardinal rule in writing these essays," he insists. "No compromises. I will make language accessible by defining or eliminating jargon; I will not simplify concepts. I can state all sorts of highfalutin, moral justifications for this approach (and I do believe in them), but the basic reason is simple and personal. I write these essays primarily to aid my own quest to learn and understand as much as possible about nature in the short time allotted."

In his own view, Gould is lucky: He is a writer carried along by a single, fascinating theme. "If my volumes work at all, they owe their reputation to coherence supplied by the common theme of evolutionary theory. I have a wonderful advantage among essayists because no other theme so beautifully encompasses both the particulars that fascinate and the generalities that instruct. . . . Each essay is both a single long argument and a welding together of particulars."

FOR DISCUSSION

1. What differences would occur naturally between the work of a scientist writing for other scientists and Gould, who writes about science for a general AUDIENCE?
2. How does the author defend himself against the possible charge that, as a popularizer of science, he trivializes his subject?

CARL SAGAN and RICHARD TURCO

Known widely as an interpreter of science to common readers (and television viewers), CARL SAGAN is himself a noted astronomer. Born in New York City in 1934, he completed four degrees at the University of Chicago. He now directs the Laboratory for Planetary Studies and holds a professorship of astronomy and space sciences at Cornell. Among his books are several nonfiction best-sellers: *The Dragons of Eden* (1977), winner of the Pulitzer Prize for literature; *Broca's Brain: Reflections on the Romance of Science* (1979); and *Cosmos* (1980), based on Sagan's PBS television series of the same title, in which he appeared as narrator. Sagan is also a novelist: In *Contact* (1985), a radio astronomer deciphers a message from another world.

RICHARD TURCO is a professor of atmospheric science at the University of California at Los Angeles. Born in New York City in 1943, he was educated at Rutgers University (B.S., 1965) and the University of Illinois (M.S., 1967; Ph.D., 1971). He has worked for NASA, published numerous articles in academic journals, and won many fellowships and awards, including a MacArthur Foundation Grant in 1986. That same year Turco published *Environmental Consequences of Nuclear War*, a book merging his research interests in atmospheric pollution, nuclear explosion, and arms limitation.

Too Many Weapons in the World

Carl Sagan and Richard Turco were part of a team of five scientists who in 1983 predicted a possible "nuclear winter": A nuclear war could spew so much smoke and dust into the atmosphere that the earth would be darkened and cooled, and its life, including humans and their civilization, would be drastically altered. This theory has engaged scientists and politicians in debate ever since. Sagan, Turco, and their colleagues have continually refined their predictions to reflect emerging evidence, and recently they have taken account of what the significant changes in American and Soviet relations may mean for the nuclear arms race. This essay first appeared in February

1990 in *Parade*, the Sunday newspaper supplement, and is based on Sagan and Turco's book, *A Path Where No Man Thought: Nuclear Winter and the End of the Arms Race* (1990).

> Great perils have this beauty, that they bring
> together the fraternity of strangers.
> —Victor Hugo

We live in astonishing times. A reawakened passion for democracy is sweeping across our planet. The present comparative warmth in relations between the United States and the Soviet Union stands in sharp contrast to the chill of the Cold War. Arms control and the elimination of at least some nuclear-weapons systems are being not only seriously discussed but actually implemented.

So there's an understandable tendency to think that the problem of nuclear war has been solved, or at least is being solved — that we can now ignore it and turn our attention to the formidable array of other pressing problems. This opinion is surprisingly widespread. It is, we believe, a dangerous illusion.

Many people first heard of nuclear winter back in 1983. The early 1980s now seem like some remote geological era, when the prospects of "fighting," "containing," and "winning" a nuclear war were deemed feasible, or even prudent, national policy. Then, merely describing the dangers of nuclear war — nuclear winter aside — was considered unpatriotic, or at least naive and foolish, eroding the will of the American people to oppose Soviet tyranny. The conclusion that nuclear war could usher in a global climatic catastrophe, causing billions of people to starve to death, ran against the grain of the prevailing wisdom.

The direct consequences of nuclear war are bad enough. How much worse can nuclear winter be?

Nuclear winter would be the delayed result — chiefly from clouds of fine, sooty particles injected into the atmosphere, especially from the burning of cities and petroleum facilities — of a nuclear war. It would entail widespread cold and dark; poison gases released from the burning of cities and chemical plants; radioactivity slowly falling out of the atmosphere; and, later, an increase in dangerous ultraviolet light at the surface of the Earth, penetrating the war-breached protective ozone layer. The high-altitude soot would prevent warming sunlight from reaching the ground. It would diminish the greenhouse effect, which is what keeps the temperature of the Earth above freezing in the first place. Smoke plumes and firestorms rising above hundreds or thousands of targets throughout the northern midlatitudes, spreading first in longitude and then in latitude, would cause temperatures to plummet, eventually over much of the Earth. A temperature drop of only a few degrees centigrade (°C) during the growing season is enough to cause massive crop failures. With no food, people starve.

Nuclear winter does not lend itself to full experimental verifi-   6
cation — at least, not more than once. The danger is explored and understood by using computer models, similar to those that correctly predict the climatic consequences of the dust from volcanic explosions and the smoke from large forest fires. Since our first findings in 1982–83, nuclear winter has received much critical scientific scrutiny, and most calculations of nuclear winter's effects now seem in reasonable agreement. Drops in land temperature for a "baseline" nuclear war are generally in the 10°C to 20°C (18°F to 36°F) range, plunging by 35°C (63°F) in some locales. There was a period when some investigators referred to a 10°C decline as "nuclear autumn" to distinguish it from a 20°C "nuclear winter." But all the scientists involved acknowledge that even a 10°C temperature drop would represent a cataclysmic threat, endangering many more people than would the direct effects of nuclear war blast, fire, radiation.

The reality of nuclear winter has now been confirmed by de-   7
tailed investigations in the United States, the Soviet Union, and many other nations; in analyses by the World Meteorological Organization and the United Nations; and in a landmark study involving hundreds of scientists in more than a dozen countries working over three years, sponsored by the Paris-based International Council of Scientific Unions. This two-volume report warns:

> The total loss of human agricultural and societal support systems would result in the loss of almost all humans on Earth,

essentially equally among combatant and noncombatant countries alike. . . . This vulnerability is an aspect not currently a part of the understanding of nuclear war; not only are the major combatant countries in danger, but virtually the entire human population is being held hostage to the large-scale of nuclear weapons. . . .

As representatives of the world scientific community, drawn together in this study, we conclude that many of the serious global environmental effects are sufficiently probable to require widespread concern. Because of the possibility of a tragedy of an unprecedented dimension, any disposition to minimize or ignore the widespread environmental effects of nuclear war would be a fundamental disservice to the future of global civilization. . . . A fundamentally different picture of global suffering among peoples in noncombatant and combatant countries alike must become the new standard perception for decision-makers throughout the world if the visions portrayed in this study are to remain just intellectual exercises and not the irreversible future of humanity.

Troubling issues are raised by the threat of nuclear winter. 8 Among them: that a major consequence of nuclear war eluded the civilian and military establishments of the contending nation-states for decades; that policies of massive retaliation, or a disarming first strike, might be catastrophic for the nation employing them (and for its allies), independent of its adversary's response; that distant nations are in jeopardy even if not a single nuclear weapon is detonated on their soil; and that the size and nature of the present nuclear arsenals — as well as the central role of nuclear weapons in the strategic relations of the United States and the Soviet Union — may be not merely imprudent but also a policy mistake unprecedented in human history. If one nation can destroy itself by a massive attack on another, how credible is it that we or the Soviets would ever launch such an attack? And if we would never launch it, how believable is the notion of nuclear deterrence — at least with the present massive nuclear arsenals?

One of the most disquieting implications of nuclear winter is 9 that only a small fraction, perhaps less than one percent, of the nearly 60,000 nuclear weapons in the world (almost all of them in American and Soviet hands) might be enough to generate a nuclear winter — depending, of course, on targeting. In a world in which people and machines can go disastrously wrong despite confident assurances of safety (as, for example, with the Challenger space shuttle and the Chernobyl nuclear power plant), and in a century in which madmen (Adolf Hitler and Joseph Stalin, for example) have acquired absolute control over modern industrial nations, is it wise to maintain nuclear arsenals of such apocalyptic power?

During the 1980s, we saw nuclear winter imagery and arguments appearing in the statements of political leaders worldwide, and a push to reduce world nuclear arsenals has gained wide currency. If Cold War tensions were high, things would be different. There would be little prospect of cutting the stockpiles, and each nation would clutch its arsenal as a security blanket, believing that the more nuclear weapons it has, the more secure it is. As long as the Soviet Union and its allies were considered to have "overwhelming superiority" in troops and nonnuclear weapons in Europe, major dismantling of nuclear weapons by the United States, even with corresponding Soviet divestitures, was unlikely.

But we are now entering a very different era.[1] In a dizzying succession of unilateral steps, the Soviets have begun massive withdrawals of troops and armor from Europe. They have announced that they will cut tank production in half, slow their modernization of nuclear weapons, and remove all overseas military bases by the year 2000. Both the U.S. and the USSR have signed and implemented the INF (Intermediate-Range Nuclear Forces) Treaty, which eliminates an entire class of nuclear-weapons systems and, even more important, demonstrates that each nation will allow inspectors from the other on its territory, monitoring compliance with an arms-control agreement. U.S. reductions in conventional forces are being seriously discussed, and further treaties to reverse the nuclear arms race are being negotiated. Even without nuclear winter, these steps make enormous sense.

[1]The changes discussed below were current as of winter 1990, when this essay was published. — Eds.

But the INF Treaty affected only some 3 percent of the   12
world's nuclear weapons — and the nuclear warheads, the explosive guts, were not dismantled but are being recycled into new nuclear weapons. The nuclear powers, with great trepidation, are now actually contemplating the fearsome step — called START, for Strategic Arms Reduction Talks — of reducing the world's nuclear arsenals from nearly 60,000 weapons to only a little more than 50,000 weapons. But if we are to escape the threat that nuclear winter portends, we will have to do much better.

Many nuclear strategists, East and West, are now researching   13
the best way to manage arms reductions down to a very small, invulnerable, retaliatory force on each side. Such a force would be enough to provide nuclear deterrence — if that's what we're after — but not enough, if the worst happens, to generate nuclear winter. Because having many nuclear warheads on a single missile is an inducement to the other side to make a preemptive attack in a time of crisis, we would all be far safer with only one warhead per missile. An important task before us is to find the safest, most stable, most rigorously verifiable path to a minimum sufficient deterrence. If we like, we can think of this as a step along the way to a much more difficult goal: the reliable, wholesale, worldwide abolition of nuclear weapons.

No significant reversal of the arms race is possible without far-   14
reaching changes in the attitudes that the United States and the Soviet Union bear toward one another. Such changes are now clearly under way. Improved U.S./Soviet relations make possible fair and verified arms reductions. And the arms reductions, particularly in conventional forces, permit enormous benefits for the economies of the two nations. Nuclear winter provides a strong common incentive for reversing the arms race — an incentive that embraces not only the nuclear-armed nations but the entire human community as well. It also offers important clues on how to go about reducing arms and what lower levels to aim for.

We have entered a most promising new decade — not just be-   15
cause the walls are tumbling down, not just because money and scientists long devoted to the military will now become available for urgent civilian concerns, but also because we finally are becoming aware of our unsuspected and awesome powers over the

environment that sustains us. Like the assault on the protective ozone layer and global greenhouse warming, nuclear winter is a looming planetwide catastrophe that is within our power to avert. It teaches us the need for foresight and wisdom as we negotiate our way through our technological adolescence. And nuclear winter also reminds us of an ancient truth: When we kill our brothers, we kill ourselves.

QUESTIONS ON MEANING

1. What is Sagan and Turco's primary PURPOSE: to explain how nuclear weapons fit into present international politics, to explain what would happen in a nuclear winter, to persuade readers not to be complacent about nuclear weapons, to persuade readers not to be concerned about nuclear war, or what?
2. What do the authors maintain would happen in a nuclear winter?
3. What is Sagan and Turco's THESIS? Do you agree with the authors?
4. Given that the Cold War is thawing, why do Sagan and Turco insist that disarmament is still an urgent priority?
5. Why do Sagan and Turco conclude that "we have entered a most promising new decade" (para. 15)?

QUESTIONS ON WRITING STRATEGY

1. What do Sagan and Turco examine the causes and/or effects of in this essay?
2. What function do paragraphs 6–7 serve in this essay?
3. Why do Sagan and Turco cite the Challenger space shuttle, the Chernobyl nuclear power plant, Adolf Hitler, and Joseph Stalin?
4. *Parade* magazine, where this essay first appeared, is a supplement to many Sunday newspapers around the country. How would you characterize *Parade*'s AUDIENCE? Is Sagan and Turco's essay appropriate for that audience? Why, or why not?
5. OTHER METHODS. Sagan and Turco take some pains to give a definition (Chap. 10) of "nuclear winter." Since they've defined the term elsewhere in print, why do you think they define it again here? Is the definition adequate?

QUESTIONS ON LANGUAGE

1. Look at the long quotation in paragraph 7. Do you find differences between it and Sagan and Turco's text in terms of DICTION and STYLE? Why do you think Sagan and Turco didn't just PARAPHRASE these two paragraphs?
2. Write short definitions of the scientific concepts in paragraph 5: atmosphere, radioactivity, ultraviolet light, protective ozone layer, greenhouse effect, firestorms, longitude, latitude.
3. Do you detect any IRONY or SARCASM in this essay? If so, is it effective?
4. If any of the following words are unfamiliar, look them up in the dictionary: formidable, array (para. 2); feasible, prevailing (3); plummet (5); verification, scrutiny, cataclysmic (6); eluded, retaliation, adversary, jeopardy, deterrence (8); disquieting, apocalyptic, divestitures (9); unilateral, compliance (11); trepidation, portends (12); inducement, preemptive (13).

SUGGESTIONS FOR WRITING

1. Consider a decision you must make in the near future — what courses to take next term, what major to select, even where to go on spring break — and, in a brief essay, analyze the possible effects of the decision.
2. Write an essay in which you detail some of the effects of the nuclear buildup other than all-out destruction and nuclear winter. How, for instance, has the buildup affected our national budget? What is the psychological effect on the populace? What effect does government secrecy about nuclear arms and preparedness have on the populace? How do our nuclear arsenal and posture affect our image abroad? Be sure to back up your assertions with EVIDENCE. (You may need to visit the library.)
3. CONNECTIONS. Bruno Bettelheim's essay in the next chapter (p. 597) defines a word often applied to nuclear war: *holocaust*. Based on Bettelheim's arguments and information, write a brief essay considering whether it is appropriate to use this word for nuclear destruction. (You might want to consult an unabridged dictionary for additional information on the word *holocaust*.)

CARL SAGAN ON WRITING

Sometimes, the prolific Carl Sagan has written first for a nonprint medium, then rewritten his work for publication in book form. *The Dragons of Eden* grew from a lecture, six chapters in *Broca's Brain* were first written to be delivered as speeches, and the best-selling *Cosmos* was based on a television series. Turning television scripts into a book produced certain unexpected improvements, Sagan found. As he noted in his introduction to *Cosmos*, "There is much more freedom for the author in choosing the range and depth of topics for a chapter in a book than for the procrustean fifty-eight minutes, thirty seconds of a noncommercial television program. This book goes more deeply into many topics than does the television series."

As a writer, Sagan told the interviewer John F. Baker, he sees his audience to be the general public: anyone seeking a better understanding of science. Such writing, he believes, gives pleasure to both writer and reader: "If you make a person understand something, you make that person happy — you communicate joy." Accepting with pride the label of a "generalist," Sagan has written in many fields (besides brain research) in which he has no professional credentials. "But such insights as I've been able to achieve have been at the borders of the sciences, where different disciplines overlap. That's where the excitement is, and that's where I want to be." He distrusts the notion that scientists are "authorities." "Experts, yes, but not authorities. In science every idea must be challenged."

FOR DISCUSSION

1. What does *procrustean* mean?
2. What subtle shade of difference does Sagan see between "authorities" and "experts"? What reason does he give for not wanting scientists to be regarded as authorities?

JAMES FALLOWS

A compelling voice in political and social journalism, JAMES
FALLOWS was born in 1949 in Philadelphia, was raised in California, graduated from Harvard College, and studied at Oxford
for two years on a Rhodes Scholarship. At Harvard, Fallows
honed his journalistic skills as president of the *Crimson*, the student daily. After Oxford, he served as a writer and editor for
Washington Monthly and *Texas Monthly*. Then for two years he
was chief speechwriter for President Jimmy Carter, a job he left
with ambivalent feelings about the thoroughness and the
power of the press. He is now the Washington editor of *The Atlantic Monthly*. His books include *The Water Lords* (1971),
about a water-pollution crisis in Savannah, Georgia; *National
Defense* (1981), about the technology of modern warfare; and
More Like Us: Making America Great Again (1989), about how
the United States can recover itself amid increasing competition from Asia.

Freedom, Control, and Success: Asia and America

For more than three years in the late 1980s, Fallows reported
for the *Atlantic* from Malaysia and Japan. His observations and
experiences inform his book *More Like Us* and the following essay, which first appeared in the *Atlantic* in November 1989
when Fallows and his family were about to return to the
United States. (The title of the essay is the editors'.)

Living in a foreign culture is, most of the time, exhilarating   1
and liberating. You don't have to feel responsible for the foibles
of your temporary home; you can forget about the foibles of
your real home for a while. Your life seems longer, because each
day is dense with new and surprising experiences. I can remember distinctly almost every week of the past three and a half
years. The preceding half dozen years more or less run together
in a blur.

But there is also distress in foreign living, particularly in living 2
in Asia at this time in its history. It comes not from daily exasper-
ations, which after all build character, but from the unsettling
thoughts that living in Asia introduces. As I head for home, let
me mention the thought that disturbs me most.

It concerns the nature of freedom: whether free societies are 3
fit to compete, in a Darwinian sense. Until the repression in
China last summer [1989], many Westerners assumed that the
world had entered an era of overall progress. True, environmental problems were getting worse rather than better, and many African and Latin American societies were still in bad shape. But in
Asia it seemed possible to believe that people had learned how to
make their societies both richer and freer year by year. As countries in Asia became more advanced and prosperous, they loosened their political controls — and as the controls came off, economic progress speeded up. This was the moral of the Korean and
Taiwanese success stories, as those countries evolved toward the
ideal set by stable, prosperous Japan. Even China, before the
summer, seemed to be loosening up, both economically and polit-
ically. China's crackdown made the spread of democracy and
capitalism seem less certain than it had seemed before, but even
this step backward confirmed the idea that political freedoms and
economic progress were naturally connected. Everyone assumes
that as China makes its political system more repressive, its economy will stagnate.

I draw a darker conclusion from the rise of the Asian econo- 4
mies. The economic success stories of Asia do not prove that political freedom and material progress go hand in hand. On the
contrary: The Asian societies are, in different ways, fundamentally more repressive than America is, and their repression is a
key to their economic success. Japan, Korea, Taiwan, and Singapore allow their citizens much less latitude than America does,
and in so doing they make the whole society, including the business sector, function more efficiently than ours does. The lesson
of the Soviet economic collapse would seem to be that a completely controlled economy cannot survive. The lesson of the rising Asian system is that economies with some degree of control
can not only survive but prevail.

The crucial concepts here are "excessive" choice and "de-   5
structive" competition. Classical free-market economic theory
says that these are impossibilities; a person can never have too
much choice, and there can never be too much competition in a
market. Asian societies approach this issue from a fundamentally
different perspective. They were built on neither an Enlightenment concept of individiual rights nor a capitalist concept of free
and open markets, and they demonstrate in countless ways that
less choice for individuals can mean more freedom and success for
the social whole.

The examples of economic efficiency are the most familiar.   6
Japanese businessmen have almost no freedom to move to another company, even if they're dissatisfied with conditions where
they're working. (Of course, they're technically free to quit, but
very few reputable big companies will hire someone who has left
another big firm.) This may be frustrating for the businessmen,
but so far it has been efficient for the companies. For instance,
they can invest in employee training programs without fear that
newly skilled workers will use their skills somewhere else. Singa-
poreans have been forced to put much of their income into a national retirement fund; Koreans have been discouraged from
squandering their money overseas on tourism (until this year,
only people planning business trips and those in a few other narrow categories were granted passports); Japanese consumers are
forced to pay inflated prices for everything they buy. All these
measures have been bad for individuals but efficient for the collective. In different ways they have transferred money from people to large institutions, which then invest it for future productivity. To illustrate the point the opposite way: Korea has in the past
two years become a more successful democracy and a less successful export economy. Precisely because workers have been going
on strike and consumers demanding a higher standard of living,
Korean companies have temporarily lost their edge against com-
petitors in Taiwan and Japan.

Yu-Shan Wu, of The Brookings Institution, has suggested a   7
useful way to think about this combination of economic freedom
and political control. In communist economies, he says, property
is owned by the state, and investment decisions are made by the

state. The result is a disaster. The style of capitalism practiced in the United States takes the opposite approach: Private owners control most property, and private groups make most investment decisions. The result over the past century has been a big success, but now some inefficiencies are showing up. Japan, Wu says, has pioneered a new approach: private ownership of property, plus public guidance of investment decisions. The big industrial combines of Japan are as private and profit-oriented as those of the United States, and therefore at least as efficiency-minded (unlike state enterprises in Russia or China). But in Japan's brand of capitalism some of the largest decisions are made by the state, not the "invisible hand."[1] This private-public approach, Wu concludes, reduces the freedom of people and single companies, but it has certain long-term advantages over the private-private system.

Last year two U.S. companies made supercomputers, the   8
Cray corporation and a subsidiary of Control Data. This year only one does. Control Data abandoned the business, finding it unprofitable. The same circumstances have applied in Japan — difficult but important technology; lean or nonexistent profits for the foreseeable future — but the results have been different, because the state occasionally overrules the invisible hand. It is inconceivable that the Japanese government would have let one of only two participants abandon an area of obvious future technical importance. If Japan left decisions to the invisible hand, there would be no aircraft engineers at work in the country, because Mitsubishi and Kawasaki cannot hope to earn a profit competing against Boeing. But the big Japanese companies keep their aerospace-engineering departments active, in part because of government-directed incentives to do so. (These range from explicit subsidies, like the FSX fighter-plane contracts, to a system of industrial organization that makes it possible for companies to subsidize unprofitable divisions for years.) Eventually, Japanese planners believe, the aerospace expertise will pay off.

Americans should not be surprised by what the private-   9
public system can accomplish. It's essentially the way our econ-

[1]An idea developed by the Scottish philosopher Adam Smith (1723–1790): As individuals pursue their own interests, their work inadvertently benefits all of society. — Eds.

omy worked during the Second World War. People were forced to save, through Liberty Bonds, and forced not to consume, through rationing. Big companies were privately owned and run, but overall goals were set by the state. Under this system the output of the U.S. economy rose faster than ever before or since. (Part of the reason for the rapid rise, of course, was that wartime production finally brought America out of the Great Depression.) For the United States this managed economy was a wartime exception. For the Japanese-style economic systems of Asia it has been the postwar rule. This is not to say that we need a wartime mentality again but, rather, to show that the connection between individual freedom and collective prosperity is more complicated than we usually think. We may not like the way the Japanese-style economic system operates, but we'd be foolish not to recognize that it does work, and in many ways works better than ours.

Here's an even harder truth to face: The most successful Asian economies employ a division of labor between men and women that we may find retrograde but that has big practical advantages for them. Despite some signs of change — for instance, the rising influence of Takako Doi at the head of the Socialist Party in Japan — the difference between a man's role and woman's is much more cut and dried in Asia than in the United States. It is tempting to conclude that a time lag is all that separates Asian practices from American, and that Japanese and Korean women will soon be demanding the rights that American women have won during the past generation. But from everything I've seen, such an assumption is as naive as imagining that Japan is about to be swept by an American-style consumer-rights movement. 10

There is a lot to dislike in this strict assignment of sex roles. It's unfair in an obvious way to women, because 99 percent of them can never really compete for business, political, academic, or other opportunities and success. I think it's ultimately just as bad for men, because most of them are cut off from the very idea of dealing with women as equals, and have what we would consider emotionally barren family lives. The average Japanese salaryman takes more emotional satisfaction in his workplace life than the average American does, but less in his relations with 11 wife and children. Nonetheless, this system has one tremendous practical advantage. By making it difficult for women to do anything except care for their families, the traditional Asian system concentrates a larger share of social energy on the preparation of the young.

The best-educated American children are a match for the best 12 in Asia, but the average student in Japan, Korea, Singapore, or Taiwan does better in school than the average American. The fundamental reason, I think, is that average students in these countries come from families with two parents, one of whom concentrates most of her time and effort on helping her children through school. Limits on individual satisfaction undergird this educational achievement in two ways: The mother is discouraged from pursuing a career outside the house, and she and the father are discouraged from even thinking about divorce. The typical Asian marriage is not very romantic. In most countries arranged marriages are still common, and while extramarital affairs are at least as frequent as they are in the United States, they seem to cause less guilt. But because most husbands and wives expect less emotional fulfillment from marriage, very few marriages end in divorce. Individual satisfaction from marriage may be lower, but the society enjoys the advantages of having families that are intact.

The Asian approach to the division of labor is not one that 13 Americans want to emulate, or can. Except in emergencies we have believed in satisfying individual desires rather than suppressing them. But, to come back to the central point, we shouldn't fool ourselves about the sheer effectiveness of the system that the Asian societies have devised. Their approach to child-rearing, as to economic development, is worse for many individuals but better for the collective welfare than ours seems to be. The Asian model is not going to collapse of its own weight, unlike the Soviet communist system. So the puzzle for us is to find ways to evoke similar behavior — moderation of individual greed, adequate attention of society's long-term interests, commitment to raising children — within our own values of individualism and free choice.

I hope somebody has figured out the answer to this while I've 14 been away.

QUESTIONS ON MEANING

1. Summarize the causes Fallows cites for "the economic success stories of Asia."
2. Why does Fallows say that "excessive" choice and "destructive" competition are crucial concepts if, as he also says, they are both impossible in classical free-market economic theory?
3. What new approach to capitalism in Japan does Fallows cite Yu-Shan Wu as pointing out? What is its significance?
4. What historical American economy does Fallows find similar to the Japanese economy? Why?
5. What is Fallows's THESIS? His PURPOSE?

QUESTIONS ON WRITING STRATEGY

1. Can you distinguish between the more immediate and more remote causes in Fallows's analysis of the success of Asian economies?
2. Paragraphs 7 and 8 both present EVIDENCE, but of different kinds. What are the differences?
3. What key AUDIENCE assumption is Fallows working against? Why is it important that he address this assumption?
4. OTHER METHODS. Fallows compares and contrasts American and Asian economies (Chap. 4). Undoubtedly, there are more differences and similarities between the two culture groups than he cites. Can you name some of them? Why does Fallows not deal with them as well?

QUESTIONS ON LANGUAGE

1. What does Fallows mean by free societies competing "in a Darwinian sense" (para. 3)?
2. Familiarize yourself with these economic terms: capitalism (para. 3); free-market (5); invest, inflated, productivity, export economy (6); communist, profit-oriented (7); division of labor, (10). What are the basic economic systems Fallows describes?
3. Consult your dictionary for any of these words that are unfamiliar: foibles (para. 1); stagnate (3); prevail (4); squandering (6); inconceivable, incentives, subsidies (8); retrograde (10); undergird (12); emulate (13).

SUGGESTIONS FOR WRITING

1. Think of a local, national, or even international situation in which you have first-hand experience: a dispute at school, a new traffic ordinance in town, the state or federal policy on student aid, trade barriers or immigration quotas between nations. Following Fallows's example, write a cause-and-effect essay about the situation, using varied EVIDENCE, including your own observations, to support your analysis.

2. In his CONCLUSION, Fallows suggests changes that Americans may need to make if they are to compete successfully in the world economy. Based on the information Fallows provides and your own library research as well, write an essay about this issue of needed change: Do you think it's important for the United States to change? If so, how? If not, why not? What about Asian societies? Should they change? How? (For library research, you might start with the *Readers' Guide to Periodical Literature*, which will direct you to recent magazine articles on this subject.)

3. CONNECTIONS. Both Fallows's essay and Sagan and Turco's "Too Many Weapons in the World" (p. 520) are fairly recent works that warn Americans against excessive optimism about peace, economic progress, and other issues. Drawing on both of these essays and your own observations and experiences, write an essay analyzing the causes and effects of this optimism. Do you share Fallows's and Sagan and Turco's concerns about it?

JAMES FALLOWS ON WRITING

How much does James Fallows love his word processor? Here's what he wrote in the *Boston Review*: "I'd sell my computer before I'd sell my children. But the kids better watch their step. When have the children helped me meet a deadline? When has the computer dragged in a dead cat it found in the back yard?"

Fallows seems to be one of those writers who like the clever technology of a word processor almost as much as they like its convenience. He tells everyone that he needs the word processor for writing, and he does; but "the truth," he confesses, "is that *I love to see it work*." Fallows has invented a new "editing step" that satisfies his addiction and helps improve his writing at the same time. "When I think I'm finished with an article," he says, "I set the print speed to *Slow*. This runs the printer at about a hundred words per minute, or roughly the pace of reading aloud. I stuff my ears with earplugs and then lean over the platen [the paper roller] as the printing begins. Watching the article print at this speed is like hearing it read; infelicities are more difficult to ignore than when you are scooting your eye over words on a page."

The chief advantage of the computer for Fallows the writer (as opposed to Fallows the gadget lover) is that it allows him more leeway for revision. "Since I now spend less time and energy retyping, I have more left over for editing and rewriting."

FOR DISCUSSION

1. What has a word processor done for Fallows? If you use a word processor, what has it done for you? In your experience, are there any disadvantages to a word processor?
2. Explain Fallows's trick of reading his material as it comes through the printer. Why are "infelicities" more difficult to ignore?

ADDITIONAL WRITING TOPICS
Cause and Effect

1. In a short essay, explain *either* the causes *or* the effects of a situation that concerns you. Narrow your topic enough to treat it in some detail, and provide more than a mere list of causes or effects. If seeking causes, you will have to decide carefully how far back to go in your search for remote causes. If stating effects, fill your essay with examples. Here are some topics to consider:

Labor strikes in professional sports
State laws mandating the use of seat belts in cars (or the wearing of helmets on motorcycles)
Friction between two roommates, or two friends
The pressure on students to get good grades
Some quirk in your personality, or a friend's
The increasing need for more than one breadwinner per family
The temptation to do something dishonest to get ahead
The popularity of a particular television program, comic strip, rock group, or pop singer
The steady increase in college costs
The scarcity of people in training for employment as skilled workers: plumbers, tool and die makers, electricians, masons, carpenters, to name a few
A decision to enter the ministry or a religious order
The fact that cigarette advertising has been banned from television
The absence of a peacetime draft
The fact that more couples are choosing to have only one child, or none
The growing popularity of private elementary and high schools
The fact that most Americans can communicate in no language other than English
Being "born again"
The grim tone of recent novels for young people (such as Robert Cormier's *I Am the Cheese* and other juvenile fiction dealing with violence, madness, and terror)
The fact that women increasingly are training for jobs formerly regarded as men's only
The pressure on young people to conform to the standards of their peers

538

The emphasis on competitive sports in high school and college

Children's watching soft-core pornography on cable television

2. In *Blue Highways* (1982), an account of his rambles around America, William Least Heat Moon asserts why Americans, and not the British, settled the vast tract of northern land that lies between the Mississippi and the Rockies. He traces what he believes to be the major cause in this paragraph:

> Were it not for a web-footed rodent and a haberdashery fad in eighteenth-century Europe, Minnesota might be a Canadian province today. The beaver, almost as much as the horse, helped shape the course of early American history. Some *Mayflower* colonists paid their passage with beaver pelts; and a good fur could bring an Indian three steel knifes or a five-foot stack could bring a musket. But even more influential were the trappers and fur traders penetrating the great Northern wilderness between the Mississippi River and the Rocky Mountains, since it was their presence that helped hold the Near West against British expansion from the north; and it was their explorations that opened the heart of the nation to white settlement. These men, by making pelts the currency of the wilds, laid the base for a new economy that quickly overwhelmed the old. And all because European men of mode simply had to wear a beaver hat.

In a Least Heat Moon–like paragraph of your own, explain how a small cause produced a large effect. You might generate ideas by browsing in a history book — where you might find, for instance, that a cow belonging to Mrs. Patrick O'Leary is believed to have started the Great Chicago Fire of 1871 by kicking over a lighted lantern — or in a collection of *Ripley's Believe It or Not*. If some small event in your life has had large consequences, you might care to write instead from personal experience.

10
DEFINITION
Tracing a Boundary

THE METHOD

As a rule, when we hear the word *definition*, we immediately think of a dictionary. In that helpful storehouse — a writer's best friend — we find the literal and specific meaning (or meanings) of a word. The dictionary supplies this information concisely: in a sentence, in a phrase, or even in a synonym — a single word that means the same thing ("**narrative** [năr - e - tĭv] *n.* **1:** story . . .").

Stating such a definition is often a good way to begin an essay when basic terms may be in doubt. A short definition can clarify your subject to your reader, and perhaps help you to limit what you have to say. If, for instance, you are going to discuss a demolition derby, explaining such a spectacle to readers who may never have seen one, you might offer at the outset a short definition of *demolition derby*, your subject and your key term.

In constructing a short definition, the usual procedure is this: First, you state the general class to which your subject belongs; then you add any particular features that distinguish it. You could say: "A demolition derby is a contest" — that is its general class — "in which drivers ram old cars into one another until only one car is left running." Short definitions may also be useful at *any* moment in your essay. If you introduce a technical term, you'll want to define it briefly: "As the derby proceeds, there's many a broken manifold — that's the fitting that connects the openings of a car engine's exhaust."

In this chapter, however, we are mainly concerned with another sort of definition. It is *extended definition*, a kind of expository writing that relies on a variety of other methods. Suppose you wanted to write an essay to make clear what *poetry* means. You would specify its elements — rhythm, images, and so on — by using DIVISION or ANALYSIS (Chap. 6). You'd probably provide EXAMPLES of each element (Chap. 3). You might COMPARE and CONTRAST poetry with prose (Chap. 4). You might discuss the EFFECT of poetry on the reader (Chap. 9). (Emily Dickinson, a poet herself, once stated the effect that reading a poem had on her: "I feel as if the top of my head were taken off.") In fact, extended definition, unlike other methods of writing discussed in this book, is perhaps less a method in itself than the application of a variety of methods to clarify a purpose. Like DESCRIPTION, extended definition tries to *show* a reader its subject. It does so by establishing boundaries, for its writer tries to differentiate a subject from anything that might be confused with it. When Tom Wolfe, in his essay in this chapter, seeks to define a certain trend he has noticed in newspapers, books, and television, he describes exactly what he sees happening, so that we, too, will understand what he calls "the pornography of violence." In an extended definition, a writer studies the nature of a subject, carefully sums up its chief characteristics, and strives to answer the question What is this? — or What makes this what it is, not something else?

An extended definition can *define* (from the Latin, "to set bounds to") a word, or it can define a thing (a laser beam), a concept (male chauvinism), or a general phenomenon (the popularity of the demolition derby). Unlike a sentence definition, or any you would find in a standard dictionary, an extended definition takes room: at least a paragraph, perhaps an entire volume. The subject may be as large as the concepts of "home" and "vulgarity."

Outside an English course, how is this method of writing used? In a newspaper feature, a sports writer defines what makes a "great team" great. In a journal article, a physician defines the nature of a previously unknown syndrome or disease. In a written opinion, a judge defines not only a word but a concept, *obscenity*. In a book review, a critic defines a newly prevalent kind of poem. In a letter to a younger brother or sister contemplating college, a student might define a "gut course" and how to recognize one.

Unlike a definition in a dictionary that sets forth the literal meaning of a word in an unimpassioned manner, some definitions imply biases. In defining *patron* to the earl of Chesterfield, who had tried to befriend him after ignoring his petitions for aid during his years of grinding poverty, Samuel Johnson wrote scornfully: "Is not a Patron, my Lord, one who looks with unconcern on a man struggling for life in the water, and, when he has reached the ground, encumbers him with help?" IRONY, METAPHOR, and short definition have rarely been wielded with such crushing power. (*Encumbers*, by the way, is a wonderfully physical word in its context: It means "to burden with dead weight.") In his extended definition of *pornoviolence*, Tom Wolfe is biased, even jaundiced, in his view of American media. In having many methods of writing at their disposal, writers of extended definitions have ample freedom and wide latitude.

THE PROCESS

Writing an extended definition, you'll want to employ whatever method or methods of writing can best answer the question What is the nature of this subject? You will probably find yourself making use of much that you have learned earlier from this book. A short definition like the one for *demolition derby* on page 542 may be a good start for your essay, especially if you think your readers need a quick grounding in the subject or in your view of it. (But feel no duty to place a dictionaryish definition in the INTRODUCTION of every essay you write: The device is overused.) In explaining a demolition derby, if your readers already have at least a vague idea of the meaning of the term and need no short, formal definition of it, you might open your extended definition with the aid of NARRATION. You could relate the events at a typical demolition derby, starting with a description of the lineup of old, beat-up vehicles:

> One hundred worthless cars — everything from a 1940 Cadillac to a Dodge Dart to a recently wrecked Thunderbird, their glass removed, their radiators leaking — assemble on a racetrack or an open field. Their drivers, wearing crash helmets, buckle themselves into their seats, some pulling at beer cans to soften the blows to come.

You might proceed by example, listing demolition derbies you have known ("The great destruction of 184 vehicles took place at the Orleans County Fair in Barton, Vermont, in the summer of '81 . . ."). If you have enough examples, you might wish to CLASSIFY them; or perhaps you might analyze a demolition derby, dividing it into its components of cars, drivers, judges, first-aid squad, and spectators, and discussing each. You could compare and contrast a demolition derby with that amusement park ride known as Bumper Cars or Dodge-'ems, in which small cars with rubber bumpers bash one another head-on, but (unlike cars in the derby) harmlessly. A PROCESS ANALYSIS of a demolition derby might help your readers understand the nature of the spectacle: how in round after round, cars are eliminated until one remains. You might ask: What causes the owners of old cars to want to smash them? Or perhaps: What causes people to watch the destruction? Or: What are the consequences? To answer such questions in an essay, you would apply the method of CAUSE and EFFECT. Perhaps an ANALOGY might occur to you, one that would explain the demolition derby to someone unfamiliar with it: "It is like a birthday party in which every kid strives to have the last unpopped balloon."

Say you're preparing to write an extended definition of anything living or in motion (a basketball superstar, for instance, or a desert, or a comet). To discover points about your subject worth noticing, you may find it useful to ask yourself a series of questions. These questions may be applied both to individual subjects, such as the superstar, and to collective subjects — institutions (like the American family, a typical savings bank, a university, the Church of Jesus Christ of Latter-Day Saints) and organizations (IBM, the Mafia, a heavy-metal band, a Little League baseball team). To illustrate how the questions might work, at least in one instance, let's say you plan to write a paper defining a male chauvinist.[1]

1. *Is this subject unique, or are there others of its kind? If it resembles others, in what ways? How is it different?* As you can see, these last two questions invite you to compare and contrast. Applied to the concept of male chauvinism, these questions might remind you that male chauvinists come in different varieties — middle-aged and college-aged, for instance — and you might care to compare and contrast the two kinds.

2. *In what different forms does it occur, while keeping its own identity?* Specific examples might occur to you: your Uncle George, who won't hire any "damned females" in his auto repair shop; some college-aged male acquaintance who regards women as nothing but *Penthouse* centerfolds. Each form — Uncle George and the would-be stud — might rate a description.

3. *When and where do we find it? Under what circumstances and in what situations?* Well, where have you been lately? At any parties where male chauvinism reared its ugly head? In any classroom discussions? Consider other areas of your experience: Did you meet any such male pigs while holding a part-time or summer job?

4. *What is it at the present moment?* Perhaps you might make the point that a few years ago male chauvinists used to be blatant tyrants and harsh critics of women. Today, wary of being recog-

---

[1]The six questions that follow are freely adapted from those first stated by Richard E. Young, Alton L. Becker, and Kenneth L. Pike, who have applied insights from psychology and linguistics to the writing process. Their procedure for generating ideas and discovering information is called *tagmemics*. To investigate subjects in greater depth, their own six questions may be used in nine possible combinations, as they explain in detail in *Rhetoric: Discovery and Change* (New York: Harcourt, 1970).

nized, they appear as ordinary citizens who now and then slip in a little tyranny, or make a nasty remark. You might care to draw examples from life.

5. *What does it do? What are its functions and activities?* Male chauvinists try to keep women in what they imagine to be women's place. These questions might even invite you to reply with a process analysis. You might show how some male chauvinist you know goes about implementing his views: how a personnel director you met, who determines pay scales, systematically eliminates women from better-paying jobs; how the *Penthouse* reader plots a seduction.

6. *How is it put together? What parts make it up? What holds these parts together?* You could apply analysis to the various beliefs and assumptions that, all together, make up a male chauvinist's attitude. This question might work well in writing about some organization: the personnel director's company, for instance, with its unfair hiring policies.

Not all these questions will fit every subject under the sun, and some may lead nowhere, but you will usually find them well worth asking. They can make you aware of points to notice, remind you of facts you already know. They can also suggest interesting points you need to find out more about.

In defining something, you need not try to forge a definition so absolute that it will stand till the mountains turn to plains. Like a mapmaker, the writer of an extended definition draws approximate boundaries, takes in only some of what lies within them, and ignores what lies outside. The boundaries, of course, may be wide; and for this reason, the writing of an extended definition sometimes tempts a writer to sweep across a continent airily and to soar off into abstract clouds. Like any other method of expository writing, though, definition will work only for the writer who remembers the world of the senses and supports every generalization with concrete evidence.

There may be no finer illustration of the perils of definition than the scene, in Charles Dickens's novel *Hard Times*, of the grim schoolroom of a teacher named Gradgrind, who insists on facts but who completely ignores living realities. When a girl whose father is a horse trainer is unable to define a horse, Grad-grind blames her for not knowing what a horse is; and he praises the definition of a horse supplied by a pet pupil: "Quadruped. Graminivorous. Forty teeth, namely twenty-four grinders, four eye-teeth, and twelve incisive. Sheds coat in the spring; in marshy countries, sheds hoofs, too. Hoofs hard, but requiring to be shod with iron. Age known by marks in mouth." To anyone who didn't already know what a horse is, this enumeration of facts would prove of little help. In writing an extended definition, never lose sight of the reality you are attempting to bound, even if its frontiers are as inclusive as those of "psychological burnout" or "human rights." Give your reader examples, tell an illustrative story, use an analogy, bring in specific description — in whatever method you use, keep coming down to earth. Without your eyes on the world, you will define no reality. You might define "ani-mal husbandry" till the cows come home, and never make clear what it means.

DEFINITION IN A PARAGRAPH:
TWO ILLUSTRATIONS

Using Definition to Write about Television

Miami Vice is at last banished to late-night syndication. Contrary to what we might have expected, this show presented a view of police work that did not belong on prime-time televi-sion: the ideal cop as lawbreaker. Crockett and Tubbs, heroes of the series, continually broke department rules and rode roughshod over civil liberties. When they set a trap for a drug dealer, using real heroin for bait, or when they kidnapped some thug and slapped him around a little, they didn't fret about not going by the book. Time and again they defied petty bureau-crats who would hamper them. They ignored mayor, district attorney, and police commissioner, and sometimes even their sympathetic, frozen-faced boss, Lieutenant Castillo. As they moved through the twilight world of big-time narcotics, Crock-ett and Tubbs, to do their jobs, needed to break the law con-stantly. Despite their puny paychecks (which in real life would be about $459 a week), they lived in high style, like the crooks they pursued. Glamorized figures in trendy clothes, they jetted away to New York or Bogotá on fat expense accounts, enjoying the sports cars and fancy mansions lent to them for disguise. Society, according to *Miami Vice*, is so corrupt and its police force so riddled with corruption that Crockett and Tubbs had to take the law into their own hands and become outlaws themselves. As ideal cops, they listened not to the law but to some higher code engraved only upon their hearts.

COMMENT. In setting forth a definition in a paragraph, this writer explores a narrow subject: the idea of the ideal cop as shown in a single TV series. This seems enough matter for one paragraph. The main point of the definition, you'll notice, is that the ideal cop in the *Miami Vice* mode is himself a lawbreaker. This point is made at the start of the paragraph and — to reinforce it and sum up — again at the end. But the writer suggests too that on *Miami Vice*, the ideal cop was idealized in other ways: Crockett and Tubbs were "glamorized figures in trendy clothes" who drove borrowed sports cars. What makes the paragraph vivid and clear is that the writer keeps supplying examples. No sooner are we told that the two cops broke the law than we learn that they set traps with real drugs. Did they violate civil liberties? An example follows: They rough up a criminal. The writer does not stop at "bureaucrats," but mentions three kinds, and names one individual, Lieutenant Castillo. Giving examples, as this paragraph shows, is one of the more effective ways to define.

Using Definition in an Academic Discipline

When the character traits found in any two species owe their resemblance to a common ancestry, taxonomists say the states are *homologous*, or are *homologues* of each other. *Homology* is defined as correspondence between two structures due to inheritance from a common ancestor. Homologous structures can be identical in appearance and can even be based on identical genes. However, such structures can diverge until they become very different in both appearance and function. Nevertheless, homologous structures usually retain certain basic features that betray a common ancestry. Consider the forelimbs of vertebrates. It is easy to make a detailed, bone-by-bone, muscle-by-muscle comparison of the forearm of a person and a monkey and to conclude that the forearms, as well as the various parts of the forearm, are homologous. The forelimb of a dog, however, shows marked differences from those of primates in both structure and function. The forelimb is used for locomotion by dogs but for grasping and manipulation by people and monkeys. Even so, all of the bones can still be matched. The wing of a bird and the flipper of a seal are even more different from each other or from the human forearm, yet they too are constructed around bones that can be matched on a nearly perfect one-to-one basis.

COMMENT. Taken from *Life: The Science of Biology*, by William K. Purves and Gordon H. Orians (1983), this paragraph sets out to define *homology* and also to show how the two related forms of the word, *homologous* and *homologues*, are used. Students need to know the meanings of all three to study biology. The authors begin with a brief definition, then emphasize that not all homologues closely resemble one another on the surface. To show the differences that species can display, as well as what they must have in common to be homologues, Purves and Orians amplify their definition with examples. The forearms of humans closely resemble those of monkeys, and the two are indeed homologous. The forelimbs of dogs, the wings of birds, and the flippers of seals, however, are homologous with the forearms of people even though they appear in many ways different. The examples are valuable here because they help to define the concepts.

JOHN BERGER

JOHN BERGER was born in London in 1926, attended art school, and became an influential art critic with a passionate interest in the social role of art. His many significant works of art criticism include *The Success and Failure of Picasso* (1965), *The Moment of Cubism and Other Essays* (1969), and *Ways of Seeing* (1972). Berger also has a reputation as a screenwriter (*Jonah Who Will Be 25 in the Year 2000* and *La Salamandre*), a documentary writer (*A Fortunate Man: The Story of a Country Doctor*, 1967), and a novelist. His most recent fiction — *Pig Earth* (1979), *Once in Europa* (1987), and *Lilac and Flag* (1990) — is a trilogy about peasant life and reflects Berger's abiding concern with class structures, particularly with the gulf between rural poor and urban rich. These books are set in the small village in the French Alps where Berger has lived for nearly two decades.

On Home

This work (titled by the editors) comes from *And Our Faces, My Heart, Brief as Photos*, a collection of poems, stories, and sketches published by Berger in 1984. In exploring the meaning of *home*, Berger reaches deeper than might be expected: Home, he says, is reality. (For another view of the same subject, see the following essay, Nikki Giovanni's "Pioneers: A View of Home.")

> "Philosophy is really homesickness,
> it is the urge to be at home everywhere."
> — Novalis

The transition from a nomadic life to a settled one is said to mark the beginning of what was later called civilization. Soon all those who survived outside the city began to be considered uncivilized. But that is another story — to be told in the hills near the wolves.

Perhaps during the last century and a half an equally important transformation has taken place. Never before our time have so many people been uprooted. Emigration, forced or chosen, across national frontiers or from village to metropolis, is the quintessential experience of our time. That industrialization and capitalism would require such a transport of men on an unprecedented scale and with a new kind of violence was already prophesied by the opening of the slave trade in the sixteenth century. The Western Front in the First World War with its conscripted massed armies was a later confirmation of the same practice of tearing up, assembling, transporting, and concentrating in a "no-man's land." Later, concentration camps, across the world, followed the logic of the same continuous practice.

All the modern historians from Marx to Spengler[1] have identified the contemporary phenomenon of emigration. Why add more words? To whisper for that which has been lost. Not out of nostalgia, but because it is on the site of loss that hopes are born. 3

The term *home* (Old Norse *Heimer*, High German *heim*, Greek *kōmi*, meaning "village") has, since a long time, been taken over by two kinds of moralists, both dear to those who wield power. The notion of *home* became the keystone for a code of domestic morality, safeguarding the property (which included the women) of the family. Simultaneously the notion of *homeland* supplied a first article of faith for patriotism, persuading men to die in wars which often served no other interest except that of a minority of their ruling class. Both usages have hidden the original meaning. 4

Originally home meant the center of the world — not in a geographical, but in an ontological sense. Mircea Eliade[2] has demonstrated how home was the place from which the world could be *founded*. A home was established, as he says, "at the heart of the real." In traditional societies, everything that made sense of the world was real; the surrounding chaos existed and was threatening, but it was threatening because it was *unreal*. Without a home at the center of the real, one was not only shelterless, but also lost in nonbeing, in unreality. Without a home everything was fragmentation. 5

[1]Karl Marx (1818–1883) and Oswald Spengler (1880–1936) were both Germans. — Eds.
[2]Eliade (1907–1986) was a Romanian-born novelist and religious historian. — Eds.

Home was the center of the world because it was the place   6
where a vertical line crossed with a horizontal one. The vertical
line was a path leading upwards to the sky and downwards to the
underworld. The horizontal line represented the traffic of the
world, all the possible roads leading across the earth to other
places. Thus, at home, one was nearest to the gods in the sky and
to the dead in the underworld. This nearness promised access to
both. And at the same time, one was at the starting point and,
hopefully, the returning point of all terrestrial journeys.

The crossing of the two lines, the reassurance their inter-   7
section promises, was probably already there, in embryo, in the
thinking and beliefs of nomadic people, but they carried the vertical line with them, as they might carry a tent pole. Perhaps at the
end of this century of unprecedented transportation, vestiges of
the reassurance still remain in the unarticulated feelings of many
millions of displaced people.

Emigration does not only involve leaving behind, crossing   8
water, living amongst strangers, but also, undoing the very meaning of the world and — at its most extreme — abandoning oneself
to the unreal which is the absurd.

Emigration, when it is not enforced at gunpoint, may of   9
course be prompted by hope as well as desperation. For example,
to the peasant son the father's traditional authority may seem
more oppressively absurd than any chaos. The poverty of the village may appear more absurd than the crimes of the metropolis.
To live and die amongst foreigners may seem less absurd then to
live persecuted or tortured by one's fellow countrymen. All this
can be true. But to emigrate is always to dismantle the center of
the world, and so to move into a lost, disoriented one of fragments.

QUESTIONS ON MEANING

1. Berger states a PURPOSE in paragraph 3. Based on the essay, would
   you say this is his complete purpose?

2. In your own words, summarize Berger's definition of *home*.
3. Why does Berger call emigration "the quintessential experience of our time" (para. 2)?
4. PARAPHRASE Berger's argument about emigration in paragraphs 5, 8, and 9. How does it relate to his definition?

QUESTIONS ON WRITING STRATEGY

1. Berger uses a fairly common technique of definition in rejecting certain familiar meanings of his subject. What meanings does he reject?
2. What is the point of Berger's opening paragraph? How does it relate to the rest of the essay?
3. OTHER METHODS. In paragraphs 6–7, Berger's definition of *home* draws on an analogy (Chap. 8). What is the analogy, and what does it accomplish?

QUESTIONS ON LANGUAGE

1. A key word in Berger's definition is *ontological* (para. 5). What does it mean in this context?
2. Examine the words Berger uses to define *home*. How do their CONNOTATIONS reinforce his definition?
3. A number of words in Berger's definition may require further definition: nomadic (para. 2); unprecedented, prophesied, conscripted (3); phenomenon, nostalgia (4); moralists, wield, keystone (5); underworld, terrestrial (7); embryo, vestiges, unarticulated, displaced (8).

SUGGESTIONS FOR WRITING

1. Do you agree with Berger's definition of *home*? Write an essay extending or contesting his definition, using examples from your reading and experience to support your ideas.
2. Write an essay about some experience you have had with emigration, whether from one nation to another, from the country to the city, or even from one neighborhood to another. What did you lose by emigrating? What did you gain? (If you prefer, write instead of the experience of some member or members of your family.)
3. Write your own definition of an ABSTRACT word, such as *health, success, friendship, honor,* or *fairness*. Use specific examples to make your meaning CONCRETE.

4. CONNECTIONS. When you have read the next essay, Nikki Giovanni's "Pioneers," write your own definition of *home*. As your starting point, agree or disagree with Berger's and Giovanni's definitions.

JOHN BERGER ON WRITING

John Berger took up residence in a tiny French mountain village in the early 1970s so that he could learn and write about the experiences of peasants. He especially wanted to understand the dislocations of peasants who migrated from their villages to cities such as those he had always lived in. Berger rents a farmhouse beneath a hayloft and next to a cow barn, his rent paid mostly in farm labor for his landlord. To a writer who visited him, Gerald Marzorati, Berger explained that he likes farm work and, besides, that "the best way to get to know peasants is not by talking but by doing things, working together. . . . If you are, as I was, prepared to get dirty with them, clean stables and work in the fields and so on — and do these things ludicrously badly, so that they are master and you the idiot — if you can do this, the distance can be overcome, a closeness felt."

But what, Marzorati wanted to know, did Berger's coworkers think when Berger left the fields to write stories? "They understand my being a writer," Berger answered, "because they understand that it is hard work, which they appreciate. Work is how one makes sense of one's life, makes sense of one's place in nature. A peasant knows that to do anything well takes time and skill — whether you are writing or felling a tree."

FOR DISCUSSION

1. How is farm labor actually research for Berger?
2. What are the parallels between writing and farming? Go beyond Berger's statements to explore the meaning of "Work is how one makes sense of one's life, makes sense of one's place in nature."

"If one writes that he is in love with a redheaded girl, I want to know if her mother and her sister are redheads. I want information about the girl's background. How did he meet her? How will this affair end? What is he envisioning?

"I'm trying to teach students to see the whole scene and bring all the information to bear on this love poem. Then we might have something, because it's insufficient to just write that you are in love. Nobody cares. We care about what's around it, what triggered the poem.

"If you are working on your own — not as part of a workshop — and if, for instance, you are writing about raindrops, have this conversation with yourself:

Question: Where does the rain go?
Answer: It falls to the ground.
Question: Then what?
Answer: The rain comes back as a bud.
Question: What does the bud do?
Answer: The bud gives off oxygen and oxygen goes back up into space.

"Follow your image as far as you can no matter how useless you think it is. Push yourself. Always ask, 'What else can I do with this image?' because you have images before you have poems. Words are illustrations of thoughts. You must think this way."

FOR DISCUSSION

1. What is the point of taking things "a little bit beyond what makes sense"? What might happen in the process?
2. How can Giovanni's advice on poetry writing be applied to writing nonfiction prose as well?

FRANCINE PROSE

Born in 1947 in Brooklyn, New York, FRANCINE PROSE received
a B.A. from Radcliffe in 1968 and an M.A. from Harvard in
1969. She has contributed short stories and essays to the *Atlantic*, *Commentary*, the *Village Voice*, *Mademoiselle*, and other periodicals and has published a volume of stories, *Women and
Children First* (1988). Her seven novels, most dealing with myth
and faith, include *Judah the Pious* (1973), *The Glorious Ones*
(1974), *Animal Magnetism* (1978), *Hungry Hearts* (1983), and
Bigfoot Dreams (1986). Prose has taught creative writing at Harvard, the University of Arizona, Warren Wilson College, and
the University of Iowa. She lives in New York State.

Gossip

Prose's fiction often explores the role of storytelling in our lives.
It seems appropriate, then, that she would write an essay on the
storytelling in common, everyday gossip. This essay first appeared in May 1985 as a "Hers" column in the *New York
Times*.

Once I met a woman who grew up in the small North Caro- 1
lina town to which Chang and Eng, the original Siamese twins,
retired after their circus careers. When I asked her how the town
reacted to the twins marrying local girls and setting up adjacent
households, she laughed and said: "Honey, that was *nothing* compared to what happened *before* the twins got there. Get the good
gossip on any little mountain town, scratch the surface, and you'll
find a snake pit!"

Surely she was exaggerating; one assumes the domestic ar- 2
rangements of a pair of Siamese twins and their families would
cause a few ripples anywhere. And yet the truth of what she said
seemed less important than the glee with which she said it, her
pride in the snake pit she'd come from, in its history, its scandals,
its legacy of "good gossip." Gossip, the juicier the better, was her

heritage, her birthright; that town, with its social life freaki:
enough to make Chang and Eng's seem mundane, was part
who she was.

Gossip must be nearly as old as language itself. It was, I ima
ine, the earliest recreational use of the spoken word. First the ca·
man learned to describe the location of the plumpest bison, th·
he began to report and speculate on the doings of his neighbors
the cave next door. And yet, for all its antiquity, gossip has rar·
received its due; its very name connotes idleness, time-wastir
frivolity and worse. Gossip is the unacknowledged poor relat·
of civilized conversation: Almost everyone does it but hardly a·
one will admit to or defend it; and of these only the smallest ·
most shameless fraction will own up to enjoying it.

My mother and her friends are eloquent on the subject
on the distinction between gossiping and exchanging infor
tion: "John got a new job," is, they say, information. "Hey
you hear John got fired?" is gossip, which is, they agree, prec
nantly scurrilous, mean-spirited. That's the conventional w·   n
on gossip and why it's so tempting to disown. Not long   I
heard myself describe a friend, half-jokingly, as "a mucł   :er
person than I am, that is, she doesn't gossip so much." I h·   my
voice distorted by that same false note that sometimes cr·   ·nto
it when social strain and some misguided notion of a·   ·ility
make me assent to opinions I don't really share. Wh·   ·n the
world was I talking about?

I don't, of course, mean rumor-mongering, outrigh·   ander,
willful fabrication meant to damage and undermine. B·   ·ather,
ordinary gossip, incidents from and analyses of the lives·   ·ur heroes and heroines, our relatives, acquaintances, and fr·   ·ls. The
fact is, I love gossip, and beyond that, I believe in it —·   its purposes, its human uses.

I'm even fond of the word, its etymology, its or·   · in the
Anglo-Saxon term godsibbe for godparent, relative,·   meaning
widening by the Renaissance to include friends, cron·   and later
what one does with one's cronies. One gossips. Parinş·   ·ay its less
flattering modern connotations, we discover a kinc·   synonym
for connection, for community, and this, it seems·   me, is the
primary function of gossip. It maps our ties, remir·   ·us of what

sort of people we know and what manner of lives they lead, confirms our sense of who we are, how we live, and where we have come from. The roots of the grapevine are inextricably entwined with our own. Who knows how much of our sense of the world has reached us on its branches, how often, as babies, we dropped off to sleep to the rhythms of family gossip? I've often thought that gossip's bad name might be cleared by calling it "oral tradition"; for what, after all, is an oral tradition but the stories of other lives, other eras, legends from a time when human traffic with spirits and gods was considered fit material for gossipy speculation?

Older children gossip; adolescents certainly do. Except in the   7
case of those rare toddler-fabulists, enchanting parents and siblings with fairy tales made upon the spot, gossip may be the way that most of us learn to tell stories. And though, as Gertrude Stein is supposed to have told Hemingway,[1] gossip is not literature, some similar criteria may apply to both. Pacing, tone, clarity, and authenticity are as essential for the reportage of neighborhood news as they are for well-made fiction.

Perhaps more important is gossip's analytical component.   8
Most people — I'm leaving out writers, psychologists, and probably some large proportion of the academic and service professions — are, at least in theory, free to go about their lives without feeling the compulsion to endlessly dissect the minutiae of human motivation. They can indulge in this at their leisure, for pleasure, in their gossip. And while there are those who clearly believe that the sole aim of gossip is to criticize, to condemn (or, frequently, to titillate, to bask in the aura of scandal as if it were one's own), I prefer to see gossip as a tool of understanding. It only takes a moment to tell what someone did. Far more mileage — and more enjoyment — can be extracted from debating why he did it. Such questions, impossible to discuss without touching on matters of choice and consequence, responsibility and will, are, one might argue, the beginnings of moral inquiry, first steps toward a moral

[1]Stein (1874–1946) was an American writer; Ernest Hemingway (1899–1961) was also an American writer, and winner of a Nobel Prize. — EDS.

education. It has always seemed peculiar that a pastime so conducive to the moral life should be considered faintly immoral.

I don't mean to deny the role of plain nosiness in all this, of 9
unadorned curiosity about our neighbors' secrets. And curiosity
(where would we be without it?) has, like gossip, come in for some
negative press. Still, it's understandable; everyone wants to gossip, hardly anyone wants to be gossiped about. What rankles is
the fear that our secrets will be revealed, some essential privacy
stripped away and, of course, the lack of control over what others
say. Still, such talk is unavoidable; it's part of human nature, of
the human community. When one asks, "What's the gossip?" it's
that community that is being affirmed.

So I continue to ask, mostly without apology and especially 10
when I'm talking to friends who still live in places I've moved
away from. And when they answer — recalling the personalities,
telling the stories, the news — I feel as close as I ever will to the
lives we shared, to what we know and remember in common, to
those much-missed, familiar, and essentially beneficent snake pits
I've lived in and left behind.

QUESTIONS ON MEANING

1. From what source does Prose take "the conventional wisdom" on
   gossip? What, in a sentence, is Prose's own meaning?
2. Why does Prose make exceptions of "writers, psychologists, and
   probably some large proportion of the academic and service professions" in paragraph 8? What is her attitude toward these people?
3. How is gossip "a tool of understanding" (para. 8)?
4. Where does Prose express her THESIS? What is it?

QUESTIONS ON WRITING STRATEGY

1. What does Prose gain from two definition techniques: saying what
   she does not mean (paras. 4–5) and providing a word history (6)?
2. What kind of EVIDENCE does Prose use in paragraph 3? Is it reliable?
   If not, what is the point of it?

3. When Prose writes that "the truth of what she said seemed less important than the glee with which she said it" (para. 2), how does the statement anticipate her thesis and her CONCLUSION?
4. OTHER METHODS. Prose introduces brief narratives, or ANECDOTES, in paragraphs 1–2 and 4. What is the function of each one?

QUESTIONS ON LANGUAGE

1. What does "scratch the surface and you'll find a snake pit" mean (para. 1)? Can you locate other COLLOQUIAL EXPRESSIONS in the essay?
2. Analyze the difference between "John got a new job" and "Hey, did you hear John got fired?" Could you rewrite the second sentence so that it would meet Prose's mother's standards of information exchange rather than gossip?
3. Consult a dictionary, if necessary, for the meanings of these words: adjacent (para. 1); legacy, mundane (2); connotes, frivolity (3); predominantly, scurrilous, amiability, assent (4); etymology, cronies, inextricably, entwined (6); fabulists, criteria, authenticity (7); minutiae, aura, conducive (8); rankles (9); beneficent (10).

SUGGESTIONS FOR WRITING

1. Write an essay agreeing or disagreeing with Prose, using as your principal support a narrative about the spreading of some item of gossip. Were the gossipers helped or hurt by gossiping, and how? What about the subject(s) of the gossip? (If you need help constructing a narrative, see Chapter 1.)
2. Choose some human activity that you feel is unfairly defined in the popular opinion: hunting, shopping, playing a sport, attending rock concerts, loitering, hitchhiking. Following Prose's example, redefine this activity in a way that makes clear what you see as its positive side. Use the popular opinion for contrast.
3. CONNECTIONS. Gossip is not the subject of Shirley Jackson's "The Lottery" (p. 100), but it figures prominently in the story's narrative and dialogue. Read or reread the story in the light of Prose's essay. Write an essay of your own in which you analyze the functions that gossip seems to serve in Jackson's fictional town. (Use quotations from the story to support your ideas.)

TOM WOLFE

TOM WOLFE, author, journalist, and cartoonist, was born in 1931 in Richmond, Virginia, and went to Washington and Lee University. After taking a Ph.D. in American Studies at Yale, he decided against an academic career and instead worked as a reporter for the *Springfield Union* in Massachusetts, then as a correspondent on Latin America for the *Washington Post*. Early in the 1960s, Wolfe began writing his electrifying, satiric articles on the American scene (with special, mocking attention to sub-cultures and trendsetters), which have enlivened *New York*, *Esquire*, *Rolling Stone*, *Harper's*, and other sophisticated magazines. Among his books are *The Electric Kool-Aid Acid Test* (1965), a memoir of LSD-spaced-out hippies; *The Kandy-Kolored Tangerine-Flake Streamline Baby* (1968), glimpses of popular follies and foibles; *The Pump House Gang* (1968), a study of California surfers; *Radical Chic and Mau-Mauing the Flak Catchers* (1970), an unflattering view of New York artists and literati; *The Right Stuff* (1979), a chronicle of America's first astronauts, which was made into a movie; *From Bauhaus to Our House* (1981), a complaint against modern architecture; and *The Purple Decades* (1983), a retrospective selection of essays. Wolfe's first novel, *The Bonfire of the Vanities* (1987), was both controversial and hugely popular.

Pornoviolence

This essay, from a collection raking over the 1970s, *Mauve Gloves & Madmen, Clutter & Vine* (1976), is vintage Tom Wolfe. He played a large part in the invention of "the new journalism" (a brand of reporting that tells the truth excitedly, as if it were fiction), and his essay is marked by certain breathless features of style: long sentences full of parenthetical asides, ellipses (. . .), generous use of italics. (For a sampling of lively reporting by Wolfe and others, see the anthology Wolfe edited with E. W. Johnson, *The New Journalism*, 1973.) In the following essay Wolfe coins a term to fit the blend of pornography and pandering to bloodlust that he finds in the media. Although not recent, his remarks have dated little since they first appeared.

"*Keeps His Mom-in-law in Chains*, meet *Kills Son and Feeds*   1
Corpse to Pigs."

"Pleased to meet you."   2

"*Teenager Twists Off Corpse's Head . . . to Get Gold Teeth*,   3
meet *Strangles Girl Friend, Then Chops Her to Pieces*."

"How you doing?"   4

"*Nurse's Aide Sees Fingers Chopped Off in Meat Grinder*, meet   5
I Left My Babies in the Deep Freeze."

"It's a pleasure."   6

It's a pleasure! No doubt about that! In all these years of jour- 7
nalism I have covered more conventions than I care to remember.
Podiatrists, theosophists, Professional Budget Finance dentists,
oyster farmers, mathematicians, truckers, dry cleaners, stamp
collectors, Esperantists, nudists, and newspaper editors —
I have seen them all, together, in vast assemblies, sloughing
through the wall-to-wall of a thousand hotel lobbies (the nudists
excepted) in their shimmering gray-metal suits and pajama-stripe
shirts with white Plasti-Coat name cards on their chests, and I
have sat through their speeches and seminars (the nudists included) and attentively endured ear baths such as you wouldn't
believe. And yet none has ever been quite like the convention of
the stringers for the *National Enquirer*.

The *Enquirer* is a weekly newspaper that is probably known   8
by sight to millions more than know it by name. No one who
ever came face-to-face with the *Enquirer* on a newsstand in its
wildest days is likely to have forgotten the sight: a tabloid with
great inky shocks of type all over the front page saying something
on the order of *Gouges Out Wife's Eyes to Make Her Ugly, Dad
Hurls Hot Grease in Daughter's Face, Wife Commits Suicide after 2
Years of Poisoning Fails to Kill Husband . . .*

The stories themselves were supplied largely by stringers, i.e., 9
correspondents, from all over the country, the world, for that
matter, mostly copy editors and reporters on local newspapers.
Every so often they would come upon a story, usually via the police beat, that was so grotesque the local sheet would discard it or
run it in a highly glossed form rather than offend or perplex its
readers. The stringers would preserve them for the *Enquirer*,
which always rewarded them well and respectfully.

One year the *Enquirer* convened and feted them at a hotel in   10
Manhattan. This convention was a success in every way. The
only awkward moment was at the outset when the stringers all
pulled in. None of them knew each other. Their hosts got around
the problem by introducing them by the stories they had supplied. The introductions went like this:

"Harry, I want you to meet Frank here. Frank did that story,   11
you remember that story, *Midget Murderer Throws Girl Off Cliff
after She Refuses to Dance with Him.*"

"Pleased to meet you. That was some story."   12

"And Harry did the one about *I Spent Three Days Trapped at*   13
*Bottom of Forty-Foot-Deep Mine Shaft and Was Saved by a Swarm
of Flies.*"

"Likewise, I'm sure."   14

And *Midget Murderer Throws Girl Off Cliff* shakes hands   15
with *I Spent Three Days Trapped at Bottom of Forty-Foot-Deep
Mine Shaft*, and *Buries Her Baby Alive* shakes hands with *Boy,
Twelve, Strangles Two-Year-Old Girl*, and *Kills Son and Feeds
Corpse to Pigs* shakes hands with *He Strangles Old Woman and
Smears Corpse with Syrup, Ketchup, and Oatmeal* . . . and . . .

. . . There was a great deal of esprit about the whole thing.   16
These men were, in fact, the avant-garde of a new genre that since
then has become institutionalized throughout the nation without
anyone knowing its proper name. I speak of the new pornography, the pornography of violence.

Pornography comes from the Greek word "*porne*," meaning   17
harlot, and pornography is literally the depiction of the acts of
harlots. In the new pornography, the theme is not sex. The new
pornography depicts practitioners acting out another, murkier
drive: people staving teeth in, ripping guts open, blowing brains
out, and getting even with all those bastards . . .

The success of the *Enquirer* prompted many imitators to enter   18
the field, *Midnight*, the *Star Chronicle*, the *National Insider*, *Inside
News*, the *National Close-up*, the *National Tattler*, the *National
Examiner*. A truly competitive free press evolved, and soon a
reader could go to the newspaper of his choice for *Kill the Re-
tarded! (Won't You Join My Movement?)* and *Unfaithful Wife?
Burn Her Bed!*, *Harem Master's Mistress Chops Him with Machete*,

Babe Bites Off Boy's Tongue, and *Cuts Buddy's Face to Pieces for Stealing His Business and Fiancée.*

And yet the last time I surveyed the Violence press, I noticed 19 a curious thing. These pioneering journals seem to have pulled back. They seem to be regressing to what is by now the Redi-Mix staple of literate Americans, mere sex. *Ecstasy and Me (by Hedy Lamarr),*[1] says the *National Enquirer. I Run a Sex Art Gallery,* says the *National Insider.* What has happened, I think, is something that has happened to avant-gardes in many fields, from William Morris and the Craftsmen to the Bauhaus group.[2] Namely, their discoveries have been preempted by the Establishment and so thoroughly dissolved into the mainstream they no longer look original.

Robert Harrison, the former publisher of *Confidential,* and 20 later publisher of the aforementioned *Inside News,* was perhaps the first person to see it coming. I was interviewing Harrison early in January 1964 for a story in *Esquire* about six weeks after the assassination of President Kennedy, and we were in a cab in the West Fifties in Manhattan, at a stoplight, by a newsstand, and Harrison suddenly pointed at the newsstand and said, "Look at that. They're doing the same thing the *Enquirer* does."

There on the stand was a row of slick-paper, magazine-size 21 publications, known in the trade as one-shots, with titles like *Four Days That Shook the World, Death of a President, An American Tragedy,* or just *John Fitzgerald Kennedy (1921–1963).* "You want to know why people buy those things?" said Harrison. "People buy those things to see a man get his head blown off."

And, of course, he was right. Only now the publishers were 22 in many cases the pillars of the American press. Invariably, these

[1]*Ecstasy,* an early, European-made Hedy Lamarr film, was notorious for its scenes of soft-core lovemaking. Later, paired with Charles ("Come with me to the Casbah") Boyer, Lamarr rose to Hollywood stardom in *Algiers* (1938). — EDS.

[2]Morris (1834–1896), an English artist, poet, printer, and socialist, founded a company of craftspeople to bring tasteful design to furniture (the Morris chair) and other implements of everyday life. The Bauhaus, an influential art school in Germany (1919–1933), taught crafts and brought new ideas of design to architecture and to goods produced in factories. — EDS.

"special coverages" of the assassination bore introductions piously commemorating the fallen President, exhorting the American people to strength and unity in a time of crisis, urging greater vigilance and safeguards for the new President, and even raising the nice metaphysical question of collective guilt in "an age of violence."

In the years since then, of course, there has been an incessant 23 replay, with every recoverable clinical detail, of those less than five seconds in which a man got his head blown off. And throughout this deluge of words, pictures, and film frames, I have been intrigued with one thing: The point of view, the vantage point, is almost never that of the victim, riding in the Presidential Lincoln Continental. What you get is . . . the view from Oswald's rifle. You can step right up here and look point-blank right through the very hairline cross in Lee Harvey Oswald's Optics Ordinance in weaponry four-power Japanese telescope sight and watch, frame by frame by frame by frame, as that man there's head comes apart. Just a little History there before your very eyes.

The television networks have schooled us in the view from 24 Oswald's rifle and made it seem a normal pastime. The TV viewpoint is nearly always that of the man who is going to strike. The last time I watched *Gunsmoke*, which was not known as a very violent Western in TV terms, the action went like this: The Wellington agents and the stagecoach driver pull guns on the badlands gang leader's daughter and Kitty, the heart-of-gold saloonkeeper, and kidnap them. Then the badlands gang shoots two Wellington agents. Then they tie up five more and talk about shooting them. Then they desist because they might not be able to get a hotel room in the next town if the word got around. Then one badlands gang gunslinger attempts to rape Kitty while the gang leader's younger daughter looks on. Then Kitty resists, so he slugs her one in the jaw. Then the gang leader slugs him. Then the gang leader slugs Kitty. Then Kitty throws hot stew in a gang member's face and hits him over the back of the head with a revolver. Then he knocks her down with a rock. Then the gang sticks up a bank. Here comes the marshal, Matt Dillon. He shoots a gang member and breaks it up. Then the gang leader shoots the guy who was guarding his daughter and the woman. Then the

marshal shoots the gang leader. The final exploding bullet signals
The End.

It is not the accumulated slayings and bone crushings that   25
make this pornoviolence, however. What makes it pornoviolence
is that in almost every case the camera angle, therefore the
viewer, is with the gun, the fist, the rock. The pornography of violence has no point of view in the old sense that novels do. You
do not live the action through the hero's eyes. You live with the
aggressor, whoever he may be. One moment you are the hero.
The next you are the villain. No matter whose side you may be
on consciously, you are in fact with the muscle, and it is you who
disintegrate all comers, villains, lawmen, women, anybody. On
the rare occasions in which the gun is emptied into the camera —
i.e., into your face — the effect is so startling that the pornography of violence all but loses its fantasy charm. There are not
nearly so many masochists as sadists among those little devils
whispering into one's ears.

In fact, sex — "sadomasochism" — is only a part of the por-   26
nography of violence. Violence is much more wrapped up, simply, with status. Violence is the simple, ultimate solution for
problems of status competition, just as gambling is the simple, ultimate solution for economic competition. The old pornography
was the fantasy of easy sexual delights in a world where sex was
kept unavailable. The new pornography is the fantasy of easy triumph in a world where status competition has become so complicated and frustrating.

Already the old pornography is losing its kick because of   27
overexposure. In the late thirties, Nathanael West published his
last and best-regarded novel, *The Day of the Locust*, and it was a
terrible flop commercially, and his publisher said if he ever published another book about Hollywood it would "have to be *My
Thirty-nine Ways of Making Love by Hedy Lamarr*." He thought he
was saying something that was funny because it was beyond the
realm of possibility. Less than thirty years later, however, Hedy
Lamarr's *Ecstasy and Me* was published. Whether she mentions
thirty-nine ways, I'm not sure, but she gets off to a flying start:
"The men in my life have ranged from a classic case history of im-
potence, to a whip-brandishing sadist who enjoyed sex only after

he tied my arms behind me with the sash of his robe. There was another man who took his pleasure with a girl in my own bed, while he thought I was asleep in it."

Yet she was too late. The book very nearly sank without a   28
trace. The sin itself is wearing out. Pornography cannot exist without certified taboo to violate. And today Lust, like the rest of the Seven Deadly Sins — Pride, Sloth, Envy, Greed, Anger, and Gluttony — is becoming a rather minor vice. The Seven Deadly Sins, after all, are only sins against the self. Theologically, the idea of Lust — well, the idea is that if you seduce some poor girl from Akron, it is not a sin because you are ruining her, but because you are wasting your time and your energies and damaging your own spirit. This goes back to the old work ethic, when the idea was to keep every able-bodied man's shoulder to the wheel. In an age of riches for all, the ethic becomes more nearly: Let him do anything he pleases, as long as he doesn't get in my way. And if he does get in my way, or even if he doesn't . . . well . . . we have *new* fantasies for that. *Put hair on the walls.*

"Hair on the walls" is the invisible subtitle of Truman Ca-   29
pote's book *In Cold Blood*. The book is neither a who-done-it nor a will-they-be-caught, since the answers to both questions are known from the outset. It does ask why-did-they-do-it, but the answer is soon as clear as it is going to be. Instead, the book's suspense is based largely on a totally new idea in detective stories: the promise of gory details, and the withholding of them until the end. Early in the game one of the two murderers, Dick, starts promising to put "plenty of hair on them-those walls" with a shotgun. So read on, gentle readers, and on and on; you are led up to the moment before the crime on page 60 — yet the specifics, what happened, the gory details, are kept out of sight, in grisly dangle, until page 244.

But Dick and Perry, Capote's killers, are only a couple of Low   30
Rent bums. With James Bond the new pornography reached a dead center, the bureaucratic middle class. The appeal of Bond has been explained as the appeal of the lone man who can solve enormously complicated, even world problems through his own bravery and initiative. But Bond is not a lone man at all, of course. He is not the Lone Ranger. He is much easier to identify

than that. He is a salaried functionary in a bureaucracy. He is a sport, but a believable one; not a millionaire, but a bureaucrat on an expense account. He is not even a high-level bureaucrat. He is an operative. This point is carefully and repeatedly made by having his superiors dress him down for violations of standard operating procedure. Bond, like the Lone Ranger, solves problems with guns and fists. When it is over, however, the Lone Ranger leaves a silver bullet. Bond, like the rest of us, fills out a report in triplicate.

Marshall McLuhan[3] says we are in a period in which it will become harder and harder to stimulate lust through words and pictures — i.e., the old pornography. In the latest round of pornographic movies the producers have found it necessary to introduce violence, bondage, torture, and aggressive physical destruction to an extraordinary degree. The same sort of bloody escalation may very well happen in the pure pornography of violence. Even such able craftsmen as Truman Capote, Ian Fleming, NBC, and CBS may not suffice. Fortunately, there are historical models to rescue us from this frustration. In the latter days of the Roman Empire, the Emperor Commodus became jealous of the celebrity of the great gladiators. He took to the arena himself, with his sword, and began dispatching suitably screened cripples and hobbled fighters. Audience participation became so popular that soon various *illuminati* of the Commodus set, various boys and girls of the year, were out there, suited up, gaily cutting a sequence of dwarfs and feebles down to short ribs. Ah, swinging generations, what new delights await? 31

QUESTIONS ON MEANING

1. Which of the following statements comes closest to summing up Tom Wolfe's main PURPOSE in writing "Pornoviolence"?

[3]Canadian English professor, author of *Understanding Media* (1964), *The Medium Is the Message* (1967), and other books, McLuhan (1911–1980) analyzed the effects on world society of television and other electronic media. — EDS.

Wolfe writes to define a word.

Wolfe writes to define a trend in society.

Wolfe writes to define a trend in the media that reflects a trend in society.

Wolfe writes to explain how John F. Kennedy was assassinated.

Wolfe writes to entertain us by mocking Americans' latest foolishness.

(If you don't find any of these statements adequate, compose your own.)

2. If you have ever read the *National Enquirer* or any of its imitators, test the accuracy of Wolfe's reporting. What is the purpose of a featured article in the *Enquirer*?

3. According to Wolfe, what POINT OF VIEW does the writer or producer of pornoviolence always take? What other examples of this point of view (in violent incidents on films or TV shows) can you supply? (Did you ever see a replay of Jack Ruby's shooting of Oswald, for instance?)

4. "Violence is the simple, ultimate solution for problems of status competition" (para. 26). What does Wolfe mean?

5. Wolfe does not explicitly pass judgment on Truman Capote's book *In Cold Blood*. But what is his opinion of it? How can you tell?

6. "No advocate of change for the sake of change, Tom Wolfe writes as a conservative moralist who, like Jonathan Swift, rankles with savage indignation." Does this critical remark fit this particular essay? What, in Wolfe's view, appears to be happening to America and Americans?

QUESTIONS ON WRITING STRATEGY

1. On first reading, what did you make of Wolfe's opening sentence, "'*Keeps His Mom-in-Law in Chains*, meet *Kills Son and Feeds Corpse to Pigs*'"? At what point did you first tumble to what the writer was doing? What IRONY do you find in the convention hosts' introducing people by the headlines of their gory stories? What advantage is it to Wolfe's essay that his INTRODUCTION (with its odd introductions) keeps you guessing for a while?

2. What is Wolfe's point in listing (in para. 7) some of the other conventions he has reported — gatherings of nudists, oyster farmers, and others?

3. At what moment does Wolfe give us his short definition of *pornoviolence*, or the new pornography? Do you think he would have

done better to introduce his short definition of the word in paragraph 1? Why, or why not?

4. What is the TONE or attitude of Wolfe's CONCLUSION (para. 31)? Note in particular the closing line.

5. OTHER METHODS. Typically for a writer of extended definition, Wolfe draws on many methods of development, including narration (para. 1–16, 24), division or analysis (29), and cause and effect (26). What is the purpose of the comparison and contrast in paragraph 30?

QUESTIONS ON LANGUAGE

1. What help to the reader does Wolfe provide by noting the source of the word *pornography* (para. 17)?

2. "The television networks have schooled us in the view from Oswald's rifle" (para. 24). What CONNOTATIONS enlarge the meaning of *schooled*?

3. Define *masochist* and *sadist* (para. 25). What kind of DICTION do you find in these terms? In "plenty of hair on them-those walls" (29)?

4. How much use does Wolfe make of COLLOQUIAL EXPRESSIONS? Point to examples.

5. What does Wolfe mean in noting that the fighters slain by the Emperor Commodus were "hobbled" and the cripples were "suitably screened" (para. 31)? What unflattering connotations does this emperor's very name contain? (If you don't get this, look up *commode* in your desk dictionary.)

SUGGESTIONS FOR WRITING

1. In a paragraph, narrate or describe some recent example of pornoviolence you have seen in the movies or on television or one that you have observed. In a second paragraph, comment on it.

2. Write an essay defining some current trend you've noticed in films or TV, popular music, sports, consumer buying, or some other large arena of life. Like Wolfe, invent a name for it. Use plenty of examples to make your definition clear.

3. CONNECTIONS. Both Tom Wolfe and Rosalind Coward, in "Naughty but Nice" (p. 374), analyze what they see as forms of pornography similar to but also different from sexual pornography. In an essay, define *pornography* by drawing on Wolfe's and Coward's ideas, information in a dictionary, and your own ideas and exam-

ples. In your definition, you may want to address Wolfe's statement that "pornography cannot exist without a certain taboo to violate" (para. 28).

TOM WOLFE ON WRITING

"What about your writing techniques and habits?" Tom Wolfe was asked by Joe David Bellamy for *Writer's Digest*. "The actual writing I do very fast," Wolfe said. "I make a very tight outline of everything I write before I write it. And often, as in the case of *The Electric Kool-Aid Acid Test*, the research, the reporting, is going to take me much longer than the writing. By writing an outline you really are writing in a way, because you're creating the structure of what you're going to do. Once I really know what I'm going to write, I don't find the actual writing takes all that long.

"*The Electric Kool-Aid Acid Test* in manuscript form was about 1,100 pages, triple-spaced, typewritten. That means about 200 words a page, and, you know, some of that was thrown out or cut eventually; but I wrote all of that in three and a half months. I had never written a full-length book before, and at first I decided I would treat each chapter as if it were a magazine article — because I *had* done that before. So I would set an artificial deadline, and I'd make myself meet it. And I did that for three chapters.

"But after I had done this three times and then I looked ahead and I saw that there were *twenty-five* more times I was going to have to do this, I couldn't face it anymore. I said, 'I cannot do this, even one more time, because there's no end to it.' So I completely changed my system, and I set up a quota for myself — of ten typewritten pages a day. At 200 words a page that's 2,000 words, which is not, you know, an overwhelming amount. It's a good clip, but it's not overwhelming. And I found this worked much better. I had my outline done, and sometimes ten pages would get me hardly an eighth-of-an-inch along the outline. It didn't bother me. Just like working in a factory — end of ten pages, I'd close my lunch pail."

FOR DISCUSSION

1. In what way is outlining really writing, according to Wolfe? (In answering, consider the implications of his statement about "creating a structure.")
2. What strategy did the author finally settle on to get himself through the toil of his first book? What made this strategy superior to the one he had used earlier?

JOSEPH EPSTEIN

Joseph Epstein, author, critic, and editor of *The American Scholar*, teaches writing and literature at Northwestern University. He was born in Chicago in 1937. A graduate of the University of Chicago, he served in the army from 1958 to 1960. Epstein's lively and incisive essays have appeared from time to time in such places as the *New York Times Book Review*, *Commentary*, *The New Criterion*, the *New York Times Magazine*, and *Harper's*. He writes regularly for *The American Scholar*. And he is the author of *Divorce in America* (1975); *Familiar Territory* (1980); *Ambition* (1981); *The Middle of My Tether* (1983); *Plausible Prejudices* (1985); *Once More Around the Block* (1987); and *Partial Payments* (1989).

What Is Vulgar?

Epstein wrote "What Is Vulgar?" in 1981 for *The American Scholar*, the magazine published by Phi Beta Kappa (the oldest American honor society for college students). Later he included it in *The Middle of My Tether*. In the essay Epstein seems to have a rollicking good time deciding what vulgarity is. He examines the history of both word and concept. He speculates about what vulgarity is *not*. He relishes colorful examples. Some aspects of his definition may surprise you; others may give you a jolt. We're sure they won't bore you.

What's vulgar? Some people might say that the contraction of the words *what* and *is* itself is vulgar. On the other hand, I remember being called a stuffed shirt by a reviewer of a book of mine because I used almost no contractions. I have forgotten the reviewer's name but I have remembered the criticism. Not being of that category of writers who never forget a compliment, I also remember being called a racist by another reviewer for observing that failure to insist on table manners in children was to risk dining with Apaches. The larger criticisms I forget, but, oddly, these goofy little criticisms stick in the teeth like sesame seeds. Yet that last trope — is it, too, vulgar? Ought I really to be picking my teeth in public, even metaphorically?

What, to return to the question in uncontractioned form, is 2 vulgar? Illustrations, obviously, are wanted. Consider a relative of mine, long deceased, my father's Uncle Jake and hence my grand-uncle. I don't wish to brag about bloodlines, but my Uncle Jake was a bootlegger during Prohibition who afterward went into the scrap-iron — that is to say, the junk — business. Think of the ar-chetypal sensitive Jewish intellectual faces: of Spinoza, of Freud, of Einstein, of Oppenheimer.[1] In my uncle's face you would not have found the least trace of any of them. He was completely bald, weighed in at around two hundred fifty pounds, and had a complexion of clear vermilion. I loved him, yet even as a child I knew there was about him something a bit — how shall I put it? — outsized, and I refer not merely to his personal tonnage. When he visited our home he generally greeted me by pressing a ten- or twenty-dollar bill into my hand — an amount of money quite im-possible, of course, for a boy of nine or ten, when what was wanted was a quarter or fifty-cent piece. A widower, he would usually bring a lady-friend along; here his tastes ran to Hungarian women in their fifties with operatic bosoms. These women wore large diamond rings, possibly the same rings, which my uncle may have passed from woman to woman. A big spender and a high roller, my uncle was an immigrant version of the sport, a kind of Diamond Chaim Brodsky.

But to see Uncle Jake in action you had to see him at table. 3 He drank whiskey with his meal, the bottle before him on the ta-ble along with another of seltzer water, both of which he supplied himself. He ate and drank like a character out of Rabelais.[2] My

---

[1]Benedict (or Baruch) Spinoza (1632–1677) was a Dutch philosopher; Sigmund Freud (1856–1939), the Austrian founder of psychoanalysis; Albert Einstein (1879–1955), the eminent physicist; and J. Robert Oppenheimer (1904–1967), an American physicist who helped develop the first atomic bomb and then opposed the government's decision to develop the hydrogen bomb. — Eds.

[2]François Rabelais (1494?–1553?), French humorist who in *Gargantua and Pantagruel* (1532–1534) depicts two giants with tremendous appetites. — Eds.

mother served him his soup course, not in a regular bowl, but in a vessel more on the order of a tureen. He would eat hot soup and drink whiskey and sweat — my Uncle Jake did not, decidedly, do anything so delicate as perspire — and sometimes it seemed that the sweat rolled from his face right into his soup dish, so that, toward the end, he may well have been engaged in an act of liquid auto-cannibalism, consuming his own body fluids with a whiskey chaser.

He was crude, certainly, my Uncle Jake; he was coarse, of course; gross, it goes without saying; uncouth, beyond question. But was he vulgar? I don't think he was. For one thing, he was good-hearted, and it somehow seems wrong to call anyone vulgar who is good-hearted. But more to the point, I don't think that if you had accused him of being vulgar, he would have known what the devil you were talking about. To be vulgar requires at least a modicum of pretension, and this Uncle Jake sorely lacked. "Wulgar," he might have responded to the accusation that he was vulgar, "so vat's dis wulgar?"

To go from persons to things, and from lack of pretension to a mountain of it, let me tell you about a house I passed one night, in a neighborhood not far from my own, that so filled me with disbelief that I took a hard right turn at the next corner and drove round the block to make certain I had actually seen what I thought I had. I had, but it was no house — it was a bloody edifice!

The edifice in question totally fills its rather modest lot, leaving no backyard at all. It is constructed of a white stone, sanded and perhaps even painted, with so much gray-colored mortar that, even though it may be real, the stone looks fake. The roof is red. It has two chimneys, neither of which, I would wager, functions. My confidence here derives from the fact that nothing much else in the structure of the house seems to function. There is, for example, a balcony over a portico — a portico held up by columns — onto which the only possible mode of entry is by pole vault. There is, similarly, over the attached garage, a sun deck whose only access appears to be through a bathroom window. The house seems to have been built on the aesthetic formula of functionlessness follows formlessness.

But it is in its details that the true spirit of the house emerges.   7
These details are not minuscule, and neither are they subtle. For
starters, outside the house under the portico, there is a chande-
lier. There are also two torch-shaped lamps on either side of the
front door, which is carved in a scallop pattern, giving it the effect
of seeming the back door to a much larger house. Along the short
walk leading up to this front door stand, on short pillars, two
plaster of paris lions — gilded. On each pillar, in gold and black,
appears the owner's name. A white chain fence, strung along
poles whose tops are painted gold, spans the front of the property;
it is the kind of fence that would be more appropriate around,
say, the tomb of Lenin. At the curb are two large cars, sheets of
plastic covering their grills; there is also a trailer; and, in the summer months, a boat sits in the short driveway leading up to the
garage. The lawn disappoints by being not Astro-Turf but, alas,
real grass. However, closer inspection reveals two animals, a
skunk and a rabbit, both of plastic, in petrified play upon the
lawn — a nice, you might almost say a finishing, touch. Sometimes, on long drives or when unable to sleep at night, I have
pondered upon the possible decor of this extraordinary house's
den and upon the ways of man, which are various beyond imagining.

You want vulgar, I am inclined to exclaim, I'll show you vul-   8
gar: The house I have just described is vulgar, patently, palpably,
pluperfectly vulgar. Forced to live in it for more than three hours,
certain figures of refined sensibility — Edith Wharton or Harold
Acton or Wallace Stevens[3] — might have ended as suicides. Yet
as I described that house, I noted two contradictory feelings in
myself: how pleasant it is to point out someone else's vulgarity,
and yet the fear that calling someone else vulgar may itself be
slightly vulgar. After all, the family that lives in this house no
doubt loves it; most probably they feel that they have a real show-
place. Their house, I assume, gives them a large measure of happi-

---

[3]Edith Wharton (1862–1937), American novelist, who frequently wrote
of well-to-do society; Harold Acton (born in 1904), British art critic, historian,
and student of Chinese culture, author of *Memoirs of an Aesthete* (1948) and
other works; Wallace Stevens (1879–1955), American poet and insurance company executive, who wrote with a philosopher's sensibility. — EDS.

ness. Yet why does my calling their home vulgar also give me such a measure of happiness? I suppose it is because vulgarity can be so amusing — other people's vulgarity, that is.

Here I must insert that I have invariably thought that the people who have called me vulgar were themselves rather vulgar. So far as I know I have been called vulgar three times, once directly, once behind my back, and once by association. In each instance the charge was intellectual vulgarity: On one occasion a contributor to a collection of essays on contemporary writing that I once reviewed called me vulgar because I didn't find anything good to say about this book of some six hundred pages; once an old friend, an editor with whom I had had a falling out over politics, told another friend of mine that an article I had written seemed to him vulgar; and, finally, having patched things up with this friend and having begun to write for his magazine again, yet a third friend asked me why I allowed my writing to appear in that particular magazine, when it was so patently — you guessed her, Chester — vulgar.

None of these accusations stung in the least. In intellectual and academic life, vulgar is something one calls people with whom one disagrees. Like having one's ideas called reductionist, it is nothing to get worked up about — certainly nothing to take personally. What would wound me, though, is if word got back to me that someone had said that my manners at table were so vulgar that it sickened him to eat with me, or that my clothes were laughable, or that taste in general wasn't exactly my strong point. In a novel whose author or title I can no longer remember, I recall a female character who was described as having vulgar thumbs. I am not sure I have a clear picture of vulgar thumbs, but if it is all the same, I would just as soon not have them.

I prefer not to be thought vulgar in any wise. When not long ago a salesman offered to show me a winter coat that, as he put it, "has been very popular," I told him to stow it — if it has been popular, it is not for me. I comb my speech, as best I am able, of popular phrases: You will not hear an unfundamental "basically" or a flying "whatever" from these chaste lips. I do not utter "bottom line"; I do not mutter "trade-off." I am keen to cut myself out from the herd, at least when I can. In recent years this has not been difficult. Distinction has lain in plain speech, plain dress, clean cheeks. The simple has become rococo, the rococo simple. But now I see that television anchormen, hairdressers, and other leaders in our society have adopted this plainer look. This is discomfiting news. Vulgar is, after all, as vulgar does.

Which returns us yet again to the question: What is vulgar? 12
The Oxford English Dictionary, which provides more than two pages on the word, is rather better at telling us what vulgar was than what it is. Its definitions run from "1. The common or usual language of a country; the vernacular. *Obs.*" to "13. Having a common and offensively mean character; coarsely commonplace; lacking in refinement or good taste; uncultured, illbred." Historically, the word *vulgar* was used in fairly neutral description up to the last quarter of the seventeenth century to mean and describe the common people. Vulgar was common but not yet contemned. I noted such a neutral usage as late as a William Hazlitt essay of 1818, "On the Ignorance of the Learned," in which Hazlitt writes: "The vulgar are in the right when they judge for themselves; they are wrong when they trust to their blind guides." Yet, according to the *OED*, in 1797 the *Monthly Magazine* remarked: "So the word *vulgar* now implies something base and groveling in actions."

From the early nineteenth century on, then, vulgar has been 13
purely pejorative, a key term in the lexicon of insult and invective. Its currency as a term of abuse rose with the rise of the middle class; its spread was tied to the spread of capitalism and democracy. Until the rise of the middle class, until the spread of capitalism and democracy, people perhaps hadn't the occasion or the need to call one another vulgar. The rise of the middle class, the spread of capitalism and democracy, opened all sorts of social doors; social classes commingled as never before; plutocracy made possible almost daily strides from stratum to stratum. Still, some people had to be placed outside the pale, some doors had to be locked — and the cry of vulgarity, properly intoned, became a most effective Close Sesame.

Such seems to me roughly the social history of the word *vul-* 14
gar. But the history of vulgarity, the thing itself even before it had a name, is much longer. According to the French art historian

Albert Dasnoy, aesthetic vulgarity taints Greek art of the fourth and third centuries B.C. "An exhibition of Roman portraits," Dasnoy writes, "shows that, between the Etruscan style of the earliest and the Byzantine style of the latest, vulgarity made its first full-blooded appearance in the academic realism of imperial Rome." Vulgarity, in Dasnoy's view, comes of the shock of philosophic rationalism, when humankind divests itself of belief in the sacred. "Vulgarity seems to be the price of man's liberation," he writes, "one might even say, of his evolution. It is unquestionably the price of the freeing of the individual personality." Certainly it is true that one would never think to call a savage vulgar; a respectable level of civilization has to have been reached to qualify for the dubious distinction of being called vulgar.

"You have surely noticed the curious fact," writes Valéry,[4]   15 "that a certain *word*, which is perfectly clear when you hear or use it in *everyday* speech, and which presents no difficulty when caught up in the rapidity of an ordinary sentence, becomes mysteriously cumbersome, offers a strange resistance, defeats all efforts at definition, the moment you withdraw it from circulation for separate study and try to find its meaning after taking away its temporary function." *Vulgar* presents special difficulties, though: While vulgarity has been often enough on display — may even be a part of the human soul that only the fortunate and the saintly are able to root out — every age has its own notion of what constitutes the vulgar. Riding a bicycle at Oxford in the 1890s, Max Beerbohm reports, "was the earmark of vulgarity." Working further backward, we find that Matthew Arnold frequently links the word *vulgar* with the word *hideous* and hopes that culture "saves the future, as one may hope, from being vulgarized, even if it cannot save the present." "In Jane Austen's novels," Lionel Trilling writes, "vulgarity has these elements: smallness of mind, insufficiency of awareness, assertive self-esteem, the wish to devalue, especially to devalue the human worth of other people." Hazlitt found vulgarity in false feeling among "the herd of pretenders to what they do not feel and to what is not natural to them, whether in high or low life."

[4]Paul Valéry (1871–1945), French poet and literary critic. — EDS.

Vulgarity, it begins to appear, is often in the eye of the be- 16
holder. What is more, it comes in so many forms. It is so multiple
and so complex — so multiplex. There are vulgarities of taste, of
manner, of mind, of spirit. There are whole vulgar ages — the
Gilded Age in the United States, for one, at least to hear Mark
Twain and Henry Adams tell it. (Is our own age another?) To
compound the complication there is even likeable vulgarity. This
is vulgarity of the kind that Cyril Connolly must have had in
mind when he wrote, "Vulgarity is the garlic in the salad of life."
In the realm of winning vulgarity are the novels of Balzac, the
paintings of Frans Hals, some of the music of Tchaikovsky (ex-
cluding the cannon fire in the 1812 Overture, which is vulgarity
of the unwinning kind).

Rightly used, profanity, normally deemed the epitome of vul- 17
gar manners, can be charming. I recently moved to a new apartment, and the person I dealt with at the moving company we
employed, a woman whose voice had an almost strident
matter-of-factness, instructed me to call back with an inventory of
our furniture. When I did, our conversation, starting with my inventory of our living room, began:

"One couch." 18
"One couch." 19
"Two lamp tables, a coffee table, a small gateleg table." 20
"Four tables." 21
"Two wing chairs and an occasional chair." 22
"Three chairs." 23
"One box of bric-a-brac." 24
"One box of shit." 25

Heavy garlic of course is not to every taste; but then again 26
some people do not much care for endive. I attended city schools,
where garlic was never in short supply and where profanity, in
proper hands, could be a useful craft turned up to the power of
fine art. I have since met people so well-mannered, so icily, elegantly correct, that with a mere glance across the table or a word
to a waiter they could put a chill on the wine and indeed on the
entire evening. Some people have more, some less, in the way of
polish, but polish doesn't necessarily cover vulgarity. As there
can be diamonds in the rough, so can there be sludge in the
smooth.

It would be helpful in drawing a definitional bead on the   27
word *vulgar* if one could determine its antonym. But I am not
sure that it has an antonym. Refined? I think not. Sophisticated?
Not really. Elegant? Nope. Charming? Close, but I can think of
charming vulgarians — M. Rabelais, please come forth and take a
bow. Besides, charm is nearly as difficult to define as vulgarity.
Perhaps the only safe thing to be said about charm is that if you
think you have it, you can be fairly certain that you don't.

If vulgarity cannot be defined by its antonym, from the rear   28
so to say, examples may be more to the point. I once heard a
friend describe a woman thus: "Next to Sam Jensen's prose, she's
the vulgarest thing in New York." From this description, I had a
fairly firm sense of what the woman was like. Sam Jensen is a
writer for one of the newsmagazines; each week on schedule he
makes a fresh cultural discovery, writing as if every sentence will
be his last, every little movie or play he reviews will change our
lives — an exhibitionist with not a great deal to exhibit. Sam Jensen is a fictitious name — made up to protect the guilty — but
here are a few sentences that he, not I, made up:

> The great Victorian William Morris combined a practical so-
> cialism with a love for the spirit of the King Arthur legends.
> What these films show is the paradox democracy has forgotten
> — that the dream of Camelot is the ultimate dream of freedom
> and order in a difficult but necessary balance.

> The screenplay by Michael Wilson and Richard Maibaum is
> not from an Ian Fleming novel; it's really a cookbook that
> throws Roger Moore as Bond into these action recipes like a cu-
> cumber tossed into an Osterizer. Osterization is becoming more
> and more necessary for Moore; he's beginning to look a bit
> puckered, as if he's been bottled in Bond.

From these sentences — with their false paradoxes, muffed metaphors, obvious puns, and general bloat — I think I can extrapolate the woman who, next to this prose, is the vulgarest thing in
New York. I see teeth, I see elaborate hairdo, much jewelry, flam-
boyant dress, a woman requiring a great deal of attention, who
sucks up most of the mental oxygen in any room she is in — a
woman, in sum, vastly overdone.

Coming at things from a different angle, I imagine myself in   29
session with a psychologist, playing the word association game.
"Vulgar," he says, "quick, name ten items you associate with the
word *vulgar*." "Okay," I say, "here goes:

1. Publicity
2. The Oscar awards
3. The Aspen Institute for Humanistic Studies
4. Talk shows
5. Pulitzer Prizes
6. Barbara Walters
7. Interviews with writers
8. Lauren Bacall
9. Dialogue as an ideal
10. Psychology."

This would not, I suspect, be everyone's list. Looking it over, I see
that, of the ten items, several are linked with one another. But let
me inquire into what made me choose the items I did.

Ladies first. Barbara Walters seems to me vulgar because for a   30
great many years now she has been paid to ask all the vulgar questions, and she seems to do it with such cheerfulness, such competence, such amiable insincerity. "What did you think when you
first heard your husband had been killed?" she will ask, just the
right hush in her voice. "What went on in your mind when you
learned that you had cancer, now for the third time?" The questions that people with imagination do not need to ask, the questions that people with good hearts know they have no right to
ask, these questions and others Barbara Walters can be depended
upon to ask. "Tell me, Holy Father, have you never regretted not
having children of your own?"

Lauren Bacall has only recently graduated to vulgarity, or at   31
least she has only in the past few years revealed herself vulgar.
Hers is a double vulgarity: the vulgarity of false candor — the
woman who, presumably, tells it straight — and the vulgarity
provided by someone who has decided to cash in her chips. In her
autobiography, Miss Bacall has supposedly told all her secrets;
when interviewed on television — by, for example, Barbara Walters — the tack she takes is that of the ringwise babe over whose
eyes no one, kiddo, is going to pull the cashmere. Yet turn the

channel or page, and there is Miss Bacall in a commercial or advertisement doing her best to pull the cashmere over ours. Vulgar stuff.

Talk shows are vulgar for the same reason that Pulitzer Prizes 32 and the Aspen Institute for Humanistic Studies are vulgar. All three fail to live up to their pretensions, which are extravagant: talk shows to being serious, Pulitzer Prizes to rewarding true merit, the Aspen Institute to promoting "dialogue" (see item 9), "the bridging of cultures," "the interdisciplinary approach," and nearly every other phony shibboleth that has cropped up in American intellectual life over the past three decades.

Publicity is vulgar because those who seek it — and even 33 those who are sought by it — tend almost without exception to be divested of their dignity. You have to sell yourself, the sales manuals used to advise, in order to sell your product. With publicity, though, one is selling only oneself, which is different. Which is a bit vulgar, really.

The Oscar awards ceremony is the single item on my list least 34 in need of explanation, for it seems vulgar prima facie.[5] It is the air of self-congratulation — of, a step beyond, self-adulation — that is so splendidly vulgar about the Oscar awards ceremony. Self-congratulation, even on good grounds, is best concealed; on no grounds whatever, it is embarrassing. But then, for vulgarity, there's no business like show business.

Unless it be literary business. The only thing worse than false 35 modesty is no modesty at all, and no modesty at all is what interviews with writers generally bring out. "That most vulgar of all crowds the literary," wrote Keats presciently — that is, before the incontestable evidence came in with the advent and subsequent popularity of what is by now that staple of the book review and little magazine and talk show, the interview with the great author. What these interviews generally come down to is an invitation to writers to pontificate upon things for which it is either unseemly for them to speak (the quality of their own work) or upon which they are unfit to judge (the state of the cosmos). Roughly a

[5](Latin) "On first sight." — Eds.

decade ago I watched Isaac Bashevis Singer,[6] when asked on a television talk show what he thought of the Vietnam War, answer, "I am a writer, and that doesn't mean I have to have an opinion on everything. I'd rather discuss literature." Still, how tempting it is, with an interviewer chirping away at your feet, handing you your own horn and your own drum, to blow it and beat it. As someone who has been interviewed a time or two, I can attest that never have I shifted spiritual gears so quickly from self-importance to self-loathing as during and after an interview. What I felt was, well, vulgar.

Psychology seems to me vulgar because it is too often overbearing in its confidence. Instead of saying, "I don't know," it readily says, "unresolved Oedipus complex" or "manic-depressive syndrome" or "identity crisis." As with other intellectual discoveries before (Marxism) and since (structuralism), psychology acts as if it is holding all the theoretical keys, but then in practice reveals that it doesn't even know where the doors are. As an old *Punch* cartoon once put it, "It's worse than wicked, my dear, it's vulgar." 36

Reviewing my list and attempting to account for the reasons why I have chosen the items on it, I feel I have a firmer sense of what I think vulgar. Exhibitionism, obviousness, pretentiousness, self-congratulation, self-importance, hypocrisy, overconfidence — these seem to me qualities at the heart of vulgarity in our day. It does, though, leave out common sense, a quality which, like clarity, one might have thought one could never have in overabundance. (On the philosophy table in my local bookstore, a book appeared with the title *Clarity Is Not Enough*; I could never pass it without thinking, "Ah, but it's a start.") Yet too great reliance on common sense can narrow the mind, make meager the imagination. Strict common sense abhors mystery, seldom allows for the attraction of tradition, is intolerant of questions that haven't any answers. The problem that common sense presents is knowing the limits of common sense. The too commonsensical 37

---

[6]Singer (born in 1904), Polish-born American writer of fiction in Yiddish and English, received the Nobel Prize for literature in 1978. — EDS.

man or woman grows angry at anything that falls outside his or her common sense, and this anger seems to me vulgar.

Vulgarity is not necessarily stupid but it is always insensi- 38 tive. Its insensitivity invariably extends to itself: The vulgar person seldom knows that he is vulgar, as in the old joke about the young woman whose fiancé reports to her that his parents found her vulgar, and who, enraged, responds, "What's this vulgar crap?" Such obvious vulgarity can be comical, like a *nouveau riche* man bringing opera glasses to a porno film, or the Chicago politician who, while escorting the then ruling British monarch through City Hall, supposedly introduced him to the assembled aldermen by saying, "King, meet the boys." But such things are contretemps merely, not vulgarity of the insidious kind.

In our age vulgarity does not consist in failing to recognize the 39 fish knife or to know the wine list but in the inability to make distinctions. Not long ago I heard a lecture by a Harvard philosophy professor on a Howard Hawks movie, and thought, as one high reference after another was made in connection with this low subject, "Oh, Santayana,[7] 'tis better you are not alive to see this." A vulgar performance, clearly, yet few people in the audience of professors and graduate students seemed to notice.

A great many people did notice, however, when, in an act of 40 singular moral vulgarity, a publisher, an editor, and a novelist recently sponsored a convicted murderer for parole, and the man, not long after being paroled, murdered again. The reason for these men speaking out on behalf of the convict's parole, they said, was his ability as a writer: His work appeared in the editor's journal; he was to have a book published by the publisher's firm; the novelist had encouraged him from the outset. Distinctions — crucial distinctions — were not made: first, that the man was not a very good writer, but a crudely Marxist one, whose work was filled with hatreds and half-truths; second, and more important, that, having killed before, he might kill again — might just be a pathological killer. Not to have made these distinctions

---

[7]George Santayana (1863–1952) was a Spanish-born American poet and philosopher. — Eds.

is vulgarity at its most vile. But to adopt a distinction new to our day, the publisher, the editor, and the novelist took responsibility for what they had done — responsibility but no real blame.

Can an entire culture grow vulgar? Matthew Arnold feared   41 such might happen in "the mechanical and material civilization" of the England of his day. Vladimir Nabokov felt it already had happened in the Soviet Union, a country, as he described it, "of moral imbeciles, of smiling slaves and poker-faced bullies," without, as in the old days, "a Gogol, a Tolstoy, a Chekhov in quest of that simplicity of truth [who] easily distinguished the vulgar side of things as well as the trashy systems of pseudo-thought." Moral imbeciles, smiling slaves, poker-faced bullies — the curl of a sneer in those Nabokovian phrases is a sharp reminder of the force that the charge of "vulgar" can have as an insult — as well as a reminder of how deep and pervasive vulgarity can become.

But American vulgarity, if I may put it so, is rather more re-   42 fined. It is also more piecemeal than pervasive, and more insidious. Creeping vulgarity is how I think of it, the way Taft Republicans[8] used to think of creeping socialism. The insertion of a science fiction course in a major university curriculum, a television commercial by a once-serious actor for a cheap wine, an increased interest in gossip and trivia that is placed under the rubric Style in our most important newspapers: So the vulgar creeps along, while everywhere the third- and fourth-rate — in art, in literature, in intellectual life — is considered good enough, or at any rate highly interesting.

Yet being refined — or at least sophisticated — American   43 vulgarity is vulnerable to the charge of being called vulgar. "As long as war is regarded as wicked," said Oscar Wilde, "it will always have its fascination. When it is looked upon as vulgar, it will cease to be popular." There may be something to this, if not for war then at least for designer jeans, French literary criticism, and other fashions. The one thing the vulgar of our day do not like to be called is vulgar. So crook your little finger, purse your lips, distend your nostrils slightly as you lift your nose in the air the bet-

---

[8]Robert A. Taft (1889–1953), U.S. senator from Ohio from 1939 to 1953, was a leading spokesperson for Republican conservatives. — Eds.

ter to look down it, and repeat after me: *Vulgar! Vulgar! Vulgar!*
The word might save us all.

———

QUESTIONS ON MEANING

1. On what basis does the author conclude that the house with the portico is vulgar and Uncle Jake is not?
2. To what events in history does Epstein attribute the growth of unfavorable CONNOTATIONS around the word *vulgar*?
3. What are the key words in Epstein's definition of *vulgarity*? Which one seems at first glance the most surprising? In which paragraph does the author most succinctly sum up his definition of vulgarity?
4. What points does Epstein make in paragraph 4 and in paragraph 38? Does he contradict himself? Explain.
5. Look up *vulgar* and *vulgarity* in your desk dictionary. In his essay, what liberties has Epstein taken with the dictionary definition? To what extent are these liberties justified? Do they hint at any PURPOSE besides definition?

QUESTIONS ON WRITING STRATEGY

1. What does Epstein's TONE contribute to his essay?
2. What proportion of Epstein's essay is devoted to illustrating what vulgarity is *not*? Of what value is this material to the essay as a whole?
3. What devices does Epstein use to give his long essay COHERENCE?
4. What segments of Epstein's AUDIENCE might be expected to enjoy his essay the most? Whom might it offend?
5. **OTHER METHODS.** Epstein takes pains to describe the appearance and behavior of Uncle Jake (paras. 2–4). What are the functions of this description?

QUESTIONS ON LANGUAGE

1. Be sure you know what the following words mean as Epstein uses them: archetypal, vermilion, sport (para. 2); modicum, pretension (4); edifice (5); portico (6); minuscule (7); patently, palpably, pluperfectly, sensibility (8); reductionist (10); rococo, discomfiting (11);

contemned (12); pejorative, lexicon, invective, commingled, plutocracy, stratum (13); aesthetic, rationalism, divests (14); epitome (17);
extrapolate (28); shibboleth (32); presciently, incontestable, advent,
pontificate (35); theoretical (36); abhors (37); nouveau riche, contretemps, insidious (38); singular, pathological (40); pervasive (41);
piecemeal (42).

2. What does the author mean by "operatic bosoms" (para. 2); "in petrified play" (7); "outside the pale" (13); "diamonds in the rough"
(26); "drawing a definitional bead" (27)?

3. What ALLUSION do you find in the name "Diamond Chaim
Brodsky" (para. 2)? In the phrases "functionlessness follows formlessness" (6); "Vulgar is . . . as vulgar does" (11); "Close Sesame" (13);
and "pull the cashmere" (31)?

4. Where in the essay does Epstein use COLLOQUIAL EXPRESSIONS?
Where does his word choice inject humor into the essay?

5. Identify the METAPHORS in paragraph 26. Do they have any function
other than as word play? If so, what?

SUGGESTIONS FOR WRITING

1. Write your own definition of some quality other than vulgarity. Possible subjects might be refinement, prudishness, generosity, classi-
ness, sensitivity, dishonesty, or snobbishness. Try to tell what the
quality is *not* as well as what it is. Load your essay with examples.

2. In paragraph 29, Epstein lists ten items he associates with the word
vulgar. The critic and essayist Paul Fussell is another distinguished
writer to ponder the subject of vulgarity. In his book *Class* (1983), in
a section of imaginary (and very funny) letters from his readers, he
answers the request, "To settle a bet, would you indicate some
things that are Vulgar?"

I'd say these are vulgar, but in no particular order: Jerry Lewis's
TV telethon; any "Cultural Center"; beef Wellington; cute
words for drinks like *drinky-poos* or *nightcaps*; dinner napkins
with high polyester content; colored wineglasses; oil paintings
depicting members of the family; display of laminated diplomas.

(Old clothes and paper napkins, he adds, aren't vulgar; neither are
fireworks on the Fourth of July.) In two paragraphs, write your own
definition of *vulgar* (borrowing from Epstein's if you like, as long as
you credit him) and provide your own examples along with your
reason(s) for including each one.

3. CONNECTIONS. One of Epstein's top ten vulgar items is the television personality Barbara Walters (see paras. 29, 30). Elsewhere in

this book, Mark Crispin Miller devotes an entire essay to Walters (see p. 365). In an essay of your own, use examples from Miller's essay to support and extend Epstein's sense of Walters's vulgarity, being sure to explain how the examples relate to Epstein's definition. Or, if you prefer, use Miller's examples or your own to refute Epstein's view of Walters.

JOSEPH EPSTEIN ON WRITING

"As a professional writer, I have this in common with the student writer," says Joseph Epstein in a statement written for *The Bedford Reader.* "I cannot sit around and wait for inspiration to arrive."

Like most of what Epstein writes, "What Is Vulgar?" was written to a deadline. He planned for the essay, following a simple, workable system, which he recommends to students assigned to write a long paper. In a file folder, he notes everything he can think of that has any connection with the proposed subject of his essay: quotations, anecdotes, other books and articles on the subject to look into, stray ideas. On index cards and odd scraps of paper, he jots down any items that occur to him as the days pass; everything swells the folder. "Sometimes, while shopping or driving around, I will think up possible opening sentences for my essay. These, too, go into the folder. When I finally do sit down to the writing of my essay, I don't sit down empty-handed — or, perhaps more precisely, empty-minded. I have a store of material before me, which I find a very great aid to composition."

Epstein never uses an outline. "I am not opposed to outlines in logic or on principle but by temperament. I have never felt comfortable with them. I wonder if many serious essayists do use outlines. Aldous Huxley once described the method of the great French essayist Montaigne as 'free association artistically controlled.' I know something similar occurs in my own writing. We all free-associate easily enough; the trick is in the artistic control. But I know I have given up on outlines because I have discovered that there is no way I can know what will be in the second paragraph of something I write until I have written the first paragraph.

My first paragraph may contain a phrase or end on a point I hadn't anticipated, and this phrase or point may send me off into an entirely unexpected direction in my second paragraph.

"When I set out to write the essay 'What Is Vulgar?' I had only a vague notion of what would go into it (apart from some of the scraps in that folder). Certainly, I was not yet clear about my thoughts on vulgarity. The chief point of the essay, for me, was to find out what I really did think about it. The essay itself, now that it is done, shows a writer in the act of thinking.

"Which is a roundabout way of saying that, for me, writing is foremost a mode of thinking and, when it works well, an act of discovery. I write to find out what I believe, what seems logical and sensible to me, what notions, ideas, and views I can live with. I don't mean to say that, when I begin an essay, I don't have some general view or feeling about my subject. I mean instead that, when I begin, I am never altogether sure how I am going to end. Robert Frost once said that whenever he knew how one of his poems was going to end, it almost invariably turned out to be a bad poem. I believe him. Writing for discovery, to find out what one truly thinks of things, may be a bit riskier than writing knowing one's conclusion in advance, but it figures to be much more interesting, more surprising, and, once one gets over one's early apprehension at the prospect of winging it, more fun."

FOR DISCUSSION

1. What makes Epstein skeptical of outlines?
2. Do you agree or disagree with Epstein's view of writing as a way of finding out what you believe? Can you think of any situations for which this approach would not work?

BRUNO BETTELHEIM

Described in his *New York Times* obituary as "a psychoanalyst of great impact" and "a gifted writer . . . with a great literary and moral sensibility," BRUNO BETTELHEIM was born in Austria in 1903 and died in the United States in 1990. Growing up in the Vienna of Sigmund Freud, Bettelheim became interested in psychoanalysis as a young teenager and trained as a psychologist at the University of Vienna. He had already earned a wide reputation when he was imprisoned by the Nazis in the Buchenwald and Dachau concentration camps. When released because of American intervention in 1939, Bettelheim immigrated to Chicago. After several research and teaching positions, in 1944 he began teaching at the University of Chicago and continued there until his retirement in 1973. Bettelheim's work concentrated on children with severe emotional disorders such as autism and psychosis, and many of his theories were provocative and controversial. Some of his well-known books, all on children, are *Love Is Not Enough* (1950), *Truants from Life* (1955), *The Children of the Dream* (1969), and *The Uses of Enchantment* (1976).

The Holocaust

In two books, *The Informed Heart* (1960) and *Surviving, and Other Essays* (1979), Bettelheim probed his and others' experiences in the Nazis' concentration camps. What follows is a freestanding slice of a much longer essay, "The Holocaust — One Generation After," from *Surviving*. Here Bettelheim, with cool passion, dissects a loaded word.

To begin with, it was not the hapless victims of the Nazis who named their incomprehensible and totally unmasterable fate the "holocaust." It was the Americans who applied this artificial and highly technical term to the Nazi extermination of the European Jews. But while the event when named as mass murder most foul evokes the most immediate, most powerful revulsion, when it is designated by a rare technical term, we must first in our minds translate it back into emotionally meaningful language. Using technical or specially created terms instead of words from our common vocabulary is one of the best-known and most widely used distancing devices, separating the intellectual from the emotional experience. Talking about "the holocaust" permits us to manage it intellectually where the raw facts, when given their ordinary names, would overwhelm us emotionally — because it was catastrophe beyond comprehension, beyond the limits of our imagination, unless we force ourselves against our desire to extend it to encompass these terrible events.

This linguistic circumlocution began while it all was only 2
in the planning stage. Even the Nazis — usually given to grossness in language and action — shied away from facing openly what they were up to and called this vile mass murder "the final solution of the Jewish problem." After all, solving a problem can be made to appear like an honorable enterprise, as long as we are not forced to recognize that the solution we are about to embark on consists of the completely unprovoked, vicious murder of millions of helpless men, women, and children. The Nuremberg judges of these Nazi criminals followed their example of circumlocution by coining a neologism out of one Greek and one Latin root: genocide. These artificially created technical terms fail to connect with our strongest feelings. The horror of murder is part of our most common human heritage. From earliest infancy on, it arouses violent abhorrence in us. Therefore in whatever form it appears we should give such an act its true designation and not hide it behind polite, erudite terms created out of classical words.

To call this vile mass murder "the holocaust" is not to give it 3
a special name emphasizing its uniqueness which would permit, over time, the word becoming invested with feelings germane to the event it refers to. The correct definition of *holocaust* is "burnt offering." As such, it is part of the language of the psalmist, a meaningful word to all who have some acquaintance with the Bible, full of the richest emotional connotations. By using the term "holocaust," entirely false associations are established through conscious and unconscious connotations between the most vi-

cious of mass murders and ancient rituals of a deeply religious nature.

Using a word with such strong unconscious religious connotations when speaking of the murder of millions of Jews robs the victims of this abominable mass murder of the only thing left to them: their uniqueness. Calling the most callous, most brutal, most horrid, most heinous mass murder a burnt offering is a sacrilege, a profanation of God and man.   4

Martyrdom is part of our religious heritage. A martyr, burned at the stake, is a burnt offering to his god. And it is true that after the Jews were asphyxiated, the victims' corpses were burned. But I believe we fool ourselves if we think we are honoring the victims of systematic murder by using this term, which has the highest moral connotations. By doing so, we connect for our own psychological reasons what happened in the extermination camps with historical events we deeply regret, but also greatly admire. We do so because this makes it easier for us to cope; only in doing so we cope with our distorted image of what happened, not with the events the way they did happen.   5

By calling the victims of the Nazis martyrs, we falsify their fate. The true meaning of *martyr* is: "One who voluntarily undergoes the penalty of death for refusing to renounce his faith" (*Oxford English Dictionary*). The Nazis made sure that nobody could mistakenly think that their victims were murdered for their religious beliefs. Renouncing their faith would have saved none of them. Those who had converted to Christianity were gassed, as were those who were atheists, and those who were deeply religious Jews. They did not die for any conviction, and certainly not out of choice.   6

Millions of Jews were systematically slaughtered, as were untold other "undesirables," not for any convictions of theirs, but only because they stood in the way of the realization of an illusion. They neither died for their convictions, nor were they slaughtered because of their convictions, but only in consequence of the Nazis' delusional belief about what was required to protect the purity of their assumed superior racial endowment, and what they thought necessary to guarantee them the   7 living space they believed they needed and were entitled to. Thus while these millions were slaughtered for an idea, they did not die for one.

Millions — men, women, and children — were processed after they had been utterly brutalized, their humanity destroyed, their clothes torn from their bodies. Naked, they were sorted into those who were destined to be murdered immediately, and those others who had a short-term usefulness as slave labor. But after a brief interval they, too, were to be herded into the same gas chambers into which the others were immediately piled, there to be asphyxiated so that, in their last moments, they could not prevent themselves from fighting each other in vain for a last breath of air.

To call these most wretched victims of a murderous delusion, of destructive drives run rampant, martyrs or a burnt offering is a distortion invented for our comfort, small as it may be. It pretends that this most vicious of mass murders had some deeper meaning; that in some fashion the victims either offered themselves or at least became sacrifices to a higher cause. It robs them of the last recognition which could be theirs, denies them the last dignity we could accord them: to face and accept what their death was all about, not embellishing it for the small psychological relief this may give us.

We could feel so much better if the victims had acted out of choice. For our emotional relief, therefore, we dwell on the tiny minority who did exercise some choice: the resistance fighters of the Warsaw ghetto, for example, and others like them. We are ready to overlook the fact that these people fought back only at a time when everything was lost, when the overwhelming majority of those who had been forced into the ghettos had already been exterminated without resisting. Certainly those few who finally fought for their survival and their convictions, risking and losing their lives in doing so, deserve our admiration; their deeds give us a moral lift. But the more we dwell on these few, the more unfair are we to the memory of the millions who were slaughtered — who gave in, did not fight back — because we deny them the only thing which up to the very end remained uniquely their own: their fate.

QUESTIONS ON MEANING

1. Why does Bettelheim feel that *holocaust* is an inappropriate term for the mass murder of Jews during World War II? Why does he say this sort of "linguistic circumlocution" is used? (What is a "linguistic circumlocution"?)
2. What is Bettelheim's PURPOSE here?
3. According to Bettelheim, what do we do besides using unemotional terms to distance ourselves from the murder of the Jews?
4. Does Bettelheim suggest an alternative term for *holocaust?*

QUESTIONS ON WRITING STRATEGY

1. Where does Bettelheim stress etymologies, or word histories, and dictionary definitions? What is their EFFECT?
2. What does Bettelheim accomplish with paragraph 8? Why is this paragraph essential?
3. How would you characterize Bettelheim's TONE? What creates it? Is it appropriate, do you think?
4. In several places Bettleheim repeats or restates passages — for instance, "By doing so . . . We do so . . . only in doing so" (para. 5), or "stood in the way of the realization of an illusion . . . in consequence of the Nazis' delusional belief . . . slaughtered for an idea" (7). Do you think such repetition and restatement is deliberate on Bettelheim's part? Why, or why not?
5. OTHER METHODS. Bettelheim's definition is an argument (Chap. 11). What is the THESIS of his argument? What EVIDENCE supports the thesis?

QUESTIONS ON LANGUAGE

1. Analyze the words Bettelheim uses to refer to the murder of the Jews. How do the words support his argument?
2. What is the effect of Bettelheim's use of *we* — for instance, in paragraphs 5 and 10?
3. Look up any unfamiliar words: hapless (para. 1); neologism, abhorrence, erudite (2); germane, psalmist (3); abominable, callous, heinous, sacrilege, profanation (4); asphyxiated (5); delusional, endowment (7); rampant, embellishing (9).

SUGGESTIONS FOR WRITING

1. For the sake of argument, write an essay in which you defend the use of "technical or specially created terms" — not for the Nazi murders but for an activity or field you're familiar with. For instance, what about the terminology of sports, dance, guitar playing, nursing, business, auto mechanics?

2. Although Bettelheim does not use the term, he is objecting to a use of EUPHEMISM, or inoffensive word, in place of a word that might wound or offend. Euphemisms abound in the speech of politicians: The economy undergoes a "slowdown" or a "downturn"; a space-based nuclear weapons system is called a "Strategic Defense Initiative." Drawing on Bettelheim's arguments as you see fit, write an essay about one or more euphemisms appearing in a daily newspaper. What do the euphemisms accomplish, and for whom? What do they conceal, and who is hurt?

3. CONNECTIONS. Read "I Have a Dream" by Martin Luther King, Jr. (p. 706). Compare it with Bettelheim's essay on the purposeful use of repetition and restatement. How does each author use this device? For what aim? What is the EFFECT? If you like, you can narrow your comparison to one representative passage of each essay. Just be sure to use quotations to support your comparison.

ADDITIONAL WRITING TOPICS
Definition

1. Write an essay in which you define an institution, a trend, a phenomenon, or an abstraction. Following are some suggestions designed to stimulate ideas. Before you begin, limit your subject as far as possible, and illustrate your essay with specific examples.

Responsibility
Fun
Sorrow
Unethical behavior
The environment
Education
Progress
Advertising
Happiness
Fads
Feminism
Marriage
Sportsmanship
Leadership
Leisure
Originality
Character
Imagination
Democracy
A smile
A classic (of music, literature, art, or film)
Dieting
Meditation
Friendship

2. In a brief essay, define one of the following. In each instance, you have a choice of something good or something bad to talk about.

A good or bad boss
A good or bad parent
A good or bad host
A good or bad TV newscaster
A good or bad physician

A good or bad nurse
A good or bad minister, priest, or rabbi
A good or bad roommate
A good or bad driver
A good or bad disk jockey

3. In a paragraph, define one of the following for someone who has never heard the term: wigged out, dweeb, awesome, fool around, wimp, preppie, "dog," druggie, snob, freak, loser, loner, freeloader, burnout, soul, quack, "chill," pig-out, gross out, winging it, "bad," "sweet."

11
ARGUMENT AND
PERSUASION
Stating Opinions and Proposals

THE METHOD

Practically every day, we try to persuade ourselves, or someone else. We usually attempt such persuasion without being
aware that we follow any special method at all. (*Persuasion*, let's
make clear, is the art of convincing people to change their minds
— perhaps also to act.) Often, we'll state an *opinion*: We'll tell
someone our own way of viewing things. We say to a friend, "I'm
starting to like Senator Clark. Look at all she's done to help the
handicapped. Look at her voting record on toxic waste. . . ."
And, having stated these opinions, we might go on to make a *proposal*, to recommend that some action to be taken. Addressing
our friend, we might suggest, "Hey, Senator Clark is talking on
campus at four-thirty. Want to come with me and listen to her?"

Sometimes you try to convince yourself that a certain way of
interpreting things is right. You even set forth an opinion in writing — as in a letter to a friend who has asked, "Now that you're at

Siwash College, how do you like the place?" You might write a letter of protest to a landlord who wants to raise your rent, pointing out that the bathroom hot water faucet doesn't work. As a concerned citizen, you may wish to speak your mind in an occasional letter to a newspaper or to your elected representatives.

In truth, we live our lives under a steady rain of opinions and proposals. Organizations that work for causes campaign with posters and direct mail, all hoping that we will see things their way. Moreover, we are bombarded with proposals from people who wish us to act. Ministers, priests, and rabbis urge us to lead more virtuous lives. Advertisers urge us to rush right out and buy the large economy size.

If you should enter certain professions, you will be expected to persuade people in writing. Before arguing a case in court, a lawyer prepares briefs setting forth all the points in favor of his or her side. Business executives regularly put in writing their ideas for new products and ventures, for improvements in cost control and job efficiency. Researchers write proposals for grants to obtain money to support their work. Scientists write and publish papers to persuade the scientific community that their findings are valid, often stating hypotheses, or tentative opinions.

Small wonder, then, that persuasion — and how to resist persuasion — may be among the most useful skills a college student can acquire. Time and again, your instructors will ask you to state an opinion, either in class or in writing. You may be asked to state your view of anything from the electoral college to animal experimentation, the desirability or undesirability of compulsory testing for AIDS, or the revision of existing immigration laws. You may be asked to propose a solution to a problem. On an examination in, say, sociology, you might be asked, "Suggest three practical approaches to the most pressing needs of disadvantaged people in urban areas." Writing your answer, you will find, helps you make clear to yourself what you think. It also gives you the chance to share what you believe.

Unlike some television advertisers, college writers don't storm other people's minds. In writing a paper for a course, you persuade by gentler means: by sharing your view with a reader willing to consider it. You'll want to learn how to express your view clearly and vigorously. But to be fair and persuasive, it is important to understand your reader's view as well.

In stating your opinion, you present the truth as you see it: "The immigration laws discourage employers from hiring nonnative workers," or, "The immigration laws protect legal aliens." To persuade your readers that your view makes sense, you need not begin by proclaiming that, by Heaven, your view is absolutely right and should prevail. Instead, you might begin by trying to state what your reader probably thinks, as best you can infer it. You don't consider views that differ from your own merely to flatter your reader. You do so to correct your own view and make it more accurate. Regarded in this light, persuasive writing isn't a cynical way to pull other people's strings. Writer and reader become two sensible people trying to find a common ground. This view of persuasion will relieve you, whenever you have to state your opinions in writing, of the terrible obligation to be 100 percent right at all times.

In trying to win over a reader who doesn't share your view, you use *argument* — a useful means of persuading. In ordinary use, the word *argument* often means a fight with words, as in the report, "After their cars crashed, the two drivers had a violent argument." But the nearly-coming-to-blows kind of argument isn't the kind we mean. Instead, we will be dealing with argument as a form of expression that, in ancient Greece, could be heard in speeches in a public forum. Today you find it in effective editorials, thoughtful articles, and other persuasive statements of a writer's view. In this sense, argument is reasoning: making statements that lead to a conclusion. (A fuller discussion of these methods is found in "A Note on Reasoning" later in this chapter.)

How do you write an argument? You assert whatever view or opinion you're going to defend. When stated in a sentence, it is sometimes called the *proposition* or THESIS of your argument, or your *claim*. It is a statement of what you believe, and, if you are writing a proposal, it is a statement of an action that you recommend on the basis of what you believe. Sometimes, but not always, you make such a statement at the beginning of your essay: "Welfare funds need to be trimmed from our state budget," or, "To cut back welfare funds now would be a mistake." To support your claim you need EVIDENCE — anything that demonstrates what you're trying to say. Evidence may include facts, statistics (or facts expressed in numbers), expert opinions, illustrations and examples, reported experience.

Often, the writer of an effective argument will appeal both to readers' intelligence and to their feelings. In appealing to reason — a RATIONAL APPEAL — the writer relies on conventional methods of reasoning (see p. 609) and supplies facts, figures, and other evidence that may be new to readers. In an EMOTIONAL APPEAL, in contrast, the writer may simply restate what readers already know well. Editorials in publications for special audiences (members of ethnic groups and religious denominations, or people whose political views are far to the left or right) tend to contain few factual surprises for their subscribers, who presumably read to have their views reinforced. In spoken discourse, you can hear this kind of emotional appeal in a commencement day speech or a Fourth of July oration. An impressive example of such emotional appeal is included in this chapter: the speech by Martin Luther King, Jr., "I Have a Dream." Dr. King's speech did not tell its audience anything new to them, for the listeners were mostly blacks disappointed in the American dream. The speaker appeals not primarily to reason, but to feelings — and to the willingness of his listeners to be inspired.

Emotional argument, to be sure, can sometimes be cynical manipulation. It can mean selling a sucker a bill of shoddy goods by appealing to pride, or shame — "Don't you really want the best for your children?" But emotional argument can also stir readers to constructive action by fair means. It recognizes that we are not intellectual robots, but creatures with feelings. Indeed, in any effective argument, a writer had better engage the readers' feelings or they may reply, "True enough, but who cares?" Argument, to succeed in persuading, makes us feel that a writer's views are close to our own.

Yet another resource in argument is ETHICAL APPEAL: impressing your reader that you are a well-informed person of goodwill, good sense, and good moral character — and, therefore, to be believed. You make such an appeal by reasoning carefully, writing well, and collecting ample evidence. You can also cite or quote respected authorities. If you don't know whether an authority is respected, you can ask a reference librarian for tips on finding out, or talk to an instructor who is a specialist in that field.

In arguing, you don't prove your assertion in the same irrefutable way in which a chemist demonstrates that hydrogen will burn. If you say, "Health insurance should be given top priority in Washington," that kind of claim isn't clearly either true or false. Argument takes place in areas that invite more than one opinion. In writing an argument, you help your reader see and understand just one open-eyed, open-minded view of reality.

A NOTE ON REASONING

When we argue rationally, we reason — that is, we make statements that lead to a conclusion. From the time of the ancient Greeks down to our own day, distinctly different methods of proceeding from statements to conclusions have been devised. This section will tell you of a recent, informal method of reasoning and also of two traditional methods. Understanding these methods, knowing how to use them, and being able to recognize when they are misused will make you a better writer *and* reader. Indeed, the analysis of arguments is a component of critical thinking, which we discussed in Chapter 6, page 337.

Data, Claim, and Warrant[1]

In recent years, a simple, practical method of reasoning has been devised by the British philosopher Stephen Toulmin. Helpfully, Toulmin has divided a typical argument into three parts:

1. The DATA, or evidence to prove something
2. The CLAIM, what you are proving with the data
3. The WARRANT, the assumption or principle that connects the data to the claim

---

[1]This discussion of data, claim, and warrant is adapted from the Kennedys' textbook, *The Bedford Guide for College Writers with Readings and Handbook* (2nd ed., 1990), pp. 527–528.

Any clear, explicit argument has to have all three parts. Toulmin's own example of such an argument is this:

Harry was born in Bermuda ——┬—— Harry is a British subject
            (*Data*)   │   (*Claim*)
                                  │
                    Since a man born in Bermuda
                    will be a British subject
                            (*Warrant*)

Of course, the data for a larger, more controversial claim will be more extensive. Here are some claims that would call for many more data, perhaps thousands of words.

> The war on drugs is not winnable.
> The United States must help to destroy drug production in South America.
> Drug addiction is a personal matter.

The warrant, that middle term, is often crucially important. It tells *why* the claim follows from the data. Often a writer won't bother to state a warrant because it is obvious: "In his bid for re-election, Mayor Perkins failed miserably. Out of 5,000 votes cast for both candidates, he received only 200." The warrant might be stated, "To make what I would consider a strong showing, he would have had to receive 2,000 votes or more," but it is clear that 200 out of 5,000 is a small minority, and no further explanation seems necessary.

A flaw in many arguments, though, is that the warrant is not clear. A clear warrant is essential. To be persuaded, a reader needs to understand your assumptions and the thinking that follows from them. If you were to argue, "Drug abuse is a serious problem in the United States. Therefore, the United States must help to destroy drug production in Latin America," then your reader might well be left wondering why the second statement follows from the first. But if you were to add, between the statements, "As long as drugs are manufactured in Latin America, they will be smuggled into the United States, and drug abuse will continue," then you supply a warrant. You show why your claim follows from your data — which, of course, you must also supply to make your case.

The unstated warrant can pitch an argument into trouble — whether your own or another writer's. Warrants usually involve assumptions or GENERALIZATIONS, which means they are valid only if readers accept or agree that they are valid. With stated warrants, any weaknesses are more likely to show. Suppose someone asserts that a certain woman should not be elected mayor because women cannot form ideas independent of their husbands and this woman's husband has bad ideas on how to run the city. At least the warrant — that women cannot form ideas independent of their husbands — is out there on the table, exposed for all to inspect. But unstated warrants can be just as absurd, or even just doubtful, and pass unnoticed because they are not exposed. Here's the same argument without its warrant: "She shouldn't be elected mayor because her husband has bad ideas on how to run the city."

Here's another argument with an unstated warrant, this one adapted from a magazine advertisement: "Scientists have no proof, just statistical correlations, linking smoking and heart disease, so you needn't worry about the connection." Now, the fact that this ad was placed by a cigarette manufacturer would tip off any reasonably alert reader to beware of bias in the claim. To discover the slant, we need to examine the unstated warrant, which runs something like this: "Since they are not proof, statistical correlations are worthless as guides to behavior." It is true that statistical correlations are not scientific proof, by which we generally mean repeated results obtained under controlled laboratory conditions — the kind of conditions to which human beings cannot ethically be subjected. But statistical correlations *can* establish connections and in fact inform much of our healthful behavior, such as getting physical exercise, avoiding fatty foods, brushing our teeth, and not driving while intoxicated. The advertiser's unstated warrant isn't valid, so neither is the argument.

Here is an extended example of how Toulmin's scheme can work in constructing an argument. In an assignment for her second-semester course in English composition, Maire Flynn was asked to set forth in three short paragraphs a condensed argument. The first paragraph was to set forth some data; the second, a claim; and the third, a warrant. The result became a kind of outline that the writer could then expand into a whole essay. Here is Flynn's argument.

> DATA
>
> Over the past five years in the state of Illinois, assistance in the form of food stamps has had the effect of increasing the number of people on welfare instead of reducing it. Despite this help, 95 percent of long-term recipients remain below the poverty line today.
>
> CLAIM
>
> I maintain that the present system of distributing food stamps is a dismal failure, a less effective way to help the needy than other possible ways.
>
> WARRANT
>
> No one is happy to receive charity. We need to encourage people to quit the welfare rolls; we need to make sure that government aid goes only to the deserving. More effective than giving out food might be to help untrained young people learn job skills; to help single mothers with small children to obtain child care, freeing them for the job market; and to enlarge and improve our state employment counseling and job-placement services. The problem of poverty will be helped only if more people will find jobs and become self-sufficient.

In her warrant paragraph, Flynn spells out her reasons for holding her opinion — the one she states in her claim. "The warrant," she found, "was the hardest part to write," but hers turned out to be clear. Like any good warrant, hers expresses those thoughts that her data set in motion. Another way of looking at the warrant: It is the thinking that led the writer on to the opinion she holds. In this statement of her warrant, Flynn makes clear her assumptions: that people who can support themselves don't deserve food stamps and that a person is better off (and happier) holding a job than receiving charity. By generating more ideas and evidence, she was easily able to expand both data paragraph and warrant paragraph, and the result was a coherent essay of 700 words.

How, by the way, would someone who didn't accept Flynn's warrant argue with her? What about old, infirm, or handicapped persons who cannot work? What quite different assumptions about poverty might be possible?

Deductive and Inductive Reasoning

Stephen Toulmin's method of argument is a fairly recent — and very helpful — way to analyze and construct arguments. Two other reliable methods date back to the Greek philosopher Aristotle, who identified the complementary processes of inductive reasoning (INDUCTION) and deductive reasoning (DEDUCTION). In *Zen and the Art of Motorcycle Maintenance*, Robert M. Pirsig gives examples of deductive and inductive reasoning:

> If the cycle goes over a bump and the engine misfires, and then goes over another bump and the engine misfires, and then goes over another bump and the engine misfires, and then goes over a long smooth stretch of road and there is no misfiring, and then goes over a fourth bump and the engine misfires again, one can logically conclude that the misfiring is caused by the bumps. That is induction: reasoning from particular experiences to general truths.
>
> Deductive inferences do the reverse. They start with general knowledge and predict a specific observation. For example if, from reading the hierarchy of facts about the machine, the mechanic knows the horn of the cycle is powered exclusively by electricity from the battery, then he can logically infer that if the battery is dead the horn will not work. That is deduction.

In *inductive reasoning*, the method of the sciences, we collect bits of evidence on which to base generalizations. From interviews with a hundred self-identified conservative Republicans (the evidence), you might conclude that conservative Republicans favor less government regulation of business (the generalization). The more evidence you have, the more trustworthy your generalization is, but it would never be airtight unless you talked to every conservative Republican in the country. Since such thoroughness is impractical if not impossible, inductive reasoning involves making an *inductive leap* from the evidence to the conclusion. The smaller the leap — the more evidence you have — the better.

Deductive reasoning works the other way, from a general state-ment to particular cases. The basis of deduction is the SYLLOGISM, a three-step form of reasoning practiced by Aristotle:

All men are mortal.
Socrates is a man.
Therefore, Socrates is mortal.

The first statement (the *major premise*) is a generalization about a large group: It is the result of inductive reasoning. The second statement (the *minor premise*) says something about a particular member of that large group. The third statement (the *conclusion*) follows inevitably from the premises and applies the generaliza-tion to the particular: If the premises are true, then the conclu-sion must be true. Here is another syllogism:

Major premise: Conservative Republicans favor less government reg-ulation of business.
Minor premise: William F. Buckley, Jr., is a conservative Republican.
Conclusion: Therefore, William F. Buckley, Jr., favors less govern-ment regulation of business.

Problems with deductive reasoning start in the premises. In 1633, Scipio Chiaramonti, professor of philosophy at the Univer-sity of Pisa, came up with this untrustworthy syllogism: "Animals, which move, have limbs and muscles. The earth has no limbs and muscles. Hence, the earth does not move." This is bad deductive reasoning, and its flaw is to assume that all things need limbs and muscles to move — ignoring raindrops, rivers, and many other moving things. In the next few pages, we'll look at some of the things that can go wrong with any kind of reasoning.

Logical Fallacies

In arguments we read and hear, we often meet LOGICAL FALLA-CIES: errors in reasoning that lead to wrong conclusions. From the time when you start thinking about your proposition or claim, and planning your paper, you'll need to watch out for them. To help you recognize logical fallacies when you see them or hear them, and so guard against them when you write, here is a list of the most common.

Non sequitur (from the Latin, "it does not follow"): stating a conclusion that doesn't follow from the first premise or premises. "I've lived in this town a long time — why, my grandfather was the first mayor — so I'm against putting fluoride in the drinking water."

Oversimplification: supplying neat and easy explanations for large and complicated phenomena. "No wonder drug abuse is out of control. Look at how the courts have hobbled police officers." Oversimplified solutions are also popular: "All these teenage kids that get in trouble with the law — why, they ought to ship 'em over to China. That would straighten 'em out!"

Either/or reasoning: assuming that a reality may be divided into only two parts or extremes; assuming that a given problem has only one of two possible solutions. "What do we do about these sheiks who keep jacking up oil prices? Either we kowtow to 'em, or we bomb 'em off the face of the earth, right?" Obviously, either/or reasoning is a kind of extreme oversimplification.

Argument from doubtful or unidentified authority: "Certainly we ought to castrate all sex offenders; Uncle Oswald says we should." Or: "According to reliable sources, my opponent is lying."

Argument ad hominem (from the Latin, "to the man"): attacking a person's views by attacking his or her character. "Mayor Burns is divorced and estranged from his family. How can we listen to his pleas for a city nursing home?"

Begging the question: taking for granted from the start what you set out to demonstrate. When you reason in a *logical* way, you state that because something is true, then, as a result, some other truth follows. When you beg the question, however, you repeat that what is true is true. If you argue, for instance, that dogs are a menace to people because they are dangerous, you don't prove a thing, since the idea that dogs are dangerous is already assumed in the statement that they are a menace. Beggars of questions often just repeat what they already believe, only in different words. This fallacy sometimes takes the form of *arguing in a circle*, or demonstrating a premise by a conclusion and a conclusion by a premise: "I am in college because that is the right thing to do. Going to college is the right thing to do because it is expected of me."

Post hoc, ergo propter hoc (from the Latin, "after this, therefore because of this"): assuming that because A follows B, A was caused by B. "Ever since the city suspended height restrictions on skyscrapers, the city budget has been balanced." (See also page 483.)

False analogy: the claim of persuasive likeness when no significant likeness exists. ANALOGY, you may recall from Chapter 8, is the method of asserting that because two things are comparable in some respects, they are comparable in other respects as well. Analogies cannot serve as evidence in a rational argument because the differences always outweigh the similarities; but analogies can reinforce such arguments *if* the subjects are indeed similar in some ways. If they aren't, the analogy is false. Many observers see the "war on drugs" as a false and damaging analogy because warfare aims for clear victory over a specific, organized enemy, whereas the complete eradication of illegal drugs is probably unrealistic and, in any event, the "enemy" isn't well defined: the drugs themselves? users? sellers? producers? the producing nations? (These critics urge approaching drugs as a social problem to be skillfully managed and reduced.)

In recent years, the study of *logic*, or systematic reasoning, has seen exciting developments. If you care to venture more deeply into its fascinating territory, a good, lively (but challenging) introductory textbook is Albert E. Blumberg's *Logic* (1976). Stephen Toulmin, in *The Uses of Argument* (1969), sets forth his own system in detail. His views are further explained and applied by Douglas Ehninger and Wayne Brockriede in *Decision by Debate* (2nd ed., 1978) and by Toulmin himself, with Richard Rieke and Allan Janik, in *An Introduction to Reasoning* (2nd ed., 1984).

THE PROCESS

In stating an opinion, you set forth and support a claim — a truth you believe. You may find such a truth by thinking and feeling, by talking to your instructors or fellow students, by scanning a newspaper or reading books and magazines, by listening to a discussion of some problem or controversy.

In stating a proposal, you already have an opinion in mind, and from there, you go on to urge an action or a solution to a problem. Usually, these two statements will take place within the same piece of writing: First, a writer will set forth a view ("Compact disks are grossly overpriced"); and then, will go right on to a proposal ("Compact disks should be discounted in the college store").

Whether your essay states an opinion, a proposal, or both, it is likely to contain similar ingredients. State clearly, if possible at the start of your essay, the proposition or claim you are going to defend. If you like, you can explain why you think it worth upholding — showing, perhaps, that it concerns your readers. If you plan to include both an opinion and proposal in your essay, you may wish to set forth your opinion first, saving your proposal for later — perhaps for your conclusion.

Your proposition stated, introduce your least important point first. Then build in a crescendo to the strongest point you have. This structure will lend emphasis to your essay, and perhaps make your chain of ideas more persuasive as the reader continues to follow it.

For every point, give evidence: facts, figures, examples, expert opinions. If you introduce statistics, make sure that they are up to date and fairly represented. In an essay advocating a law against smoking, it would be unfair to declare that "in Pottsville, Illinois, last year, 50 percent of all deaths were caused by lung cancer," if only two people died in Pottsville last year — one of them struck by a car.

If you are arguing fairly, you should be able to face potential criticisms fairly, and give your critics due credit, by recognizing the objections you expect your assertion will meet. This is the strategy H. L. Mencken uses in "The Penalty of Death," and he introduces it in his essay right at the beginning. (You might also tackle the opposition at the end of your essay or at relevant points throughout.) Notice that Mencken takes pains to dispense with his opponents: He doesn't just dismiss them; he reasons with them.

In your conclusion, briefly restate your claim, if possible in a fresh, pointed way. (For example, see the concluding sentence in the essay by William F. Buckley in this chapter.) In emotionally persuasive writing, you may want to end with a strong appeal. (See "I Have a Dream" by Martin Luther King, Jr.)

Finally, don't forget the power of humor in argument. You don't have to crack gratuitous jokes, but there is often an advantage in having a reader or listener who laughs on your side. When Abraham Lincoln debated Stephen Douglas, he triumphed in his reply to Douglas's snide remark that Lincoln had once been a bartender. "I have long since quit my side of the bar," Lincoln declared, "while Mr. Douglas clings to his as tenaciously as ever."

In arguing — doing everything you can to bring your reader around to your view — you can draw on any method of writing you have already learned. Arguing for or against welfare funding, you might give EXAMPLES of wasteful spending, or of neighborhoods where welfare funds are needed. You might analyze the CAUSES of social problems that call for welfare funds, or foresee the likely EFFECTS of cutting welfare programs, or of keeping them. You might COMPARE and CONTRAST the idea of slashing welfare funds with the idea of increasing them. You could use NARRATION to tell a pointed story; you could use DESCRIPTION to portray certain welfare recipients and their neighborhoods. If you wanted to, you could employ several of these methods in writing a single argument.

You will rarely find, when you begin to write a persuasive paper, that you have too much evidence to support your claim. But unless you're writing a term paper and have months to spend on it, you're limited in how much evidence you can gather. Begin by stating your claim. Make it narrow enough to support in the time you have available. For a paper due a week from now, the opinion that "our city's downtown area has a serious litter problem" can probably be backed up in part by your own eyewitness reports. But to support the claim, "Litter is one of the worst environmental problems of North American cities," you would surely need to spend time in a library.

In rewriting, you may find yourself tempted to keep all the evidence you have collected with such effort. Of course, some of it may not support your claim; some may seem likely to persuade the reader only to go to sleep. If so, throw it out. A stronger argument will remain.

ARGUMENT AND PERSUASION
IN A PARAGRAPH: FOUR ILLUSTRATIONS
Stating an Opinion about Television

Television news has a serious failing: It's show business. Unlike a newspaper, its every word has to entertain the average beer drinker. To score high ratings and win advertisers, it must find drama, suspense, and human interest in each story, turning every kidnapping into a hostage crisis. A visual medium, it favors the spectacular: riots, tornados, air crashes. The fire that tore through six city blocks has more eye-appeal than ten fires prevented. Now that satellite transmission invites live coverage, newscasters go for the fast-breaking story at the expense of thoughtful analysis. "The more you can get data out instantly," says media critic Jeff Greenfield, "the more you rely on instant data to define the news." TV zooms in on people who make news, but, to avoid boredom, won't let them argue or explain. (How can they, in speeches limited to fifteen seconds?) On one infamous *Today* show, Senator Proxmire's ideas about nuclear attack were cut short so that viewers might see Seattle Slew waking up in his stall after his Kentucky Derby victory. On NBC late news for September 12, 1987, President Reagan blasted a plan to end war in Nicaragua. His address was clipped to sixty seconds, then an anchorwoman digested the opposition in one quick line: "Democrats tonight were critical of the President's remarks." Americans who rely on television for their news (64 percent, according to 1984 Roper polls) exist on a starvation diet.

COMMENT. The writer states an opinion in the opening line, then proceeds to back up the claim with evidence: examples from specific television shows and a quotation from Jeff Greenfield, a professional critic of the media (and an author represented elsewhere in this book; see page 258). Some of the writer's evidence — the bit about President Reagan's condensed address — came from the direct experiences of watching TV newscasts.

In the last sentence, the writer restates the opening opinion in a fresh way. The next step is to propose a cure.

Stating a Proposal about Television

To make television news more responsible to people who depend on it for full and accurate information, I propose that commercials be banned from local and network news programs. This ban would have the effect of freeing newscasters from the obligation to score high ratings. Since 1963, when NBC and CBS began the first thirty-minute evening newscasts, television news has dwindled in integrity. Back then, according to television historian Daniel C. Hallin, the news was designed to earn prestige for the networks, not money. Today the priorities have been reversed. We need a return to the original situation. Eliminating commercials would hurt revenues, it is true, but stations could make up their losses from selling spots on prime-time shows clearly labeled "entertainment." No longer forced to highlight fires, storms, and other violent scenes, no longer tempted to use live coverage (even though the story covered may be trivial), news teams would no longer strive to race with their rivals to break a story. At last there would be time for more analysis, for the thoughtful follow-up story. Television news would become less entertaining, no doubt, and fewer people would watch it. The reader might object that, as a result, the mass of American viewers would be even less well informed. But sheer entertainment that passes for news is, I believe, more insidious than no news at all.

COMMENT. Continuing the argument about television news (begun in the paragraph stating an opinion), the writer makes a radical proposal for greatly improving television news. We get less evidence than in the opinion paragraph, but then, less evidence seems necessary. We do, however, hear from a television historian, and the next sentence ("Today the priorities have been reversed") contrasts present and past. Showing an awareness for the skeptical reader, the writer recognizes two possible objections to the proposal: (1) stations would suffer losses; and (2) people would be less well informed. To each objection, the writer offers an answer and leaves us to ponder it.

Stating an Opinion in an Academic Discipline

We need wilderness, I believe, as an environment of humility. Civilization breeds arrogance. A modern human, armed with checkbook, television, and four-wheel drive, feels like a demigod. It is good to be reminded in wilderness of our true status as member — not master — of the natural world. It is good to rekindle the sense of restraint and limits that has been obscured by technological optimism. It is good to see natural powers and processes greater than our own. The lessons of such experiences are precisely what are needed if human-environment relations are to be harmonious and stable in the long run. Wilderness, then, is a profound educational resource, schooling overcivilized humans in what we once knew but unfortunately forgot.

COMMENT. *Living in the Environment*, by G. Tyler Miller, Jr. (2nd ed., 1979), is an unusual textbook because many of its chapters contain guest editorials written by respected experts. This paragraph by Roderick Nash, a professor of history and environmental studies at the University of California, Santa Barbara, is taken from one of the editorials. Nash has stated his opinion that wilderness areas are vitally important to all Americans for several reasons. One of those reasons is detailed in the paragraph cited here. Notice how briefly, concretely ("armed with checkbook, television, and four-wheel drive"), and effectively Nash sets it forth. He makes a convincing case for the usefulness of an "environment of humility."

Stating a Proposal in an Academic Discipline

Individual acts of consumption, litter, and so on, have contributed to the mess [in our environment]. When you are tempted to say this little bit won't hurt, multiply it by millions of others saying the same thing. Picking up a single beer can, not turning on a light, using a car pool, writing on both sides of a piece of paper, and not buying a grocery product with more packages inside the outer package are all very significant acts. Each small act reminds us of ecological thinking and leads to other ecologically sound practices. Start now with a small con-

crete personal act and then expand your actions in ever widening circles. Little acts can be used to expand our awareness of
the need for fundamental changes in our political, economic,
and social systems over the next few decades. These acts also
help us to avoid psychological numbness when we realize the
magnitude of the job to be done.

COMMENT. Also from *Living in the Environment,* here is a
paragraph in which the author of the book, G. Tyler Miller, Jr.,
makes a proposal. This paragraph in fact is labeled number seven
in a whole list of proposals under the title "What Can You Do?"
The list is designed to convey a sense that the world's environmental problems are not so overwhelming that individual efforts
can't contribute to solving them. "You can do little things" is
this paragraph's claim. Notice that almost every sentence gives
concrete suggestions for dealing in a small but meaningful way
with problems of great magnitude. The paragraph ends effectively, with the author supplying compelling reasons for taking
his advice.

H. L. MENCKEN

Henry Louis Mencken (1880–1956) was a native of Baltimore, where for four decades he worked as newspaper reporter, editor, and columnist. In the 1920s, his boisterous, cynical observations on American life, appearing regularly in *The Smart Set* and later in *The American Mercury* (which he founded and edited), made him probably the most widely quoted writer in the country. As an editor and literary critic, Mencken championed Sinclair Lewis, Theodore Dreiser, and other realistic writers. As a social critic, he leveled blasts at pomp, hypocrisy, and the middle classes (whom he labeled "the booboisie"). (Recently, the publication of *The Diary of H. L. Mencken* [1989] revealed its author's outspoken opinions and touched off a controversy: was Mencken a bigot? The debate goes on.) In 1933, when Mencken's attempts to laugh off the Depression began to ring hollow, his magazine died. He then devoted himself to revising and supplementing *The American Language* (4th ed., 1948), a learned and highly entertaining survey of a nation's speech habits and vocabulary. Two dozen of Mencken's books are now in print, including *A Mencken Chrestomathy* (1949), a representative selection of his best writings of various kinds; and *A Choice of Days* (1980), a selection from his memoirs.

The Penalty of Death

Above all, Mencken was a humorist whose thought had a serious core. He argues by first making the reader's jaw drop, then inducing a laugh, and finally causing the reader to ponder, "Hmmmm — what if he's right?" The following still-controversial essay, from *Prejudices, Fifth Series* (1926), shows Mencken the persuader in top form. No writer is better at swinging from ornate and abstract words to salty and concrete ones, at tossing a metaphor that makes you smile even as it kicks in your teeth.

Of the arguments against capital punishment that issue from   1
uplifters, two are commonly heard most often, to wit:

1. That hanging a man (or frying him or gassing him) is a dreadful business, degrading to those who have to do it and revolting to those who have to witness it.
2. That it is useless, for it does not deter others from the same crime.

The first of these arguments, it seems to me, is plainly too   2
weak to need serious refutation. All it says, in brief, is that the
work of the hangman is unpleasant. Granted. But suppose it is? It
may be quite necessary to society for all that. There are, indeed,
many other jobs that are unpleasant, and yet no one thinks of
abolishing them — that of the plumber, that of the soldier, that
of the garbageman, that of the priest hearing confessions, that of
the sandhog, and so on. Moreover, what evidence is there that
any actual hangman complains of his work? I have heard none.
On the contrary, I have known many who delighted in their ancient art, and practiced it proudly.

In the second argument of the abolitionists there is rather   3
more force, but even here, I believe, the ground under them is
shaky. Their fundamental error consists in assuming that the
whole aim of punishing criminals is to deter other (potential)
criminals — that we hang or electrocute A simply in order to so
alarm B that he will not kill C. This, I believe, is an assumption
which confuses a part with the whole. Deterrence, obviously, is
one of the aims of punishment, but it is surely not the only one.
On the contrary, there are at least a half dozen, and some are
probably quite as important. At least one of them, practically
considered, is *more* important. Commonly, it is described as revenge, but revenge is really not the word for it. I borrow a better
term from the late Aristotle: *katharsis*. *Katharsis*, so used, means a
salubrious discharge of emotions, a healthy letting off of steam. A
schoolboy, disliking his teacher, deposits a tack upon the pedagogical chair; the teacher jumps and the boy laughs. This is *ka-*
tharsis. What I contend is that one of the prime objects of all judi-
cial punishments is to afford the same grateful relief (*a*) to the
immediate victims of the criminal punished, and (*b*) to the general
body of moral and timorous men.

These persons, and particularly the first group, are concerned   4
only indirectly with deterring other criminals. The thing they
crave primarily is the satisfaction of seeing the criminal actually
before them suffer as he made them suffer. What they want is the
peace of mind that goes with the feeling that accounts are
squared. Until they get that satisfaction they are in a state of emotional tension, and hence unhappy. The instant they get it they
are comfortable. I do not argue that this yearning is noble; I simply argue that it is almost universal among human beings. In the
face of injuries that are unimportant and can be borne without
damage it may yield to higher impulses; that is to say, it may yield
to what is called Christian charity. But when the injury is serious
Christianity is adjourned, and even saints reach for their side-
arms. It is plainly asking too much of human nature to expect it
to conquer so natural an impulse. A keeps a store and has a book-
keeper, B. B steals $700, employs it in playing at dice or bingo,
and is cleaned out. What is A to do? Let B go? If he does so he will
be unable to sleep at night. The sense of injury, of injustice, of
frustration will haunt him like pruritus. So he turns B over to the
police, and they hustle B to prison. Thereafter A can sleep. More,
he has pleasant dreams. He pictures B chained to the wall of a
dungeon a hundred feet underground, devoured by rats and scor-
pions. It is so agreeable that it makes him forget his $700. He has
got his *katharsis*.

The same thing precisely takes place on a larger scale when   5
there is a crime which destroys a whole community's sense of security. Every law-abiding citizen feels menaced and frustrated until the criminals have been struck down — until the communal
capacity to get even with them, and more than even, has been
dramatically demonstrated. Here, manifestly, the business of deterring others is no more than an afterthought. The main thing is
to destroy the concrete scoundrels whose act has alarmed everyone, and thus made everyone unhappy. Until they are brought to
book that unhappiness continues; when the law has been executed upon them there is a sigh of relief. In other words, there is
katharsis.

I know of no public demand for the death penalty for ordi-   6
nary crimes, even for ordinary homicides. Its infliction would

shock all men of normal decency of feeling. But for crimes involving the deliberate and inexcusable taking of human life, by men
openly defiant of all civilized order — for such crimes it seems, to
nine men out of ten, a just and proper punishment. Any lesser
penalty leaves them feeling that the criminal has got the better of
society — that he is free to add insult to injury by laughing. That
feeling can be dissipated only by a recourse to *katharsis*, the invention of the aforesaid Aristotle. It is more effectively and economically achieved, as human nature now is, by wafting the criminal to realms of bliss.

The real objection to capital punishment doesn't lie against   7
the actual extermination of the condemned, but against our brutal American habit of putting it off so long. After all, every one of
us must die soon or late, and a murderer, it must be assumed, is
one who makes that sad fact the cornerstone of his metaphysic.
But it is one thing to die, and quite another thing to lie for long
months and even years under the shadow of death. No sane man
would choose such a finish. All of us, despite the Prayer Book,
long for a swift and unexpected end. Unhappily, a murderer, under the irrational American system, is tortured for what, to him,
must seem a whole series of eternities. For months on end he sits
in prison while his lawyers carry on their idiotic buffoonery with
writs, injunctions, mandamuses, and appeals. In order to get his
money (or that of his friends) they have to feed him with hope.
Now and then, by the imbecility of a judge or some trick of juridic
science, they actually justify it. But let us say that, his money all
gone, they finally throw up their hands. Their client is now ready
for the rope or the chair. But he must still wait for months before
it fetches him.

That wait, I believe, is horribly cruel. I have seen more than   8
one man sitting in the death-house, and I don't want to see any
more. Worse, it is wholly useless. Why should he wait at all? Why
not hang him the day after the last court dissipates his last hope?
Why torture him as not even cannibals would torture their victims? The common answer is that he must have time to make his
peace with God. But how long does that take? It may be accomplished, I believe, in two hours quite as comfortably as in two
years. There are, indeed, no temporal limitations upon God. He

could forgive a whole herd of murderers in a millionth of a second. More, it has been done.

QUESTIONS ON MEANING

1. Identify Mencken's main reasons for his support of capital punishment. What is his THESIS?
2. In paragraph 3, Mencken asserts that there are at least half a dozen reasons for punishing offenders. In his essay, he mentions two, deterrence and revenge. What others can you supply?
3. For which class of offenders does Mencken advocate the death penalty?
4. What is Mencken's "real objection" to capital punishment?

QUESTIONS ON WRITING STRATEGY

1. How would you characterize Mencken's humor? Point to examples of it. In the light of his grim subject, do you find it funny?
2. In his first paragraph, Mencken pares his subject down to manageable size. What techniques does he employ for this purpose?
3. At the start of paragraph 7, Mencken shifts his stance from concern for the victims of crime to concern for prisoners awaiting execution. Does the shift help or weaken the effectiveness of his earlier justification for capital punishment?
4. Do you think the author expects his AUDIENCE to agree with him? At what points does he seem to recognize the fact that some readers may see things differently?
5. OTHER METHODS. In paragraphs 2 and 3, Mencken uses analogies (Chap. 8) in an apparent attempt to strengthen his argument. What are the analogies? Do they seem false to you (see page 616 for a discussion of false analogy)? Do you think Mencken would agree with your judgment?

QUESTIONS ON LANGUAGE

1. Mencken opens his argument by referring to those who reject capital punishment as "uplifters." What CONNOTATIONS does this word

have for you? Does the use of this "loaded" word strengthen or weaken Mencken's position? Explain.

2. Be sure you know the meanings of the following words: refutation, sandhog (para. 2); salubrious, pedagogical, timorous (3); pruritus (4); wafting (6); mandamuses, juridic (7).

3. What emotional overtones can you detect in Mencken's reference to the hangman's job as an "ancient art" (para. 2)?

4. What does Mencken's argument gain from his substitution of the word *katharsis* for *revenge*?

SUGGESTIONS FOR WRITING

1. Write a paper in which you state an opinion about one current method of apprehending, trying, or sentencing criminals. Supply EV-IDENCE to persuade readers to accept your idea.

2. Write an essay refuting Mencken's case; or, take Mencken's side but use different arguments. Be sure to defend your stance, point by point.

3. CONNECTIONS. Write an essay in which you compare and contrast Mencken's "The Penalty of Death" with George Orwell's "A Hanging" (p. 54). Pay particular attention to the essays as arguments, by analyzing their assertions and evidence. On the basis of this analysis, which do you think presents the stronger case?

H. L. MENCKEN ON WRITING

"All my work hangs together," wrote H. L. Mencken in a piece called "Addendum on Aims," "once the main ideas under it are discerned. Those ideas are chiefly of a skeptical character. I believe that nothing is unconditionally true, and hence I am opposed to every statement of positive truth and to every man who states it. Such men seem to me to be either idiots or scoundrels. To one category or the other belong all theologians, professors, editorial writers, right-thinkers, etc. . . . Whether [my work] appears to be burlesque, or serious criticism, or mere casual controversy, it is always directed against one thing: unwarranted pretension."

Mencken cheerfully acknowledged his debts to his teachers: chiefly writers he read as a young man and newspaper editors he worked under. "My style of writing is chiefly grounded upon an early enthusiasm for Huxley,[1] the greatest of all masters of orderly exposition. He taught me the importance of giving to every argument a simple structure. As for the fancy work on the surface, it comes chiefly from an anonymous editorial writer in the *New York Sun*, circa 1900. He taught me the value of apt phrases. My vocabulary is pretty large; it probably runs to 25,000 words. It represents much labor. I am constantly expanding it. I believe that a good phrase is better than a Great Truth — which is usually buncombe. I delight in argument, not because I want to convince, but because argument itself is an end."

In another essay, "The Fringes of Lovely Letters," Mencken wrote that "what is in the head infallibly oozes out of the nub of the pen. If it is sparkling Burgundy the writing is full of life and charm. If it is mush the writing is mush too." He recalls the example of President Warren G. Harding, who once sent a message to Congress that was quite incomprehensible. "Why? Simply because Dr. Harding's thoughts, on the high and grave subjects he discussed, were so muddled that he couldn't understand them himself. But on matters within his range of customary meditation he was clear and even charming, as all of us are. . . . Style cannot go beyond the ideas which lie at the heart of it. If they are clear, it too will be clear. If they are held passionately, it will be eloquent."

FOR DISCUSSION

1. According to Mencken, what PURPOSE animates his writing?
2. What relationship does Mencken see between a writer's thought and his STYLE?
3. Where in his views on writing does Mencken use FIGURES OF SPEECH to advantage?

---

[1]Thomas Henry Huxley (1825–1895), English biologist and educator, who wrote many essays popularizing science. In Victorian England, Huxley was the leading exponent and defender of Charles Darwin's theory of evolution. — EDS.

BARBARA EHRENREICH

Barbara Ehrenreich was born in 1941 in Butte, Montana. After she graduated from Reed College, she took her Ph.D. at Rockefeller University, then taught at the State University of New York in Old Westbury in the early 1970s. Since 1981 she has been an editor for *Ms.* magazine, and since 1974 she has edited *Seven Days* magazine in Washington, D.C. As a writer, Ehrenreich has been a hard-hitting investigative reporter, a popular historian, and an astute social commentator. Her books include *The American Health Empire* (with her first husband, John Ehrenreich; 1970); *Complaints and Disorders: The Sexual Politics of Sickness* (1973); *For Her Own Good: 150 Years of the Experts' Advice to Women* (with Deirdre English; 1978); *The Hearts of Men: American Dreams and the Flight from Commitment* (1983); *Re-making Love: The Feminization of Sex* (with Elizabeth Hess and Gloria Jacobs; 1986); and *Fear of Falling: The Inner Life of the Middle Class* (1989). *The Worst Years of Our Lives* (1990) is a collection of Ehrenreich's essays.

Hope I Die before I Get Rich

Ehrenreich's essay first appeared in 1986 in *Mother Jones,* a magazine of social commentary with a liberal bias. ("Mother" Mary Harris Jones was an early twentieth-century labor organizer.) What Ehrenreich finds lamentably missing from contemporary life is a counterculture, and she sets forth her opinion in a lively essay. See if you think it applies to the 1990s as well as the 1980s.

What America needs is a good strong counterculture, or at least a few square blocks of bohemia for our youth to loiter in before making the plunge into a career of investment banking or futures trading. The fifties had the beats; the sixties had the hippies; the seventies had subsistence farming in Vermont. But the eighties are about as barren of countercultural impulse as Boston under Cotton Mather's administration. Sure, there are still artists in

SoHo, but they're busy discussing tax shelters over their decaf cappuccino.

A true counterculture requires at least three things: (1) a distinctive mode of dress, which can include anything from recycled velvet to torn T-shirts, so long as no part of it can be purchased at Benetton; (2) some attempt at artistic or literary creativity, even if the only product is an occasional mimeographed disquisition on love, death, and other current issues; and (3) (this is indispensable) an absolute contempt for the bourgeoisie, which can be defined flexibly as the ruling class, any class that lets itself be ruled by it, or one's parents.

The key thing, underlying all of the above, is a massive, uncompromising indifference to money and all known methods of acquiring it, storing it, and displaying it. This is where members of today's artistic subculture fall down so grievously. Yes, they have a distinctive style of dress, generally modeled after Madonna with a hangover. And yes, they have artistic pretensions, and are mightily productive of items such as silk-screened renditions of Kraft grape jelly jars. But they love money, and this is why they thrive wherever art and real estate intersect in that special frenzy of speculation that defines New York's SoHo or San Francisco's SoMa.

The problem is that our educated young people have never heard of anyone — outside of certain monastic orders — subsisting voluntarily on less than $50,000 a year. The result is that middle-class youth have come to expect to leap directly from a college dorm to a condominium, eliminating that entire stage of the human life cycle known as "finding yourself." And that phase, now as in Jack Kerouac's day, is best conducted in a run-down sixth-floor walk-up apartment and on a diet of peanut butter and day-old bread.

You can't really blame today's young people for failing to invent their own counterculture. First, it's almost impossible these days to find low-rent sixth-floor walk-up apartments that are not subject to constant incendiary attacks by landlords bent on condominiumizing. Second, it's hard to find the personnel. All great countercultures arose from the intimate mixing of people of different classes and races (not to mention sexual orientations). But

outside of Miller beer commercials, this doesn't happen much
anymore.

Then there's the problem of coming up with something en-   6
tirely new — post-Zen, post-LSD, post-punk, post-vegetarian,
and (although the new art entrepreneurs don't know it yet) post-
Warhol. I don't know what the shape of the next counterculture
will be, or whether an aging ex-Ginsberg groupie like myself
would feel comfortable in it. But I have confidence that the generation that invented Live Aid and constructed shantytowns on
campus lawns to protest apartheid before even reaching the legal
drinking age will figure something out.

QUESTIONS ON MEANING

1. Who was Cotton Mather (para. 1)?
2. What does Ehrenreich criticize about young people? What does she
   have to say in their favor?
3. What does the author reveal about herself when she confesses that
   she's "an aging ex-Ginsberg groupie" (para. 6)?
4. Where in her essay does Ehrenreich make clear her reasons for advocating "a good strong counterculture"?
5. What present-day trends besides the lack of a counterculture does
   Ehrenreich's humor target?

QUESTIONS ON WRITING STRATEGY

1. Is "Hope I Die before I Get Rich" a humorous essay, or does the author use humor to make a serious point? Explain.
2. Where in her essay does Ehrenreich make expert use of TRANSI-
   TIONS?
3. Ehrenreich presents her claim right at the beginning, in the first sentence. Do you think this is an effective strategy?
4. OTHER METHODS. Ehrenreich's argument depends in part on a definition (Chap. 10). What does she define?

QUESTIONS ON LANGUAGE

1. Be sure you know what Ehrenreich means by the following: bohemia, subsistence, cappuccino (para. 1); disquisition (2); massive, subculture (3); incendiary (5); entrepreneurs (6).
2. Compare Ehrenreich's definition of *bourgeoisie* (para. 2) with the dictionary definition. How do you account for the differences?

SUGGESTIONS FOR WRITING

1. Write an essay in which you agree or disagree with Ehrenreich's apparent assumption that today's college students are all preparing to "plunge into a career of investment banking or futures trading." Be sure to back up your position with plenty of EVIDENCE.
2. If you had the power to invent a counterculture for your generation, of what ingredients would it consist? Write a paper in which you set forth those ingredients.
3. CONNECTIONS. Gail Sheehy's "Predictable Crises of Adulthood" also addresses the attitudes and activities of young adults (see "Pulling Up Roots" and "The Trying Twenties," pp. 347–350). In an essay, play these two essays off against each other. Does Sheehy's illuminate Ehrenreich's, or vice versa? Do they contradict each other? Does either seem truer to you, or more effective? Your essay should include specific evidence from each essay to back up your opinions.

BARBARA EHRENREICH ON WRITING

The printed word, in the view of Barbara Ehrenreich, should be a powerful instrument for reform. In an article in *Mother Jones*, though, she complains about a tacit censorship in American magazines that has sometimes prevented her from fulfilling her purpose as a writer. Ehrenreich recalls the difficulties she had in trying to persuade the editor of a national magazine to assign her a story on the plight of Third World women refugees. "Sorry," said the editor, "Third World women have never done anything for me."

Ehrenreich infers that writers who write for such magazines must follow a rule: "You must learn not to stray from your assigned socio-demographic stereotype." She observes, "As a woman, I am generally asked to write on 'women's topics,' such as cooking, divorce, how to succeed in business, diet fads, and the return of the bustle. These are all fine topics and give great scope to my talents, but when I ask, in faltering tones, for an assignment on the arms race or on the trade deficit, I am likely to be told that *anyone* (Bill, Gerry, Bob) could cover that, whereas my 'voice' is *essential* for the aerobic toothbrushing story. This is not, strictly speaking, 'censorship' — just a division of labor in which white men cover politics, foreign policy, and the economy, and the rest of us cover what's left over, such as the bustle."

Over the years Ehrenreich has had many manuscripts rejected by editors who comment, "too angry," "too depressing," and "Where's the bright side?" She agrees with writer Herbert Gold, who once deduced that the American media want only "happy stories about happy people with happy problems." She concludes, "You can write about anything — death squads, AIDS, or the prospect for a Pat Robertson victory in '88 — so long as you make it 'upbeat.'" Despite such discouragements, Ehrenreich continues her battle to "disturb the stupor induced by six straight pages of Calvin Klein ads."

FOR DISCUSSION

1. Is Ehrenreich right about what she calls "a tacit censorship in American magazines"? Check some recent issue of a magazine that prints signed articles. How many of the articles *not* on "women's topics" are written by women? How many are written by men?
2. How many women can you name who write serious newspaper and magazine articles reporting on or arguing matters of general interest, as opposed to those meant to appeal chiefly to women?
3. To what extent do you agree with Ehrenreich — and with Herbert Gold — that the American media are interested only in "upbeat" stories?

CURTIS CHANG

A 1990 graduate of Harvard University, CURTIS CHANG majored in government and was active in a variety of student organizations. He was born in Taiwan and immigrated to the United States in 1971 with his family. He attended public school near Chicago. At Harvard, Chang helped found the Minority Student Alliance, belonged to the debating society, wrote for the *Harvard Political Review*, and was a leader of the Harvard-Radcliffe Christian Fellowship. Winner of the Michael C. Rockefeller Fellowship for Travel Abroad, Chang plans to go to South Africa, where he will work with local churches and explore the relations between Asians and blacks. After that, he plans to attend graduate school or to enter the ministry.

Streets of Gold:
The Myth of the Model Minority

This essay, like Linnea Saukko's (p. 314) and Margot Harrison's (p. 357), won a Bedford Prize in Student Writing and was published in *Student Writers at Work* (3rd ed., 1989), edited by Nancy Sommers and Donald McQuade. Written when Chang was a freshman at Harvard, the essay grew out of his friendship with black students, his increasing interest in issues of racial identity, and his realization that Asian-Americans had at best an ambiguous position in American society. "Streets of Gold" states and supports an opinion forcefully and, we think, convincingly. And it has something else to recommend it as well: It provides a model of research writing and documentation. The documentation style is that of the Modern Language Association.

Over 100 years ago, an American myth misled many of my ancestors. Seeking cheap labor, railroad companies convinced numerous Chinese that American streets were paved with gold. Today, the media portray Asian-Americans as finally mining those golden streets. Major publications like *Time*, *Newsweek*,

U.S. News & World Report, Fortune, The New Republic, the *Wall Street Journal,* and the *New York Times Magazine* have all recently published congratulatory "Model Minority" headline stories with such titles as

> America's Super Minority
> An American Success Story
> A "Model Minority"
> Why They Succeed
> The Ultimate Assimilation
> The Triumph of Asian-Americans.

But the Model Minority is another "Streets of Gold" tale. It 2 distorts Asian-Americans' true status and ignores our racial handicaps. And the Model Minority's ideology is even worse than its mythology. It attempts to justify the existing system of racial inequality by blaming the victims rather than the system itself.

The Model Minority myth introduces us as an ethnic minor- 3 ity that is finally "making it in America," as stated in *Time* (Doerner 42). The media consistently define "making it" as achieving material wealth, wealth that flows from our successes in the workplace and the schoolroom. This economic achievement allegedly proves a minority can, as *Fortune* says, "lay claim to the American dream" (Ramirez 149).

Trying to show how "Asian-Americans present a picture of 4 affluence and economic success," as the *New York Times Magazine* puts it (Oxnam 72), 9 out of 10 of the major Model Minority stories of the last four years relied heavily on one statistic: the family median income. The median Asian-American family income, according to the U.S. Census Survey of Income and Education data, is $22,713 compared to $20,800 for white Americans. Armed with that figure, national magazines such as *Newsweek* have trumpeted our "remarkable, ever-mounting achievements" (Kasindorf et al. 51).

Such assertions demonstrate the truth of the aphorism "Sta- 5 tistics are like a bikini. What they reveal is suggestive, but what they conceal is vital." The family median income statistic conceals the fact that Asian-American families generally (1) have more children and live-in relatives and thus have more mouths to feed; (2) are often forced by necessity to have everyone in the family work, averaging *more* than two family income earners (whites only have 1.6) (Cabezas 402); and (3) live disproportionately in high cost of living areas (i.e., New York, Chicago, Los Angeles, and Honolulu) which artificially inflate income figures. Dr. Robert S. Mariano, professor of economics at the University of Pennsylvania, has calculated that

> when such appropriate adjustments and comparisons are made, a different and rather disturbing picture emerges, showing indeed a clearly disadvantaged group. . . . Filipino and Chinese men *are no better off than black men with regard to median incomes.* (55)[1]

Along with other racial minorities, Asian-Americans are still scraping for the crumbs of the economic pie.

Throughout its distortion of our status, the media propagate   6
two crucial assumptions. First, they lump all Asian-Americans into one monolithic, homogeneous, yellow-skinned mass. Such a view ignores the existence of an incredibly disadvantaged Asian-American underclass. Asians work in low-income and low-status jobs two to three times more than whites (Cabezas 438). Recent Vietnamese refugees in California are living like the Appalachian poor. While going to his Manhattan office, multimillionaire architect I. M. Pei's car passes Chinese restaurants and laundries where 72% of all New York Chinese men still work (U.S. Bureau of the Census qtd. in Cabezas 443).

But the media make an even more dangerous assumption.   7
They suggest that (alleged) material success is the same thing as basic racial equality. Citing that venerable family median income figure, magazines claim Asian-Americans are "obviously nondisadvantaged folks," as stated in *Fortune* (Seligman 64). Yet a 1979 United States Equal Employment Opportunity Commission

---

[1]The picture becomes even more disturbing when one realizes the higher income figures do not necessarily equal higher quality of life. For instance, in New York Chinatown, more than 1 out of 5 residents work more than 57 hours per week, almost 1 out of 10 elderly must labor more than 55 hours per week (Nishi 503).

study on Asian-Americans discovered widespread anti-Asian hiring and promotion practices. Asian-Americans "in the professional, technical, and managerial occupations" often face "modern racism — the subtle, sophisticated, systemic patterns and practices . . . which function to effect and to obscure the disciminatory outcomes" (Nishi 398). One myth simply does not prove another: Neither our "astonishing economic prosperity" (Ramirez 152) nor a racially equal America exist.

An emphasis on material success also pervades the media's   8
stress on Asian-Americans' educational status at "the top of the class" ("Asian Americans" 4). Our "march into the ranks of the educational elite," as *U.S. News & World Report* puts it (McBee et al. 41), is significant, according to *Fortune*, because "all that education is paying off spectacularly" (Ramirez 149). Once again, the same fallacious assumptions plague this "whiz kids" image of Asian-Americans.

The media again ignore the fact that class division accounts   9
for much of the publicized success. Until 1976, the U.S. Immigration Department only admitted Asian immigrants that were termed "skilled" workers. "Skilled" generally meant college educated, usually in the sciences since poor English would not be a handicap. The result was that the vast majority of pre-1976 Asian immigrants came from already well-educated, upper-class backgrounds — the classic "brain drain" syndrome (Hirschman and Wong 507–10).

The post-1976 immigrants, however, come generally from   10
the lower, less educated classes (Kim 24). A study by Professor Elizabeth Ahn Toupin of Tufts University matched similar Asian and non-Asian students *along class lines* and found that Asian-Americans "did not perform at a superior academic level to non-Asian students. Asian-Americans were more likely to be placed on academic probation than their white counterparts. . . . Twice as many Asian-American students withdrew from the university" (12).

Thus, it is doubtful whether the perceived widespread educa-   11
tional success will continue as the Asian-American population eventually balances out along class lines. When 16.2% of all Chinese have less than four years of schooling (*four times* the percentage of whites) (Azores 73), it seems many future Asian-Americans

will worry more about being able to read a newspaper rather than a Harvard acceptance letter.

Most important, the media assume once again that achieving a   12
certain level of material or educational success means achieving real equality. People easily forget that to begin with, Asians invest heavily in education since other means of upward mobility are barred to them by race. Until recently, for instance, Asian-Americans were barred from unions and traditional lines of credit (Yun 23–24).[2] Other "white" avenues to success, such as the "old boy network," are still closed to Asian-Americans.

When *Time* claims "as a result of their academic achievement   13
Asians are climbing the economic ladder with remarkable speed," it glosses over an inescapable fact: There is a white ladder and then there is a yellow one. Almost all of the academic studies on the *actual returns Asians receive* from their education point to prevalent discrimination. A striking example of this was found in a City University of New York research project which constructed résumés with equivalent educational backgrounds. Applications were then sent to employers, one group under an Asian name and a similar group under a Caucasian name. Whites received interviews five times more than Asians (Nishi 399). The media never headline even more shocking data that can be easily found in the U.S. Census. For instance, Chinese and Filipino males only earned respectively 74% and 52% as much as their *equally educated* white counterparts. Asian females fared even worse. Their salaries were only 44% to 54% as large as equivalent white males' paychecks (Cabezas 391). Blacks suffer from this same statistical disparity. We Asian-Americans are indeed a Model Minority — a perfect model of racial discrimination in America.

Yet this media myth encourages neglect of our pressing needs.   14
"Clearly, many Asian-Americans and Pacific peoples are invisible to the governmental agencies," reported the California State Advisory Committee to the U.S. Commission on Civil Rights. "Discrimination against Asian-Americans and Pacific peoples is as much the result of omission as commission" (qtd. in Chun 7). In 1979, while the president praised Asian-Americans' "successful in-

---

[2]For further analysis on the role racism plays in Asian-Americans' stress on education and certain technical and scientific fields, see Suzuki 44.

tegration into American society," his administration revoked Asian-Americans' eligibility for minority small business loans, devastating thousands of struggling, newly arrived small businessmen. Hosts of other minority issues, ranging from reparations for the Japanese-American internment to the ominous rise of anti-Asian violence, are widely ignored by the general public.

The media, in fact, insist to the general populace that we are 15 not a true racial minority. In an attack on affirmative action, the *Boston Globe* pointed out that universities, like many people, "obviously feel that Asian-Americans, especially those of Chinese and Japanese descent, are brilliant, privileged, and wrongly classified as minorities" ("Affirmative Non-actions" 10). Harvard Dean Henry Rosovsky remarked in the same article that "It does not seem to me that as a group, they are disadvantaged. . . . Asian-Americans appear to be in an odd category among other protected minorities."

The image that we Asians aren't like "other minorities" is fun- 16 damental to the Model Minority ideology. Any elementary-school student knows that the teacher designates one student the model, the "teacher's pet," in order to set an example for others to follow. One only sets up a "model minority" in order to communicate to the other "students," the blacks and Hispanics, "Why can't you be like that?" The media, in fact, almost admit to "grading" minorities as they headline Model Minority stories "Asian-Americans: Are They Making the Grade?" (McBee et al.). And Asians have earned the highest grade by fulfilling one important assignment: identifying with the white majority, with its values and wishes.

Unlike blacks, for instance, we Asian-Americans have not vig- 17 orously asserted our ethnic identity (a.k.a. Black Power). And the American public has historically demanded assimilation over racial pluralism.[3] Over the years, *Newsweek* has published titles from "Success Story: Outwhiting the Whites" to "The Ultimate Assimilation," which lauded the increasing number of Asian-white mar-

---

[3]A full discussion of racial pluralism versus assimilation is impossible here. But suffice it to say that pluralism accepts ethnic cultures as equally different; assimilation asks for a "melting" into the majority. An example of the assimilation philosophy is the massive "Americanization" programs of the late 1880s, which successfully erased Eastern Europe immigrants' customs in favor of Anglo-Saxon ones.

riages as evidence of Asian-Americans' "acceptance into American society" (Kantrowitz et al. 80).

Even more significant is the public's approval of how we have succeeded in the "American tradition" (Ramirez 164). Unlike the blacks and Hispanics, we "Puritan-like" Asians (Oxnam 72) disdain governmental assistance. A *New Republic* piece, "The Triumph of Asian-Americans," similarly applauded how "Asian-Americans pose no problems at all" (Bell 30). The media consistently compare the crime-ridden image of other minorities with the picture of law-abiding Asian parents whose "well-behaved kids" hit books and not the streets ("Asian Americans" 4). [18]

Some insist there is nothing terrible about whites conjuring up our "tremendous" success, divining from it model American traits, then preaching, "Why can't you blacks and Hispanics be like that?" After all, one might argue, aren't those traits desirable? [19]

Such a view, as mentioned, neglects Asian-Americans' true and pressing needs. Moreover, this view completely misses the Model Minority image's fundamental ideology, an ideology meant to falsely grant America absolution from its racial barriers. [20]

David O. Sears and Donald R. Kinder, two social scientists, have recently published significant empirical studies on the underpinnings of American racial attitudes. They consistently discovered that Americans' stress on "values, such as 'individualism and self-reliance, the work ethic, obedience, and discipline' . . . can be invoked, however perversely, to feed racist appetites" (qtd. in Kennedy 88). In other words, the Model Minority image lets Americans' consciences rest easy. They can think: "It's not our fault those blacks and Hispanics can't make it. They're just too lazy. After all, look at the Asians."[4] Consequently, American society never confronts the systemic racial and economic factors underlying such inequality. The victims instead bear the blame. [21]

---

[4]This phenomenon of blaming the victim for racial inequality is as old as America itself. For instance, southerners once eased their consciences over slavery by labeling blacks as animals lacking humanity. Today, America does it by labeling them as inferior people lacking "desirable" traits. For an excellent further analysis of this ideology, actually widespread among American intellectuals, see *Iron Cages: Race and Culture in 19th-Century America* by Ronald T. Takaki.

This ideology behind the Model Minority image is best seen   22
when we examine one of the first Model Minority stories, which
suddenly appeared in the mid-1960s. It is important to note that
the period was marked by newfound, strident black demands for
equality and power.

> At a time when it is being proposed that hundreds of billions
> be spent to uplift Negroes and other minorities, the na-
> tion's 300,000 Chinese-Americans are moving ahead on
> their own — with no help from anyone else. . . . Few Chinese-
> Americans are getting welfare handouts — or even want them.
> . . . They don't sit around moaning. ("Success Story of One
> Minority Group" 73)

The same article then concludes that the Chinese-American history and accomplishment "would shock those now complaining
about the hardships endured by today's Negroes."

Not surprisingly, the dunce-capped blacks and Hispanics re-   23
sent us apple-polishing, "well-behaved" teacher's pets. Black comedian Richard Pryor performs a revealing routine in which new
Asian immigrants learn from whites their first English word:
"Nigger." And Asian-Americans themselves succumb to the
Model Minority's deceptive mythology and racist ideology.[5] "I
made it without help," one often hears among Asian circles; "why
can't they?" In a 1986 nationwide poll, only 27% of Asian-American students rated "racial understanding" as "essential." The figure plunged 9% in the last year alone (a year marked by a torrent
of Model Minority stories) (Hune). We "whitewashed" Asians
have simply lost our identity as a fellow, disadvantaged minority.

But we don't even need to look beyond the Model Minority   24
stories themselves to realize that whites see us as "whiter" than
blacks — but not quite white enough. For instance, citing that familiar median family income figure, *Fortune* magazine of 17 May
1982 complained that the Asian-American community is in fact

---

[5]America has a long history of playing off one minority against the other.
During the early 1900s, for instance, mining companies in the west often hired
Asians solely as scabs against striking black miners. Black versus Asian hostility and violence usually followed. This pattern was repeated in numerous industries. In a larger historical sense, almost every immigrant group has assimilated, to some degree, the culture of antiblack racism.

"getting *more* than its share of the pie" (Seligman 64). For decades, when white Americans were leading the nation in every single economic measure, editorials arguing that whites were getting more than *their* share of the pie were rather rare.

No matter how "well-behaved" we are, Asian-Americans are 25 still excluded from the real pie, the "positions of institutional power and political power" (Kuo 289). Professor Harry Kitano of UCLA has written extensively on the plight of Asian-Americans as the "middleman minority," a minority supposedly satisfied materially but forever racially barred from a ture, *significant* role in society. Empirical studies indicate that Asian-Americans "have been channeled into lower-echelon white-collar jobs having little or no decision making authority" (Suzuki 38). For example, in *Fortune's* 1,000 largest companies, Asian-American nameplates rest on a mere half of one percent of all officers' and directors' desks (a statistical disparity worsened by the fact that most of the Asians founded their companies) (Ramirez 152). While the education of the upper-class Asians may save them from the bread lines, their race still keeps them from the boardroom.

Our docile acceptance of such exclusion is actually one of our 26 "model" traits. When Asian-Americans in San Francisco showed their first hint of political activism and protested Asian exclusion from city boards, the *Washington Monthly* warned in a long Asian-American article, "Watch out, here comes another group to pander to" ("The Wrong Way" 21). *The New Republic* praised Asian-American political movements because

> Unlike blacks or Hispanics, Asian-American politicians have the luxury of not having to devote the bulk of their time to an "Asian-American agenda," and thus escape becoming prisoners of such an agenda. . . . The most important thing for Asian-Americans . . . is simply "being part of the process." (Bell 31)

This is strikingly reminiscent of another of the first Model Minority stories:

> As the Black and Brown communities push for changes in the present system, the Oriental is set forth as an example to be followed — a minority group that has achieved success through adaptation rather than confrontation. (*Gidra* qtd. in Chun 7)

But it is precisely this "present system," this system of subtle, 27
persistent racism that we all must confront, not adapt to. For example, we Asians gained our right to vote from the 1964 Civil
Rights Act that blacks marched, bled, died, and, in the words of
that original Model Minority story, "sat around moaning for."
Unless we assert our true identity as a minority and challenge racial misconceptions and inequalities, we will be nothing more
than techno-coolies — collecting our wages but silently enduring
basic political and economic inequality.

This country perpetuated a myth once. Today, no one can af- 28
ford to dreamily chase after that gold in the streets, oblivious to
the genuine treasure of racial equality. When racism persists, can
one really call any minority a "model"?

Works Cited

"Affirmative Non-actions." Op-ed. *The Boston Globe* 14 January 1985: 10.
"Asian Americans, The Drive to Excel." *Newsweek on Campus* April
　　1984: 4–13.
Asian American Studies: Contemporary Issues. Proc. from East Coast
　　Asian American Scholars Conference. 1986.
Azores, Fortunata M. "Census Methodology and the Development of
　　Social Indicators for Asian and Pacific Americans." United States
　　Commission on Civil Rights 70–79.
Bell, David A. "The Triumph of Asian-Americans." *The New Republic*
　　15 & 22 July 1985: 24–31.
Cabezas, Armado. "Employment Issues of Asian Americans." United
　　States Commission on Civil Rights.
Chun, Ki-Taek. "The Myth of Asian American Success and Its Educa-
　　tional Ramifications." *IRCD Bulletin* Winter/Spring 1980.
Doerner, William R. "To America with Skills." *Time* 8 July 1985: 42–44.
Dutta, Manoranjan. "Asian/Pacific American Employment Profile:
　　Myth and Reality — Issues and Answers." The United States Com-
　　mission on Civil Rights 445–489.
Hirschman, Charles, and Morrison G. Wong. "Trends in Socio-
　　economic Achievement Among Immigrants and Native-Born
　　Asian-Americans, 1960–1976." *Sociological Quarterly* 22.4 (1981):
　　495–513.
Hune, Shirley. Keynote address. East Coast Asian Student Union Con-
　　ference. Boston University. 14 Feb. 1987.

Kahng, Anthony. "Employment Issues." The United States Commission on Civil Rights 1980.

Kantrowitz, Barbara, et al. "The Ultimate Assimilation." *Newsweek* 24 Nov. 1986: 80.

Kasindorf, Martin, et al. "Asian-Americans: A 'Model Minority.'" *Newsweek* 6 Dec. 1982: 39–51.

Kennedy, David M. "The Making of a Classic. Gunnar Myrdal and Black-White Relations: The Use and Abuse of *An American Dilemma.*" *Atlantic* May 1987: 86–89.

Kiang, Peter. Personal interview. 1 May 1987.

Kim, Illsoo. "Class Divisions Among Asian Immigrants: Its Implications for Social Welfare Policy." *Asian American Studies* 24–25.

Kuo, Wen H. "On the Study of Asian-Americans: Its Current State and Agenda." *Sociological Quarterly* 20.2 (1979): 279–290.

Mariano, Robert S. "Census Issues." United States Commission on Civil Rights 54–59.

McBee, Susanna, et al. "Asian-Americans: Are They Making the Grade?" *US News and World Report* 2 Apr. 1984: 41–47.

Nishi, Setsuko Matsunaga. "Asian American Employment Issues: Myths and Realities." United States Commission on Civil Rights 397–399, 495–507.

Oxnam, Robert B. "Why Asians Succeed Here." *New York Times Magazine* 30 Nov. 1986: 72+.

Ramirez, Anthony, "America's Super Minority." *Fortune* 24 November 1986: 148–149.

Seligman, Daniel. "Keeping Up: Working Smarter." *Fortune* 17 May 1982: 64.

"Success Story of One Minority Group in the US." *U.S. News and World Report* 26 Dec. 1966: 73–76.

"Success Story: Outwhiting the Whites." *Newsweek* 21 June 1971: 24–25.

Sung, Betty Lee. *A Survey of Chinese American Manpower and Employment.* NY: Praeger, 1976.

Suzuki, Bob H. "Education and the Socialization of Asian Americans: A Revisionist Analysis of the 'Model Minority' Thesis." *Amerasia Journal* 4.2 (1977): 23–51.

Toupin, Elizabeth Ahn. "A Model University for a Model Minority." *Asian American Studies* 10–12.

"The Wrong Way to Court Ethnics." *Washington Monthly* May 1986: 21–26.

United States. Commission on Civil Rights. *Civil Rights Issues of Asian and Pacific Americans: Myths and Realities.* 1980.

Yun, Grace. "Notes from Discussions on Asian American Education." *Asian American Studies* 20–24.

QUESTIONS ON MEANING

1. What is Chang's THESIS? Why does he introduce it where he does?
2. What "two crucial assumptions" do the media mistakenly propagate about Asian-Americans?
3. What exactly does Chang mean by the "pressing needs" of Asian-Americans?
4. Summarize Chang's ideas about the "Model Minority ideology" (beginning in para. 16). What is an "ideology"? What does this one do?

QUESTIONS ON WRITING STRATEGY

1. Is Chang's argument based more on EMOTIONAL APPEAL or on RATIONAL APPEAL? Why do you say so?
2. Try to summarize Chang's argument in a SYLLOGISM (as demonstrated on p. 614). What part of the syllogism corresponds to Chang's thesis?
3. What types of EVIDENCE does Chang base his argument on? Is the evidence adequate?
4. Analyze Chang's POINT OF VIEW. With whom does he ally himself? How does his position affect the essay?
5. Where does Chang acknowledge and address possible objections to his argument?
6. OTHER METHODS. How does Chang use division or analysis (Chap. 6) to develop his argument?

QUESTIONS ON LANGUAGE

1. What is the "old boy network" (para. 12)? What are the implications of this phrase?
2. In paragraph 27, Chang uses the term "techno-coolies." What ALLUSION is he making? Why is it especially suitable at this point in the essay?
3. Chang refers in paragraphs 5, 24, and 25 to an "economic pie." What images does this METAPHOR evoke?
4. Consult your dictionary if any of the following words are unfamiliar: allegedly (para. 3); median (4); aphorism (5); propagates, monolithic (6); venerable, systemic (7); fallacious (8); prevalent, disparity (13); reparations, internment (14); assimilation, lauded (17); absolu-

tion (20); empirical (21); succumb, torrent (23); lower-echelon (25); docile, pander (26); perpetuated (28).

SUGGESTIONS FOR WRITING

1. Do you know of an issue or an incident when the media have distorted or omitted facts? (The subject could be a local fire, a demonstration, an arrest, a legislative debate, anything.) Write an argument in which you analyze and correct the media record.
2. Do you agree with Chang's argument? Write an essay supporting or contesting his opinion that the "Model Minority" is a harmful myth.
3. Take Chang's essay further: Write a concrete proposal for correcting the situation he describes.
4. CONNECTIONS. William Ouchi's "Japanese and American Workers" (p. 250) and James Fallows's "Freedom, Control, and Success" (p. 529) both address differences between Americans and Asians, mainly Japanese. Analyze the possible connections between these essays and Chang's. For instance, what characteristics of Asians identified by Ouchi and Fallows show up in the stereotypes Chang disputes? What characteristics don't get translated into stereotypes?

CURTIS CHANG ON WRITING

For Curtis Chang, a word processor is an "essential" writing tool. Once he completes and outlines his research, he explains in *Student Writers at Work*, "I must see my thoughts on the computer screen. I find it difficult to manipulate thoughts unless I can physically manipulate the words that represent them."

But the word processor can be a mixed blessing, for it supports Chang's "urge to perfect each sentence as I am writing. One is especially vulnerable when working on a word processor. I often have to force myself to continue getting the basic facts out first." Once he does have his thoughts on screen, Chang turns to global revision, an important part of his writing process. Although he strives for perfect sentences, Chang thinks of revision as "more than just the usual forms of correcting grammar and spelling and using one adjective instead of another." For Chang,

"Revising means acting as devil's advocate and trying to pick apart my paper's argument. Then I have to answer to those criticisms."

Like many writers, Chang is rarely satisfied with his work. For each paper, he reports, "I average about three drafts, but it is usually determined by time constraints. I never really finish an essay; I just tire of tinkering with it."

FOR DISCUSSION

1. Why does Chang try not to perfect his sentences until the entire essay is written? What is the advantage of "getting the basic facts out first"?
2. Curtis Chang considers the word processor essential for writing. Would his extensive revisions be possible without one?

ISHMAEL REED

Born in Chattanooga, Tennessee, in 1938 and raised in Buffalo, New York, ISHMAEL REED began writing in elementary school and as a teenager had work published. He attended the State University of New York at Buffalo. In the years since, Reed has become known as a writer given to experimentation and provocation. He has produced eight novels, four volumes of poetry, three plays, and countless songs. Some notable works include the poetry collections *catechism of d neoamerican hoodoo church* (1971) and *Conjure* (1972); the novels *The Free-Lance Pallbearers* (1967), *Mumbo Jumbo* (1972), and *The Terrible Threes* (1989); and the essay collection *Writin' Is Fightin'* (1988). A supporter of young writers from all cultures through his publishing imprint, I. Reed Books, Reed has also taught writing at many colleges and universities. He now lives in California and teaches at the University of California at Berkeley.

America:
The Multinational Society

As its title suggests, this essay holds that Americans have nothing to fear from immigrants and others who may seem to threaten unity and stability: The transformation to a multicultural society is already occurring; and, Reed thinks, it is making us a stronger nation. Reed's opinion is perhaps unsurprising from one whose own ancestry is part African-American, part Native American, part French, and part Irish. The essay was first published in a periodical, *San Francisco Focus*, and was then collected in *Writin' Is Fightin'*.

> At the annual Lower East Side Jewish Festival yesterday, a Chinese woman ate a pizza slice in front of Ty Thuan Duc's Vietnamese grocery store. Beside her a Spanish-speaking family patronized a cart with two signs: "Italian Ices" and "Kosher by Rabbi Alper." And after the pastrami ran out, everybody ate knishes.
> —*New York Times*, 23 June 1983

On the day before Memorial Day, 1983, a poet called me to 1
describe a city he had just visited. He said that one section included mosques, built by the Islamic people who dwelled there.
Attending his reading, he said, were large numbers of Hispanic
people, forty thousand of whom lived in the same city. He was
not talking about a fabled city located in some mysterious region
of the world. The city he'd visited was Detroit.

A few months before, as I was leaving Houston, Texas, I 2
heard it announced on the radio that Texas's largest minority was
Mexican-American, and though a foundation recently issued a
report critical of bilingual education, the taped voice used to
guide the passengers on the air trams connecting terminals in Dallas Airport is in both Spanish and English. If the trend continues,
a day will come when it will be difficult to travel through some
sections of the country without hearing commands in both English and Spanish; after all, for some western states, Spanish was
the first written language and the Spanish style lives on in the
western way of life.

Shortly after my Texas trip, I sat in an auditorium located on 3
the campus of the University of Wisconsin at Milwaukee as a Yale
professor — whose original work on the influence of African cultures upon those of the Americas has led to his ostracism from
some monocultural intellectual circles — walked up and down
the aisle, like an old-time southern evangelist, dancing and drum-
ming the top of the lectern, illustrating his points before some serious Afro-American intellectuals and artists who cheered and
applauded his performance and his mastery of information. The
professor was "white." After his lecture, he joined a group of Mil-
waukeeans in a conversation. All of the participants spoke Yoru-
ban, though only the professor had ever traveled to Africa.

One of the artists told me that his paintings, which included 4
African and Afro-American mythological symbols and imagery,
were hanging in the local McDonald's restaurant. The next day I
went to McDonald's and snapped pictures of smiling youngsters
eating hamburgers below paintings that could grace the walls of any
of the country's leading museums. The manager of the local Mc-
Donald's said, "I don't know what you boys are doing, but I like it,"
as he commissioned the local painters to exhibit in his restaurant.

Such blurring of cultural styles occurs in everyday life in the United States to a greater extent than anyone can imagine and is probably more prevalent than the sensational conflict between people of different backgrounds that is played up and often encouraged by the media. The result is what the Yale professor Robert Thompson referred to as a cultural bouillabaisse, yet members of the nation's present educational and cultural Elect still cling to the notion that the United States belongs to some vaguely defined entity they refer to as "Western civilization," by which they mean, presumably, a civilization created by the people of Europe, as if Europe can be viewed in monolithic terms. Is Beethoven's Ninth Symphony, which includes Turkish marches, a part of Western civilization, or the late nineteenth- and twentieth-century French paintings, whose creators were influenced by Japanese art? And what of the Cubists, through whom the influence of African art changed modern painting, or the Surrealists, who were so impressed with the art of the Pacific Northwest Indians that, in their map of North America, Alaska dwarfs the lower forty-eight in size?

Are the Russians, who are often criticized for their adoption of "Western" ways by Tsarist dissidents in exile, members of Western civilization? And what of the millions of Europeans who have black African and Asian ancestry, black Africans having occupied several countries for hundreds of years? Are these "Europeans" members of Western civilization, or the Hungarians, who originated across the Urals in a place called Greater Hungary, or the Irish, who came from the Iberian Peninsula?

Even the notion that North America is part of Western civilization because our "system of government" is derived from Europe is being challenged by Native American historians who say that the founding fathers, Benjamin Franklin especially, were actually influenced by the system of government that had been adopted by the Iroquois hundreds of years prior to the arrival of large numbers of Europeans.

Western civilization, then, becomes another confusing category like Third World, or Judeo-Christian culture, as man attempts to impose his small-screen view of political and cultural reality upon a complex world. Our most publicized novelist

recently said that Western civilization was the greatest achievement of mankind, an attitude that flourishes on the street level as
scribbles in public restrooms: "White Power," "Niggers and Spics
Suck," or "Hitler was a prophet," the latter being the most telling,
for wasn't Adolf Hitler the archetypal monoculturalist who, in
his pigheaded arrogance, believed that one way and one blood
was so pure that it had to be protected from alien strains at all
costs? Where did such an attitude, which has caused so much misery and depression in our national life, which has tainted even
our noblest achievements, begin? An attitude that caused the incarceration of Japanese-American citizens during World War II,
the persecution of Chicanos and Chinese-Americans, the near-
extermination of the Indians, and the murder and lynchings of
thousands of Afro-Americans.

Virtuous, hardworking, pious, even though they occasionally   9
would wander off after some fancy clothes, or rendezvous in the
woods with the town prostitute, the Puritans are idealized in our
schoolbooks as "a hardy band" of no-nonsense patriarchs whose
discipline razed the forest and brought order to the New World (a
term that annoys Native American historians). Industrious, responsible, it was their "Yankee ingenuity" and practicality that
created the work ethic. They were simple folk who produced a
number of good poets, and they set the tone for the American
writing style, of lean and spare lines, long before Hemingway.
They worshiped in churches whose colors blended in with the
New England snow, churches with simple structures and ornate
lecterns.

The Puritans were a daring lot, but they had a mean streak.   10
They hated the theater and banned Christmas. They punished
people in a cruel and inhuman manner. They killed children who
disobeyed their parents. When they came in contact with those
whom they considered heathens or aliens, they behaved in such a
bizarre and irrational manner that this chapter in the American
history comes down to us as a late-movie horror film. They exterminated the Indians, who taught them how to survive in a world
unknown to them, and their encounter with the calypso culture
of Barbados resulted in what the tourist guide in Salem's Witches'
House refers to as the Witchcraft Hysteria.

The Puritan legacy of hard work and meticulous accounting 11 led to the establishment of a great industrial society; it is no wonder that the American industrial revolution began in Lowell, Massachusetts. But there was the other side, the strange and paranoid attitudes toward those different from the Elect.

The cultural attitudes of that early Elect continue to be 12 voiced in everyday life in the United States: the president of a distinguished university, writing a letter to the *Times*, belittling the study of African civilizations; the television network that promoted its show on the Vatican art with the boast that this art represented "the finest achievements of the human spirit." A modern up-tempo state of complex rhythms that depends upon contacts with an international community can no longer behave as if it dwelled in a "Zion Wilderness" surrounded by beasts and pagans.

When I heard a schoolteacher warn the other night about the 13 invasion of the American educational system by foreign curriculums, I wanted to yell at the television set, "Lady, they're already here." It has already begun because the world is here. The world has been arriving at these shores for at least ten thousand years from Europe, Africa, and Asia. In the late nineteenth and early twentieth centuries, large numbers of Europeans arrived, adding their cultures to those of the European, African, and Asian settlers who were already here, and recently millions have been entering the country from South America and the Caribbean, making Yale Professor Bob Thompson's bouillabaisse richer and thicker.

One of our most visionary politicians said that he envisioned 14 a time when the United States could become the brain of the world, by which he meant the repository of all of the latest advanced information systems. I thought of that remark when an enterprising poet friend of mine called to say that he had just sold a poem to a computer magazine and that the editors were delighted to get it because they didn't carry fiction or poetry. Is that the kind of world we desire? A humdrum homogeneous world of all brains and no heart, no fiction, no poetry; a world of robots with human attendants bereft of imagination, of culture? Or does North America deserve a more exciting destiny? To become a place where the cultures of the world crisscross. This is possible because the United States is unique in the world: The world is here.

QUESTIONS ON MEANING

1. How does Reed see *Western civilization* being defined by those who champion it as the dominant culture? In his eyes, what is wrong with this definition?
2. What do you take to be Reed's PURPOSE in this essay?
3. What does Reed mean by the two key and contrasting terms *mono-cultural* (paras. 3, 8) and *bouillabaisse* (5, 13)?
4. How does Reed interpret the notion that "the United States could become the brain of the world" (para. 14)? What is his objection?

QUESTIONS ON WRITING STRATEGY

1. Where do most of Reed's examples come from? Are they adequate as EVIDENCE? Why, or why not?
2. Why does Reed wait until the fifth paragraph to present his THESIS? Does he arrive at it through INDUCTION or DEDUCTION?
3. How does Reed's CONCLUSION promote his argument?
4. What assumptions does the author make about the attitudes and beliefs of his AUDIENCE? How do his use of evidence and his TONE support your answer?
5. OTHER METHODS. In paragraphs 8–12, Reed analyzes causes and effects (Chap. 9). What is the point of this analysis in his argument?

QUESTIONS ON LANGUAGE

1. Look up the definitions of any words below that you are unfamiliar with: mosques (para. 1); ostracism (3); Elect (noun), Cubists, Surrealists (5); dissidents (6); archetypal, incarceration, lynchings (8); razed (9); repository, bereft (14).
2. What is the EFFECT of the "scribbles in public restrooms" (para. 8)? What do they represent to Reed?
3. Analyze Reed's use of language in discussing the Puritans (paras. 9–11). What attitude(s) toward the Puritans does the language convey?

SUGGESTIONS FOR WRITING

1. Reed asserts that a "blurring of cultural styles . . . is probably more prevalent [in the United States] than the sensational conflict between people of different backgrounds that is played up and often encouraged by the media." Is this true in your experience? Compare and contrast the image and reality of a community you either live in or visit. Support your essay with examples.

2. Reed calls Western civilization "another confusing category like Third World, or Judeo-Christian culture" (para. 8). How confusing are these other terms? In social-science encyclopedias, dictionaries of culture, and other library references (but not abridged dictionaries), find at least three definitions of either term. Write a brief essay that specifies the similarities and differences in the definitions.

3. "The dreams and fears of a community can be found written on the walls of its restrooms." Check out some restrooms in your community and write an essay that supports or rejects the above statement.

4. CONNECTIONS. Both Reed's essay and the following one, Richard Rodriguez's "Aria," address problems of difference and assimilation in American culture. When you have read both essays, write an essay in which you argue for or against the need for a unified, unilingual American culture. Consider the implications of your opinion, such as what would bind a highly diverse, multilingual culture, or which of America's many cultural groups would predominate in a unified culture.

ISHMAEL REED ON WRITING

Ishmael Reed describes himself as someone with a "prolific writing jab" — a knack for starting fights, or at least stirring up controversy, with his pen. In fiction and nonfiction, he has taken on governments, literary intellectuals, the media, feminists — any person or any group he felt needed correcting. As he told the writer William C. Brisick, he sees himself as part "trickster," a term he learned from Native Americans for a figure common to many folk traditions who exposes pretension and dishonesty. Essays for Reed are a means of "talking back, a way of including in the national dialogue another point of view, one not present in the media."

Reed does not disdain using his talents for even more practical purposes. To publicize the deterioration of his crack-infested neighborhood in Oakland, California, Reed wrote an article for a local newspaper that gained wide attention, both pro and con. In addition to this piece, Reed composed press releases for the neighborhood association — writing that "really moved the community," he says. "It's become functional art."

FOR DISCUSSION

1. Would you say that writing that has a practical goal (a press release, for instance) can be valued for its own sake as writing? Is it art?
2. What of the "trickster" do you see in Reed's essay, "America: The Multinational Society"?

and back again. What is the overall EFFECT of these shifts? Do they strengthen or weaken the author's stance against bilingual education?

3. Twice in his essay (in paras. 1 and 40) the author mentions schoolbooks wrapped in shopping-bag paper. How does the use of this detail enhance his argument?

4. What AUDIENCE probably would not like this essay? Why would they not like it?

5. OTHER METHODS. Rodriguez makes extensive use of comparison and contrast (Chap. 4) — for instance, in contrasting the sounds of Spanish and of English (paras. 10, 11, 13, 14, 18, 33, 37). What other uses of comparison and contrast do you find?

QUESTIONS ON LANGUAGE

1. Consult the dictionary if you need help defining these words: counterpoint (para. 8); polysyllabic (10); guttural, syntax (11); falsetto, exuberance (13); inconsequential (14); cloistered, lacquered (18); diffident (21); intrinsically (22); incongruity (23); bemused (29); effusive (35); assimilated (38); paradoxically, tenuous, decadent (39).

2. In Rodriguez's essay, how do the words *public* and *private* relate to the issue of bilingual education? What important distinction does the author make between *individuality* and *separateness* (para. 39)?

3. What exactly does the author mean when he says, "More and more of my day was spent hearing words, not sounds" (para. 40)?

SUGGESTIONS FOR WRITING

1. Try to define the distinctive quality of the language spoken in your home when you were a child. Explain any ways in which this language differed from what you heard in school. How has the difference mattered to you? (This language need not be a foreign language; it might include any words used in your family but not in the world at large: a dialect, slang, ALLUSIONS, sayings, FIGURES OF SPEECH, or a special vocabulary.)

2. Bilingual education is a controversial issue with evidence and strong feelings on both sides. In a page or so of preliminary writing, respond to Rodriguez's essay with your own gut feelings on the issue. Then do some library research to extend, support, or refute your views. (Consult the *Readers' Guide to Periodical Literature* as a first step.) In a well-reasoned and well-supported essay, give your opinion

on whether or not public schools should teach children in their "family language."

3. CONNECTIONS. Rodriguez and Ishmael Reed, in "America: The Multinational Society" (p. 649), not only express different views of assimilation and diversity in the United States but also approach the issues differently. In an essay, compare and contrast these two selections in terms of their content, OBJECTIVE/SUBJECTIVE emphasis, and TONE. Which essay states its argument more effectively? Support your answer with EVIDENCE.

RICHARD RODRIGUEZ ON WRITING

For *The Bedford Reader*, Richard Rodriguez has described the writing of "Aria":

"From grammar school to college, my teachers offered perennial encouragement: 'Write about what you know.' Every year I would respond with the student's complaint: 'I have nothing to write about . . . I haven't done anything.' (Writers, real writers, I thought, lived in New York or Paris; they smoked on the back jackets of library books, their chores done.)

"Stories die for not being told. . . . My story got told because I had received an education; my teachers had given me the skill of stringing words together in a coherent line. But it was not until I was a man that I felt any need to write my story. A few years ago I left graduate school, quit teaching for political reasons (to protest affirmative action). But after leaving the classroom, as the months passed, I grew desperate to talk to serious people about serious things. In the great journals of the world, I noticed, there was conversation of a sort, glamorous company of a sort, and I determined to join it. I began writing to stay alive — not as a job, but to stay alive.

"Even as you see my essay now, in cool printer's type, I look at some pages and cannot remember having written them. Or else I can remember earlier versions — unused incident, character, description (rooms, faces) — crumbled and discarded. Flung from possibility. They hit the wastebasket, those pages, and yet, defying gravity with a scratchy, starchy resilience, tried to reopen themselves. Then they fell silent. I read certain other sentences now and they recall the very day they were composed — the afternoon of rain or the telephone call that was to come a few moments after, the house, the room where these sentences were composed, the pattern of the rug, the wastebasket. (In all there were about thirty or forty versions that preceded this final 'Aria.') I tried to describe my experiences exactly, at once to discover myself and to reveal myself. Always I had to write against the fear I felt that no one would be able to understand what I was saying.

"As a reader, I have been struck by the way those novels and essays that are most particular, most particularly about one other life and time (Hannibal, Missouri; one summer; a slave; the loveliness of a muddy river) most fully achieve universality and call to be cherished. It is a paradox apparently: The more a writer unearths the detail that makes a life singular, the more a reader is led to feel a kind of sharing. Perhaps the reason we are able to respond to the life that is so different is because we all, each of us, think privately that we are different from one another. And the more closely we examine another life in its misery or wisdom or foolishness, the more it seems we take some version of ourselves.

"It is, in any case, finally you that I end up having to trust not to laugh, not to snicker. Even as you regard me in these lines, I try to imagine your face as you read. You who read 'Aria,' especially those of you with your theme-divining yellow felt pen poised in your hand, you for whom this essay is yet another assignment, please do not forget that it is my life I am handing you in these pages — memories that are as personal for me as family photographs in an old cigar box."

FOR DISCUSSION

1. What seems to be Rodriguez's attitude toward his AUDIENCE when he writes? Do you think he writes chiefly for his readers, or for himself? Defend your answer.
2. Rodriguez tells us what he said when, as a student, he was told, "Write about what you know." What do you think he would say now?

WILLIAM F. BUCKLEY, JR.

Born in New York in 1925, WILLIAM FRANK BUCKLEY, JR., is one of the most articulate proponents of American conservatism. Shortly after his graduation from Yale, he published *God and Man at Yale* (1951), a memoir espousing conservative political values and traditional Christian principles. Since then, he has written more than twenty works on politics and government, published a syndicated newspaper column, and founded and edited *The National Review*, a magazine of conservative opinion. In addition, Buckley has written three books on sailing and eight spy novels. With all his publications, however, Buckley is probably best known for his weekly television debate program, *Firing Line*. As the program's several million viewers know, he is a man of wry charm. When he was half-seriously running for mayor of New York City in 1965, someone asked him what he would do if elected. "Demand a recount," he replied.

Why Don't We Complain?

Most people riding in an overheated commuter train would perspire quietly. For Buckley, this excess of warmth sparks an indignant essay, first published in *Esquire* in 1961, in which he takes to task both himself and his fellow Americans. Does the essay appeal mainly to reason or to emotion? And what would happen if everyone were to do as Buckley urges?

It was the very last coach and the only empty seat on the entire train, so there was no turning back. The problem was to breathe. Outside, the temperature was below freezing. Inside the railroad car the temperature must have been about 85 degrees. I took off my overcoat, and a few minutes later my jacket, and noticed that the car was flecked with the white shirts of the passengers. I soon found my hand moving to loosen my tie. From one end of the car to the other, as we rattled through Westchester County, we sweated; but we did not moan.

I watched the train conductor appear at the head of the car.   2
"Tickets, all tickets, please!" In a more virile age, I thought, the passengers would seize the conductor and strap him down on a seat over the radiator to share the fate of his patrons. He shuffled down the aisle, picking up tickets, punching commutation cards. *No one addressed a word to him.* He approached my seat, and I drew a deep breath of resolution. "Conductor," I began with a considerable edge to my voice. . . . Instantly the doleful eyes of my seatmate turned tiredly from his newspaper to fix me with a resentful stare: What question could be so important as to justify my sibilant intrusion into his stupor? I was shaken by those eyes. I am incapable of making a discreet fuss, so I mumbled a question about what time we were due in Stamford (I didn't even ask whether it would be before or after dehydration could be expected to set in), got my reply, and went back to my newspaper and to wiping my brow.

The conductor had nonchalantly walked down the gauntlet   3
of eighty sweating American freemen, and not one of them had asked him to explain why the passengers in that car had been consigned to suffer. There is nothing to be done when the temperature *outdoors* is 85 degrees, and indoors the air conditioner has broken down; obviously when that happens there is nothing to do, except perhaps curse the day that one was born. But when the temperature outdoors is below freezing, it takes a positive act of will on somebody's part to set the temperature *indoors* at 85. Somewhere a valve was turned too far, a furnace overstocked, a thermostat maladjusted: something that could easily be remedied by turning off the heat and allowing the great outdoors to come indoors. All this is so obvious. What is not obvious is what has happened to the American people.

It isn't just the commuters, whom we have come to visualize   4
as a supine breed who have got on to the trick of suspending their sensory faculties twice a day while they submit to the creeping dissolution of the railroad industry. It isn't just they who have given

up trying to rectify irrational vexations. It is the American people everywhere.

A few weeks ago at a large movie theater I turned to my wife and said, "The picture is out of focus." "Be quiet," she answered. I obeyed. But a few minutes later I raised the point again, with mounting impatience. "It will be all right in a minute," she said apprehensively. (She would rather lose her eyesight than be around when I make one of my infrequent scenes.) I waited. It was *just* out of focus — not glaringly out, but out. My vision is 20-20, and I assume that is the vision, adjusted, of most people in the movie house. So, after hectoring my wife throughout the first reel, I finally prevailed upon her to admit that it *was* off, and very annoying. We then settled down, coming to rest on the presumption that: a) someone connected with the management of the theater must soon notice the blur and make the correction; or b) that someone seated near the rear of the house would make the complaint in behalf of those of us up front; or c) that — any minute now — the entire house would explode into catcalls and foot stamping, calling dramatic attention to the irksome distortion.

What happened was nothing. The movie ended, as it had begun *just* out of focus, and as we trooped out, we stretched our faces in a variety of contortions to accustom the eye to the shock of normal focus.

I think it is safe to say that everybody suffered on that occasion. And I think it is safe to assume that everyone was expecting someone else to take the initiative in going back to speak to the manager. And it is probably true even that if we had supposed the movie would run right through the blurred image, someone surely would have summoned up the purposive indignation to get up out of his seat and file his complaint.

But notice that no one did. And the reason no one did is because we are all increasingly anxious in America to be unobtrusive, we are reluctant to make our voices heard, hesitant about claiming our rights; we are afraid that our cause is unjust, or that if it is not unjust, that it is ambiguous; or if not even that, that it is too trivial to justify the horrors of a confrontation with Authority; we will sit in an oven or endure a racking headache before undertaking a head-on, I'm-here-to-tell-you complaint. That tendency to passive compliance, to a heedless endurance, is something to keep one's eyes on — in sharp focus.

I myself can occasionally summon the courage to complain, but I cannot, as I have intimated, complain softly. My own instinct is so strong to let the thing ride, to forget about it — to expect that someone will take the matter up, when the grievance is collective, in my behalf — that it is only when the provocation is at a very special key, whose vibrations touch simultaneously a complexus of nerves, allergies, and passions, that I catch fire and find the reserves of courage and assertiveness to speak up. When that happens, I get quite carried away. My blood gets hot, my brow wet, I become unbearably and unconscionably sarcastic and bellicose; I am girded for a total showdown.   9

Why should that be? Why could not I (or anyone else) on that railroad coach have said simply to the conductor, "Sir" — I take that back: that sounds sarcastic — "Conductor, would you be good enough to turn down the heat? I am extremely hot. In fact, I tend to get hot every time the temperature reaches 85 degr——." Strike that last sentence. Just end it with the simple statement that you are extremely hot, and let the conductor infer the cause.   10

Every New Year's Eve I resolve to do something about the Milquetoast in me and vow to speak up, calmly, for my rights, and for the betterment of our society, on every appropriate occasion. Entering last New Year's Eve I was fortified in my resolve because that morning at breakfast I had had to ask the waitress three times for a glass of milk. She finally brought it — after I had finished my eggs, which is when I don't want it any more. I did not have the manliness to order her to take the milk back, but settled instead for a cowardly sulk, and ostentatiously refused to drink the milk — though I later paid for it — rather than state plainly to the hostess, as I should have, why I had not drunk it, and would not pay for it.   11

So by the time the New Year ushered out the Old, riding in on my morning's indignation and stimulated by the gastric juices of resolution that flow so faithfully on New Year's Eve, I rendered my vow. Henceforward I would conquer my shyness, my despica-   12 ble disposition to supineness. I would speak out like a man against the unnecessary annoyances of our time.

Forty-eight hours later, I was standing in line at the ski re- 13 pair store in Pico Peak, Vermont. All I needed, to get on with my skiing, was the loan, for one minute, of a small screwdriver, to tighten a loose binding. Behind the counter in the workshop were two men. One was industriously engaged in servicing the complicated requirements of a young lady at the head of the line, and obviously he would be tied up for quite a while. The other — "Jiggs," his workmate called him — was a middle-aged man, who sat in a chair puffing a pipe, exchanging small talk with his working partner. My pulse began its telltale accelera-tion. The minutes ticked on. I stared at the idle shopkeeper, hoping to shame him into action, but he was impervious to my telepathic reproof and continued his small talk with his friend, brazenly insensitive to the nervous demands of six good men who were raring to ski.

Suddenly my New Year's Eve resolution struck me. It was 14 now or never. I broke from my place in line and marched to the counter. I was going to control myself. I dug my nails into my palms. My effort was only partially successful.

"If you are not too busy," I said icily, "would you mind hand- 15 ing me a screwdriver?"

Work stopped and everyone turned his eyes on me, and I ex- 16 perienced that mortification I always feel when I am the center of centripetal shafts of curiosity, resentment, perplexity.

But the worst was yet to come. "I am sorry, sir," said Jiggs 17 deferentially, moving the pipe from his mouth. "I am not sup-posed to move. I have just had a heart attack." That was the sig-nal for a great whirring noise that descended from heaven. We looked, stricken, out the window, and it appeared as though a cy-clone had suddenly focused on the snowy courtyard between the shop and the ski lift. Suddenly a gigantic army helicopter materi-alized, and hovered down to a landing. Two men jumped out of the plane carrying a stretcher, tore into the ski shop, and lifted the shopkeeper onto the stretcher. Jiggs bade his companion good-bye was whisked out the door, into the plane, up to the heavens, down — we learned — to a nearby army hospital. I looked up manfully — into a score of man-eating eyes. I put the experience down as a reversal.

As I write this, on an airplane, I have run out of paper and 18
need to reach into my briefcase under my legs for more. I cannot do this until my empty lunch tray is removed from my lap. I arrested the stewardess as she passed empty-handed down the aisle on the way to the kitchen to fetch the lunch trays for the passengers up forward who haven't been served yet. "Would you please take my tray?" "Just a *moment*, sir!" she said, and marched on sternly. Shall I tell her that since she is headed for the kitchen *anyway*, it could not delay the feeding of the other passengers by more than two seconds necessary to stash away my empty tray? Or remind her that not fifteen minutes ago she spoke unctuously into the loudspeaker the words undoubtedly devised by the airline's highly paid public relations counselor: "If there is anything I or Miss French can do for you to make your trip more enjoyable, *please* let us ——" I have run out of paper.

I think the observable reluctance of the majority of Ameri- 19
cans to assert themselves in minor matters is related to our increased sense of helplessness in an age of technology and centralized political and economic power. For generations, Americans who were too hot, or too cold, got up and did something about it. Now we call the plumber, or the electrician, or the furnace man. The habit of looking after our own needs obviously had something to do with the assertiveness that characterized the American family familiar to readers of American literature. With the technification of life goes our direct responsibility for our material environment, and we are conditioned to adopt a position of helplessness not only as regards the broken air conditioner, but as regards the overheated train. It takes an expert to fix the former, but not the latter; yet these distinctions, as we withdraw into helplessness, tend to fade away.

Our notorious political apathy is a related phenomenon. 20
Every year, whether the Republican or the Democratic Party is in office, more and more power drains away from the individual to feed vast reservoirs in far-off places; and we have less and less say about the shape of events which shape our future. From this alienation of personal power comes the sense of resignation with

which we accept the political dispensations of a powerful government whose hold upon us continues to increase.

An editor of a national weekly news magazine told me a few 21 years ago that as few as a dozen letters of protest against an editorial stance of his magazine was enough to convene a plenipotentiary meeting of the board of editors to review policy. "So few people complain, or make their voices heard," he explained to me, "that we assume a dozen letters represent the inarticulated views of thousands of readers." In the past ten years, he said, the volume of mail has noticeably decreased, even though the circulation of his magazine has risen.

When our voices are finally mute, when we have finally sup- 22 pressed the natural instinct to complain, whether the vexation is trivial or grave, we shall have become automatons, incapable of feeling. When Premier Khrushchev first came to this country late in 1959 he was primed, we are informed, to experience the bitter resentment of the American people against his tyranny, against his persecutions, against the movement which is responsible for the great number of American deaths in Korea, for billions in taxes every year, and for life everlasting on the brink of disaster; but Khrushchev was pleasantly surprised, and reported back to the Russian people that he had been met with overwhelming cordiality (read: apathy), except, to be sure, for "a few fascists who followed me around with their wretched posters, and should be horsewhipped."

I may be crazy, but I say there would have been lots more 23 posters in a society where train temperatures in the dead of winter are not allowed to climb to 85 degrees without complaint.

QUESTIONS ON MEANING

1. How does Buckley account for his failure to complain to the train conductor? What reasons does he give for not taking action when he notices that the movie he is watching is out of focus?

2. Where does Buckley finally place the blame for the average American's reluctance to try to "rectify irrational vexations"?
3. By what means does the author bring his argument around to the subject of political apathy?
4. What THESIS does Buckley attempt to support? How would you state it?

QUESTIONS ON WRITING STRATEGY

1. In taking to task not only his fellow Americans but also himself, does Buckley strengthen or weaken his charge that, as a people, Americans do not complain enough?
2. Judging from the vocabulary displayed in this essay, would you say that Buckley is writing for a highly specialized AUDIENCE or an educated but nonspecialized general audience.
3. As a whole, is Buckley's essay an example of appeal to emotion or of reasoned argument? Give EVIDENCE for your answer.
4. OTHER METHODS. Buckley includes as evidence four narratives (Chap. 1) of his personal experiences. What is the point of the narrative about Jiggs (paras. 13–17)?

QUESTIONS ON LANGUAGE

1. Define the following words: virile, doleful, sibilant (para. 2); supine (4); hectoring (5); unobtrusive, ambiguous (8); intimated, unconscionably, bellicose (9); ostentatiously (11); despicable (12); impervious (13); mortification, centripetal (16); deferentially (17); unctuously (18); notorious, dispensations (20); plenipotentiary, inarticulated (21); automatons (22).
2. What does Buckley's use of the capital A in *Authority* (para. 8) contribute to the sentence in which he uses it?
3. What is Buckley talking about when he alludes to "the Milquetoast in me" (para. 11)? (Notice how well the ALLUSION fits into the paragraph, with its emphasis on breakfast and a glass of milk.)

SUGGESTIONS FOR WRITING

1. Write about an occasion when you should have registered a complaint and did not; or, recount what happened when you did in fact protest against one of "the unnecessary annoyances of our time."

2. Write a paper in which you take issue with any one of Buckley's ideas. Argue that he is wrong and you are right.

3. Think of some disturbing incident you have witnessed, or some annoying treatment you have received in a store or other public place, and write a letter of complaint to whomever you believe responsible. Be specific in your evidence, be temperate in your language, make clear what you would like to come of your complaint (your proposal), and be sure to put your letter in the mail.

4. CONNECTIONS. The "speaker" in both Buckley's "Why Don't We Complain?" and Jonathan Swift's "A Modest Proposal" (p. 713) makes a strong ethical appeal, going out of his way to convince readers of his good will, reasonableness, and authority. Write an essay in which you analyze the "speaker" created by each writer, its character, its functions, and its EFFECT. Use quotations, PARAPHRASES, and summaries from both essays to support your analysis.

WILLIAM F. BUCKLEY, JR., ON WRITING

In the autobiographical *Overdrive*, Buckley recalls a conversation with a friend and fellow columnist: "George Will once told me how deeply he loves to write. 'I wake in the morning,' he explained to me, 'and I ask myself: Is this one of the days I have to write a column? And if the answer is yes, I rise a happy man.' I, on the other hand, wake neither particularly happy nor unhappy, but to the extent that my mood is affected by the question whether I need to write a column that morning, the impact of Monday-Wednesday-Friday" — the days when he must write a newspaper column — "is definitely negative. Because I do not like to write, for the simple reason that writing is extremely hard work, and I do not 'like' extremely hard work."

Still, in the course of a "typical year," Buckley estimates that he produces not only 150 newspaper columns, but also a dozen longer articles, eight or ten speeches, fifty introductions for his television program, various editorial pieces for the magazine he edits, *The National Review*, and a book or two. "Why do I do so much? . . . It is easier to stay up late working for hours than to take one tenth the time to inquire into the question whether the work is worth performing."

In the introduction to another book, *A Hymnal: The Controversial Arts*, Buckley states an attitude toward writing that most other writers would not share. "I have discovered, in sixteen years of writing columns," he declares, "that there is no observable difference in the quality of that which is written at very great speed (twenty minutes, say), and that which takes three or four times as long. . . . Pieces that take longer to write sometimes, on revisiting them, move along grumpily."

FOR DISCUSSION

1. Given that he so dislikes writing, why does Buckley do it?
2. Buckley's attitude toward giving time to writing is unusual. What is the more usual view of writing?

LEWIS THOMAS

For a biographical note, see page 445.

On the Need for Asylums

Medical miracles can cause as many problems as they solve:
That is the message of this essay by a distinguished medical scientist and writer. As a result of the case Thomas examines, desperately ill people are going uncared for.

From time to time, medical science has achieved an indisputable triumph that is pure benefit for all levels of society and deserving of such terms as "breakthrough" and "medical miracle." It
is not a long list, but the items are solid bits of encouragement for
the future. The conquests of tuberculosis, smallpox, and syphilis
of the central nervous system should be at the top of anyone's list.
Rheumatic fever, the most common cause of heart disease forty
years ago, has become a rare, almost exotic disorder, thanks to
the introduction of antibiotics for treating streptococcal sore
throat. Some forms of cancer — notably childhood leukemias,
Hodgkin's disease, and certain sarcomas affecting young people —
have become curable in a high proportion of patients. Poliomyeli-
tis is no longer with us.

But there is still a formidable agenda of diseases for which
there are no cures, needing much more research before their underlying mechanisms can be brought to light. Among these diseases are some for which we have only halfway technologies to
offer, measures that turn out to be much more costly than we had
guessed and only partly, sometimes marginally, effective. The
transplantation of major organs has become successful, but only
for a relatively small number of patients with damaged kidneys
and hearts, and at a financial cost much too high for applying the
technologies on a wide scale. Very large numbers of patients with
these fatal illnesses have no access to such treatments. Renal dial-

ysis makes it possible to live for many months, even a few years, with failed kidneys, but it is a hard life.

The overestimation of the value of an advance in medicine can lead to more trouble than anyone can foresee, and a lot of careful thought and analysis ought to be invested before any technology is turned loose on the marketplace. It begins to look as if coronary bypass surgery, for example, is an indispensable operation for a limited number of people, but it was probably not necessary for the large number in whom the expensive procedure has already been employed.

There are other examples of this sort of premature, sweeping adoption of new measures in medicine. Probably none has resulted in more untoward social damage than the unpredicted, indirect but calamitous effects of the widepsread introduction twenty or so years ago of Thorazine and its chemical relatives for the treatment of schizophrenia. For a while, when it was first used in state hospitals for the insane, the new line of drugs seemed miraculous indeed. Patients whose hallucinations and delusions impelled them to wild, uncontrollable behavior were discovered to be so calmed by the treatment as to make possible the closing down of many of the locked wards in asylums. Patients with milder forms of schizophrenia could return, at least temporarily, to life outside the institutions. It was the first real advance in the treatment of severe mental disease, and the whole world of psychiatry seemed to have been transformed. Psychopharmacology became, overnight, a bright new discipline in medicine.

Then came the side effect. Not a medical effect (although there were some of these) but a political one, and a disaster. On the assumption that the new drugs made hospitalization unnecessary, two social policies were launched with the enthusiastic agreement of both the professional psychiatric community and the governmental agencies responsible for the care of the mentally ill. Brand-new institutions, ambitiously designated "community mental health centers," were deployed across the country. These centers were to be the source of the new technology for treating schizophrenia, along with all other sorts of mental illness: In theory, patients would come to the clinics and be given the needed drugs, and, when necessary, psychotherapy. And at the same time orders came down that most of the patients living in the state hospitals be discharged forthwith to their homes or, lacking homes, to other quarters in the community.

For a while it looked like the best of worlds, on paper, any- 6 way. Brochures with handsome charts were issued by state and federal agencies displaying the plummeting curves of state hospital occupancy, with the lines coinciding marvelously with the introduction of the new drugs. No one noted that the occupancy of private mental hospitals rose at the same time — though it could not rise very high, with the annual cost of such hospitalization running around $40,000 per bed. The term "breakthrough" was used over and over again, but after a little while it came to be something more like a breakout. The mentally ill were out of the hospital, but in many cases they were simply out on the streets, less agitated but lost, still disabled but now uncared for. The community mental health centers were not designed to take on the task of custodial care. They could serve as shelters only during the hours of appointment, not at night.

All this is still going on, and it is not working. To be sure, the 7 drugs do work — but only to the extent of allaying some of the most distressing manifestations of schizophrenia. They do not turn the disease off. The evidences of the mind's unhinging are still there, coming and going in cycles of remission and exacerbation just as they have always done since schizophrenia was first described. Some patients recover spontaneously and for good, as some have always done. The chronically and permanently disabled are better off because they are in lesser degrees of mental torment when they have their medication; but they are at the same time much worse off because they can no longer find refuge when they are in need of it. They are, instead, out on the streets, or down in the subways, or wandering in the parks, or confined in shabby rooms in the shabbiest hotels, alone. Or perhaps they are living at home, but not many of them living happily; nor are many of their families happy to have them at home. One of the high risks of severe mental disease is suicide, and many of these abandoned patients choose this way out, with no one to stop them. It is an appalling situation.

It is claimed that the old state hospitals were even more ap- 8 palling. They were called warehouses for the insane, incapable of curing anything, more likely to make it worse by the process known in psychiatric circles as "institutionalization," a steady downhill course toward total dependency on the very bleakness of the institution itself. The places were badly managed, always understaffed, repellent to doctors, nurses, and all the other people needed for the care of those with sick minds. Better off without them, it was said. Cheaper too, although this wasn't said so openly.

What never seems to have been thought of, or at least never   9
discussed publicly, was changing the state hospitals from bad to good institutions, given the opportunity for vastly improved care that came along with the drugs. It was partly the history of such places that got in the way. For centuries the madhouses, as they were called, served no purpose beyond keeping deranged people out of the public view. Despite efforts at reform in the late nineteenth and early twentieth centuries, they remained essentially lockups.

But now it is becoming plain that life in the state hospitals,   10
bad as it was, was better than life in the subways or in the doorways of downtown streets, late on cold nights with nothing in the shopping bag to keep a body warm, and no protection at all against molestation by predators or the sudden urge for self-destruction. What now?

We should restore the state hospital system, improve it, expand it if necessary, and spend enough money to ensure that the   11
patients who must live in these institutions will be able to come in off the streets and live in decency and warmth, under the care of adequately paid, competent professionals and compassionate surrogate friends.

If there is not enough money, there are ways to save. There   12
was a time when many doctors were glad to volunteer their services on a part-time basis, indeed competed to do so, unpaid by state or federal funds and unreimbursed by insurance companies, in order to look after people unable to care for themselves. We should be looking around again for such doctors, not necessarily specialists in psychiatric medicine, but well-trained physicians possessing affection for people in trouble — a quality on which re-

cruitment to the profession of medicine has always, we hope, been based. We cannot leave the situation of insane human beings where it is today.

A society can be judged by the way it treats its most disad- 13 vantaged, its least beloved, its mad. As things now stand, we must be judged a poor lot, and it is time to mend our ways.

QUESTIONS ON MEANING

1. What two social policies resulted from the treatment of schizophrenics with drugs?
2. Why, according to Thomas, did these policies fail?
3. What problems do deinstitutionalized schizophrenics face?
4. What solution does Thomas propose? What does he propose as an alternative to money?

QUESTIONS ON WRITING STRATEGY

1. Why does Thomas begin his essay by citing medical "breakthroughs"? What EFFECT does this have?
2. Where does Thomas state his THESIS? Why there?
3. What possible objection to his proposal does Thomas address?
4. To what does Thomas appeal in the final paragraph? What does this paragraph reveal of Thomas's assumptions about his AUDIENCE?
5. OTHER METHODS. As part of the support for his argument, Thomas traces causes and effects (Chap. 9). Diagram the causal chain he identifies in paragraphs 4–7.

QUESTIONS ON LANGUAGE

1. What are the implications of the phrase "side effect" applied to the new policies (para. 5)?
2. Consult a psychology textbook or encyclopedia for a definition of *schizophrenia*. Why does Thomas wait until paragraph 7 to elaborate on the illness's effects on its victims?
3. What is the effect of Thomas's language in paragraph 7? What attitude does he convey?

4. You may find it worthwhile to look up some of the diseases and other medical terms Thomas mentions in his opening paragraphs. In addition, consult your dictionary if any of these words are unfamiliar: indisputable (para. 1); untoward, calamitous (4); deployed, forthwith (5); plummeting, custodial (6); allaying, unhinging, manifestations, exacerbation, chronically, appalling (7); bleakness (8); predators (10); surrogate (11); unreimbursed (12).

SUGGESTIONS FOR WRITING

1. Do you agree with Thomas's proposal? Write an essay responding to it, considering (as much as you are able) the likely perspectives of the severely mentally ill, state governments, and "normal" citizens.
2. As an alternative to the first suggestion, agree or disagree with Thomas's proposal solely from the perspective of a severe schizophrenic. For this, you should do some research to try to understand that perspective. One possible source is a moving and disturbing book about schizophrenia, *Is There No Place on Earth for Me?* by Susan Sheehan (Random House, 1983).
3. Is there something that has been abolished or outlawed that you think should be allowed — for example, cars without seatbelts, school prayer, burning leaves, liquor or cigarette advertising on television? Write an essay arguing your position and making a specific proposal.
4. CONNECTIONS. Barbara Lazear Ascher's "On Compassion" (p. 183) also looks at the problem of the mentally ill homeless, but from a closer and more personal POINT OF VIEW. Compare and contrast Ascher's and Thomas's essays on matters of detail and EFFECT. Do the two complement or contradict each other? Support your ideas in part with specific quotations from each essay.
5. CONNECTIONS. Another essay by Lewis Thomas, "The Attic of the Brain," appears in Chapter 8 (p. 445). In an essay of your own, analyze both that essay and this one, considering how the two are similar and different. To what extent do their different PURPOSES account for their other differences?

Note: Some comments by Lewis Thomas on writing appear on page 451.

GEORGE ORWELL

For a biographical note, see page 54.

Politics and
the English Language

In Orwell's novel *1984*, a dictatorship tries to replace spoken
and written English with Newspeak, an official language that
limits thought by reducing its users' vocabulary. (The words
light and *bad*, for instance, are suppressed in favor of *unlight*
and *unbad*.) This concern with language and with its importance to society is constant in George Orwell's work. (See
"George Orwell on Writing," p. 61.) First published in 1946,
"Politics and the English Language" still stands as one of the
most devastating attacks on muddy writing and thinking ever
penned. Orwell's six short rules for writing responsible prose
are well worth remembering.

Most people who bother with the matter at all would admit 1
that the English language is in a bad way, but it is generally assumed that we cannot by conscious action do anything about it.
Our civilization is decadent and our language — so the argument
runs — must inevitably share in the general collapse. It follows
that any struggle against the abuse of language is a sentimental archaism, like preferring candles to electric light or hansom cabs to
airplanes. Underneath this lies the half-conscious belief that language is a natural growth and not an instrument which we shape
for our own purposes.

Now, it is clear that the decline of a language must ulti- 2
mately have political and economic causes: It is not due simply
to the bad influence of this or that individual writer. But an effect
can become a cause, reinforcing the original cause and producing
the same effect in an intensified form, and so on indefinitely. A
man may take to drink because he feels himself to be a failure,
and then fail all the more completely because he drinks. It is

rather the same thing that is happening to the English language. It becomes ugly and inaccurate because our thoughts are foolish, but the slovenliness of our language makes it easier for us to have foolish thoughts. The point is that the process is reversible. Modern English, especially written English, is full of bad habits which spread by imitation and which can be avoided if one is willing to take the necessary trouble. If one gets rid of these habits one can think more clearly, and to think clearly is a necessary first step toward political regeneration: so that the fight against bad English is not frivolous and is not the exclusive concern of professional writers. I will come back to this presently, and I hope that by that time the meaning of what I have said here will have become clearer. Meanwhile, here are five specimens of the English language as it is now habitually written.

These five passages have not been picked out because they   3
are especially bad — I could have quoted far worse if I had chosen — but because they illustrate various of the mental vices from which we now suffer. They are a little below the average, but are fairly representative samples. I number them so that I can refer back to them when necessary:

> (1) I am not, indeed, sure whether it is not true to say that the Milton who once seemed not unlike a seventeenth-century Shelley had not become, out of an experience ever more bitter in each year, more alien [sic] to the founder of that Jesuit sect which nothing could induce him to tolerate.
> Professor Harold Laski (Essay in *Freedom of Expression*).

> (2) Above all, we cannot play ducks and drakes with a native battery of idioms which prescribes such egregious collocations of vocables as the Basic *put up with* for *tolerate* or *put at a loss* for *bewilder*.   Professor Lancelot Hogben (*Interglossa*).

> (3) On the one side we have the free personality: By definition it is not neurotic, for it has neither conflict nor dream. Its desires, such as they are, are transparent, for they are just what institutional approval keeps in the forefront of consciousness; another institutional pattern would alter their number and intensity; there is little in them that is natural, irreducible, or culturally dangerous. But *on the other side*, the social bond itself is nothing but the mutual reflection of these self-secure in-

tegrities. Recall the definition of love. Is not this the very picture of a small academic? Where is there a place in this hall of mirrors for either personality or fraternity?

Essay on psychology in *Politics* (New York).

(4) All the "best people" from the gentlemen's clubs, and all the frantic fascist captains, united in common hatred of Socialism and bestial horror of the rising tide of the mass revolutionary movement, have turned to acts of provocation, to foul incendiarism, to medieval legends of poisoned wells, to legalize their own destruction of proletarian organizations, and rouse the agitated petty-bourgeoisie to chauvinistic fervor on behalf of the fight against the revolutionary way out of the crisis.

Communist pamphlet.

(5) If a new spirit *is* to be infused into this old country, there is one thorny and contentious reform which must be tackled, and that is the humanization and galvanization of the B.B.C. Timidity here will bespeak cancer and atrophy of the soul. The heart of Britain may be sound and of strong beat, for instance, but the British lion's roar at present is like that of Bottom in Shakespeare's *Midsummer Night's Dream* — as gentle as any sucking dove. A virile new Britain cannot continue indefinitely to be traduced in the eyes or rather ears, of the world by the effete languors of Langham Place, brazenly masquerading as "standard English." When the Voice of Britain is heard at nine o'clock, better far and infinitely less ludicrous to hear aitches honestly dropped than the present priggish, inflated, inhibited, school-ma'amish arch braying of blameless bashful mewing maidens!   Letter in *Tribune*.

Each of these passages has faults of its own, but, quite apart   4
from avoidable ugliness, two qualities are common to all of them. The first is staleness of imagery: The other is lack of precision. The writer either has a meaning and cannot express it, or he inadvertently says something else, or he is almost indifferent as to whether his words mean anything or not. The mixture of vagueness and sheer incompetence is the most marked characteristic of modern English prose, and especially of any kind of political writing. As soon as certain topics are raised, the concrete melts into the abstract and no one seems to think of turns of speech that are not hackneyed: Prose consists less and less of *words* chosen for the

sake of their meaning, and more and more of *phrases* tacked together like the sections of a prefabricated hen-house. I list below, with notes and examples, various of the tricks by means of which the work of prose-construction is habitually dodged:

Dying Metaphors. A newly invented metaphor assists thought 5
by evoking a visual image, while on the other hand a metaphor which is technically "dead" (e.g., *iron resolution*) has in effect reverted to being an ordinary word and can generally be used without loss of vividness. But in between these two classes there is a huge dump of worn-out metaphors which have lost all evocative power and are merely used because they save people the trouble of inventing phrases for themselves. Examples are: *Ring the changes on, take up the cudgels for, toe the line, ride roughshod over, stand shoulder to shoulder with, play into the hands of, no axe to grind, grist to the mill, fishing in troubled waters, rift within the lute, on the order of the day, Achilles' heel, swan song, hotbed.* Many of these are used without knowledge of their meaning (what is a "rift," for instance?), and incompatible metaphors are frequently mixed, a sure sign that the writer is not interested in what he is saying. Some metaphors now current have been twisted out of their original meaning without those who use them even being aware of the fact. For example, *toe the line* is sometimes written *tow the line.* Another example is *the hammer and the anvil,* now always used with the implication that the anvil gets the worst of it. In real life it is always the anvil that breaks the hammer, never the other way about: A writer who stopped to think what he was saying would be aware of this, and would avoid perverting the original phrase.

Operators or Verbal False Limbs. These save the trouble of 6
picking out appropriate verbs and nouns, and at the same time pad each sentence with extra syllables which give it an appearance of symmetry. Characteristic phrases are: *render inoperative, militate against, make contact with, be subjected to, give rise to, give grounds for, have the effect of, play a leading part (role) in, make itself felt, take effect, exhibit a tendency to, serve the purpose of,* etc., etc. The keynote is the elimination of simple verbs. Instead of be-

ing a single word, such as *break, stop, spoil, mend, kill*, a verb becomes a *phrase*, made up of a noun or adjective tacked on to some general-purpose verb such as *prove, serve, form, play, render*. In addition, the passive voice is wherever possible used in preference to the active, and noun constructions are used instead of gerunds (*by examination of* instead of *by examining*). The range of verbs is further cut down by means of the *-ize* and *de-* formation, and the banal statements are given an appearance of profundity by means of the *not un-* formation. Simple conjunctions and prepositions are replaced by such phrases as *with respect to, having regard to, the fact that, by dint of, in view of, in the interests of, on the hypothesis that*; and the ends of sentences are saved from anticlimax by such resounding commonplaces as *greatly to be desired, cannot be left out of account, a development to be expected in the near future, deserving of serious consideration, brought to a satisfactory conclusion*, and so on and so forth.

Pretentious Diction. Words like *phenomenon, element, individual* (as noun), *objective, categorical, effective, virtual, basic, primary, promote, constitute, exhibit, exploit, utilize, eliminate, liquidate*, are used to dress up simple statements and give an air of scientific impartiality to biased judgments. Adjectives like *epochmaking, epic, historic, unforgettable, triumphant, age-old, inevitable, inexorable, veritable*, are used to dignify the sordid processes of international politics, while writing that aims at glorifying war usually takes on an archaic color, its characteristic words being: *realm, throne, chariot, mailed fist, trident, sword, shield, buckler, banner, jackboot, clarion*. Foreign words and expressions such as *cul de sac, ancien régime, deus ex machina, mutatis mutandis, status quo, gleichschaltung, weltanschauung*, are used to give an air of culture and elegance. Except for the useful abbreviations *i.e., e.g.*, and *etc.*, there is no real need for any of the hundreds of foreign phrases now current in English. Bad writers, and especially scientific, political, and sociological writers, are nearly always haunted by the notion that Latin or Greek words are grander than Saxon ones, and unnecessary words like *expedite, ameliorate, predict, extraneous, deracinated, clandestine, subaqueous* and hundreds of others constantly gain ground from their Anglo-Saxon opposite numbers.[1] The jargon peculiar to Marxist writing (*hyena, hangman, cannibal, petty bourgeois, these gentry, lackey, flunkey, mad dog, White Guard,* etc.) consists largely of words and phrases translated from Russian, German, or French; but the normal way of coining a new word is to use a Latin or Greek root with the appropriate affix and, where necessary, the *-ize* formation. It is often easier to make up words of this kind (*deregionalize, impermissible, extramarital, nonfragmentatory,* and so forth) than to think up the English words that will cover one's meaning. The result, in general, is an increase in slovenliness and vagueness.

Meaningless Words. In certain kinds of writing, particularly in art criticism and literary criticism, it is normal to come across long passages which are almost completely lacking in meaning.[2] Words like *romantic, plastic, values, human, dead, sentimental, natural, vitality,* as used in art criticism, are strictly meaningless in the sense that they not only do not point to any discoverable object, but are hardly ever expected to do so by the reader. When one critic writes, "The outstanding feature of Mr. X's work is its living quality," while another writes, "The immediately striking thing about Mr. X's work is its peculiar deadness," the reader accepts this as a simple difference of opinion. If words like *black* and *white* were involved, instead of the jargon words *dead* and *living,* he would see at once that language was being used in an improper way. Many political words are similarly abused. The word *fascism* has now no meaning except in so far as it signifies "something not desirable."

---

[1]An interesting illustration of this is the way in which the English flower names which were in use till very recently are being ousted by Greek ones, *snapdragon* becoming *antirrhinum, forget-me-not* becoming *myosotis,* etc. It is hard to see any practical reason for this change of fashion: It is probably due to an instinctive turning-away from the more homely word and a vague feeling that the Greek word is scientific.

[2]Example: "Comfort's catholicity of perception and image, strangely Whitmanesque in range, almost the exact opposite in aesthetic compulsion, continues to evoke that trembling atmospheric accumulative hinting at a cruel, an inexorably serene timelessness. . . . Wrey Gardiner scores by aiming at simple bull's-eyes with precision. Only they are not so simple, and through this contented sadness runs more than the surface bitter-sweet of resignation." (*Poetry Quarterly.*)

The words *democracy, socialism, freedom, patriotic, realistic, justice,* have each of them several different meanings which cannot be reconciled with one another. In the case of a word like *democracy,* not only is there no agreed definition, but the attempt to make one is resisted from all sides. It is almost universally felt that when we call a country democratic we are praising it: Consequently the defenders of every kind of regime claim that it is a democracy, and fear that they might have to stop using the word if it were tied down to any one meaning. Words of this kind are often used in a consciously dishonest way. That is, the person who uses them has his own private definition, but allows his hearer to think he means something quite different. Statements like *Marshal Pétain was a true patriot, The Soviet Press is the freest in the world, The Catholic Church is opposed to persecution,* are almost always made with intent to deceive. Other words used in variable meanings, in most cases more or less dishonestly, are: *class, totalitarian, science, progressive, reactionary, bourgeois, equality.*

Now that I have made this catalog of swindles and perver-   9
sions, let me give another example of the kind of writing that they lead to. This time it must of its nature be an imaginary one. I am going to translate a passage of good English into modern English of the worst sort. Here is a well-known verse from *Ecclesiastes:*

> I returned and saw under the sun, that the race is not to the swift, nor the battle to the strong, neither yet bread to the wise, nor yet riches to men of understanding, nor yet favor to men of skill; but time and chance happeneth to them all.

Here it is in modern English:

> Objective consideration of contemporary phenomena compels the conclusion that success or failure in competitive activities exhibits no tendency to be commensurate with innate capacity, but that a considerable element of the unpredictable must invariably be taken into account.

This is a parody, but not a very gross one. Exhibit (3), above,   10
for instance, contains several patches of the same kind of English. It will be seen that I have not made a full translation. The beginning and ending of the sentence follow the original meaning fairly

closely, but in the middle the concrete illustrations — race, battle, bread — dissolve into the vague phrase "success or failure in competitive activities." This had to be so, because no modern writer of the kind I am discussing — no one capable of using phrases like "objective consideration of contemporary phenomena" — would ever tabulate his thoughts in that precise and detailed way. The whole tendency of modern prose is away from concreteness. Now analyze these two sentences a little more closely. The first contains forty-nine words but only sixty syllables, and all its words are those of everyday life. The second contains thirty-eight words of ninety syllables: eighteen of its words are from Latin roots, and one from Greek. The first sentence contains six vivid images, and only one phrase ("time and chance") that could be called vague. The second contains not a single fresh, arresting phrase, and in spite of its ninety syllables it gives only a shortened version of the meaning contained in the first. Yet without a doubt it is the second kind of sentence that is gaining ground in modern English. I do not want to exaggerate. This kind of writing is not yet universal, and outcrops of simplicity will occur here and there in the worst-written page. Still, if you or I were told to write a few lines on the uncertainty of human fortunes, we should probably come much nearer to my imaginary sentence than to the one from *Ecclesiastes*.

As I have tried to show, modern writing at its worst does not 11 consist in picking out words for the sake of their meaning and inventing images in order to make the meaning clearer. It consists in gumming together long strips of words which have already been set in order by someone else, and making the results presentable by sheer humbug. The attraction of this way of writing is that it is easy. It is easier — even quicker once you have the habit — to say *In my opinion it is a not unjustifiable assumption that* than to say *I think*. If you use ready-made phrases, you not only don't have to hunt about for words; you also don't have to bother with the rhythms of your sentences, since these phrases are generally so arranged as to be more or less euphonious. When you are composing in a hurry — when you are dictating to a stenographer, for instance, or making a public speech — it is natural to fall into a pretentious, Latinized style. Tags like *a consideration which we should do well to bear in mind* or *a conclusion to which all of us would readily assent* will save many a sentence from coming down with a bump. By using stale metaphors, similes, and idioms, you save much mental effort, at the cost of leaving your meaning vague, not only for your reader but for yourself. This is the significance of mixed metaphors. The sole aim of a metaphor is to call up a visual image. When these images clash — as in *The fascist octopus has sung its swan song, the jackboot is thrown into the melting pot* — it can be taken as certain that the writer is not seeing a mental image of the objects he is naming; in other words he is not really thinking. Look again at the examples I gave at the beginning of this essay. Professor Laski (1) uses five negatives in fifty-three words. One of these is superfluous, making nonsense of the whole passage, and in addition there is the slip *alien* for akin, making further nonsense, and several avoidable pieces of clumsiness which increase the general vagueness. Professor Hogben (2) plays ducks and drakes with a battery which is able to write prescriptions, and, while disapproving of the everyday phrase *put up with*, is unwilling to look *egregious* up in the dictionary and see what it means. (3), if one takes an uncharitable attitude toward it, is simply meaningless: Probably one could work out its intended meaning by reading the whole of the article in which it occurs. In (4), the writer knows more or less what he wants to say, but an accumulation of stale phrases chokes him like tea leaves blocking a sink. In (5), words and meaning have almost parted company. People who write in this manner usually have a general emotional meaning — they dislike one thing and want to express solidarity with another — but they are not interested in the detail of what they are saying. A scrupulous writer, in every sentence that he writes, will ask himself at least four questions, thus: What am I trying to say? What words will express it? What image or idiom will make it clearer? Is this image fresh enough to have an effect? And he will probably ask himself two more: Could I put it more shortly? Have I said anything that is avoidably ugly? But you are not obliged to go to all this trouble. You can shirk it by simply throwing your mind open and letting the ready-made phrases come crowding in. They will construct your sentences for you — even think your thoughts for you, to a certain extent — and at need they will perform the important service of partially concealing your meaning even from yourself. It is at this point that the special connection between politics and the debasement of language becomes clear.

In our time it is broadly true that political writing is bad writ- 12 ing. Where it is not true, it will generally be found that the writer is some kind of rebel, expressing his private opinions and not a "party line." Orthodoxy, of whatever color, seems to demand a lifeless, imitative style. The political dialects to be found in pamphlets, leading articles, manifestos, White Papers, and the speeches of under-secretaries do, of course, vary from party to party, but they are all alike in that one almost never finds in them a fresh, vivid, homemade turn of speech. When one watches some tired hack on the platform mechanically repeating the famil- iar phrases — *bestial atrocities, iron heel, bloodstained tyranny, free peoples of the world, stand shoulder to shoulder* — one often has a curious feeling that one is not watching a live human being but some kind of dummy; a feeling which suddenly becomes stronger at moments when the light catches the speaker's spectacles and turns them into blank discs which seem to have no eyes behind them. And this is not altogether fanciful. A speaker who uses that kind of phraseology has gone some distance toward turning him- self into a machine. The appropriate noises are coming out of his larynx, but his brain is not involved as it would be if he were choosing his words for himself. If the speech he is making is one that he is accustomed to make over and over again, he may be al- most unconscious of what he is saying, as one is when one utters the responses in church. And this reduced state of conscious- ness, if not indispensable, is at any rate favorable to political con- formity.

In our time, political speech and writing are largely the de- 13 fense of the indefensible. Things like the continuance of British rule in India, the Russian purges and deportations, the dropping of the atom bombs on Japan, can indeed be defended, but only by arguments which are too brutal for most people to face, and which do not square with the professed aims of political parties. Thus political language has to consist largely of euphemism, ques- tion-begging and sheer cloudy vagueness. Defenseless villages are bombarded from the air, the inhabitants driven out into the countryside, the cattle machine-gunned, the huts set on fire with incendiary bullets: This is called *pacification*. Millions of peasants are robbed of their farms and sent trudging along the roads with no more than they can carry: This is called *transfer of population* or *rectification of frontiers*. People are imprisoned for years without trial, or shot in the back of the neck or sent to die of scurvy in Arctic lumber camps: This is called *elimination of unreliable elements*. Such phraseology is needed if one wants to name things without calling up mental pictures of them. Consider for instance some comfortable English professor defending Russian totalitarianism. He cannot say outright, "I believe in killing off your opponents when you can get good results by doing so." Probably, therefore, he will say something like this:

"While freely conceding that the Soviet régime exhibits certain features which the humanitarian may be inclined to deplore, we must, I think, agree that a certain curtailment of the right to political opposition is an unavoidable concomitant of transitional periods, and that the rigors which the Russian people have been called upon to undergo have been amply justified in the sphere of concrete achievement."

The inflated style is itself a kind of euphemism. A mass of Latin words fall upon the facts like soft snow, blurring the outlines and covering up all the details. The great enemy of clear language is insincerity. When there is a gap between one's real and one's declared aims, one turns as it were instinctively to long words and exhausted idioms, like a cuttlefish squirting out ink. In our age there is no such thing as "keeping out of politics." All issues are political issues, and politics itself is a mass of lies, evasions, folly, hatred, and schizophrenia. When the general atmosphere is bad, language must suffer. I should expect to find — this is a guess which I have not sufficient knowledge to verify — that the German, Russian, and Italian languages have all deteriorated in the last ten or fifteen years, as a result of dictatorship.

But if thought corrupts language, language can also corrupt thought. A bad usage can spread by tradition and imitation, even among people who should and do know better. The debased language that I have been discussing is in some ways very convenient. Phrases like *a not unjustifiable assumption, leaves much to be desired, would serve no good purpose, a consideration which we should do well to bear in mind,* are a continuous temptation, a packet of aspirins always at one's elbow. Look back through this essay, and for certain you will find that I have again and again committed the very faults I am protesting against. By this morning's post I have received a pamphlet dealing with conditions in Germany. The author tells me that he "felt impelled" to write it. I open it at random, and here is almost the first sentence that I see: "(The Allies) have an opportunity not only of achieving a radical transformation of Germany's social and political structure in such a way as to avoid a nationalistic reaction in Germany itself, but at the same time of laying the foundations of a co-operative and unified Europe." You see, he "feels impelled" to write — feels, presumably, that he has something new to say — and yet his words, like cavalry horses answering the bugle, group themselves automatically into the familiar dreary pattern. This invasion of one's mind by ready-made phrases (*lay the foundations, achieve a radical transformation*) can only be prevented if one is constantly on guard against them, and every such phrase anesthetizes a portion of one's brain.

I said earlier that the decadence of our language is probably 17 curable. Those who deny this would argue, if they produced an argument at all, that language merely reflects existing social conditions, and that we cannot influence its development by any direct tinkering with words and constructions. So far as the general tone or spirit of a language goes, this may be true, but it is not true in detail. Silly words and expressions have often disappeared, not through any evolutionary process but owing to the conscious action of a minority. Two recent examples were *explore every avenue* and *leave no stone unturned,* which were killed by the jeers of a few journalists. There is a long list of flyblown metaphors which could similarly be got rid of if enough people would interest themselves in the job; and it should also be possible to laugh the *not un-* formation out of existence,[3] to reduce

---

[3] One can cure oneself of the *not un-* formation by memorizing this sentence: *A not unblack dog was chasing a not unsmall rabbit across a not ungreen field.*

the amount of Latin and Greek in the average sentence, to drive
out foreign phrases and strayed scientific words, and, in general,
to make pretentiousness unfashionable. But all these are minor
points. The defense of the English language implies more than
this, and perhaps it is best to start by saying what it does *not*
imply.

   To begin with it has nothing to do with archaism, with the   18
salvaging of obsolete words and turns of speech, or with the setting up of a "standard English" which must never be departed
from. On the contrary, it is especially concerned with the scrap-
ping of every word or idiom which has outworn its usefulness. It
has nothing to do with correct grammar and syntax, which are of
no importance so long as one makes one's meaning clear, or with
the avoidance of Americanisms, or with having what is called a
"good prose style." On the other hand it is not concerned with
fake simplicity and the attempt to make written English colloquial. Nor does it even imply in every case preferring the Saxon
word to the Latin one, though it does imply using the fewest and
shortest words that will cover one's meaning. What is above all
needed is to let the meaning choose the word, and not the other
way about. In prose, the worst thing one can do with words is to
surrender to them. When you think of a concrete object, you
think wordlessly, and then, if you want to describe the thing you
have been visualizing you probably hunt about till you find the
exact words that seem to fit. When you think of something abstract you are more inclined to use words from the start, and unless you make a conscious effort to prevent it, the existing dialect
will come rushing in and do the job for you, at the expense of
blurring or even changing your meaning. Probably it is better to
put off using words as long as possible and get one's meaning as
clear as one can through pictures or sensations. Afterwards one
can choose — not simply *accept* — the phrases that will best cover
the meaning, and then switch round and decide what impression
one's words are likely to make on another person. This last effort
of the mind cuts out all stale or mixed images, all prefabricated
phrases, needless repetitions, and humbug and vagueness generally. But one can often be in doubt about the effect of a word or

phrase, and one needs rules that one can rely on when instinct fails. I think the following rules will cover most cases:

(i) Never use a metaphor, simile, or other figure of speech which you are used to seeing in print.
(ii) Never use a long word where a short one will do.
(iii) If it is possible to cut a word out, always cut it out.
(iv) Never use the passive where you can use the active.
(v) Never use a foreign phrase, a scientific word or a jargon word if you can think of an everyday English equivalent.
(vi) Break any of these rules sooner than say anything outright barbarous.

These rules sound elementary, and so they are, but they demand a deep change in attitude in anyone who has grown used to writing in the style now fashionable. One could keep all of them and still write bad English, but one could not write the kind of stuff that I quoted in those five specimens at the beginning of this article.

I have not here been considering the literary use of language, 19 but merely language as an instrument for expressing and not for concealing or preventing thought. Stuart Chase and others have come near to claiming that all abstract words are meaningless, and have used this as a pretext for advocating a kind of political quietism. Since you don't know what Fascism is, how can you struggle against Fascism? One need not swallow such absurdities as this, but one ought to recognize that the present political chaos is connected with the decay of language, and that one can probably bring about some improvement by starting at the verbal end. If you simplify your English, you are freed from the worst follies of orthodoxy. You cannot speak any of the necessary dialects, and when you make a stupid remark its stupidity will be obvious, even to yourself. Political language — and with variations this is true of all political parties, from Conservatives to Anarchists — is designed to make lies sound truthful and murder respectable, and to give an appearance of solidity to pure wind. One cannot change this all in a moment, but one can at least change one's own habits, and from time to time one can even, if one jeers loudly enough, send some worn-out and useless phrase — some *jackboot,*

Achilles' heel, hotbed, melting pot, acid test, veritable inferno, or other lump of verbal refuse — into the dustbin where it belongs.

QUESTIONS ON MEANING

1. Orwell states his THESIS early in his essay. What is it?
2. What two common faults does Orwell find in all five of his horrible examples (para. 3)?
3. What questions does Orwell provide for scrupulous writers to ask themselves?
4. How does Orwell support his contention that there is a direct relationship between bad writing and political injustice? Why, in his view, is vague and misleading language necessary to describe acts of oppression?
5. What, according to Orwell, can *you* do to combat the decay of the English language?

QUESTIONS ON WRITING STRATEGY

1. Identify Orwell's AUDIENCE.
2. Taking his own advice, Orwell seeks fresh phrases and colorful, concrete FIGURES OF SPEECH. Point to some of these.
3. Is the appeal of Orwell's argument mainly rational, mainly emotional, or both?
4. OTHER METHODS. Orwell's primary EVIDENCE consists of examples (Chap. 3). Some of these examples are dated, such as a few dying metaphors (para. 5) that have mercifully disappeared, or the reference to British rule of India (13), which ended in 1947. Does the age of the essay weaken it? Can you think of examples to replace any of Orwell's that are dated?

QUESTIONS ON LANGUAGE

1. In plainer words than Lancelot Hogben's, what are "egregious collocations of vocables" (in Orwell's second example in para. 3)?
2. Mixed metaphors, such as "the fascist octopus has sung its swan song" (para. 11), can be unintentionally funny. Recall or invent

some more examples. What, according to Orwell, is the cause of such verbal snafus?

3. Does Orwell agree that "all abstract words are meaningless" (para. 20)?

4. Define decadent, archaism (para. 1); slovenliness, regeneration, frivolous (2); inadvertently, hackneyed, prefabricated (4); evocative (5); symmetry, banal, profundity (6); sordid (7); reconciled (8); parody, tabulate (10); euphonious, superfluous, scrupulous, debasement (11); orthodoxy, phraseology (12); purges, euphemism, totalitarianism (13); curtailment, concomitant (14); impelled (16); colloquial, barbarous (18); quietism (19).

SUGGESTIONS FOR WRITING

1. From browsing in current newspapers and magazines, find a few passages of writing as bad as the ones George Orwell quotes and condemns in "Politics and the English Language." Analyze what you find wrong with them.

2. Like Orwell, who in "Politics and the English Language" deliberately worsens a verse from Ecclesiastes, take a passage of excellent prose and try rewriting it in words as abstract and colorless as possible. For passages to work on, try paragraph 2 from Thoreau's "The Battle of the Ants" in Chapter 8, paragraph 12 from Martin Luther King's "I Have a Dream" in this chapter, or any other passage you admire. If you choose an unfamiliar passage, supply a copy of it along with your finished paper. What does your experiment demonstrate?

3. CONNECTIONS. Apply Orwell's do's and don't's to his other essay in this book, "A Hanging" (p. 54). Does Orwell do as Orwell teaches? Be specific, using quotations and PARAPHRASES from both essays to support your analysis and evaluation.

Note: Some comments by George Orwell on writing appear on page 61.

MARTIN LUTHER KING, JR.

MARTIN LUTHER KING, JR., (1929–1968) was born in Atlanta, the son of a Baptist minister, and was himself ordained in the same denomination. Stepping to the forefront of the civil rights movement in 1955, King led blacks in a boycott of segregated city buses in Montgomery, Alabama; became first president of the Southern Christian Leadership Conference; and staged sit-ins and mass marches that helped bring about the Civil Rights Act passed by Congress in 1964 and the Voting Rights Act of 1965. He received the Nobel Peace Prize in 1964. In view of the fact that King preached "nonviolent resistance," it is particularly ironic that he was himself the target of violence. He was stabbed in New York, pelted with stones in Chicago; his home in Montgomery was bombed; and finally in Memphis he was assassinated by a sniper. On his tombstone near Atlanta's Ebenezer Baptist Church are these words from the spiritual he quotes at the conclusion of "I Have a Dream": "Free at last, free at last, thank God almighty, I'm free at last." Martin Luther King's birthday, January 15, is now a national holiday.

I Have a Dream

In Washington, D.C., on August 28, 1963, King's campaign of nonviolent resistance reached its historic climax. On that date, commemorating the centennial of Lincoln's Emancipation Proclamation freeing the slaves, King led a march of 200,000 persons, black and white, from the Washington Monument to the Lincoln Memorial. Before this throng, and to millions who watched on television, he delivered this unforgettable speech.

Five score years ago, a great American, in whose symbolic 1 shadow we stand, signed the Emancipation Proclamation. This momentous decree came as a great beacon light of hope to millions of Negro slaves who had been seared in the flames of withering injustice. It came as a joyous daybreak to end the long night of captivity.

But one hundred years later, we must face the tragic fact that the Negro is still not free. One hundred years later, the life of the Negro is still sadly crippled by the manacles of segregation and the chains of discrimination. One hundred years later, the Negro lives on a lonely island of poverty in the midst of a vast ocean of material prosperity. One hundred years later, the Negro is still languishing in the corners of American society and finds himself an exile in his own land. So we have come here today to dramatize an appalling condition.

In a sense we have come to our nation's capital to cash a check. When the architects of our republic wrote the magnificent words of the Constitution and the Declaration of Independence, they were signing a promissory note to which every American was to fall heir. This note was a promise that all men would be guaranteed the unalienable rights of life, liberty, and the pursuit of happiness.

It is obvious today that America has defaulted on this promissory note insofar as her citizens of color are concerned. Instead of honoring this sacred obligation, America has given the Negro people a bad check; a check which has come back marked "insufficient funds." But we refuse to believe that the bank of justice is bankrupt. We refuse to believe that there are insufficient funds in the great vaults of opportunity of this nation. So we have come to cash this check — a check that will give us upon demand the riches of freedom and the security of justice. We have also come to this hallowed spot to remind America of the fierce urgency of *now*. This is no time to engage in the luxury of cooling off or to take the tranquilizing drugs of gradualism. *Now* is the time to make real the promises of Democracy. *Now* is the time to rise from the dark and desolate valley of segregation to the sunlit path of racial justice. *Now* is the time to open the doors of opportunity to all of God's children. *Now* is the time to lift our nation from the quicksands of racial injustice to the solid rock of brotherhood.

It would be fatal for the nation to overlook the urgency of the moment and to underestimate the determination of the Negro. This sweltering summer of the Negro's legitimate discontent will not pass until there is an invigorating autumn of freedom and equality. 1963 is not an end, but a beginning. Those who hope that the Negro needed to blow off steam and will now be content will have a rude awakening if the nation returns to business as usual. There will be neither rest nor tranquillity in America until the Negro is granted his citizenship rights. The whirlwinds of revolt will continue to shake the foundations of our nation until the bright day of justice emerges.

But there is something that I must say to my people who 6 stand on the warm threshold which leads into the palace of justice. In the process of gaining our rightful place we must not be guilty of wrongful deeds. Let us not seek to satisfy our thirst for freedom by drinking from the cup of bitterness and hatred. We must forever conduct our struggle on the high plane of dignity and discipline. We must not allow our creative protest to degenerate into physical violence. Again and again we must rise to the majestic heights of meeting physical force with soul force. The marvelous new militancy which has engulfed the Negro community must not lead us to a distrust of all white people, for many of our white brothers, as evidenced by their presénce here today, have come to realize that their destiny is tied up with our destiny and their freedom is inextricably bound to our freedom. We cannot walk alone.

And as we walk, we must make the pledge that we shall 7 march ahead. We cannot turn back. There are those who are asking the devotees of civil rights, "When will you be satisfied?" We can never be satisfied as long as the Negro is the victim of the unspeakable horrors of police brutality. We can never be satisfied as long as our bodies, heavy with the fatigue of travel, cannot gain lodging in the motels of the highways and the hotels of the cities. We cannot be satisfied as long as the Negro's basic mobility is from a smaller ghetto to a larger one. We can never be satisfied as long as a Negro in Mississippi cannot vote and a Negro in New York believes he has nothing for which to vote. No, no, we are not satisfied, and we will not be satisfied until justice rolls down like waters and righteousness like a mighty stream.

I am not unmindful that some of you have come here out of 8 great trials and tribulations. Some of you have come fresh from narrow jail cells. Some of you have come from areas where your quest for freedom left you battered by the storms of persecution and staggered by the winds of police brutality. You have been the veterans of creative suffering. Continue to work with the faith that unearned suffering is redemptive.

Go back to Mississippi, go back to Alabama, go back to 9
South Carolina, go back to Georgia, go back to Louisiana, go back to the slums and ghettos of our northern cities, knowing that somehow this situation can and will be changed. Let us not wallow in the valley of despair.

I say to you today, my friends, that in spite of the difficulties 10
and frustrations of the moment I still have a dream. It is a dream deeply rooted in the American dream.

I have a dream that one day this nation will rise up and live 11
out the true meaning of its creed: "We hold these truths to be self-evident; that all men are created equal."

I have a dream that one day on the red hills of Georgia the 12
sons of former slaves and the sons of former slaveowners will be able to sit down together at the table of brotherhood.

I have a dream that one day even the state of Mississippi, a 13
desert state sweltering with the heat of injustice and oppression, will be transformed into an oasis of freedom and justice.

I have a dream that my four little children will one day live in 14
a nation where they will not be judged by the color of their skin but by the content of their character.

I have a dream today. 15

I have a dream that one day the state of Alabama, whose gov- 16
ernor's lips are presently dripping with the words of interposition and nullification, will be transformed into a situation where little black boys and black girls will be able to join hands with little white boys and white girls and walk together as sisters and brothers.

I have a dream today. 17

I have a dream that one day every valley shall be exalted, every 18
hill and mountain shall be made low, the rough places will be made plain, and the crooked places will be made straight, and the glory of the Lord shall be revealed, and all flesh shall see it together.

This is our hope. This is the faith with which I return to the 19
South. With this faith we will be able to hew out of the mountain of despair a stone of hope. With this faith we will be able to transform the jangling discords of our nation into a beautiful symphony of

brotherhood. With this faith we will be able to work together, to pray together, to struggle together, to go to jail together, to stand up for freedom together, knowing that we will be free one day.

This will be the day when all of God's children will be able to 20 sing with new meaning

> My country, 'tis of thee,
> Sweet land of liberty,
>   Of thee I sing:
> Land where my fathers died,
> Land of the pilgrims' pride,
> From every mountainside
>   Let freedom ring.

And if America is to be a great nation this must become true. 21 So let freedom ring from the prodigious hilltops of New Hampshire. Let freedom ring from the mighty mountains of New York. Let freedom ring from the heightening Alleghenies of Pennsylvania!

Let freedom ring from the snowcapped Rockies of Colorado! 22

Let freedom ring from the curvaceous peaks of California! 23

But not only that; let freedom ring from Stone Mountain of 24 Georgia!

Let freedom ring from Lookout Mountain of Tennessee! 25

Let freedom ring from every hill and molehill of Mississippi. 26 From every mountainside, let freedom ring.

When we let freedom ring, when we let it ring from every vil- 27 lage and every hamlet, from every state and every city, we will be able to speed up that day when all of God's children, black men and white men, Jews and Gentiles, Protestants and Catholics, will be able to join hands and sing in the words of the old Negro spiritual, "Free at last! free at last! thank God almighty, we are free at last!"

QUESTIONS ON MEANING

1. What is the apparent PURPOSE of this speech?
2. What THESIS does King develop in his first four paragraphs?

3. What does King mean by the "marvelous new militancy which has engulfed the Negro community" (para. 6)? Does this contradict King's nonviolent philosophy?
4. In what passages of his speech does King notice events of history? Where does he acknowledge the historic occasion on which he is speaking?

QUESTIONS ON WRITING STRATEGY

1. Analyze King's ETHICAL APPEAL (see pp. 608–609). Where in the speech, for instance, does he present himself as reasonable despite his passion? To what extent does his personal authority lend power to his words?
2. What examples of particular injustices does King offer in paragraph 7? In his speech as a whole, do his observations tend to be GENERAL or SPECIFIC?
3. What indicates that King's words were meant primarily for an AUDIENCE of listeners, and only secondarily for a reading audience? To hear these indications, try reading the speech aloud. What use of PARALLELISM do you notice?
4. Where in the speech does King acknowledge that not all of his listeners are black?
5. How much EMPHASIS does King place on the past? How much does he place on the future?
6. OTHER METHODS. Like many inspirational speakers and writers, King develops analogies (Chap. 8) to drive his points home. Explain the analogy of the bad check (paras. 3–4). What similarity do you find between it and any of the parables in the Bible, such as those of the lost sheep, the lost silver, and the prodigal son (Luke 15:1–32)?

QUESTIONS ON LANGUAGE

1. In general, is the language of King's speech ABSTRACT or CONCRETE? How is this level appropriate to the speaker's message and to the span of history with which he deals?
2. Point to memorable FIGURES OF SPEECH.
3. Define momentous (para. 1); manacles, languishing (2); promissory note (3); defaulted, hallowed, gradualism (4); inextricably (6); mobility, ghetto (7); tribulations, redemptive (8); interposition, nullification (16); prodigious (21); curvaceous (23); hamlet (27).

SUGGESTIONS FOR WRITING

1. Has America (or your locality) today moved closer in any respects to the fulfillment of King's dream? Discuss this question in an essay, giving specific examples.

2. Propose some course of action in a situation that you consider an injustice. Racial injustice is one possible area, or unfairness to any minority, or to women, children, the old, ex-convicts, the handicapped, the poor. If possible, narrow your subject to a particular incident or a local situation on which you can write knowledgeably.

3. CONNECTIONS. King's "I Have a Dream" and Jonathan Swift's "A Modest Proposal" (the following essay) both seek to arouse an AUDIENCE to action, and yet they take very different approaches to achieve this PURPOSE. Compare and contrast the authors' persuasive strategies, considering especially their effectiveness for the situation each writes about and the audience each addresses.

JONATHAN SWIFT

Jonathan Swift (1667–1745), the son of English parents who had settled in Ireland, divided his energies among literature, politics, and the Church of England. Dissatisfied with the quiet life of an Anglican parish priest, Swift spent much of his time in London hobnobbing with writers and producing pamphlets in support of the Tory Party. In 1713 Queen Anne rewarded his political services with an assignment the London-loving Swift didn't want: to supervise St. Patrick's Cathedral in Dublin. There, as Dean Swift, he ended his days — beloved by the Irish, whose interests he defended against the English government.

Although Swift's chief works include the remarkable satires *The Battle of the Books* and *A Tale of a Tub* (both 1704) and scores of fine poems, he is best remembered for *Gulliver's Travels* (1726), an account of four imaginary voyages. This classic is always abridged when it is given to children because of its frank descriptions of human filth and viciousness. In *Gulliver's Travels* Swift pays tribute to the reasoning portion of "that animal called man," and delivers a stinging rebuke to the rest of him.

A Modest Proposal

Three consecutive years of drought and sparse crops had worked hardship upon the Irish when Swift wrote this ferocious essay in the summer of 1729. At the time, there were said to be 35,000 wandering beggars in the country: Whole families had quit their farms and had taken to the roads. Large landowners, of English ancestry, preferred to ignore their tenants' sufferings and lived abroad to dodge taxes and payment of church duties. Swift had no special fondness for the Irish, but he hated the inhumanity he witnessed.

Although printed as a pamphlet in Dublin, Swift's essay is clearly meant for English readers as well as Irish ones. When circulated, the pamphlet caused a sensation in both Ireland and England and had to be reprinted seven times in the same year. Swift is an expert with plain, vigorous English prose, and "A Modest Proposal" is a masterpiece of satire and irony. (If you

are uncertain what Swift argues for, see the discussion of SATIRE
and IRONY in Useful Terms.)

For Preventing the Children of Poor People in Ireland
from Being a Burden to Their Parents or Country,
and for Making Them Beneficial to the Public

It is a melancholy object to those who walk through this great   1
town[1] or travel in the country, when they see the streets, the
roads, and cabin doors, crowded with beggars of the female sex,
followed by three, four, or six children, all in rags and importuning every passenger for an alms. These mothers, instead of being
able to work for their honest livelihood, are forced to employ all
their time in strolling to beg sustenance for their helpless infants,
who, as they grow up, either turn thieves for want of work, or
leave their dear native country to fight for the Pretender in Spain,
or sell themselves to the Barbados.[2]

I think it is agreed by all parties that this prodigious number   2
of children in the arms, or on the backs, or at the heels of their
mothers, and frequently of their fathers, is in the present deplor-
able state of the kingdom a very great additional grievance; and
therefore whoever could find out a fair, cheap, and easy method
of making these children sound, useful members of the commonwealth would deserve so well of the public as to have his statue set
up for a preserver of the nation.

But my intention is very far from being confined to provide   3
only for the children of professed beggars; it is of a much greater
extent, and shall take in the whole number of infants at a certain
age who are born of parents in effect as little able to support them
as those who demand our charity in the streets.

[1]Dublin. — EDS.
[2]The Pretender was James Stuart, exiled in Spain; in 1718 many Irishmen
had joined an army seeking to restore him to the English throne. Others wishing to emigrate had signed papers as indentured servants, agreeing to work for
a number of years in the Barbados or other British colonies in exchange for
their ocean passage. — EDS.

As to my own part, having turned my thoughts for many   4
years upon this important subject, and maturely weighed the several schemes of other projectors,[3] I have always found them
grossly mistaken in their computation. It is true, a child just
dropped from its dam may be supported by her milk for a solar
year, with little other nourishment; at most not above the value
of two shillings, which the mother may certainly get, or the value
in scraps, by her lawful occupation of begging; and it is exactly at
one year that I propose to provide for them in such a manner as
instead of being a charge upon their parents or the parish, or
wanting food and raiment for the rest of their lives, they shall on
the contrary contribute to the feeding, and partly to the clothing,
of many thousands.

There is likewise another great advantage in my scheme, that   5
it will prevent those voluntary abortions, and that horrid practice
of women murdering their bastard children, alas, too frequent
among us, sacrificing the poor innocent babes, I doubt, more to
avoid the expense than the shame, which would move tears and
pity in the most savage and inhuman breast.

The number of souls in this kingdom being usually reckoned   6
one million and a half, of these I calculate there may be about two
hundred thousand couples whose wives are breeders; from which
number I subtract thirty thousand couples who are able to maintain their own children, although I apprehend there cannot be so
many under the present distress of the kingdom; but this being
granted, there will remain an hundred and seventy thousand
breeders. I again subtract fifty thousand for those women who
miscarry, or whose children die by accident or disease within the
year. There only remain an hundred and twenty thousand children of poor parents annually born. The question therefore is,
how this number shall be reared and provided for, which, as I
have already said, under the present situation of affairs, is utterly
impossible by all the methods hitherto proposed. For we can neither employ them in handicraft or agriculture; we neither build
houses (I mean in the country) nor cultivate land. They can very

[3]Planners. — Eds.

seldom pick up a livelihood stealing till they arrive at six years old, except where they are of towardly parts;[4] although I confess they learn the rudiments much earlier, during which time they can however be looked upon only as probationers, as I have been informed by a principal gentleman in the country of Cavan, who protested to me that he never knew above one or two instances under the age of six, even in a part of the kingdom so renowned for the quickest proficiency in that art.

I am assured by our merchants that a boy or a girl before 7 twelve years old is no salable commodity; and even when they come to this age they will not yield above three pounds, or three pounds and half a crown at most on the Exchange; which cannot turn to account either to the parents or the kingdom, the charge of nutriment and rags having been at least four times that value.

I shall now therefore humbly propose my own thoughts, 8 which I hope will not be liable to the least objection.

I have been assured by a very knowing American of my ac- 9 quaintance in London, that a young healthy child well nursed is at a year old a most delicious, nourishing, and wholesome food, whether stewed, roasted, baked, or boiled; and I make no doubt that it will equally serve in a fricassee or a ragout.[5]

I do therefore humbly offer it to public consideration that of 10 the hundred and twenty thousand children, already computed, twenty thousand may be reserved for breed, whereof only one fourth part to be males, which is more than we allow to sheep, black cattle, or swine; and my reason is that these children are seldom the fruits of marriage, a circumstance not much regarded by our savages, therefore one male will be sufficient to serve four females. That the remaining hundred thousand may at a year old be offered in sale to the persons of quality and fortune through the kingdom, always advising the mother to let them suck plentifully in the last month, so as to render them plump and fat for a good table. A child will make two dishes at an entertainment for friends; and when the family dines alone, the fore or hind quarter will make a reasonable dish, and seasoned with a little pepper

[4]Teachable wits, innate abilities. — Eds.
[5]Stew. — Eds.

or salt will be very good boiled on the fourth day, especially in winter.

I have reckoned upon a medium that a child just born will 11 weigh twelve pounds, and in a solar year if tolerably nursed increaseth to twenty-eight pounds.

I grant this food will be somewhat dear, and therefore very 12 proper for landlords, who, as they have already devoured most of the parents, seem to have the best title to the children.

Infant's flesh will be in season throughout the year, but more 13 plentiful in March, and a little before and after. For we are told by a grave author, an eminent French physician,[6] that fish being a prolific diet, there are more children born in Roman Catholic countries about nine months after Lent than at any other season; therefore, reckoning a year after Lent, the markets will be more glutted than usual, because the number of popish infants is at least three to one in this kingdom; and therefore it will have one other collateral advantage, by lessening the number of Papists among us.

I have already computed the charge of nursing a beggar's 14 child (in which list I reckon all cottagers, laborers, and four-fifths of the farmers) to be about two shillings per annum, rags included; and I believe no gentleman would repine to give ten shillings for the carcass of a good fat child, which, as I have said, will make four dishes of excellent nutritive meat, when he hath only some particular friend or his own family to dine with him. Thus the squire will learn to be a good landlord, and grow popular among the tenants; the mother will have eight shillings net profit, and be fit for work till she produces another child.

Those who are more thrifty (as I must confess the times re- 15 quire) may flay the carcass; the skin of which artificially[7] dressed will make admirable gloves for ladies, and summer boots for fine gentlemen.

As to our city of Dublin, shambles[8] may be appointed for this 16

---

[6]Swift's favorite French writer, François Rabelais, sixteenth-century author; not "grave" at all, but a broad humorist. — Eds.

[7]With art or craft. — Eds.

[8]Butcher shops or slaughterhouses. — Eds.

purpose in the most convenient parts of it, and butchers we may be assured will not be wanting; although I rather recommend buying the children alive, and dressing them hot from the knife as we do roasting pigs.

A very worthy person, a true lover of his country, and 17 whose virtues I highly esteem, was lately pleased in discoursing on this matter to offer a refinement upon my scheme. He said that many gentlemen of his kingdom, having of late destroyed their deer, he conceived that the want of venison might be well supplied by the bodies of young lads and maidens, not exceeding fourteen years of age nor under twelve, so great a number of both sexes in every county being now ready to starve for want of work and service; and these to be disposed of by their parents, if alive, or otherwise by their nearest relations. But with due deference to so excellent a friend and so deserving a patriot, I cannot be altogether in his sentiments; for as to the males, my American acquaintance assured me from frequent experience that their flesh was generally tough and lean, like that of our schoolboys, by continual exercise, and their taste disagreeable; and to fatten them would not answer the charge. Then as to the females, it would, I think with humble submission, be a loss to the public, because they soon would become breeders themselves; and besides, it is not improbable that some scrupulous people might be apt to censure such a practice (although indeed very unjustly) as a little bordering upon cruelty; which, I confess, hath always been with me the strongest objection against any project, how well soever intended.

But in order to justify my friend, he confessed that this expedient was put into his head by the famous Psalmanazar,[9] a native of the island Formosa, who came from thence to London above twenty years ago, and in conversation told my friend that in his country when any young person happened to be put to death, the executioner sold the carcass to persons of quality as a prime dainty; and that in his time the body of a plump girl of fifteen,

---

[9]Georges Psalmanazar, a Frenchman who pretended to be Japanese, author of a completely imaginary *Description of the Isle Formosa* (1705), had become a well-known figure in gullible London society. — Eds.

who was crucified for an attempt to poison the emperor, was sold to his Imperial Majesty's prime minister of state, and other great mandarins of the court, in joints from the gibbet, at four hundred crowns. Neither indeed can I deny that if the same use were made of several plump young girls in this town, who without one single groat to their fortunes cannot stir abroad without a chair, and appear at the playhouse and assemblies in foreign fineries which they never will pay for, the kingdom would not be the worse.

Some persons of a desponding spirit are in great concern 19 about that vast number of poor people who are aged, diseased, or maimed, and I have been desired to employ my thoughts what course may be taken to ease the nation of so grievous an encumbrance. But I am not in the least pain upon that matter, because it is very well known that they are every day dying and rotting by cold and famine, and filth and vermin, as fast as can be reasonably expected. And as to the younger laborers, they are now in almost as hopeful a condition. They cannot get work, and consequently pine away for want of nourishment to a degree that if any time they are accidentally hired to common labor, they have not strength to perform it; and thus the country and themselves are happily delivered from the evils to come.

I have too long digressed, and therefore shall return to my 20 subject. I think the advantages by the proposal which I have made are obvious and many, as well as of the highest importance.

For first, as I have already observed, it would greatly lessen 21 the number of Papists, with whom we are yearly overrun, being the principal breeders of the nation as well as our most dangerous enemies; and who stay at home on purpose to deliver the kingdom to the Pretender, hoping to take their advantage by the absence of so many good Protestants, who have chosen rather to leave their country than to stay at home and pay tithes against their conscience to an Episcopal curate.

Secondly, the poorer tenants will have something valuable of 22 their own, which by law may be made liable to distress,[10] and help to pay their landlord's rent, their corn and cattle being already seized and money a thing unknown.

[10]Subject to seizure by creditors. — EDS.

Thirdly, whereas the maintenance of an hundred thousand 23
children, from two years old and upwards, cannot be computed
at less than ten shillings a piece per annum, the nation's stock will
be thereby increased fifty thousand pounds per annum, besides
the profit of a new dish introduced to the tables of all gentlemen
of fortune in the kingdom who have any refinement in taste. And
the money will circulate among ourselves, the goods being entirely of our own growth and manufacture.

Fourthly, the constant breeders, besides the gain of eight shil- 24
lings sterling per annum by the sale of their children, will be rid of
the charge of maintaining them after the first year.

Fifthly, this food would likewise bring great custom to tav- 25
erns, where the vintners will certainly be so prudent as to procure
the best receipts for dressing it to perfection, and consequently
have their houses frequented by all the fine gentlemen, who justly
value themselves upon their knowledge in good eating; and a
skillful cook, who understands how to oblige his guests, will contrive to make it as expensive as they please.

Sixthly, this would be a great inducement to marriage, which 26
all wise nations have either encouraged by rewards or enforced by
laws and penalties. It would increase the care and tenderness of
mothers toward their children, when they were sure of a settle-
ment for life to the poor babes, provided in some sort by the public, to their annual profit instead of expense. We should see an
honest emulation among the married women, which of them
could bring the fattest child to the market. Men would become as
fond of their wives during the time of their pregnancy as they are
now of their mares in foal, their cows in calf, or sows when they
are ready to farrow; nor offer to beat or kick them (as is too frequent a practice) for fear of a miscarriage.

Many other advantages might be enumerated. For in- 27
stance, the addition of some thousand carcasses in our exportation of barreled beef, the propagation of swine's flesh, and improvements in the art of making good bacon, so much wanted
among us by the great destruction of pigs, too frequent at our
tables, which are no way comparable in taste or magnificence
to a well-grown, fat, yearling child, which roasted whole will
make a considerable figure at a lord mayor's feast or any other

public entertainment. But this and many others I omit, being studious of brevity.

Supposing that one thousand families in this city would be 28
constant customers for infants' flesh, besides others who might have it at merry meetings, particularly weddings and christenings, I compute that Dublin would take off annually about twenty thousand carcasses, and the rest of the kingdom (where probably they will be sold somewhat cheaper) the remaining eighty thousand.

I can think of no one objection that will possibly be raised 29
against this proposal, unless it should be urged that the number of people will be thereby much lessened in the kingdom. This I freely own, and it was indeed one principal design in offering it to the world. I desire the reader will observe, that I calculate my remedy for this one individual kingdom of Ireland and for no other that ever was, is, or I think ever can be upon earth. Therefore let no man talk to me of other expedients: of taxing our absentees at five shillings a pound: of using neither clothes nor household furniture except what is of our own growth and manufacture: of utterly rejecting the materials and instruments that promote foreign luxury: of curing the expensiveness of pride, vanity, idleness, and gaming in our women: of introducing a vein of parsimony, prudence, and temperance: of learning to love our country, in the want of which we differ even from Laplanders and the inhabitants of Topinamboo:[11] of quitting our animosities and factions, nor acting any longer like the Jews, who were murdering one another at the very moment their city was taken:[12] of being a little cautious not to sell our country and conscience for nothing: of teaching landlords to have at least one degree of mercy toward their tenants: lastly, of putting a spirit of honesty, industry, and skill into our shopkeepers; who, if a resolution could now be taken to buy only our native goods, would immediately unite to cheat and exact upon us in the price, the measure, and the goodness, nor could ever yet be brought to make one

---

[11]District of Brazil inhabited by primitive tribes. — EDS.
[12]During the Roman siege of Jerusalem (A.D. 70), prominent Jews were executed on the charge of being in league with the enemy. — EDS.

fair proposal of just dealing, though often and earnestly invited to it.

Therefore I repeat, let no man talk to me of these and the like 30 expedients, till he hath at least some glimpse of hope that there will ever be some hearty and sincere attempt to put them in practice.

But as to myself, having been wearied out for many years 31 with offering vain, idle, visionary thoughts, and at length utterly despairing of success, I fortunately fell upon this proposal, which, as it is wholly new, so it hath something solid and real, of no expense and little trouble, full in our own power, and whereby we can incur no danger in disobliging England. For this kind of commodity will not bear exportation, the flesh being of too tender a consistence to admit a long continuance in salt, although perhaps I could name a country which would be glad to eat up our whole nation without it.

After all, I am not so violently bent upon my own opinion as 32 to reject any offer proposed by wise men, which shall be found equally innocent, cheap, easy, and effectual. But before something of that kind shall be advanced in contradiction to my scheme, and offering a better, I desire the author or authors will be pleased maturely to consider two points. First, as things now stand, how they will be able to find food and raiment for an hundred thousand useless mouths and backs. And secondly, there being a round million of creatures in human figure throughout this kingdom, whose sole subsistence put into a common stock would leave them in debt two millions of pounds sterling, adding those who are beggars by profession to the bulk of farmers, cottagers, and laborers, with their wives and children who are beggars in effect; I desire those politicians who dislike my overture, and may perhaps be so bold to attempt an answer, that they will first ask the parents of these mortals whether they would not at this day think it a great happiness to have been sold for food at a year old in this manner I prescribe, and thereby have avoided such a perpetual scene of misfortunes as they have since gone through by the oppression of landlords, the impossibility of paying rent without money or trade, the want of common sustenance, with neither house nor clothes to cover them from the inclemencies of the weather, and the most inevitable prospect of entailing the like or greater miseries upon their breed forever.

I profess, in the sincerity of my heart, that I have not the least 33 personal interest in endeavoring to promote this necessary work, having no other motive than the public good of my country, by advancing our trade, providing for infants, relieving the poor, and giving some pleasure to the rich. I have no children by which I can propose to get a single penny; the youngest being nine years old, and my wife past childbearing.

QUESTIONS ON MEANING

1. On the surface, what is Swift proposing?
2. Beneath his IRONY, what is Swift's argument?
3. What do you take to be the PURPOSE of Swift's essay?
4. How does the introductory paragraph serve Swift's purpose?
5. Comment on the statement, "I can think of no one objection that will possibly be raised against this proposal" (para. 29). What objections can you think of?

QUESTIONS ON WRITING STRATEGY

1. Describe the mask of the personage through whom Swift writes.
2. By what means does the writer attest to his reasonableness?
3. At what point in the essay did it become clear to you that the proposal isn't modest but horrible?
4. As an essay in argument, does "A Modest Proposal" appeal primarily to reason or to emotion?
5. OTHER METHODS. Although not serious, Swift's proposal is worked out in detailed paragraphs of process analysis (Chap. 5). What is the EFFECT of paragraphs 10–16? Why do you think Swift took such trouble with the process?

QUESTIONS ON LANGUAGE

1. How does Swift's choice of words enforce the monstrousness of his proposal? Note especially words from the vocabulary of breeding and butchery.

2. Consult your dictionary for the meanings of any of the following words not yet in your vocabulary: importuning, sustenance (para. 1); prodigious, commonwealth (2); computation, raiment (4); apprehend, rudiments, probationers (6); nutriment (7); fricassee (9); repine (14); flay (15); scrupulous, censure (17); mandarins (18); desponding, encumbrance (19); per annum (23); vintners (25); emulation, foal, farrow (26); expedients, parsimony, animosities (29); disobliging, consistence (31); overture, inclemencies (32).

SUGGESTIONS FOR WRITING

1. Consider a group of people whom you regard as mistreated or victimized. (If none come immediately to mind, see today's newspaper — or write, less seriously, about college freshmen.) Then write either:

   a. A straight argument, giving EVIDENCE, in which you set forth possible solutions to their plight.

   b. An ironic proposal in the manner of Swift. If you do this one, find a device other than cannibalism to eliminate the victims or their problems. You don't want to imitate Swift too closely; he is probably inimitable.

2. In an encyclopedia, look into what has happened in Ireland since Swift wrote. Choose a specific contemporary aspect of Irish-English relations, research it in books and periodicals, and write a report on it.

3. CONNECTIONS. Analyze the ways Swift and Martin Luther King, Jr. (in "I Have A Dream," p. 706), create sympathy for the oppressed groups they are concerned about. Concentrate not only on what they say but on the words they use and their TONE. Then write a process analysis (Chap. 5) explaining techniques for portraying oppression so as to win the reader's sympathy. Use quotations or PARAPHRASES from Swift's and King's essays as examples. If you can think of other techniques that neither author uses, by all means include and illustrate them as well.

JONATHAN SWIFT ON WRITING

Although surely one of the most inventive writers in English literature, Swift voiced his contempt for writers of his day who bragged of their newness and originality. In *The Battle of the Books*, he compares such a self-professed original to a spider who "spins and spits wholly from himself, and scorns to own any obligation or assistance from without." Swift has the fable-writer Aesop praise that writer who, like a bee gathering nectar, draws from many sources.

> Erect your schemes with as much method and skill as you please; yet if the materials be nothing but dirt, spun out of your own entrails (the guts of modern brains), the edifice will conclude at last in a cobweb. . . . As for us Ancients, we are content, with the bee, to pretend to nothing of our own beyond our wings and our voice, that is to say, our flights and our language. For the rest, whatever we have got has been by infinite labor and search, and ranging through every corner of nature; the difference is, that, instead of dirt and poison, we have rather chosen to fill our hives with honey and wax, thus furnishing mankind with the two noblest of things, which are sweetness and light.

Swift's advice for a writer would seem to be: Don't just invent things out of thin air; read the best writers of the past. Observe and converse. Do legwork.

Interestingly, when in *Gulliver's Travels* Swift portrays his ideal beings, the Houyhnhnms, a race of noble and intelligent horses, he includes no writers at all in their society. "The Houyhnhnms have no letters," Gulliver observes, "and consequently their knowledge is all traditional." Still, "in poetry they must be allowed to excel all other mortals; wherein the justness of their description are indeed inimitable." (Those very traits — striking comparisons and detailed descriptions — make much of Swift's own writing memorable.)

In his great book, in "A Modest Proposal," and in virtually all he wrote, Swift's purpose was forthright and evident. He declared in "Verses on the Death of Dr. Swift,"

As with a moral view designed
To cure the vices of mankind: . . .
Yet malice never was his aim;
He lashed the vice but spared the name.
No individual could resent,
Where thousands equally were meant.
His satire points at no defect
But what all mortals may correct.

FOR DISCUSSION

1. Try applying Swift's parable of the spider and the bee to our own day. How much truth is left in it?
2. Reread thoughtfully the quotation from Swift's poem. According to the poet, what faults or abuses can a satiric writer fall into? How may these be avoided?
3. What do you take to be Swift's main PURPOSE as a writer? In your own words, summarize it.

ADDITIONAL WRITING TOPICS
Argument and Persuasion

1. Write a persuasive essay in which you express a deeply felt opinion. In it, address a particular person or audience. For instance, you might direct your essay:

   To a friend unwilling to attend a ballet performance (or a wrestling match) with you on the grounds that such an event is for the birds

   To a teacher who asserts that more term papers, and longer ones, are necessary

   To a state trooper who intends to give you a ticket for speeding

   To a male employer skeptical of hiring women

   To a developer who plans to tear down a historic house

   To someone who sees no purpose in studying a foreign language

   To a high-school class whose members don't want to go to college

   To an older generation skeptical of the value of "all that noise" (meaning current popular music)

   To an atheist who asserts that religion is a lot of pie-in-the-sky

   To the members of a library board who want to ban a certain book

2. Write a letter to your campus newspaper, or to a city newspaper, in which you argue for or against a certain cause or view. Perhaps you may wish to object to a particular feature, column, or editorial in the paper. Send your letter and see if it is published.

3. Write a short letter to your congressional or state representative, arguing in favor of (or against) the passage of some pending legislation. See a news magazine or a newspaper for a worthwhile bill to champion. Or else write in favor of some continuing cause: for instance, saving whales, reducing (or increasing) armaments, or providing aid to the arts.

4. Write an essay arguing that something you feel strongly about should be changed, removed, abolished, enforced, repeated, revised, reinstated, or reconsidered. Be sure to propose some plan for carrying out whatever suggestions you make. Possible topics, listed to start you thinking, are:

   The drinking age

   Gun laws

   The draft

Low-income housing
Graduation requirements
The mandatory retirement age
ROTC programs in schools and colleges
The voting age
Movie ratings (G, PG, PG-13, R, X)
School prayer
Fraternities and sororities
Dress codes
TV advertising

5. On the model of Maire Flynn's three-part condensed argument on page 612, write a condensed argument in three paragraphs demonstrating data, warrant, and claim. For a topic, consider any problem or controversy in this morning's newspaper and form an opinion on it.

USEFUL TERMS

Abstract and **concrete** are names for two kinds of language. *Abstract* words refer to ideas, conditions, and qualities we cannot directly perceive: *truth, love, courage, evil, wealth, poverty, progressive, reactionary. Concrete* words indicate things we can know with our senses: *tree, chair, bird, pen, motorcycle, perfume, thunderclap, cheeseburger.* The use of concrete words lends vigor and clarity to writing, for such words help a reader to picture things. See IMAGE.

Writers of expository essays tend to shift back and forth from one kind of language to the other. They often begin a paragraph with a general statement full of abstract words ("There is *hope* for the *future* of *motoring*"). Then they usually go on to give examples and present evidence in sentences full of concrete words ("Inventor *Jones* claims his *car* will go from *Fresno* to *Los Angeles* on a *gallon* of *peanut oil*"). Beginning writers often use too many abstract words and not enough concrete ones.

Allusion refers a reader to any person, place, or thing in fact, fiction, or legend that the writer believes is common knowledge. An allusion (a single reference) may point to a famous event, a familiar saying, a noted personality, a well-known story or song. Usually brief, an allusion is a space-saving way to convey much meaning. For example, the statement "The game was Coach Johnson's Waterloo" informs the reader that, like Napoleon meeting defeat in a celebrated battle, the coach led a confrontation resulting in his downfall and that of his team. If the writer is also showing Johnson's character, the allusion might further tell us that the coach is a man of Napoleonic ambition and pride. To observe "He is our town's J. R. Ewing" concisely says that a prominent citizen is like that lead character in *Dallas*: unscrupulous, deceptive, merciless, rich, eager to become richer — and perhaps superficially charming and promiscuous as well. To make an effective allusion, you have to be aware of your audience. If your readers do not recognize the allusion, it will only confuse. Not everyone, for example, would understand you if you alluded to a neighbor, to a seventeenth-century Russian harpsichordist, or to a little-known stock car driver.

Analogy is a form of exposition that uses an extended comparison based on the like features of two unlike things: one familiar or easily understood, the other unfamiliar, abstract, or complicated. See Chapter 8. For the logical fallacy called **false analogy**, see page 616.

Analysis, also called **division**, is a form of expository writing in which the writer separates a subject into its elements or parts. See Chapter 6. See also CRITICAL THINKING.

Anecdote is the name for a brief narrative, or retelling of a story or event. Anecdotes have many uses: as essay openers or closers, as ex amples, as sheer entertainment. See Chapter 1.

Appeals are resources writers draw on to connect with and persuade readers.

A **rational appeal** asks readers to use their intellects and their powers of reasoning. It relies on established conventions of logic and evidence.

An **emotional appeal** asks readers to respond out of their beliefs, values, or feelings. It inspires, affirms, frightens, angers.

An **ethical appeal** asks readers to look favorably on the writer. It stresses the writer's intelligence, competence, fairness, morality, and other qualities desirable in a trustworthy debater or teacher. See also Chapter 11, pages 608–609.

Argument is a principal mode of writing, whose function is to convince readers. See Chapter 11.

Audience, for a writer, means readers. Having in mind a particular audience helps the writer in choosing strategies. Imagine, for instance, that you are writing two reviews of the French movie *Jean de Florette*: one for the students who read the campus newspaper, the other for amateur and professional filmmakers who read *Millimeter*. For the first audience, you might write about the actors, the plot, and especially dramatic scenes. You might judge the picture and urge your readers to see it — or to avoid it. Writing for *Millimeter*, you might discuss special effects, shooting techniques, problems in editing and in mixing picture and sound. In this review, you might use more specialized and technical terms. Obviously, an awareness of the interests and knowledge of your readers, in each case, would help you decide how to write. If you told readers of the campus paper too much about filming techniques, you would lose most of them. If you told *Millimeter*'s readers the plot of the film in detail and how you liked its opening scene, probably you would put them to sleep.

You can increase your awareness of your audience by asking yourself a few questions before you begin to write. Who are to be your readers? What is their age level? Background? Education? Where do they live? What are their beliefs and attitudes? What interests them? What, if anything, sets them apart from most people? How familiar are they with your subject? Knowing your audience can help you write so that your readers will not only understand you better, but more deeply care about what you say.

Cause and effect is a form of exposition in which a writer analyzes reasons for an action, event, or decision, or analyzes its consequences. See Chapter 9. See also EFFECT.

Chronological order is the arrangement of events as they occurred or occur in time, first to last. Most narratives and process analyses use chronological order.

Claim is the proposition that an argument demonstrates. Stephen Toulmin favors this term in his system of reasoning. See page 607. In some discussions of argument, the term THESIS is used instead.

Classification is a form of exposition in which a writer sorts out plural things (contact sports, college students, kinds of music) into categories. See Chapter 7.

Cliché (French) is a name for any worn out, trite expression that a writer employs thoughtlessly. Although at one time the expression may have been colorful, from heavy use it has lost its luster. It is now "old as the hills." In conversation, most of us sometimes use clichés, but in writing they "stick out like sore thumbs." Alert writers, when they revise, replace a cliché with a fresh, concrete expression. Writers who have trouble recognizing clichés generally need to read more widely. Their problem is that, so many expressions being new to them, they do not know which ones are full of moths.

Coherence is the clear connection of the parts in a piece of effective writing. This quality exists when the reader can easily follow the flow of ideas between sentences, paragraphs, and larger divisions, and can see how they relate successively to one another.

In making your essay coherent, you may find certain devices useful. TRANSITIONS, for instance, can bridge ideas. Reminders of points you have stated earlier are helpful to a reader who may have forgotten them — as readers tend to do sometimes, particularly if your essay is long. However, a coherent essay is not one merely pasted together with transitions and reminders. It derives its coherence from the clear relationship between its thesis (or central idea) and all its parts.

Colloquial expressions are those which occur primarily in speech and informal writing that seeks a relaxed, conversational tone. "My favorite chow is a burger and a shake" or "This math exam has me wired" may be acceptable in talking to a roommate, in corresponding with a friend, or in writing a humorous essay for general readers. Such choices of words, however, would be out of place in formal writing — in, say, a laboratory report or a letter to your senator. Contractions (*let's, don't, we'll*) and abbreviated words (*photo, sales rep, TV*) are the shorthand of spoken language. Good writers use such expressions with an awareness that they produce an effect of casualness.

Comparison and contrast, two writing strategies, are usually found together. They are a form of exposition in which a writer examines the similarities and differences between two things to reveal their natures. See Chapter 4.

Conclusions are those sentences or paragraphs that bring an essay to a satisfying and logical end. They are purposefully crafted to give a sense of unity and completeness to the whole essay. The best conclusions evolve naturally out of what has gone before and convince the reader that the essay is indeed at an end, not that the writer has run out of steam.

Conclusions vary in type and length depending on the nature and scope of the essay. A long research paper may require several paragraphs of summary to review and emphasize the main points. A short essay, however, may benefit from a few brief closing sentences.

In concluding an essay, beware of diminishing the impact of your writing by finishing on a weak note. Don't apologize for what you have or have not written, or cram in a final detail that would have been better placed elsewhere.

Although there are no set formulas for closing, the following list presents several options:

1. Restate the thesis of your essay, and perhaps your main points.
2. Mention the broader implications or significance of your topic.

3. Give a final example that pulls all the parts of your discussion together.

4. Offer a prediction.

5. End with the most important point as the culmination of your essay's development.

6. Suggest how the reader can apply the information you have just imparted.

7. End with a bit of drama or flourish. Tell an ANECDOTE, offer an appropriate quotation, ask a question, make a final insightful remark. Keep in mind, however, that an ending shouldn't sound false and gimmicky. It truly has to conclude.

Concrete: See ABSTRACT and CONCRETE.

Connotation and **denotation** are names for the two types of meanings most words have. *Denotation* is the explicit, literal, dictionary definition of a word. *Connotation* refers to the implied meaning, resonant with associations, of a word. The denotation of *blood* is "the fluid that circulates in the vascular system." The word's connotations range from *life force* to *gore* to *family bond*. A doctor might use the word *blood* for its denotation, and a mystery writer might rely on the rich connotations of the word to heighten a scene.

Because people have different experiences, they bring to the same word different associations. A conservative Republican's emotional response to the word *welfare* is not likely to be the same as a liberal Democrat's. And referring to your senator as a *diplomat* evokes a different response, from the senator and from others, than would *baby-kisser*, or even *politician*. The effective use of words involves knowing both what they mean literally and what they are likely to suggest.

Critical thinking, one of the most important skills for college work and beyond, seeks the meaning beneath the surface of a statement, poem, editorial, picture, advertisement, or other "text." Using analysis, the critical thinker separates this text into its elements in order to see meanings, relations, and assumptions that might otherwise remain buried. See also pages 337–338.

Data, another name for EVIDENCE, is a term favored by logician Stephen Toulmin in his system of reasoning. See page 609.

Deductive reasoning, or **deduction,** is the method of reasoning from the general to the particular: From information about what we already know, we deduce what we need or want to know. See Chapter 11, page 614.

Definition may refer to a statement of the literal and specific meaning or meanings of a word (**short definition**), or to a form of expository writing (**extended definition**). In the latter, the writer usually explains the nature of a word, a thing, a concept, or a phenomenon; in doing so the writer may employ narration, description, or any of the expository methods. See Chapter 10.

Denotation: See CONNOTATION and DENOTATION.

Description is a mode of writing that conveys the evidence of the senses: sight, hearing, touch, taste, smell. See Chapter 2.

Diction is a choice of words. Every written or spoken statement contains diction of some kind. To describe certain aspects of diction, the following terms may be useful:

Standard English: words and grammatical forms that native speakers of the language use in formal writing.

Nonstandard English: words and grammatical forms such as *theirselves* and *ain't* that occur mainly in the speech of people from a particular area or social background.

Slang: certain words in highly informal speech or writing, or in the speech of a particular group. For example, *blow off, dis, dweeb.*

Colloquial expressions: words and phrases from conversation. See COLLOQUIAL EXPRESSIONS for examples.

Regional terms: words heard in a certain locality, such as *spritzing* for "raining" in Pennsylvania Dutch country.

Dialect: a variety of English based on differences in geography, education, or social background. Dialect is usually spoken, but may be written. Maya Angelou's essay in Chapter 1 transcribes the words of dialect speakers: people waiting for the fight broadcast ("He gone whip him till that white boy call him Momma").

Technical terms: words and phrases that form the vocabulary of a particular discipline (*monocotyledon* from botany), occupation (*drawplate* from die-making), or avocation (*interval training* from running). See also JARGON.

Archaisms: old-fashioned expressions, once common but now used to suggest an earlier style, such as *ere, yon,* and *forsooth.* (Actually, *yon* is still current in the expression *hither and yon*; but if you say "Behold yon glass of beer!" it is an archaism.)

Obsolete diction: words that have passed out of use (such as the verb *werien,* "to protect or defend," and the noun *isetnesses,* "agreements"). *Obsolete* may also refer to certain meanings of words no longer current (*fond* for foolish, *clipping* for hugging or embracing).

Pretentious diction: use of words more numerous and elaborate than necessary, such as *institution of higher learning* for college, and *partake of solid nourishment* for eat.

Archaic, obsolete, and pretentious diction usually has no place in good writing unless a writer deliberately uses it for ironic or humorous effect: H. L. Mencken delighted in the hifalutin use of *tonsorial studio* instead of barber shop. Still, any diction may be the right diction for a certain occasion: The choice of words depends on a writer's purpose and audience.

Division, also called **analysis**, is a form of expository writing in which the writer separates a subject into its elements or parts. See Chapter 6.

Dominant impression is the main idea a writer conveys about a subject through description — that an elephant is gigantic, for example, or an experience scary. See also Chapter 2.

Effect, the result of an event or action, is usually considered together with *cause* as a form of exposition. See the discussion of cause and effect in Chapter 9. In discussing writing, the term *effect* also refers to the impression a word, sentence, paragraph, or entire work makes on the reader: how convincing it is, whether it elicits an emotional response, what associations it conjures up, and so on.

Emotional appeal: See APPEALS.

Emphasis is stress or special importance given to a certain point or element to make it stand out. A skillful writer draws attention to what is most important in a sentence, paragraph, or essay by controlling emphasis in any of the following ways:

Proportion: Important ideas are given greater coverage than minor points.

Position: The beginnings and ends of sentences, paragraphs, and larger divisions are the strongest positions. Placing key ideas in these spots helps draw attention to their importance. The end is the stronger position, for what stands last stands out. A sentence in which less important details precede the main point is called a **periodic sentence**: "Having disguised himself as a guard and walked through the courtyard to the side gate, the prisoner made his escape." A sentence in which the main point precedes less important details is a **loose sentence**: "Autumn is orange: gourds in baskets at roadside stands, the harvest moon hanging like a pumpkin, and oak and beech leaves flashing like goldfish."

Repetition: Careful repetition of key words or phrases can give them greater importance. (Careless repetition, however, can cause boredom.)

Mechanical devices: Italics (underlining), capital letters, and exclamation points can make words or sentences stand out. Writers sometimes fall back on these devices, however, after failing to show significance by other means. Italics and exclamation points can be useful in reporting speech, but excessive use sounds exaggerated or bombastic.

Essay refers to a short nonfiction composition on one central theme or subject in which the writer may offer personal views. Essays are sometimes classified as either formal or informal. In general, a **formal essay** is one whose diction is that of the written language (not colloquial speech), serious in tone, and usually focused on a subject the writer believes is important. (For example, see Bruce Catton's "Grant and Lee.") An **informal essay**, in contrast, is more likely to admit colloquial expressions; the writer's tone tends to be lighter, perhaps humorous, and the subject is likely to be personal, sometimes even trivial. (See James Thurber's "University Days.") These distinctions, however, are rough ones: An essay such as Judy Brady's "I Want a Wife" may use colloquial language and speak of personal experience, though it is serious in tone and has an undeniably important subject.

Ethical appeal: See APPEALS.

Euphemism is the use of inoffensive language in place of language that readers or listeners may find hurtful, distasteful, frightening, or otherwise objectionable. *A euphemism* is an example of the following usage: someone *passed on* rather than *died*; a politician calls for *revenue enhancement* rather than *taxation*. Writers sometimes use euphemism out of consideration for readers' feelings, but just as often they use it to deceive readers or shirk responsibility.

Evaluation is judging merits. In evaluating a work of writing, you suspend personal preference and judge its success in fulfilling the writer's apparent purpose. For instance, if an essay tells how to tune up a car and you have no interest in engines, you nevertheless decide how clearly and effectively the writer explains the process to you.

Evidence is the factual basis for an argument or an explanation. In a courtroom, an attorney's case is only as good as the evidence marshaled to support it. In an essay, a writer's opinions and generalizations also must rest upon evidence. The common forms of evidence are **facts**, verifiable statements; **statistics**, facts stated numerically; **examples**, specific instances of a generalization; **reported experience**, usually eyewitness accounts; and **expert testimony**, the opinions of people considered very skilled or knowledgeable in the field. In critical writing, especially writing about literature, the evidence usually consists of **quotations** from the work being discussed.

Example, also called **exemplification** or **illustration**, is a form of exposition in which the writer provides instances of a general idea. See Chapter 3. *An example* is a verbal illustration.

Exposition is the mode of prose writing that explains a subject. Its function is to inform, to instruct, or to set forth ideas. Exposition may call various methods to its service: example, comparison and con-

trast, process analysis, and so on. Expository writing exposes information: the major trade routes in the Middle East, how to make a
dulcimer, why the United States consumes more energy than it
needs. Most college writing is exposition, and most of the essays in
this book are mainly expository.

Fallacies: See pages 614–616.

Figures of speech occur whenever a writer, for the sake of emphasis or
vividness, departs from the literal meanings (or denotations) of
words. To say "She's a jewel" doesn't mean that the subject of praise
is literally a kind of shining stone; the statement makes sense because its connotations come to mind: rare, priceless, worth cherishing. Some figures of speech involve comparisons of two objects
apparently unlike. A **simile** (from the Latin, "likeness") states the
comparison directly, usually connecting the two things using *like*, *as*,
or *than*: "The moon is like a snowball," "He's lazy as a cat full of
cream," "My feet are flatter than flyswatters." A **metaphor** (from
the Greek, "transfer") declares one thing *to be* another: "A mighty
fortress is our God," "The sheep were bolls of cotton on the hill." (A
dead metaphor is a word or phrase that, originally a figure of
speech, has come to be literal through common usage: "the *hands* of
a clock.") **Personification** is a simile or metaphor that assigns
human traits to inanimate objects or abstractions: "A stoop-
shouldered refrigerator hummed quietly to itself," "All of a sudden
the solution to the math problem sat there winking at me."

Other figures of speech consist of deliberate misrepresentations.
Hyperbole (from the Greek, "throwing beyond") is a conscious exaggeration: "I'm so hungry I could eat a horse and saddle," "I'd wait
for you a thousand years." Its opposite, **understatement**, creates
an ironic or humorous effect: "I accepted the ride. At the moment, I
didn't much feel like walking across the Mojave Desert." A **paradox** is a seemingly self-contradictory statement that, on reflection,
makes sense: "Children are the poor man's wealth" (wealth can be
monetary, or it can be spiritual). *Paradox* may also refer to a situation that is inexplicable or contradictory, such as the restriction of
one group's rights in order to secure the rights of another group.

Flashback, a technique of narrative, involves interrupting the sequence
of events to recall an earlier event.

Focus is the narrowing of a subject to make it manageable. Beginning
with a general subject, you concentrate on a certain aspect of it. For
instance, you may select crafts as a general subject, then decide your
main interest lies in weaving. You could focus your essay still further
by narrowing it to operating a hand loom. You can also focus your
writing according to who will read it (AUDIENCE) or what you want it
to achieve (PURPOSE).

General and **specific** refer to words and describe their relative degrees
of abstractness. *General* words name a group or class (*flowers*); *specific* words limit the class by naming its individual members (*rose, vi-
olet, dahlia, marigold*). Words may be arranged in a series from more
general to more specific: *clothes, pants, jeans, Levis*. The word *cat* is
more specific than *animal*, but less specific than *tiger cat*, or *Gar-
field*. See also ABSTRACT and CONCRETE.

Generalization refers to a statement about a class based on an examination of some of its members: "Lions are fierce." The more members examined and the more representative they are of the class, the
sturdier the generalization. Insufficient or nonrepresentative evidence often leads to a hasty generalization. The statement "Solar
heat saves homeowners money" would be challenged by homeowners who have yet to recover their installation costs. "Solar heat can
save homeowners money in the long run" would be a sounder generalization. Words such as *all, every, only,* and *always* have to be used
with care. "Some artists are alcoholics" is more credible than "Artists are always alcoholics." Making a trustworthy generalization involves the use of INDUCTIVE REASONING (discussed on p. 613).

Hyperbole: See FIGURES OF SPEECH.

Illustration is another name for the expository method of giving examples. See Chapter 3.

Image refers to a word or word sequence that evokes a sensory experience. Whether literal ("We picked two red apples") or figurative
("His cheeks looked like two red apples, buffed and shining"), an
image appeals to the reader's memory of seeing, hearing, smelling,
touching, or tasting. Images add concreteness to fiction — "The
farm looked as tiny and still as a seashell, with the little knob of a
house surrounded by its curved furrows of tomato plants" (Eudora
Welty in a short story, "The Whistle") — and are an important element in poetry. But writers of essays, too, find images valuable to
bring ideas down to earth. See also FIGURES OF SPEECH.

Inductive reasoning, or **induction**, is the process of reasoning to a
conclusion about an entire class by examining some of its members.
See page 613.

Introductions are the openings of written works. Often they state the
writer's subject, narrow it, and communicate an attitude toward it
(TONE). Introductions vary in length, depending on their purposes.
A research paper may need several paragraphs to set forth its central
idea and its plan of organization; on the other hand, a brief, informal essay may need only a sentence or two for an introduction.
Whether long or short, good introductions tell us no more than we
need to know when we begin reading. Here are a few possible ways
to open an essay effectively:

    1. State your central idea, perhaps showing why you care about it.

    2. Present startling facts about your subject.

    3. Tell an illustrative ANECDOTE.

    4. Give background information that will help your reader understand your subject, or see why it is important.

    5. Begin with an arresting quotation.

    6. Ask a challenging question. (In your essay, you'll go on to answer it.)

Irony is a manner of speaking or writing that does not directly state a discrepancy, but implies one. **Verbal irony** is the intentional use of words to suggest a meaning other than literal: "What a mansion!" (said of a shack); "There's nothing like sunshine" (said on a foggy morning). (For more examples, see the essays by James Thurber, Jessica Mitford, Judy Brady, and Fran Lebowitz.) If irony is delivered contemptuously with an intent to hurt, we call it **sarcasm:** "Oh, you're a real friend!" (said to someone who refuses to lend the speaker a quarter to make a phone call). With **situational irony,** the circumstances themselves are incongruous, run contrary to expectations, or twist fate: Juliet regains consciousness only to find that Romeo, believing her dead, has stabbed himself. See also SATIRE.

Jargon, strictly speaking, is the special vocabulary of a trade or profession; but the term has also come to mean inflated, vague, meaningless language of any kind. It is characterized by wordiness, abstractions galore, pretentious diction, and needlessly complicated word order. Whenever you meet a sentence that obviously could express its idea in fewer words and shorter ones, chances are that it is jargon. For instance: "The motivating force compelling her to opt continually for the most labor-intensive mode of operation in performing her functions was consistently observed to be the single constant and regular factor in her behavior patterns." Translation: "She did everything the hard way."

Metaphor: See FIGURES OF SPEECH.

Narration is the mode of writing that tells a story. See Chapter 1.

Nonstandard English: See DICTION.

Objective and **subjective** are names for kinds of writing that differ in emphasis. In *objective* writing, the emphasis falls on the topic; in *subjective* writing, it falls on the writer's view of the topic. Objective writing occurs in factual reporting, certain process analyses (such as recipes, directions, and instructions), and logical arguments in which the writer attempts to downplay personal feelings and opinions. Subjective writing sets forth the writer's feelings, opinions, and interpretations. It occurs in friendly letters, journals, editorials, by-lined feature stories and columns in newspapers, personal essays, and arguments that appeal to emotion. Very few essays, however, contain one kind of writing exclusive of the other.

Paradox: See FIGURES OF SPEECH.

Paragraph refers to a group of closely related sentences that develop a central idea. In an essay, a paragraph is the most important unit of thought because it is both self-contained and part of the larger whole. Paragraphs separate long and involved ideas into smaller parts that are more manageable for the writer and easier for the reader to take in. Good paragraphs, like good essays, possess unity and coherence. The central idea is usually stated in the TOPIC SEN- TENCE, often found at the beginning of the paragraph. All other sentences in the paragraph relate to this topic sentence, defining it, explaining it, illustrating it, providing it with evidence and support. Sometimes you will meet a unified and coherent paragraph that has no topic sentence. It usually contains a central idea that no sentence in it explicitly states, but that every sentence in it clearly implies.

Parallelism, or **parallel structure**, is a name for a habit of good writers: keeping ideas of equal importance in similar grammatical form. A writer may place nouns side by side ("*Time* and *tide* wait for no man") or in a series ("Give me *wind, sea,* and *stars*"). Phrases, too, may be arranged in parallel structure ("*Out of my bed, into my shoes, up to my classroom* — that's my life"); or clauses ("Ask not what your country can do for you; ask what you can do for your country").

Parallelism may be found not only in single sentences, but in larger units as well. A paragraph might read: "Rhythm is every- where. It throbs in the rain forests of Brazil. It vibrates ballroom floors in Vienna. It snaps its fingers on street corners in Chicago." In a whole essay, parallelism may be the principle used to arrange ideas in a balanced or harmonious structure. See the famous speech given by Martin Luther King, Jr. (Chapter 11), in which each para- graph in a series (paragraphs 11 through 18) begins with the words "I have a dream" and goes on to describe an imagined future. Not only does such a parallel structure organize ideas, but it also lends them force.

Paraphrase is putting another writer's thoughts into your own words. In writing a research paper or an essay containing evidence gathered from your reading, you will find it necessary to paraphrase — unless you are using another writer's very words with quotation marks around them. In paraphrasing, you rethink what the other writer has said, decide what is essential, and determine how you would say it otherwise. (Of course, you still acknowledge your source.) The purpose of paraphrasing is not merely to avoid copying word for word, but to adapt material to the needs of your own paper.

Although a paraphrase sometimes makes material briefer, it does not always do so; in principle, it rewrites and restates, sometimes in the same number of words, if not more. A condensation of longer material that renders it more concise is called a **summary**: for instance, a statement of the plot of a whole novel in a few sentences.

Person is a grammatical distinction made between the speaker, the one spoken to, and the one spoken about. In the first person (*I, we*), the subject is speaking. In the second person (*you*), the subject is being spoken to. In the third person (*he, she, it*), the subject is being spoken about. The point of view of an essay or work of fiction is often specified according to person: "This short story is told from a first-person point of view." See POINT OF VIEW.

Personification: See FIGURES OF SPEECH.

Persuasion is the technique of changing people's minds or causing people to take action. See Chapter 11.

Point of view, in an essay, is the physical position or the mental angle from which a writer beholds a subject. Assuming the subject is starlings, the following three writers have different points of view. An ornithologist might write objectively about the introduction of these birds into North America. A farmer might advise other farmers how to prevent the birds from eating seed. A bird-watcher might subjectively describe a first glad sighting of an unusual species. Furthermore, the person of each essay would probably differ: The scientist might present a scholarly paper in the third person; the farmer might offer advice in the second; the bird-watcher might recount the experience in the first. See PERSON.

Premise is a name for a proposition or assumption that supports a conclusion. See page 614 for examples.

Prewriting generally refers to the stage or stages in the process of composition before the first draft. It is the activity of the mind before setting pen or typewriter keys to paper, and may include evoking ideas, deciding on a topic, narrowing the topic, doing factual reading and research, defining your audience, planning and arranging material. An important stage of prewriting usually comes first: **invention**, the creation or discovery of ideas. Invention may follow from daydreaming or meditation, reading, keeping a journal, or perhaps carefully ransacking your memory.

In practice, prewriting usually involves considerable writing. And the prewriting stage often continues well into drafting: Reading, research, taking into account your audience, and further discovery take place even while you write.

Process analysis is a form of exposition that most often explains step by step how something is done or how to do something. See Chapter 5.

Purpose is a writer's reason for writing; it is whatever the writer of any work tries to achieve. To achieve unity and coherence, a writer often identifies a purpose before beginning to write. The more clearly defined the purpose, the better the writer can concentrate on achieving it.

In trying to define the purpose of an essay you read, ask yourself, Why did the writer write this? or, What was this writer trying to achieve? Even though you cannot know the writer's intentions with absolute certainty, an effective essay generally makes some purpose clear.

Rational appeal: See APPEALS.

Rhetoric is the study (and the art) of using language effectively. Often the modes of prose discourse (narration, description, exposition, and argument) and the various methods of exposition (exemplification, comparison and contrast, and the others) are called **rhetorical forms**.

Rhetoric also has a negative connotation of empty or pretentious language meant to waffle, stall, or even deceive. This is the meaning in "The President had nothing substantial to say about taxes. Just the usual rhetoric."

Rhetorical question indicates a question posed for effect, one that requires no answer. Instead, it often provokes thought, lends emphasis to a point, asserts or denies something without making a direct statement, launches further discussion, introduces an opinion, or leads the reader where the writer intends. Sometimes a writer throws one in to introduce variety in a paragraph full of declarative sentences. The following questions are rhetorical: "When will the United States learn that sending people to the moon does not feed them on earth?" "Shall I compare thee to a summer's day?" "What shall it profit a man to gain the whole world if he lose his immortal soul?" Both reader and writer know what the answers are supposed to be. (1) Someday, if the United States ever wises up. (2) Yes. (3) Nothing.

Sarcasm: See IRONY.

Satire is a form of writing that employs wit to attack folly. Unlike most comedy, the purpose of satire is not merely to entertain, but to bring about enlightenment — even reform. Usually, satire employs irony — as in Jonathan Swift's "A Modest Proposal" (Chapter 11). See also IRONY.

Sentimentality is a quality sometimes found in writing that fails to communicate. Such writing calls for an extreme emotional response on the part of an audience, although its writer fails to supply adequate reason for any such reaction. A sentimental writer delights in waxing teary over certain objects: great-grandmother's portrait, the first stick of chewing gum baby chewed (now a shapeless wad), an empty popcorn box saved from the World Series of 1952. Sentimental writing usually results when writers shut their eyes to the actual world, preferring to snuffle the sweet scents of remembrance.

Simile: See FIGURES OF SPEECH.

Slang: See DICTION.

Specific: See GENERAL and SPECIFIC.

Standard English: See DICTION.

Strategy refers to whatever means a writer employs to write effectively. The methods set forth in each chapter of this book are strategies; but so are narrowing a subject, organizing ideas clearly, using transitions, writing with an awareness of your reader, and other effective writing practices.

Style is the distinctive manner in which a writer writes; it may be seen especially in the writer's choice of words and sentence structure. Two writers may write on the same subject, even express similar ideas, but it is style that gives each writer's work a personality.

Subjective: See OBJECTIVE and SUBJECTIVE.

Suspense is often an element in narration: the pleasurable expectation or anxiety we feel that keeps us reading a story. In an exciting mystery story, suspense is constant: How will it all turn out? Will the detective get to the scene in time to prevent another murder? But there can be suspense in less melodramatic accounts as well.

Syllogism is a name for a three-step form of reasoning that employs deduction. See page 614 for an illustration.

Symbol is a name for a visible object or action that suggests some further meaning. The flag suggests country, the crown suggests royalty — these are conventional symbols familiar to us. Life abounds in such relatively clear-cut symbols. Football teams use dolphins and rams for easy identification; married couples symbolize their union with a ring.

In writing, symbols usually do not have such a one-to-one correspondence, but evoke a whole constellation of associations. In Herman Melville's *Moby Dick*, the whale suggests more than the large mammal it is. It hints at evil, obsession, and the untamable forces of nature. Such a symbol carries meanings too complex or elusive to be neatly defined.

Although more common in fiction and poetry, symbols can be used to good purpose in exposition because they often communicate an idea in a compact and concrete way.

Thesis is the central idea in a work of writing, to which everything else in the work refers. In some way, each sentence and paragraph in an effective essay serves to support the thesis and to make it clear and explicit to an audience. Good writers, before they begin to write, often set down a **thesis sentence** or **thesis statement** to help them define their purpose. They may also write this statement into their essay as a promise and a guide to readers.

Tone refers to the way a writer expresses his or her regard for subject, audience, or self. Through word choice, sentence structures, and what is actually said, the writer conveys an attitude and sets a prevailing spirit. Tone in writing varies as greatly as tone of voice varies in conversation. It can be serious, distant, flippant, angry, enthusiastic, sincere, sympathetic. Whatever tone a writer chooses, usually it informs an entire essay and helps a reader decide how to respond. For works of strong tone, see the essays by Joan Didion, Annie Dillard, Jessica Mitford, Judy Brady, Alice Walker, A. M. Rosenthal, and Martin Luther King, Jr.

Topic sentence is a name for the statement of the central idea in a paragraph. Often it will appear at (or near) the beginning of the paragraph, announcing the idea and beginning its development. Because all other sentences in the paragraph explain and support this central idea, the topic sentence is a way to create UNITY.

Transitions are words, phrases, sentences, or even paragraphs that relate ideas. In moving from one topic to the next, a writer has to bring the reader along by showing how the ideas are developing, what bearing a new thought or detail has on an earlier discussion, or why a new topic is being introduced. A clear purpose, strong ideas, and logical development certainly aid COHERENCE, but to ensure that the reader is following along, good writers provide signals, or transitions.

To bridge paragraphs and to point out relationships within them, you can use some of the following devices of transition:

1. Repeat words or phrases to produce an echo in the reader's mind.

2. Use PARALLEL STRUCTURES to produce a rhythm that moves the reader forward.

3. Use pronouns to refer back to nouns in earlier passages.

4. Use transitional words and phrases. These may indicate a relationship of time (*right away, later, soon, meanwhile, in a few minutes, that night*), proximity (*beside, close to, distant from, nearby, facing*), effect (*therefore, for this reason, as a result, consequently*), comparison (*similarly, in the same way, likewise*), or contrast (*yet, but, nevertheless, however, despite*). Some words and phrases of transition simply add on: *besides, too, also, moreover, in addition to, second, last, in the end.*

Understatement: See FIGURES OF SPEECH.

Unity is the quality of good writing in which all parts relate to the THE-SIS. In a unified essay, all words, sentences, and paragraphs support the single central idea. Your first step in achieving unity is to state your thesis; your next step is to organize your thoughts so that they make your thesis clear.

Voice, in writing, is the sense of the author's character, personality, and attitude that comes through the words. See TONE.

Warrant, the thinking, or assumption that leads from DATA to CLAIM, is a term favored in Stephen Toulmin's system of reasoning. See pages 609–613.

ESSAYS ARRANGED
BY SUBJECT

CAPITAL PUNISHMENT

CHILDREN AND FAMILY

CLASS

COMMUNITY

THE CONDUCT OF LIFE

DEATH

ENVIRONMENT

MANNERS AND MORALS

MEDIA

MEDICINE AND ILLNESS

MINORITY EXPERIENCE

THE NATURAL WORLD

OTHER PEOPLES, OTHER COUNTRIES

PLACES

PSYCHOLOGY AND BEHAVIOR

READING, WRITING, AND LANGUAGE

SCHOOL AND COLLEGE

SCIENCE AND TECHNOLOGY

SELF-DISCOVERY

SOCIAL CUSTOMS

SPORTS AND LEISURE

WARFARE AND WEAPONS

WOMEN AND MEN

WORK

Acknowledgments (continued from page iv)

Michael J. Arlen. "Ode to Thanksgiving." From *The Camera Age* by Michael J. Arlen. Originally appeared in *The New Yorker*. Copyright © 1978, 1981 by Michael J. Arlen. Reprinted by permission of Farrar, Straus and Giroux, Inc.

Barbara Lazear Ascher. "On Compassion." From *The Habit of Loving* by Barbara Ascher. Copyright © 1989 by Barbara Lazear Ascher. Reprinted by permission of Random House, Inc.

John Berger. "On Home." From *And Our Faces, My Heart, Brief as Photos* by John Berger. Copyright © 1984 by John Berger. Reprinted by permission of Pantheon Books, a Division of Random House, Inc. In "John Berger on Writing," excerpts from an interview with John Berger in Gerald Marzorati, "Living and Writing the Peasant Life," *The New York Times* (Magazine), November 29, 1987. Copyright © 1987 by The New York Times Company. Reprinted by permission.

Wendell Berry. "Solving for Pattern." Excerpted from *The Gift of Good Land*, copyright © 1981 by Wendell Berry. Published by North Point Press and reprinted by permission. In "Wendell Berry on Writing," excerpts from "Standing by Words." Excerpted from *Standing by words*. Copyright © 1983 by Wendell Berry. Published by North Point Press and reprinted by permission.

Bruno Bettelheim. "The Holocaust." Excerpted from "The Holocaust" from *Surviving and Other Essays* by Bruno Bettelheim. Copyright © 1979 by Bruno Bettelheim. Reprinted by permission of Alfred A. Knopf, Inc.

Tom Bodett. "Wait Divisions." From Tom Bodett, *Small Comforts*, © 1987 by Tom Bodett. Pages 53–56 and (in "Tom Bodett on Writing") Introduction excerpts. Reprinted with permission of Addison-Wesley Publishing Co., Inc., Reading, Massachusetts.

Judy Brady. "I Want a Wife," *Ms.*, Vol. 1, No. 1, December 31, 1971. Reprinted by permission of the author.

Suzanne Britt. "Neat People vs. Sloppy People." From *Show and Tell* by Suzanne Britt. Copyright © 1982 by Suzanne Britt. Reprinted by permission of the author. "Suzanne Britt on Writing," copyright © 1984 by St. Martin's Press, Inc.

William F. Buckley, Jr. "Why Don't We Complain?" *Esquire*, January 1961. Reprinted by permission of the Wallace Literary Agency, Inc. Copyright © 1960 by Esquire. Renewed. In "William F. Buckley, Jr. on Writing," excerpts from *Overdrive: A Personal Documentary* by William F. Buckley, Jr. Copyright © 1983 N. R. Resources, Inc. Reprinted by permission of Doubleday, a division of Bantam, Doubleday, Dell Publishing Group, Inc. Excerpt from *Hymnal: The Controversial Arts* by William F. Buckley, Jr. Copyright © 1978 by William F. Buckley, Jr. Reprinted by permission of G. P. Putnam's Sons.

Bruce Catton. "Grant and Lee: A Study in Contrasts." Copyright 1956 U.S. Capitol Historical Society. All rights reserved. Reprinted with permission. In "Bruce Catton on Writing," excerpts from Oliver Jensen's Introduction to *Bruce Catton's America.* Copyright 1979 by American Heritage Publishing Co., Inc. Reprinted with permission from *Bruce Catton's America.*

Curtis Chang. "Streets of Gold: The Myth of the Model Minority" and excerpts in "Curtis Chang on Writing." From Nancy Sommers and Donald McQuade, *Student Writers at Work and in the Company of Other Writers,* 3rd ed. Copyright © 1989 by St. Martin's Press, Inc. Reprinted by permission.

Rosalind Coward. "Naughty but Nice: Food Pornography." From *Female Desires* by Rosalind Coward. Copyright © 1985 by Rosalind Coward. Reprinted by permission of Grove Weidenfeld.

Richard N. Current, T. Harry Williams, Frank Freidel, and Alan Brinkley. Excerpt from *American History: A Survey,* 6th ed., Knopf, 1983. Reprinted by permission of McGraw-Hill, Inc.

Emily Dickinson. "A narrow Fellow in the Grass" and (in "Emily Dickinson on Writing") "A word is dead . . ." Reprinted by permission of the publishers and the Trustees of Amherst College from *The Poems of Emily Dickinson,* Thomas H. Johnson, ed., Cambridge, Mass.: The Belknap Press of Harvard University Press. Copyright 1951, © 1955, 1979, 1983 by the President and Fellows of Harvard College.

Joan Didion. "In Bed." From *The White Album* by Joan Didion. Copyright © 1968, 1979, 1989 by Joan Didion. Reprinted by permission of Farrar, Straus and Giroux, Inc. "The Liquid City." Excerpted from *Miami* by Joan Didion. Copyright © 1987 by Joan Didion. Reprinted by permission of Simon & Schuster, Inc. In "Joan Didion on Writing," excerpts from "Why I Write" by Joan Didion. Copyright © 1976 by Joan Didion. Reprinted by permission of The Wallace Literary Agency, Inc. First appeared in *The New York Times Book Review,* December 5, 1976.

Annie Dillard. "Death of a Moth," *Harper's* Magazine, May 1976. Reprinted by permission of the author and her agent, Blanche C. Gregory, Inc. Copyright © 1976 by Annie Dillard. "Writing and Vision," excerpts from *The Writing Life* by Annie Dillard. Copyright © 1989 by Annie Dillard. Reprinted by permission of HarperCollins Publishers. "Annie Dillard on Writing," copyright © 1985 by St. Martin's Press, Inc.

Barbara Ehrenreich. "Hope I Die before I Get Rich." Reprinted with permission from *Mother Jones* magazine, © 1986, Foundation for National Progress. In "Barbara Ehrenreich on Writing," excerpts from "Put on a Happy Face." Reprinted with permission from *Mother Jones* magazine, © 1987, Foundation for National Progress.

Peter Elbow. "Desperation Writing." From *Writing Without Teachers* by Peter

1968 by Sonia Brownell Orwell. Reprinted by permission of Harcourt Brace Jovanovich, Inc., the estate of the late Sonia Brownell Orwell, and Secker & Warburg Ltd.

William Ouchi. "Japanese and American Workers: Two Casts of Mind." From William Ouchi, *Theory Z*, © 1981, by Addison-Wesley Publishing Co., Inc., Reading, Massachusetts. Reprinted with permission of the publisher.

Diane E. Papalia and Sally Wendkos Olds. Excerpts from *Psychology* (1985). Reprinted by permission of the publisher, McGraw-Hill, Inc.

Robert Pirsig. Excerpt from *Zen and the Art of Motorcycle Maintenance* by Robert Pirsig. Copyright © 1974 by Robert Pirsig. Reprinted by permission of William Morrow & Company, Inc.

Neil Postman. "The Parable of the Ring around the Collar" and (in "Neil Postman on Writing") Preface excerpts. From *Conscientious Objections* by Neil Postman. Copyright © 1988 by Neil Postman. Reprinted by permission of Alfred A. Knopf, Inc.

Francine Prose. "Gossip," *The New York Times*, May 16, 1985. Reprinted by permission of Georges Borchardt, Inc. for the author. Copyright © 1985 by Francine Prose.

William K. Purves and Gordon H. Orians. Excerpt from *Life: The Science of Biology*. Copyright © 1983 by Sinauer Associates, Inc. Reprinted by permission of the publisher.

Anna Quindlen. "Homeless" and (in "Anna Quindlen on Writing") selected excerpts from "In the Beginning." From *Living Out Loud* by Anna Quindlen. Copyright © 1988 by Anna Quindlen. Reprinted by permission of Random House, Inc.

Ishmael Reed. "America: The Multinational Society." Reprinted with permission of Atheneum Publishers, an imprint of Macmillan Publishing Company, from *Writin' Is Fightin'* by Ishmael Reed. Copyright © 1988 Ishmael Reed. In "Ishmael Reed on Writing," excerpts from William C. Brisick, "Ishmael Reed," *Publishers Weekly*, July 1, 1988.

Robert B. Reich. "Why the Rich Are Getting Richer and the Poor Poorer." Excerpted from *The New Republic*, May 1, 1989. Reprinted by permission of *The New Republic*, Copyright © 1989 by The New Republic, Inc. In "Robert B. Reich on Writing," excerpts from Introduction to *Tales of a New America* by Robert B. Reich. Copyright © 1987 by Robert B. Reich. Reprinted by permission of Times Books, a Division of Random House, Inc.

James C. Rettie. " 'But a Watch in the Night': A Scientific Fable". From *Forever the Land*, edited by Russell and Kate Lord. Copyright 1950 by Harper & Row, Publishers, Inc. Copyright renewed 1978 by Russell and Kate Lord. Reprinted by permission of HarperCollins Publishers.

John Rockwell. "Why Rock Remains the Enemy," *The New York Times*, January 21, 1990. Copyright © 1990 by The New York Times Company. Reprinted by permission. In "John Rockwell on Writing," excerpts from Jean W. Ross's interview with John Rockwell from *Contemporary Authors*, vol. 126, edited by Susan M. Trosky. Copyright © 1989 by Gale Research Inc. All rights reserved. Reprinted by permission of the author.

Richard Rodriguez. "Aria: A Memoir of a Bilingual Childhood," *The American Scholar*, Winter 1980. Copyright © 1980 by Richard Rodriguez. Reprinted by permission of Georges Borchardt, Inc. for the author. "Richard Rodriguez on Writing," copyright © 1985 by St. Martin's Press, Inc.

A. M. Rosenthal. "The Case for Slavery," *The New York Times*, September 26, 1989. Copyright © 1989 by The New York Times Company. Reprinted by permission. In "A. M. Rosenthal on Writing," excerpts from "Learning on the Job," *The New York Times*, December 4, 1986. Copyright © 1986 by The New York Times Company. Reprinted by permission.

Murray Ross. "Football Red and Baseball Green." Copyright © 1991 by Murray Ross. An earlier version of this article appeared in *Chicago Review*, January/February 1971. Reprinted by permission of the author.

Oliver Sacks. "The President's Speech." From *The Man Who Mistook His Wife for a Hat* by Oliver Sacks. Copyright 1970, 1981, 1983, 1984, 1985 by Oliver Sacks. Reprinted by permission of Summit Books, a division of Simon & Schuster, Inc. In "Oliver Sacks on Writing," brief quotations from interviews in *New Statesman*, November 28, 1986, *Publishers Weekly*, May 26, 1989, and *Interview*, October 1989, and excerpt from *Seeing Voices* by Oliver Sacks (University of California Press, 1989).

Carl Sagan and Richard Turco. "Too Many Weapons in the World." Excerpted from *A Path Where No Man Thought: Nuclear Winters and Its Implications* by Carl Sagan. Copyright © 1990 by Carl Sagan and Richard Turco. Reprinted by permission of Random House, Inc. In "Carl Sagan on Writing," excerpt from *Cosmos* by Carl Sagan. Copyright © 1980 by Carl Sagan. All rights reserved. Reprinted by permission of the author. Excerpt from John F. Baker interview with Carl Sagan, *Publishers Weekly*, May 2, 1977.

Linnea Saukko. "How to Poison the Earth" and (in "Linnea Saukko on Writing") excerpts from *Student Writers at Work*. Copyright © 1984 by St. Martin's Press, Inc. Reprinted by permission.

Michael A. Seeds. Excerpt from *Foundations of Astronomy*, 1986 Edition. © 1986, 1984 by Wadsworth, Inc. Reprinted by permission of the publisher.

Richard Selzer. "The Discus Thrower." From *Confessions of a Knife* by Richard Selzer. Copyright © 1979 by David Goldman and Janet Selzer, Trustees. Reprinted by permission of William Morrow & Company. In "Richard Selzer on Writing," excerpts from Richard Selzer, "The Pen and the Scalpel," *The New York Times* (Magazine), August 21, 1988. Copyright © 1988 by The New York Times Company. Reprinted by permission.

Gail Sheehy. "Predictable Crises of Adulthood." Excerpted from *Passages: Predictable Crises of Adult Life* by Gail Sheehy. Copyright © 1974, 1976 by Gail Sheehy. Reprinted by permission of the publisher, E. P. Dutton, an imprint of New American Library, a division of Penguin Books USA Inc.

John Simpson. "Tiananmen Square." From *Granta*, vol. 28, Autumn 1989. Reprinted by permission.

L. C. Solmon. Excerpt from L. C. Solmon, *Microeconomics*, 3rd edition. © 1980, by Addison-Wesley Publishing Co., Inc., Reading, Massachusetts. Reprinted by permission of the publisher.

Brent Staples. "Black Men and Public Space." *Harper's* Magazine, December 1986. Reprinted by permission of the author. "Brent Staples on Writing," copyright © 1991 by St. Martin's Press, Inc.

Lewis Thomas. "The Attic of the Brain" and "On the Need for Asylums." From *Late Night Thoughts on Listening to Mahler's Ninth Symphony* by Lewis Thomas. Copyright © 1980 by Lewis Thomas. Reprinted by permission of Viking Penguin, a Division of Penguin Books USA Inc. In "Lewis Thomas on Writing," excerpts from David Hellerstein, "The Muse of Medicine," *Esquire*, March 1984.

James Thurber. "University Days." From *My Life and Hard Times*, published by Harper & Row. Copyright 1933, © 1961 James Thurber. Reprinted by permission. In "James Thurber on Writing," excerpts from George Plimpton and Max Steele's interview with James Thurber in *Writers at Work: The Paris Review Interviews*. First Series, edited by Malcolm Cowley. Copyright © 1957, 1958 by The Paris Review, Inc. Reprinted by permission of Viking Penguin, a Division of Penguin Books USA Inc. Excerpt from "What's So Funny?" by James Thurber. Copyright 1953 James Thurber. Copyright © 1981 Helen Thurber and Rosemary A. Thurber. From *Thurber Country*, published by Simon & Schuster. Reprinted by permission.

Calvin Trillin. "It's Just Too Late." From his book *Killings*, published by Ticknor & Fields. Copyright © 1984 by Calvin Trillin. Reprinted by permission of Lescher & Lescher, Ltd. In "Calvin Trillin on Writing," excerpts from Alice Trillin, "A Writer's Process: A Conversation with Calvin Trillin," *Journal of Basic Writing*, Fall/Winter 1981, Volume 3, Number 3. © 1982, Journal of Basic Writing, Instructional Resource Center, Office of Academic Affairs, The City University of New York, 535 East 80 Street, New York, NY 10021. Reprinted by permission.

Robert M. Veatch. Excerpt from "Models for Medicine in a Revolutionary Age," *Hastings Center Report*, June 1972. Reprinted by permission.

Gore Vidal. "Drugs." From *Homage to Daniel Shays: Collected Essays, 1952–1972* by Gore Vidal. Copyright © 1972 by Gore Vidal. Reprinted by permission of Random House, Inc. In "Gore Vidal on Writing," excerpts from Gerald Clarke's interview with Gore Vidal in *Writers at Work: The*

INDEX

Page numbers in bold type refer to
definitions in the glossary.

765

To the Student

We regularly revise the books we publish in order to make them better. To do this well we need to know what instructors and students think of the previous edition. At some point your instructor will be asked to comment on *The Bedford Reader*, Fourth Edition; now we would like to hear from you.

Please take a few minutes to complete this questionnaire and send it to Bedford Books of St. Martin's Press, 29 Winchester St., Boston, Massachusetts 02116. We promise to listen to what you have to say. Thanks.

School _____

School location (city, state) _____

Course title _____

Instructor's name _____

Please rate the selections.	Liked a lot	Okay	Didn't like	Didn't read
Joan Didion, *In Bed*	____	____	____	____
Maya Angelou, *Champion of the World*	____	____	____	____
Ralph Ellison, *On Being the Target of Discrimination*	____	____	____	____
George Orwell, *A Hanging*	____	____	____	____
James Thurber, *University Days*	____	____	____	____
Calvin Trillin, *It's Just Too Late*	____	____	____	____
John Simpson, *Tiananmen Square*	____	____	____	____
Shirley Jackson, *The Lottery*	____	____	____	____
Virginia Woolf, *The Death of the Moth*	____	____	____	____
Annie Dillard, *Death of a Moth*	____	____	____	____

	Liked a lot	Okay	Didn't like	Didn't read
Michael J. Arlen, *Ode to Thanksgiving*	___	___	___	___
Joan Didion, *The Liquid City*	___	___	___	___
Richard Selzer, *The Discus Thrower*	___	___	___	___
E. B. White, *Once More to the Lake*	___	___	___	___
Emily Dickinson, *A narrow Fellow in the Grass*	___	___	___	___
Barbara Lazear Ascher, *On Compassion*	___	___	___	___
Anna Quindlen, *Homeless*	___	___	___	___
Lance Morrow, *Advertisements for Oneself*	___	___	___	___
Brent Staples, *Black Men and Public Space*	___	___	___	___
Edward T. Hall, *Proxemics in the Arab World*	___	___	___	___
Suzanne Britt, *Neat People vs. Sloppy People*	___	___	___	___
Bruce Catton, *Grant and Lee*	___	___	___	___
Ellen Goodman, *Sin, Salvation, and a Good Shrink*	___	___	___	___
William Ouchi, *Japanese and American Workers: Two Casts of Mind*	___	___	___	___
Jeff Greenfield, *The Black and White Truth about Basketball*	___	___	___	___
Murray Ross, *Football Red and Baseball Green*	___	___	___	___
Jessica Mitford, *Behind the Formaldehyde Curtain*	___	___	___	___

	Liked a lot	Okay	Didn't like	Didn't read
Marvin Harris, *How Our Skins Got Their Color*	——	——	——	——
Oliver Sacks, *The President's Speech*	——	——	——	——
Linnea Saukko, *How to Poison the Earth*	——	——	——	——
Peter Elbow, *Desperation Writing*	——	——	——	——
Annie Dillard, *Writing and Vision*	——	——	——	——
Judy Brady, *I Want a Wife*	——	——	——	——
Gail Sheehy, *Predictable Crises of Adulthood*	——	——	——	——
Margot Harrison, *The Death of a Moth: Two Visions*	——	——	——	——
Mark Crispin Miller, *Barbara Walters's Theater of Revenge*	——	——	——	——
Rosalind Coward, *Naughty but Nice: Food Pornography*	——	——	——	——
Tom Bodett, *Wait Divisions*	——	——	——	——
Fran Lebowitz, *The Sound of Music: Enough Already*	——	——	——	——
Wendell Berry, *Solving for Pattern*	——	——	——	——
Robert B. Reich, *Why the Rich Are Getting Richer and the Poor Poorer*	——	——	——	——
Ralph Whitehead, Jr., *Class Acts: America's Changing Middle Class*	——	——	——	——
Alice Walker, *Oppressed Hair Puts a Ceiling on the Brain*	——	——	——	——

	Liked a lot	Okay	Didn't like	Didn't read
Lewis Thomas, *The Attic of the Brain*	___	___	___	___
Henry David Thoreau, *The Battle of the Ants*	___	___	___	___
James C. Rettie, *"But a Watch in the Night": A Scientific Fable*	___	___	___	___
Neil Postman, *The Parable of the Ring around the Collar*	___	___	___	___
Gore Vidal, *Drugs*	___	___	___	___
A. M. Rosenthal, *The Case for Slavery*	___	___	___	___
John Rockwell, *Why Rock Remains the Enemy*	___	___	___	___
Stephen Jay Gould, *Sex, Drugs, Disasters, and the Extinction of Dinosaurs*	___	___	___	___
Carl Sagan and Richard Turco, *Too Many Weapons in the World*	___	___	___	___
James Fallows, *Freedom, Control, and Success: Asia and America*	___	___	___	___
John Berger, *On Home*	___	___	___	___
Nikki Giovanni, *Pioneers: A View of Home*	___	___	___	___
Francine Prose, *Gossip*	___	___	___	___
Tom Wolfe, *Pornoviolence*	___	___	___	___
Joseph Epstein, *What Is Vulgar?*	___	___	___	___
Bruno Bettelheim, *The Holocaust*	___	___	___	___
H. L. Mencken, *The Penalty of Death*	___	___	___	___

_____

_____

_____

_____

_____

_____

Name _____

Mailing address _____

Date _____

	Liked a lot	Okay	Didn't like	Didn't read
Barbara Ehrenreich, *Hope I Die before I Get Rich*	___	___	___	___
Curtis Chang, *Streets of Gold: The Myth of the Model Minority*	___	___	___	___
Ishmael Reed, *America: The Multinational Society*	___	___	___	___
Richard Rodriguez, *Aria: A Memoir of a Bilingual Childhood*	___	___	___	___
William F. Buckley, Jr., *Why Don't We Complain?*	___	___	___	___
Lewis Thomas, *On the Need for Asylums*	___	___	___	___
George Orwell, *Politics and the English Language*	___	___	___	___
Martin Luther King, Jr., *I Have a Dream*	___	___	___	___
Jonathan Swift, *A Modest Proposal*	___	___	___	___

Are there any writers not included you would like to see added? _____

_____

_____

Did you read the comments by the writers on writing? _____

Were they useful? _____

_____

Any general comments or suggestions? _____

_____